Edinburgh

timeout.com/edinburgh

Published by Time Out Guides Ltd, a wholly owned subsidiary of Time Out Group Ltd.
Time Out and the Time Out logo are trademarks of Time Out Group Ltd.

© Time Out Group Ltd 2004
Previous editions 1998, 2000, 2002

10 9 8 7 6 5 4 3 2 1

This edition first published in Great Britain in 2004 by Ebury
Ebury is a division of The Random House Group Ltd,
20 Vauxhall Bridge Road, London SW1V 2SA

Random House Australia Pty Limited, 20 Alfred Street, Milsons Point, Sydney, New South Wales 2061, Australia
Random House New Zealand Limited, 18 Poland Road, Glenfield, Auckland 10, New Zealand
Random House South Africa (Pty) Limited, Endulini, 5A Jubilee Road, Parktown 2193, South Africa

Random House UK Limited Reg. No. 954009

Distributed in USA by Publishers Group West
1700 Fourth Street, Berkeley, California 94710

Distributed in Canada by Penguin Canada Ltd
10 Alcorn Avenue, Toronto, Ontario, Canada M4V 3B2

For further distribution details, see www.timeout.com

ISBN 1-904978-17-7

A CIP catalogue record for this book is available from the British Library

Colour reprographics by Icon, Crowne House, 56-58 Southwark Street, London SE1 1UN

Printed and bound by Cayfosa-Quebecor, Ctra. De Caldes, KM 3 08 130 Sta, Perpètua de Mogoda, Barcelona, Spain

Time Out Edinburgh

Edited and designed by
Time Out Guides Limited
Universal House
251 Tottenham Court Road
London W1T 7AB
Tel + 44 (0)20 7813 3000
Fax + 44 (0)20 7813 6001
Email guides@timeout.com
www.timeout.com

Editorial
Editors Dan Lerner and Helen Pidd
Deputy Editor Edoardo Albert
Listings Checker Ruth Lewis
Proofreader John Watson
Indexer Anna Norman

Editorial/Managing Director Peter Fiennes
Series Editor Ruth Jarvis
Deputy Series Editor Lesley McCave
Guides Co-ordinator Anna Norman
Accountant Sarah Bostock

Design
Art Director Mandy Martin
Acting Art Director Scott Moore
Acting Art Editor Tracey Ridgewell
Acting Senior Designer Astrid Kogler
Designer Sam Lands
Junior Designer Oliver Knight
Digital Imaging Dan Conway
Ad Make-up Charlotte Blythe

Picture Desk
Picture Editor Jael Marschner
Deputy Picture Editor Kit Burnet
Picture Researcher Ivy Lahon
Picture Desk Assistant/Librarian Laura Lord

Advertising
Sales Director Mark Phillips
International Sales Manager Ross Canadé
International Sales Executive James Tuson
Advertising Sales (Edinburgh) Christie Dessy
Advertising Assistant Lucy Butler

Marketing
Marketing Manager Mandy Martinez
US Publicity & Marketing Associate Rosella Albanese

Production
Guides Production Director Mark Lamond
Production Controller Samantha Furniss

Time Out Group
Chairman Tony Elliott
Managing Director Mike Hardwick
Group Financial Director Richard Waterlow
Group Commercial Director Lesley Gill
Group Marketing Director Christine Cort
Group General Manager Nichola Coulthard
Group Art Director John Oakey
Online Managing Director David Pepper
Group Production Director Steve Proctor
Group IT Director Simon Chappell

Contributors
Introduction Helen Pidd. **History** Christine Ure. **Edinburgh Today** Dan Lerner, Neil Cooper (*Book ends* Neil Cooper). **Architecture** Neil Cameron. **Festival Edinburgh** Robin Lee. **Where to Stay** Maureen Ellis. **Sightseeing Introduction** Phil Maynard. **Old Town** Phil Maynard (*Ian Rankin* Neil Cooper; *Ghosts, trust us* Anna Burkey; *Burning down the town* Phil Maynard). **New Town** Phil Maynard. **Stockbridge** Phil Maynard. **Calton Hill & Broughton** Phil Maynard. **Arthur's Seat & Duddingston** Phil Maynard. **South Edinburgh** Phil Maynard (*City Walks* Phil Maynard; *Edinburgh Uni: Fame Academy* Phil Maynard; *JK Rowling* Neil Cooper). **West Edinburgh** Phil Maynard. **Leith** Phil Maynard (*Star for a night* Phil Maynard; *Irvine Welsh* John Lyndon). **Restaurants** Keith Davidson. **Café-Bars & Cafés** Keith Davidson (*Kevin Williamson* Neil Cooper). **Pubs** Keith Davidson. **Shops and Services** Katey Dixon. **By Season** Robin Lee. **Children** Mark Fisher. **Comedy** Jason Hall. **Film** Michael Creek (*Reel to real* Michael Creek; *Beer Monsters, Inc* Michael Creek; *Sean Connery* John Lyndon). **Galleries** Phyllis Martin. **Gay & Lesbian** Michael Creek. **Music** Neil Cooper. **Nightlife** James Smart. **Sport & Fitness** Daniel Schofield. **Theatre & Dance** Neil Cooper. **Getting Started** Mark Fisher. **Glasgow** Stephen Phelan. **Around Edinburgh** Mark Fisher. **Directory** Daniel Schofield.

Maps JS Graphics (john@jsgraphics). Edinburgh street maps are based on material supplied by Alan Collinson through Copyright Exchange. Hillhead map based on material supplied by XYZ Digital Map Co Ltd. Blackford Hill's walk map based on material supplied by Netmaps.

Photography Muir Vidler, except: page 6 National Gallery of Scotland; page 11 Hulton Getty; pages 13, 184, 208 Rex Features; page 35 Douglas Robertson; page 35 Lucia Trujillo; page 39 Brooke Pegram; page 39 Mike Pinches; page 43 Melvin House Hotel; page 73 Pete Goddard; pages 74, 127 Rankin; page 114 Bloomsbury Publishing; page 122 Getty Images/MTV; pages 194, 196, 262, 271 Scottish Viewpoint; page 194 Isla Leaver-Yap; page 197 Edinburgh and Lothians Tourist Board; page 206 Entertainment Film Distributors; page 220 East West Records; page 220 SL Records; page 232 Simon Deviller; page 260 Canongate. The following pictures were supplied by the featured establishments/artists: pages 24, 25, 26, 51, 53, 55, 209, 210, 211, 254.

The Editors would like to thank Neil Cooper, Michael Creek, Nicola Gilbert, Tomas Caro Jimenez, Keith Davidson, Douglas Fraser and all contributors to previous editions.

Contents

Introduction

Wee it may well be, but Edinburgh is still a fabulously capricious little city. A stroll around town entails so many rapid scenery changes, it's like wandering on to a multi-purpose film set. Arrive via Princes Street and you'll admire the jagged skyline and the awesome sense of space – from the Gothic spire of the Scott Monument to the neo-classical columns of the National Gallery and the monolithic bulk of the Castle, all kept in their place by the rolling lawns of Princes Street Gardens. Wheeze up the steeply cobbled Cockburn Street into the Old Town and suddenly you're closed in on all sides by imposing tenements, higgledy piggledy wynds and secret passages. All that before you've meandered through the once boho and now chichi Stockbridge district, jiggled about in lively Broughton, mingled with the students in South Edinburgh, got gritty in Leith or climbed Arthur's Seat, the city's extinct volcano.

Unsurprisingly, given Edinburgh's long and colourful past, the city is renowned for its history. Indeed, a good chunk of town has been declared a World Heritage Site. Now, however, thanks in part to an injection of cash and confidence from both devolution and a slew of high profile media events, the capital has shimmied right into the here and now. When Justin Timberlake and Beyoncé sang Edinburgh's praises at the 2003 MTV awards held in the city, it was a deserved stamp of approval from the cool kids. No longer just a mecca for architecture geeks and tourists on the tartan trail, Edinburgh has undergone a radical metamorphosis: it is now a truly European city with nightlife and sass to match – as a visit during August's ever-expanding festival season will prove.

So the once reserved Edinburgh now has an extra spring in its step. Admittedly, Glasgow still wins on the clubbing and music front, but head out to the bars and bistros any night of the week and you'll feel that change is afoot – be it a new gallery opening, a club night or an up-and-coming band. That's not to say that traditions are dying out. Far from it. The historic Old Town remains inebriated with whisky shops; cosy old pubs still ring with the sound of Celtic folk sessions; and you'll never be far from a busking bagpiper.

Whether you're into the old or the new, now is the time to get over any lingering preconceptions and enjoy the Edinburgh of the new millennium. Scotland's capital has shed its fusty, tight-lipped reputation to become a lively, cultural, cosmopolitan and stylish city at the forefront of European metropolitan life.

ABOUT THE TIME OUT CITY GUIDES

This fourth edition of *Time Out Edinburgh* is one of an expanding series of Time Out City Guides, now numbering over 45, produced by the people behind London and New York's successful listings magazines. Our guides are all written and updated by resident experts who have striven to provide you with all the most up-to-date information you'll need to explore the city or read up on its background, whether you're a local or a first-time visitor.

THE LOWDOWN ON LISTINGS

Above all, we've tried to make this book as useful as possible. Addresses, telephone numbers, websites, transport information, opening times, admission prices and credit card details have all been included in the listings. And, as far as possible, we've given details of facilities, services and events, all checked and correct as we went to press. However, owners and managers can change their arrangements at any time, and they often do. Before you go out of your way, we'd advise you to telephone and check opening times, ticket prices and other particulars. While every effort has been made to ensure the accuracy of the information contained in this guide, the publishers cannot accept responsibility for any errors it may contain.

PRICES AND PAYMENT

We have noted where venues such as shops, hotels, restaurants, museums and the like accept the following credit cards: American Express (AmEx), Diners Club (DC), MasterCard (MC) and Visa (V). Many will also accept other credit cards (including JCB, Discover or Carte Blanche), travellers' cheques issued by a major financial institution, and debit cards such as Switch and Delta.

The prices we've supplied should be treated as guidelines, not gospel. If prices vary wildly from those we've quoted, please write and let us

know. We aim to give the best and most up-to-date advice, so we want to know if you've been badly treated or overcharged.

THE LIE OF THE LAND
In order to make the book (and the city) as easy to navigate as possible, we have divided Edinburgh into areas that are convenient to walk around, and assigned each one its own chapter in our Sightseeing section starting on page 65. Although these area designations are a simplification of Edinburgh's geography, we hope they will help you to understand the city's layout and to find its most interesting sights. For consistency, the same areas are used in addresses and chapters throughout the guide. We've included only bus services operated by Lothian Buses in our city listings. Edinburgh's bus system is extensive and surprisingly efficient, with some central destinations served by as many as 20 different routes. For convenience, we've grouped buses for some of these busy destinations together; for details, see page 275. We've given postcodes for those venues you might want to write to and website addresses wherever possible.

TELEPHONE NUMBERS
The area code for Edinburgh is 0131. All telephone numbers printed in this guide take this code unless otherwise stated. Glasgow and other destinations in our Trips Out of Town section are also listed with their full code. Numbers preceded by 0800 in the listings can be called free of charge from within the UK; some of them are obtainable from outside the UK, but are unlikely to be free of charge. If you are dialling from abroad, follow the country code (44) with the area code without its initial zero, then the number.

ESSENTIAL INFORMATION
For all the practical information you might need for visiting the city – including visa and customs information, advice on facilities and access for the disabled, emergency telephone numbers, health services, a lowdown on the local transport network and information on studying and working in the city – turn to the Directory chapter at the back of the guide. It starts on page 273.

MAPS
Wherever possible, map references have been provided for all the places listed in the guide, indicating the page and grid reference at which they can be found on our maps. These fully indexed colour maps are located at the back of the book (starting on page 302), and include an overview of the areas we have used in the guide, a detailed map of Princes Street, street maps of Edinburgh and Leith, overview maps of Edinburgh and Glasgow, street maps of central Glasgow and a map of Scotland.

LET US KNOW WHAT YOU THINK
We hope that you enjoy the *Time Out Edinburgh Guide*, and we'd like to know what you think of it. We welcome tips for places that you consider we should include in future editions of the guide and take note of your criticism of our choices. You can email us at guides@timeout.com.

There is an online version of this book, along with guides to 45 other international cities, at **www.timeout.com**.

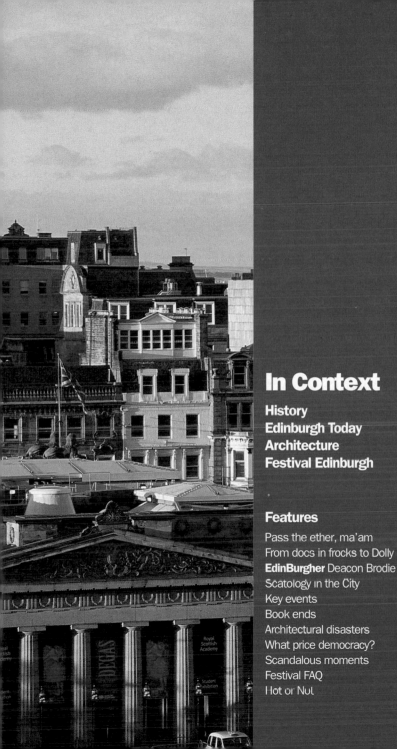

In Context

Features

History

Half Old, half New: invention and reinvention.

Approach Edinburgh from any direction and what dominates the horizon is Edinburgh Castle, welded to its basalt outcrop. Catching the rays of the westering sun, visible from half way to Glasgow and the opposite shores of Fife, here is a natural fortress whose occupants, secure on their dizzying heights, could survey the flowing waters of the Firth of Forth and watch for the approach of distant raiders. It was on this natural vantage point that Edinburgh began, first with the fortress on the rock, and later followed by the city that flowed down the castle's ridge, eventually spilling northwards across the intervening valley to the New Town and beyond.

Edinburgh's dramatic setting is the result of a landscape shaped by fire and ice. Over 300 million years ago, volcanoes spewed their molten lava across desolate landscapes to form the hills of the city. Creeping northwards across the globe as the continents played their slow game of marriage and divorce, and engulfed by successive ice ages, Scotland vanished under vast rivers of grinding, groaning ice, which carved out a mountainous landscape. With the disappearance of the final glaciers some 15,000 years ago, the stage was set, the backdrop ready for the emergence of that most visually striking of cities, Edinburgh.

IN THE BEGINNING

It is not known when people first began to colonise the area that would become Edinburgh, but traces of human occupation go back seven millennia. Rewind five thousand years and you would see hunter-gatherers foraging along the Water of Leith; go back just three thousand and you would witness the introduction of farming, traces of which can still be detected in the terraces on the flanks of Arthur's Seat. It was two thousand years ago that metal tools began to replace stone and bone. The hills of Edinburgh all bear traces of early fortification and hut settlements, while the waters of Duddingston Loch, when dredged in the 18th century, revealed caches of Bronze Age weapons.

While there is no direct evidence that the Romans occupied the Castle Rock, they did establish ports at the mouths of the rivers Almond and Esk, and are thought to have established trading relationships with the native tribes, the Votadini, whose fortress originally occupied the Castle Rock. By the seventh century, the Votadini were transformed into the Goddodin, an early British tribe who shared a language and tradition with the peoples of south-west Scotland, Cumbria and Wales. The juicy exploits of these British warriors and their king, Mynyddog, eventually became woven into the stuff of Arthurian legend. The fortress on the rock was named Dun Eidyn, meaning 'hill fort', and was captured several times. In 638 AD, southern Scotland was conquered by the Northumbrians, who built on the rock and anglicised its name to Edinburgh. In the middle of the tenth century, the MacAlpin kings repelled the Northumbrians southwards again and, in 1018, Malcolm II (1005-34) defeated them at Carham. The Castle Rock and the surrounding area became Scottish.

THE FIRST CASTLE

It was Malcolm III who established the first known castle on the hill. Malcolm, known as 'Canmore' ('big head' or 'great leader'), is best known for his appearance in Shakespeare's *Macbeth* and for his marriage to Margaret, the Saxon princess who, fleeing the arrival of the Normans to England, arrived on the shores of the Forth in 1070 and shortly afterwards married the king. This romantic tale does conveniently forget his first queen, the Norwegian Ingeborg. Nevertheless, Margaret proved a pious but energetic and fertile queen. In between producing nine children she played a central role in the introduction of Roman Catholicism to Scotland, founded a priory at Dunfermline in Fife, established a ferry service for pilgrims across the Forth, and worked several miracles. She died in the royal residence on the Rock in 1093, having learned of the death of her husband and son in a raid at Alnwick. Under the cover of a sea mist, or haar, supporters smuggled her body from the castle, which was then beseiged by Malcolm's brother, Donald Bane (also featured in *Macbeth*), for burial in Dunfermline. The oldest extant building on the Rock, the 12th-century St Margaret's Chapel, is dedicated to her (*see p70*). Three of Malcolm and Margaret's sons, Edgar, Alexander and David, went on to rule Scotland.

DAVID I MADE A MINT

The last of Margaret's sons ruled as King David I (1084-1153) and, having inherited his mother's piety, established religious foundations throughout Scotland. With the help of some construction-savvy Augustinian friars, David founded Holyrood Abbey. The church was built to commemorate David's lucky and rather miraculous escape from a stag, which attacked him as he hunted in the forests below the Salisbury Crags. Miraculous, so legend has it, because of the sudden appearance of the crucifix, or 'rood', between its antlers. The Gothic ruins of the Abbey can still be seen in

the grounds of Holyrood House today. David was kept busy on the throne for nearly thirty years, during which period he introduced feudalism to Scotland and established the first royal burghs. The burghs were towns that were granted charters to hold markets and fairs and whose inhabitants were known as burgesses. Edinburgh was a burgh, although the now-vanished Borders town of Roxburgh and the currently English Berwick then had greater status. David was also the first Scottish king to introduce coinage, and by 1153 had established a royal mint in Edinburgh.

GETTING MY RELIGION

Holyrood Abbey was completed in 1141 and Augustinian monks were brought from St Andrews to fill it. The lower half of what is now the Royal Mile became known as the Canongate, a separate burgh named after the canons at Holyrood. Canongate was separated from the city of Edinburgh by the defensive Netherbow Port and did not officially become part of Edinburgh until 1856. On the long rocky ridge that runs down behind the Castle hill, the city of Edinburgh began to develop.

> **'The succession of Stewart child-kings left Scotland vulnerable to the machinations of rival court factions.'**

The burgess's houses faced on to the High Street, with long gardens rolling down the slopes behind them, their lower garden walls being used as part of the city defences. Parallel to the Canongate, the deep valley of the Cowgate gave access to grazing areas outside the city walls for cattle. Other religious foundations were established throughout the city: in 1230 the Dominicans or 'Black Friars' founded a friary at the eastern end of the Cowgate, while the Franciscans set up their monastery outside the city boundary, at Greyfriars. While there are references to a church dedicated to St Giles from the ninth century, the great church of St Giles was actually established on its present High Street site in 1120 by Alexander II and formally dedicated by Bishop Bernham of St Andrews in 1243.

SCOTS WHA HAE WI' WALLACE BLED

In 1286, Alexander III, riding one stormy night to be with his new French bride, fell to his unfortunate death over a cliff at Kinghorn. He left no living children to inherit his throne, only

a little granddaughter, the 'Maid of Norway', who died before she could be brought to Scotland and the throne. Thus began a long and sombre chapter in Scotland's history of warfare with her nearest neighbour, England.

Repeatedly ravaged by English armies, Scotland had nevertheless managed to secure its independence after Robert the Bruce's victory at Bannockburn in 1314. In 1328, the Treaty of Edinburgh was signed, formally ending, alas not permanently, hostilities between the two kingdoms. In 1329, the year of his death, Bruce granted Edinburgh the status of royal burgh, giving its burgesses important fiscal privileges.

Bruce's successor, David II, was only five years old in 1329, leaving the kingdom vulnerable to renewed strikes by the English. Edward III attacked first, followed by Richard II in 1380, whose offensive saw the castle besieged and the burning of both the Canongate and St Giles. Edinburgh, however, with just 2,000 residents, was emerging as Scotland's most populous burgh, a position it was to hold for the next 400 years until it was overtaken by the population explosion of 19th-century industrial Glasgow. David II died in 1371 with no heir, and was succeeded by Robert II, son of Walter the Steward who, through his dynastic marriage to Marjorie, daughter of Robert the Bruce, was able to start a dynasty of his own: the House of Stewart.

A DRAMATIC DYNASTY

The Stewarts proved to be dynastically tenacious, and ruled Scotland until 1688. As individuals, however, they were somewhat short-lived, and the ensuing succession of Stewart child-kings left Scotland vulnerable to the machinations of rival court factions. They also proved unimaginative in their choice of royal baby names. James I (1406-37) tried to curb the power of the nobles but himself became a victim of their power struggles and was murdered at Blackfriars in Perth in 1437. His six-year-old son was hastily crowned James II (1430-60) by his mother at Holyrood Abbey.

Three years later, the boy-king was to witness the 'Black Dinner' at Edinburgh Castle, where his young cousins, the Earl of Douglas and his brother, were murdered on the orders of the governor, the Earl of Crichton. James II himself later murdered the eighth Earl of Douglas in the course of a quarrel at Stirling Castle. His turbulent reign ended abruptly when, besieging the English occupiers of Roxburgh Castle, he was killed by an exploding cannon. Ironically, James had been the king whose lively interest in firearms had seen him welcome to Scotland the great cannon, Mons

Meg, on display today at the Castle. Throughout James's tumultuous reign, the Old Town was expanded and the city's defences strengthened. The first defensive wall, the King's Wall, surrounded the Old Town, running eastward from halfway down the Castle Rock above the Grassmarket and the Cowgate to the Netherbow, before dipping down to the Nor' Loch. The Loch was a sort of natural moat in the valley north of the castle, whose water levels had risen after the damming of the Craig Burn in the mid-15th century.

Along the Royal Mile the familiar herringbone pattern of narrow closes and wynds between densely packed houses began to emerge. Running down the steep sides of the ridge, these were muddy and slippery, covered with animal and human ordure. None too pleasant, especially given that soap was not manufactured in Edinburgh until 1554. The main city landmarks were the Castle, the High Kirk of St Giles, the trading post at the Mercat Cross, and the Tolbooth to the east of St Giles. The tollbooth was, literally, where taxes were paid and the council met; by the 15th century the Scottish Parliament and the Court of Session met there and a prison had been added.

> ## 'As part of his marriage settlement, James signed the Treaty of Perpetual Peace with England, a treaty which failed to live up to its name.'

James III (1452-88), like his father and grandfather, inherited the throne as a child, and once again the kingdom was riven by warring factions and power struggles. James alienated support by cultivating 'favourites' and ignoring his nobles, who took revenge by lynching the King's friend Robert Cochrane and his associates from a Borders bridge at Lauder. Despite political unrest, it was during James III's reign that the Cowgate developed as a fashionable quarter, the French writer Froissart remarking on the fine aristocratic mansions of the Cowgate with their gardens and orchards. Commerce was also flourishing. Edinburgh's port at Leith, the major port between the rivers Tweed and Forth, offered opportunities to capitalise on trade with the Continent. In 1469, the town ceased to be governed by its merchant burgesses and became a self-electing corporation, and, in 1477, James established a livestock market in the Grassmarket. In 1482 he granted the 'Blue Blanket' to the guilds of

Pass the ether, ma'am

That Edinburgh's beating heart has survived, despite the onslaught of all the high culture and low pleasure that the city has to offer is, perhaps, testament to its medical roots. Ever since James IV awarded a charter to the Barber Surgeons of Edinburgh in 1567, the city has been recognised as an important centre of medical research. That tradition continues today: the city is home to a number of biotech firms and research labs.

Dr James Young Simpson, the pioneer of modern anaesthetics, was one of the most notable of Edinburgh's many medical path-breakers. Until the mid-19th century, the only relief from the pains of surgery was a very stiff drink or a session of hypnosis. Appalled by the suffering he witnessed in theatre, big-hearted Dr Simpson resolved to find a means of making operations and childbirth safer and less traumatic.

A graduate of Edinburgh University, by 1835 Simpson was Professor of Midwifery and had begun to explore the potential of anaesthetics, often experimenting on himself. By 1847 he had found what he believed to be the ideal method: chloroform.

The conservative medical profession viewed Simpson's findings with suspicion. Intent on demonstrating chloroform's effectiveness and safety, he invited colleagues to dinner at his Queen Street house. There, abandoning the Victorian tradition of passing the port after dinner, he casually passed the ether instead. Finding themselves abandoned in the drawing room, Mrs Simpson and the other ladies hastened to the dining room and found all three doctors sprawled asleep and snoring over the table. His point was proven.

Simpson faced more opposition from the (all-male) clergy, who decreed that painless childbirth was against the Biblical commandment that women should 'bring forth children in sorrow'. Simpson, every girl's hero, countered this by reminding the churchmen that when creating Eve 'from Adam's rib', God first considerately rendered Adam unconscious.

Support for anaesthesia eventually came from an exalted if unexpected quarter. In 1847 Simpson was appointed Royal Physician in Scotland. Queen Victoria, already a mother of seven and the wiser for it, would not be deterred from enlisting chloroform in giving birth to her eighth. Prince Leopold's safe arrival proved the endorsement Simpson needed, especially when the grateful Queen created him baronet, the first ever appointed for medical services.

One of Dr Simpson's first non-royal patients to give birth with the help of chloroform was so delighted she saddled her unfortunate daughter with the name Anaesthesia.

Edinburgh, a flag symbolising the exclusive rights of the town's craftsmen. Despite intermittent support from the Edinburgh mob, James ultimately faced a rebellion of Border nobles who enlisted the support of his son and heir, another James, the Duke of Rothesay, and was mysteriously murdered after his defeat at the Battle of Sauchieburn in 1488.

JAMES IV

Implicated in the overthrowing of his father, James IV (1473-1513) suffered from life-long guilt, reputedly wearing an iron chain which he increased in weight with each passing year in penance. Aged just 15 at his coronation, and in spite of his murky beginning, James set about enhancing the status and reputation of his crown and his kingdom. Well educated, speaking several languages (including Gaelic), and with a lively interest in the arts and scientific research, James is often described as a 'Renaissance prince'. Embarking on an extensive architectural programme, James's reign saw the construction of the Great Halls of Stirling and Edinburgh castles and the addition of a gold-tipped crown spire to St Giles Cathedral. Workaholic James also founded the Scottish navy and commissioned the greatest ship of its age, the *Great Michael*, constructed in a specially built harbour at Newhaven.

In 1503 he married Margaret Tudor, sister of Henry VIII of England, and ordered the construction of a fine royal palace at Holyrood to receive his bride. Education and literature flourished during his reign, which saw the discovery of the poets Henryson, Dunbar and Alexander Douglas. In 1507 James granted a patent, or licence, to Scotland's first printing press, founded by Chapman and Myllar, at the foot of Blackfriars Wynd. Edinburgh's reputation for medical research began with James, who authorised the foundation of the Guild of Barbers and Surgeons and allowed anatomical research on the body of one hanged criminal a year. As part of his marriage settlement, James had signed the Treaty of

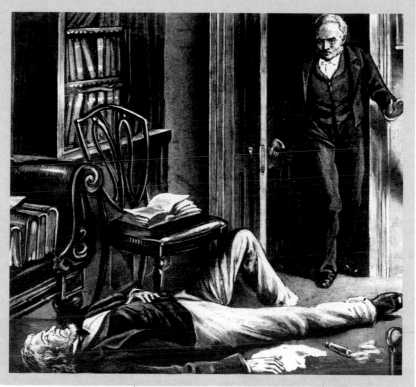

Perpetual Peace with England, a treaty which unfortunately failed to live up to its name. In 1513, in support of his French allies, James led his army into Northumberland. Despite numerical superiority, the Battle of Flodden was a disaster for the Scots, 10,000 of whom were killed, James among them. Learning the ghastly news, Edinburgh was thrown into panic and despair. In a desperate attempt to repel any attack by the English, the Flodden Wall was hastily constructed around the city, built, it is said, by widows, orphans and old men. Finally completed in 1560, this wall formed the city boundary for a further two centuries.

JAMES V – THE FRANCOPHILE

Despite, or perhaps because of, his English mother, James V (1512-42) turned his back on alliances with England and encouraged relations with France. His first wife was Madeleine, daughter of Francis I, and, after her death, his second was the more robust widow, Marie of Guise, a member of the

powerful French family of Guise-Lorraine. Travelling to France for his first wedding, James was impressed by the French king's new Renaissance palaces and had French masons brought to Scotland to work on the new royal residences at Stirling, Linlithgow and Falkland. It was during James' reign that the first tower of Holyrood Palace was built.

Mary of Guise bore James two sons but, by the end of 1541, both were dead. The following December, Mary gave birth to a third child, a girl, at Linlithgow Palace. News of the new arrival could not console James after the defeat of his army by the English at Solway Moss. He subsequently sank into a profound depression and died at Falkland Palace, leaving his six-day old daughter Mary Queen of Scots.

MOST BEAUTIFUL AND MOST CRUEL PRINCESS

The accession of yet another child, this one younger than ever, left Scotland open to another bout of in-fighting and turmoil, exacerbated by the rival claims from the French and English kings for a dynastic marriage with their sons. Henry VIII sent the Earl of Hertford with an army to 'persuade' the Scots to agree to a marriage of Mary with his son, Edward. In what came to be known as the 'rough wooing', Hertford landed at Leith in 1544 and looted the Abbey and Palace of Holyrood. Three years later the English army returned, led by the Earl of Somerset. They set up a base at Haddington, 18 miles south of Edinburgh, and, in 1547, the Battle of Pinkie Cleuch was fought at Musselburgh. The Scots lost and were driven back to the city but retained control of the castle. This harassment only ended in 1548 when French and Dutch reinforcements landed at Leith and the port was fortified against further attack. Mary, aged five, was sent to France and grew up at the court of Henri II, marrying his son and briefly ruling France as consort of Francis II. Francis, a sickly boy, died in 1560 and Mary, an 18 year-old widow, returned to her Scottish kingdom.

MARRIAGE AND MURDER

The Scotland to which Mary returned was riven by religious dissent, with churchman John Knox leading the movement for Reformation in Scotland. In 1560 Protestantism became Scotland's official religion and Mary's reign saw much friction between the Royal pro-Catholic faction and the Protestant Church.

In 1565 Mary married her cousin Henry Darnley, who was also a grandchild of Margaret Tudor – a fact which made Elizabeth I even more suspicious of their claims on the English throne. What was probably a true love-match for Mary seems to have been more of an exercise in self-promotion for Darnley. It has been suggested that the brutal assassination of Mary's Italian secretary, David Rizzio, at Holyrood in 1566, was an attempt engineered by Darnley to bring about a miscarriage and the possible death of the Queen, thus leaving the throne vacant for his assumption. The royal couple's relationship became increasingly estranged. In 1567, while Darnley was recuperating from illness at Kirk o' Field on the site of the present-day Old College, his house was blown up and Darnley's body was found. He had died in mysterious circumstances, but not so mysterious as to disguise the fact that he had been murdered. While no proof of the Queen's involvement in this murder can be definitively laid at Mary's feet, strong suspicion fell upon Lord Bothwell, one of her most loyal supporters. Mary's subsequent marriage to Bothwell turned public opinion violently against her. Forced to abdicate in favour of her infant son, the future James VI, Mary escaped

from imprisonment at Loch Leven castle, only to have her army defeated near Glasgow. Mary took refuge in England, where she spent 19 years as the prisoner of Elizabeth I before her execution in 1587.

THE WISEST FOOL IN CHRISTENDOM

Born in a tiny room in Edinburgh castle, James VI spent barely a year with his mother. On Mary's abdication, at the age of just thirteen months, he was crowned at Stirling, with John Knox preaching the coronation sermon. Brought up by Protestant tutors, alienated from his mother, and subject to several kidnapping attempts, poor old James was a suspicious and wary man by the time he assumed the reins of government. His reign was a permanent headache, thanks to hassles with the economy, the nobles and, above all, the Church.

James VI's long-term strategy was to inherit the English crown from the childless Elizabeth I. Elizabeth was reluctant to formally recognise 'that false Scotch urchin' as her heir, but on her death in 1603, James's dream came true when Sir Robert Carey galloped up from London to Holyrood in an incredible 36 hours to announce that James was now king of Great Britain. James, once described as 'the wisest fool in Christendom', left gleefully for London, promising to return to Scotland every three years, but sixteen passed before Scotland saw the return of its monarch.

ABSENTEE RULE

The Edinburgh James deserted had, in 1582, acquired a university, the 'Townis College'. On a less positive note, James also left behind an unpleasant legacy of persecution of witches that would result in the death of some 300 unfortunates. Suspected witches were tried first by immersion in the Nor' Loch. Those who managed to escape drowning were then burned at the stake.

James died in 1625 and was succeeded by his son, Charles I, who was crowned King of Scots in 1633 at Holyrood. A Parliament House was built beside St Giles, to be the home of the Scottish parliament until the Union of Parliaments in 1707. The commercial life of the city flourished, with arcaded buildings such as Gladstone's Land, built for wealthy merchant Thomas Gledstanes, running the length of the High Street.

MERRY MONARCHS

Charles I made it his mission to impose uniformity throughout the kingdom, but his controversial attempt to impose bishops on the Presbyterian Scottish church met with strong resistance. In 1637 a riot broke out in St Giles, with an old cabbage seller by the name of Jenny

From docs in frocks to Dolly

Edinburgh's doctors have made and continue to make important medical discoveries.
James Lind (1716-94) discovered that lime juice prevented scurvy.
Edinburgh-born **Dr George Cleghorn** (1716-94) discovered quinine as a cure for malaria, ensuring the restorative reputation of gin and tonic.
Andrew Duncan (1744-1828) established the first humane asylum for the insane.
James Miranda Barry (c1795-1865), the world's first woman doctor, graduated from Edinburgh University. She spent her army medical career, serving as Inspector-General of military hospitals in Montreal and Quebec, disguised as a man.
James Syme (1799-1870) performed the first operations to reconstruct damaged tissue, paving the way for plastic surgery.
William Gregory (1803-58) perfected chemical compounds such as chloroform and morphia which led to the mass production of synthesised drugs. Edinburgh today is still a world centre for opiates production.
New Town doctor **Alexander Wood** (1817-84) invented the hypodermic syringe.
Sophia Jex-Blake (1840-1912) set up the UK's first mother and child dispensary
Developed by **Sir Robert Philip** (1857-1938), the Edinburgh System was adopted world-wide for the prevention and management of tuberculosis. The system treated the entire family for TB. Continuing his work, Edinburgh launched the UK's first community X-ray campaign in 1954.
Birth-control pioneer **Marie Stopes** (1880-1958) was born and brought up in Edinburgh. The world's bitterest taste, **Bitrex**, was developed by the Edinburgh pharmaceutical company Macfarlan Smith in 1958 and is used in drugs and chemical products to prevent people being poisoned.
The first successful UK kidney transplant was performed in 1960 at Edinburgh Royal Infirmary by **Sir Michael Woodruff**.
Europe's first lung transplant was carried out in 1968 at Edinburgh Royal Infirmary by **Andrew Logan**.
Amniocentesis, the pregnancy screening test, was pioneered in the 1970s by **Professor David Brock** of Edinburgh University.
In 1978, **Sir Kenneth Murray**, former Professor of Molecular Biology at Edinburgh University, developed the first artificial vaccine for Viral Hepatitis B.

In 1993, the first bionic arm in the world was fitted by biomedical engineers at the now defunct Princess Margaret Rose hospital.
In 1997 it was announced that the Edinburgh-based Roslin Institute had cloned a sheep, the first mammal to be successfully reproduced from an adult cell. The announcement sparked a storm of protest and a vigorous debate about the ethics of cloning. **Dolly**, who was born in 1996, was put down in 2003. The debate continues.

EdinBurgher Deacon Brodie

Robert Louis Stevenson's childhood dreams were haunted by the sinister creakings of an old cabinet in his bedroom, the handiwork of the notorious criminal Deacon Brodie. For Stevenson, Brodie came to embody the hypocrisy of the bourgeois Edinburgh society of his day and the contrasting worlds of the genteel New Town and the squalid old city, a theme which was to inspire his account of the double life of Dr Jekyll and Mr Hyde.

William Brodie (born 1741) was the son of a wealthy Edinburgh craftsman and grew up in the tenement block owned by his family at the foot of the Lawnmarket. By 1773 he had already joined his father in the family cabinet-making business, rising rapidly to become Deacon of the Guild of Wrights and Masons. Following his election in 1781, at the relatively young age of 40, to the City Council, Brodie became a veritable pillar of respectable Victorian society. But behind this worthy veneer, Brodie was leading a secret double life in the gambling and drinking dens and brothels of old Edinburgh. When his income failed to keep pace with his expenses, he took to crime.

His trade offered perfect opportunities: while visiting clients' houses to take measurements, Brodie would take an imprint of their keys in a ball of wax, returning later with a counterfeit key to break into the house. As the number of burglaries grew, Edinburgh seethed with suspicion, none, of course, directed at the respectable Councillor. His raid on the Canongate Excise Offices in Chessels Court, however, proved to be his downfall. Brodie and his accomplices were disturbed in the act, and although Brodie escaped, a co-conspirator was arrested and revealed the identity of the ringleader behind the Edinburgh burglaries.

Brodie fled to Amsterdam but rather unwisely sent a letter to one of his mistresses, betraying his whereabouts. Officers of the Law travelled to Holland to bring the miscreant to justice, and in 1788 he was hanged at Edinburgh's Tolbooth. Brodie's mechanical skills had previously been directed at devising an improved form of gallows; ironically, he was one of the first to test their effectiveness. Unfortunately for him, they worked.

Geddes throwing her stool at Dean Hanna, shouting, 'Dost thou say mass in my lug?' In an effort to assert the rights of religious and civil liberty, the National Covenant was drawn up and read from the pulpit of Greyfriars Church. Resolute citizens queued over the next two days to add their names to this document, sometimes signing in their own blood. Thus began the turmoil of the Covenanting Wars, which were to continue into the reign of Charles II.

Civil War had broken out in England and by 1649 Oliver Cromwell was in power and Charles had been executed at Westminster. The Scots were outraged that their Parliament had not been consulted – Charles, after all, had been their king too – and six days later proclaimed his son, Charles II, King of Scots, on condition he accepted the Covenanters' demands.

Instead, Charles II enlisted the Marquis of Montrose, who had been loyal to his father, to conquer Scotland for him. Initially successful in his campaign against the Covenanters, Montrose was subsequently captured and executed at the Mercat Cross. Undeterred by Montrose's fate, Charles came to Scotland in 1650, the last monarch to come to Edinburgh until George IV in 1822. Cromwell's response was to invade and, after a victory at Dunbar, to burn down Holyrood House. Charles, crowned at Scone, fled south and into exile abroad.

RESTORATION, RESTORATION
Although Cromwell's government and the Scots' Presbyterian church shared the same values, Cromwell's Scottish occupation proved increasingly unpopular – thanks in part to the swingeing taxes imposed for the maintenance of Cromwell's army. Charles II's return to the throne after Cromwell's death in 1658 – the Restoration – was therefore greeted with relief.

'The result was an urban landscape unrivalled anywhere in Europe.'

Discontent simmered again when the King reneged on acts he had made in favour of the Covenanters. Thus began the 'Killing Times', with revolts breaking out in the south-west. The Covenanters' victory at Drumclog (1679) was followed by their defeat later that year at the Battle of Bothwell Brig. Greyfriars Churchyard was transformed into a squalid open-air prison, where many Covenanters died of disease or exposure. Others met their death on the gallows in the Grassmarket or were transported as slaves to Barbados.

In 1685 Charles II was succeeded by his brother, James VII (1633-1701), but his intransigence and Catholicism made him unpopular. James fled to France and was replaced on the throne by his daughter, Mary, and her husband, William, the Protestant Prince of Orange. Although the majority of Scots supported this 'Glorious Revolution', there remained significant backing for the exiled James, particularly among the Catholic Highland chiefs. This in turn led to another half-century of rebellion and civil war, until the final defeat of Stuart aspirations in 1746 on the battlefield of Culloden near Inverness.

AN END TO AN OLD SONG
Supporters of James VII (James II to the English), named 'Jacobites' from the Latin for James (*Jacobus*), mounted resistance to the new regime almost as soon as he had gone into exile. The misery of civil war was exacerbated by wretched living conditions, the result of numerous failed harvests throughout the 1690s, and the negative impact on trade of England's war with France. Scottish attempts to establish a trading colony in Central America with the so-called Darien Scheme proved a financial disaster. Ill-advised and over-promoted, the Scheme led to multiple bankruptcies When news of this financial disaster reached Edinburgh, the distraught citizens rioted, storming the Tolbooth and setting fire to the Cowgate. The collapse of the Darien Scheme strengthened the hand of those who promoted a union of the Scottish and Westminster parliaments, and after many machinations – not to mention the lavish bribery of hesitant MPs by those who saw their fortune beckoning in London – the Act of Union became law in January 1707. The Scots Parliament dissolved the following April. Far from being an occasion for rejoicing, the Union was viewed with misgivings and suspicion. It was to be nearly 300 years before a Scots Parliament sat again in Edinburgh.

REBELLION AND ENLIGHTENMENT
Gradually, southern Scottish cities such as Edinburgh and Glasgow came to realise that the Union with Great Britain offered beneficial opportunities for commerce and trade. Although Edinburgh was initially seduced by the glamour of Charles Edward Stuart (Bonnie Prince Charlie) who, in 1745, with the assistance of a number of Highland clans, 'took' the city before heading southwards in an attempt to claim the British throne, Edinburgh's sympathies ultimately remained British.

Shortly after the Stuarts' last fateful stand at Culloden, the city embarked on an incredibly ambitious building programme: the planning of the New Town. This scheme was certainly influenced by the living conditions in the plague and epidemic prone old town, but it also had a political basis: to demonstrate to the world that here was a civilised, cultured European city. For this reason, the 18th century is known in Edinburgh as the 'Age of Improvement'. The elegant classicism of the New Town was in keeping with urban developments throughout Europe (*see p91* **The making of the New Town**). Even street names were chosen to demonstrate Edinburgh's affiliation to the Union and to the British Royal family – George Street for the King (George III) and Charlotte Square for his Queen. Even the artisans' streets were named not just for Scotland's national flower, the thistle, but also for England's rose.

The competition to design this new suburb was won by James Craig, aged 22. Work began in 1767 on a site entirely outside the confines of the old city, across the valley north of the castle. Craig's plan was simple, elegant and harmonious; or, according to Robert Louis Stevenson, a set of 'draughty parallelograms'. The original New Town consisted of three main streets – Princes, George and Queen – positioned between two imposing squares. As part of the scheme, the Nor' Loch was drained and, in 1763, work on the North Bridge spanning the valley began. The earth dug from the foundations of the New Town formed the basis for the Mound, linking the Old and New towns, some two million cartloads of earth going into its construction. South of the Old Town the elegant George Square was laid out and a new college for the university (now known, confusingly, as Old College) was built at the old Kirk o' Fields by Robert Adam. Adam was also responsible for Register House (1771), the oldest building in Europe specially designed for the preservation of national archives, and the palatial facades of Charlotte Square, one of his last uncompleted masterpieces. The combined result was an urban landscape unrivalled anywhere in Europe.

Conceived as entirely residential, the New Town was soon attracting citizens of means to its elegant residences and, by 1792, some 7,000 people were already residing within its graceful confines.

NEW TOWN, NEW AGE

18th-century Edinburgh was the setting not only for this architectural masterpiece but also for an extraordinary intellectual flowering that in later times came to be known as the 'Scottish Enlightenment', peopled by intellectual colossi such as the economist Adam Smith, author of *The Wealth of Nations*, philosopher David Hume and the geologist James Hutton. The number of Edinburgh University students doubled between 1763 and 1783, the year the Royal Edinburgh Society was founded. Long an important legal centre, Edinburgh now expanded as a centre of medical research. In 1725, Provost George Drummond drew up plans for a new medical school; the first infirmary

Pillars in the sky. The **National Monument**. *See p18.*

Scatology in the City

Robinson Crusoe author Daniel Defoe may have praised Edinburgh's High Street as 'the largest, longest and finest street in the world', but he certainly couldn't have described it as fragrant. Life cooped up in the 17th-century tenements was grotty and cramped. Plumbing was non-existent and the stairs of the tenements were steep and inconvenient, so the city's resourceful residents evolved a simple system of waste disposal. At the sound of the evening curfew bell, windows all over the town were opened and pails emptied directly into the street. Passers-by were warned of an imminent deluge by cries of 'Gardey-loo', an expression derived from the French expression of the 1600s *Gare a l'eau!* (Beware of the water!) which, if somewhat euphemistic, demonstrated that the citizens of Edinburgh were multilingual – if unsanitary.

But out of great civic uncleanliness was born a great civic cleaner: **Sir James Dick**, the then Lord Provost of Edinburgh. In 1677 Dick acquired the Priestfield estate on the southern slopes of Arthur's Seat and commissioned Sir William Bruce, recent architect of Holyrood Palace, to build the fine mansion of Prestonfield. Keen and clean, Sir James then took it upon himself to cleanse the highways of Edinburgh, all at his own expense. This heroic undertaking was no act of pure charity, however, as the waste was conveyed to Prestonfield and used to enrich the lands of his estate.

His descendant, Sir Alexander Dick, went one step further in improving Edinburgh's health when in 1746 he inherited the family estate. Seven times elected President of the Royal College of Physicians, he got together with Edinburgh University's Professor of Medicine, a volatile Aberdonian called James Gregory. Dr Gregory was then studying the purgative properties of rhubarb, a plant long known to canny Chinese herbalists but only recently introduced to Britain. Sir Alexander was persuaded to bring this new crop to Scotland, where it flourished on the lands manured by his ancestors. It grew so successfully that, in 1774, Sir Alexander's rhubarb was awarded a gold medal by the London Society for Promoting Arts and Commerce. Combined with magnesium and ginger, rhubarb provided the essential ingredient for the celebrated 'Gregory's Mixture', which brought relief to costive generations to come.

opened in 1729 and was granted a Royal Charter in 1736. Social life in the New Town centred around the new Assembly Rooms, opened in 1787 in George Street. Lucky revellers were carried to elegant balls and concerts there, snugly encased in sedan chairs, protected from the ravages of Edinburgh's chill winds.

With the moneyed classes occupying the fine new residences of the New Town, the lands and tenements of Old Edinburgh were abandoned to artisans and the poor. A sort of social apartheid developed, with Edinburgh becoming a city with two faces. The contrast between the respectable gentility of the New Town and the squalid low-life of the Old Town, with its cock-fighting dens, oyster taverns and brothels, became a theme attributed to Edinburgh society to this day. The duality of Edinburgh life is perhaps best embodied in Deacon William Brodie (*see p14* **EdinBurgher Deacon Brodie**), whose double life as pillar of society and burglar was to inspire Robert Louis Stevenson's classic tale, *Dr Jekyll and Mr Hyde*.

Not only a centre for science and philosophy, Edinburgh had also developed a vibrant literary scene. Poets such as Allan Ramsay (whose statue now adorns Princes Street) and Robert Fergusson rescued the old and composed new Scottish ballads and songs. Robert Burns was a frequent visitor, penning love poems to his beloved Clarinda, drinking with the Crochallan Fencibles club and mixing with Edinburgh society, among them a youthful Walter Scott. Music-lovers could attend performances of new compositions by Sir John Clerk of Penicuik, pupil of Corelli, in St Cecilia's Hall, built in 1763 by Robert Mylne for the Edinburgh Musical Society.

GREAT SCOTT

Edinburgh-born Sir Walter Scott (1771-1832) was a titan of the later years of this era. The most influential literary figure of his day, his blockbuster poems and novels introduced readers to the hitherto neglected landscape and heritage of the Scottish Borders and Highlands. Born in Edinburgh in 1771, educated at the Royal High School and the Law Faculty of the University, Scott's destiny was sealed by time spent as a child in the Borders, where he had been sent to recuperate from the polio that would leave him forever with a limp. The stark history of his Borders forebears and the romance of Borders legend and ballad was to enthral the imaginative child; the collection of such stories from all parts of Scotland became a life-long passion. Embarking on a legal career that would see him become Deputy Sheriff of Selkirk and Principal Clerk to the Court of Session in Edinburgh, Scott nevertheless managed to combine legal duties with a prodigious literary output. Epic poems such as *The Lay of the Last Minstrel* and *The Lady of the Lake*, and novels such as *The Heart of Midlothian* and *Rob Roy,* communicated Scott's deep knowledge of and love for his Scottish heritage to the literary world of the early 19th century. Scott's wider influence cannot be underestimated: he almost single-handedly awakened the world to the romantic potential of Scotland and paved the way for its rehabilitation after the Jacobite debacle.

It was thanks to Scott's enthusiasm and perseverance that the long-lost 'Honours of Scotland' – the crown, sceptre and sword of state – were uncovered from their hiding place in Edinburgh Castle and put on public display. Scott was also responsible for the first visit to Scotland of a British monarch since the reign of Charles II, when, in 1822, he persuaded George IV to visit the capital of 'North Britain'. So well had Scott succeeded in restoring Highland

traditions that lowland Edinburgh was awash with tartan for the King's visit (kilts, the dress of the Highland rebels, had been banned after Culloden). In fact, even portly George appeared before his subjects swathed in tartan, albeit with the precautionary addition of pink silk tights to shield the Royal knees from impious gazes. This prompted the remark from one Edinburgh lady – always a formidable breed – that since there were so few opportunities to admire the Royal personage, it was just as well the King revealed so much of it during his visit.

'Burke and Hare spurned the established – if unsavoury – practice of digging up recently buried bodies in favour of providing fresh ones.'

Throughout the first three decades of the new century, Edinburgh had been adding to its townscape: the National Monument on Calton Hill above Hamilton's new Royal High School, Waterloo Bridge in the east, and, in the west, Melville Street. The National Monument, incomplete and so dubbed 'Scotland's Disgrace',

Walking the **Royal Mile**. *See p9.*

Holyrood, Batman! Who destroyed our church? *See p7.*

was the work of William Playfair, who was also responsible for the Royal Scottish Academy (1826) on Princes Street. Playfair was later to contribute the National Gallery (1854) on the Mound and, in a departure from his usual classical inspiration, Donaldson's Hospital (1850) near Murrayfield.

VICTORIAN EDINBURGH

Donaldson's Hospital, a school for deaf children, was formally opened by Queen Victoria, who was sufficiently impressed by its 'Jacobethan' splendours to remark that Playfair's school was finer than any of her Scottish palaces. It was during Victoria's reign that Edinburgh underwent further expansion, when suburbs such as Morningside, Marchmont and Bruntsfield were built for the burgeoning middle classes. At the start of the 19th century, the population of Edinburgh and Leith was just over 100,000. By 1881, over 320,000 people lived in Greater Edinburgh. Irish refugees and Highlanders displaced by the Clearances moved to the city in search of work.

Indeed, the infamous Burke and Hare were both Irish labourers who came to work on the Union Canal to the west of the city. They abandoned digging ditches in favour of the more lucrative trade of supplying corpses to the Anatomy School of the University. Burke and Hare, however, spurned the established – if unsavoury – practice of digging up recently buried bodies in favour of providing fresh ones, unfortunate by-products of a killing spree the

pair carried out from their lodgings in the West Port off the Grassmarket. Convicted of some 16 murders, in 1829 Burke was hanged on the evidence of his turncoat partner. A purse made from his skin is still on display in the somewhat grisly medical museum behind Surgeon's Hall on South Bridge (*see p115*).

This immigration swelled the population of the already crowded tenements of the Old Town, which fell victim to repeated epidemics of cholera and typhoid. In 1824, many lives were lost in a great fire which destroyed much of the High Street and which led to the formation of the world's first municipal fire service. Concern over living conditions in the Old Town led to investigations by Dr George Bell, who found that 159 of the Old Town closes lacked drainage and fresh water and that Blackfriar's Wynd was home to 1,000 people crammed into 142 houses. A separate study by Dr William Tait in 1842 revealed that an impressive 200 brothels were concentrated in the Old Town. When the neglected Paisley Close on the High Street collapsed in 1861, killing 35 people, public outrage caused the Town Council to agree to the adoption of proper health and safety regulations. Dr Henry Littlejohn was appointed as the first Medical Officer of Health in Scotland. Littlejohn's report on sanitary conditions in Edinburgh coincided with the election of the philanthropic publisher William Chamber as Lord Provost, resulting in the improvement scheme of 1866 that cleared some of the congested slums of the Old Town and created new streets such as St Mary's and Blackfriars, both of which provided housing for artisans.

In 1843 Edinburgh was the setting for yet another religious revolution, this time bloodless, known today as the 'Disruption', which began when 474 ministers upheld their belief in the right of congregations to choose their own ministers. Led by Dr Thomas Chalmers, the dissenters left St Andrew's Church in George Street to march to Tanfield Hall in Canonmills to form a breakaway group, the Free Church of Scotland. This split was not resolved until 1929.

FASTER THAN WITCHES

In the early 17th century London was 13 days away by coach; by the end of the century, the journey could be done in four. Waverley Station was built in 1846, the first public train from London to Edinburgh ran in 1850 and, in 1862, the *Flying Scotsman* completed the journey in ten and a half hours. The construction of the Forth Bridge in 1890, hailed as the eighth wonder of the world, linked the city with towns beyond the Forth, while a network of suburban lines made possible the expansion of Edinburgh into outlying villages. Medical advances brought international renown to James Young Simpson (*see p10* **Pass the ether, ma'am**) and Joseph Lister, famous for their work on anaesthetics and antiseptics respectively.

THE 20TH CENTURY

The history of the first half of the 20th century was dominated by the two world wars. In 1914, battalions of Edinburgh citizens volunteered to serve in the Great War. Scots made up ten per cent of British recruitment, with 25 per cent of the Scottish male population marching off to war. Long lists of the many who did not return can be seen on Lorimer's Scottish National War Memorial at the Castle. Edinburgh itself suffered very few direct attacks in the first war, although a Zeppelin raid in 1916 caused damage in Leith and also, with ironic accuracy, scored a direct hit on the German Church at Bellevue. Edinburgh, unlike the major industrial centre of Glasgow's Clydebank, was spared the worst of aerial attacks in World War II. However, the city was a peripheral victim of the first air raid of the war in October 1939, when the Luftwaffe attacked Royal Navy cruisers off Inchgarvie in the Forth.

Between the wars, and again unlike Glasgow, Edinburgh's lack of heavy industry meant the city escaped the worst ravages of the Depression in the 1930s. A concern for improving living conditions led to the establishment of new housing in areas such as Craigmillar, Niddrie and Pilton, when the population of the decaying Old Town was moved to the periphery of the city. Visitors to the prosperous business centre and middle-class suburbs of Edinburgh may be unaware that the city is ringed by poorly resourced housing schemes, which have in turn fallen victim to urban decay. The dual face of Edinburgh lives on, though less obviously than in the days of the Old Town/New Town divide – all displayed against the dramatic backdrop of this most visually impressive of cities.

Rock and bone. **Edinburgh Castle**. *See p7.*

Key events

c1-c300AD Castle Rock is fortress of Votadini, tribal allies of Romans.
c300-c700 Rock is stronghold of British tribe, the Gododdin.
638 Northumbrians take over southern Scotland.
c950 Northumbrians are defeated by Kenneth MacAlpin.
1018 Battle of Carham; Malcolm II drives Northumbrians from Lothian.
1070 Malcolm Canmore marries Margaret. First castle built on Castle Rock.
1093 Malcolm III killed; Margaret dies.
1084-1153 David I founds Augustinian Priory at Holyrood; establishes Royal Mint.
1243 High Kirk of St Giles consecrated.
1286 Alexander III killed. Scotland invaded by Edward I of England.
1314 Thomas Randolph retakes Edinburgh Castle from English occupation.
1329 Robert the Bruce gives Royal Charter to Edinburgh.
1333 Berwick falls to the English
1349 The Black Death arrives; further epidemics in **1362** and **1379**. Around a third of the Scottish population die of the plague.
1477 James III charters livestock market in Grassmarket.
1488-1513 Reign of James IV; Great Hall built at Castle, crown spire added to St Giles, Royal Palace of Holyrood House begun.
1513 Edinburgh citizens muster at Mercat Cross to march to Flodden. Scots defeated, James IV killed. Flodden Wall built round city.
1513-42 Reign of James V. Holyrood House extended.
1542 Mary Queen of Scots inherits throne. Holyrood House and Abbey attacked in 'Rough Wooing'.
1560 John Knox declares Protestantism the official religion of Scotland.
1561-67 Mary Queen of Scots returns from France to rule Scotland.
1565 Mary marries Henry Darnley.
1566 Mary's secretary, David Rizzio, murdered at Holyrood. Mary gives birth to future James VI at Edinburgh Castle.
1582 Edinburgh University founded.
1603 James VI accedes to the English throne; the Court moves to London.
1638 National Covenant signed in Greyfriars Graveyard.
1639 Parliament House completed; remains seat of Scots Parliament till 1707.

1650 Marquis of Montrose executed at Mercat Cross.
1681 James Dalrymple publishes *Institutions of the Law of Scotland*.
1695 Bank of Scotland established.
1699 Collapse of Darien Scheme.
1707 Act of Union; Parliament moves to Westminster.
1726 Last burning of a witch in Edinburgh.
1727 Royal Bank of Scotland founded.
1736 Porteous Riots.
1767 Construction of New Town begins.
1771 *Encyclopaedia Britannica* published by William Smellie. Walter Scott born in College Wynd.
1784 Last execution in the Grassmarket.
1787 Edinburgh edition of Burns' poems published.
1788 Deacon Brodie hanged at Tolbooth.
1817 *Blackwood's Magazine* and the *Scotsman* are founded.
1824 The Great Fire destroys much of the High Street and results in formation of world's first municipal fire brigade. Botanic Garden established at Inverleith.
1836 Waverley Station begun.
1843 Church split by the Disruption.
1847 Alexander Graham Bell, inventor of the telephone, born in South Charlotte Street.
1864 Last public hanging in Edinburgh.
1871 First international rugby match played at Raeburn Park.
1874 Heart of Midlothian Football Club founded.
1875 Hibernian Football Club founded.
1890 Forth Rail Bridge opens.
1895 Electric street lighting introduced.
1903 Edinburgh Zoo opens.
1925 Murrayfield Stadium opens.
1947 First Edinburgh International Festival.
1964 Heriot-Watt University founded.
1996 Stone of Destiny returns to Edinburgh Castle.
1997 Scotland votes for Scottish Parliament.
1998 Holyrood announced as site of new Scottish Parliament building. Royal Yacht *Britannia* berthed permanently at Leith.
1999 The Queen opens the Scottish Parliament.
2000 Death of Donald Dewar, first First Minister of Scotland.
2002 Fire destroys part of Old Town and Cowgate.
2003 MTV Music Awards held in Leith.

Edinburgh Today

Parliamentary passion gives way to the painstaking task of nation building.

Half a decade after the triumphant Scottish victory in the centuries-old battle for devolution, Edinburgh is beginning to adjust to its role as capital city, festival paradise, financial centre and tourist mecca. The new parliament building is nearly ready, visitor numbers to the festival break new records every year, MTV Europe decided to hold its music awards here and local politics are beginning to settle into the humdrum routine of an established regional administration.

Scotland's devolved government has proven to be a major reality check for the flag-waving, bagpipe-playing proponents of self-rule. That's not to say that the new parliament has been unsuccessful. The battle to gain regional autonomy was hard fought and the early years of the parliament have seen some key successes.

The story of the New Scotland began in 1999. The Queen ended almost 300 years of English dominance on 1st July when she opened the Scottish parliament in its temporary home. Buoyed by the (irrational) exuberance of

commentators and the hyperbole of politicians, many believed the spirit of the warrior William Wallace (Hollywood's *Braveheart*) was finally upon them. To the believers, it was as if all their Burns Suppers and St Andrew's Days had marched into town at once. Edinburgh was again to be a proper capital city.

But, of course, the real story of how Edinburgh came to be at the heart of such a radical political innovation in a country with no written constitution begins much earlier. For some it begins with the establishment of the first Scottish parliament in 1290. The inglorious political history that has seen England trample repeatedly on the wishes of its northern neighbours since then has left political and cultural firebrands with a collective chip on their shoulders that transcends generations.

The recent history of devolution began with a referendum in 1979 which failed to gain a sufficient mandate for devolution from a lukewarm populace. Only after years of swingeing attacks from a hostile Conservative government in Westminster, including the testing of the iniquitous Poll Tax a year ahead of England, were the Conservatives electorally banished from Scotland. Their defeat ushered in a Labour government at Westminster under the young, charismatic, Tony Blair. Whether ideologically or pragmatically, the new administration was committed to devolution and immediately began drawing up plans for a new Scottish parliament.

Under the terms of the devolution agreement – the 1999 Scotland Act – the parliament is allowed to go its own way on a vast number of issues, with only a few powers 'reserved' to Westminster. Defence and foreign policy, along with macroeconomics and taxation, are all left in the hands of the grown-ups down south.

FALLING INTO THE FUTURE

As the Scottish capital, Edinburgh is at the heart of the devolution experiment, and there's a two-way exchange of ideas and people between the rest of the country and the capital. But the years since 1999 have seen the city stumble rather than stride across the obstacle-course of adjustment to capital city status. Just as Scotland is learning that the white heat of devolution excitement must give way to smoulderingly steady progress, so is Edinburgh.

Neither the adjustment of the capital nor the country has been eased by the speed with which the devolved administration appears to have got through First Ministers. In just two electoral terms, the country has had three Labour chiefs. Donald Dewar, the long-time driving force of the devolution project, died just fifteen months after the opening of the parliament; his successor, Henry McLeish, shamefacedly resigned in 2001 over an expenses scandal, leaving the jocular but wooden figure of Jack McConnell at the helm. He governs in a coalition of Labour and the Liberal Democrats and is opposed by the Scottish Nationalists, Conservatives, Socialists, Greens and a clutch of independents.

The devolution naysayers were always keen to find a stick with which to beat the settlement. They have seized on the low quality of debate in the parliamentary chamber and point to the depressingly adversarial politics that seems to have emerged despite early and optimistic promises to the contrary. But their point of reference is faulty. The electrifying debates of Westminster, the mother of all parliaments, often generate more heat than light and, anyway, the snake oil of consensual, non-adversarial politics was peddled by self-interested purveyors. It may be less exciting, but other regions make more appropriate

comparisons: Québec, for instance. To the believers, the fruits of the parliament are many: culture, healthcare and education have all benefited from Tartan policy solutions. Scotland's elderly are entitled to free long-term healthcare and its students have (thus far) escaped tuition fees – 'top-up' or otherwise.

If nothing else, the new bureaucracies created by the Parliament have been a boon for the Edinburgh economy, with hundreds of millions of pounds of new buildings and well-paid paper-pushing jobs created. With politicians come lobbyists, PR people, journalists and advisors, all contributing to the life of the city. Businesses, too, are flocking to the capital, keen to be close to the seat of power.

The jostle for positions among political aspirants in the Parliament has also thrown open the doors of the New Town dinner parties, where the real political meat was carved up in the old Edinburgh. Edinburgh is still a small place, though, and its famously well networked elite still meet, dine and conspire with a regularity that would be unimaginable in a larger country. This looks set to continue as 2004 saw the opening of the Hallion on Picardy Place, the city's attempt at a private members' club in the Soho House or Groucho mode.

Newly present on the Edinburgh dinner party scene are the Scottish Socialists. Long moribund in the rest of the UK, they have emerged as a credible parliamentary force in left-leaning Scotland. Staffed by feisty attention-hungry parliamentarians, the party has won influence above and beyond its six seats. It even has representation in the traditionally staid Lothians area, which takes in Edinburgh. A particularly memorable piece of political theatre saw Socialist MSP Rosie Kane don jeans to swear allegiance to the Queen, raising her palm dubbed with 'my oath is to the people' in protest.

The success of the Scottish Socialists under their irrepressible leader Tommy Sheridan has as much to do with the mixed first-past-the-post and proportional electoral system as with anything else; the system has also benefited the Green Party, which holds seven seats at time of writing. The Tories have also gained from the system and, according to some observers, are beginning the long and arduous path back from electoral purdah.

MONEY, MONEY, MONEY

Not all of Edinburgh's successes are a result of devolution, though. The city is a financial powerhouse in its own right, third only to Frankfurt and London in Europe. It hosts the Royal Bank of Scotland, a truly global super-bank. RBoS is a major employer in the city and

Book ends

When Yann Martel's *The Life Of Pi* won the Booker Prize in 2002, it proved that it was perfectly possible to win an international audience without being based in London. Edinburgh-based publisher Canongate's ability to tap into the zeitgeist has helped make literature hipper than a box of rare funk 12" singles, reinvigorating publishing in a city whose printing history stretches all the way back to the first edition of the *Encyclopedia Britannica*.

Long before Canongate boss Jamie Byng introduced a youthful readership to The Bible via miniatures of each book with introductory essays by the likes of Nick Cave, he worked as a volunteer at the then ailing independent publishing house. Under the tenure of founders Angus and Stephanie Wolfe Murray, Canongate had built up an impressive back catalogue, having been the first to publish works by the new wave of Glasgow writers, including James Kelman, as well as Alasdair Gray's seminal 1981 post-modern classic, *Lanark*.

By the time Byng arrived, however, Canongate was in decline. So, with a wad of family money in his pocket, the young buck set about refashioning the company with a maverick spirit born of Beat literature. Just as the wave of post-Irvine Welsh writers were being wooed by London publishing houses, Byng teamed up with *Rebel Inc*, Kevin Williamson's punk/Beat inspired litzine, which first helped put Welsh and co on the map. Together, the pair produced *Children Of Albion Rovers*, an anthology of

has been the source of much local wealth. Likewise the Bank of Scotland (merged with Halifax to form HBoS) is based here. If these financial beasts ever decided to quit the city in favour of gold-paved London, it would be a massive blow to local prestige and the economy. A clutch of highly ranked fund management firms have also made Edinburgh home.

With banks come bankers. Well-heeled city slickers are drawn to Edinburgh's tremendously high standard of living. Bored of the tiring commutes in London, they can swap Broadgate for the West End financial district, which is just a couple of city-strides away from the plush New Town.

Publishing is also strong in the city that gave birth to the *Encyclopedia Britannica* in 1771. Canongate Books, once a small, ailing independent publishing house has been revitalised under the management of former work experience boy Jamie Byng and won the 2002 Man Booker Prize with Yann Martel's *The Life Of Pi* (*see above* **Book ends**). It's lucky for Canongate they don't take up much space, or else they might find themselves bought by developers and turned into flats. The property boom that has gone hand in hand with the development of the Parliament has already

been responsible for the enforced closure of the self generated Bongo Club and Out Of The Blue complex of club and studio spaces, both of which have recently moved to new premises. Property prices are such that commentators worry about how Edinburgh is to cope with this prosperity, and what will happen when the property bubble finally inevitably bursts.

Edinburgh is finally getting away from its chocolate box image with plans to pedestrianise Princes Street, introduce road tolls and eventually re-establish a tram service. In a recent study, tourists who hadn't been to the city were asked where they would compare it to: most named places like Bath and York, two pretty cathedral towns. But after having visited Edinburgh, most said they would compare it to Barcelona, Europe's unchallenged centre of the hedonistic culture consumer.

Whether the 21st century reaches beyond the city boundaries, however, is another matter. Away from the gleaming counting houses of the West End and the hazy drinking houses of the Old Town, Edinburgh remains a tale of two cities. As old working-class areas such as the Cowgate morph into late-night playgrounds for international pleasure seekers, so the housing estates on the outskirts of the city have become novellas by Welsh, *Morvern Callar* author Alan Warner and others.

In tandem, Payback Press was launched to bring the fiction of rap poet Gil Scott Heron and new writers to the wider marketplace, while other ventures made Canongate the coolest publishing house on the planet. An early run of Kevin Williamson's pro-cannabis polemic, *Drugs And The Party Line*, came bound with hemp paper. Similarly, a deluxe edition of Robert Sabbag's novel of adventures in the drugs trade came complete with a customised credit card and a (fake) $100 bill.

Canongate has since divorced itself from *Rebel Inc*, but the rakish approach remains. Byng teamed up with *Mojo* magazine to publish a series of music biographies and, from the *Rebel Inc* years, kept hold of brilliant Edinburgh-based novelist Laura Hird, whose dry, streetwise vernacular is one of the most refreshing voices for years.

More recently, Canongate has published novels by convicted murderer Hugh Collins and situationist prankster Stuart Home, as well as the memoirs of colourful ex-footballer Frank McAvennie. Having ventured into deals with fellow travellers in New York, rumours abound that Canongate are about to jump ship to – eek! – London. While Byng denies such a move, he's also gone on record as saying, 'It's not where you publish that matters, it's how.'

increasingly marginalised ghettoes for the culturally and economically disenfranchised. The sticking-plaster of social inclusion policies, however worthily intentioned, has come too late for some: Edinburgh is host to pockets of grinding poverty. Over a decade since Irvine Welsh chronicled the lives of the city's heroin junkies in his best-selling *Trainspotting* (*see p127* **EdinBurgher Irvine Welsh**), the city is still struggling to kick a major drug problem. The number of drug addicts injecting heroin in the capital has more than doubled over five years, raising fears of a new wave of HIV and Aids. On a less alarming note, January 2004 saw the opening of Scotland's first cannabis café, Purple Haze, on Dalmeny Street in Leith. It may not last long though, vigilant police officers have already raided it.

WHERE IS EVERYBODY?

While Scotland in general, and Edinburgh in particular, suffers from a happy surfeit of tourists (about 4.8 million a year), it has real trouble hanging on to its own. In common with the rest of Europe, Scotland seems set on demographic suicide, its population down to just over 5 million at the last count. The problem is so serious that the Executive (as the government at Holyrood is known) has launched a series of drives to boost population. One newspaper urged its readers to have more sex. The message has to be carefully targeted, though: Scotland is home to the highest rate of teenage pregnancy in Western Europe. Immigration is contentious in the rest of the UK, and asylum seekers are the least favourite group of much of the press, but Scotland is making an effort to attract immigrants with plans for favourable visa conditions.

Elsewhere, despite enlightenment amongst the majority, a little-Scotlander mentality lingers among a mindless few. For all Scotland's official emphasis on cultural diversity, where derogatory remarks about other ethnic minorities are officially frowned upon, in some circles anti-English jokes are considered *de rigueur*.

Riven as it is with cultural insecurity which, given its history is perfectly understandable, the trick for Scotland and Edinburgh now is to get over itself and join the 21st century. A culturally mature nation that's big enough to embrace other influences as well as recognise its own strengths and shortcomings, should start to emerge. It's advisable, however, not to hold your breath just yet.

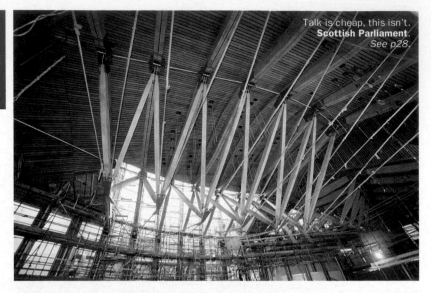

Talk is cheap, this isn't.
Scottish Parliament.
See p28.

Architecture

Order and disorder.

Often described as the 'Athens of the North' for its magnificent setting, grand architecture and history of intellectual and artistic endeavour, Edinburgh is justifiably classed as one of Europe's finest cities. A 'dream of a great genius', wrote one 1820s visitor, while Mary Shelley had the narrator of *Frankenstein* comment on 'the beauty and regularity of the New Town of Edinburgh, its romantic castle and its environs, the most delightful in the world…' For the visitor interested in architecture, Edinburgh's array of great buildings – from the twelfth century to the twentieth – is endlessly rewarding.

Topographically, the city has been dealt a spectacular hand. The Pentland Hills lie to the south and a coastal plain stretches north and east to the Firth of Forth, while Arthur's Seat and Castle Rock, along with Calton Hill and the Salisbury Crags, lend geographical drama to the capital. This setting has helped shape a city of two distinct characters. The architectural chaos of the Old Town looks across to the regularity of the New Town, a triumph of classical formality played out in a gridiron of

well-disciplined streets. In 1995, UNESCO designated the Old Town and New Town a World Heritage Site, an honour that underlines this city's knack for seducing the visitor.

PREHISTORIC TO MEDIEVAL

Bronze Age settlers first colonised the natural citadel of Castle Rock around 900 BC. Under the ambitious rule of the House of Canmore, Castle Rock emerged as a fortified stronghold (today's Edinburgh Castle). St Margaret's Chapel (c1120), with its chevron-decorated chancel arch, is the earliest architectural survivor.

In 1125AD, the expanding settlement was declared a royal burgh and, in 1128, **Holyrood Abbey** (*see p7*) was founded. Linear development gradually linked Holyrood to the Castle Rock, defining the route of today's Royal Mile. Of the handful of medieval stone structures, **St Giles** (today's High Kirk of St Giles on the Royal Mile) dates from the 12th century (*see p77*), but only fragments of the original building remain. It was extensively remodelled in the late 14th century, when Gothic transepts and chapels were added.

SCOTTISH RENAISSANCE

As its national stature grew during the reign of James III (1460-88), Edinburgh witnessed a surge in confidence and building activity. Holyrood Abbey became a royal residence and was expanded, leading to grand additions to the **Palace of Holyroodhouse** (*see p84*) and **Edinburgh Castle** (*see p70*) which was augmented by Crown Square and its baronial Great Hall, topped with a hammerbeam roof.

Money was pumped into churches, most notably the now-demolished Trinity College Church, which housed a magnificent altarpiece by Hugo van der Goes, now on display in the National Gallery of Scotland (*see p93*). Similar grand gestures resulted in a crown steeple being added to the central tower of St Giles around 1500; it became a template for the numerous crown steeples to be found on churches across Scotland.

THE RISE OF THE TENEMENT

As the population of the city increased more housing was required, but the rocky and uneven terrain of the Old Town, combined with the ancient 'feu' system of land tenure (which granted leases in perpetuity) made horizontal development problematic. Thus expansion was forced upwards, leading to the birth of the tenement; dwellings stacked in storeys, linked by a common stairwell.

Lanes, known locally as wynds and closes, developed rib-like from the spine of the Royal Mile. Existing houses had extra storeys tacked on to them, often haphazardly, in addition to jutting windows and a confusion of roof levels. **John Knox's House** (c1490) is one of the few remaining examples (*see p79*), but it's a relatively restrained one – some timber-framed structures protruded as far as seven feet (two metres) into the street. Building regulations, however, reined in the property speculators, stipulating, from the 1620s onwards, tile or slate roofs and, in 1674, stone façades as fire precautions. Daringly exploiting the ridge of the Old Town, tenements frequently bridged different levels down the side of the slope, making them some of the tallest domestic buildings in Europe, on the side away from the road at least. Standing cheek-by-jowl along the Royal Mile, the sandstone or harling (a mix of small stones and lime plaster) tenements had more in common with the architecture of northern Europe than that of England. The five-storey **Gladstone's Land** (c1620-30; *see p75*) retains the once-commonplace street arcade and an oak-panelled interior. With the upper Royal Mile awash with merchants, its lower reaches became the choice location of the nobility, their mansions flanking the approach to the Palace of Holyroodhouse. **Moray House** (c1628), with its pyramid-topped gate-piers, and the vast **Queensberry House** (c1634), currently redundant but to be converted into offices for the new Scottish Parliament, are the grandest of the buildings that survive.

The Palace itself was rebuilt in the 1670s in a triumphant blend of Scottish and European influences, to create a thick-set façade with turreted towers fronting an inner courtyard lined with classical arcades. New wealth brought along in its well-heeled wake a new **Parliament House** (*see p76*). The building was given a classical overhaul in the early 19th century. Elsewhere the city flaunted its internationalism, exemplified by its easy if rather tardy handling of the Renaissance 'palace' style in the grandly ornamented **George Heriot's School** (1628; *see p104* **Schools rule**), south of the Royal Mile. Along the Royal Mile itself churches were being built, namely John Mylne's handsome **Tron Kirk** (1663, today the Old Town Information Centre, *see p79*) and the aristocratic and Dutch-looking **Canongate Kirk** (1688; *see p83*), with its delicate, curving gables.

Top five Architectural disasters

St James Centre

A beautiful Georgian square was bulldozed to make way for this arrogantly brutal shopping precinct.

Radisson SAS Hotel

A modern hotel lamely masquerading as an original Old Town building. Why bother?

Sheraton Grand Hotel

Is it possible to build a blander building?

Harvey Nichols

Unimaginative filler architecture that adds nothing to one of the key sites for new building in central Edinburgh.

Waverley Shopping Centre

Edinburgh's planners seem to think Princes Street is the Champs-Elysées. It isn't; in fact, this depressing shopping mall is one of the worst offenders.

TIME FOR A MAKEOVER

The 1707 Act of Union with England provoked an identity crisis for Edinburgh, and some dubbed the city 'a widowed metropolis'. But Edinburgh soon came to see architecture as an essential way of asserting the city's character.

The collapse in 1751 of a Royal Mile tenement highlighted the old-fashioned and run-down state of the Old Town and the need for 'modern' living quarters. In 1752 the city's Lord Provost, George Drummond, drew up proposals to expand Edinburgh, creating the grandiose Exchange (now the City Chambers) on the

Royal Mile and, in 1765, the North Bridge. The bridge, which was the first to cross Nor' Loch, gave easy access towards the port of Leith and, importantly, to a swathe of redundant land to the north of the Old Town. This was to become the site of the 'new towns', collectively known as today's New Town (*see p91* **The making of the New Town**).

Conceived as Edinburgh's 'civilised' face, the first New Town, designed in 1766 by James Craig, was built to a regimented layout. Influenced by the growing Europe-wide fascination with classical civilisation,

What price democracy?

£420 million and rising. That's the price of democracy, Scotland style, as voters contemplate the cost of the soon-to-be-opened Scottish parliament building. The construction of Scotland's first parliament for 300 years has been dogged by controversy and allegations of gross incompetence. Its troubled construction wasn't helped by the deaths of Catalan architect Enric Miralles and devolution driving-force Donald Dewar within months of each other, when work had barely started on the site.

If you've decided you're going to have a devolved administration, then you need a parliament building to house it. In 1997, government spokesmen conjured up the suspiciously low figure of £40 million as the cost of creating such an iconic structure. But to anyone in the know, that's the kind of money you'd pay for a medium-sized office block, not for one of the most significant buildings ever to be erected in Scotland's capital. By 2004, the £420 million mark was reached and there is every possibility that the final bill will exceed this substantially. Nevertheless, the new building promises to be one of the most extraordinary public buildings ever created in Scotland, and in the long-term the money may have been worth it. Its fan-like windows and the sinuous organic forms of the roof mark this out as a building that loudly proclaims its unique architectural identity. It can, at least, never be accused of being bland. In Edinburgh, with its tendency to celebrate the past rather than the present, that surely has to be welcomed wholeheartedly. But the cost to the reputation of Scotland's new political identity may be higher still, and if the new building is in any sense a national metaphor, it is already a seriously compromised one.

The story of the parliament's construction is one of Shakespearean intrigue and Byzantine complexity. Miralles, although apparently not strictly eligible according to the guidelines, won an opaquely organised 'competition' in 1998 to design the great new building and set up a partnership with the Edinburgh-based firm RMJM. At that stage, Miralles' designs were in a state of considerable flux and were largely inspired by some upturned boats he apparently spotted on the coastline of Northumberland – in England. But the fact that an international architect had been chosen at least showed that there was an untypical willingness to engage with something new. When he died, it was left to his local partners to interpret his visions.

Public reaction to the initial designs was predictable. A fair proportion of the Scottish media and the public decided the whole business was fanciful, and the building costs only added fuel to their fire. In summer 1999, the cost was set at £109 million.

But members of parliament demanded more space in their new building, which had knock-on effects on the costing and these necessitated further revisions to Miralles' design. Add in building industry inflation and an alleged willingness to allow contractors to revise estimates upwards without penalty and, not surprisingly, the costs rose quite spectacularly: by 2000 £200 million was being mentioned. The project suffered two major setbacks later that year when Miralles and First Minister Donald Dewar died. By the end of 2001 estimates stood at £275 million and, in spring 2002, they punched through the £300 million mark, with completion not planned until 2003. At time of writing, the parliament is set to open at the end of 2004, two years late and many millions over budget.

Edinburgh's **Old Town** in all its grey granite glory. *See p27.*

Edinburgh's new architecture adopted proportion and grandeur as its hallmarks. The city has the largest area of neo-classical domestic architecture in the world.

A leading practitioner, Robert Adam, designed **Charlotte Square** (from 1792), a residential enclave acting as a grand full stop to the west end of George Street. **Register House** (c1788; *see p92*), on the axis of North Bridge, is another example of Adam's well-mannered classicism. Its cupolas and pedimented portico are a gracious retort to the haphazard gables of the Old Town.

CLASSICAL REINVENTION

By the early 1800s, architecture had taken on an increasingly crucial role in expressing the city's newly cultivated identity. As early as 1762, it was dubbed the 'Athens of the North'. The city's topography made the analogy plausible and, besides, Edinburgh liked the idea of being an intellectual 'Athenian' metropolis compared to the imperial 'Roman' capital, London.

As the Scottish Enlightenment held sway, the architect William Playfair provided a stone and mortar representation of Calton Hill's status as Edinburgh's 'Acropolis'. His **City Observatory** (1818; *see p105*), a cruciform mini-temple capped by a dome, stands next to his Parthenon-inspired **National Monument** (*see p104*). Begun in 1826 to commemorate the Napoleonic Wars, its 12 huge columns, set on a vast stepped plinth, were an attempt to provide

the classical illusion to end all classical illusions. But it remained unfinished due to a funding crisis – earning it the nickname 'Edinburgh's Disgrace'. Later it formed a visual link to Thomas Hamilton's **Royal High School** (1825; *see p103*), on the lower slopes of Calton Hill. Described as the 'noblest monument of the Scottish Greek revival', the structure was neo-classicism at its most authoritative, with a central 'temple' flanked by grand pavilions.

On the Mound, meanwhile, the prolific Playfair produced further classical expression in the form of the **Royal Scottish Academy** (1823, *see p93*) and the **National Gallery of Scotland** (1850, *see p93*), a monumental, temple-inspired duo parading an army of columns and classical trimmings.

SCOTTISH BARONIAL – TRIUMPH OF THE FICTIONAL

In 1822, George IV visited Edinburgh dressed in pink stockings and a kilt. His sartorial advisor was Sir Walter Scott, author and campaigner for the 'tartanisation' of Scotland. Scott's campaign bore fruit in brick and stone when the 1827 Improvement Act advised that new buildings and those in need of a facelift should adopt the 'Old Scot' style. Turrets, crenellations and crows' feet elbowed their way past Doric columns and back into the city's architecture; **Cockburn Street**, the first vehicular link between the Royal Mile and what is today Waverley Station, is a determined example.

How the mighty have fallen. The **Scotsman**'s new offices. See p31.

Elsewhere, new public buildings masqueraded as rural piles airlifted from the Scottish Highlands. The **Royal Infirmary** (1870; see p86), to the south of the Royal Mile, sports a central clock-tower and an array of turrets. **Fettes College** (1865-70, see p104 **Schools rule**), north of the New Town, is an exuberant intermarriage of Highland baronial seat and French chateau, and inspiration of Hogwarts School of Witchcraft and Wizardry.

This growing adventurousness soon gave way to architectural promiscuity. The city's well-off institutions showed confident but sometimes florid excess, with a pick-and-mix approach to building style. The headquarters of the **Bank of Scotland** (see p94), grandly posed on the precipice of the Mound, was given a neo-Baroque makeover; the British Linen Bank (now a Bank of Scotland branch) on St Andrew's Square opted for the Renaissance palazzo look, its Corinthian columns topped by six colossal statues.

The Gothic revival also made its mark. The master of the decorated pinnacle and soaring spire, Augustus Pugin, designed the Tolbooth Church (1844) below Castle Esplanade. Today it is the **Hub** (see p72), a café and ticket centre run by the Edinburgh International Festival. But the finest line in romantic Gothic came in George Meikle Kemp's **Scott Monument** (1840; see p93) on Princes Street, a fitting memorial to the man who reinvented Scotland's medieval past.

PRETTY VACANT

1930s modernism made little impression on Edinburgh, save in the authoritarian government edifice **St Andrew's House** (1939; see p102), on the lower reaches of Calton Hill. Designed by Thomas Tait, it is a true architectural heavyweight, with an imposing, symmetrical façade.

By the inter-war years, residents were being encouraged to decamp to a series of council-built satellite townships on the periphery of the city, first among them the Craigmillar Estate. This social engineering, achieved through town planning, was a crude mirror of the earlier and socially exclusive New Town.

In 1949, the Abercrombie Plan saw slum tenements demolished, along with the grander George Square, to create space for a new university campus. The sacrifice of George Square in particular, its buildings replaced by unpopular 1960s-style architecture, sent a rallying call to the preservation troops. Much of the Old Town was saved as a result. But other parts of the city instead suffered some explosions of 1960s Brutalism, as seen in the ugly, blocky St James Centre just off Princes Street. The subsequent backlash sent the city planners retreating into cautious mode, inviting accusations of architectural timidity. These complaints reached their height in 1989 when a prime redundant site on the Royal Mile was occupied by the then Scandic Crown Hotel (now the Radisson SAS Hotel; see p47), constructed in a Disneyfied Old Town-imitation style (*see p27* **Architectural disasters**). A flirtation with late 20th-century architecture is shown in the **Exchange**, the city's new financial quarter to the west side of Lothian Road. Terry Farrell's Edinburgh International Conference Centre (1995) on Morrison Street forms the nucleus, with big-name companies moving in to inhabit the surrounding office blocks. Edinburgh is the fourth-largest financial centre in Europe, thanks to the sterling efforts of actuaries and fund managers among others – not species often renowned for their adventurous artistic spirit. Indeed, the central parabolic sweep of the Scottish Widows building (1998) on Morrison Street, while hardly the stuff of no-holds-barred invention, offers the only credible design gesture in the whole Exchange precinct.

THE MODERN AGE

The downside to Edinburgh's fight to save itself from the ravages of town planners was the creation of a visual culture antagonistic towards anything which had the taint of the contemporary: the number of major buildings dating from the last two decades is small. But a new generation of Scottish architects is attempting to drag the burghers of Edinburgh kicking and screaming into the 21st century.

One of the key sites has been on and around Holyrood Road, near the site of the new Parliament. Opposite the Parliament site Michael Hopkins' **Our Dynamic Earth** (*see p84*), a vast tent-like structure that opened in 1999. And in the closes and hidden streets between Holyrood Road and the Royal Mile there are a couple of seriously contemporary interventions. The **Scottish Poetry Library** in Crichton's Close was designed by Malcolm Fraser Architects and shortlisted for the Channel 4 Building of the Year Award in 2000. But the boldest flourish so far is the **Tun** in Holyrood Road (2002), a mix of offices and a café-bar in a former brewery building. This design by Allan Murray Architects stands out as a funkily projecting glass challenge to the desperate blandness of the new *Scotsman* newspaper offices over the way.

Leith has also seen major changes, with the arrival of the **Ocean Terminal** shopping centre (2001, *see p177*) near the Scottish Executive. Vast amounts of money are being spent on the redevelopment of the whole of the seafront of Edinburgh from Leith to Granton, and this promises to be one of the most exciting contemporary developments in the city.

Perhaps the most conspicuous attempt by Edinburgh to engage with the contemporary is the **Museum of Scotland** (*see p88*). Situated next to the grand Victorian edifice of

the Royal Museum of Scotland on the fringes of the Old Town, it was designed by architects Benson and Forsyth and opened in 1998. It attempts to flatter its location with references to traditional Scottish forms and the great curve of the Half Moon Battery of Edinburgh Castle. But it has been an effective stalking horse for advancing the cause of modern building design. Resolutely contemporary architecture in key locations within Edinburgh city centre is now something the city fathers and its conservative citizenry are far more likely to accept.

But the truth is that new buildings of international significance are thin on the ground and the jury is still out on the late Enric Miralles' **Parliament** building (*see p28* **What price democracy?**). With little private or corporate taste for the new, funky or just plain stupid, younger architects with more adventurous aspirations have been kept afloat by the odd Lottery-funded public commission. Many of the best new buildings are out of the town centre, such as Gareth Hoskins' stylish new Visitor Centre at Saughton Jail on the western outskirts and Zoo Architects' arts centre at Wester Hailes to the north.

In the city centre, you have to look closely to spot any oasis of newness. Richard Murphy's slick **Oloroso** bar and restaurant (*see p139*), with magnificent views to the Old Town and across to Fife, is perched on the top storey of an unremarkable block at the corner of George Street and Castle Street. In Hart Street near the top of Leith Walk stands **Barlass House**, a rare New Town example of a punchy new domestic property, designed by up-and-coming architects Zone. And if you wander through the Old Town towards Tollcross you'll catch Andrew Doolan's cleverly understated but colourful revamp of a '30s department store as the **Point Conference Centre**.

From the Old Town to Leith, luxury residential developments continue to spring up, aimed mainly at young professionals working in the city's booming financial and commercial sectors. The **Old Royal Infirmary** on Lauriston Place (*see p86*), for centuries the city's main hospital, is currently being converted into hundreds of luxury apartments, and the fashion for loft-style living has been exploited by the conversion of various historic warehouses near the waterfront at Leith.

In the city centre, however, lost opportunities are numerous and sadly often very conspicuous but the recent fire in the Old Town's Cowgate will provide an exceptional opportunity to introduce new architecture into a key site in the heart of Edinburgh (*see p73* **Burning down the town**). Whether the city and its architects are up to the challenge remains to be seen.

Festival Edinburgh

Join in the party at the world's biggest knees-up.

Every August, great chunks of the performing, visual and literary art worlds decamp to a city on the edge of Europe with unreliable weather and too many hills. They parade their artistic visions, from multi-million pound stagings in grand theatres to shows in church halls, and the world watches. As with prison sentences for the over active criminal, seven main separate festivals run concurrently to embrace the broadest of artistic spectrums. Squeezed together in an uncharacteristic display of auld reekie intimacy, they make up the biggest arts festival on the planet.

The Royal Mile, the cobbled street running through Edinburgh's Old Town, is a riot: street performers juggle, walk high wires and ride unicycles, and over-excited comedians press flyers into your hand for the ubiquitous 'best show of the festival'. It's a spectacle more tight-lipped residents don't always appreciate. Dodging the dawn till dusk bustle, you can sometimes see their point. Yet a city known

more for its uptight Presbyterian reserve than its propensity for fun would be a lot duller without the festivals. Edinburgh's population doubles and there's plenty of mileage in people-watching: some rare and exotic creatures flock towards this parade of free artistic expression and its unique vibe.

Many festival-goers will herd towards the bigger venues housing well-known TV faces. It's far more in the spirit of things, however, to take a chance on the unknown. There are some hidden gems out there, and this is the one time of year where press reviews really count. Careers are born (and sink) here, so keep an eye out for four- and five-star reviews and try to catch these shows above all. Some smaller productions can be awful – it's not unheard of to be the solitary audience member – but take a chance on the unknown and you might see something or someone that goes on to be really big. For some more information on getting started, *see p36.*

In Context

THE MAGNIFICENT SEVEN

Confusingly, the 'festival' is not one festival but many. In 1947, the **Edinburgh International Festival** (EIF) began with the ambition of providing Europe and the world with a new centre for the very best in drama, music and the visual arts. It was intended to unite the continent's culture while the great festivals of Salzburg and Munich found their feet again in the aftermath of World War II.

EIF events are programmed by the festival's director, currently the recently knighted Sir Brian McMaster. McMaster has a sizeable pot of money at his disposal – the whole festival had a performance budget of £5.3m in 2003. He has brought the likes of composer Pierre Boulez and theatre directors Peter Stein and Ivo Van Hove to Edinburgh in past years. Audiences are often caricatured as the great and good of Edinburgh society, but McMaster has worked hard to broaden access to the festival, with outreach work and discounted ticket schemes for the young. Its programme is published at the beginning of April.

There wasn't a welcoming space in the first EIF programme for everyone. Eight companies held unofficial performances on the fringes of the festival, and the anarchic **Fringe** was born. From modest beginnings it has grown to dwarf the other festivals, with 298 venues playing host to 1,541 shows in 2003. Comedy and

theatre are the Fringe's mainstays, but dance, music, and, to a lesser degree, art are all featured in the programme prominently too.

In 1998, the Fringe broke away further from the International Festival and now starts a week earlier. It differs from the other festivals in that nobody decides what's on: anyone can put on a show provided they can hire a venue, find accommodation and live on air for a month. Practically all pay £300-odd to the Festival Fringe Society and get listed in the Fringe guide, the comprehensive 200-page brochure that comes out in mid-June.

The Fringe attracts a bewildering, heady array of aspiring young talent, consummate crowd pleasers, once-in-a-lifetime amateurs and old pros looking for a career boost. Despite the sheen of amateurism, it has become a well-oiled machine that produces regular artistic revelations. Some of the big venues are permanent, but the majority are used for something else during the rest of the year. In recent times the triumvirate of the Pleasance, the Gilded Balloon and the Assembly Rooms has been challenged by exciting new spaces like the Underbelly and C Venues. However it doesn't end there – in 2003, intrepid punters could see shows in cars, a lift, or even, for those with high a olfactory tolerance, a public toilet.

The first incarnation of the **Edinburgh International Film Festival** also occurred in

Top five ▶ Scandalous moments

Whether challenging society's boundaries or shamelessly aiming for free publicity, shows at the festival like to cause a stir.

1. Jesus is gay

In the 1999 play, *Corpus Christi,* Terence McNally pursued that most tired of publicity tactics: blasphemy. Surprisingly some religious leaders and councillors still fell for the sucker punch but then the desire for headlines is not limited to playwrights.

2. Jim Rose's nose

Purveyor of wonderfully distasteful freak show comedy, Jim Rose appeared on a festival radio show in 1993 and proceeded to bash a nail up his nose. He was admitted to hospital but it turned out to be a rather clever stunt – not his last that year.

3. Five-star performance

Journalists used to phone in reviews to meet deadlines, and comedian Malcolm Hardee

found out what number to call. Cue a gushing review of his show in the next day's *Scotsman* and bumper audiences – especially when the stunt was exposed.

4. Osama likes it not

'Comedy terrorist' Aaron Barschak came up with a cunning publicity stunt in 2003 – he invaded Prince William's 21st birthday party at Windsor Castle dressed in a ballgown and sporting a pubic wig. His show bombed but the notoriety lived on.

5. Futz tuts

In prim 1967, Rochelle Owens caused a stir with a play about Farmer Futz and his love affair with a pig. Under the headline 'Filth on the Fringe', the Scottish *Daily Express*'s critic described it as 'the most shocking play I have ever seen' – achieving such a notice may well be the summit of aspiration for some Fringe performers.

1947, the Edinburgh Film Guild being somewhat piqued that the International Festival had omitted film from its remit. It has since become an important industry jamboree as well as a public event: successful Brit flicks *Morvern Callar* and *Young Adam* received their world premières in Edinburgh in 2002 and 2003 respectively.

In 1950, the armed forces joined in the fun with the **Edinburgh Military Tattoo**, a soldiers' parade of music, dance and athleticism held outside on the Castle Esplanade. It is the festival's most popular single event, selling 200,000 tickets each year, and home to the world's longest queue. Plans are mooted to move the Tattoo to a new arena in Princes Street Gardens, built on the site of the dilapidated Ross Bandstand.

As the festival grew, others were attracted to the delights of August. The **Edinburgh Jazz and Blues Festival**, which takes place a week before the Fringe festival, began in 1979 and is the longest-running jazz festival in the UK. The intellectual hub of the festival is the **Edinburgh International Book Festival**, established in 1983, and now the largest book festival in the world.

Every single one of the festivals reported record-breaking ticket sales in 2003 as punters paid up, perused performances and partied harder than ever. But rising ticket prices and the increasing commercialisation of festival events has led some to argue that the festival's spirit has disappeared. Some say the Fringe is too big and that it should be regulated so that art wins out over light entertainment and entrepreneurs trying out shows for London's West End or television; others suggest that it only serves the moneyed, well-educated metropolitan classes.

In response to the latter, the **Edinburgh People's Festival** was re-established in 2002. It echoes the first People's Festival, which ran from 1951-54 and claimed to be 'by working people for working people'. The new version aims to 'bring the arts to the ignored indigenous communities across the city' by staging performances in the city's deprived areas.

Comedy

The Fringe is the home for comedy at the festival, and the programme is vast: 355 shows were listed in 2003. The largest comedy festival in the world is also the most gruelling for performers: where other comedy festivals may last for no more than a week and consist of showcases where acts have to make you laugh for only 20 minutes, Edinburgh demands more. Comedians commonly get on stage six days out

of seven for three weeks, and some perform on their own for an hour – an expectation that stretches the best joke-tellers and highlights the deficiencies in others. The toughest test for the live comedian is the **Gilded Balloon's Late and Live** show, a bear pit of a comedy club that starts at 1am every night. It welcomes boozed-up hecklers and their attempts to waylay the four performers, who each have half an hour to impress. Expect no script.

Some of the greatest comic talents have got their first breaks and moved on to world renown over the history of the festival. Peter Cook, Dudley Moore, Eric Idle, Michael Palin, Terry Jones, Rowan Atkinson, Stephen Fry, Emma Thompson, Eddie Izzard, Steve Coogan, Greg Proops, Scott Capurro and Rich Hall all kick-started their careers in Edinburgh.

The main venues for comedy are the **Assembly Rooms**, the **Pleasance**, the **Gilded Balloon** and the **Underbelly**, who produce their own brochures in addition to the Bible-like Fringe guide (available from the Festival Fringe Society, *see p41*). Don't limit yourself, though – numerous acts appear at **C Venues** and a multitude of smaller venues. The intimate **Stand** is one of only two permanent comedy clubs in Edinburgh (*see p203*).

Theatre & Dance

Theatre is a deeper, more enduring art form than comedy, and is served by both the International Festival and the Fringe. At the International Festival the programme is small, grand and expensively staged. Recently, Shakespeare, modern Scottish playwrights and drama from around the world have formed the core, treating viewers to the spectacle of naked figures writhing in mud, *Macbeth* in Dutch, and flesh-eating in David Greig's *San Diego*.

'Shock and controversy are touchstones – the more attention a show receives, the more tickets it sells.'

Efforts in recent years have increased attendance amongst the young and less well-off through discounted ticket schemes, and productions have become more challenging, with acclaimed international acts making their UK debut at the EIF. However, you won't see brand-new acts breaking through at the International Festival – the highest highs and lowest lows come from the Fringe.

Everybody from posh private school ensembles to well-known companies from

Hands up if you love your mummy.
Canadian Opera Company's *Oedipus Rex*.

Some Fringe venues are
a little cramped. *See p33.*

abroad come to the party. As with comedy, there is no set format: it can be classic, modern, funny, silent, physical or surreal. Shock and controversy are touchstones – the more attention a show receives, the more tickets it sells. This may not be related to quality.

Among the venues, Scotland's new-writing theatre the **Traverse** (*see p238*) prides itself on staging cutting-edge drama, and is perhaps the beating heart of Fringe theatre. *Gagarin Way, The People Next Door* and *Outlying Islands* all started at the Traverse, and its bar is the hangout for many a luvvie, especially the don't-you-know-who-I-am crowd.

Dance bridges the gap between theatre and music, and is well represented at both the International and Fringe festivals. It is at the edgier end of proceedings at the International Festival – sometimes veering towards art installation and taking in world dance – but there is usually some classical ballet too. Again, the Fringe is where dance can express itself freely, spanning belly dancing, physical theatre and all points between.

Music

Rock, indie, dance, opera, jazz, musicals, cabaret, classical and world music are all represented at the festival, and there is a large programme of traditional Scottish and Celtic music too. Edinburgh is hoping to benefit from an 'MTV bounce' after the awards staged in Leith (*see p122* **Star for a night**), and the expectation is that the amount of music at the Fringe will increase. Young, fashionable, thrusting types are represented by **T on the Fringe** – Interpol, the Super Furry Animals and Grandaddy all sold out in 2003. The success of T on the Fringe has meant that other Fringe music festivals – Planet Pop, Flux Festival and Biorhythm – are no longer running. However, the **Underbelly** is looking to expand its music programme – featuring rock, indie, beats and funkiness – in its tie-up with local radio station Forth One. Free festival newspaper *Fest* (*see p40*) is also planning an exciting mini-festival of alternative music.

Festival FAQ

How much are tickets?
Free to £33 (for operas at the International Festival). On average, £8.

How quickly do things sell out?
Depends. If any of the following diddle your skittle, join the queue asap:
- The Tattoo (*see p41*).
- The firework concert at the end of the Festival (*see p38*).
- Anything involving a celebrity.
- All big films at the Film Festival and big names at the Book Festival (for both *see p41*).
- International Festival operas (*see p41*).

How far ahead do you need to book?
For the above, as soon as the programmes are announced (*see p38*). Otherwise, if you arrive towards the beginning of August, you should be okay buying tickets on the day. Later on, you'd be wise to book at least a couple of days in advance.

When is the best week to come to the Festival?
The third week in August, when all the key festivals are in full swing, tends to be the busiest and buzziest.

Can you book online?
Yes. *See p41.*

How early do you need to book accommodation?
If you're planning on staying somewhere nice in the centre of town, then definitely before August. The earlier the better.

Is it possible to stay out of town and commute?
Yes, but you'll miss out on the festival vibe and waste precious time and money on the journeys into town. Not recommended.

Should you book restaurants ahead?
Only if you're planning to go somewhere really special and want a table at 8pm. If you're not fussy, you'll always find a table somewhere.

What's the best way to get around town during the Festival?
Walk. Edinburgh is a compact city. Just bear in mind that the venues are quite spread out and it could take you half an hour to get from one to the next if you get caught up in a crowd on the way. The bus services aren't bad, but congestion on main thoroughfares can absorb precious show-seeing time. Take a velo taxi if you're feeling decadent.

The rest of the Fringe programme is a wide-ranging mix of everything. The International Festival's programme is a lot more focused, concentrating on classical music and half a dozen operas, Wagner being a fixture in recent years. The ever-popular **Fireworks Concert** in Princes Street Gardens closes the International Festival with suitable pomp and circumstance. In the week leading up to the Tattoo, the Castle Esplanade arena has seen concerts from the likes of Rod Stewart, Paul Simon, Tom Jones and Status Quo.

Not to be found in any festival programme, the clubs and music venues that do business all year round take advantage of the influx of hedonists and book big-name DJs for sessions that often last until 5am, when you can emerge blinking into the dawn. Promoters try to attract the Festival crowd, but in the transitory world of dance music only the most mainstream can book DJs far enough ahead to get into the Fringe brochure. Check out the flyers in bars for an idea of what is going on, *see p226*.

The **Edinburgh Jazz and Blues Festival** has seen performances from Dionne Warwick, Wynton Marsalis, Van Morrison and the nascent Jamie Cullum recently. The emphasis of the festival is trad jazz and R&B fused with dance, hip hop, drum 'n' bass, funk and reggae. Occurring a week before the Fringe descends on Edinburgh, it's a relaxed way to warm up.

Film

The **Edinburgh International Film Festival** started life as a gala for documentaries, but now presents a mix of feature films, world cinema, short films, animation, retrospective and documentary. John Huston, the late actor and director most famous for *The African Queen*, described it in 1972 as 'the only film festival worth a damn', and it's an important date in the cinema calendar. The festival has been overtaken in prominence by Cannes and Sundance but there remains a strong industry presence – spot the delegates with their laminated passes, glasses of white wine and predilection for black clothes.

The Film Festival is sometimes referred to as a 'hoover festival', picking up the best movies from the previous twelve months' international festivals and giving them their UK premières, alongside some world and European premières. There is a strong hand guiding the selections – the management of the festival choose a Directors' Showcase each year, and the 'Rosebud' section for first- and second-time directors has assumed great importance since it was introduced in 1995. Artistic principles are to the fore, the festival aiming 'to surprise and

challenge with a bold, independent, eclectic and inclusive programme'. Short films and animations are becoming increasingly prominent, and every year the *List* Surprise Movie plays to an unprepared audience. The last three have been *The Bourne Identity, Planet of the Apes* and *Spirited Away*, suggesting that a capricious hand leads the surprise selection.

Adventurous cinema-goers and earnest film buffs can expect to see the future hits of intelligent cinema up to a year before they take their bow at the box office, as well as a few that will vanish without trace. *Belleville Rendez-vous, Crimson Gold, Mystic River* and *Swimming Pool* are examples of recent successes. Unfortunately few films get more than two public screenings, although this is mitigated by the fact that punters can sometimes chat with the director or actors involved after the showing.

Books

Pitching its well-appointed marquees on Robert Adam-designed Charlotte Square in the West End, the **Edinburgh International Book Festival** is a calm haven set apart from the thronged festival hub in the Old Town. This may appear unusual, given that cars race round the square and two or three thousand people are on site at one time, but it's clear that the tranquility alone attracts a sizeable minority.

You can't call the festival staid though – Mo Mowlam and Germaine Greer both cheekily pontificated on Tony Blair's sex life in 2002, and '80s New York brat pack author Tama Janowitz made her entrance in 2003 in Ali Baba shoes, a Napoleon hat, pantaloons and a coat clearly inspired by Joseph's Amazing Technicolor one. Legendary loudmouth and keen rambler Janet Street-Porter even had the chutzpah to decry Arthur's Seat as 'full of awful people strumming on guitars and American tourists' when she appeared in 2003.

Events include hour-long talks, readings and discussions grouped into broad themes that change each year. The festival is keen to encourage participation: debates are an increasingly prominent part of the programme, as are events for children, who can romp safely in the enclosed gardens.

Most authors make solitary appearances but the stellar – or tenacious – may make several. Big names in recent years include Susan Sontag, Harold Pinter, Doris Lessing, Seamus Heaney, Candace Bushnell – the list goes on. Aspiring writers are encouraged, with writers' workshops and a writers' retreat hidden among the trees. The festival's bars and cafés are open late too, if you like to read with a glass in your hand as the summer sun goes down.

Festival Cavalcade

Dates 8 August 2004; 7 August 2005.

Opening the Edinburgh Festival is a two-hour parade of noise and colour through the centre of Edinburgh. The cast of the Military Tattoo leads the way down Princes Street and is followed by floats bobbing with the casts of plays and shows eager to dazzle spectators into buying a ticket, festival organisations, and the wider Edinburgh community.

Fringe Sunday

Information: www.edfringe.com. **Dates** 15 August 2004; 14 August 2005.

On the second Sunday of the Fringe, the Meadows (*see p115*) plays host to a showcase of the talent performing at the festival: a free sample of the many comedies, shows and plays to demonstrate the enchanting variety that characterises the Fringe. Street performers, displays and stalls add to the mix as 15,000 people turn up and participate in the largest, most vibrant garden party of the summer.

International Festival Fireworks Concert

Information: 473 2003/www.eif.co.uk.

The International Festival's closing concert in Princes Street Gardens is followed by some spectacular explosions lighting up the night sky above the Castle. The concert is ticketed and always sold out, but the fireworks are free and best viewed from North Bridge, Princes Street, or Salisbury Crags. 150,000 revellers watched 100,000 fireworks in 2003.

Edinburgh Mela

Information: 557 1400/www.edinburgh-mela.co.uk. **Dates** 4-5 September 2004; 2005 tbc.

Representing the increasing influence of the Pakistani, Bangladeshi and Indian communities on the capital's life, the Edinburgh Mela is a two-day event celebrating Asian culture in vivid colour. It's set in Pilrig Park to the north of the city centre on the last weekend of the festival, and most events are free. Expect music, dance, arts and crafts, fashion, food, sports, children's activities and a bazaar.

Festival Erotique

Information: 477 3500/www.festivalerotique.co.uk. **Dates** tbc.

The Festival Erotique began in 2003, on the last Friday, Saturday and Sunday of the festival. Fifty exhibitors drew 3,500 people a day to snap up DVDs, sex toys, fetish gear and erotic art from noon to 9pm.

Edinburgh International Games Festival

Information www.eigf.co.uk. **Dates** 8-22 August 2004; 2005 dates tbc.

Embarking on its second year of operation in 2004, the International Games Festival is a two-week public game-playing exhibition held in the Royal Museum of Scotland (*see p88*).

Festival Directory

Make like Darwin: in silly season, only the strongest survive.

This directory aims to help you along every step of the way.

● For how to back a winning show, *see below.*
● For how to book tickets, *see p41.*
● For how to book accommodation, *see p41.*
● For contact details and dates for the individual festivals, *see p41.*
● For our Festival FAQ, *see p36.*
● For other events, *see above.*

How to back a winner

Firstly: don't be scared. Even the festival organisers themselves are probably confused when it comes to making sense of the umpteen programmes. Approach the festivals logically. Military precision isn't absolutely essential, but it certainly helps. You might think of yourself as a fly-by-the-seat-of-your-pants kind of guy or gal, but the festival is no place for lackadaisical cool cats. By all means rock up ticketless and let nature take its inexorable course, but don't come crying to us when the only show you can get into is the Aberystwyth Amateur Dramatics Society production of *Carousel* (mimed, in Welsh).

If you're in town for more than a weekend, however, or the hipness factor of the shows you see means a great deal to you, hang around in the bar after a show to find out the best tips. Word of mouth is by far the most effective form of promotion, and a chance conversation struck up in a pub can send you off to some unexpectedly groovy treats. But however eager a Festival darling you are, remember to take it easy. You're here for enjoyment, it shouldn't become a chore. Also accept the fact that you will make mistakes. No one can back a winner every single time. And there's nothing stopping you walking out.

But never fear: help is at hand in the form of an indispensable website ready to soothe your fevered brow during the festival nightmare. At **www.edinburghfestivals.co.uk** you can access each individual Festival website, as well as the pages for events that occur during the other eleven months of the year (*see p194*). From there, you can scrutinise programmes or order your own copies. When they arrive, make brief notes of the highlights of the different festivals and add those to your wish list. Once the must-have hard copies have arrived in the post, equip yourself with a highlighter pen, the tipple of your choice and peruse them

Visit the festival. Lives depend on it.

thoroughly. At this stage select only the shows that you consider to be completely unmissable. Deliberations on secondary choices can be made once you get to Edinburgh. For information on which tickets get snapped up first, *see p36*.

So, how do you sort out the duff from the diamonds? Well, this is the one time of the year when press coverage really counts, so getting media savvy is a good idea. Ignore the publicity stunts, read the reviews. The *Scotsman*, Scotland's Edinburgh-based daily newspaper, prints a festival supplement every day and is a decent read – although cost-cutting in recent years has lowered the quality of the reviews.

Fest, a free festival newspaper, contains news, reviews, interviews, features, listings, scurrilous gossip and a handy map of all the venues. It comes out every Monday, Wednesday and Friday and prides itself on being irreverent, incisive and fun. Copies can be found in venues, bars, shops and on the Royal Mile. Check out the website at **www.festonline.co.uk** for exclusive online content too. Another pertinent purchase is the *List*, Glasgow and Edinburgh's entertainment and listings magazine, which comes out every Thursday during the festival.

The *Herald*, Scotland's Glasgow-based daily newspaper, is forced east despite itself for the duration of the festival and carries a number of reviews, as do the *Guardian* and the other London-based broadsheets. The *Scotsman* and the *Herald* newspapers award Fringe Firsts and Angel Awards, respectively, to new plays, comedies, concerts and film that have particularly impressed their critics, and the tickets for these become like gold dust.

Hot or Not

The festival is notorious for making and breaking careers. We assess which stars and starlets have shone under the festival spotlight and which losers have been left out in the dark.

1. Gregory Burke

In 1999, *Gagarin Way* arrived as an unsolicited script on the desk of the Traverse Theatre's then literary director, John Tiffany. It dealt with how the decay of traditional political ideology effects ordinary people. The author, Burke, claimed to have never been in a theatre before, and yet two years later his play had become the hottest ticket at the Fringe – allegedly not even Kate Winslet could get in – and Burke was the beau of the ball at every party in town. He returned in 2003 with *The Straits*, cementing his reputation as an international force in theatre.

2. Sarah Kendall

Australian Kendall left Sydney to join the British comedy circuit in 2000, saying that life was too good down-under for her comedy to succeed. Making intelligent observations but never passing up an opportunity to joke about poo, she's one of a new generation of confident yet self-deprecating comedians who can turn their hands to anything, tackling themes from war and mental illness to hyenas and the need for 'sky sharks' to make the walk to work more interesting.

3. Steven Berkoff

Known to many as the bad guy in *Octopussy*, Steven Berkoff made his writing debut on the Fringe in 1975 with the drama *East*, and has gone on to be described by some commentators as theatre's greatest living exponent. For others, a mere whiff of the name sends them running. In 1997, he received a Total Theatre Lifetime Achievement Award, and more often than not there's a Berkoff play on during the festival. However, his 9/11 monologue *Requiem for Ground Zero* was widely panned by the critics for its lack of insight.

4. Jo Brand

Married, and with children, Jo Brand came to the Fringe in 2003 with a stand-up show and also a play, *Mental*, about her experiences as a psychiatric nurse. But it was her comedy routine that disappointed, commenting on hackneyed issues such as the banality of *Big Brother*, and dragging out old material about how useless men are, how much she weighs, and how low her breasts sag.

5. Paul Daniels

The darling of light entertainment on British television in the late '80s and early '90s, diminutive magician Daniels brought two shows to the Fringe in 2003. *An Audience With...* and *The Magic of Max Malini* revealed a man reinventing himself for a new festival generation, unfamiliar with his previous status as the king of Saturday night television. But the show went on, and if you didn't see him and his wife – the lovely Debbie McGee – traipsing around town then you were one of the few.

How to book tickets

Now comes the part that's second only in the fun stakes to the Festival itself: booking tickets and planning your itinerary. Bookings can be made by telephone or post, and most festivals now have a facility to book online. When planning your itinerary, a top tip is to base it around the Book Festival and Film Festival events, which are mostly one-offs. You might even consider booking ahead for both these festivals, as they are renowned for being places where authors and directors get to meet their public.

For fans of the more populist Fringe, another insider's tip is to get there early. On the first weekend of the Fringe, you can buy two tickets for the price of one for most shows – a godsend for the financially stretched. Some shows have previews too, when tickets are discounted and performances are not quite so polished. Hang around the main comedy and theatre venues in the early evening to catch excited promoters handing out free tickets for shows that are selling poorly in an attempt to conjure up an audience. One show even offered free beer in 2000. The International Festival has also recently provided free tickets for the young, and cheap tickets for those who turn up an hour before the performance. However, the schemes are not a fixture – it's hoped that money can be found for them again in 2004 and 2005.

The Book Festival and the Film Festival also offer discounts for multiple ticket purchases, but if all else fails, get on the Royal Mile and practise your party trick. There's always someone willing to throw money into a hat in the hope that you'll pack up and go away.

Where to stay

Hotels book up very quickly during the Festival, and prices skyrocket. Along with hostels to hotels, there are a sizeable number of flats and university rooms for rent over the Festival, their owners either students who have gone home for the vacation or locals off on holiday. *See p58 for a list of agencies.* The Fringe website also has a message board where offers of accommodation are posted.

Directory

The Fringe
Information, programmes & tickets: Fringe Office, 180 High Street, Old Town, EH1 1QS (information 226 0026/box office 226 0000/www.edfringe.com). Bus 35/Nicolson Street–North Bridge buses. **Open** *Postal & internet bookings* from early June. *Box office* (in person) mid June-July 9am-2pm daily; Aug 9am-9pm daily. *Telephone* mid June-Aug 9am-9pm daily.

Tickets prices vary; consult the Fringe programme for details. **Credit** MC, V. **Map** p309 F5. **Dates** 8-30 Aug 2004; 7-29 Aug 2005.

Edinburgh International Book Festival
Charlotte Square Gardens, New Town (information 228 5444/box office 624 5050/www.edbookfest. co.uk). Bus 13, 19, 29, 30, 41/Princes Street buses. **Open** 9.30am-late daily. **Tickets** prices vary; see website or phone for details. **Credit** MC, V. **Map** p309 D5. **Dates** 14-30 Aug 2004; 2005 dates tbc; 2006 dates tbc.
During the festival, the Book Festival takes place at the above address. The rest of the year it can be contacted at 137 Dundee Street, Edinburgh, EH11 1BG.

Edinburgh International Festival
Tickets & information: The Hub, Castlehill, Old Town, EH1 2NE (administration 473 2099/box office 473 2000/www.eif.co.uk). Bus 23, 27, 28, 35, 41, 42, 45. **Open** *Internet bookings* from mid April. *Box office* mid Apr-late July 10am-5pm Mon-Sat; late July-31 Aug 9am-7.30pm Mon-Sat; 10am-7.30pm Sun. **Tickets** prices vary; see website or phone for details. **Credit** AmEx, MC, V. **Map** p304 C3. **Dates** 15 Aug-4 Sept 2004; 14 Aug-3 Sept 2005; 13 Aug-2 Sept 2006.

Edinburgh International Film Festival
Information & tickets: Filmhouse, 88 Lothian Road, Old Town, EH3 9BZ (information 229 2550/ administration 228 4051/box office 623 8030/www. edfilmfest.org.uk). Bus 1, 10, 15, 16, 17, 22, 24, 34. **Tickets** (also available from The Hub; see p72) £5-£12; £5-£7 concessions. **Credit** MC, V. **Map** p309 D6. **Dates** 18-29 Aug 2004; 2005 dates tbc.

Edinburgh Jazz and Blues Festival
Information: 467 5200/tickets 668 2019/www.jazz music.co.uk. **Open** *Information* 9am-5.30pm Mon-Fri, daily during the Festival. *Ticket line* 10am-6pm daily. **Tickets** prices vary; phone for details. **Credit** MC, V. **Dates** 30 July-8 Aug 2004; 29 July-7 Aug 2005.

Edinburgh Military Tattoo
Castle Esplanade, Old Town (information & tickets 225 1188/www.edintattoo.co.uk). Bus 23, 27, 28, 35, 41, 42, 45. **Open** *Information* Sept-July 10am-4.30pm Mon-Fri. Aug 10am-9pm Mon-Fri, 10am-10.30pm Sat, 10am-4.30pm Sun. *Box office* Mar-Aug. *Telephone bookings* mid Dec-Aug. *Internet bookings* mid Dec-Aug. **Tickets** £9-£30; £2.50 supplement for 10.30pm Sat. *Tickets also available from the Tattoo Office, 32 Market Street, Old Town, EH1 1QB (08707 555 1188).* **Open** *Sept-June* 10am-4.30pm Mon-Fri. *July* 10am-4.30pm Mon-Sat, 1am-start of performance daily. **Credit** AmEx, MC, V. **Map** p309 E5. **Dates** 6-28 Aug 2004; 2005 dates tbc.

Edinburgh People's Festival
c/o Communication Workers Union, 15 Brunswick Street, EH7 (information 556 8869/www.edinburgh peoplesfestival.org.uk). **Dates** 7-14 Aug 2004; 2005 dates tbc.

Where to Stay

Where to Stay   **44**

Where to Stay

Book early or pay dearly.

Where's the kilt? The **Scotsman**. *See p45*.

A three-fold weight now rests on the shoulders of Edinburgh's hotels, and they're rising to the challenge. In addition to the existing demands of local people (weddings, business conferences and the like) and a year-round stream of visitors on city breaks, extra pressure is exerted by the city's future as an 'event' destination. The Festivals, the MTV awards, rugby internationals and Hogmanay revelries all have a part to play in swelling the demand for hotel accommodation.

And so it is that new hotels pop up and old hotels reinvent themselves. It's a win-win situation for the tourist: a better class of establishment at busy intervals and some killer savings to be made in quieter periods.

Large hotel groups manage many of Edinburgh's hotels, particularly the biggest. With the chains, you know what you're getting. But if you want to capture something of the spirit of Edinburgh, look elsewhere. Converted Georgian and Edwardian townhouses abound in the city: from the cool elegance of the **Howard** (*see p51*) to the **Albany Hotel**'s (*see p51*) rich historical tapestry, both grand and

homely. Even if you can only afford to pay budget prices, you still have the opportunity to stay in a converted townhouse – try **Ailsa Craig Hotel** (*see p55*) or the **Inverleith Hotel** (*see p54*).

However, room size and views can be a lottery. Some hotels, such as the **Roxburghe** (*see p52*) and the **Apex** (*see p46*), charge a supplement for bigger rooms with views of the Castle. With others, it's the luck of the draw. Instead of paying through the nose for a sight of the big building on the rock, why not look elsewhere? The **Bonham** (*see p51*) has striking vistas over the Dean Village and the Forth, **Prestonfield** (*see p57*) has the looming expanse of Arthur's Seat as a backdrop and Orocco Pier the awe-inspiring architectural majesty of the Forth Rail Bridge.

Edinburgh is a compact city; if you stay near the centre, you'll find that many places are accessible on foot. But if being in the heart of town isn't crucial, you may prefer to opt for the coast – the regenerated Leith Docks, home to the landmark **Malmaison** (*see p63*) is only a 10-minute drive from the town centre.

RATES AND RESERVATIONS

At certain times of the year, significant savings can be made if you're prepared to wait until the last minute before booking. Most clued-up hoteliers would rather sell their beds at a discount than leave them empty, so always ask if stand-by rates are available. Some hotels offer this as standard, others will recognise it as a coded way of saying 'do me a deal'. This applies equally to the more expensive hotels: they may command top rates from business clients from Monday to Thursday, but at the weekends they rely on budget-conscious leisure travellers. Bargain deals are increasingly commonplace – particularly from October to April when rates can drop by more than 50 per cent. But watch out for those major events that book out the whole city. If you're planning your visit during a major rugby international, Hogmanay, an international conference or during August (see p32 and p194), the advice is simple: book early or pay dearly.

Hotels in this chapter have been arranged by area and placed into different categories according to the price of the cheapest double room with breakfast – usually continental. We've noted where breakfast costs extra. Room prices include VAT and are the standard, year-round rate. Rates for hostel accommodation are given per person per night unless stated otherwise. The independent hostels get very busy, so try to book ahead if at all possible. If you intend staying out late, it's worth remembering to check about curfews when booking.

OTHER INFORMATION

Parking in Edinburgh can be both difficult and expensive, particularly in the centre of town and in residential areas. If you're travelling by car, you should check out the parking situation with the hotel before you arrive, especially if the parking is listed below as 'on street'.

Many hotels have disabled access and specially adapted rooms; the **Edinburgh & Lothians Tourist Board** (see below) will send you a list. Other advice is available from **Edinburgh City Council** and **Grapevine**, the former Lothian Coalition of Disabled People (for both, see p279).

Edinburgh & Lothians Tourist Board

Top floor of Waverley Shopping Centre, 3 Princes Street, New Town (473 3800/fax 473 3881/ www.edinburgh.org). Princes Street buses. **Open** *Nov-Mar* 9am-5pm Mon-Wed; 9am-6pm Thur-Sat; 10am-5pm Sun. *Apr, Oct* 9am-6pm Mon-Sat; 10am-6pm Sun. *May, June, Sept* 9am-7pm Mon-Sat; 10am-7pm Sun. *July, Aug* 9am-8pm Mon-Sat; 10am-8pm Sun. **Booking fee** £3 plus 10% deposit (£1 per head for 4+). **Credit** MC, V. **Map** p309 F5.

The Tourist Board is a useful resource for the bed-seeking visitor: it can make reservations across the city from its office, and grades accommodation using a star-rating system based on the standard of furnishings and overall welcome.

Scottish Youth Hostel Association

7 Glebe Crescent, Stirling, FK7 2JA (01786 891 400/fax 01786 891 333/www.syha.org.uk). **Open** 9am-5pm Mon-Fri. **Membership** £6. **Credit** MC, V. The SYHA will provide information on accommodation in its hostels around Scotland. You have to be a member to stay in them, but you can join when you arrive for £6. In addition to the Bruntsfield (see p61) and the Eglinton (see p63), the SYHA operates the seasonal Pleasance Youth Hostel on New Arthur Place, South Edinburgh (open Aug only) and the new Edinburgh International Youth Hostel on Kincaids Court in the city centre (open July, Aug only). Phone for further information.

Hotels & Hostels

Old Town

Deluxe (over £185)

Scotsman

20 North Bridge, EH1 1YT (556 5565/fax 652 3652/www.thescotsmanhotel.co.uk). Nicolson Street–North Bridge buses. **Rates** (breakfast not included) from £160 single; from £200 double; £395-£1500 suite. **Credit** AmEx, DC, MC, V. **Map** p304 D2.

This hotel has expertly married the pursuits of business and pleasure since it opened in the former home of the *Scotsman* newspaper in 2001. It has transformed the paper's previous grand reception on North Bridge into a buzzing bar and bistro. The designers have preserved and restored the historic building's original features – elaborate cornicing, marble floors, walnut panelling and stained-glass windows. Add to these features a state-of-the-art gym, 16m pool, the Vermilion fine dining restaurant (see p135) and ten choices of sausage for breakfast and the result is a broadsheet property of distinct quality. Each room is individually decorated with original art and exclusive estate tweeds; each has a well-stocked and competitively priced private wine bar (full bottles – not halves); and all have a hatch to deliver room service. Of course, the all-work, all-play attitude permeates to the rooms – an Edinburgh Monopoly boardgame comes as standard.

Hotel services *Air conditioning (12). Babysitting. Bars (2). Beauty salon. Business services. Concierge. Disabled: access, adapted rooms (2). Gym. No-smoking rooms. Parking (£15/night). Restaurants (2). Swimming pool (16m).* **Room services** *Bathrobe. Dataport. DVD. Ethernet. Hifi. Iron. Minibar. Newspapers. Room service (24hr). Turndown. TV: cable.*

Witchery by the Castle

Castlehill, EH1 2NF (225 5613/fax 220 4392/
www.thewitchery.com). Bus 23, 27, 35, 41, 42.
Rates £250 suite. **Credit** AmEx, DC, MC, V.
Map p304 C3.

Warm, incredibly romantic, charismatic and filled
with history, the Witchery is not so much a hotel as
a restaurant with seven suites attached. Taking its
name from the witches burned at the stake during
the reign of James VI, the Witchery's suites are located in two buildings straddling the Royal Mile: two
in the 16th-century building in Boswell's Court, and
five in the more recently opened 17th-century
dwelling off Sempill's Court.

Each of the suites is lavishly furnished with original antiques, sumptuous leather and velvet upholstery, claw-foot Victorian baths and grand,
wood-carved beds. The style is dark, Gothic and
thoroughly theatrical. Five of the suites have
kitchens attached. Many hotels – particularly in
Edinburgh – try to replicate this level of traditional
elegance, but this is the real deal. If you have the
means – and if you can get a room – the Witchery
is *the* place to indulge yourself.
Hotel services *Air conditioning. Cooking facilities*
(5). Restaurants (2). **Room services** *Bathrobe.*
Complimentary champagne. Dataport. DVD. Hifi.
Iron. Kitchenette (5). Newspapers. TV: cable, VCR.

Top five Four posters

Albany Hotel
For a romantic getaway, look no further
than the intimate environs of the Albany.
Two lavishly furnished rooms have four
poster beds (*see p51*).

Malmaison
Boasting three rooms with more minimalist
four poster beds, Malmaison is best suited
to those with an eye for stylish detail
(*see p63*).

Inverleith Hotel
One mahogany bed dominates the grand
front room overlooking the Royal Botanic
Gardens (*see p54*).

Howard
For a taste of Georgian splendour, the
Howard's junior suite has a restored four
poster bed to complement its romantic
setting (*see p51*).

Bonham
Old school romantics should take solace
that the Bonham's contemporary designs
allow for one four poster bed and four
rooms with canopy beds (*see p51*).

Expensive (£115-£185)

Apex International Hotel

31-35 Grassmarket, EH1 2HS (300 3456/fax 220
5345/www.apexhotels.co.uk). Bus 23, 27, 35, 41, 42.
Rates £170 single; £180 double. **Credit** AmEx, DC,
MC, V. **Map** p309 E6.

Only the bijou size of the Apex Hotel's 175 rooms
betray its past as a budget chain hotel. Refurbished,
restyled and relaunched in spring 2002, the
Edinburgh-based Apex hotel group has undergone
a transformation from comfortable but bland, mid-
market residence to sleek, stylish, designer luxury.
With black rubberised floors, brown leather furnishings, American cherrywood panelling and shiny
chrome fittings, the Apex International is the epito-
me of contemporary style with a retro twist. All
rooms are decorated with identical furnishings in
plums, whites and beiges, while gadgetry includes
Playstation consoles, DVDs, CDs and interactive
TVs. Superior rooms, and the fifth-floor restaurant,
the Heights, boast stunning views of Edinburgh
Castle. The lively Metro bistro on the ground floor
is perfect for a lighter bite in relaxed surroundings.
Hotel services *Bars (3). Business services.*
Concierge. Disabled: access, adapted rooms (6).
Laundry. No-smoking rooms. Parking (free).
Restaurants (2). **Room services** *Bathrobe. Dataport.*
DVD. Hairdryer. Iron. Newspapers. Minibar.
Refrigerator. Room service (24hr). TV: satellite.
Other location: Apex City, 61 Grassmarket, Old
Town (243 3456).

Bank Hotel

1 South Bridge, EH1 1LL (556 9940/fax 622 6822/
www.festival-inns.co.uk). Nicolson Street–North
Bridge buses. **Rates** £120 double; £140 suite.
Credit AmEx, MC, V. **Map** p304 D3.

The Bank Hotel consists of nine rooms above Logie
Baird's Bar, accessed through a hidden doorway at
the rear of the bar. The mood is determinedly Gaelic,
with wood panelling and dark tartan furnishings.
Each bedroom is individually named after, and
themed around, a famous Scot: the James Young
Simpson room (*see p10* **Pass the ether, ma'am**),
for example, plays on the anaesthetic motif with
anatomical sketches, bookcases and old potion bottles, while the Thomas Telford room is dominated
by a black four-poster construction over the bed.
The lively bar is open round the clock and the staff
are friendly and helpful.
Hotel services *Air conditioning. Bar. Restaurant.*
Room services *Hairdryer. Hifi. Iron. Newspapers.*
Room service (8am-9pm daily). TV: satellite.

Carlton

North Bridge, EH1 1SD (472 3000/fax 556 2691/
www.paramount-hotels.co.uk). Nicolson Street–North
Bridge buses. **Rates** (breakfast not included) £100
single; £132 double. **Credit** AmEx, DC, MC, V.
Map p304 D2.

Straddling North Bridge, the Carlton offers fine
views of the city from each and every room – some-

Be**Witchery by the Castle**. See p46.

thing that even its five-star competitors cannot match. It has also, and not before time, undergone a dramatic transformation: guests are greeted by a grand reception with contemporary lighting, pale marble flooring and an imposing staircase. Every room has been gutted and revamped. The rooms are homely and comfortable so the decor may not suit those seeking cutting-edge style or all mod cons.
Hotel services *Air conditioning. Babysitting. Bar. Beauty salon. Business services. Concierge. Disabled: access, adapted rooms (4). Gym. Limousine. Laundry. No-smoking floors (140 rooms). Parking (£15/day). Restaurant. Swimming pool (10m). Valet parking.* **Room services** *Bathrobe (premium). Dataport. Minibar. Hairdryer. Iron. Minibar. Newspapers. Room service (24hr). TV: satellite.*

MacDonald Holyrood Hotel

81 Holyrood Road, EH8 6AE (550 4500/fax 550 4545/www.holyroodevents.co.uk). Bus 30, 35.
Rates from £90 single; from £120 double; £120-£195 suite. **Credit** AmEx, DC, MC, V.
Map p310 H5.
The MacDonald is across the road from the *Scotsman* offices and just a stone's throw from the new Scottish Parliament, so it comes as no surprise to find it was built with business travellers in mind. That said, it is also near the Royal Mile, Dynamic Earth and Holyrood Palace. The rooms are furnished with splashes of Harris tweed, maple wood finishings and even a heated mirror to banish the post-shower haze. There's an impressive fine-dining restaurant, a well-equipped gym, a 14m pool, and, on the Club Floor, the services of a private butler to attend to your every whim.

Hotel services *Air conditioning. Bars (2). Beauty salon. Business services. Concierge. Cooking facilities. Disabled: access, adapted rooms (12). Gym. No-smoking rooms (26). Parking (£9.50/day). Restaurant. Pool (14m).* **Room services** *Bathrobe. Dataport. ISDN. Hairdryer. Iron. Minibar. Newspapers. Room service (24hr). TV: cable.*

Radisson SAS Hotel

80 High Street, EH1 1TH (557 9797/fax 557 9789/www.radissonsas.com). Bus 35/Nicolson Street–North Bridge buses. **Rates** £95-£230.
Credit AmEx, DC, MC, V. **Map** p304 D3.
This turreted hotel may look like one of the original stone buildings on the Royal Mile but it was only actually built in 1989. From its chequered marble flooring in reception to its faux-Victorian windows in the lounge, it attempts to blend in with its historic neighbours, its efforts attracting only the scorn of architectural modernists (*see p27*). The public areas are modern and bustling. The newly refurbished Carrubbers restaurant is bright and modern, and Dickson's Bar in the basement has regular live music. Wood panelling and heavy fabrics effect a cosy, comfortable style in the rooms, while views of Arthur's Seat and the new Parliament from the top-floor rooms are impressive. The Radisson also boasts rare ample car-parking space.
Hotel services *Air conditioning. Bars (2). Beauty salon. Business services. Concierge. Disabled: access, adapted rooms (3). Gym. Internet access. No-smoking rooms & floors. Parking (£2/hr). Restaurant. Pool (10m).* **Room services** *Dataport. Ethernet. Hairdryer. Iron. Minibar. Refrigerator. Room service (24hr). TV: cable.*

Moderate (£65-£115)

Jurys Inn

43 Jeffrey Street, EH1 1DG (200 3300/fax 200 0400/www.jurysdoyle.com). Nicolson Street–North Bridge buses. **Rates** (breakfast not included) £78-£98 single/double. **Credit** AmEx, DC, MC, V. **Map** p310 G5.

Few hotels can match the ideal location of this former office block. To the front lies Waverley station, Calton Hill and the New Town, while the wynd to the rear leads up into the heart of the Royal Mile. **Hotel services** *Air conditioning. Bar. Business services. Disabled: access, adapted rooms (6). No-smoking rooms (64). Parking (on street). Restaurant.* **Room services** *Dataport. Hairdryer. Iron. Newspapers. TV.*

Tailors Hall Hotel

139 Cowgate, EH1 1JS (622 6801/fax 622 6818/ www.festival-inns.co.uk). Nicolson Street–North Bridge buses. **Rates** £90 single; £110 double/twin; £135 triple. **Credit**: AmEx, MC, V. **Map** p304 D3.

Anyone wishing to turn up the volume on their Festival experience should make this their base. With its central Cowgate location, Tailors Hall is only yards from the Fringe's hippest new late-night venue, the Underbelly, and a further five minute amble from the Pleasance. The Three Sisters bar – if not the most popular bar in town, then certainly one of the busiest – lies right under its feet. Built around a courtyard that acts as overspill for the bar, the 17th-century building houses a thoroughly modern interior. Rooms vary greatly in size and shape, but all are comfortable and clean. If you value your sleep, ask for the new wing, which is less noisy. Take note, though, many of Edinburgh's visiting hordes of stags and hens also choose to make this their base. **Hotel services** *Bars (3). Business services. Disabled: access, adapted rooms (4).* **Room services** *Room service (9am-9pm daily). TV.*

Travelodge

33 St Mary's Street, EH1 1TA (08701 911 637/ fax 557 3681/www.travelodge.co.uk). Nicolson Street–North Bridge buses. **Rates** (breakfast not included) £49.95-£69.95 single/double. **Credit** AmEx, DC, MC, V. **Map** p310 G5.

Hotel services *Bar. Business services. Disabled: access, adapted rooms (10). No-smoking rooms (148). Parking (limited, £5 per exit). Restaurant.* **Room services** *Dataport. Iron. Newspapers. TV.*

Budget (under £65)

Hotel Ibis

6 Hunter Square, EH1 1QW (240 7000/fax 240 7007/www.ibishotel.com) Nicolson Street–North Bridge buses. **Rates** (breakfast not included) Oct-Apr £49.95 per room (single/double). May £59.95. June-Sept £69.95. **Credit** AmEx, DC, MC, V. **Map** p304 D3.

The Ibis chain has a reputation for efficiency and good value, but the downside is a certain tendency to bland anonymity. There are plans to create a restaurant late in 2004. **Hotel services** *Bar. Concierge. Disabled: access, adapted rooms (6). No-smoking rooms (54).* **Room services** *Dataport. Newspapers. TV: cable.*

No, this is not the Queen's pad, honest. The **Balmoral**. *See p49.*

Hostels

Brodies Backpackers

12 & 93 High Street, EH1 1TB (556 6770/
www.brodieshostels.co.uk). Nicolson Street–North
Bridge buses. **Open** *Reception* 7am-midnight. No
curfew. **Rates** £9.50-£12.50 dorm; £35-£39 double;
£45-£49 triple. **Credit** MC, V. **Map** p304 D3.
Hostel services *Internet access. Laundry service.*
No-smoking rooms. Payphone.

Budget Backpackers

15 Cowgatehead, EH1 1JY (226 6351/www.budget
backpacker.com). Princes Street buses. **Beds** 110.
Open *Reception* 24hrs. No curfew. **Rates** £10-£16
dorm; £16-£25 double. **Credit** MC, V. **Map** p304 C3.
Hostel services *Garden (rooftop from Jan 2005).*
Internet access. Laundry service. No-smoking rooms.
Payphone. TV room.

Castle Rock Hostel

15 Johnston Terrace, EH1 2PW (225 9666/fax 226
5078/www.scotlands-top-hostels.com). Bus 23, 27,
35, 41, 42. **Beds** 280. **Open** 24hrs. No curfew.
Rates £12 dorm; doubles available. **Credit** AmEx,
DC, MC, V. **Map** p304 B3.

Edinburgh Backpackers Hostel

65 Cockburn Street, EH1 1BU (reception 220 1717/
fax 220 5143/reservations 220 2200/reservations
fax 539 8695/www.hoppo.com). Nicolson Street–
North Bridge buses. **Beds** 100 dorms; 6 twins; 6
doubles; 3 triples. **Open** 24hrs. No curfew. **Rates**
from £13 dorm; from £44.50 doubles/triples.
Credit DC, MC, V. **Map** p304 D2.

Edinburgh Central Youth Hostel (SYHA)

Robertson's Close, Cowgate, EH1 1LY (556 5566/
central reservations 08701 553255/www.syha.
org.uk). Nicolson Street–North Bridge buses. **Open**
July, Aug only. No curfew. *Reception* 7am-11.30pm
daily. **Rates** (membership not included) *July* £20.
Aug £21. **Credit** MC, V. **Map** p304 D3.

Royal Mile Backpackers

105 High Street, EH1 1SG (557 6120/fax 556
3999/www.scotlands-top-hostels.com). Bus 35/
Nicolson Street–North Bridge buses. **Open** *Reception* 7am-3 am.
No curfew. **Rates** £12. **Credit** AmEx, DC, MC, V.
Map p304 D3.

New Town

Deluxe (over £185)

Balmoral

1 Princes Street, EH2 2EQ (556 2414/fax 557 3747/
www.thebalmoralhotel.com). Princes Street buses or
Nicolson Street–North Bridge buses. **Rates** £225-
£275 single/double; £465-£927 suite. **Credit** AmEx,
DC, MC, V. **Map** p304 D2.
Still the most prestigious short-term address in
Edinburgh, the Balmoral recently underwent a

Top five # Hotels

Balmoral

Edinburgh's oldest and grandest hotel
looks better than ever thanks to a £7
million facelift. Style and substance
combine to devastating effect (*see below*).

Scotsman

Boasting a wealth of facilities for business
and pleasure, the Scotsman is a hotel that
recognises the importance of work, rest
and play (*see p45*).

Channings

Despite a quieter residential location,
Channings is fighting fit with a blend of
traditionalism, fine dining and dedication
to personal service (*see p54*).

Prestonfield

Arguably Edinburgh's most exciting hotel
development in recent years, this converted
manor house exudes opulent individual
style that is unrivalled anywhere in the
city (*see p57*).

Roxburghe Hotel

A thoroughly relaxed atmosphere and
friendly attitude make a visit here a
pleasure – let the hotel's fusion of old
and new speak for itself (*see p52*).

£7 million investment to cement its reputation.
Protruding from the junction of Princes Street and
North Bridge, this former railway hotel exudes
majesty from its grand six-floor exterior, which is
replicated inside. The Balmoral has all the trappings
you would expect from a top-drawer hotel: marble
floors, fine art, crystal chandeliers and service that
is always attentive but rarely intrusive.

Each of the 180 rooms has been completely refurbished with the emphasis on cool, earthy colours,
geometric shapes and, above all, comfort. Exterior
rooms are popular with tourists seeking panoramic
views, while business customers may be more at
home in the quieter interior rooms, overlooking Palm
Court. Tradition merges with modernity in the
suites, which are an assortment of ornaments, paintings and furniture pieces. Hadrian's Brasserie benefited from a revamp early in 2004, but still retains
its breezy feel. The darkened, salubrious core of
Palm Court bustles with visitors and guests, savour-
ing the fare from the kitchen and bar. The real ace
in the Balmoral's catering pack, though, is Number
One, its Michelin starred fine-dining restaurant.
Throw in a newly refurbished spa and you have a
residence worthy of its five-star standing.

Splash out at the **Howard**.

Hotel services *Air conditioning. Babysitting. Bars (3). Business services. Concierge. Disabled: access, adapted rooms (4). Gym. Limousine. No-smoking rooms. Parking (valet). Restaurants (3). Spa. Swimming pool.* **Room services** *Bathrobes. Dataport. DVD. Fax. Hairdryer. Hifi. Iron. Minibar. Newspapers. Refrigerator. Room service (24hr). TV. satellite.*

Howard

34 Great King Street, EH3 6QH (557 3500/ reservations 315 2220/fax 557 6515/www.the howard.com). Bus 19A, 23, 27, 28. **Rates** £145 single; £240-£265 double; £325-£365 suite. **Credit** AmEx, DC, MC, V. **Map** p306 E3.

This discreet terraced residence only reveals its identity through the brass plaque on the front door. Built in 1829, the Howard is a perfect example of how to successfully combine Georgian style and architecture with comfort and luxury. The breakfast room, with its sumptuous arrangement of red Victorian chairs, overlooks Great King Street, a cobbled thoroughfare that was built as Edinburgh's 'second New Town'. Each of the 15 rooms is named after an area in Edinburgh; large bathrooms, state-of-the-art showers with steam jets and roll-top baths are luxurious bonuses. The Terraced Suites in the basement are popular with honeymooning couples and have separate entrances from the street. The service is second to none – a butler checks in guests in the lavishly decorated drawing room, and even a weather forecast is left on pillows every night. **Hotel services** *Air conditioning. Business services. Concierge. Garden. Laundry. No-smoking rooms. Parking. Restaurant.* **Room services** *Dataport. DVD. Hairdryer. Hifi. Minibar. Room service (24hr). Turndown. TV: cable.*

Expensive (£115-£185)

Albany Hotel

39-43 Albany Street, EH1 3QY (556 0397/fax 557 6633/www.albanyhoteledinburgh.co.uk). Bus 8/ Playhouse buses. **Rates** £95-£125 single; £130-£235 double; £235 suite. **Credit** AmEx, MC, V. **Map** p306 F4.

Tucked away in a corner of the New Town, yet only minutes from Princes Street and Broughton, the Albany is a discreet and charming hotel. Converted from three Georgian townhouses, its interior decor is designed to match: rich red fabrics and warm mahogany tones are inviting and homely. Haldanes Restaurant in the basement of the hotel is lauded with a host of awards and welcomes a varied clientele. This is a good hotel for a romantic weekend. **Hotel services** *Air conditioning. Babysitting. Business services. Laundry. No-smoking rooms. Parking (on street).* **Room services** *Dataport. Hairdryer. Minibar. Newspapers. Room service (7-10am, 6-9pm daily). Turndown. TV: satellite.*

Bonham

35 Drumsheugh Gardens, EH3 7RN (226 6050/ reservations 623 6060/fax 226 6080/www. thebonham.com). Bus 19, 29, 29A, 37, 37A, 41, 42. **Rates** £145 single; £165-£240 double; £325 suite. **Credit** AmEx, DC, MC, V. **Map** p308 C5.

Ever-popular with style-conscious visitors, the townhouse exterior of the Bonham gives way to a contemporary blend of comfortable, light minimalism that however avoids becoming too Starck. The elaborately carved, wood-panelled reception area, complete with original telephone booths that serve to bookend the entrance, is particularly welcoming. Neutral colours, with some bright splashes, and art deco furniture in public areas complement the soaring ceilings and cornices of the original Victorian building. Many of the 48 individually decorated rooms boast original art by local students. All this, plus a restaurant with a £60 per table of four lunch menu at weekends: no wonder it is a recipient of the AA Hotel of the Year award in Scotland. **Hotel services** *Air conditioning. Babysitting. Business services. Concierge. Disabled: access, adapted room (1). Limousine. No-smoking rooms. Parking (on street). Restaurant.* **Room services** *Dataport. DVD. Hairdryer. Hifi. Iron. Minibar. Room service (24hr). Turndown. TV: cable.*

Edinburgh Residence

7 Rothesay Terrace, EH3 7RY (623 9304/fax 226 3381/www.theedinburghresidence.com). Bus 13. **Rates** £150-£395 suite. **Credit** AmEx, MC, V. **Map** p308 B5.

The Edinburgh Residence is easy to miss: only a gold plaque reveals its identity. Inside, the reception area is beautifully traditional, with dark, red furnishings, wood panelling, a grandfather clock and a

Top five Little luxuries

Witchery by the Castle

A bottle of champagne lies chilling in the ice bucket on your arrival, complemented by some home-made cookies and *petits fours*. Five of the Gothic suites also have kitchens (*see p46*).

Edinburgh Residence

A relaxing stay is guaranteed here – all meals are delivered and served in the suites. Should you venture out, make the most of the honesty bar in the Drawing Room (*see above*).

Minto Hotel

If the drone of the pipes is music to your mind, then you might want to stay at the Minto, where a piper serenades the guests every Saturday during summer (*see p57*).

Sheraton Grand Hotel

In the spirit of the Theatre of Live Cooking, a chef will whip up your ingredients to order in the Terrace Restaurant. Then why not work off those extra calories in one of Europe's most advanced city spas, One Spa (*see p61*)?

Dunstane House Hotel

The hotel has a licence to hold civil marriage ceremonies. The romantic experience could only be bettered by a stay in one of its four poster beds (*see p62*).

reverent atmosphere. There is no bar or restaurant on the premises – a legacy of its previous life as a block of rented flats – so meals are served in the suites. Only in the Drawing Room, with a self-serve honesty bar, can guests socialise freely. There are three categories of suites: the Town House, the Grand and the Classic. All vary in size and facilities, but each has their own idiosyncrasies: the Town House suites have bookcases concealing fold down beds, and some Classics have separate entrances onto Rothesay Terrace. **Hotel services** *Babysitting service (outside company). Bar (honesty). Concierge. Disabled: access, adapted room (1). No-smoking rooms. Parking.* **Room services** *Bathrobe. Dataport. DVD. Hairdryer. Hifi. Iron. Minibar. Newspapers. Room service (24hr). Turndown. TV: cable.*

Hilton Caledonian

4 Princes Street, EH1 2AB (222 8888/fax 222 8889/www.hilton.com/caledonian). Princes Street buses. **Rates** from £130 single; from £160 double; from £250 suite. **Credit** AmEx, DC, MC, V. **Map** p304 A2.

Recently acquired as the Scottish flagship of the Hilton chain, the *grande dame* of Princes Street was once in danger of losing her lustre. Trading primarily on reputation, the hotel had a hard time convincing the public that she had more to offer than a grandiose Edwardian façade and an enviable position at the foot of Edinburgh Castle. Following extensive refurbishment, however, the huge Caledonian has been brought back to its former glory. It steadfastly refuses to follow any current design trends, retaining instead a sense of a bygone era throughout: huge arched corridors lead past broad staircases with stained-glass windows. Elegant, opulent and more than a little ostentatious, the Caledonian has a warm, luxurious feel. A high standard of service has made it a favourite of auspicious guests over the years, including Sean Connery and Nelson Mandela. After an investment of £8 million, the old dame is back to her best. **Hotel services** *Air conditioning. Babysitting. Bar (3). Beauty salon. Business services. Concierge. Disabled: access, adapted rooms (4). Garden. Gym. Laundry service. Limousine. No-smoking rooms. Parking. Restaurants (3). Swimming pool.* **Room services** *Dataport. Hairdryer. Hifi. Minibar. Room service (24hr). Turndown. TV: satellite.*

Roxburghe Hotel

38 Charlotte Square, EH2 4HG (240 5500/fax 240 5555/www.roxburghe-hotel.co.uk). Princes Street buses. **Rates** £90 single; £140 double; £180 suite. **Credit** AmEx, DC, MC, V. **Map** p304 A1.

Despite costing more than building a new hotel from scratch, the major refurbishment of the 197-room Roxburghe has paid off. The façade of this cornerstone of Charlotte Square is still faithful to Robert Adam's Georgian design, but the interior has been totally transformed into an almost seamless blend of 19th-century elegance and 21st-century style. The huge leather armchairs sit comfortably on the beech-

Scanning **Channings**. See p54.

wood floors in the lobby, and the open courtyard in the centre is bustling during the Book Festival, catering to a gaggle of high tea demands (*see p37*). Some of the rooms in the extension at the back are a little featureless, but views of Edinburgh Castle from higher floors compensate. Plans are underway to refurbish the Melrose restaurant in mid 2004.
Hotel services *Bars (2). Beauty salon. Concierge. Disabled: access, adapted rooms (10). Gym. Internet access. Laundry. No-smoking rooms. Parking (limited). Restaurants (2). Swimming pool.* **Room services** *Dataport. Hairdryer. Room service (24hr). TV: satellite.*

Royal Scots Club
30 Abercromby Place, EH3 6QE (556 4270/fax 558 3769/www.royalscotsclub.com). Bus 23, 27, 28. **Rates** £110 single; £140 double; £160 king-size double; £200 four poster.* **Credit** AmEx, DC, MC, V. **Map** p306 E4.
The gentlemen's club vibe is very much in evidence on entering this classic Georgian townhouse. The Royal Scots Club was founded in 1919 as a tribute to those who fell in the Great War, and today the air of tranquillity and strong sense of history is palpa-

ble and genuine. The recently refurbished rooms are all tastefully furnished in a traditional style, some with four-poster beds and fine views towards the Forth. The cosy atmosphere and classic features extend into every room, from the lounge with the real fire, to the elegant restaurant. The Scots Club is minutes away from Princes Street yet a million miles from the commercial modernity of that thoroughfare.
Hotel services *Bar (3). Beauty salon. Business services. Gym. Laundry. No-smoking rooms. Parking (on street). Restaurant.* **Room services** *Dataport. Hairdryer. Newspapers. Room service (7.30am-8.30pm daily). TV: cable.*

Rick's
55a Frederick Street, EH2 1HL (622 7800/www. ricksedinburgh.co.uk). Princes Street buses. **Rates** £130 double.* **Credit** AmEx, MC, V. **Map** p304 B1.
Nightlife and style both come high on the agenda at Rick's. A bar and restaurant with ten boutique rooms attached, it has been the 'in' place to be in Edinburgh since its inception in 1998. Located amid the New Town's hive of activity, and overlooking a quiet cobbled street, the rooms are well placed for venturing out into the city's many eateries and

watering holes. If you can bear to leave, that is. Furnished to a high modern standard with lilac lambs' wool, walnut headboards and cream angora blankets, the mammoth beds demand to be lounged on. A tempting room service menu could further hamper any pre-arranged bookings. Location is everything – and Rick's has that, and style, in spades. **Hotel services** *Bar. Concierge. Restaurant.* **Room services** *DVD. Hairdryer. Hifi. Room service (24hr). TV: satellite.*

Budget (under £65)

Frederick House Hotel
42 Frederick Street, EH2 1EX (226 1999/fax 624 7064/www.townhousehotels.co.uk). Bus 28, 29, 37. **Rates** *£40-£90 single; £60-£150 double; £140-£190 suite.* **Credit** AmEx, DC, MC, V. **Map** p304 B1.
Centrally located near St Andrew Square bus station and Waverley train station, this listed building has been transformed from offices into five floors of bedrooms in patterned greens, golds and reds. The best rooms are at the front of the hotel, while the Skyline suite has views across to the Forth. Breakfast is taken in Rick's bar, opposite the hotel (*see p154*), and is included in the tariff.
Hotel services *Parking (on street). Payphone.* **Room services** *Dataport. Hairdryer. Refrigerator. TV: satellite.*

Top five Hip hotels

Rick's
A buzzing basement bar specialising in cocktails could be a tempting diversion from the stylish rooms (*see p53*).

Borough Hotel
Fast becoming the southside's hippest hangout, the Borough's retro bar provides the perfect place to wind down before cosying into the snug boutique hotel (*see p57*).

Point Hotel
Monboddo is every inch the city style bar – much like the metropolitan rooms above (*see p59*).

Scotsman
Friday nights are the liveliest in the Scotsman's bistro – get there early to bag a pew (*see p45*).

Orocco Pier
Relax in a leather-clad booth while drinking in the views of the Forth Rail Bridge. Orocco Pier brings city centre ambience to South Queensferry (*see p62*).

Hostels

Princes Street East Backpackers
5 West Register Street, EH2 2AA (556 6894/fax 557 3236/www.edinburghbackpackers.com). Princes Street buses or Nicolson Street–North Bridge buses. **Beds** 110 dorm beds (one female only dorm); 4 doubles; 2 quads. **Open** *Reception* 24-hrs daily. No curfew. **Rates** £11 dorm, £30 double; 7th night free. **Credit** MC, V. **Map** p304 D1.
Hostel services *Cooking facilities. Internet access. Laundry (self-service). No-smoking rooms. Payphone. TV room.*

Stockbridge

Deluxe (over £185)

Channings
15 South Learmonth Gardens, EH4 1EZ (315 2226/reservations 623 9302/fax 332 9631/ www.channings.co.uk). Bus 19, 29, 37, 41, 42. **Rates** £140 single; £185 double/twin; £260 suite. **Credit** AmEx, DC, MC, V. **Map** p305 B4.
Channings has an ace in its pack: as well as offering up market, comfortable accommodation and an acclaimed restaurant, this Edwardian hotel boasts a buzzing bar, Ochre Vita. The Mediterranean-themed bistro is bright, lively and attracts a discerning crowd. Upstairs, the lounges incorporate a scant maritime theme amid rich cream fabrics and gold finishes. The bedrooms feature stylish chequer board carpets and single-colour fabrics in mushrooms and creams. The upper floors have been updated rather than redesigned but have the advantage of terrific views of Fettes School – Tony Blair's alma mater – at the front and extras such as roll-top baths and jacuzzis at the rear.
Hotel services *Babysitting. Bar. Beauty salon. Business services. Concierge. Garden. Internet access (free). Laundry service. No-smoking rooms. Parking (on street). Restaurant (2).* **Room services** *Bathrobe. Dataport. DVD. Hairdryer. Iron. Newspapers. Room service (24hr). TV: cable.*

Budget (under £65)

Inverleith Hotel
5 Inverleith Terrace, EH3 4NS (556 2745/www. inverleithhotel.co.uk). Bus 8, 17, 23, 27. **Rates** from £40 single; £60-£120 double. **Credit** MC, V. **Map** p306 D2.
The Inverleith Hotel offers a home away from home experience. Set in a discreet Victorian townhouse adjacent to the Botanic Garden, its furnishings and facilities are designed with maximum comfort in mind. A family-run residence, it marries the best of hotel services with the intimacy of a guest house. Rooms at the rear are compact but exude warmth and homeliness, with thick bedspreads and luxurious furnishings. There is one four poster bed in the hotel's grandest room, overlooking the Botanics.

Be a bed head at **Inverleith Hotel**. *See p54.*

Hotel services Babysitting. Bar. Internet access. No-smoking rooms. Parking (on street). **Room services** *Hairdryer. Newspapers. TV.*

Calton Hill & Broughton

Expensive (£115-£185)

Parliament House Hotel

15 Calton Hill, EH1 3BJ (478 4000/fax 478 4001/ www.parliamenthouse-hotel.co.uk). Playhouse buses. **Rates** (breakfast not included) £120 single; £170 double; £250 suite. **Credit** AmEx, DC, MC, V. **Map** p307 G4.

This hotel's rather grandiose name belies a welcoming residence. Located in a quiet nook of Calton Hill, the hotel itself is comprised of three buildings – a Georgian frontage, a Jacobean side building, and the rear section, which is a mere architectural pup at just over 100 years old. The rooms vary in size: some cavernous, with views of Arthur's Seat and the Old Town, others cosy and looking out over Leith and the Forth. The MPs' Bistro is a colourful and roomy dining space.

Hotel services *Bar. Disabled: access, adapted rooms (3). Laundry. No-smoking rooms. Parking (on street). Restaurant.* **Room services** *Dataport. Hairdryer. Minibar. Refrigerator. Room service (7-10am, 6-9.30pm daily). TV.*

Royal Terrace Hotel

18 Royal Terrace, EH7 5AQ (557 3222/fax 557 5334/www.theroyalterracehotel.co.uk). Playhouse buses. **Rates** (breakfast not included) £115 single; £175 double/twin; £240-£270 suite. **Credit** AmEx, DC, MC, V. **Map** p307 H4.

A change of ownership and the Royal Terrace has reverted to its original name. Designed by William Playfair in 1822, this quiet terrace sits beneath Calton Hill with views towards Leith and the Forth. The Georgian opulence is echoed in the swags and flounces of the soft furnishings and chandeliers, but contemporary touches include a small gym and pool in the basement. The garden, with its life-size chess board and fountain is popular in summer. Rooms on the top floor are small due to the sloped attic ceilings.

Hotel services *Babysitting. Bar. Business services. Concierge. Garden. Gym. Limousine. No-smoking rooms. Parking (on street). Restaurant. Swimming pool.* **Room services** *Dataport. Hairdryer. Minibar (on request). Room service (24hr). TV: satellite.*

Budget (under £65)

Ailsa Craig Hotel

24 Royal Terrace, EH7 5AH (556 1022/fax 556 6055/www.townhousehotels.co.uk). Playhouse buses. **Rates** £35-£75 single; £60-£150 double. **Credit** AmEx, DC, MC, V. **Map** p307 H4.

Like its sister hotel, Greenside, just a few doors down (9 Royal Terrace; 557 0022), Ailsa Craig boasts big, clean rooms that have retained their original Georgian features. Though they're a bit on the basic side, some have views towards the Forth and all enjoy the quiet of this residential crescent. Some rooms are kitted out with five beds. The public areas were refurbished in 2003, but these all retain a traditional character and unassuming comfort.
Hotel services *Bar. Garden. No-smoking rooms. Parking (on street). Payphone.* **Room services** *Hairdryer. TV.*

Balfour Guest House

90-92 Pilrig Street, EH6 5AY (554 2106/fax 554 3887). Bus 7, 10, 11, 12, 14, 16, 22. **Rates** £25 single; £50 double. **Credit** AmEx, DC, MC, V. **Map** p307 G1.
The hospitality, central location and free parking, with a mini-bus to ferry visitors around, makes this a popular choice for groups, who can take advantage of dinner in the basement dining room and packed lunches on request.
Hotel services *Bar. Garden. Mini-bus taxi service. Packed lunches. Parking (on street). Restaurant.* **Room services** *Room service (8am-9pm daily).*

Claremont

14-15 Claremont Crescent, EH7 4HX (556 1487/fax 556 7077). Bus 8. **Rates** £25-£40 single; £45-£70 double. **Credit** AmEx, DC, MC, V. **Map** p306 F2.
This hotel comprises two huge Georgian houses knocked into one. Rooms are clean, comfortable and very large, with views of Arthur's Seat or the Forth. The place is a hive of activity, with quiz nights in the public bar and a disco downstairs.
Hotel services *Bar. Business services. Garden. Parking. Payphone.* **Room services** *TV.*

South Edinburgh

Deluxe (over £185)

Prestonfield

Priestfield Road, Prestonfield, EH16 5UT (668 3346/fax 668 3976/www.prestonfieldhouse.com). Bus 2, 14, 21, 33. **Rates** from £195 single; from £195 double; from £250 suite. **Credit** AmEx, DC, MC, V.
Like its sister hotel the Witchery, Prestonfield has recently benefited from the James Thomson treatment. Following the investment of £2 million, the parkland-set hotel is more grand European chateaux than staid Jacobean manor. Much of the character of the 1687 building has been retained – from its winding, tree-lined drive to its heavy ceiling cornicing – but the new European flavour extends from the antique furniture and upholstery imported from France, Germany and Holland. The Rhubarb restaurant (*see p146*) typifies the style – a cornucopia of blood-red chairs, opulent matching wallpaper and scarlet flowers (imported daily from Amsterdam). The amber and gold-infused Yellow Room and the

red nubuck-strewn Leather Room are furnished with materials from the 16th and 17th centuries: the effect is a palatial, historical gem. Rooms are located in the newly built extension to the rear of the property. In keeping with the sumptuous splendour of the public areas, they exemplify the happy coupling of comfort and history – antique pieces next to a plasma screen TV for example. All rooms have views over the extensive gardens or golf course – and don't be surprised to see the odd peacock or Highland cow saunter past: it's all part of the utterly decadent experience. Simply without comparison.
Hotel services *Air conditioning. Bar (butler service). Business services. Disabled: access, adapted rooms (2). Garden. No-smoking rooms. Parking. Restaurant.* **Room services** *Bathrobe. Dataport. DVD. Hairdryer. Hifi. Iron. Minibar. Newspapers. Turndown. Wifi. Room service (24hr). TV: satellite.*

Moderate (£65-£115)

Best Western Edinburgh City

79 Lauriston Place, EH3 9HZ (622 7979/fax 622 7900/www.bestwesternedinburghcity.co.uk). Bus 23, 27. **Rates** from £60 single; from £80 double. **Credit** AmEx, DC, MC, V. **Map** p309 E7.
Unfussy and unpretentious, this is a smart, no-frills establishment. Built in 1879, the building was once a maternity hospital dedicated to James Young Simpson, the discoverer of chloroform. Rooms are all of a fair size.
Hotel services *Babysitting. Bar. Business services. Concierge. Disabled: access, adapted rooms (3). Parking (on street). Restaurant.* **Room services** *Dataport. Room service (24hr). TV: satellite.*

Borough Hotel

72-80 Causewayside, EH9 1PY (668 2255/fax 667 6622/www.boroughhotel.com). Bus 42. **Rates** from £70. **Credit** AmEx, DC, MC, V.
The Borough is now the haunt of a discerning, stylish set, eager to sample its spacious, retro-tinged bar area or its moderately priced, yet beautifully varied restaurant. A boutique hotel in every sense, its rooms are located upstairs in surprisingly serene environs. Much is made of beechwood panelling and bold blocks of colour – the effect is sumptuous, stylish and utterly relaxing. No expense is spared on the bathrooms: contemporary finishes, a monsoon shower and even rubber ducks complete the look. The Borough is ideal for those who want to keep their options open: a buzzing bar downstairs, the city centre a ten-minute walk away, yet with this contemporary snug as a base.
Hotel services *Air conditioning. Bar. Business services. Internet access. No-smoking rooms. Parking (on street). Restaurant.* **Room services** *Bathrobe. DVD. Hairdryer. Room service (24hr). TV: satellite.*

Minto Hotel

16-18 Minto Street, EH9 9RQ (668 1234/fax 662 4870/www.edinburghmintohotel.co.uk). Bus 7, 8, 31, 80. **Rates** £50-£60 single; £70-£95 double; £95-£125 family room. **Credit** AmEx, DC, MC, V.

Alternative accommodation

In addition to hotels and hostels, Edinburgh offers a variety of other accommodation options, including campsites and caravan parks, private apartments and seasonal lets. As with hotels, watch out for good deals. And remember: venturing just a few streets outside the city centre often means stumbling upon better value accommodation.

Camping & caravanning

Edinburgh Caravan Club Site

Marine Drive, Silverknowes, EH4 5EN (312 6874/fax 336 4269/www.caravan club.co.uk). Bus 16, 27, 28, 29. **Open** *Reception 8am-8pm daily.* **Rates** £9.50-£11.50 pitch; plus £3.80-£5 per adult; £1.10-£1.60 per child; other prices vary. **Credit** MC, V.

Mortonhall Caravan Park

Frogston Road East, EH16 6TJ (664 1533/fax 664 5387/www.meadowhead. co.uk/mortonhall). Bus 11, 32, 52. **Open** *Reception low season 8am-6pm daily; high season 8am-9pm daily.* **Rates** £9.75-£15.25 pitch & 2 adults; £1 per extra person/dogs. **Credit** MC, V.

Letting

Hotel accommodation works well for a few nights' stay, but for longer-term visits they can be restrictive and pricey. Renting a private flat is a popular form of cheap accommodation if you're planning on hanging around Edinburgh for some time. During the Festival and Hogmanay it's especially busy and the prices of many residences will inflate with demand – it's best to book early.

Below is a list of serviced accommodation that is available year-round. Much like a hotel with enhanced facilities, it's a luxurious option if you're travelling as a group or just prefer a bit more space. Self-catering accommodation tends to be a cheaper option; a selection of properties are listed below. Bear in mind, though, that some flats have a minimum let period of a few nights. A number of private landlords let properties throughout the city on a short-term basis – perhaps one week or one month. Most of the bookings are driven through websites, and some of the best are listed below. The city's many accommodation agencies tend to let flats on long-term contracts only, but we've listed a choice of organisations that specialise in shorter-term rentals. If you're staying during the summer period, and you think youth hostelling equates with slumming it, then the city's universities offer good value accommodation in their halls of residence.

If something longer-term still is required, and you're on a budget, then flatshares are a comfortable option. Look in the *Scotsman*'s accommodation section on a Thursday for rooms available in shared flats. The *List* magazine, which tends to have a younger readership, publishes a selection of flatshare ads on a fortnightly basis. Most are bound by a six-month lease, but a few ads crop up for one week or month-long lets. For an extensive online selection of longer-term lets, the ESPC website (**www.espc.co.uk**) has a variety of flatshare and flat-to-let ads. There are a number of specific flatshare sites, including www.accommodationforstudents.com, www.uk.easyroommate.com and www.flatmatesedinburgh.net.

A less methodical approach to letting is to keep an eye out around town. **Real Foods** on Broughton Street (*see p185*), **Helios Fountain** on the Grassmarket (*see p192*) and newsagents around the universities often have cards in the windows offering rooms for rent. There's no quality control mechanisms in place, of course, so exercise vigilance when viewing properties.

The Minto Hotel provides a cheap stopover for groups. There's invariably a wedding or party taking place in the hotel's function suite. And while the establishment falls into the fairly basic but comfortable category it's the warmth of the welcome that keeps the regulars flocking back.

Hotel services *Bar. Business services. Disabled: access, adapted rooms (15). Garden. No-smoking rooms. Parking. Restaurant.* **Room services** *Hairdryer. TV.*

Novotel Edinburgh Centre

80 Lauriston Place, EH3 9DE (656 3500/fax 656 3510/www.accor-hotels.com). Bus 1, 10, 11, 15, 15A, 16, 17, 23, 24, 27, 28, 34, 35, 45. **Rates** from £100 single; from £100 double. **Credit** AmEx, DC, MC, V. **Map** p309 E7.

One of the newest additions to Edinburgh's hotel family, and a welcome addition to the range of more moderately priced hotels in this expensive to stay in capital city. Accommodation is the standard typical

Serviced accommodation

An interesting alternative that offers the best of hotel services and luxury, coupled with the privacy and freedom of your own apartment. It's not cheap, however.

Canon Court Apartments

20 Canonmills, New Town, EH3 5LH (474 7000/fax 474 7001/www. canoncourt.co.uk). Bus 8, 23, 27. **Open** *Reception 8am-8pm Mon-Fri; 8.30am-2pm Sat, Sun.* **Rates** (per night) £67-£170. **Credit** AmEx, DC, MC, V. **Map** p306 E2.

Chester Residence

9 Chester Street, New Town, EH3 7RF (226 2075/fax 226 2191/ www.chester-residence.com). Bus 13. **Open** *9am-10pm daily.* **Rates** (per night) £120-£230. **Credit** AmEx, MC, V. **Map** p308 D5.

Fountain Court Apartments

123 Grove Street, West Edinburgh, EH3 8AA (622 6677/www.fountaincourt apartments.com). Bus 1, 2, 22, 34. **Open** 8.30am-7pm Mon-Fri. **Rates** (per night) from £60. **Credit** MC, V. **Map** p308 C7.

Glen House Apartments

101 Lauriston Place, South Edinburgh, EH3 9JB (228 4043/fax 229 8873/www. edinburgh-apartments.co.uk). Bus 23, 28, 45. **Open** 9.30am-4.30pm Mon-Fri. **Rates** (per night) £45-£220. **Credit** AmEx, MC, V. **Map** p309 E7.

Kew Apartments

1 Kew Terrace, West Edinburgh, EH12 5JE (313 0700/fax 313 0747/ www.kewhouse.com). Bus 26, 31. **Open** 8am-10pm daily. **Rates** (per night) £90-£275. **Credit** AmEx, MC, V. ▶

to the mid-market Novotel chain: good-sized rooms are furnished in a contemporary, minimalist style. Like the welcoming reception area, the Garden Brasserie is light and informal.
Hotel services *Air conditioning. Babysitting. Bar. Business services. Concierge. Disabled: access, adapted rooms (5). Gym. Internet access. No-smoking rooms. Parking. Pool. Restaurant.* **Room services** *Bathrobe. Dataport. Ethernet. Hairdryer. Iron. Minibar. Newspaper. TV: satellite.*

Point Hotel

34 Bread Street, EH3 9AF (221 5555/fax 221 9929/www.point-hotel.co.uk). Bus 1, 10, 11, 16, 17, 28, 34, 35. **Rates** £60-£90 double/twin; £90-£300 suite. **Credit** AmEx, DC, MC, V. **Map** p309 D6.
Owned and designed by architect Andrew Doolan, this 140-room hotel – most with excellent views of the Castle – has represented state-of-the-art metropolitan minimalism since 1995. The clean lines,

No.5 Self-catering Apartments
3 Abercorn Terrace, Portobello, EH15 2DD (tel/fax 669 1044/www.numberfive.com). Bus 2, 15, 19, 26, 32. **Open** *Reception* 9am-10pm daily. **Rates** £75-£400 per wk. **No credit cards.**

Royal Garden Apartments
York Buildings, Queen Street, New Town, EH2 1HY (625 1234/fax 625 5678/www. royal-garden.co.uk). Bus 4, 8, 10, 12, 15, 16, 17, 26. **Open** 7am-7pm Mon-Fri; 8am-8pm Sat, Sun. **Rates** (per night) £130-£365. **Credit** AmEx, MC, V. **Map** p306 D4.

West End Apartments
2 Learmonth Terrace, Stockbridge, EH4 1PQ (332 0717/fax 226 6513/www.edinburgh apartments.biz). Bus 19, 41. **Open** 9am-11pm daily. **Rates** £280-£700 per wk. **No credit cards. Map** p305 B4.

Self-catering flats

Not as luxurious as serviced accommodation, self catering flats ars designed to be let in the short term for holiday or business guests. They are generally a less pricey alternative, particularly for a medium or long stay.

AEM Apartments, Morningside
663 3291.

Ardmor Apartment
554 4944/www.ardmorapartments.com.

Calton Apartments
556 3221/www.townhousehotels.co.uk.

Gladstone's Land (NTS property)
243 9331/www.nts.org.uk.

3 Great King Street (JM Barrie's former lodging)
01750 32213/www.ashkirk.demon.co.uk.

12 Abercromby Place
556 4374/http://home.btconnect.com/ jayrobertson.

21 Hanover Street
01383 853358/http://members. edinburgh.org/21hanover.

Royal Mile Apartment
554 1301/www.edinburghroyalmile.co.uk.

Royal Mile Mansions
669 3771/www.apartmentscentral.co.uk.

Swanston Cottages
445 5744/www.swanston.co.uk.

Private letting websites

Independent landlords who let properties for short- or long-term stays in Edinburgh.

Apartments in Edinburgh
www.apartmentsinedinburgh.com. Central flats for long and short term lets.

Edinburgh Holiday Flats
www.edinburghholidayflats.com. A variety of stylish properties.

Glen House Apartments
www.edinburgh-apartments.co.uk. No online booking, but a good range of flats.

Agencies

Clouds
26 Forth Street, EH1 3LH (550 3808/www. clouds.co.uk). Playhouse buses. **Open** 9am-5pm Mon-Fri. **Credit** MC, V. **Map** p307 G3. An Edinburgh-based agency that manages a host of affordable and luxury properties in the city. Prices start at a very reasonable £200 per week. Clouds specialises in short term lets, particularly during the Festival.

sweeping curved walls and blocks of soft colour give a feeling of futuristic fluidity and space. The white bedrooms – some with wide stripes of colour – plus black leather furniture and low-level beds swathed in white linen, have an understated simplicity, but there's no compromise on comfort. The executive suites are all huge, as are the bathrooms; some have square, internally lit Jacuzzis. Environmentally friendly sensor-activated heating clicks on as you enter the rooms. The ground-floor Point Restaurant serves mainly modish European dishes with a local flavour – three courses for a mere £14.90. The glass-fronted Monboddo bar is stylish and popular, and it also showcases the work of the American artist, Beckerman Balken.

Hotel services *Babysitting. Bar. Disabled: access, adapted rooms. No-smoking rooms. Restaurant.* **Room services** *Internet access: executive rooms. Newspapers. Room service (10am-10pm daily). TV.*

Factotum

63 Dublin Street, New Town, EH3 6NS (539 1100/fax 539 1110/www.factotum.co.uk). Bus 23, 27, 28. **Open** 9am-5.30pm Mon-Fri. **Credit** MC, V.

Festival Beds

Information & reservations 225 1101/fax 225 2724/www.festivalbeds.co.uk. **Open** *Mar-Oct* 9am-5.30pm Mon-Fri. Closed Nov-Feb. **Credit** MC, V.

If you arrive when the Festival is in full swing and have nowhere to stay, then this is the place to contact for bed and breakfast in a private house; around 60 properties contribute. In the past, the occupancy rate has been as low as 50% during the Festival season, so you're more than likely to find a proper bed. Less clued-up visitors have been spotted sleeping on the streets - not recommended, even in the summer.

Festival flats

Mackay's Agency

30 Frederick Street, New Town, EH2 2JR (225 3539/fax 226 5284/www.mackays-scotland.co.uk). Bus 10A, 23, 27, 28. **Open** Office 9am-5pm Mon-Fri; 9am-4pm Sat; 10am-2pm Sun. *Phone enquiries* 9am-7pm Mon-Fri. **Credit** MC, V. **Map** p304 B1.

3 Linkylea Cottages

Gifford, East Lothian, EH41 4PE (01620 810 620/fax 01620 810619/www.festivalflats. com). **Open** 9am-5pm Mon-Fri. **No credit cards.**

Seasonal lets

Universities let out their halls of residence during student holidays. They can be some way out of town, but are a useful form of basic accommodation.

Carberry Tower Conference Centre

Musselburgh, EH21 8PY (665 3135/ fax 653 2930/www.carberry.org.uk). Bus 15, 26, 44. **Rates** B&B £26-£36. **Credit** MC, V.

Edinburgh University Accommodation Service

18 Holyrood Park Road, South Edinburgh, EH16 5AY (667 1971/fax 668 3217/ www.accom.ed.ac.uk). Bus 2, 14, 21, 23. **Rates** £28-£49 single; £80-£98 twin. **Credit** MC, V. **Map** p310 J8.

Fet-Lor Youth Centre

122 Crewe Road South, Cragleith, EH4 2NY (332 4506). Bus 19, 29, 37. **Rates** £10 per person. **No credit cards.** Available during Festival only.

Heriot-Watt University Conference Office

Heriot-Watt University, Riccarton Campus, Riccarton, EH14 4AS (451 3669/fax 451 3199/www.eccscotland.com). Bus 25, 34, 35, 45. **Rates** B&B £37.50 single; £55 double. **Credit** MC, V.

Napier University Conference & Letting Services

219 Colinton Road, Craiglockhart, West Edinburgh, EH14 4DJ (455 3738/fax 455 3739/www.napier.ac.uk). Bus 4, 10, 18, 27, 45. **Rates** £335-£535 per wk. **Credit** MC, V.

Queen Margaret University College

Hospitality Services Department, Clerwood Terrace, Corstorphine, EH12 8TS (317 3310/fax 317 3169/www.qmuc.ac.uk). Bus 26, 103, 203. **Rates** B&B £27 single; £38 twin. **Credit** MC, V.

Hostels

Edinburgh Bruntsfield Youth Hostel (SYHA)

7 Brunstfield Crescent, EH10 4EZ (447 2994/ central reservations 08701 553255/fax 452 8588/ www.syha.org.uk). Bus 11, 15, 16, 17, 23. **Beds** 126. **Open** *Reception* 7am-11pm daily. No curfew. **Rates** (membership not included) *Sept-May* £11.75. *June* £13.50. *July* £14. *Aug* £16. **Credit** MC, V.

West Edinburgh

Deluxe (over £185)

Sheraton Grand Hotel

1 Festival Square, Lothian Road, EH3 9SR (229 9131/fax 228 4510/www.sheraton.com). Bus 10, 11, 16, 17. **Rates** £180 single; £220 double; £400 £700 suite. **Credit** AmEx, DC, MC, V. **Map** p309 D6.

This imposing concrete hotel block in the heart of Edinburgh's business district once swarmed with a peculiar mix of officious suits and less adventurous travellers. Now, thanks to recent investments, its delectable One Spa has become the hotel's unique selling point. Widely regarded as one of the best city spas in the world, its extensive treatments and facilities have locals and tourists booking time in their diaries months in advance. Despite these advances, the feeling that you could be anywhere in the world remains. Its two restaurants (the informal Terrace and fine dining area the Grill Room) are enticing. **Hotel services** *Air conditioning. Babysitting. Bar. Beauty salon. Business services. Concierge. Disabled: access, adapted rooms (2). Gym. Internet access. Limousine. No-smoking rooms. Parking (£8). Restaurants (4). Swimming pool.* **Room services** *Dataport. Hairdryer. Minibar. Refrigerator. Room service (24hr). TV: satellite.*

Expensive (£115-£185)

Ramada Jarvis Edinburgh Murrayfield Hotel

Ellersly Road, EH12 6HZ (337 6888/fax 313 2543/ www.ramadajarvis.co.uk). Bus 12, 26, 31, 38. **Rates** £120 single; £145 double; £165 executive. **Credit** AmEx, DC, MC, V.

It's easy to forget that you're just moments from Murrayfield Stadium here. Park the car on the gravel drive in front of the hotel's moss-covered exterior, and then stroll inside to relax in front of the open fire in the bar. The patio doors at the back of the building lead onto a croquet lawn, which adds to the overall impression that you've stumbled into a Merchant Ivory production. The small and rather ordinary rooms are somewhat out of kilter with the rest of the hotel, but for a quiet retreat this is a popular business and tourist choice.

Hotel services *Babysitting. Bar. Business services. Concierge. Disabled: access, adapted rooms (2). Garden. Internet access. No-smoking rooms. Parking. Restaurant.* **Room services** *Bathrobe. Ethernet. Hairdryer. Room service (24hr). TV: satellite.*

Moderate (£65-£115)

Dunstane House Hotel

4 West Coates, Haymarket, EH12 5JG (337 6169/ fax 337 6060/www.dunstane-hotel-edinburgh. co.uk). Bus 2, 12, 26, 31. **Rates** from £49 single; from £88 double. **Credit** AmEx, MC, V. **Map** p308 A6.

Designed by architect William Playfair in 1852, Dunstane House is a converted mansion located in the western reaches of the city. Before becoming a hotel in 1969, its previous incarnations included a base for the Royal Bank of Scotland. Now owned by Orkney-born couple Shirley and Derek Mowat, the Orcadian theme is represented in the Skerries Restaurant (fresh produce from Orkney is delivered twice-weekly) and the Stane Bar, which specialises

in malt whiskies. A quaint country feel to the bedrooms complements the traditional decor of the luxuriant public rooms – floral bedspreads and decorative wallpaper in autumnal colours are cosy without being straining on the eyes. A visit in summer is highly recommended – the tempting patio tables in the front gardens are perfect for sipping a cool Chardonnay and gazing out over the Edinburgh skyline while the sun slowly sets in the northern sky. **Hotel services** *Bar. Business services. Garden. Internet access. No-smoking rooms. Parking. Restaurant.* **Room services** *Hairdryer. Iron. Room service (noon-9.30pm daily). TV.*

Orocco Pier

17 High Street, South Queensferry, EH30 9PP (331 1298/fax 331 4731/www.oroccopier.co.uk). Bus 43. **Rates** from £70 single; from £90 double. **Credit** MC, V.

Few city centre hotels could offer any of the individualisms of Orocco Pier. Located just ten miles west of the city centre, in South Queensferry, Orocco Pier's ethos is 'eat, drink, dream', and the hotel's designers have pulled out every stop to ensure guests do just that. Following a half million pounds' investment in the former coaching inn, the white-fronted building has been transformed into a striking and stylish bistro and bar with rooms – think secluded booths and subdued lighting. The extensive menu is typically Scots fusion with some unexpected twists – one being moderate pricing for such salubrious surrounds.

However, the hotel's *pièce de résistance* is location: it occupies a space directly between the Forth road and rail bridges – expansive windows and clever lighting maximise the striking vista. The contemporary-styled bedrooms to the rear benefit from a relaxing soundtrack of waves lapping against the shore; those to the front look onto the quaint cobbled High Street. All rooms, in addition to the usual TV/DVD gadgetry, are furnished with a fibre optic lighting device that produces an ethereal display of sleep-inducing coloured swirls. A dream of a hotel. **Hotel services** *Bar. Business services. Internet access. No-smoking rooms. Parking (on street). Restaurant.* **Room services** *DVD. Hairdryer. Minibar. TV.*

Budget (under £65)

Travel Inn

1 Morrison Link, EH3 8DN (228 9819/fax 228 9836/www.travelinn.co.uk). Bus 12, 21, 22, 25, 26. **Rates** £52.95. **Credit** AmEx, DC, MC, V. **Map** p308 C6.

One of the cheapest room rates in the city. All 282 rooms are priced at £52.95, and can squeeze in two adults and two kids. The informal ground-floor restaurant is open all day. However, there's no room service or phones.

Hotel services *Bar. Disabled: access, adapted rooms (15). No-smoking rooms. Parking. Restaurant.* **Room services** *Dataport. No phone. TV.*

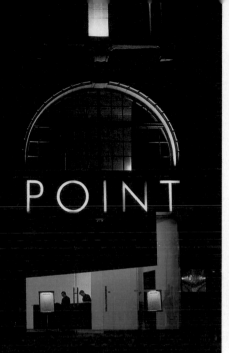

What's the **Point**? *See p59.*

Hostels

Edinburgh Eglinton Youth Hostel (SYHA)

18 Eglinton Crescent, West End, EH12 5DD (337 1120/central reservations 08701 553255/fax 313 2053/www.syha.org.uk). Bus 12, 21, 25, 26, 31, 33. **Beds** 150. **Open** *Reception* 7am-11pm daily. No curfew. **Rates** (membership not included) *Jan* £11.75. *Feb-Mar; Oct-Dec* £12.50. *Apr, May* £13. *June, Sept* £13.50. *July* £14. *Aug* £16. Under-18 prices £10.50-£14. **Credit** MC, V. **Map** p308 A6.

Leith & the coast

Expensive (£115-£185)

Malmaison

1 Tower Place, EH6 7DB (555 6868/fax 468 5002/ www.malmaison.com). Bus 10A, 16, 22, 35. **Rates** £130 single/double; £145-£165 suite. **Credit** AmEx, DC, MC, V. **Map** p311 Jx.

The first home of the Malmaison chain, this hotel opened in September 1994. Designer Amanda Rosa transformed this ex-seamen's mission on the Leith dockside. The subtle style and sexy sophistication of this award-winning hotel have helped to breathe new life into Edinburgh's hotel trade by setting a new standard in chic sleek décor at affordable prices.

All bedrooms are decorated in either checks or wide stripes, using a muted but effective palette of coffee and cream through to navy and olive. The best rooms are the suites at the front, the four-poster rooms and the max rooms (double doubles). Attention to detail is clearly a priority. There's a 24-hour gym, should you be struck by a sudden urge to work out at four in the morning and Chef Yannick Grospellier serves up uncomplicated French-style food, while the adjacent café serves wholesome vegetarian fare (*see p159*).

Hotel services *Babysitting. Bar. Business services. Disabled: access, adapted rooms (2). Gymnasium. Parking (on street). Restaurant. Terrace.* **Room services** *Dataport. Hifi. Minibar. Refrigerator. Room service (24hr). TV: satellite.*

Moderate (£65-£115)

Express by Holiday Inn

Britannia Way, Ocean Drive, EH6 6LA (555 4422/fax 555 4646/www.hiex-edinburgh.com). Bus 10, 16, 22, 34. **Rates** £79-£110 twin/ double/family. **Credit** AmEx, DC, MC, V. **Map** p311 Hx.

Guests at the Holiday Inn Express enjoy views of one of the city's most popular tourist attractions, the Royal Yacht *Britannia*. Ocean Terminal, the megalithic retail and entertainment complex, is also near at hand (*see p177*). The accommodation itself has all the pros and cons that go with a purpose-built hotel. At the time of writing, a city centre Holiday Inn was being constructed on Picardy Place, opposite the Omni Centre and Playhouse Theatre.

Hotel services *Bar. Business services. Disabled: access, adapted rooms (6). No-smoking rooms. Parking.* **Room services** *Dataport. Hairdryer. Radio. TV: satellite.*

Other locations: Picardy Place, Old Town, EH1 (668 2300); 132 Corstorphine Road, EH12 (0870 400 9026); 107 Queensferry Road, EH4 3HL (332 2442).

Budget (under £65)

Bar Java

48-50 Constitution Street, EH6 6RS (553 2020/ fax 554 1299/www.hotelbarjava.com). Bus 16, 22, 34. **Rates** £25-£50 double. **Credit** MC, V. **Map** p311 Jz.

Near the rejuvenated Leith dock area and popular with Festival and Hogmanay performers for obvious reasons given its reasonable rates. Bar Java has nine rooms – eight doubles with one family room suitable for four or five guests – are each named after a different island. Plans are underway to build en suite facilities in eight of its nine rooms. Below the accommodation is a funky bar with a beer garden. Snacks and a wide variety of flavoured teas, coffees and smoothies are available all day, along with an excellent brunch on Sundays. Guests can make full use of the bar, café and satellite TV lounge.

Hotel services *Bar. Garden. Parking (on street).* **Room services** *TV.*

Sightseeing

Features

Map

Introduction

Where to begin?

Edinburgh is well on its way to becoming a genuine European capital city. By the end of 2004, its hot-to-trot new **Parliament** building (*see p28* **What price democracy?**) will finally be unveiled at Holyrood (near the Queen's official residence), providing a stylish home for Scotland's newly devolved government. This transformation from the starched primness of the past to the shiny modernity of the future has brought a wealth of opportunities for sightseers. Museums and historical buildings abound, juxtaposed with the new splashes of colour and culture that come from development.

Despite the city's increasing population, its multi-million pound constructions and the increasing traffic, the so-called 'city of seven hills' is very much in tune with its natural surroundings. Suburban villages like Stockbridge, Broughton, Leith and Duddingston have been gradually incorporated into the main body of the city but their distinct characters still remain intact.

Much of Edinburgh's enchanting neo-classical architecture is best viewed from natural beauty spots such as the top of Arthur's Seat, an unspoiled extinct volcano. The best way to see Edinburgh is to simply get lost in its maze of bridges, crescents and wynds – almost every street has something of unique interest.

ORIENTATION

The best way to negotiate your way around Edinburgh is to pay almost no attention to the street names. Instead, navigate according to the compass points in relation to the city's three major landmarks of **Arthur's Seat** (*see p107*), the **Castle** (*see p70*) and **Calton Hill** (*see p102*). South Edinburgh's major thoroughfare is a case in point. Step out of the **Scotsman Hotel** (*see p45*) and you're on North Bridge. You've hardly had time to admire the view before it becomes South Bridge, then Nicolson Street, then Clerk Street. By the time you reach Craigmillar Park two miles along the same street, its name has already changed a further four times.

This is annoyingly common in Edinburgh – the Royal Mile manages to cram in four different monikers, switching from Castlehill to Lawnmarket to High Street to Canongate, in 1,600 cobbled metres. Similarly, the best map in the world won't get you out of the muddle that

is the Cowgate, which despite not being a tunnel, runs happily under both South and George IV Bridges – neither of which, incidentally, seem like bridges at all when you're strolling along them.

The best place to start any tour is the **Old Town** (*see p68*). This is the area immediately south of Princes Street, dominated by the glowering silhouette of Edinburgh Castle. The Old Town was the original settlement of medieval Edinburgh and is bound to the north by Princes Street Gardens, and to the east and south by the Flodden Wall, which goes up to the Pleasance and has its south boundary just past where the Museum of Scotland now stands.

Looking north from the Castle eminence, the **New Town** (*see p89*) is the succession of magnificently regular 18th-century planned developments that stretch from Princes Street down the hill towards the Forth, and end at the Water of Leith. They are bounded to the east by Calton Hill, identifiable by the telescope-shaped Nelson Monument and the pillars of the National Monument, and to the west by the triple towers of St Mary's Episcopal Cathedral.

As Edinburgh extended, the New Town reached the leafy village of **Stockbridge** (*see p98*) and the rather less regimented developments of the Raeburn Estate, the Dean Village, with its two modern art galleries, and the Royal Botanic Garden.

To the south, Arthur's Seat dominates the skyline, with the tiny Duddingston village tucked behind it. **South Edinburgh** (*see p111*) stretches inland from the Meadows up towards the Pentland Hills. It includes the so-called villages of Bruntsfield and Marchmont, as well as Craigmillar Castle in Little France, and the Royal Observatory on Blackford Hill. **West Edinburgh** (*see p117*) goes from Lothian Road and the New Town out towards the airport, including the Union Canal, the new financial district, the Zoo and the old Roman port of Cramond on the Forth.

The port of **Leith** (*see p121*), at the north edge of the city, is a district in its own right and despite being part of Edinburgh, has traditions very much of its own, fiercely protected by its residents. Leith is flanked by the fishing village of Newhaven to the west and the seaside town of Portobello to the east.

Sightseeing

Great **Scott**! Stop the pigeon. *See p93.*

PLACES OF INTEREST

First-time visitors often make an immediate beeline for Edinburgh Castle, and in many ways this is justifiable – the Castle has a central role in the city's history and it's an ideal venue for playing 'King of the Castle'. However, the city has many better (and cheaper) alternatives for those on a short visit. Edinburgh's museums are all free to enter and, as a whole, offer a guide to Edinburgh's history better than any book. The recently refurbished **Royal Museum** and **Museum of Scotland** (*see p88*) on Chambers Street are the largest and widest in scope. The latter contains a thematically arranged exploration of Scottish history from its beginnings to the present day.

The **Museum of Edinburgh** on the Canongate (*see p84*), and the **People's Story Museum** across the road (*see p85*), are good guides to the city and its people. For those with strong stomachs, the **Museum of Pathology & Anatomy** is an absorbing display devoted to disease and other matters of the body (*see p115*).

There is a wealth of vibrant art galleries in the city to help digest the complexities of Edinburgh's history and art. Many of these are also free to enter and there is an invaluable courtesy bus link between the National Galleries. The **National Gallery** on the Mound (*see p93*) contains many Renaissance masters and the **Scottish National Gallery of Modern Art** (*see p101*) contains most of the big names in surrealism and abstract impressionism. The **Stills Gallery** (*see p212*) and the **Collective Gallery** (*see p210*), on Cockburn Street, are the best places to go to check out what is going on in the contemporary art scene.

Sightseeing tours

If walking round Edinburgh gets too much – and there are enough hills for that to be likely – three operators run open-top bus tours around the Old and New Towns. All start from Waverley Bridge and, while each offers a slightly different route, there is not a lot to choose between them. All tours take about an hour, and leave every ten to 20 minutes from about 9am to 7pm in the summer, 9am to 5pm in the spring and autumn, and 10am to 4pm in the winter. All go past most of the major sights and offer a one-day, 'hop on, hop off' ticket, which allows passengers to alight or rejoin the tour at any point along the way.

Edinburgh Classic Tour

Information 555 6363. **Tickets** £7.50; £2.50-£6 concessions. **Credit** MC, V.
The driver provides a commentary but all passengers also have their own headphones, with a choice of pre-recorded commentaries.

Guide Friday

Information 556 2244. **Tickets** £8.50; £2.50-£7 concessions. **Credit** MC, V.
A guide provides a running commentary on these green and cream buses, and can answer questions.

MacVintage Tours

Information 220 0770. **Tickets** *Red route* £8; £2.50-£7 concessions. *Blue route* £7.50; £2-£6.50 concessions. *Grand Tour* phone for details. *Royal Edinburgh* phone for details. **Credit** MC, V.
The over 30 years old, red and cream buses come with a conductor as well as a guide. It's worth asking about the Royal Edinburgh Ticket, which includes entry to Holyroodhouse, the Castle and *Britannia* in the price of the tour.

Old Town

The rock of history beneath your feet.

Calling Captain Kirk. **High Kirk of St Giles**.
See p77.

Edinburgh's Old Town is roughly defined as the area between Princes Street to the north and the Grassmarket/Cowgate to the south. More historic attractions are packed into this area than anywhere else in Scotland. The overcrowded feel of the Old Town is enhanced still by the wynds (alleys), closes (entries closed at one end), burrows and tunnels that are evident all around the Royal Mile. As the area, constrained by the defensive **Flodden Wall**, became more and more congested, expanding into these closes was the only option. Construction began on the wall in 1513 after the Scottish army suffered its worst ever defeat at Flodden that year. It was 50 years before it was completed, boxing in the Old Town and running east from the foot of Nor' Loch, now the site of Waverley Station, then south over the ridge of the Royal Mile, up the Pleasance and west along Drummond Street. The population grew quickly and the crammed infrastructure, coupled with the dire state of sanitation, led to a third of the city's residents being wiped out by plague by the end of the 16th century. The city recovered though, and by 1851 the population was a massive 40,000. For many it became too

much and a mass exodus, first called 'the Great Flitting', began towards the New Town.

The residential population is currently relatively low and the area is now more of a commercial and tourist centre. Walking around this historic square mile can at times be like perusing an open-air museum – most of its points of interest are open all year round and are free to enter. Jam-packed with buildings of immense historical interest, it was no suprise that the devastating Old Town fire in December 2002 was reported so widely around the world (*see p73* **Burning down the town**). Overlooking it all is Scotland's most visited landmark, the world-famous **Edinburgh Castle** (*see p70*). Officially, this was Edinburgh's first registered building but much of the original structure is long gone and what remains dates mostly from the 18th and 19th centuries.

The Old Town is linked to the south of the city by two bridges. **George IV Bridge**, upon which reside the **National Library of Scotland** and a series of trendy bars and restaurants, and **South Bridge**, which doesn't look like a bridge, but is made up of hidden arches. Looking north from South Bridge is the beautifully lit **North Bridge**, which gives walkers excellent views of Calton Hill and Arthur's Seat to the east.

Walking east, old Edinburgh continues down to the **Palace of Holyroodhouse** via the **Canongate**, once a separate burgh, but now a distinct part of the Old Town. A brewery and gas works once occupied the eastern end of the Royal Mile, but these have been replaced by the controversial new **Scottish Parliament** building, offices for the *Scotsman* newspaper and the high-tech **Our Dynamic Earth** attraction (*see p84*).

The Royal Mile

Edinburgh's most famous street runs from the top of Castlehill changing its name three times before it concludes at the Palace of Holyroodhouse. It is flanked on both sides by over 60 closes and wynds, which contain highly sought-after residential tenements and provide the eerie atmosphere for many of Edinburgh's popular ghost tours (*see p80* **Ghosts, trust us**).

During the height of the tourist season, the street becomes the focal point of the Festival, thronged with street performers, temporary stalls and masses of desperate thespians keen for you to see their shows. It is only too common for the unwary tourist to become the unwitting star/victim of an amateur juggling act or the bombarded paperweight for thousands of fliers and free newspapers (*see p32*). The unique drone of fully kitted out bagpipers provides the street's soundtrack throughout the year making it well nigh impossible to travel its length without having to hear at least one rendition of 'Flower of Scotland' (adopted by the Scots as their de facto national anthem).

Castlehill

The Royal Mile begins with Castlehill, home to Edinburgh Castle. There is evidence to suggest that the volcanic basalt of **Castle Rock** (which stands at 435feet/130metres) has been inhabited by humans since at least the ninth century BC. The Castle was a royal residence until the Lang Siege of 1571-73 when Mary, Queen of Scots' supporters in the Castle were bombarded by the Regent, who governed on behalf of her son, the infant King James VI of Scotland (James I of England). The royal home was then moved to Holyroodhouse at the other end of the Mile and the Castle was extensively refurbished and heavily fortified. The Castle was last involved in battle in 1745 when the

cannons were used to repel the invading forces of the Young Pretender, Charles Edward Stuart – or 'Bonnie Prince Charlie' as he was popularly known – the son of the deposed Catholic King James II (of England) and VII (of Scotland). Today the cannon's only use is to mark the striking of one o'clock, which has been done with precision by local hero 'Tam the Gun' for the past 20 years. The gun itself is not visible from the Esplanade but provides a daily fright for non-Edinburghers.

The approach to the Castle is through the Esplanade, where the world-famous and nearly always sold-out **Edinburgh Military Tattoo** has been held every Festival since 1950 (*see p41*), although there have been persistent suggestions that the Tattoo may move in the near future. During the rest of the year (when the temporary seating is not in place), the imposing Half Moon Battery dominates the Esplanade. Built after the Lang Siege to defend the east side of the castle (the other sides are all protected by sheer cliffs), it provided the basis for the Castle's massive artillery strength. Behind it on the left is the Palace, now one of the Castle's museums.

The view from the southern parapet of the Esplanade looks out over the suburbs of Edinburgh, which were once open heath, as far as the Pentland Hills. The northern aspect is over the New Town, across the Firth of Forth to Fife. A small gate at the eastern end of the north side leads down winding paths to Princes Street Gardens. There are various military memorials on the Esplanade serving as sombre remembrance to the many Scottish soldiers killed in action overseas.

A less welcome reminder comes in the shape of the Witches' Memorial, a lasting epitaph to the shameful history Edinburgh shares with much of Europe – burning women as witches. Although usually attributed to the Middle Ages, burning old ladies was, in fact, a sport of Renaissance and Enlightenment, rather than Medieval, Man. This bronze, wall-mounted well marks the place where over 300 women were burned as witches between 1479 and 1722.

On the extreme left, as you face away from the Castle, is **Ramsay Gardens**, an irregular complex of romantic baronial buildings bristling with spiral staircases and overhangs. Constructed around the poet Alan Ramsay's octagonal 'goose-pie' house, the buildings were mostly erected in the late 19th century to lure the upper classes back into the Old Town. The buildings, some of the city's most expensive real estate, are all privately owned. The low, flat building beside them was once the Castlehill reservoir, built in 1851, which supplied water to Princes Street. Nowadays, it

Sightseeing

houses the **Edinburgh Old Town Weaving Company** (*see p70*). Another popular tourist feature, the **Camera Obscura**, is really only worth a visit on clear days, and even then, it is only mildly diverting at best. Housed in the striking black and white tower on the left as you look down Castlehill, it contains a system of lenses and mirrors that project images of the surrounding area onto a disc inside. **Cannonball House**, nearby, is so called because of the two cannon balls lodged in the west gable end wall, about halfway up. They are said to have been placed there to mark the level to which water piped from Comiston Springs in the Pentland Hills would rise, proving that it could be used to feed the Castlehill reservoir.

Opposite this is the **Scotch Whisky Heritage Centre** (*see p72*), which occupies an old school building. As well as offering tours explaining the history of whisky-making, there is also a well-stocked shop, with samples, and an educational amusement ride. **The Hub** (*see p72*), standing where Castlehill meets the top of Johnston Terrace, was designed by Augustus Pugin, famed for the Houses of Parliament in London, and was completed in 1844 as the Victoria Hall, later becoming the Tolbooth St John's Kirk. Its 240-foot (73-metre) Gothic spire is the highest point in Edinburgh. The church was bought by the Edinburgh International Festival in 1998 as its headquarters.

Camera Obscura

Castlehill (226 3709). Bus 23, 27, 28, 35, 41, 42, 45. **Open** *Nov-Mar* 10am-5pm daily. *Apr-Oct* 9.30am-6pm daily. **Admission** £5.95; £3.80-£4.75 concessions; 10% discounts for families. **Credit** MC, V. **Map** p82 (Royal Mile) A1.

Created by the optician Maria Short in the 1850s, the Camera Obscura is a system of mirrors that projects a periscope image of the city onto a white disc in the centre of a small darkened room. Main landmarks are pointed out by the guides as they pan the lens across the city. Essentially, the Camera Obscura is of interest as a historical relic rather than a genuine attraction in its own right. Children will love it but, despite the tagline on the door ('Seeing is not believing'), the technology involved doesn't stretch your credulity very far. More impressive is the set of powerful telescopes on the roof that allow superb views across the city. One thing is for sure: once you have heard the guides tell you that with these lenses you can watch people going about their lives obliviously, you really begin to notice the CCTV cameras on the city's street corners.

Edinburgh Castle

Castlehill (inquiries 668 8800/ticket office 225 9846/ www.historic-scotland.gov.uk). Bus 23, 27, 28, 35, 41, 42, 45. **Open** (last entry 45 mins before closing) *Apr-Sept* 9.30am-6pm daily. *Oct-Mar* 9.30am-5pm

daily. **Admission** £9.50; £7 concessions; £2 under-16s. *Guided tour* free. *Audio guide* £3, £2 concessions, £1 under-16s. **Credit** AmEx, DC, MC, V. **Map** p82 (Royal Mile) A1.

Officially Scotland's most visited tourist attraction, despite its inflated entrance fee, Edinburgh Castle sits high on Castle Rock at the top of the Royal Mile. Its lofty position is extremely useful as a navigational guide once you have inevitably become lost in Edinburgh's warren of streets and closes.

The Castle is actually made up of a series of buildings, the oldest (St Margaret's Chapel) dates from the early 12th century. Most visitors use the audio guides (available in six languages) to lead them around the main sights. The Great Hall is situated on nearby Crown Square, which was created as the Castle's focal point during the reign of King James III (1460-88). Also on Crown Square is the Palace. This was the main royal residence before Holyroodhouse took over the role and was where Mary, Queen of Scots gave birth to James VI of Scotland in 1566. On the Palace's first floor is an exhibition built around the Honours of Scotland – the Scottish crown jewels, with the addition of the Stone of Scone, or Stone of Destiny, which is the ancient coronation stone of Scotland. It was stolen by Edward I in 1296 and finally brought here from Westminster Abbey in 1996. On the immediate right of the Square is the Scottish National War Memorial. A converted barracks, designed in 1924 by Sir Robert Lorimer, one of Scotland's leading restoration architects, it has been a shrine to Scotland's war dead since its opening by the Prince of Wales (who became Edward VIII) in 1927. The Castle is steeped in military history and is a fitting home for the National War Museum of Scotland. The history of Scotland's involvement in wars dating back 400 years is charted here, and in other regimental museums, in a humbling and mostly objective way. On show are a variety of uniforms, weapons, medals and Mons Meg – a giant 500-year-old cannon.

With the constant flow of tourists in and out of the old gates it is easy to forget that the Castle is still a working barracks (although this role has greatly diminished since 1923). In fact, the Castle has had to be adapted to many uses in its long history, including a records office, an ordnance factory and, during World War I, a military prison. Aside from the obvious points of interest in the grounds, the vantage point on top of Castle Rock holds breathtaking views. And in case you forget you're a tourist, the gift shops stacked with tartan tat should remind you.

Edinburgh Old Town Weaving Company

555 Castlehill (226 1555/www.scotweb.co.uk/ edinburgh/weaving). Bus 23, 27, 28, 35, 41, 42, 45. **Open** *Exhibition* 9am-5.30pm daily. *Shop* 9am-5.30pm Mon-Sat; 10am-5.30pm Sun. **Admission** *Building* free. *Tour* Mon-Fri (over 10 people, must be booked in advance) £3.60; £2.80 concessions; £2 under-16s. **Credit** AmEx, MC, V. **Map** p82 (Royal Mile) A1.

OLD FISHMARKET CLOSE

Been there. Got the T-shirt. The **Royal Mile**. See p69

No grass for sale. **Lawnmarket**.

plaster statues by Jill Watson representing people who have performed in the International Festival over the years. The ground floor and terrace café serves excellent, if rather pricey, food (*see p153*).

Scottish Whisky Heritage Centre

354 Castlehill (220 0441/www.whisky-heritage.co.uk). Bus 23, 27, 28, 35, 41, 42, 45. **Open** *Apr-Sept* 9am-6.30pm daily. *Oct-Mar* 10am-5pm daily. **Admission** £7.95; £4.25-£5.95 concessions; £18 family. **Credit** AmEx, DC, MC, V. **Map** p82 (Royal Mile) A1.
The shop inside the tourist-orientated whisky centre alone is worth a visit, with a huge selection of popular and less well-known blends and malts available. The most expensive is a 64-year-old whisky costing £10,000. The tour is the main attraction, though, and lasts about an hour. You are guided through a series of video displays, exhibitions and finally a theme-park style ride, all of which chart the history of whisky production, which was first recorded in 1497. Scotland's national drink is shown in all its constituent parts, with the tastes, smells and noises of its production cleverly intertwined in an educational, if light-hearted, sensory journey. Also included in the cover charge is a whisky glass designed to give serious whisky drinkers the ultimate Scotch experience and entice them down to the pleasant well-stocked bar below the exhibition.

Lawnmarket

The section of the Royal Mile between the Hub and the intersection of George IV Bridge is known as the Lawnmarket. Nothing to do with grass, the name comes from the fine linen cloth called 'lawn' that was sold here.

More interesting than the street itself are the closes that lead off it. On the left as you head down the High Street is **Gladstone's Land** (*see p75*), a well-maintained example of a plush 17th-century townhouse. The property dates from 1550 and was extensively rebuilt 70 years later by an ancestor of Prime Minister William Gladstone. Now it is owned by the National Trust for Scotland and visitors should note that it is only open between April and October. Similarly grand is the nearby **Lady Stair's House** (also dating from the 17th century). It currently holds the **Writers' Museum** which celebrates the work of Burns, Walter Scott and Robert Louis Stevenson. Its location is fitting, as Robert Burns stayed in Lady Stair's Close on his first visit to Edinburgh. The area itself is known collectively as Makars' Court, from 'makar', the archaic Scots word for poet; 17 Scottish writers of note are commemorated in paving stones approaching the Writers' Museum.

Also leading off the Lawnmarket is Mylne's Court, the temporary home for the **Scottish Parliament Debating Chamber** until it moves to Holyrood in the summer of 2004.

Behind the extensive tartan-stacked shop, paying visitors can see the processes that go into producing Scotland's national dress. Skilled workers attend noisy working looms whose output appears for sale at the front of the shop. There is a 'through the ages' guide to tartan and also the unique opportunity for you to have a go at tartan-weaving yourself. Whether you're in the market for kilts or not, the process of their manufacture is genuinely fascinating.

The Hub

348 Castlehill (473 2000/www.eif.co.uk/thehub). Bus 23, 27, 28, 35, 41, 42, 45. **Open** *Shop & Café* 9.30am-6pm Mon, Sun; 9.30am-9.30pm Tue-Sat. *Ticket office* 10am-5pm Mon-Fri. *Festival office* 9am-7.30pm Mon-Sat, 10am-7.30pm Sun. **Admission** free. **Credit** AmEx, MC, V, DC. **Map** p82 (Royal Mile) A1.
The Tolbooth St John's Church was built as the Victoria Hall for the Established Church General Assembly in 1844, in response to the religious 'Disruption' of the previous year (*see p20*). Having fallen out of use as a church during the 1960s, it was lovingly refurbished in 1999 for the Edinburgh International Festival, which has its offices under the roof. The bold colour scheme of the Assembly Hall upstairs – said to adhere to architect Augustus Pugin's original palette – is worth seeing all by itself. The rich red stairwell is decorated with some 200

Burning down the town

On Friday 7 December 2002, Edinburgh's Old Town hit the headlines the world over. As smoke and flames rose high into the night sky, photographers and journalists outnumbered fire engines, and crowds gathered to see a World Heritage Site dramatically burn to the ground. Miraculously, there was not a single injury despite the proximity of the blaze to some of the area's most popular nightclubs, concentrated with boozed-up youngsters.

As the embers cooled the next day, stakeholders in the ruined buildings began counting their losses. The blaze itself cost the fire brigade £300,000 and the redevelopment of the area is estimated at £100m. Having initially feared arson, the fire brigade eventually attributed the fire to a faulty fuse-box.

Among the buildings destroyed were the popular live music venue La Belle Angele, the infamous Fringe venue the Gilded Balloon, and a section of residential flats. The University of Edinburgh's Informatics Department, situated on South Bridge, lost its entire library in the blaze. Art in Partnership, Scotland's leading public art commissions agency, who had offices in a neighbouring building, lost one of the best databases of artworks in Scotland.

The area on the Cowgate was a popular nightspot for clubbers but was notoriously unpopular with local residents, who objected to the late-night noise and the accompanying anti-social behaviour. For this reason, there has been much debate about what should replace the destroyed buildings, with residents starkly opposed to the granting of licences for replacement nightclubs.

The fire has also raised concerns for other property owners in the area. Fire officials described it as an accident waiting to happen. The cramped nature of the former buildings and the pockets of air provided by the hive of winding closes were ideal conditions for the inferno.

Today, the destruction is still plain to see since the plans to redevelop the area were delayed due to wrangling over the future of the site. Eventually the key owners enlisted the help of leading city architect Malcolm Fraser to form a development company. The latest plan envisages a central square forming the heart of a new development, complete with stunning closes and wide steps linking the site to the Cowgate and surrounding streets.

Members of the public are allowed in the public gallery; schedules can be obtained from the Scottish Parliament Visitor Centre on George IV Bridge. Also accessible from Mylne's Court is **James's Court**, where James Boswell (biographer of the dictionary writer Dr Johnson) lived. In the restored 18th-century courtyard at the bottom of James's Court is the Jolly Judge (225 2669), a convenient and cosy pub with an open fire, and a favourite with thirsty politicians. **Riddles Close** is the most interesting entry to explore, leading into two courtyards; it was from here that philosopher David Hume published his *Political Discourses*. **Brodie's Close** was the home of the notorious Deacon Brodie, a respected member of

Edinburgh society who led a double life as a burglar (*see p14* **EdinBurgher Deacon Brodie**). He was put to death outside St Giles' on gallows he had designed himself – an irony remembered in the plaque on the wall of Deacon Brodie's Tavern.

Bank Street, which winds round to the left to become the Mound, is home to the grand **Bank of Scotland** head office. Designed in the 1860s along classical lines but embellished with baroque flourishes it is topped off by a gold statue on its roof that is a highlight of Edinburgh's central skyline. It is here that the **Museum on the Mound** can be found – a section of the bank given over to coin collections, maps and other monetary

EdinBurgher Ian Rankin

When hard-boiled pulp lit icon James Ellroy dubbed Ian Rankin the 'King of Tartan Noir', it was praise indeed for a writer who only a few years earlier had baulked at his books being dumped on the crime shelves. But, as with Ellroy, Raymond Chandler and co, the dour existentialist heart that drives Rankin's series of Inspector Rebus novels (all set in Edinburgh) has transcended genre fiction to become an international brand. At home, Edinburgh-based Ian Rankin is the UK's biggest-selling crime writer, his raincoat weighed down by assorted doctorates and crime writing awards that make him a very serious writer indeed.

Such highfalutin' accolades are a far cry from Cardenden, Fife, the library-less mining town where Rankin misspent his youth inventing make-believe bands and putting together his own comic books. His first book, *The Flood*, was published by Polygon in 1986, but it wasn't until a year later when Rebus was born in *Knots & Crosses* that Rankin hit pay dirt.

The appeal of Rebus and all his flaws isn't hard to grasp. He's a classic anti-hero, a mess of neuroses and an in-built disdain for authority – all shot through with classic Presbyterian self-loathing.

It is Edinburgh, however, that became the real star of the show. Rankin takes care to use genuine city locations, from the bleak desolation of Salisbury Crags (*see p107*) to the down-at-heel bonhomie of the **Oxford Bar**, a favourite real life haunt of Rankin (*see p169*). Like carelessly discarded clues,

there are traces of Rankin the Renaissance Man everywhere. One minute he's hanging out with the plain clothes squad in the Oxford, the next he's in **Avalanche Records** (*see p189*) picking up the latest Mogwai album. Turn on the telly and he's dropping pithy *bon mots* as a pundit on highbrow arts programme, *Newsnight Review*.

Given such hip ubiquity, it was a surprise to many when, in 2002, the Queen's Golden Jubilee year no less, the old punk accepted the ultimate pat on the head from the English establishment, an OBE. Better watch your back, there, Rankin. If you're not careful you'll have Rebus joining the Masons.
www.ianrankin.net

memorabilia. The Mound leads down on to Princes Street, Edinburgh's busiest thoroughfare, and is the best place to catch one of the city's many tour buses. It is flanked by Prince's Street Gardens, upon which the **National Gallery** and the **Royal Scottish Academy** can be found.

The road that intersects the Lawnmarket from the south is George IV Bridge. It was opened in 1834 to complement the parallel South Bridge and crosses the Cowgate. Three libraries dominate: the **National Library of Scotland**, the **Central Library** and the **Music Library**. The tone is lowered by the ugly Scottish Parliament buildings, though these will be demolished once the new debating chambers at Holyrood are completed.

George IV Bridge leads to the statue of Greyfriars Bobby, and the famous **Greyfriars Kirk** cemetery where the dog is buried. The sculpture of the faithful Skye terrier is often kissed by sentimental tourists as they pass by. On the left of the bridge is Chambers Street, home to the **Royal Museum of Scotland**.

Central Library

George IV Bridge (242 8020/www.edinburgh.gov.uk/ libraries). Bus 23, 27, 28, 35, 41, 42, 45. **Open** 10am-8pm Mon-Thur, 10am-5pm Fri; 9am-1pm Sat. **Admission** free. **Map** p82 B2.

The headquarters of Edinburgh's library service was built in 1870 and houses the Edinburgh room, Scottish department and reference, fiction and lending libraries. The Edinburgh room is for reference only, but contains over 100,000 individual items pertaining to the city, from newspaper cuttings to historical records and prints. Some of these are available on loan from the Scottish department below. The children's and music libraries are housed in the next building along as you walk across the bridge. The latter has an extensive selection of sheetmusic, biographies and CDs from all genres. You have to be a resident of Edinburgh to borrow books but the library is free for all to browse.

Gladstone's Land

477b Lawnmarket (226 5856). Bus 23, 27, 28, 35, 41, 42, 45. **Open** Apr-Oct 10am-5pm Mon-Sat; 2-5pm Sun. *Guided tour* 1-2pm Sun (no booking; max 10). Closed Nov-Mar. **Admission** £5; £3.75 concessions; £13.50 family. **No credit cards**. **Map** p82 A1.

This National Trust for Scotland property is kept in the 17th-century style of its former owner, Thomas Gledstanes. Gledstanes bought the six-storey house in 1617 and extended it into the street to create room for an arcade and booths at the front. The displays of Dutch and Chinese porcelain are not really suited to such confined rooms, but the guides are always helpful. This is an essential stop in any tour of the Royal Mile that hopes to get under the un-soaped skin of historic Edinburgh.

Museum on the Mound

Bank of Scotland Head Office, The Mound (529 1288/www.bankofscotland.co.uk). Bus 23, 27, 28, 41, 42, 45. **Open** June-Sept 10am-4.45pm Mon-Fri. By appointment at other times. **Admission** free. **Map** p82 B1.

This small museum displays some of the Bank of Scotland's old documents, artefacts, notes and coins. The bank was founded by the Parliament of Scotland in 1695 and is one of the few institutions created by that parliament to have survived. To this day, the Bank of Scotland continues to issue its own banknotes, as do the country's other main banks, which are legal tender in England too.

National Library of Scotland

George IV Bridge (226 4531/www.nls.uk). Bus 23, 27, 28, 41, 42, 45. **Open** *Exhibition hall* June-Oct 10am-5pm Mon-Sat; 2-5pm Sun. Closed Nov-May. *Reading rooms* 9.30am-8.30pm Mon, Tue, Thur, Fri; 10am-8.30pm Wed; 9.30am-1pm Sat. *Shop* 10am-8.15pm Mon-Fri; 9.30am-12.45pm Sat. **Admission** free. **Map** p82 B2.

Surprisingly, Scotland did not have a national library until 1925, because this function was fulfilled by the Faculty of Advocates Library at Parliament House. The NLS is one of the UK's deposit libraries and contains seven million printed books, 1.6 million maps, 120,000 volumes of manuscripts, and over 20,000 newspaper and magazine titles. These are available to view for research purposes here and in the Causewayside Building to those 'requiring material not readily available elsewhere'. Admission to the reading rooms is by ticket only, for which identification is required. During the summer and autumn, the Exhibition Hall just inside the main door houses small exhibitions pertaining to Scottish books and writers; no ticket is required for this.

Scottish Parliament Debating Chamber

Mylne's Court, Lawnmarket (348 5411/ www.scottish.parliament.uk). Bus 23, 27, 28, 41, 42, 45. **Open** (last admission 15 mins before close) 10am-12.30pm, 1.45-4.15pm Mon, Tue, Fri; 9.30am-12.30pm, 1.45-end of parliamentary session (usually approx 5pm) Wed, Thur. **Admission** free. **Map** p82 A1.

Since Scotland voted for devolution from the British government in 1999, the Scottish Parliament has met on the Lawnmarket. The parliament has powers to pass laws on devolved matters in Scotland and has taken over most of the duties previously held by the Scottish Office. The venue on Mylne's Court will continue to be used for debates until the building work is completed on the new Parliament at the other end of the Royal Mile (expected to be in 2004). Tickets for the public gallery are free and available on a first come, first served basis, bookable up to seven days in advance. The best time to see the 129 MSPs in action is on a Thursday afternoon for First Minister's Question Time, but the chamber is open to the public at the above times.

Writers' Museum

*Lady Stair's House, Makars' Court, Lawnmarket
(529 4901/www.cac.org.uk). Bus 23, 27, 28, 35,
41, 42, 45.* **Open** *Sept-July* 10am-5pm Mon-Sat.
Aug 10am-5pm Mon-Sat; noon-5pm Sun.
Admission free. **Map** p82 A1.

Perhaps the most interesting thing about the
Writers' Museum is the building itself. Lady Stair's
House, built by William Gray in 1622, is remarkable
for its steep spiral staircases and maze-like layout.
It was gifted to the City of Edinburgh in 1907 and
now contains curiosities and memorabilia from
Scotland's three premier writers: Sir Walter Scott,
Robert Burns and Robert Louis Stevenson. Glass
cases are filled with early editions of the writers'
works and are complemented by models of the writers themselves with appropriate voiceover tapes.

Also on display is a selection of the writers' personal effects, including a large ornate pipe once
belonging to Walter Scott and one of Burns' snuff-
boxes. For those looking to make a day of it, there
is a relaxation area with a selection of the authors'
works and comfy chairs.

High Street, above the Bridges

The bronze statue of David Hume, the
Edinburgh-born philosopher and historian,
watches over this section of the Royal Mile.
Absurdly, for a 1997 statue of an 18th-century
figure, he appears to be clothed in classical
dress. Hume was a hugely influential figure in
the Scottish Enlightenment and his works are
still highly regarded today. The three brass
bricks laid into the pavement opposite Hume
mark the place where the last public hanging in
Edinburgh took place: on 21 June 1864, George
Bruce was put to death in front of 20,000 people.

The section of the Royal Mile above the
North and South Bridges is undeniably
impressive and was used in the film version
of Thomas Hardy's *Jude the Obscure* as a
stand-in for the fictional Oxford-like town of
Christminster. It is dominated by the **High
Kirk of St Giles**, where Scottish Reformer
John Knox once preached. In front of this,
in Parliament Square, is the **Heart of
Midlothian**, a heart shape set in the
cobblestones of the street. This marks the spot
where Edinburgh's Tolbooth prison stood (not
to be confused with the Canongate Tolbooth
which still survives). The Tolbooth was built
as a town hall and was used in the 16th and
17th centuries as a meeting place for the
Scottish Parliament until Charles I demanded
that a separate building be constructed for this
use. The prison often displayed the severed
heads of its executed criminals and this,
coupled with the dire state of its waste disposal
system, made it a pretty grim place to be. It was
eventually demolished in 1817 and, due to the

criminal fraternity's habit of spitting on the
ground outside the Tolbooth, the tradition is
carried on today with locals spitting on the
stones that make up the Heart of Midlothian.

A church has stood on this site from as far
back as the ninth century although the oldest
parts of the present structure date from around
1120. Newer features include the 1911 Thistle
Chapel, an intricately decorated chamber
designed by Robert Lorimer, the prominent
architect who also designed the Scottish War
Memorial at Edinburgh Castle (*see p70*). For
the pedantic, the fabric of the building itself
is referred to as St Giles, while the church is
known as the High Kirk of Edinburgh. The
Lower Aisle Restaurant, entered round the
corner of the church on the south side, is good
for a reasonably priced lunchtime bite, and is
popular with the city's lawyers who come
from the nearby courts.

Parliament Square was a bustling scene of
commerce in the 15th century, crammed with
shops and 'lucken booths' – lockable stalls.
Now, however, it stands empty. **Parliament
House** runs along the back of the square; its
plush Parliament Hall is worth a visit. Formerly
used by the Scottish Parliament in the 17th
century, it is now used by lawyers discussing
cases from the adjoining District Court, Court
of Session and High Court. Traditionally,
solicitors have marched up and down
Parliament Hall (usually in pairs) engaged in
dialogue about cases they are working on.

To the east of the Cathedral is the **Mercat
Cross**, identified by the white unicorn holding
the Saltire flag that stands proudly at the top of
the turret. Legend has it that a ghostly figure
spoke the names of those about to die in the
Battle of Flodden in 1513 from here (*see p11*).
Many executions were carried out at Mercat
Cross including the Marquis of Montrose in
1650, a royalist who, on returning to Britain
to avenge the death of Charles I, was hung,
drawn and quartered by Oliver Cromwell's
army. The Mercat Cross is also the spot where
royal proclamations were traditionally read out.

Across the High Street from St Giles are the
City Chambers where the city council sits.
Completed in 1761, and thus one of the first
truly Georgian buildings in Edinburgh, it was
originally part of the Royal Exchange, a trading
place for small businesses, but failed because
traders still preferred to do their business in the
open air at the Mercat Cross. The city council
moved into the building in 1811 but did not
have exclusive use until 1893. The Chambers
were built on top of three closes, the most
famous of which, Mary King's, is used today
as a spooky museum accessible as part of a
walking tour (*see p80* **Ghosts, trust us**). The

building of the City Chambers was a concerted effort to bury the horrific memories of disease, starvation and desperation that lurked in Mary King's Close when it was quarantined during the plague that struck in 1645. The whole close was blocked up and all its inhabitants left to die. Butchers were sent in later to dismember the corpses. Large sections of the close are still intact amid the City Chambers' foundations and it is reputed to be one of the most haunted places in Scotland; even sceptics find it eerie. In one room, the ghost of a little girl has been placated with gifts – dolls, sweets and coins – left by visitors.

Among several wynds and closes that lead off the High Street down onto Cockburn Street is Advocates Close. Further along the High Street is the **Police Information Centre**, an operational branch of the Lothians Police Force, which houses a small museum of local policing. There is also the Festival Fringe office and gift shop, where souvenirs can be purchased all year round. During the Fringe itself, the office has tickets on sale and is one of the busiest places in the city (see p41).

High Kirk of St Giles

High Street (225 4363/visitor services 335 9442). Bus 23, 27, 28, 35, 41, 42, 45/Nicolson Street–North Bridge buses. **Open** *Apr-Sept* 9am-7pm Mon-Sat. *Oct-Mar* 9am-5pm Mon-Sat. *Services* noon Mon-Sat; 8am, 10am, 11.30am, 6pm, 8pm Sun. **Admission** free; donations welcome. **Map** p82 (Royal Mile) B1.

Although nothing remains of the earliest structures there has been a church on the site of St Giles since 854. However, the four pillars surrounding the Holy Table in the centre have stood firm since around 1120, surviving the destructions of marauding English armies during the Reformation in the 16th century. The Kirk was considerably refurbished in the 19th century and much of what can be seen today dates from this period.

John Knox, the principal figure in Scotland's Reformation era, became minister here in 1560, 12 years before his death. This was a tumultuous time for religion in Scotland, with Edinburgh very much at the heart of the Scottish Reformation. The Kirk has changed its status many times and is often referred to as a cathedral today, even though it has only had two bishops in its history. Charles I first made it a cathedral in 1633 and it was still referred to as such even after the bishops were banished in the Glorious Revolution of 1688, although as a Presbyterian place of worship it cannot technically be considered a cathedral at all.

Inside, a great vaulted ceiling shelters a medieval interior dominated by the banners and plaques of many Scottish regiments. The main entrance takes visitors past the West Porch screen, originally designed as a royal pew for Queen Victoria. The dazzling West Window is by Icelandic stained-glass artist Leifur Breidfjord and was dedicated to Robert Burns' memory in 1984. The organ is an even more recent addition, from 1992, with a glass back revealing the workings. The Knights of the Thistle – an order of chivalry founded in 1687 – has its own chapel, an intimate panelled room with intricate wooden carvings of thistles, roses and shamrocks, divided into knights' stalls.

Police Information Centre

188 High Street (226 6966). Bus 23, 27, 28, 35, 41, 42, 45/North Bridge buses. **Open** *Mar-Apr* 10am-8pm daily. *May-Aug* 10am-10pm daily. *Sept-Feb* 10am-6pm daily. **Admission** free. **Map** p82 B1.

You name it, Edinburgh has a museum for it. This small room off the main street is staffed by working police officers and has a few fascinating exhibits including a macabre business-card holder made out of the cured skin of the infamous grave-robber William Burke (see p19). The small centre provides everything you should want to know about policing in Edinburgh, and the friendly city bobbies are only too happy to give you directions, advice, etc.

Scottish Parliament Visitor Centre

George IV Bridge (348 5411/www.scottish. parliament.uk). Bus 23, 27, 28, 35, 41, 43, 45. **Open** 9.30am Tue-Thur when Parliament is sitting; 10am-5pm Mon-Fri at other times. **Admission** free. **Map** p82 B1.

In these security conscious days, be prepared to put whatever you are carrying through an x-ray machine before being allowed to experience democracy Scotland-style. The exhibition is much like the parliament itself – it has obviously been assembled through a lot of hard work, with plenty of information on show, and there is a certain amount of technological wizardry involved. However, there doesn't appear to be any coherent arrangement of the data and instead the walls are choc full of dizzying statistics that attack you at every turn. There are fascinating exhibits, though, and, if you are prepared to put a bit of work in, plenty to be learned. The shop also takes bookings for the public gallery in the debating chamber on the Mound.

Cockburn Street & the Bridges

Cockburn Street is the city-centre's home to alternative culture. Its streets can usually be found ornamented by skiving youths loitering outside the record shops and counter-culture clothing stores (see p180). The street's two modern art galleries (the **Collective Gallery** and the **Stills Gallery**, see p210 and p212) add some class to the surroundings and provide an ideal starting point for a tour that can be continued on Market Street with the Fruitmarket Gallery and the City Art Centre. Music enthusiasts can easily spend a lot of time and money browsing in Cockburn Street's record shops: **Avalanche** and **Fopp** (see p189)

Sightseeing

Urban anthropology: how many tribes can you identify? **Cockburn Street**. *See p77.*

both offer a cheap alternative to the corporate superstores on Princes Street, with **Underground Solu'shn** aiming more at the vinyl-heavy dance market (*see p190*).

At the bottom of Cockburn Street is the Lothian Buses information centre, where timetables can be obtained and tickets can be booked for day trips around Scotland. Next door to this is the **Edinburgh Dungeon**, a popular attraction luring tourists in with ghoulishly dressed staff.

During August, Market Street is often lined with people queuing for tickets for the Edinburgh Military Tattoo. The event's offices are next to the Edinburgh Dungeon and are open all year round for the sale of related souvenirs. At the top of the street, on the corner with South Bridge, is the Tron Kirk. This area was the traditional gathering place for revellers seeing in the New Year until Edinburgh's official Hogmanay celebrations began in 1993 and the focus moved down to Princes Street. Just behind is Hunter Square, a pleasant place for a breather and usually busy at lunchtime.

At the traffic lights here, the High Street is cut in two by North Bridge and South Bridge, known together as 'the Bridges'. They were built to provide access to the south of the city and hastened expansion into the New Town in the late 18th century. Although South Bridge looks like a continuous street, it is in fact supported by 19 massive arches, only one of which is visible. The last building on the left

of North Bridge, looking towards the New Town, is the rugged, iconic edifice that housed Scotsman Publications (publishers of the *Scotsman*) throughout the 20th century. Purpose-built for the company in 1905, it was vacated in 1999 in favour of new premises at Holyrood and has since been transformed into a luxury hotel. At the front of the building is an enclosed spiral staircase that provides a short cut down to Market Street and Waverley Station; don't use it unless you enjoy the stench of stale urine. This dank stairway is the entirely believable setting for foul murder in several Edinburgh-set detective thrillers.

Edinburgh Dungeon

31 Market Street (240 1000/www.thedungeons.com). Princes Street buses. **Open** *Apr-Oct* 10am-5pm daily. *Nov-Mar* 11am-4pm daily. **Admission** £10.45; £6.45-£9.45 concessions. **Credit** AmEx, MC, V. **Map** p82 B1.

The history of Edinburgh is littered with grisly murders, ghoulish bodysnatching and horrific diseases, so it seems natural enough that the makers of the London and York Dungeons wanted to set up shop here. Much effort has gone into making the experience genuinely gruesome, with role-playing tour guides waiting to jump out at any opportunity. The exhibits concentrate mainly on events and figures of local history, and the infamous grave-robbing duo Burke and Hare are well represented. There are all sorts of diabolical torture instruments on show, too, and a reconstruction of the cave which was home to notorious 14th-century cannibal Sawney Bean.

There could, perhaps, have been more attention to historic detail but there is plenty of opportunity for that elsewhere in the city. If it's subtlety and quiet reflection you're after, then this is the wrong place.

Old Town Information Centre

Tron Kirk, High Street (225 8408). Bus 35/Nicolson Street–North Bridge buses. **Open** *Nov-Apr* noon-5pm daily. *May-Oct* 10am-5.30pm daily. **Admission** free. **Map** p82 C2.

This frankly surreal centre is fairly short on actual hard information. It does, however, contain a shop from which tickets to city attractions can be bought alongside what can only be described as a jumble-sale stall. The main attraction though is the reclaimed underground remains of Mary's Wynd – an early 1600s alley that was demolished later in the century. All of this resides uneasily under the roof of the Tron Kirk – a 17th-century church that has survived the development of South Bridge in 1785 and the 'Great Conflagration' of 1824.

High Street, below the Bridges

Beyond the traffic lights, just behind the welcoming Bank Hotel, **Niddry Street** dips steeply down towards the Cowgate. Its shabby walls have been done up to represent 19th-century Edinburgh in at least one BBC drama, and behind them is a rabbit warren of cellars built into the arches of South Bridge. These subterranean expanses are atmospheric places and are brought to life through a number of guided tours (*see p80*), but are gradually being taken over by pubs like Nicol Edwards. The Honeycomb, just up Niddry Street from the cellars, is a popular night spot (*see p228*). The **Medieval Torture Museum** is here too, displaying instruments of torture that were used on suspected witches in Germany during the Middle Ages. Its range of devices is steadily expanding, and it hopes soon to be the largest museum of its kind in the world, although at the moment it is only accessible on the Mercat tour of the vaults (*see p80* **Ghosts, trust us**).

The Crowne Plaza Edinburgh has been much maligned for its individual interpretation of Scottish baronial style. Actually, it is a valiant and largely successful attempt by the hotel to blend into its Old Town surroundings. On the right is Blackfriars Street, a thoroughfare well known to backpackers and hostellers. It also boasts **Black Bo's** (*see p166*), an atmospheric pub that is well on its way to becoming a fully fledged Edinburgh institution.

A tasteful glass façade fronts the **Museum of Childhood** (*see p82*), opened in 1955 as the first museum in the world to examine the history of childhood. Its founder made sure that visitors understood the difference between a museum of childhood and a museum for children, and the displays are handled in such a way as to fascinate both kids and adults. The **Brass Rubbing Centre** (*see below*), which is also popular with kids, is on Chalmers Close, just opposite the museum.

Opposite this is the **John Knox House Museum**. The house is currently closed for refurbishment and is due to re-open in 2005. The house has an odd history – it was saved from demolition in 1830 out of reverence for its former resident but there is little evidence that Scotland's founder of Presbyterianism and father of the Reformation, John Knox, ever lived here at all. The house was first built by goldsmith James Mossman, whose workbench is reconstructed inside. Today the museum is connected to the Netherbow Arts Centre, which contains a 75 seat theatre, storytelling centre and café. However, this will also be closed for refurbishment until 2005.

The east gate of the city, the Netherbow, used to stand at this point on the High Street. Along **Tweeddale Court** is a surviving length of the city wall and sheds that were once used to store sedan chairs. Back on the High Street, there's a reference to the city boundary in the name of the pub on the corner: the World's End, which serves reasonable food and well-kept beer.

Brass Rubbing Centre

Trinity Apse, Chalmers Close, High Street (556 4364/www.cac.org.uk). Bus 30, 35/Nicolson Street–North Bridge buses. **Open** *Apr-July, Sept* 10am-5pm Mon-Sat. *Aug* 10am-5pm Mon-Sat; noon-5pm Sun. Closed Oct-Mar. **Admission** free; but costs to make a rubbing. **Map** p82 C1.

Just up from John Knox House Museum, the Brass Rubbing Centre is housed in the atmospheric location of the apse which is the only surviving remnant of the Gothic Trinity College Church, which was founded in 1460. The centre demonstrates that, although brass-rubbing might be a good kids' activity, it has an artistic side, too, particularly when Celtic knots are involved. Cheery, friendly staff and good schematic guides show how it's done.

John Knox House Museum

43 High Street (556 9579). Bus 30, 35/Nicolson Street–North Bridge buses. **Open** 10am-4.30pm Mon-Sat. **Admission** £2.25; £1.75 concessions. **Credit** MC, V. **Map** p82 C1.

The museum will be closed until 2005 as the old house, built in 1450, undergoes some much-needed renovations. Although it is only probable that the religious reformer John Knox died here in 1572, the belief that he did has been enough to stop one of Edinburgh's oldest residences from being razed. The house now holds a detailed exhibition on the Scottish Reformation, complete with an audio re-enactment of Knox's famous debate with the Catholic Mary, Queen of Scots.

Ghosts, trust us

With its underground caverns and locked-up graveyards, Edinburgh is widely regarded as one of the world's most haunted cities. All tourist-baiting nonsense, surely? Former ghost tour guide **Anna Burkey** isn't so sure.

"Ghost tour punters expect to be scared; they have paid at least a fiver for the pleasure. The cynical customers might be ready with logical explanations for every unusual happening – it's all in the imagination, the tour company set it up – but they're still filled with anticipation, hoping to witness the supernatural. As the intrepid guide, you are doing a job and are blasé, fearless. You know the territory well, fully expecting the blood-curling shriek made by a hidden colleague to spook the tourists. It is when the guide becomes uneasy that the customers should worry. We know if it is a set-up or not, and so we know if something odd is going on.

"Different evenings, different groups – yet visitors instinctively avoid certain areas, patches said by psychics to be 'cold spots', scientifically proven not to be draughts. I've seen, night after night, two or three – unrelated – people become restless, their gazes drawn to the same spot, colour draining from their features, not sure what they have seen, but agitated by something. Their sudden and co-ordinated looks of sheer terror can't have been faked. A woman is shoved to the ground, claiming she was pushed by the man behind her – only I can see that there was no one behind her. OK, so perhaps she was trying to make a scene, but as the guide, you know that this has happened before, and in exactly the same location. Many times.

"Parts of Greyfriars' graveyard have become known for such activity, with tourists fainting, or emerging bruised and scratched, not knowing how they came by that black eye or cut arm. The South Bridge Vaults have become notorious for such paranormal behaviour. Dark rooms have been filled with sudden flashes of light, too bright for cameras. Heavy footsteps are heard, when you know the vaults to be otherwise deserted. Rasping breathing sounds that follow you around the room, reported by many tourists. All the lights went out on one tour as we entered a particular chamber, and the torch failed to work. The lighting was later checked,

and no electrical fault found – but this same scenario happened to two separate guides on two other occasions that night, each time with their individual torches failing, though they had been working properly earlier.

"This kind of corroboration is particularly unnerving. Not just you, but other guides too have seen the malevolent, shadowy spectre said to be lingering in the Vaults, angry that his territory has been disturbed. If you have seen it, and a friend has, and a tourist who has never been to Edinburgh – surely there must be something there?"

Auld Reekie Tours

Medieval Torture Museum, 45 Niddry Street, Old Town (557 4700). Nicolson Street–North Bridge buses. **Open** 10am-10pm daily. **Tours** *Underground city* Sept-June 12.30-3.30pm hourly daily. *Ultimate ghost and torture* Sept-June 7-10pm on the hour daily. July-Aug 6-10pm on the hour daily. **Meeting point** (all tours) Tron Kirk, High Street, Old Town. **Tickets** *Underground city* £5. *Ultimate ghost and torture* £6; £5 concessions. **Credit** AmEx, MC, V.

Guides you through the streets of Edinburgh to a section of the Underground Vaults, where you'll allegedly find a working pagan temple. Not the most accurate of tours, but it does offer the opportunity of visiting Auld Reekie's Medieval Torture Exhibition, and it all ends in a local pub.

City of the Dead Tours

(225 9044). Bus 23, 27, 28, 28A, 35, 41, 42, 45. **Meeting point** Mercat Cross, St Giles', High Street, Old Town. **Open** 10am-10pm daily. **Tours** *Nov-Mar* 7.30pm, 8.30pm daily. *Apr-Oct* 8.30pm, 9.15pm, 10pm daily. **Tickets** £6; £5 concessions. **No credit cards**.

Dips into Edinburgh's history, with the guide's own personal take on Scotland's past, but the focus is all on the trip to Greyfriars' graveyard. Many a visitor, paranoid after the guide's careful build up, faints upon entering the secluded section of the cemetery where the MacKenzie Poltergeist reportedly lingers.

Mercat Walking Tours

Mercat House, Niddry Street South, Old Town (557 6464/www.mercattours.com). Bus 23, 27, 28, 28A, 35, 41, 42, 45. **Open** 9am-6pm daily. **Tours** *Hidden underground vaults* May-Sept 12am-4pm hourly daily. Oct-Apr 2pm,

Sightseeing

4pm daily. *Ghosts and ghouls* Apr-Sept 7pm, 8pm, 9pm daily. Oct-Mar 7pm, 8pm. *Ghost hunter trail* Apr-Sept 9.30pm, 10.30pm daily. Oct-Mar 9.30pm daily. *Secrets of the Royal Mile* 10.30am daily. **Meeting point** Mercat Cross, St Giles, High Street, Old Town. **Tickets** *Hidden underground vaults* £6.50, £6 concessions, £4 children; *all other tours* £7.50, £7 concessions, £4 children. **Credit** AmEx, MC, V.

The longest established and most professional, priding itself on historical accuracy. Don't expect a lecture, though: the black-cloaked guides feed the customers a grisly portrait of Old Edinburgh. The earlier tours are a little less sinister than those from 9.30pm onwards but all Mercat's walks pass through the extensive Underground Vaults. The one hour tour is entirely concerned with the paranormal goings-on in the vaults.

The Real Mary King's Close

2 Warrison's Close, Writers' Court, Old Town (0870 243 0160/www.realmarykings close.com). North Bridge–Nicolson Street buses. **Tours** *(every 20 mins) Apr-Oct 10am-9pm daily. Nov-Mar 10am-4pm daily.* **Admission** £7; £5-6 concessions; £21 family. **Credit** MC, V.

The remains of a street beneath the City Chambers have been turned into an historical attraction, where a costumed guide ushers around visitors. A fascinating look at life in Edinburgh over the centuries, but with only the barest whisper of supernatural possibilities – the focus here is on the historical rather than the paranormal. More supernaturally focused tours are run around Hallowe'en – call for details.

Witchery Tours

84 West Bow, Victoria Street, Old Town (225 6745/www.witcherytours.com). Bus 23, 27, 28, 28A, 35, 41, 42, 45. **Open** 10am-9pm daily. **Tours** *Ghost & Gore May-Sept 7pm, 7.30pm daily. Murder & Mystery 9pm, 9.30pm daily.* **Meeting point** outside Witchery restaurant, Castlehill, Old Town. **Tickets** £7; £4 concessions (Ghost & Gore only). **Credit** AmEx, MC, V.

A little more light-hearted. Moving from the Castle through the Cowgate, a character guide entertains, with his costumed mad monk sidekick, or other characters including Burke and Hare the body snatchers, frequently popping up to startle the unwary tourist. An amusing evening out, though not the scariest of the tours on offer.

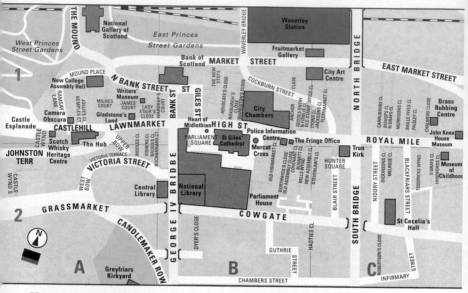

Museum of Childhood

*42 High Street (529 4142/www.cac.org.uk). Bus
30, 35/Nicolson Street–North Bridge buses.* **Open**
Sept-June 10am-5pm Mon-Sat. *July, Aug* 10am-5pm
Mon-Sat; noon-5pm Sun. **Admission** free. **Credit**
Shop MC, V. **Map** p82 C2.

As you walk around this extensive collection of toys
and childhood mementos, the grins of recognition
are apparent on the faces of kids-at-heart of all ages.
In fact, there's reason to suggest that older generations will enjoy it far more than younger children as
the trip down memory lane unfolds with train sets,
dolls' houses and literally hundreds of retro toys.
The museum was founded in 1955 by local councillor Patrick Murray and has been regularly updated.
Much of it evokes a rose-tinted impression of bygone
innocence, and many of the exhibits display a level
of craftsmanship unimaginable in toys today.
However, for those getting overly sentimental, there
is the stark image of a child-sized World War II gas
mask set beside a lurid Ed The Duck lunchbox. The
museum has occasional guest exhibitions and a
small shop at the entrance.

Canongate

The Canongate, once a burgh in its own right,
is the subject of constant regeneration and
home to an array of diverse small businesses.
The area takes its name from the route used by
Augustinian canons, who arrived at Holyrood
Abbey in 1141, to reach the gates of Edinburgh.
Situated outside the old city walls it was
separate from Edinburgh until as recently

as 1856. The buildings are largely residential
but among them stand some fascinating
museums and independent shops selling
everything from Christmas paraphernalia
to bagpipes and traditional fudge.

The **Canongate Tolbooth** served as
a council chamber, a police station and a prison.
It was built in 1592 to collect tolls from visitors
to the city and is recognisable from its clock,
bell tower and outside stairway. It now serves
as the **People's Story Museum** – a
lively interpretation of working class life in
Edinburgh through the years. Next to it lies
the Tolbooth Tavern, a classic Edinburgh
watering hole (556 5348). Huntly House,
opposite, comprises three timber-framed houses
joined into one in 1570 and is surmounted by
three overhanging white-painted gables of a
kind that were once common in the Old Town.
It is also home to the **Museum of Edinburgh**,
a fascinating insight into the other end of
the social spectrum, with well-maintained
grandfather clocks, Victorian silver and many
other artefacts collected from the city's earliest
known habitation. Bakehouse Close, under
Huntly House, leads through to the offices of
the Royal Fine Art Commission for Scotland.
This is not, as the name might suggest, a fine
art exhibition space, but the national body
for promoting the fine arts of planning
and architectural design.

Few know of **Dunbar's Close Garden**, a
secret little park at the end of an unassuming

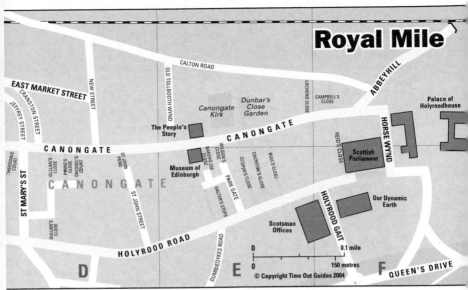

close on the north side of the Canongate. It
is laid out in the manner of a 17th-century
garden, with ornamental flower beds and
manicured hedges, and is a beautiful refuge
from the summer crowds. There's a fine view
of the old Royal High School from here (*see
p101* **Schools rule**), which was for many
years mooted as the site for the new Scottish
Parliament but is now the planned site for the
new National Photography Centre for Scotland.

Canongate Church stands out from the
tenement buildings on the Royal Mile with its
bell-shaped Dutch design. It was built for the
displaced congregation of Holyrood Abbey,
which was destroyed in 1688. Canongate is
Edinburgh's official military church and the
royal family often worship here when they are
staying in the Palace of Holyroodhouse.

The church is best known for its graveyard,
which is the resting place for the Scottish
Enlightenment economist Adam Smith; David
Rizzio, the murdered secretary of Mary, Queen
of Scots; and Robert Burns' beloved 'Clarinda'
(Mrs Agnes McLehose). The cemetery offers
excellent views of Calton Hill and is one of the
city's most exclusive burial sites.

Burns' muse is also commemorated by a tearoom, **Clarinda's** (*see p161*), a little further
down. Just the right side of twee, with patterned
plates on the wall and flowers on the tables, it
provides the best chance of a light meal at this
end of the Canongate. Poetry by Burns and
many other poets through the ages can be found

at the **Scottish Poetry Library** down
Crichton's Close. There are some attractive
houses near the gates of Holyrood, most
obviously the two well-kept, gleaming
white edifices of **Canongate Manse** and
Whiteford House, now a Scottish war
veterans' residence. White Horse Close is pretty
too; the gabled building at the end was once a
coaching inn and the departure point for the
stage coach to London. In 1745, it was called
into service as the officers' quarters of Prince
Charles Edward Stuart's army.

At the bottom of the Royal Mile is the
Palace of Holyroodhouse, one of the
Queen's official residences. It is open to the
public for guided audio tours throughout the
year when the royals are not in residence. From
a distance it looks perfectly symmetrical but on
closer inspection you can see that the left tower
is much older than the right. The palace was
damaged considerably by Cromwell's forces,
who accidentally burned down the south wing.
It was, however, restored in the reign of Charles
II and lovingly decorated by Queen Victoria,
whose influence can still be seen today.

The purpose of the strange, squat building
just inside the fence by the main road is
unknown. It might have been a bathhouse, or
perhaps a doocot (where 'doos', or pigeons,
nest). Holyrood Abbey, now an irreparable ruin,
was founded by David I in 1128. It was sacked
by Edward II in 1322, damaged in 1544 and
again in 1570 with the loss of the choir and

transepts, and violated yet further by a mob of Presbyterian vandals in 1688.

The massive building site opposite the palace is the much-maligned new **Scottish Parliament** building (*see p28* **What price democracy?**). Work was due to be completed in 2001 but this has proved to be wildly optimistic. The building is now on course to be handed over in late 2004, although it will clock in at more than £400 million (which is ten times over budget).

The ambitious design is the work of the late Spanish architect Enric Miralles and is to take the form of a collection of upturned boats. The project was criticised from the beginning – many thought the motif was too Scandinavian while others soon picked up on the unfortunate imagery of a plan that has gone 'belly-up'. However, once completed, the building is likely to draw visitors and tourists alike and will lend an exciting new view from the overlooking Salisbury Crags.

In anticipation of the move, a sizeable portion of this end of the Royal Mile is being renovated and rebuilt to exciting new designs. With buildings like the attractive new premises of the *Scotsman* publications and the modern glass façade of the Tun (the new BBC headquarters in Edinburgh) already in place, this is one of the most fashionable office addresses in Edinburgh.

Another of the buildings already in place and extremely popular with school groups is **Our Dynamic Earth**. It has drawn inevitable comparisons with London's own domed white elephant, the Millennium Dome, in both appearance and subject matter, but is seen largely as a success. It is, ostensibly, a science museum that combines natural history with simulated natural disasters, and is aimed specifically at children.

Back on Holyrood Road is the new site for the **Bongo Club** (*see p227*), a regular left-field music club and venue, and also the University of Edinburgh's Moray House buildings for teacher training and sports science. While the Dumbiedykes estate, off Holyrood Road, may have spectacular views looking out onto Salisbury Crags it is one of Edinburgh's poorest estates, an area of desperate poverty tucked away at the centre of the capital rather than being shuffled away into the suburbs. Although significant investment and redevelopment is now underway, it is best avoided at night.

Museum of Edinburgh

Huntly House, 142-146 Canongate (529 4143/ www.cac.org.uk). Bus 30, 35/Nicolson Street–North Bridge buses. **Open** *Sept-July* 10am-5pm Mon-Sat. *Aug* 10am-5pm Mon-Sat; noon-5pm Sun. **Admission** free. **Map** p83 E2.

If the People's Story Museum across the road is a tribute to hardship and Edinburgh's sturdy working classes through the ages, then the Museum of Edinburgh is a shrine to its patricians. Set over two floors and combining three tenement buildings, there is a wealth of fascinating artefacts and documents, from Roman coins to Victorian silverware. With so much on show, the dispays can be overwhelming but the house itself is worthy of close attention. It is one of Edinburgh's original tenements and dates from 1570. The original version of the National Covenant of 1638 is housed here, and tradition has it that, such was the importance of the document, some of the signatures are in blood. Among the other items on show are Greyfriar's Bobby's collar and bowl.

Our Dynamic Earth

Holyrood Road (550 7800/www.dynamicearth.co.uk). Bus 30, 35. **Open** *Apr-Jul, Sept, Oct* 10am-5pm daily (last entry 3.50pm). *July, Aug* 10am-6pm daily (last entry 5.15pm). *Nov-Mar* 10am-5pm Wed-Sun (last entry 3.50pm). **Admission** £8.95; £6.50 concessions; £5.45 5-15s; free under-5s; £16.50-£28.50 family. **Credit** MC, V. **Map** p83 F2.

Another of the new constructions in the area, Our Dynamic Earth is located near the former home of James Hutton, the Edinburgh-born 'Father of Geology'. Like London's Millennium Dome, its architecture is tent-like in appearance, but Edinburgh's version is here to stay. The tour begins by taking you back to the creation of the universe 15 billion years ago and works its way forward to the present day. Along the way you are invited to take part in the simulation of an earthquake, which involves a shuddering platform to accompany the explanatory video. Then there is a virtual helicopter ride through glaciers that can be dizzying for even the sternest constitutions. Exhibition staff play different roles at each stage as you are led through the ageing world, and it is worth going slowly as there is only one way round. The scientific explanations for each of the naturally occurring events/disasters you witness are simplistic yet not patronising; as you near the end there are philosophical musings from the French anthropologist Claude Levi-Strauss, Polish scientist Jacob Bronowski, and, er, Sting. There are also occasional events on offer and the giant dome in the centre has been used for Edinburgh Festival shows.

Palace of Holyroodhouse

Holyrood Road (524 1120/www.royalresidences.com). Bus 30, 35. **Open** *Apr-Oct* 9.30am-6pm daily (last entry 5.15pm). *Nov-Mar* 9.30am-4.30pm daily (last entry 3.45pm). **Admission** £8; £6.50 concessions; £4 5-15s; free under-5s; £20 family. **Credit** AmEx, MC, V. **Map** p83 F1.

The Palace of Holyroodhouse has its origins in the Abbey of Holyrood (now picturesque ruins), established in 1128 by David I. When Edinburgh was confirmed as the nation's capital city, royal quarters were built adjacent to the abbey and have been gradually upgraded and renovated over the years into what today stands proudly as an official residence of the Queen. The Palace has played an important role in Scottish history and it was here that the Queen appointed the late Donald Dewar as First Minister following Scotland's devolution from the British parliament in 1999. When the Queen is not in residence, parts of the Palace are open to the public and an audio tour guides you round the series of plush bedrooms, galleries and dining rooms and details their accompanying history.

Among the episodes of Scottish history most associated with the Palace, the sad life of Mary, Queen of Scots is the most poignant. The tour takes you back to 1576 when, six months pregnant, she watched as four Scottish noblemen murdered her secretary David Rizzio with the consent of her husband Lord Darnley, who wanted to kill the baby she was carrying (the future James IV). Darnley died soon after in suspicious circumstances.

Holyroodhouse Palace is also the setting for the famous scene in Sir Walter Scott's *Waverley* in which he recreates the entrance of Bonnie Prince Charlie after his forces were victorious in Perth in 1745. His popular army was eventually defeated at Culloden a year later and the rooms his soldiers had used at Holyroodhouse were destroyed.

Having acquired the estate at Balmoral, Queen Victoria used Holyroodhouse as a stop-off on the long journey and extensively redecorated its drab walls with the paintings and tapestries that remain on view today. These now form part of the extensive Royal Collection that is housed in the Palace and are on view to the public when the Royals are not in residence. The Palace's gift shop, in an unusual new twist, is to offer for sale Her Majesty's own selection of beers and spirits.

People's Story

Canongate Tolbooth, 163 Canongate (529 4057/ www.cac.org.uk). Bus 30, 35/Nicolson Street–North Bridge buses. **Open** *Sept-July* 10am-5pm Mon-Sat. *Aug* 10am-5pm Mon-Sat; noon-5pm Sun. **Admission** free. **Map** p83 E1.

The Canongate Tolbooth was once one of the most symbolically frightening buildings in Edinburgh. Many was the robber or murderer whose crime spree ended here with their heads removed from their bodies. Now the old prison is used as a museum dedicated to telling the story of the working classes in Edinburgh's colourful history. Beginning with gruesome tales of massacres and civil unrest, you are led upstairs to mock-ups of austere wartime living quarters and relics from Edinburgh's ship-building past. The exhibits continue to the present day, through Thatcher's Scotland of the 1980s (complete with an amusing mannequin punk-rocker) to testimonies from fans of the city's football teams, Hearts and Hibs. The museum really touches a nerve with its wall-mounted presentations – many of the people quoted are still living in near poverty on the outskirts of the city, on the council estates of Niddrie, Gorgie and Craigmillar.

Three steps to... **Grassmarket**. *See p86.*

Scottish Poetry Library

5 Crichton's Close, Canongate (557 2876/ www.spl.org.uk). Bus 30, 35/Nicolson Street–North Bridge buses. **Open** 11am-6pm Mon-Fri; 1-5pm Sat. **Admission** free; donations welcome. *Annual membership £20; £10 concessions.* **No credit cards. Map** p83 E2.

While Robert Burns remains Scotland's best known poet (and he is well represented on the library's shelves), there are many more that have had a significant impact on the nation's culture. Whether they have written in Scots, English, Gaelic or a surreal language of their own making (cf. Glasgow's poet laureate Edwin Morgan), you can count on finding an obscure volume of theirs here. The library also has a small selection of books for sale, including works from local poets, and the friendly staff are happy to help with recommendations.

The Cowgate & south

At the junction of the Cowgate and Holyrood Road, you can turn left, up the Pleasance towards the famous Fringe super-venue of the same name (*see p223*). Halfway up is the edge of the Old Town, marked by a remaining corner of the **Flodden Wall** (*see p11*). Turning from here along Drummond Street provides a neat shortcut to the **Museum of Scotland** and the **Royal Museum** on Chambers Street (*see p88*).

George Heriot's school days. *See p88.*

Turning right from the end of Holyrood Road up St Mary's Street leads back to the Netherbow. This crossroads was at one time an entrance to the Old Town: the Cowgate Port, through which cattle passed.

The Cowgate

The Cowgate was originally a thoroughfare used by cows and their keepers passing to and from the fields. In December 2002, many of its old buildings (part of a World Heritage Site) were engulfed in the Old Town fire (*see p73* **Burning down the town**) and had to be demolished. The rebuilding of the area has been delayed since the blaze and there has been much debate in the local press about what would be a suitable replacement.

Up until the mid-20th century the Cowgate was known locally as the 'Irish quarter' due to the thousands of Irish immigrants who settled here following the Great Famine in 1846. The Irish feel to the area is borne out in the church of **St Patrick** (5 South Gray's Close; 556 3030) – a Catholic Church which had already been built in 1771 and was one reason the Irish settled in this area in the first place.

Its gardens, accessible from South Gray's Close, are a tranquil place to pause. Nearby, on the corner of Blackfriars Street, is St Cecilia's Hall, which houses the **Russell Collection of Early Keyboard Instruments**. The hall is owned by the University of Edinburgh and is occasionally used as a live music venue. Infirmary Street, opposite, leads up to the Old High School (1777), Old Surgeon's Hall (1697), and the Victorian premises that once housed the Royal Infirmary, where Joseph Lister discovered the benefits of antiseptic surgery. At the end of Infirmary Street, on Nicolson Street, is New Surgeon's Hall, built in 1832.

By the middle of the 19th century, the Cowgate had become one of the most densely populated parts of the city, and the physical reality of its location below the Bridges was accentuated by the poverty of its inhabitants. Today, it is a popular centre for alcholic hedonism. Come the weekend, the huge Three Sisters pub takes the lion's share of the street's punters, with the nearby Subway nightclub providing cheap and cheerful competition to the similar establishments on Lothian Road. In an attempt to reduce the (alarmingly high) number of drink-related accidents, the Cowgate is now closed to traffic at night.

Beyond the towering backs of the new court buildings, the Cowgate passes under George IV Bridge. Immediately on the left is the **Magdalen Chapel**. Dwarfed by the surrounding tenements, it is supposedly where the first General Assembly of the Church of Scotland was held in 1578. In the bloody days of the late 17th century the chapel served as a mortuary for those executed Covenanters whose bodies were to be buried round the corner, in **Greyfriars Kirkyard** (*see p88*).

Magdalen Chapel

41 Cowgate (220 1450/www.scottishreformation. co.uk). Bus 2, 23, 27, 28, 41, 42, 45. **Open** 9.30am-4pm Mon-Fri. **Admission** free. **Map** p82 B2.

Built between 1541 and 1547, with the steeple added in 1626, the Chapel is the headquarters of the Scottish Reformation Society, but is still open to visitors. Of note is the only surviving pre-Reformation stained glass window in Scotland. More interesting are the 'brods' (receipts for gifts of money or goods to the chapel) dating from the 16th to the 19th centuries that wrap round the walls like a frieze, and the Deacon's Chair (1708).

Grassmarket

There has been a market in the Grassmarket since at least 1477 – a 1977 plaque on a rock here commemorates the 500th anniversary of the date when the area first received its charter from James III. Along **King's Stables Road** at the north-west corner of the Grassmarket, gardens provided the raw material for a vegetable market from the 12th century, while the Grassmarket itself held livestock sales. When England's Edward III occupied the Castle in the 1330s, King's Stables Road also became the site of a medieval tournament ground. This practice was short-lived: David II put a stop to it when Scotland regained the Castle in the mid-14th century (*see p9*).

But the Grassmarket also has a darker history as a regular venue for executions. Among the victims were many Covenanters, who are remembered in the small, walled memorial at its east end. The most famous execution to take place here, however, was the Porteous lynching in 1736, given literary form in Sir Walter Scott's *The Heart of Midlothian*. John Porteous was an unpopular captain of the town guard, who, on 14 April 1736, was in charge of the hanging of two smugglers in the Grassmarket. Sensing trouble, he sealed off the area with guardsmen so that the execution could take place. The mob reacted by throwing stones and Porteous ordered his men to open fire: three in the crowd were killed and a dozen wounded. Porteous was tried for murder and found guilty. He was to be hanged on 20 July, but a royal warrant from Queen Caroline reprieved him. Not for long, though. An angry mob broke into the Old Tolbooth on the Royal Mile on 19 July, dragged Porteous down to the Grassmarket and hanged him there. He was buried in Greyfriars Churchyard. There's still an entrance called Porteous Pend at the south-west corner of the Grassmarket, next to Mary Mallinson Antiques.

The north side of the Grassmarket is now dominated by a row of pubs and restaurants. Among them is the **White Hart Inn**, where

Robert Burns supposedly wrote 'Ae Fond Kiss'. It is also where the protagonist in Iain Banks' *Complicity* gets some hints about the whereabouts of a dismembered body.

Since 2001, the Grassmarket has been home to **Dance Base** – Scotland's National Centre For Dance (*see p239*). The independent company offers year-round classes in dance for all ages and abilities, and its state-of-the-art studios and facilities reflect how important dance has become to the programme of the Edinburgh Festival.

At the west end of the row are the new Granny's Green Steps, which lead up to Johnston Terrace and a possible walk around the base of Castle Rock. More direct routes are straight up Castle Wynd at the centre of the row or up the West Bow (confusingly at the east end of the row). West Bow quickly becomes Victoria Street – a fairly steep, bending road with Victoria Terrace sat at the top of it. With shops selling all sorts of cultish curiosities, interesting bars and the popular live music venue the Liquid Room, it is one of Edinburgh's quirkiest streets.

Greyfriars & Chambers Street

Candlemaker Row, off the Cowgate, leads up to where **Greyfriars Kirk** overlooks George IV Bridge. At the top of Candlemaker Row stands a small statue of Greyfriars Bobby. So the story goes: when a man named John Gray was buried in the kirk's graveyard, his loyal Skye terrier Bobby kept constant watch over his grave for 14 years until his own death in 1872. For some reason, this story continues to touch the hearts of visitors and locals alike and it is not uncommon to see passers-by kiss the doggy-statue. This is far from the strangest occurrence at Greyfriars Kirk, though. If stories are to be believed, the churchyard is one of the most haunted in Britain (*see p80* **Ghosts, trust us**). Not only have there been scores of reported sightings, but some of its night time visitors have reported scratches and bruises. This has been locally attributed to the ghost of a 17th-century nobleman called Sir George Mackenzie, with even hardened sceptics admitting to finding the place spooky.

Greyfriars Kirkyard has played a pivotal role in the history of Scotland. It is where the National Covenant was signed in 1638 and where the bodies of executed Covenanters were buried alongside common criminals. Later the survivors of the Battle of Bothwell Brig (1679), were kept in the south-west corner of the yard in the Covenanters' Prison, under desperate living conditions, for five months. Not all of them survived their incarceration. The Martyrs'

Sightseeing

Monument, with its chilling inscription, 'Halt passenger, take heed of what you do see, This tomb doth shew for what some men did die', is their memorial and can be found in the north-east part of the yard.

Opposite Greyfriars, the plain but graceful lines of the **Museum of Scotland** (*see p88*) mask a warren of winding corridors that open up on to spectacular drops and huge spaces. The roof and the **Tower** restaurant (*see p135*) – one of the finest in the city – give fantastic views of Arthur's Seat and the Castle. Next door, along Chambers Street, is the **Royal Museum** (*see p88*), which was designed by Captain Francis Fowke along conventional, Victorian lines and completed in 1888. Although they are distinct institutions, the two museums are linked inside. Across from the imposing steps of the Royal Museum is the Matthew Architecture Gallery (closed to the public).

Old College, which backs on to Chambers Street, is the oldest of Edinburgh's university buildings. It was built by Robert Adam, who started the work in 1789, and William Playfair, who finished it after the interruption of the Napoleonic Wars. Rowand Anderson added the landmark dome in 1883.

Entrance to the main courtyard is either through the small entrance of the Talbot Rice Gallery, up West College Street, or through the monumental arch on Nicolson Street. Certain areas of Old College are accessible to the public, notably the Playfair Library (where guided tours in the Easter and summer vacations at 1pm show off one of the city's finest classical interiors) and the old Upper Museum (now part of the Talbot Rice Gallery). The Upper Museum features a table from Napoleon's lodgings on St Helena with a cigar burn made, allegedly, by the little Corsican himself.

For details of how to join these tours, the place to contact is the University of Edinburgh Centre on North Bridge (650 2252).

Two of the Edinburgh University student unions are situated nearby, on either side of Bristo Square. Teviot Row House is the grander of the two while Potterrow is easily identifiable by its domed roof. The structure hasn't aged very well in its short life thus far but bizarrely it is now being considered for listed status. Next door to Teviot Row House is the Reid Concert Hall (Bristo Square; 225 6293), which hosts classical concerts and houses the Edinburgh University Collection of Historic Musical Instruments.

George Heriot's School (*see p104* **Schools rule**), off Lauriston Place, was used in its early days as a military hospital for Cromwell's troops. School prefects give historical tours of this fine 17th-century building that bears the legacy of George Heriot, a goldsmith and jeweller to James VI and I.

Greyfriars Kirk

2 Greyfriars Place, Candlemaker Row (226 5429/ www.greyfriarskirk.com). Bus 2, 23, 27, 28, 41, 42, 45. **Open** *Apr-Oct* 10.30am-4.30pm Mon-Fri; 10.30am-2.30pm Sat. *Nov-Mar* 1.30-3.30pm Thur or by appointment. **Admission** free. **Map** p309 F6.
Greyfriars Kirk pulls off the trick of being simple but not austere. Formerly the site of a Franciscan friary, it dates from 1620 but was severely damaged, then rebuilt, after a fire in 1845. The small visitors' exhibition on the church's 400-year history contains a display about the National Covenant, but most people go to see the original portrait of Greyfriars Bobby (John MacLeod, 1887). The church was undergoing considerable maintenance on the roof and outer walls at the time of writing.

Museum of Scotland & Royal Museum

Chambers Street (225 7534/www.nms.ac.uk). Bus 2, 23, 27, 28, 41, 42, 45. **Open** 10am-5pm Mon, Wed-Sat; 10am-8pm Tue; noon-5pm Sun. **Admission** free. **Credit** *Shop* MC, V. **Map** p309 F6.
It is necessary to set aside at least a couple of hours to experience the two conjoined museums in anything like their entirety. The Royal Museum has a beautiful, spacious atrium encompassing a pleasant café. The thousands of artefacts are grouped into rough sections – on the ground floor there is a sizeable natural history section comprising glass cases filled with stuffed animals (many of which are now extinct). There is also an entertaining 20th-century exhibition charting the changes in fashions and the technological leaps of the past 100 years. Upstairs there are old-fashioned steam engines, relics from Scotland's industrial age and much else. The adjacent Museum of Scotland houses all the Scottish artefacts owned by the National Museums of Scotland. Designed by architects Benson and Forsyth, the museum was judged to be the Scottish Building of the Year after its opening in 1999.

Talbot Rice Gallery

Old College, South Bridge (650 2211/www. trg.ed.ac.uk). Nicolson Street–North Bridge buses. **Open** 10am-5pm Tue-Sat. **Admission** free. **Map** p310 G6.
Situated just off William Playfair's stately, grand Old Quad is the relatively recent addition of the Talbot Rice Gallery. Opened in 1975, the gallery is named after the Watson Gordon Professor of Fine Art, David Talbot Rice, famed for his writings on Islamic art. Although it houses the University's Torrie Collection, consisting of Dutch and Italian Old Masters, the greatest part of this vast and lofty space is given over to temporary exhibitions, ranging from solo shows by established Scottish artists to group shows by recent graduates.

New Town

Enlightenment: a state and a place.

On a clear day...

The regimented rectangle that covers the four square miles of Edinburgh's New Town makes up Britain's biggest and best example of 18th-century town planning. The ingeniously simple design was the work of the (then unknown) 22-year-old architect **James Craig** (*see p91* **The making of the New Town**).

The new *quartier* was in fact initially shunned by Edinburgh's residents, who considered it to be over-exposed to the high winds blowing in off the Firth of Forth. But they soon saw the error of their ways and started flocking to its beautifully regimented architecture, abandoning the chaotic jumble of the Old Town.

Today, the New Town is a haven for Edinburgh's richest and snootiest residents – from arriviste self-made traders and trust-fund students to the most distinguished members of the Scottish aristocracy. The richest can afford pricey townhouses (just under £1 million on average) with immense rooms, luxuriant period decor and the key to the fabulous communal gardens situated at the centre of many blocks. Those of smaller wallet stick to the massive tenement flats that fill the area. It is here that Scotland's reputation for having a small

conspiratorial elite is founded. The parties and gatherings of the New Town set see the decision makers and their acolytes gather to gossip, conspire and decide.

The abundance of influential people hasn't stopped the New Townies from getting into an almighty row with Edinburgh Council though. At time of writing they were locked in a long-running (but prosaic) battle over whether they should be forced to suffer the indignity of having wheelie-bins on their streets. The rest of the (less well connected) city has succumbed to the inevitable practicality and efficiency of communal waste disposal. But New Town residents are (for bizarre reasons) fighting to keep their right to deposit rubbish in bin-bags by the side of the road. At last count, the New Townies were on the verge of embroiling the UN heritage agency UNESCO in the row.

In addition to being an architectural haven, the New Town plays host to some impressive boutiques and intimate cafés (*see p178* and *p154*), as well as the usual gamut of high-street shopping emporiums. It is an engaging place for a wander – even if the forbidding grey of the Enlightenment façades give little hint of the dramas that unfold within.

The second thing that strikes you about Princes Street – right after you see how lopsided it looks with buildings on one side only – is the amount of building work underway. Edinburgh's main shopping thoroughfare is getting a facelift. The Scottish broadcaster Moray MacLaren famously described Princes Street as 'one of the most chaotically tasteless streets in the United Kingdom.' In recent times, identikit chain stores have become ever more dominant; they are the only companies who can afford the exorbitant leases.

But hope is at hand: fifteen of the poorer quality buildings are due to be demolished and replaced with new shopping centres and luxury flats. However, since Princes Street is a World Heritage Site any changes to the landscape are fraught with complications. But work is underway and in ten years time Edinburgh should have a centrepiece to be proud of. A range of traffic control measures that have also been proposed include the return of a tram system to the city centre (due to launch in 2009) and the possible introduction of London-style congestion charging. Princes Street, like a number of Edinburgh's central roads, already has a one-way traffic system in place.

The verdant expanse of **Princes Street Gardens** acts as a buffer between New and Old Towns and is one part of Princes Street that everyone agrees shouldn't be changed. The stretch of land was protected by an Act of Parliament in 1816 after property developers in the late 18th century began encroaching onto it with what is now Princes Mall. During the summer months, the gardens are packed with festival-goers sunbathing in front of the picturesque skyline and bands play on rotation on the stage. In winter the traditional German Christmas market is set up behind the Scott Monument and an ice-rink is installed (*see p93* and *p200*).

At the extreme west end of Princes Street Gardens is the Episcopalian church of **St John's** (*see below*). Consecrated in 1818, it is reckoned to hold one of the finest collections of stained glass in Scotland; the café below the church is a quiet oasis from the bustling street. Behind is the Presbyterian **St Cuthbert's** (*see below*), surrounded by a large, tree-crowded graveyard where many famous people are interred.

Numerous statues of famous city residents edge the gardens. At the west end is Sir James Young Simpson (*see p10* **Pass the ether, ma'am**), the Victorian pioneer of the use of chloroform in childbirth who was frequently found self-anaesthetised on the floor of his lab.

Allegedly. He stands opposite the coolly classical 1930s building that houses Fraser's department store at No.145 (*see p175*), the first of Princes Street's architecturally inconsistent parade of shops.

St Cuthbert's

5 Lothian Road (229 1142/www.st-cuthberts.net). Princes Street buses. **Open** *Apr-Sept* 10am-4pm Mon-Sat. Closed Oct-mid Mar. **Admission** free. **Map** p304 A2.

Along with Duddingston Kirk and Kirkliston's parish church, St Cuthbert's has claim to being the oldest place of worship in Edinburgh. The building's current incarnation, however, only dates from 1894, although the steeple was built in 1789. The graveyard is the resting place of some notable names: the artist Alexander Naysmith, the logarithm inventor John Napier and the city's original drugs writer Thomas de Quincey (*Confessions of an English Opium Eater*) are all buried here.

St John's Episcopal Church

3 Lothian Road (229 7565/www.stjohns-edinburgh. org.uk). Princes Street buses. **Open** 9am-5pm daily. **Admission** free. **Map** p304 A2.

Designed in the perpendicular Gothic style by William Burn (a prominent architect of his day), St John's Episcopal Church took two years to complete and opened in 1818. Its erection began just before the Act of Parliament in 1816 forbidding further building on the surrounding Princes Street Gardens, thus leaving the church with a legally protected view of Edinburgh Castle. The building's stained glass is said to be the finest collection under one roof in the whole of Scotland, although its relentless, 19th-century worthiness and sheer Victorian vulgarity can be overwhelming.

East end of Princes Street

Opponents of the current redevelopment of Princes Street need look no further than the St James Centre to point out what can happen if you leave town planning to fashionable architects. What may have seemed a good idea in 1964 now looks like the kind of concrete monstrosity cooked up in a JG Ballard novel. Thankfully, this is the worst offender on the street and, as you head west, despite the cheap and nasty bookshops and the endless fast-food restaurants, Princes Street gets a lot prettier.

General Register House is one of the numerous buildings currently undergoing refurbishment. It was built in 1774 by Robert Adam (the key member of the famous Adam dynasty of architects), and still houses the National Archives of Scotland. In front of Register House stands a glorious statue of the Duke of Wellington on his horse Copenhagen. Sculptor James Gowans managed to set the horse on hind legs as his master points

The making of the New Town

The wide and grand George Street forms the backbone of Edinburgh's original New Town – the first of the series of developments planned to provide extra and more gracious living space to those who could afford it.

In the first half of the 18th century it was realised that Edinburgh was getting too cramped and, in 1752, a long and wordy pamphlet was published setting out proposals to enlarge the town to the north and south. The proposals were largely down to the work of George Drummond, the Lord Provost, and were – for the most part – put into effect over the next 80 years.

The first stage was the building of North Bridge, which started in 1765. The following year, an architectural competition was held to find a plan for the New Town. It was won by 22-year-old James Craig's simple and sensible solution. The layout of three parallel roads – Princes, George and Queen streets – ended by two squares, replaced Craig's earlier design of radial roads, which was inspired by the Union Jack – a symbol that was a bit too highly charged for the Scots after the 1707 Act of Union. Craig, however, was obviously keen for royal approval. He dedicated his final plan to George III, who in turn had an influence on the names of the streets. George Street is named after the monarch and Princes Street after his sons. The story goes that the original name of St Giles was dropped as it reminded the King of a sleazy quarter of London. The architectural plans are on view in the **Museum of Edinburgh** (*see p84*) on the Canongate in the Old Town.

Before work could commence on the new site, action needed to be taken in order to make it easily accessible. It was decided that the Nor' Loch (which ran the length of what is now Princes Street) should be drained, a process that took 60 years, and a bridge needed to be built over the valley. There were initial plans to retain the loch as a much smaller stream but in the end these were dropped in favour of the landscape of Princes Street Gardens, which has remained largely unchanged. The North Bridge was completed in 1772, providing the link to the New Town, and was eventually replaced in 1895 by the sturdier steel arches that you can see today.

One of the first people to realise the commercial (and aesthetic) advantages of a

relocation to the New Town was Sir Laurence Dundas. He acquired a plot of land on the east side of St Andrew Square from the town council in 1767. He promptly built the Dundas Mansion, New Town's first great house (now the Royal Bank of Scotland). It was only once work had started that the council realised that the plot of land had already been earmarked for the site of St Andrew's Church (which now sits on the other side of the square).

Although the slope of the hill down from George Street seems smooth now, a considerable amount of landscaping went into the construction of the New Town streets. Between 1781 and 1830, as the New Town expanded, it is reckoned that over two million cartloads of earth were removed and taken to create the Mound. You can get a good sense of the formidable construction work at the spot where the end of India Street looms over North West Circus Place. A proper junction would have made too much of a gradient, and the raised end of India Street shows just how much the roads were lifted above ground level to give the houses basements and to flatten out the land.

Sightseeing

Run away to the **Royal Circus**.

symbolically towards Waterloo Place. West Register Street leads past New Register House (housing the **General Register Office**; *see p93*) through to St Andrew Square and George Street and, conveniently, passes the **Café Royal** (*see p167*). This is not just a good pub for a spot of refreshment but is also an extravagantly dressed late 19th-century building. The spectacular central bar is offset by a succession of tiled murals depicting famous Scottish inventors including Michael Faraday and James Watt.

Across the road is the exclusive **Balmoral Hotel** (*see p49*), a huge Victorian edifice with a clock facing the Old Town that famously runs three minutes fast to hurry passengers to the adjacent Waverley Station. During the 2003 MTV awards, the hotel was staked out by hundreds of devoted fans hoping to catch a glimpse of pop star Beyoncé Knowles, who was a guest. **Jenners**, the world's oldest privately owned department store (*see p175*), commands a corner position on Princes Street and St Andrew Street. Founded in 1838 by two Leith drapers, it was extravagantly rebuilt in 1893 after a fire destroyed the original building. An estimated 25,000 people crowded the streets for the unveiling of its elaborately carved, statue-encrusted frontage, which was inspired by the façade of Oxford's Bodleian Library.

It is further up Princes Street, however, that 19th-century extravagance is fully exemplified. The colossal **Scott Monument** stands at 200 feet (61 metres) high (*see p93*). The Gothic steeple by draughtsman George Meikle Kemp was completed in 1846 and contains a white marble statue of Sir Walter (by Edinburgh sculptor John Steell) along with statuettes of characters from his novels. Dubbed the city's 'medieval space rocket', it was originally to have been sited in the somewhat less public residential enclave of Charlotte Square, but instead the statue dominates the skyline on the corner of Waverley Bridge (named after Scott's Waverley novels).

Overshadowed somewhat by the mammoth Scott Monument is the statue of David Livingstone. The explorer of Africa was born in Lanarkshire and, after a failed expedition to discover the source of the Nile, he was found emaciated and ill by journalist Henry Morton Stanley, who introduced himself with the famous words, 'Dr Livingstone, I presume.' Also eclipsed by the Scott Monument are statues of Adam Black, twice Lord Provost of Edinburgh and founder of the *Edinburgh Review* and John Wilson, a professor of moral philosophy at the University of Edinburgh and a respected journalist.

General Register House

2 Princes Street (535 1314/www.nas.gov.uk).
Princes Street buses. **Open** 9am-4.30pm Mon-Fri.
Admission free. **Map** p304 D1.
Designed by Robert Adam and planned while North Bridge was still being built, General Register House

Sightseeing

was first opened in 1789, although only part of the building was completed, but was not finished until the 1820s under Robert Reid. It is home to the National Archives of Scotland and is also the oldest purpose-built archive repository still in use in Europe, holding public records of government, churches, the law and businesses; access to the archives for historical research purposes is free.

General Register Office

New Register House, 3 West Register Street (334 0380/www.gro-scotland.gov.uk). Princes Street buses. **Open** 9am-4.30pm Mon-Fri. **Admission** £17 day pass; £10 part-day pass (after 1pm); £65 week pass. **Credit** MC, V. **Map** p304 D1.

The purpose-built General Register Office for Scotland contains records of all births, marriages and deaths in Scotland since 1855, census records up to 1901, and 3,500 old parish registers from between 1553 and 1854. Designed by Robert Mathieson, who also designed the old GPO building across the road, it is modelled on the General Register House next door (*see p92*) and was completed in 1863. A pass is needed to view the records and, as there are only 100 search places available, it is advisable to book ahead.

Scott Monument

East Princes Street Gardens (529 4068/ www.cac.org.uk). Princes Street buses. **Open** *Apr-Sept* 9am-6pm Mon-Sat; 10am-6pm Sun. *Oct-Mar* 9am-3pm Mon-Sat; 10am-3pm Sun. **Admission** £2.50. **No credit cards. Map** p304 C2.

Anyone emerging from Edinburgh's Waverley Station expecting to see austere classical architecture will gawp in disbelief at the ostentatious soot blackened Scott Monument. Designed by the self-taught architect George Meikle Kemp, the monument manages to incorporate statuettes of 64 of Scott's characters and was completed in 1846, 14 years after Scott's death. The funds for the monument were raised by public donations, showing how dearly the people of Edinburgh held their most famous author. The views from this 200ft (61m) city-centre landmark are quite superb, but the final flight of steps up to the very pinnacle are a tight squeeze and can be claustrophobic.

The Mound

On the west side of the junction between the Mound and Princes Street stands a statue of the wig-maker turned poet, Allan Ramsay, dating from 1903. But the area is dominated by the twin Doric temples of the **Royal Scottish Academy** (*see p94*), and the **National Gallery of Scotland** (*see below*). These were designed by William Playfair, the 19th-century architect behind many of Edinburgh's classical revival buildings. The plainer and more refined National Gallery was built 20 years after the rather more embellished Royal Scottish Academy, which is topped by sphinxes and an

incongruous statue of the young Queen Victoria. Originally the statue was displayed at street level, but it is said that Victoria was displeased by her chubby appearance and demanded its roof-top elevation to avoid close scrutiny by her subjects.

Extensive work on the two galleries and surrounding area, known as the Playfair Project, is finally nearing its completion. For the last five years the National Gallery and the Royal Scottish Academy have been building sites and, for much of this, the Royal Scottish Academy was closed for refurbishment. However, in time for the Festival in 2003 it reopened to critical acclaim with an exhibition of major works by Monet.

The second phase will see the completion of the underground link between the two buildings and will top off what has been an extremely successful and much-needed renovation for the buildings. It will also mean further integration for Edinburgh's galleries, which are already linked by a free bus service that picks up passengers at half-hour intervals from outside the National Gallery on the Mound and goes to the National Portrait Gallery, the Dean Gallery and the National Gallery of Modern Art (*see p94, p101 and p101*).

National Gallery of Scotland

The Mound (624 6200/www.nationalgalleries.org). Princes Street buses. **Open** 10am-5pm Mon-Wed, Fri-Sun; 10am-7pm Thur. Extended hours during the festival; phone for details. **Admission** free; £1-£5 for special exhibitions. **Credit** *Shop* AmEx, MC, V. **Map** p304 C2.

Edinburgh has a wealth of institutions serving the visual arts but perhaps none so grand as the National Gallery. Built by William Playfair in 1848, the gallery opened in 1859 and has since acquired an excellent collection of paintings and sculptures. Originally housing both the Royal Scottish Academy and the National Gallery, it became the latter's exclusive home in 1911.

The gallery has taken some criticism for over-crowding its walls with paintings and, like many of the city's art collections, there appears to be an aim to cater for every taste. However, the sheer wealth of great works is undeniable. Florentine and Renaissance art is well represented; Raphael's *Bridgewater Madonna* is a highlight. There is also a good selection of Impressionist and post-Impressionist work including Monet's *Haystacks* and Cézanne's *Montagne Sainte-Victoire*.

Where the gallery really comes into its own, though, is with its permanent collection of Scottish art. Housed in the basement, the largest collection of Scottish paintings in the world contains all the prominent figures: notably Ramsay, Raeburn, Wilkie and McTaggart. Among the favourites is Raeburn's so-called 'skating minister' (properly known as *The Reverend Walker Skating on*

Duddingston Loch). It has however been pointed out that the background landscape looks distinctly unlike any view possible at Duddingston. This clearly does not concern the management of the gallery's shop – you can buy prints of Raeburn's famous painting on mugs, jigsaws and fridge-magnets.

Royal Scottish Academy
The Mound (624 6200/www.royalscottish academy.org). Princes Street buses. **Open** 10am-5pm Mon-Wed, Fri-Sun; 10am-7pm Thur. **Admission** prices vary with exhibitions. **Credit** MC, V. **Map** p304 C2.

Following its multi-million pound renovation (the Playfair Project), the Royal Scottish Academy reopened with a successful Monet exhibition, which attracted 173,000 visitors. The final stages of the £30m project are due to be completed in the summer of 2004, and the occasion will be marked by a major exhibition titled 'The Age of Titian: Venetian Renaissance Art from Scottish Collections'. Converted in 1911 into the headquarters of the Royal Scottish Academy, the building now fills the role of a large-scale temporary exhibition space.

The RSA was completed in 1826, to the Doric design of William Playfair. Its 16 columns give it a Grecian air and the building contributes to the city's 'Athens of the North' nickname. On the roof there is a statue of Queen Victoria, added in 1844 by John Steell. The Aberdeen-born sculptor is responsible for many statues around Edinburgh and he is buried in the Old Calton Cemetery.

St Andrew Square

Named after Scotland's patron saint, St Andrew Square sits at the eastern end of George Street and is home to a tranquil grass area in the middle of upmarket thoroughfares. Right in the centre is the **Melville Monument**, a 135-feet (40-metre) Doric column inspired by Rome's Trajan Column and topped by a statue of Henry Dundas, first Earl of Melville and a notorious 18th-century political wheeler dealer. The square was for a long time the financial heart of Edinburgh, until regeneration programmes encouraged key institutions to expand in to West Edinburgh. The Royal Bank of Scotland has its headquarters in a former mansion on its east side. The edifice was built in 1772 for Sir Laurence Dundas on the site that, in Craig's plan, was reserved for St Andrew's Church, and is set back from the square with a private lawn – a rare sight in the New Town. It is a mark of Sir Laurence's political muscle that he was able to overrule the council's planning orders.
The bank is still a working branch and the sumptuously decorated iron dome of the Telling Room (1860) is open during banking hours. Next door, the Bank of Scotland is housed in an outlandishly loud pseudo palazzo with rooftop

statues built in 1851. The banking hall is likewise very fine and is also open during banking hours. This row was also formerly the home of the British Linen Bank and the National Bank of Scotland before they were taken over by the Bank of Scotland and Royal Bank of Scotland respectively.

The north-east corner of the square has been the site of recent multi-million pound redevelopments. First to be completed was Edinburgh's branch of Harvey Nichols, the pricey and ultra-trendy department store. Following this, Edinburgh's new bus station opened, albeit without attracting the same media coverage or celebrity visitors. To the north of the square, an explosion of Gothic-cum-medieval architecture is delivered by the **Scottish National Portrait Gallery** (*see below*), at the east end of Queen Street. A confident, late-19th-century building dotted with pinnacles and sculptures of intellectual heroes from down the ages, its red sandstone façade is best seen in the late-evening summer sun. It does not, however, fit in well with the classical constraint of much of the New Town. The huge foyer, decorated with murals that recount Scotland's history, is definitely worth a look. It seems fitting that Sir Henry Raeburn, portrait artist to Edinburgh's Enlightenment luminaries, lived over the way at 32 York Place.

Scottish National Portrait Gallery
1 Queen Street (624 6200/ www.national galleries.org). Bus 4, 8, 10, 12, 15, 16, 17, 26. **Open** 10am-5pm Mon-Sat; noon-5pm Sun. Extended hours during festival; phone for details. **Admission** free; £1-£5 for special exhibitions. **Credit** *Shop* AmEx, MC, V. **Map** p306 F4.

The massive red sandstone edifice that stands incongruously on Queen Street is home to the Scottish National Portrait Galley, part of the National Galleries of Scotland. It was built in the closing stages of the 19th century and was completed with financial help from *Scotsman* owner JR Findlay and originally housed the National Museum of Antiques.

The building, a mixture of Italianate and Gothic architectural styles, contains portraits of Scottish heroes, heroines and notable historical figures from the 16th century through to the present day. The foyer is decorated with stunning murals of important moments in Scottish history, while paintings of kings and queens, including Mary, Queen of Scots and Bonnie Prince Charlie, give a brilliant visual guide to the rise and fall of the Scottish monarchy.

Notable portraits of key Scottish characters include the poet Robert Burns, the philosopher David Hume, the author Sir Walter Scott and, from more recent times, snooker player Stephen Hendry, James Bond actor and GLS Sir Sean Connery, and *Trainspotting* author Irvine Welsh.

George Street

George Street may only be a stone's throw away from the rampant consumerism of Princes Street, but it couldn't be more different. Although chain stores like Starbucks are quietly surfacing behind toned down façades, it has retained its dignity remarkably well and remains the lynch-pin in Edinburgh's claim to truly continental style.

Built as the New Town's main thoroughfare, George Street quickly became Edinburgh's financial district. While there are still a number of banks on and around it, many of the former financial houses have been transformed for alternative uses. More often than not, these buildings provide a suitably stylish austerity to the wide range of trendy restaurants and bars that have moved in. On any given night of the week, the likes of Est Est Est and the **Opal Lounge** (*see p154*) attract Edinburgh's young and upwardly mobile revellers.

Named after King George IV, George Street was built on a ridge overlooking the New Town. It presents excellent views of the steep descent down in to Stockbridge and, on clear days, the hills of Fife, particularly down Dundas Street. At the junction of Hanover Street and George Street is a bronze statue of the celebrated monarch, erected in 1822.

The Assembly Hall and New College, which share sites, were built on a direct axis with Tolbooth Church (now the Hub information centre for Edinburgh International Festival; *see p72*), which stands at the top of the Lawnmarket. Further west along George Street, between Hanover Street and Frederick Street, is the **Assembly Rooms**, one of the most popular venues during the Edinburgh Festival (*see p34*). Built by public subscription in 1787, the rooms themselves became a favoured haunt of Edinburgh's Regency partying set. It was here that in 1827 Sir Walter Scott revealed that he was the author of the Waverley novels, having remained anonymous until then. Many of the novels were written at his nearby George Street home. Charles Dickens was among many other famous literary figures to have delighted their audiences here. The Assembly Rooms has remained an extremely popular venue for concerts, plays and performances of all kinds since its construction, though it did briefly serve as a labour exchange and recruiting centre during World War I.

This stretch of George Street was once a popular quarter for Edinburgh's literary types. The poet Shelley and his first wife Harriet Westbrook honeymooned at 84 George Street, and Scott lived around the corner at 39 North Castle Street. No.45 George Street was the headquarters of the influential literary journal, *Blackwood's Magazine*, which counted Henry James and Oscar Wilde among its contributors.

St Andrew's Church (built in 1787 on George Street) was originally intended for the plot of

The bright lamp of Enlightenment values, shining in the New Town.

land on the east side of the square. However, the site had been quickly snapped up by the entrepreneur and politician Sir Lawrence Dundas. The church was the New Town's first and became the site of what became known as 'the Disruption' of the Church of Scotland. In 1843, it was from here that 472 ministers marched down Dundas Street to the Tanfield Hall to establish the Free Church of Scotland.

Opposite St Andrew's Church is the **Dome** bar/restaurant (*see p169*). Like many buildings on George Street, this was once a bank and, although it is now a roomy public house, much of the interior decoration has still been retained. Epitomising the grandiose aspirations of Edinburgh's 19th-century banks, its richly decorated, domed interior is worth seeing. It may even have prompted John Ruskin's 1853 onslaught on the city's liberal use of classical columns: 'Your decorations are just as monotonous as your simplicities.'

Charlotte Square

Designed by Kirkcaldy-born architect Robert Adam in 1791 (the year before his death), Charlotte Square is one of the most pleasant spaces to be found in the city-centre. Initially named St George's Square, it was designed in New Town architect James Craig's original plan to mirror St Andrew Square to the east. But when George III's daughter Charlotte was born it was renamed in her honour, helping to clear up confusion with George Square in Newington. Adam originally conceived and designed the frontages – discreetly ornamented with sphinxes and pediments – to create a coherent whole, but each house was also designed and built separately, thus creating an effect of harmony in diversity.

During August, Charlotte Square plays host to the tented village of the **Edinburgh International Book Festival** (*see p37*), which attracts many prominent literary figures from around the globe. Recent big-names have included playwright Harold Pinter and *Sex in the City* creator Candace Bushnell.

The head office of the **National Trust for Scotland** is at Nos.26-31, on the south side of the square, and is open to the public. The north side of the square has the best-preserved façade, with the Trust's **Georgian House**, at No.7, offering the chance to see how the interior of a domestic house would have looked when the square was built. No.6 is the official residence of Scotland's first minister and consequently the square is awash with lobbyists and parliamentary hangers-on. Also on Charlotte Square is the **West Register Office** (535 1314; free entry), a stuffy edifice

containing the National Archive's collection of maps. A monument to Prince Albert, husband of Queen Victoria, sits in the central grassy area overlooked by West Register House, a grandly domed and porticoed affair originally built as St George's Church. The square has been home to numerous illustrious residents, the most notable being Alexander Graham Bell, the inventor of the telephone, who was born in 1847 at 16 South Charlotte Street.

Tucked away from the grander streets, Young Street is where the less financially fortunate lived. It is also a favoured haunt of one Inspector John Rebus, who drinks at the **Oxford Bar** (*see p169*) in Ian Rankin's best-selling detective novels.

To the north of Young Street, and parallel to George Street, is Queen Street and its accompanying Queen Street Gardens. These gardens, like the many others that punctuate the New Town, were created as stretches of disciplined ruralness for the residents of the grand squares and terraces to enjoy, and remain accessible only to residents. Further along Queen Street, at No.8, is a townhouse built by Robert Adam and at No.9 is Thomas Hamilton's Royal College of Physicians.

Georgian House
7 Charlotte Square (226 3318/www.nts.org.uk). Princes Street buses. **Open** *Mar-Nov* 10am-6pm daily. Closed Dec-Feb. **Admission** £5; £3.75 concessions. **Credit** *Shop* MC, V. **Map** p304 A1.
When John Lamont, the 18th Chief of Clan Lamont, bought the house in 1796, it cost him £1,600 (around £200,000 in today's money). The house is an excellent example of what upper-class living conditions were like in the 18th century. It was restored by the National Trust before being opened to the public, and the rooms contain period furnishings right down to the newspapers. The guides in each room are happy to answer any questions.

National Trust for Scotland
26-31 Charlotte Square (243 9300/restaurant reservations 243 9339/www.nts.org.uk). Princes Street buses. **Open** *Gallery* 10am-5pm Mon-Sat; noon-5pm Sun. *Shop/Coffeehouse* 10am-6pm Mon-Sat. noon-5pm Sun. *Restaurant* 6-11pm daily. **Admission** free. **Credit** *Shop* MC, V. **Map** p304 A1.
Although in many ways resembling the ubiquitous work of Edinburgh architect Robert Adam, this neo-classical building is the work of Thomas Russell. The National Trust for Scotland has spent some £13.6 million restoring these four townhouses to their original state and making them suitable for modern offices. The public rooms, which are entered at No. 28, allow visitors to see many of the original features, such as plasterwork and wallpaper. Three galleries upstairs give the NTS the opportunity to show off some of its art collection, including major works by 20th-century Scottish artists.

More hills than San Francisco? Walk up **Dundas Street** and decide.

Dundas Street

Considered to be the residential heart of the New Town, Dundas Street is home to some of the most sought-after properties in the city. It is one of six developments built in the early 19th century as speculative ventures on the part of landowners cashing in on Edinburgh's need for upmarket dwellings. Scottish property laws allowed landowners to stipulate architectural style, so the New Town's cohesive classical formality is played out with little interruption. Resolutely residential and exclusive, these new areas were designed to deter outsiders or Old Town hoi polloi. Churches aside, there were originally no public buildings, squares or markets: only in recent decades have shops and restaurants opened along the main roads. Dundas Street itself also contains a number of private art galleries (*see p209*). There is still a classy air to the area, but it is now home to a wider social mix. The best way to explore this part of the New Town is simply to follow your feet; it is nearly impossible to get lost.

The area has, like much of Edinburgh, something of a literary heritage. Robert Louis Stevenson's former residence at 17 Heriot Row is marked by a stone-carved inscription. It is said that when he was a sickly child these gardens provided inspiration for his novel *Treasure Island*. Another famous New Town resident, JM Barrie, author of *Peter Pan*, lodged as a student at 3 Great King Street. Just beyond lies Drummond Place, a crescent-shaped street with a central garden; Compton Mackenzie, author of *Whisky Galore* lived at No. 31. Over the intersection is Scotland Street, the setting for successful Edinburgh novelist Alexander McCall Smith's latest novel (serialised in 2004 in the *Scotsman*). Further west is the Moray Estate, one of the grandest of the New Town's residential quarters.

Western New Town

While the western end of the New Town is a quiet and pleasant place for a wander, it is almost entirely bereft of activity. With most of the buildings either high-rent offices, flats or hotels, it pales in comparison to the east side of the New Town. Of the more notable buildings, the Hilton Caledonian Hotel is a colossal red-brick edifice built in 1903.

The only street of any real distinction is Melville Street, which ends in the area's only construction of any real note: the episcopal cathedral of **St Mary's**, entered from Palmerston Place (*see p218*). The main building was completed in 1879 on land gifted for the purpose by the sisters Barbara and Mary Walker, but the triple spires, which form an integral part of Edinburgh's skyline, were not finished until World War I. Edinburgh has many beautiful churches but perhaps none more so than St Mary's.

Stockbridge

Edinburgh's tranquil and affluent bourgeois district.

The crème. **Edinburgh Academy**. *See p99.*

Although Stockbridge still enjoys its feeling of quiet superiority over the rest of Edinburgh, the division between this attractive bohemian suburb and its neighbours is gradually fading. This is due mainly to the recently cleaned up **Water of Leith Walkway**, a picturesque riverside path that connects Stockbridge with its less salubrious surroundings and cuts through the city, meandering down to the Firth of Forth. The suburb's character is very much still in transition: previously so rich in churches, it has now started sprouting homeopathy shops and partaking in large-scale feng shui.

Once a village independent of Edinburgh, Stockbridge was traditionally a working-class community. The nearby **Dean Village** was an industrial centre of small-scale mills and tanneries. The 'stock bridge' itself, until its stone replacement in 1785, was a precarious wooden crossing over the Water of Leith, which carts and stock movers paid a toll to use.

Now, however, Stockbridge is a culturally rich and upwardly mobile community with a popular selection of specialist shops. Even though it has been recently infiltrated by some of the bigger retail chains, it still hosts a number of attractive delicatessens and independent arts and crafts shops. If you happen to be in the vicinity as the school bell rings you cannot fail to notice that Stockbridge is also home to some spectacular centres of private (and state) education (*see p104* **Schools rule**).

From St Stephen Street to the Botanics

In the late 1960s and early 1970s an abundance of cheap rented accommodation turned Stockbridge into a student heartland and the legacy remains with several second-hand shops dotted around the area. However, the economic boom of the 1990s brought in a more affluent set of residents and it is they who now own the property and, to a great extent, determine the atmosphere of Stockbridge.

St Stephen Street in its hippest heyday once accommodated Nico (of Velvet Underground fame) but it now bears little resemblance to its former self: the bric-a-brac junk shops for which it was best known have nearly all been replaced with more up-market and functional establishments. The street is dominated by the imposing **St Stephen's Church**, a useful landmark in the area and one that dates from 1828, when Stockbridge was particularly thick with churches and their attendant schools, halls and out-buildings.

Further along are Regency-style shops and a marooned old gateway that is the last vestige of Stockbridge's meat and vegetable market. The market was built in 1826 after a public campaign led by Captain Carnegie, the legendary philanthropist who made his fortune from the iron and steel industry in Pennsylvania. This was a coup for local shoppers as stuffy town officials had hoped that Stockbridge, like neighbouring New Town, would aspire to residential classiness and strive to be a market-free zone.

Along **India Place** is **Duncan's Land**, constructed in the late 1790s and one of the area's oldest buildings. It was the birthplace,

Sightseeing

in 1796, of artist David Roberts, the painter of Middle Eastern souks and Pharaonic temples, known for his penchant for dressing up as a sheikh. The stone for Duncan's Land, including the carved lintel inscribed with the phrase 'Fear Only God 1650', was recovered from buildings in the Lawnmarket that were demolished to open up the Mound. Opposite Duncan's Land, a mass of modern flats stands on the site of a series of streets demolished in the name of slum tenement clearance in the 1960s and '70s.

Along Hamilton Place, past the Theatre Workshop and Saxe-Coburg Street, is the low-slung, neo-classical **Edinburgh Academy** on Henderson Row. Built in 1824, it was, for 150 years, a school for deaf and dumb children. In 1968, it provided a fittingly austere location for the film version of *The Prime of Miss Jean Brodie* – originally a novella by Edinburgh's own Muriel Spark (*see p207* **Reel to real**). In 1977 it was sold to Edinburgh Academy and remains part of the school today.

Not all building in 19th-century Edinburgh was as classically regimented as the New Town. The **Colonies**, which lie on the north side of Glenogle Road, between Saxe-Coburg Place and the Water of Leith, are the first of a series of artisan dwellings that were built by the Edinburgh Co-operative Building Company from the 1860s onwards. They defy Edinburgh's usual preference for tenements. Eleven narrow streets (named after members and supporters of the co-operative) are lined with two-storey stone terraces. Unusually, they are double-sided, in that the entrance to the upper level dwelling is from external steps that run from one street, with access to the ground floor dwelling from the opposite side.

The **Royal Botanic Garden** ('Botanics'; *see below*), with its collections of world importance and well-kept beds, is at the north end of Arboretum Avenue. At its heart is **Inverleith House** (*see below*) and the **Terrace Café** (*see p162*). The lawns at the front of the house give an alternative view of the castle. Offering equally magnificent views, Inverleith Park occupies the 54 acres directly across Arboretum Road. Its breezy fields are used for a number of sports all year round, and the purpose-built pond attracts model boat fanatics from around the country.

Inverleith House

Royal Botanic Garden, Inverleith Row (552 7171/www.rbge.org.uk). Bus 8, 17, 23, 27. **Open** *Nov-Feb* 10am-4pm daily. *Mar, Oct* 10am-6pm daily. *Apr-Sept* 10am-7pm daily. **Admission** free. **Map** p305 C1.
A sturdy but stately stone mansion with brilliant views of Edinburgh's skyline, Inverleith House dates from the late 18th century. It was converted to

a gallery in 1960 and was, until 1984, home to the Scottish National Gallery of Modern Art. It is situated in and run by the Botanic Garden, which is why the shows make frequent reference to the natural world, though there are often broader exhibitions.

Edinburgh-born Turner nominee Callum Innes has shown here, along with abstract-loving Myron Stout, minimalist Agnes Martin and famed bricklayer Carl Andre. As well as showing work by international artists, Inverleith House has a good relationship with the Edinburgh School of Art and keeps a sharp eye on local up-and-coming artists, by curating group shows of home-grown talent and hosting the Absolut Scotland Open art competition. The gallery is due to reopen after refurbishment in July 2004 with a major retrospective exhibition.

Royal Botanic Garden

Inverleith Row (552 7171/www.rbge.org.uk). Bus 8, 17, 23, 27. **Open** *Nov-Feb* 10am-4pm daily. *Mar, Oct* 10am-6pm daily. *Apr-Sept* 10am-7pm daily. **Admission** *Garden* free. *Glasshouses* £3.50, £1-£3 concessions; £8 family. **Credit** *Shop* V. **Map** p306 D2.
Edinburgh has a rich botanical history, dating from 1670 when the Royal Botanic Garden opened on the site now cemented over with the sprawling Waverley Station (there is a commemorative plaque on platform 11). Now, however, it resides on the far more tranquil Inverleith Row, from which the hustle and bustle of capital city life could be light years away. Still, though, it is steeped in history and contains Britain's oldest botanical library ensuring that, as well as providing a peaceful diversion for tourists, it remains a thriving centre for research.

The main attraction is the huge glasshouse complex that provides a suitable home for tropical plants. On a route through the Orchid and Cycad House (containing 200 year old specimens), and through the rainforest conditions of the Fern House, you arrive finally at the tallest palm house in Britain, a humid octagonal cornucopia that, at 70ft (21m), keeps proud watch over its neighbours.

By no means playing second fiddle is the ornate Pringle Chinese Collection, the speciality of the Botanics. Assembled by a succession of intrepid Scottish explorers over the last 150 years, it is modelled on the mountainous regions of south-west China and incorporates a particularly lovely water feature. Research work in this field is very much ongoing and they are on schedule to complete the 25 volume *Flora of China* by 2010. In the middle of the garden is Inverleith House and the Terrace Café. The gift shop has a selection of plants for sale as well as an excellent range of publications about the Garden and the native plants of Scotland.

The Raeburn Estate

Back in Stockbridge, just off Deanhaugh Street at the top of Leslie Place, lies the **Raeburn Estate**. An early 19th-century speculative property development by the artist Sir Henry Raeburn (born in Stockbridge in 1756), it seduced the moneyed classes to move down the hill. Its main focal point was St Bernard's House, which does not survive; but **St Bernard's Crescent**, which does, is an architectural heavyweight with thick Grecian columns and vast front doors. Over the way is the rather more delicate **Danube Street**, lined with wrought-iron balconies and rooftop balustrades. Behind this show of architectural propriety, an enterprising lady by the name of Dora Noyce ran a brothel until the 1980s. Known for serving liquid refreshment from a silver teapot, the infamous Mrs Noyce described her establishment as 'more of a YMCA with extras'.

Overlooking the Water of Leith is Dean Terrace, which rises up to Ann Street. Quaint and unassuming, **Ann Street** is today one of Edinburgh's most exclusive residential addresses. Named after Raeburn's wife, it is thought to have been designed by the architect James Milne and has dolls' house-like proportions compared with the lofty heights of New Town.

There is a country cottage ambience to the street, with each terraced house fronted by a small garden. Many famous residents have found refuge here, including Thomas de Quincey, the 19th-century author of *Confessions of an English Opium Eater*. The nearby Georgian terrace of Comely Bank was

the first home of writers Thomas and Jane Carlyle. Raeburn Place is home to the exclusive Grange Club (for lawn-tennis, cricket and hockey). Since acceptance into the National Cricket League in 2003, the Scottish Saltires now play a series of colourful competitive fixtures here throughout the summer.

The Dean

To the west, and just half a mile from the city's West End, lies Dean Village. The leafy surroundings and the almost faultless architecture gives the area a Disney film-set quality, and the tranquil atmosphere contributes to the timeless feel of the place. Originally known as the Village of the Water of Leith, it has grown from its origins in the meal-milling and bakery industries to a quiet residential suburb. From the Dean Bridge there are breathtaking views of the deep valley ('dean' literally means gorge) and also the city skyline. In the early 19th century the stretch of water that runs through the valley was a hive of industry. At one stage there were 11 operational mills along the banks.

Bought in 1825 by Edinburgh's Lord Provost, John Learmonth, the one-time Dean Estate did not prove as financially lucrative as he had hoped, and as the grain and baking industries declined they were replaced at the end of the 19th century with with a large number of distilleries and breweries.

Ann Street.

What a 'Landform' installation looks like. **Scottish National Gallery of Modern Art.**

Along Queensferry Road, look north down Learmonth Avenue for a view of **Fettes College**, a private school built in the 1860s. According to espionage fiction, James Bond was sent to Fettes after an 'incident' with a maid at his former educational establishment, Eton College. Back in reality, it is also the alma mater of Prime Minister Tony Blair. A flamboyant coupling of the French chateau and Scots Baronial styles, it is topped by a soaring clock tower. Back on Queensferry Road is the private school, **Stewart's Melville College.** Another architectural flight of fancy, this is an 1848 hybrid of Renaissance and Jacobean styles marched out in a sea of leaded domes.

The main attraction of Dean Village today is its two art galleries: the **Dean Gallery** and the **Scottish National Gallery of Modern Art** (*see below*). Both are accessible from the Water of Leith Walkway and their grounds are open to the public.

Dean Gallery

Belford Road (624 6200/www.nationalgalleries.org). Bus 13. **Open** 10am-5pm Mon-Wed, Fri, Sat; 10am-7pm Thur; noon-5pm Sun. **Admission** free; £1-£5 for special exhibitions. **Credit** *Shop* AmEx, MC, V. **Map** p308 A5.

Opened in 1999, the Dean Gallery is situated directly across the road from the National Gallery of Modern Art, and you can easily combine a visit to both in one day. Like its neighbour, the gallery is housed in a grand 19th century building. Despite frequently enlightening exhibitions, the Dean has a rather sterile layout and dedicates an excessive amount of space to work by Edinburgh-born artist Sir Eduardo Paolozzi (there is an indulgent mock-up of the sculptor's cluttered studio and he has donated a large body of his work to the gallery). An influential figure in the Pop Art movement, Paolozzi was

highly influenced by the surrealists of the early 20th century as much of his displayed work shows. The gallery does redeem itself to some extent, though, with the quality of its other pieces. The Dean currently holds one of Britain's largest collections of surrealist and Dada artworks including works from Dalí, Giacometti, Miró and Picasso.

Scottish National Gallery of Modern Art

Belford Road (624 6200/www.nationalgalleries.org). Bus 13. **Open** 10am-5pm Mon-Wed, Fri-Sun; 10am-7pm Thur. **Admission** free; £1-£5 for special exhibitions. **Credit** *Shop* AmEx, MC, V. **Map** p308 A5.

Since 1984, Scotland's national collection of modern art has been housed in this neo-classical structure originally built in the 19th century as an institution for fatherless children. Designed by William Burn, the gallery has been well adapted and is set impressively in the middle of plush parkland. In front of the building is a swirling 'Landform' installation designed, and eventually completed in 2002, by the American landscape architect Charles Jencks. The grounds are a perfect location for a picnic and are dotted with sculptures by Henry Moore, Paolozzi and Dan Graham. Inside, the permanent collection features mainly well-established artists with a strong showing of the so-called 1980s Glasgow Boys the likes of Peter Howson, Steven Campbell, Adrian Wiszniewski and Ken Currie.

On the way upstairs, the entire supporting wall is given over to Douglas Gordon, who has neatly printed the names of every person he has ever met and whose name he can remember. The ground level is usually devoted to special exhibitions: a collection of Andy Warhol's self-portraits is confirmed for 2005. Upstairs is occupied by the big names in international modern art with examples of fauvism, surrealism and abstract expressionism from artists such as Matisse, Magritte, Picasso and Pollock.

Calton Hill & Broughton

The classical anomaly at the heart of an Enlightenment city.

It was from the top of Calton Hill that Robert Louis Stevenson drew much of the inspiration that fuelled his writing on Edinburgh. Although *The Strange Case of Dr Jekyll and Mr Hyde* was set in London, its atmosphere of moral hypocrisy was charged with what Stevenson saw from the hill: it was a prime location for procuring the services of local prostitutes and hence an ideal place to bear witness to the seamier side of the city. Calton Hill, according to Stevenson in his 1878 work *Edinburgh: Picturesque Notes*, is the best vantage point over Edinburgh, 'since you can see the Castle, which you lose from the Castle, and Arthur's Seat, which you cannot see from Arthur's Seat.'

The hill is a favoured and atmospheric spot. Though the smoking chimneys are long gone since the advent of the Clean Air Act, when a sunny summer afternoon turns chilly and a sea mist, known on the east coast of Scotland as a 'haar', sweeps up from the Forth, the view of mist-torn chimneys and tenements creates an impression of what Edinburgh was like when it was called 'Auld Reekie'. This hill is on the edge of old Edinburgh; it's where you'll find the **City Observatory**, from which 19th-century science regimented time. But it also lies in the heart of new Edinburgh and is the site of the modern **Beltane** celebrations (*see p194*), when revived pagan rituals mark time's passage. The area is also a popular cruising ground.

Waterloo Place

Calton Hill is approached by most visitors from the west: along Princes Street or across North Bridge. Looking up, the succession of neo-classical monuments that crown the hill make it easy to understand why Edinburgh retains the accolade of the 'Athens of the North'. What is rather more strange is that the name came before the Grecian architecture was built, instead resulting from the city's inclusion in the itineraries of the grand tours of the late 18th century, and its relationship with imperial, 'Roman' London. It was only later that the classical-styled architecture followed to justify and immortalise the phrase.

Turning the corner from North Bridge into Waterloo Place brings the visitor face to face with the full impact of Edinburgh's 19th-century neo-classical architecture. The austere grey buildings clash acutely with the intricately designed extravagances elsewhere in the city. It is buildings like these that fuel Edinburgh's reputation for dour rectitude, even if it is slightly less strong than in the past.

A few yards further along, Waterloo Place bisects the **Old Calton Burying Ground**. The steps to the right lead up to the largest part of the graveyard, the last resting place of many of the main figures of the Enlightenment. The two most imposing memorials are Robert Adam's tower for the philosopher and historian David Hume and the tall Cleopatra's needle, the obelisk to the political reformers of 1793-4 who were transported for having the outrageous audacity to demand the vote for the Scots. The graveyard also contains a monument (featuring a statue of Abraham Lincoln) to the Scots who died during the American Civil War. Up against the burial ground's east wall, there is what little remains of Calton Jail – the turreted ruins are often mistaken for Edinburgh Castle by over excited tourists when disembarking at Waverley train station.

The Burying Ground was divided into two in 1815, when Princes Street was extended and the North Bridge built. Before then, access to Calton Hill had been via the steep road of the same name, which now runs from the end of Waterloo Place down to Leith Street. Rock House, set back above the road on the north side, is one of the only houses in Edinburgh to have good views both north and south and was home to a succession of photographers from the 1830s until 1945. These included David Octavius Hill, whose work, in collaboration with Robert Adamson, gave photography credibility as a modern art form. Some 5,000 of their calotype photographs form the basis for the extensive photographic collection at the **Museum of Scotland** (*see p88*).

The most direct route up Calton Hill from here is via the steps at the end of Waterloo Place. After the first flight, go straight ahead and meander up the side of the hill or, if you have more energy, take the steep steps to the right.

Regent Road

St Andrew's House is the first point of interest on the right as Waterloo Place becomes Regent Road. The site was originally host to

Beware Gaols bearing gifts. Scotland's incomplete **National Monument**. *See p104.*

Calton Gaol, described by Robert Louis Stevenson as 'castellated to the point of folly'. Its most famous prisoners were the 'Red Clydesiders', who were convicted during World War I for publicly opposing conscription. The prison was demolished to make way for St Andrew's House but one of its turreted walls remains in place and is visible from Waverley Station. St Andrew's House was originally the home of the Scottish Office and, since the Scotland Act of 1998, is now a building of the Scottish Executive.

On the left of Regent Road, just before the vehicular access to Calton Hill and next door to the Royal High School, was the site of the permanent vigil for a Scottish Parliament, where pro-devolution campaigners protested. It seemed an auspicious location: the Royal High School was fully expected to house the new Scottish Parliament, since it had already been converted into a debating chamber before the failed referendum for a Scottish Assembly in 1976. However, after the 'yes-yes' vote of autumn 1997, the government said 'no-no' to the Royal High School and chose the Holyrood site. At the top of the road there is now a permanent memorial to the vigil in the form of a cairn supporting a brazier basket for a beacon. The tarmac of the pavement, long since replaced, had been scorched and burned by the braziers that were the only source of warmth for those keeping watch during the long, cold nights between 1992 and 1997. The memorial recalls the 1,980 days of the vigil and contains stones brought from the streets of Paris, from the home of Robert Burns, and from the top of Ben Nevis.

The old **Royal High School** building (*see p104* **Schools rule**) is perhaps the finest example of neo-classical architecture in the city. Completed in 1829, the building was designed by the Glasgow-born architect Thomas Hamilton, an internationally renowned leader in the Greek revivalist school. He modelled the school building on the Temple of Theseus – since reassigned to the god of fire and called the Hephaisteion – in Athens, and it consists of a massive Doric central block with pillared wings. Because of its monumental size, it is difficult to get a proper perspective on it, even when walking past on the other side of Regent Road, so it's best to notice the detail here and then contemplate its grandeur from one of the closes at the lower end of the Royal Mile. Plans

Schools rule

It is no coincidence that some of the finest architecture in Edinburgh can be seen at the city's well-funded private schools. Scotland has long had an excellent reputation for the quality of its education, and the inspiring edifices of its fee-paying schools reflect this.

The **Royal High School**, where Sir Walter Scott was educated, was seen as the cream of the crop. The neo-classical building on Calton Hill was built in 1829 by Thomas Hamilton and resembles (like much on Calton Hill) a Greek temple. It is no longer used by the Royal High School as the growing population meant the premises became too confined and the school is now situated in Barnton in the north-west of the city. With the Scottish National Photography Centre set to move in, though, the school is due to once again be a focal point for visitors, and to resume its role as a place for learning.

In 1824, the **Edinburgh Academy** was set up as a reaction from a number of influential citizens to the way the classics were being taught at the High School. Similarly Grecian in architectural style (although by no means in the same league as the old Royal High School building), the Academy remains one of the city's top schools; famous former pupils include the founder of BBC's *Mastermind*, Magnus Magnusson.

Fettes College is the huge Disney-like edifice in Stockbridge's Comely Bank.

Probably the best example of neo-Gothic architecture in the city, its breathtaking silhouette against the far-off hills of Fife is one that should be witnessed by any visitor to Edinburgh. Up close, you can see the painstaking craftsmanship that has gone into the many gargoyles, giving it a hint of Notre Dame in Paris. It is one of the city's most exclusive and pricey schools, and counts Prime Minister Tony Blair among its former pupils. Its most famous charge, however, was Ian Fleming's fictional spy James Bond. It is also rumoured to have been the inspiration for JK Rowling's Hogwarts (*see p114* **EdinBurgher JK Rowling**). The similarly grand **Stewart's Melville College** is also located in Stockbridge.

In the heart of the Old Town is **George Heriot's School**. Originally set up by George Heriot, a prominent figure in the court of James VI who was nicknamed the 'Jinglin' Geordie', its purpose was to provide an education for fatherless boys.

A wonderful mixture of neo-classical, Gothic and English domestic-style architecture, the sheer size of the place makes it look tremendously imposing from behind its vast gardens. Its huge octagonal chimneys mark it out as one of Edinburgh's finest architectural achievements. The school is open to the public for tours, given by the school's prefects (229 7263).

are currently underway to transform the building into a venue for the National Photographic Society for Scotland, the work being due for completion in 2006.

Just across the road from the Royal High School is Hamilton's **Robert Burns Memorial**, a small circular Greek temple that seems completely out of tune with its purpose. The large collection of Burns memorabilia that was once displayed here can now be seen in the **Writers' Museum** (*see p76*). It's worth straying this far in order to take in the view up to the **Castle** (*see p70*) and down to the **Palace of Holyroodhouse** (*see p84*), the dome of **Our Dynamic Earth** (*see p84*) and the **Canongate Churchyard** (*see p83*). The paths on the right lead down to Calton Road and provide a suitable shortcut to Holyrood if you're not going back up the hill. A few steps past the Burns Memorial is the entrance to the New Calton Graveyard, which is large but not overly fascinating.

Calton Hill

Calton Hill is best known for its bizarre selection of architecture. Its centrepiece is the **Nelson Monument**, the telescope-shaped tower on the top of the hill. Nearby is a set of 12 Doric columns that form the **National Monument** to those who lost their lives in the Napoleonic Wars. The project was designed by William Playfair, the architect responsible for some of Edinburgh's finest neo-classical architecture, as a replica of the Parthenon in Athens, but the funds ran out and it remains incomplete. Known locally as 'Scotland's Disgrace', it is set to be overtaken by the new **Scottish Parliament** (*see p28* **What price democracy?**) as Edinburgh's most famous monument to poor budgeting. In keeping with the surreal nature of the structures on the hill is Playfair's Monument to Dugald Stewart, designed in homage to the Lysicrates Monument on the Acropolis in Athens.

But Stewart was no classical hero. He was an obscure professor of philosophy at the University of Edinburgh but, for reasons best known to Playfair, was nonetheless given pride of place on Calton Hill.

Another of Playfair's buildings is the **City Observatory** (1774), based on the Temple of the Winds in Athens. Various attempts have been made to open the observatory and its grounds as a visitor attraction, but none has so far been successful. At present, the only way to visit it is through the Astronomical Society of Edinburgh (556 4365). The Observatory consists of three buildings, the Old, New and City observatories, and comprises some of Edinburgh's oldest surviving edifices. Built as a commercial venture, the Observatory was granted status as a Royal Observatory in 1822 during the visit of George IV. However, as the city became increasingly polluted, views from Calton Hill diminished and the institution was moved to Blackford Hill in 1895 where it

remains today (*see p112* **City walks**). Although members of the public are free to wander around and enjoy the views from most parts of Calton Hill, the Regent Gardens to the east are private and belong to the residents of the Regent, Carlton and Royal Terraces. These New Town terraces are unique in that they follow the contours of the hill and not a grid pattern, and are regarded as being fine examples of New Town architecture.

Nelson Monument

Calton Hill (556 2716/www.cac.org.uk). Bus 30, 40. **Open** *Apr-Sept* 1-6pm Mon; 10am-6pm Tue-Sat. *Oct-Mar* 10am-3pm Mon-Sat. **Admission** £2.50. **No credit cards. Map** p307 G4.

If the views from Calton Hill aren't grand enough, you can get an even better vantage point from the top of the Nelson Monument. Be warned, though: despite its sturdy structure the viewing deck can feel very exposed on windy days and the parapet is not very high. The monument was designed in the shape of Nelson's telescope by Robert Burn in 1807. In 1852 a time ball was erected at the top of the monument and, in 1861, a steel wire over 4,000ft (1,220m) long was attached between the monument and the Castle to facilitate the firing of the 1pm gun that still shocks the unwary to this day.

Broughton

Broughton has been the home of Edinburgh's gay community for many years now, and the area defined by Broughton Street, Picardy Place and the top of Leith Walk has been nicknamed 'the pink triangle' (see p213). However, there's far more to Broughton than this; it has steadily become one of the most bohemian and trendy areas of the city in recent years. The atmosphere has always been cultured and unconventional: it was once a notorious centre for witchcraft in Edinburgh. Before it relocated to its current site next to Inverleith Park, Broughton High School was graced with the skills of poet Hugh McDairmid when he was a student teacher. The tone of Broughton (once a village in its own right) has been lowered somewhat in recent years since the opening of the monstrous Omni Complex at the top of Leith Walk. The massive glass-fronted edifice that towers over Broughton is filled with chain restaurants and a cinema multiplex (see p208). On top of the complex is the Glass House Hotel, which boasts beautiful views over Calton Hill on one side and the city on the other. Just down the road is the **Playhouse** theatre (see p237). Picardy Place,

the huge roundabout at the top of Leith Walk, was once home to a colony of Protestant French silk weavers who fled to Edinburgh from Picardy in 1685. Today it is the site of a statue of Sherlock Holmes, whose creator, Sir Arthur Conan Doyle, was born at 11 Picardy Place (now demolished). At number 12, Edinburgh's swankiest and newest private members' club, the Hallion, has taken up residence. For a bit of light relief, there are also two outsize sculptures of a foot and a grasshopper by the Leith-born artist Sir Eduardo Paolozzi in front of the Roman Catholic cathedral of St Mary's.

Broughton Street itself has excellent delicatessens, including Edinburgh's best butcher: **Crombie's** (97-101 Broughton Street; 557 0111/www.sausages.co.uk). At the bottom of the street, across the roundabout, is **Mansfield Church**, with walls covered in murals by Phoebe Traquair. The church was bought by the Mansfield Traquair Trust and, although the building is being turned into offices, the murals are being restored for public display. Continuing down the hill, a look down Bellevue Crescent on the left reveals one of the more elegant and least triumphal of New Town façades. Further north, on Warriston Road (off Broughton Road), is Warriston Cemetery. It was here that cremation first became available in Edinburgh in 1929. To the west of the cemetery lie the **Royal Botanic Gardens** (see p99) and **Stockbridge** (see p98).

Pouting in the heart of the pink triangle.
Planet Out. See p215.

Arthur's Seat & Duddingston

An inactive volcano and quaint little village a stone's throw from the city.

Climbing up on **Salisbury Crags**, I could see the city lights.

Rising high out of Holyrood Park, Arthur's Seat is the tallest of Edinburgh's seven hills. It's well worth getting out of puff on the 20- to 30 minutes walk to the summit (*see p108* **You versus the volcano**). On a clear day the view over the Lothians is unrivalled, while watching sunrise from the top is an otherworldly – and highly recommended – experience.

The peak's intriguing title hints at myth and legend, but there is no reason to suggest any connection with King Arthur. The most plausible explanation is that the hill is named after Arthur, Prince of Strathclyde (sixth century), but a more romantic notion is that the name comes from a corruption of the Gaelic

Ard-na-Said, meaning 'the height of arrows' – the area was used as a hunting ground in the 12th century.

The history of Arthur's Seat, however, dates back a lot further than this. A now extinct volcano, it was last active around 350 million years ago. The effect this has had on the geology of the area continues to fascinate scientists today, and everyone can appreciate the natural beauty of Salisbury Crags. **Our Dynamic Earth** (*see p84*) is the most recent addition to the geography of the area. An impressive, child-friendly museum, it recreates how the famous landmark was formed and is located near the home of Edinburgh's 'Father

You versus the volcano

Arthur's Seat looks out over the city and is visible from almost all over town. The novelty of having an extinct volcano in the middle of Edinburgh is not lost on locals, and taking on Vulcan's domain is a popular Sunday afternoon pastime for families. Drink-fortified teenagers have also been known to climb the peak to watch the dawn breaking over the Forth after a night-out on the tiles.

The peak of Arthur's Seat (823feet/ 251metres), along with its lower neighbour, Whinney Hill, is at the centre of the 650-acre (260-hectare) Holyrood Park. The hill is crossed by numerous paths and walkways and encircled by Queen's Drive, which has

entrances off Holyrood Road, London Road and the top of Dalkeith Road. Arthur's Seat can also be approached from the south-east via Duddingston Road West.

Enter the park by the Albert Gate near the Commonwealth swimming pool. There are many different routes to the top; the best is to take the newly opened zig-zagging set of steps that snake up the west side of the hill. The walk takes about 20 minutes and allows superb views out over the south of the city and, on a clear rain washed day, beyond. Once you are at the very top, providing you can resist the wind, the whole of Edinburgh is visible before you in a glorious panorama.

of Geology', James Hutton, whose evolutionary theory predated Darwin's *Origin of Species* by some 50 years.

Hutton's studies of the rocks at Arthur's Seat led him to conclude that Salisbury Crags had been formed by molten lava. He fought long and hard to ensure that the igneous rock (known as 'whim' by quarrymen) used for cobbling the streets of the city was taken in moderation from Salisbury Crags. One point of particular geological interest is Hutton's Rock,

which displays a deep vein of iron ore running through the stone.

The area around the hill – often likened to a 'sleeping lion' – has been in use since pre-historic times: there are mounds and hollows on the eastern slopes, indicating where people once lived. Above Salisbury Crags are the remains of Iron-Age ramparts that were part of a stockade-type fort some time in the period 500-100 BC. By the 12th century, the area was jointly owned by the Scottish royal family and the Church.

To find out more about the park, the Rangers' Lodge by the gates of the Palace of Holyroodhouse has an interesting display of its history. It also publishes guides about the park and can give advice about its wildlife and uses over the years. From the Lodge, the walk to the summit looks the most daunting, but is in fact a less strenuous route than the walk from the Albert Gate. Turn left on to Queen's Drive and take the gently sloping path up to the right, beyond the more steeply ascending start of the Radical Road. This comes out on to a path that divides at the beginning of the valley known as Hunter's Bog; you can take the right turn for the top of Salisbury Crags and a great view of the new Parliament buildings, or continue straight ahead towards the south end of Piper's Walk. The best way to the summit from here, though, is to go up the grassy incline to the left, which rises by way of slopes and paths to the top of the steps above Piper's Walk.

Once on the summit, the views are stunning on a fair day. The vista encompasses the outer suburbs of Edinburgh in the west, Bass Rock protruding from the waves in the east, the hills of Fife in the north and the Pentland Hills in the south. Head back down the path to the right of Dunsapie Loch car park to Duddingston, where the **Sheep Held Inn** (see p170) is conveniently placed for a restorative pint.

Even though it is in the centre of the city, the park has seen its share of tragic accidents: wear strong shoes that will not slip on the grass and, even on mild days, it is wise to take an extra layer of clothing as there is no shelter from the wind off the Forth.

Historic Scotland Ranger Service

Holyrood Park Information Centre, 140 Holyrood Road, Old Town (652 8150/ www.historic-scotland.gov.uk). Bus 30. **Open** 8am-4pm Mon-Thur; 8am-3.30pm Fri. **Admission** free. **Map** p310 H5.

One holy day in 1128, King David I, who was staying in Edinburgh Castle, went hunting on Arthur's Seat and was attacked by a large stag. In a dream that night he is said to have been told to found an Abbey; he did, and called it Holyrood (see p7). He also bequeathed his lands on Arthur's Seat to the Abbey, in whose ownership they remained until the Reformation, when the whole park came into the hands of the Crown. Nowadays the extensive grounds of Holyrood Park are perfect for an afternoon's walk and play host to the rather surreal husky dog races every New Year's Day.

Unsurprisingly for a piece of natural history so prominent in the city, Arthur's Seat has starred in numerous films, novels and TV dramas. There is a famous scene in James Hogg's *Private Memoirs and Confessions of a Justified Sinner* that takes place at the top of the hill, and the landmark figures in many of Ian Rankin's novels (*see p74* **EdinBurgher Ian Rankin**). Indeed, his novel *The Falls* deals with the real life case of the 17 miniature coffins that were found on the hill in 1836. Each of the 'coffins' contained a tiny detailed doll; the mystery of their origin has never been solved.

Turning left at the Holyrood Palace entrance to the park, Queen's Drive passes St Margaret's Loch, with the ruined St Anthony's Chapel perched above it. Just before the loch, there is a grille set into the wall on the right. This is St Margaret's Well, which, during the plague years, was relied upon as a source of clean and safe drinking water.

Duddingston

Despite its proximity to main roads and large shopping centres, there is a village community feel to Duddingston that can't be found anywhere else in Edinburgh. Traditionally, Duddingston was a busy hub for the weaving of a coarse linen cloth known as 'Duddingston hardings'. Its parishioners also made use of the advantageous natural conditions: farming was a common occupation as the land surrounding Arthur's Seat is extremely fertile; there was also a small salt industry.

The best way to approach the village is on foot from Newington. From the gate next to Edinburgh University's Pollock Halls (next-door to the Royal Commonwealth Pool on Holyrood Park Road), you can follow the footpath that flanks the west side of Arthur's Seat straight into the village. It is here that you can take the Innocent Railway walkway and cycle track, or catch views over Bawsinch Nature Reserve. On the right-hand side is the popular **Prestonfield Golf Club**. This is a private club but non-members are welcome to experience one of the most picturesque rounds in Scotland (*see p233*). Further on is Duddingston Golf Course, located in the grounds of Mansion House, a neo-classical building built in 1768 by Sir William Chambers. From the 16th tee you can see the folly known as the Temple, which gave the club its logo. On the left is the jutting rock at the base of Arthur's Seat. Here you can see a geological feature called 'columnar jolting', in this case known as 'Solomon's Ribs'. The columns are usually hexagonal and are formed in lava flows during cooling and contraction.

Duddingston Village is tiny, consisting mainly of the Causeway and Old Church Road, set back off the main thoroughfare of Duddingston Road West. The village and its surrounding green belt were declared a conservation area in 1975, and it remains a little slice of countryside in the midst of a big city. Its most striking feature is **Duddingston Loch**, famously captured by the Edinburgh artist Sir

Henry Raeburn in his wry painting *The Reverend Robert Walker Skating* (1784), which now hangs in the National Gallery (*see p93*). Edinburgh has three stretches of fresh water that can be legitimately described as lochs, all of which lie within the boundaries of Holyrood Park. Duddingston Loch is the biggest and most prestigious, and is nowadays extremely popular with families, who come to feed the ducks and amuse the children, or vice versa.

Today Duddingston Loch is a nature reserve managed by the Scottish Wildlife Trust. In 1961, 13 Greylag geese were released into the reserve; today there are over 200. There have also been the first sightings of otters for over 100 years in the area. The loch was also the site of a significant Bronze-Age discovery in 1778. A collection of broken tools and instruments was found buried at the bottom, and archaeologists continue to debate whether they have uncovered a ceremonial burial site or merely a Bronze-Age landfill.

The small octagonal building at the edge of the loch is **Thomson's Tower**, named after Reverend John Thomson (1778-1840), the most famous of the parish's ministers. It was Thomson who gave rise to the enduring Scots phrase 'we're a Jock Tamson's bairns', meaning that everyone shares the same humanity and none is innately better than any other. Sir Walter Scott was a friend of Thomson's and he wrote part of *The Heart of Midlothian* in the tower at the foot of the Manse's garden.

Duddingston Kirk is one of Scotland's oldest churches still in use. It dates from 1124 and has a Norman arch separating the chancel and the nave. The north aisle was added in 1631, and many alterations have been made to the building since. To the left of the church gates there is a two-storey tower, now called Session House, used as a graveyard look-out point. During the 19th century, most churches in Edinburgh used similar towers to keep guard against grave-robbers like Burke and Hare (*see p19*), who sold recently buried bodies to medical schools.

Across the road is the west entrance to the Causeway, the centre of Duddingston. The **Sheep Heid Inn** (*see p170*) on the Causeway is one of the oldest public houses in Scotland and was a favourite of James VI and I. In 1580, the King presented the landlord with a ram's head, which was later stolen.

Duddingston's proudest claim to fame is having played host to Bonnie Prince Charlie on 19 September 1745. Where he actually slept, though, has long been the subject of much conjecture – it was finally decided that the white pebble-dashed cottage at the end of the Causeway was the most likely place.

South Edinburgh

Sleepy suburbs and student central.

The south side of Edinburgh stretches back from Lauriston Place to Blackford Hill and takes in two universities (Edinburgh and Napier), the Edinburgh College of Art and all of the attendant student residences, second-hand book shops, pubs and take-away joints. While the student population continues to grow (30,000 at last count), the south side's prim and proper middle-class character still dominates the backstreets – especially in areas like Bruntsfield and Morningside. Walk along any leafy crescent off Dalkeith Road, for instance, and you'll find huge Georgian houses with driveways packed full of top-of-the-range cars.

Lothian Road & Tollcross

It's at night that Lothian Road shows its true colours: the bright and gaudy neon of the entertainment industry. A favourite haunt of the young Robert Louis Stevenson, Lothian Road and its surrounding area has a Jekyll and Hyde quality all of its own. On the one hand there is a wealth of internationally renowned theatres and, on the other, a horde of seedy nightclubs and strip bars.

At the heart of the theatre district is the **Traverse** (*see p238*). The Traverse's café-bar is usually bustling with artists, writers and performers and is very popular with theatre-goers and posers alike. It is especially jumping during the Festival (*see p32*). Two further top-rate theatres lie almost within touching distance of the Traverse. The **Royal Lyceum** (*see p238*) hosts plays, musicals and concerts behind its opulent glass façade, while the **Usher Hall** (*see p218*), with its superb acoustics, is Edinburgh's specialist concert hall.

As soon as darkness falls the nightly rituals of drinking, fighting and vomiting are all too visible outside the less salubrious clubs and bars on Lothian Road. Despite the increased competition from similar establishments on the Cowgate and at Fountainpark, Lothian Road's reputation for late-night hedonism and debauchery remains intact (*see p228* **Saturday night fevers**).

At the top of Lothian Road is Tollcross. Traditionally a hive of activity and industry, Tollcross had lost some of its sparkle until a recent investment drive saw the opening of the **Princes Exchange**, the large modern office

Sightseeing

Old school. **Old College**. See p115.

City walks

Despite Edinburgh's bustling inner city and increasing traffic problems, you are never far away from stress-busting greenery and breathtaking views. As much as Edinburgh has to offer in the way of exhibitions, museums and shopping, a great way to appreciate the city is from up high in the clean air of the Braid Hills.

Beginning at the Harrison Arch at the foot of Blackford Hill, walk up towards the observatory (unfortunately now closed to the public). As well as the expansive view of Arthur's Seat and Salisbury Crags, you can look straight down Lothian Road and see Edinburgh Castle. Walk south over the heath following the dirt trail and turn left at the Braid Burn (sturdy shoes are recommended, especially when the trails are wet). Follow the path as it curves around Blackford Quarry (now disused except for the occasional mid summer semi-legal party); off the track on your left is the sign-posted Agassiz Rock. In 1840, Louis Agassiz, a Swiss geologist, discovered that the polished and grooved

properties of the rock were consistent with it having come into contact with a glacier during an ice age. The impressive effects of glacial erosion have been somewhat lost on those who have chosen to graffiti it.

The path continues steeply up to a wooden bridge (signed Howe Dean Path) and, once this is crossed, the path climbs reasonably quickly up to a flight of wooden steps. At the top of these is the busy Braid Hills Drive and, directly opposite the path's opening, on the other side of the road, is a gate to the Braid Hills Public Golf Course. Walkers can follow the path between the 10th hole and the 11th tee and continue straight ahead until a stone dyke comes into view. The golf course is constantly in use but is quite safe so long as you keep an eye on who's playing around you (golfers shout "Fore!" on the rare occasions when there is danger). Turn right and keep to the track, and climb gradually to the summit of Braid Hills. From here the magnificent view takes in Berwick Law, the Firth, Costorphine Hill and, on a clear day, all the way right over

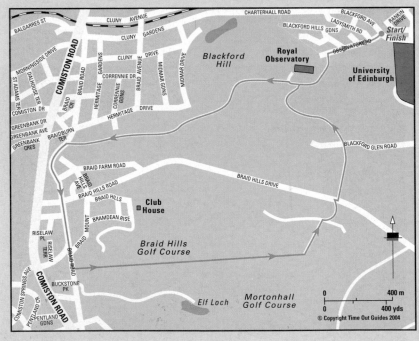

to the green hills of Fife glowing on the other side of the Firth of Forth.

The path continues gradually downhill to the west and opens out onto Braid Road. Turn left down Riselaw Crescent and onto Comiston Springs Avenue. Edinburgh's first piped water was drawn from the Comiston Springs in the late 17th century and the water still runs clear.

Turn into the Braidburn Valley Park and follow the stream north. Cross over into Hermiston of Braid and you will see a water pump which helped serve the old stone house (a gift to the city by John McDougal). This can be reached by following the path through the heath and, with a slight detour to your left, the Dovecots (called 'Doocots' in Scotland) are visible. Walking through the Hermitage of Braid nature reserve brings into view a huge selection of interesting plant life, all of it left to grow wild. The bird life is also flourishing and walkers are encouraged to look out for the reserve's resident pair of sparrow hawks, which can

sometimes be seen swooping above the trees hoping to catch their prey.

For the less adventurous, a shorter alternative can be equally refreshing. Instead of crossing over the golf course at the top of Howe Dean Path, walk 1,650 feet (500m) to your right along Braid Hills Road and you will get great views over the quarry and down into the gorge. Eventually you come to a sign posted trail with a kissing-gate at the entrance. This is the Lang Linn Path and leads down into the gorge and over the Braid burn on a sturdy wooden bridge. The ascent is fairly steep and the footing not always

easy, but on a dry day this will not be a problem. There are many excellent spots for picnics, and strategically positioned benches for those in need of a breather while they take in the views. The reserve is used widely by the locals; hardened dog walkers can be found in any weather extreme.

The walk through the Hermitage of Braid will eventually lead you back to the Royal Observatory and the full view of the city. The increasing pollution spewed out by the city traffic may pose its own problems but the smog often makes for beautiful sunsets and there is no better place to see them than on Blackford Hill.

block on Earl Grey Street currently inhabited by the Bank of Scotland. However, its bland architecture has been widely criticised; especially since it lies in the vicinity of the beautifully Gothic **Barclay Church** (at the foot of Bruntsfield Place).

To the east of Lothian Road, is the red-brick Lothian & Borders Fire Station (228 2401), built in 1898. The station isn't open to the public, but fire officers will give a tour of the small collection of historic fire-fighting equipment to those with a special interest.

Edinburgh College of Art

Lauriston Place (221 6000/www.eca.ac.uk). Bus 23, 27, 28, 45. **Open** *College* 10am-5pm Mon-Fri; 10am-2pm Sat; open later during festival. *Exhibitions* check website for details. **Admission** free. **Map** p309 E7.
The Edinburgh College of Art operates a year-round programme of exhibitions. For many, the highlight is the annual degree show in June, when the public can eye up (and, artists hope, purchase) the works of future art stars. The college puts on regular shows by artists from all over the world and the Wee Red Bar hosts a range of club nights and live music events (*see p229*).

EdinBurgher JK Rowling

While you're indulging in café society largesse, spare a thought for JK Rowling, whose Harry Potter series has become one of the biggest franchises on the planet, making her a multi-millionairess in the process. After all, it was over long afternoons in Nicolsons (now Buffet King Chinese Dining; *see p146* **The China syndrome**) where the then penniless single-mum Rowling first penned a longhand draft of *Harry Potter and the Philosopher's Stone* while her baby daughter napped. Born Joanne Kathleen Rowling in the magnificently named village of Chipping Sodbury near Bristol, Rowling began writing aged a precocious six, when she knocked off her first 'book' about the adventures of a pet rabbit, called, unsurprisingly enough, 'Rabbit'.

With a temperament that swithered between shy swot and bossy boots, Rowling has herself admitted that her childhood self was not unlike Harry's sidekick Hermione Grainger, while the thick, round NHS specs she hid behind were an obvious antecedent for everybody's favourite boy wizard. Rowling has admitted too that Harry's smart-alec confidence stems from fantasy-wish-fulfilment following her own physical insecurities as what she describes as a 'spherical' child.

After studying at Exeter University, Rowling taught for a stint, and by the time the breakdown of her first marriage prompted a move to Edinburgh, two unpublished grown-up novels were lining her bottom drawer.

The idea for Harry Potter first popped into her head on a train journey between Manchester and London. Even then it was conceived as a seven-part series, charting young Harry's travails from the ages of 11 to 17 while a pupil at Hogwarts.

She may have taken five years to finish her debut – aided, in a rare display of foresight

from a government quango, by a Scottish Arts Council grant – but its publication immediately tapped into a cross-generational readership already weaned on a steady diet of teenage witches and ass-kicking vampire slayers, and hungry for some magic to call their own.

Since Harry Potter's big-screen outings, and with five volumes enthralling a global army of would-be necromancers, these days Rowling is pretty much a self-made fairytale princess. Especially now that wishes have come true via a second marriage and happy ever afters in the Perthshire castle and Morningside mansion she calls home. With a new Harry Potter volume pending, Rowling looks set to cast her spell awhile yet.

George & Nicolson Squares

George Square is home to the arts and
social science faculties of the **University
of Edinburgh** and, in contrast with the
elegance of Old College (off Nicolson Street), is
populated with monstrous concrete blocks. The
University's main library can be found on
the south side of the square. The huge cuboid
building looks like a multi-storey car-park from
the outside but was designed in the mid 1960s
(when else?) to take over from the spectacular
William Playfair library in Old College.

Despite the ugly concrete behemoths, there
is beauty in the area. The central gardens are
open to the public (from 9am to 4.30pm) and
facing onto the neighbouring Bristo Square is
Teviot Row House, Britain's oldest purpose-
built student union (opened in 1889). **Bristo
Square** has become a favourite spot for skaters
and is packed all year round with big-trousered
youths and their entourages. All of this is
overlooked by McEwan Hall, built by Sir
William McEwan, the founder of the famous
brewery and also a one-time Edinburgh MP.

Surgeons Hall in the eastern part of the area,
around Nicolson Street, is where Burke and
Hare took their freshly deceased victims. The
troubled history of anatomy is remembered in
the Playfair Hall, home to the Royal College of
Surgeons of Edinburgh and the **Museum of
Pathology & Anatomy**, whose displays are
not for the weak of stomach (*see below*).
Another William Playfair design, its elegantly
proportioned façade is balanced by the glass
wall of the **Festival Theatre** opposite (*see
p239*). Access to the Playfair Hall is limited
and can only be gained via the Museum and
the **Sir Jules Thorn Exhibition of the
History of Surgery** on Hill Square (*see
below*). If all the gruesome sights get too
much, the historic **Pear Tree House** on West
Nicolson Street has a huge beer garden which is
perfect for those rare sunny days (*see p171*).

Museum of Pathology & Anatomy

*Playfair Hall, Royal College of Surgeons of
Edinburgh, 18 Nicolson Street (527 1649/www.rcsed.
ac.uk). Nicolson Street–North Bridge buses.* **Open** by
appointment only to groups of 12-24. **Admission**
phone for details. **Map** p310 G6.

Housed in Playfair's magnificent and well-preserved
Royal College of Surgeons (opened in 1832), this is
a working museum for the study of human disease.
The collections of pathological anatomy are there to
display diseases, abnormalities and deformities.
Close perusal by the lay person with a sense of imagination is quite distressing. Public admission is only
by booking well in advance and in groups of at least
12. The guide is chosen according to the knowledge
of the visitors. No admission for under-15s.

Sir Jules Thorn Exhibition of the History of Surgery/Dental Museum

*9 Hill Square (527 1649/www.rcsed.ac.uk). Nicolson
Street–North Bridge buses.* **Open** noon-4pm Mon-Fri
(except diploma days, Fridays monthly). **Admission**
free. **Map** p310 G6.

Tucked away in the square behind Surgeons' Hall,
this hidden treasure tells the history of surgery in
the city since 1505, when the Barber Surgeons were
granted a Charter. In providing the links between
the growth of Edinburgh and increases in the medical knowledge of its surgeons and anatomists, the
exhibition manages to say a lot about both city and
profession. There's a lot to read, but the exhibits are
well displayed – if occasionally macabre. The floor
above the Sir Jules Thorn Exhibition is dedicated to
modern surgical practice. The insightful Dental
Museum takes up an adjoining room.

Southern suburbs

The centrepiece of Edinburgh's south is the
Meadows, a large grassy area stretching east
to west from Newington to Tollcross and north
to south from the site of the old Royal Infirmary
to Marchmont. Tree-lined paths (with cycle
lanes) cut through it in every direction and it is
a popular spot for joggers and amateur sports
enthusiasts. Despite the fact that the Meadows
is often used as a short cut by those in a hurry
to get across town, it is poorly lit and some
caution should be taken at night. However, it is
generally a safe place to walk around and for
one Sunday every August it is packed out for
the Fringe Sunday carnival.

In 1886 the Meadows was the site of the
ambitious International Exhibition of Industry,
which was housed in a huge temporary
structure at the western end. The Exhibition
left the city several permanent souvenirs.
Among them are the whale jawbones of
Jawbone Walk, which were a gift from Zetland,
and the memorial pillars where Melville Drive
joins Brougham Place. Also to the east lies St
Leonard's. This largely residential area is fairly
unremarkable, but was home to Ian Rankin's
fictional detective, Inspector Rebus, who was
stationed at St Leonard's Police Station until a
real-life shake up in the city's force saw all
its detectives being re-located (*see p74*
EdinBurgher Ian Rankin).

Marchmont is composed almost entirely of
tenement buildings and is one of the desirable
residential areas in south Edinburgh. The
nearby **Warrender Swim Centre** (55
Thirlestane Road; 447 0052) is housed in a
beautiful Victorian building and is open to the
public. The cobbled sweep of Warrender Park
Road gives a general flavour of the district,
although the area now has a student ghetto

Edinburgh Uni: Fame Academy

The University of Edinburgh is one of the best in the country and its standing is exemplified by the calibre of its alumni. From scientists to spacemen, from authors to actors, Edinburgh's graduates and drop-outs have left, and continue to leave, their marks on history.

Between 1825 and 1827 the English naturalist and co-founder of the theory of evolution, Charles Darwin, studied medicine at Edinburgh before deciding that his true calling lay elsewhere. In 1859, his epoch-making work *The Origin of Species by Means of Natural Selection* was published and its conclusions are still debated today.

Another figure who was no stranger to controversy was David Hume, the Scottish philosopher, after whom one of the ugly tower blocks in George Square is named. Like Darwin he studied at Edinburgh but did not graduate. His first work (*A Treatise of Human Nature*) was published anonymously but is the one for which he is now most famous. It followed the work of fellow British philosophers John Locke and George Berkeley in the empiricist tradition and focused on problems of identity, causation and perception, famously waking Immanuel Kant from his dogmatic slumber.

Among the numerous professional authors who count Edinburgh as their alma mater, the most famous is 19th century novelist Sir Walter Scott. His numerous classics include *Ivanhoe*, *Waverley* and *Rob Roy*. Also Edinburgh students at some point were *Treasure Island* author Robert Louis Stevenson and Sherlock Holmes creator Sir Arthur Conan Doyle. It remains to be seen if popular current novelists and Edinburgh-graduates Jenny Colgan and Ian Rankin (*see p74* **EdinBurgher Ian Rankin**) have as much staying power. It is, however, certain that they will, at some stage, have utilised the revolutionary work of graduate Mark Peter Roget: his *Thesaurus of English Words and Phrases* was originally published in 1852.

Edinburgh also has a rich history of political influence. The current Chancellor of the Exchequer, Gordon Brown, was a student in the city during the 1970s; his characteristic hard work and determination led to him being elected to the prestigious position of Rector, aged just 21. Going back in time, John Witherspoon, one of the original signatories of the American Declaration of Independence, studied at Edinburgh. As did Sir David Steel, Jim Wallace and Robin Cook. Going some way to redress the balance for women, Stella Rimmington, the former director-general of MI5, studied English at Edinburgh. She retired in 1996 and was the first spy chief to have her position acknowledged by the government: before that, officials even denied the existence of the agency.

Not all famous graduates have put their Edinburgh degree to immediate academic effect: Daisy Donovan has presented a string of cult TV series and Ewan McIntosh plays 'Keith' the duke of dullards and accountant supreme in *The Office*.

atmosphere. Further west, the Meadows opens out into the Bruntsfield Links which, since it does not lie next to the sea, isn't strictly speaking 'links' ground. However, it is used as a 'pitch and putt' golf course and is free to play between May and September, provided you have your own clubs and balls. Bruntsfield itself is a mine of specialist independent shops selling everything from surf boards to designer cakes. Like Marchmont, it is almost wholly residential, but a clutch of classy bars and restaurants set it stand apart.

Morningside, despite being famous for its snobbery and pretensions, is not the place it once was. The notoriously snobby 'Morningside Ladies' look and act no differently from anyone else and, when in 1994 a TV company put the Morningside reputation to the test, they couldn't find anyone nearly snooty enough and had to use actors instead. The area was built over the old Burgh Muir, where the victims of epidemics would be banished to expire. Its other role was as a rallying ground for Scottish armies. The royal standard was pitched in the **Bore Stone** (a rock with a hole in it), then carried off at the head of the army. The Bore Stone is now displayed on a plinth on Morningside Road next to the old church at the corner of Newbattle Terrace. Just around the corner, on Newbattle Terrace itself, is the art deco **Dominion Cinema** (*see p205*).

In addition to this, there are a disproportionate number of churches. At the top of Morningside Road (nearest Bruntsfield) there are more churches in one place than in the Vatican City. The area, known locally as 'Holy Corner', also has an ever-growing number of Christian fellowship centres and yoga classes.

West Edinburgh

Exciting redevelopments and panoramic views off the beaten track.

Sightseeing

Greed is good. The **Exchange**.

Visitors rarely explore the western suburbs of Edinburgh. Tourist attractions are thin on the ground and much of the area is made up of busy roads and residential tower blocks. But the area between Lothian Road and the airport has seen huge investment in recent years as Edinburgh's financial powerhouse gradually migrates westwards. There is the odd sight to see, and the views from Corstorphine Hill are as impressively panoramic as anywhere in the city.

The Exchange

Having deserted the grand telling halls of the New Town – leaving them to be turned into grown-up drinking dens – many of Edinburgh's large banking institutions have moved to the West End of the city, to the new financial district called the **Exchange**. The term originally referred to the redeveloped area off Lothian Road that includes the Clydesdale Bank Plaza and the Edinburgh International Conference Centre but it now refers to the wider district as modern financial office blocks spring up in all directions.

First on the scene, in 1985 (before a formal development strategy had been hatched), was the almost Eastern European façade of the Sheraton Grand Hotel. This was followed in 1988 by a city council plan to promote the area as a new financial district.

At the end of the 1990s, the area around the West Approach Road and Lothian Road saw a £350-million construction extravaganza, described by the city's public relations team at the time, in predictably overblown terms, as Edinburgh's most important development since the New Town.

The Exchange's centrepiece is the **Edinburgh International Conference Centre**. Designed by Terry Farrell, this opened on Morrison Street in 1995 and the ambitious shape resembles an upturned engine part.

With this in place, the big names began moving in. The overall effect is reminiscent of London's Broadgate but with less Gordon Gecko sociopathy. At least the Standard Life building, by the Michael Laird Partnership, made an attempt to incorporate more creative elements, courtesy of sculptor John Maine

Rolling out the barrels. **Caledonian Brewery**. *See p120.*

(gates, entrance) and artist Jane Kelly (lights, railings). But beating them all for sheer verve is the Scottish Widows headquarters on Semple Street by Glasgow's Building Design Partnership. Completed in 1998, the main crescent block begs to house something a little more interesting than a pensions' management company.

Proof of the paucity of imagination that afflicts modern buildings can be seen by contrasting these big and brash 1990s upstarts with the late-Victorian **FT Pilkington** tenements, along Fountainbridge at the corner of Grove Street. Although blackened with grime, the touch of a Gaudí-esque imagination is still unmistakable. The area is a popular dining-out spot with a cosmopolitan selection of good restaurants (*see p146*).

Gorgie & Dalry

Edinburgh, west of the Castle, was once a bucolic stretch of farms and small hamlets. From the 12th century, at the latest, the area in immediate proximity to the Castle was given over to market gardening. Such rural tranquillity hardly seems credible given the riot of tenements and late-20th-century developments that are crammed into the area now. But seek out some of the older buildings, and the picture of a time when life was rather slower than today gradually emerges. Down Distillery Lane, for instance, off Dalry Road at

Haymarket, there's a beautiful 18th-century mansion called **Easter Dalry House** (now an office). Hidden away in a residential warren, it is hard to imagine this beige-harled effort as an old Scots manor with extensive grounds. Although it is thoroughly respectable these days (it is run by Age Concern), one former owner, John Chiesley, wasn't quite as douce. He was executed for murder in 1689, then buried in his own back garden.

Further out is the rather dejected area of Gorgie, where **Heart of Midlothian** (or 'Hearts') play their football at Tynecastle Stadium (*see p231*). During the football season (August to May) home games are played on average every second weekend. Opposite is the child-pleasing **Gorgie City Farm** (*see p201*). At the junction of Gorgie Road and Balgreen Road is the hidden surprise of **Saughton Park**. Here, there are beautifully kept winter gardens, centred round a public greenhouse, and a formal rose garden. This is also a good point to access the Water of Leith Walkway that meanders right through the city.

Even further out, just off the western end of Gorgie Road, sits the architectural mishmash of **Saughton Prison**, Edinburgh's lock-up since 1919. Its ghoulish claim to fame is that it was the site of the city's most recent execution. A total of four men have been dispatched at Saughton. The last to go, George Alexander Robertson, was found guilty of murder and hanged in June 1954. His body and three others lie buried inside the precincts of the jail. Still at the end of Gorgie Road, but behind the petrol station, is **Stenhouse Mansion**. This three-storey block was built in 1623 and would once have stood out from the surrounding countryside along the Water of Leith. Now it is run by Historic Scotland (668 8600) as a conservation and restoration centre, and is so well hidden that few locals even know it's there. The motto above the door reads, 'Blisit be God for all his giftis', a grace from the days when the master of the house, Patrick Eleis, could have looked back at the Castle, two and a half miles (four kilometres) away over open land.

Fountainbridge

Heading west from Lothian Road brings you to what was once Edinburgh's brewery centre. At the height of the 19th-century beer frenzy, Edinburgh had over 40 breweries. Now there's only the Caledonian brewery (the massive Fountain brewery is set to close late in 2004).

The alcoholic fug is contributed to in no small part by the Fountainpark leisure complex on the opposite side of Dundee Street. Its themed nightclubs change hands regularly, though they continue to set a similar tone to their counterparts on Lothian Road and the Cowgate. Also housed in this architectural monstrosity – a shock of glass and composite synthetics – is a large bowling alley, a gymnasium, a 13-screen cinema (one of the main venues for Edinburgh's annual film festival), and the **Shaping a Nation** visitor attraction (*see p120*).

At the end of Dundee Street on Angle Park Terrace is the **Athletic Arms** (*see p171*), a pub which sadly no longer serves the best pint of McEwan's 80/- in town, but which is still fondly known as the Diggers on account of the workers from the nearby graveyard who used to frequent it after work. For a great pint in the area it is better to visit the Caley Sample Room (*see p171*), which sells beer from the independent Caledonian Brewery (*see p120*), situated nearby on Slateford Road. The brewery has been going from strength to strength, winning prizes and plaudits for its beers: Caledonian 80/, Deuchers IPA and the organic Golden Promise.

Books and bonking

During the Scottish Enlightenment academics flocked to Edinburgh to join the likes of Adam Smith and David Hume in discussing politics, philosophy and economics. Nowadays, stag parties from around Britain and Europe take advantage of Edinburgh's relaxed attitude towards late-night drinking, porno and strip-joints. These two competing – though by no means mutually exclusive – cultures meet head-to-head in Edinburgh's West End in the area known locally as the 'Pubic Triangle'. With second-hand bookshops and topless bars in equal supply, the atmosphere is an odd one and neither side looks set to give way anytime soon.

The second-hand bookshops are, save for a few dusty copies of the *Kama Sutra*, entirely wholesome. **West Port Books** (*see p178*) specialises in artistic and philosophical volumes, though it has a small, over-priced fiction section. Bossy signs nag you at every shelf to leave your bag at the desk and to put books back exactly where you found them, and the legendary Edinburgh austerity is ever present. **Main Point Books** (8 Lauriston Street, South Edinburgh; 228 4837), on the other hand, is friendlier and less specialised though it is more random in its opening hours. At the other end of the social spectrum entirely, yet only a few doors down, is the **Erogenous Zone** licensed sex-shop. Its opaque windows hide a trove of eclectic continental pornography, bondage gear and 'marital aids'. Its literature is the diametric opposite of its dowdy neighbours: where next-door has musty grey hardbacks, here we have glitzy wipe-clean paperbacks.

In this world of soft porn, it's easy to forget that the real thing is on display at reasonable prices right across the road. The triangle's trinity of strip-bars boast broadly the same attractions: ladies willing to slowly remove their clothes for the benefit of the paying punter – a particular instance of more buying less. The three pubs face each other in a seedy showdown, and lurid window ads promise what next-door's DH Lawrence completists can only fantasise about albeit without the wilful illiteracy of phrases like 'One-2-one sessions!'

Edinburgh was dubbed among other things 'The Amsterdam of the North' when it tried introducing prostitution tolerance zones but these have since been abandoned, and the bars on the Pubic Triangle all operate within the law and are not brothels. The area is safe at night although it is more often than not packed full of boozy fancy-dress stag parties.

Caledonian Brewery

42 Slateford Road (brewery 337 1286/tours 623 8066/www.caledonian-brewery.co.uk). Bus 4, 28, 35, 35A, 44/Slateford rail. **Open** tours by appointment. **Tickets** phone for details. **Credit** MC, V.

A near-disastrous fire in 1994 allowed this forward-thinking brewery, which still uses original brewing methods, to build a visitors' centre and let the public in. Nowadays the brewery is doing so well that visits can be arranged for groups of five or more by appointment only. The only exception is during the Caledonian Beer Festival, held annually over a weekend in early June, when a vast number of ales are there for the sampling.

Shaping a Nation

Fountainpark, Dundee Street (229 0300). Bus 28, 34, 35. **Open** 2.30-9.30pm Mon; noon-7pm Tue-Thur; noon-9.30pm Fri-Sun. **Admission** £4.50; £3 concessions. **Credit** MC, V. **Map** p308 B7.

For those who like their history to be loud, flashing and interactive, the Shaping a Nation computerised theme park is a must. Pass through the various zones for exhibitions exploring the lives of famous Scottish scientists, up-to-date issues like the new – although very late – Scottish Parliament, and more flippant examples of Scotland's cultural contributions like the deep-fried Mars bar. The tour ends with a ten-minute flight simulator-type ride over Scotland's lochs and monuments; the simulator is used for amusement-style rides, too.

Corstorphine & Cramond

Scotland's home of rugby union, and an extraordinary place during any Six Nations match, is the **Murrayfield Stadium** (*see p232*) off Corstorphine Road. With a capacity of 68,500 it is one of Britain's biggest sporting arenas and is steeped in history. Further out is **Edinburgh Zoo** (*see below*). Like most modern zoos, Edinburgh's is actively involved in continuing work on conservation.

For good views, climb **Corstorphine Hill**, behind the zoo. Best accessed via the steep Kaimes Road, the wooded hill is a favourite with mountain bikers and dog walkers. The trees hide the best views around Corstorphine Hill Tower on the peak, but there are good lookout points to the east of the higher reaches of the zoo. This is the point known as 'Rest-and-be-thankful', where travellers could get their first real view of Edinburgh when travelling in from the west.

Still further north, towards the Firth of Forth, the road to Cramond village passes **Lauriston Castle**. Originally a 1590s tower house, the castle was built for Sir Archibald Napier and extended during the 1820s. Overlooking the Firth of Forth and close to the centre of Edinburgh, Lauriston is typical of the large villas that once provided rural seclusion for Edinburgh's powerful and wealthy families. The croquet lawns at the front of the house are home to the Edinburgh Croquet Club (Cramond Road South; 661 9994).

Cramond, home to the fictional Mr Lowther to whom Muriel Spark's Miss Jean Brodie paid visits on Sunday afternoons, was actually the earliest settlement in the Lothians. Waste has been found from the camps of Mesolithic people who inhabited the area in 4,000 BC. The Romans arrived in about 140 AD and their remains have been excavated behind the sea-wall car park, in the Manse gardens, where there are boards giving information about the second-century bathhouse. The finds, including a remarkable white lion discovered in the River Almond, are displayed in the **Museum of Edinburgh** (*see p84*).

During the 20th century Cramond became a commuter town and summer retreat for Edinburgh residents, but before this it had been a thriving port. In the 18th century the water power available from the Almond proved irresistible to industrialists, who built iron mills along its banks; the village became an exporter of nails around the world. The small Cramond Heritage Trust Museum offers an intriguing slant on local history and is open on the quayside during summer weekends.

Edinburgh Zoo

Corstorphine Road, Murrayfield (334 9171/ www.edinburghzoo.org.uk). Bus 12, 26, 31. **Open** *Apr-Sept* 9am-6pm daily. *Oct, Mar* 9am-5pm daily. *Nov-Feb* 9am-4.30pm daily. **Admission** £8; £5 concessions; free under-3s; family £24-£30. **Credit** MC, V.

Opened in 1913, Edinburgh Zoo is now home to over 1,000 different species of animal. It sits high on top of Corstorphine Hill and, while it is principally a family-orientated attraction, the lunch-time penguin parade is one of the most bizarre and hilarious things you will ever see and for that reason alone is completely unmissable. Watch out too for the sealion demonstrations and the keeper talks.

Lauriston Castle

Cramond Road South, Davidsons Mains, Cramond (336 2060/www.cac.org.uk). Bus 1, 41, 42. **Open** *House* Apr-Oct 11am-5pm Mon-Thur, Sat, Sun; Nov-Mar 2-4pm Sat, Sun. *Grounds* 9am-dusk daily. **Admission** *House* (by guided tour only) £4.50; £3 concessions. *Grounds* free. **No credit cards**.

Set in large, reasonably well kept grounds on the way to Cramond, this 16th-century neo-Jacobean fortified house was left in trust to the nation by William Reid in 1926. He and his wife were enthusiastic antiques collectors who furnished the house throughout with their collections. The house interior can only be viewed on the 50-minute tour, which starts at 20 past the hour (during opening hours).

Leith

Take the waters by the Shore.

Scottish Executive.
See p125.

Having been the centre of the world's media attention for a week in 2003, when it hosted the celebrity-packed MTV Europe Awards (*see p122* **Star for a night**), Leith was expected to kick on and cement its place in the 21st century. Now that the temporary marquees have been dismantled and the short economic boom brought back down to earth, Leithers are taking stock and beginning to wonder if the much vaunted rebranding of their town is a case of mutton dressing up as lamb. It is certainly true that trendy hotels, bars and clubs are springing up in the city's docklands; what is less clear is whether it is Leith itself that is providing the attraction or its favourable lease rates. Not that this necessarily matters, especially with major arts projects like the Out of the Blue studios (formerly on New Street, near Calton Hill) relocating to a new £650,000 home on Dalmeny Street (formerly a Territorial Army centre).

After the demise of the ship-building industry, Leith is undoubtedly undergoing a remarkable regeneration. The waterfront is now home to some of the trendiest bars and restaurants in the city. On Tower Place, the cheap-chic award-winning hotel **Malmaison** (*see p63*) has attracted a lot of positive attention for its constantly changing menu and neo-French cuisine – it was a major coup for Leith to attract the hotel in 2002. Competition in the area is keen, thanks to the likes of the highly rated **Martin Wishart** restaurant on the Shore and **Daniel's** (for both; *see p150*) on Commercial Street. In the less salubrious surroundings of Portland Street (opposite the Social Security office) is the highly controversial 'cannabis café', Purple Haze. Since 2004, cannabis has been effectively decriminalised and Purple Haze, with its greasy spoon image has become popular with members of the cannabis smoking culture. It should be stressed that no drugs are on sale here and, indeed, the buying, selling and possession of cannabis is still a criminal offence in Britain, albeit an ironically hazy one.

The multi-million pound **Ocean Terminal** shopping centre (*see p177*) has successfully opened on the waterfront and Leith was chosen to be the retirement dock of the **Royal Yacht Britannia** (*see p125*). Despite a slow and highly criticised start, the shopping centre is finally beginning to establish itself in the hearts of Leith's residents.

The Leith skyline is however still blighted by unsightly 1960s tower blocks and the social problems of the 1980s and '90s have by no means vanished overnight, but the town motto 'persevere' is much in evidence.

Traditionally, there has never been any love lost between Leithers and their counterparts from Edinburgh. Despite the fact that, at first appearance, Leith looks like nothing more than a different postal district of Edinburgh, it has a fiercely preserved attitude and history of its own. In 2002 the Westminster government tried unsuccessfully to change the name of the Leith electoral constituency to 'North Edinburgh', an idea that they soon realised was not just a simple 'tidying up' exercise but part of a centuries-old conflict that still stirs up strong emotions in the locals, even sparking a furious 'Keep Leith' campaign from the *Edinburgh Evening News*. The rivalry dates from 1329, when Edinburgh was granted a Royal Charter by Robert the Bruce. Under the charter, Leith was given over to Edinburgh, meaning that every captain that docked in its port would have to pay a toll (nearly three miles away) at Edinburgh's Tolbooth before his vessel was allowed to unload its cargo. Until 1833, all of

Star for a night

If evidence was needed that Leith has come a long way from Irvine Welsh's junkie den of the 1980s and '90s, then there is none better than MTV's decision to host its prestigious 2003 European Music Awards ceremony in the dockland town. The event was the hottest ticket of the year in Edinburgh as the stars of world show business descended with their huge entourages on newly vibrant Leith. The night saw performances from the Darkness, Missy Elliot and the White Stripes, but it was the arrival of Justin Timberlake (who was later spotted DJing at the cheesy student club Massa) and Beyoncé Knowles (who went for a private shopping trip in Harvey Nichols) that brought the city to a standstill.

The event was broadcast live around the world to 1 billion people in 28 countries from a purpose-built marquee in the heart of Leith. However, despite the boost for local businesses and the prestige associated with hosting such an event, there were still those who complained about the hidden price for local taxpayers. The cost of the arena that was set up near the new Ocean Terminal was in the hundreds of thousands of pounds, a sizeable portion of which was absorbed by Edinburgh council. But tourist chiefs say it was well worth it.

The main point of dissent, however, was the fact that less than half of the allotted tickets to the media event were available to the public, and no priority was given to the people of Edinburgh. Most vocal among the

killjoys were the representatives of the Scottish Socialist Party (who eventually backed down), and there was also a defiant 'Fuck MTV' rival club night at Cabaret Voltaire (*see p227*). On the evening itself, thieves made off with thousands of pounds worth of computer equipment from the MTV site containing irreplaceable records, which somewhat confirmed the area's dodgy reputation...

The event was nevertheless deemed a huge success, with the spotlight of the world's media shining exclusively on the Western Harbour. The city's hotels were mobbed with young fans, standing vigil for their heroes, and, for one night at least, Leith was the centre of the entertainment world.

Leith's foreign trade was controlled by Edinburgh, causing bitter resentment.

There were, however, a few years of independence for Leith. When the first modern docks were laid out in the early 1800s, they cost so much to construct that Edinburgh had to declare itself bankrupt. The docks were effectively nationalised in 1825 and, in 1833, an act of parliament made Leith an independent parliamentary borough. Independence was short-lived, however. The town never managed to generate enough income to sustain itself and amalgamation became increasingly likely after World War I, despite its unpopularity among Leithers. They voted 29,891 to 5,357 against amalgamation in a last-ditch, toothless referendum in 1919, but financial constraints were against them, and Edinburgh and Leith were merged in 1920.

Leith Walk

Entering Leith along Leith Walk from the city centre brings you straight to the **Kirkgate**. Historically, this was the hub of the town, but the original buildings have been torn down and replaced with a faceless shopping arcade backing on to high-rise flats. In Leith, you're never far from a town planner's bungle. Diagonally across from the Kirkgate are a supermarket and the aquatic playground **Leith Waterworld** (*see p199*), which both stand on the site once occupied by Leith Central Station. Before the station was demolished, its abandoned buildings gave **Irvine Welsh** (*see p127* **EdinBurgher Irvine Welsh**) the name of his book, *Trainspotting* – a typically sardonic euphemism for scoring heroin at the (derelict) station. The hard drugs scene of the 1980s, as featured in the novel, threatened to tar Leith's reputation permanently, but the town's regeneration is helping it to shake off its image as a junkie-ridden place of permanent industrial decline. Leith Walk itself (the main thoroughfare between Leith and the rest of Edinburgh) contains a mixture of specialist shops. There are several of the best Indian stores in the city as well as numerous pawn brokers and a well stocked Chinese supermarket. Every other Saturday during the football season the street fills with fans adorned in the green and white of **Hibernian**, who play at the nearby Easter Road stadium (*see p231*).

Leith Links

To the east of the Kirkgate, at the foot of Easter Road, lie the green spaces of **Leith Links**. As Leith's traditional common land, the Links have been used for everything from cattle-grazing to archery contests. Despite the efforts of residents and local politicians, the Links remains a favourite area for prostitutes and should be avoided at night, especially by lone women.

During the Stuart era, Leith and St Andrews (in Fife) were Britain's main centres for golf. The Royal & Ancient Club at St Andrews is known as the 'home of golf' but the oldest golf club in the world is the Honourable Company of Edinburgh Golfers who first competed on Leith Links on 7 March 1744; it was that same club that devised the set of rules which was subsequently adopted by the Royal & Ancient ten years later. Golf has been banned from the Links since 1907 but the grassy space is currently used for a number of amateur sports.

The Links also have more tragic associations. In 1560, the English army dug in here and besieged the town. Two of the 16th-century gun emplacements, Giant's Brae and Lady Fyfe's Brae, can still be seen as grassy mounds.

Signs of civic prosperity are visible in buildings such as the Leith Assembly Rooms and, round the corner in Bernard Street, the elegant, domed Old Leith Bank. This is Leith's financial centre, where many of the new businesses that flooded into Leith during its regeneration in the 1980s are concentrated.

The Shore

The Shore has claims on being Leith's oldest street and is at the forefront of its recent regeneration. The nearby neo-classical buildings of Bernard Street remain a focal point but the Shore now boasts a range of classy restaurants and bars that offer alfresco drinking, and comes into its own on summer evenings. Despite the smart new apartment blocks and offices it is still possible to imagine the haphazard tangle of narrow alleys from centuries past. It is here that the port's first loft spaces opened, and were quickly snapped up by affluent professionals with bohemian aspirations. Historically, the most notable building is **Lamb's House** on Burgess Street, a 17th-century tenement that was restored by the National Trust and is now run as an old people's home.

On the quayside itself, rather hidden by the sculpted wrought-iron railings and young trees opposite No.30 Shore, there is a plaque commemorating the place where George IV in 1822 first set foot in Scotland with the words 'Geo IV Rex O Felicem Diem' ('George IV rules on this happy day'; *see p18*).

The area around the Shore has not fully shaken off its rough image, however, and late at night the docks are not a safe place to wander around. Visitors to the city should also use

Sightseeing

Rhubarb

"Divine decadence. Rich ripe and
dangerously close to dissolute."
Tatler

"...a Baroque extravaganza where
more is most certainly more!"
Gillian Glover, the Scotsman

discretion before entering some pubs, as the traditional welcoming Scots attitude is not always in evidence. As with most of Edinburgh, when the pubs close (usually 1am) crowds spill out and there is occasionally trouble.

Leith's Coburg Street and Coalhill make up the city's red-light district and should definitely be avoided at night, particularly by women. For several years these streets were the centre of the Leith 'tolerance zone', a scheme for managing street prostitution that was withdrawn in 2001 due to complaints from residents. Attempts to create a new zone elsewhere in the city have so far been met with similar protest.

North Leith

Leith is divided by the **Water of Leith**; the area to the west of the river mouth is paradoxically called North Leith and to the east is South Leith. Described by Robert Louis Stevenson as 'that dirty Water of Leith' it has been cleaned up over the last 25 years and now the Water of Leith Walkway is a tourist attraction as well as a pleasant thoroughfare for dog-walkers. Starting at the northern end of the Sandport Place Bridge and following the riverbank right to the heart of Edinburgh, it is one of the best walks in the city.

Great Junction Street connects the north with the south and is home to an assortment of grocers, down market clothing shops, funeral directors and a couple of grim indoor markets. During shopping hours, it is usually thronged with senior citizens; many of Leith's younger residents have been rehoused in outlying council estates referred to locally as 'schemes'. One of the few sights off Great Junction Street is **Leith Victoria Swimming Pool**, which opened in 1896 (Junction Place, Leith; 555 4728).

Over Junction Bridge, the corner of Ferry Road and North Junction Street is overlooked by a gable-end mural depicting the history of Leith as a jigsaw puzzle. Portrayed as the final piece of the jigsaw is a picture of a Sikh man reaching to take the outstretched hand of the community. Most of the Sikhs in Edinburgh live in Leith, and their temple (*see p288*) is in a converted church just back over the bridge and down Mill Lane towards the Shore. To the left of the mural are two grand but unfussy buildings, **Leith Library** and **Leith Theatre**. They both opened in 1932 and are superb examples of economical design, with the theatre's portico following the curve of the library's semicircular reading room. Straight ahead is North Junction Street, where Leith School of Art inhabits the oldest Norwegian seamen's church outside Norway, a small Lutheran kirk dating from 1868.

On Commercial Quay, the developments have been far more dramatic. A row of bonded warehouses running almost the entire length of Commercial Street has been renovated into desirable apartments, upmarket shops, glass-fronted restaurants and stylish offices. Facing them across the quayside is an imposing piece of post-modern architecture that houses the **Scottish Executive**. Its design is certainly uncompromising, and is not to everyone's taste, but its brash boldness epitomises the spirit of the redevelopment that has been taking place here, where the old and new interlock with a surprising ease.

On the north side of the Executive, the whole port area is being reclaimed, with building underway for a huge new 'village' of flats and gardens, and in 2009 the waterfront will be included in the tram loop. The first major part of the development is Terence Conran's **Ocean Terminal** (*see p177*), a huge shopping centre and cinema complex built in the style of an ocean liner. Inside is the usual array of chain-stores along with the entry point to the **Royal Yacht *Britannia*** (*see below*).

Royal Yacht *Britannia*

Ocean Terminal, Ocean Drive (555 5566/www.royal yachtbritannia.co.uk). Bus 11, 22, 34, 35, 36. **Open** *Apr-Sept* 9.30am-6pm daily (last admission 4.30pm). *Oct-Mar* 10am-5pm daily (last admission 3.30pm). **Admission** £8.50; £6.50 OAPs; £4.50 concessions; free under-5s; £23 family. **Credit** AmEx, DC, MC, V. **Map** p311 Hx.

Launched in 1953, the year of Queen Elizabeth II's coronation, the Royal Yacht *Britannia* was used by the Royal family for state visits, holidays and diplomatic functions. It was decommissioned in 1997 and now resides permanently in Leith.

Entry to the yacht is from the top floor of the newly built Ocean Terminal shopping centre. The visitor centre contains many photographs and a mock-up of a sergeants' mess room. Stepping on board the yacht itself is like stepping back into the 1950s. The interior is still meticulously cleaned each day and the flowery decor, combined with the tiny living quarters for the staff, make it appear strangely class bound. The entry price also includes an informative audio guide packed with interesting anecdotes and points of reference.

Newhaven

Following the shoreline west along Lindsay Road, and on past the gleaming white silos of Chancelot Mill, leads you to the old fishing village of **Newhaven**. Much of the original village has been pulled down, but there are still some original fishermen's cottages in the streets near the shore. Up until the 20th century, Newhaven was a very insular community,

whose residents are thought to have descended from the intermarriage of locals and the shipbuilding craftsmen brought over from France, Scandinavia, Spain and Portugal by James II. Newhaven became famous for its sturdy and colourfully dressed fishwives, who used to carry their creels full of fresh fish up to Edinburgh to sell every morning. The once-flourishing fishmarket, built in 1896, now uses up only a fraction of the space that it once covered; instead, the long red building has become home to a branch of Harry Ramsden's fish and chip shop and the **Newhaven Heritage Museum** (*see below*). Although small, this is a vibrant child-friendly community museum.

Across the road, the former St Andrew's Church building is now used by **Alien Rock** (*see p234*) as an indoor climbing centre. Newhaven is also seeing some of the money being invested in the city's waterfront. The Next Generation Club, a high-tech leisure complex, has recently opened, and building work is going on at a furious rate for a new block of apartments with sea views called the Platinum Point development.

Newhaven Heritage Museum

24 Pier Place, Newhaven Harbour (551 4165/ www.cac.org.uk). Bus 7, 10, 11, 16, 22, 32. **Open** noon-4.45pm daily. **Admission** free. **Map** p311 Ex.

Set entirely within one room, this museum may be small but it is alive with the history of the harbour village. It occupies a former school building and is crammed completely full of local history, right back to when Newhaven was operating as a naval dock-yard in the 16th century. The Newhaven Living History Project has done its job well: the recorded memories are vibrant and telling, although the accents might prove a little difficult for non-locals. Other exhibits are a little wordy but, if time is not an issue, this can be a fascinating out of the way place to get an idea of the 'real' Edinburgh.

Portobello

Once a proper Victorian holiday resort – Portobello was referred to without irony as 'the Brighton of the North' – the town is now a slightly sad shadow of its former self. Nevertheless, on sunny days the long stretch of sand can get very busy with a summer atmosphere of pale bodies, ice-cream, slot machines and determined enjoyment whatever the weather that is peculiarly British.

The small town was founded in 1739 by a retired sailor, George Hamilton, although then it consisted solely of his own home. Having fought in Panama against the Spanish, he was part of the successful capture of Puerto Bello.

A ship stranded on the **Shore**. See p123.

So when he retired to the shore of Edinburgh he called his house 'Portobello' and it became a staging post for passengers on the stagecoach to Musselburgh and on towards London.

Today there is little for the tourist but the stereotypical British attractions of fish and chip shops, arcade machines and fairground rides. However Portobello does have something of a musical heritage: the 1970s punk band the Valves mock the traditional family resort and calm seas with their classic song 'Ain't No Surf in Portobello'. It also boasts the birthplace of Sir Harry Lauder (1870-1950), the Scottish entertainer who became known as the 'Laird of the Music Hall' and wrote such classics as 'Roamin' in the Gloamin' and 'I Love a Lassie'. He was born at 4 Bridge Street and a plaque commemorates him there.

Portobello Baths

Portobello Swim Centre, 57 Promenade, off Bellfield Street (669 6888). Bus 2, 15, 19, 26, 42. **Open** *Pool* 7am-9pm Mon-Thur; 7am-7.40pm Fri; 9am-3.40pm Sat, Sun. *Turkish Baths* (women only) 3-9pm Mon; 9am-9pm Wed; (men only) 9am-9pm Tue, Thur; (mixed) 9am-9pm Fri; 9am-4pm Sat, Sun. **Admission** *Pool* £1.80-£2.20; free under-5s. *Baths* (over-16s only) £5.60. **Credit** MC, V.
Housed in a beautifully designed Hispanic-style building, the baths have a long reputation for the quality of their swimming and water polo clubs. They have recently received a big-budget makeover and the Victorian building now contains a well-equipped gym as well as excellent Turkish baths and swimming pools. The centre is family-friendly, if a little on the expensive side. Phone ahead if you plan to take advantage of the Turkish baths as there are frequent men/women only days.

EdinBurgher Irvine Welsh

Trainspotting author Irvine Welsh is Edinburgh's dark side. More than anyone else in the contemporary life of the city, he is the cultural representative of the blue-collar working man, the drug-addled no-hoper, and the just-for-the-thrill-of-it thug. But Edinburgh is seen by many as prone to bourgeois complacency, so perhaps it needs a man like Welsh, a man whose loathing of all things smug is equal to the scale of smugness that can occur in this old burg.

Welsh was born in 1958 in the shadow of Easter Road, home to his much loved Hibs FC (*see p231*), before he later decamped to the grim housing estate peripheries of Muirhouse. It wasn't until 1993 that his literary venom first came to public attention, with the publication of his debut novel, *Trainspotting*. Chronicling the life and misadventures of four working class junkies, it was written in phonetic Leith dialect and portrayed a way of life that was very much at odds with Edinburgh's preferred image of respectability, aloof elegance and nobility. His position as an icon of alternative Edinburgh was cemented when *Trainspotting* was translated into a critically acclaimed and massively successful film, starring Ewan McGregor and directed by Danny Boyle.

His subsequent works may not have achieved quite the same level of success (perhaps explaining his decision to write a sequel to *Trainspotting*, called *Porno*), but he's remained a hugely influential figure in

British counter-culture, featuring on a Primal Scream record; railing against the middle class emphasis of the Edinburgh Festival; bemoaning the gentrification of his beloved Leith; and working for a time as the supposedly left-wing sass-mouth columnist for the *Daily Telegraph*.

Popular opinion remains very much divided when it comes to Irvine Welsh. Many see him as a bloated pub bore, trying to eke a career out of low grade controversy; while others truly believe that he is some kind of messianic post-junkie visionary for an apocalyptic age. Not that it matters much either way – his notoriety is assured.

Eat, Drink, Shop

Restaurants

Class acts and Chinese canteens.

Ooh, la, **La Garrigue**. *See p131.*

In the last few years, investment at the top end of the Edinburgh restaurant scene has been unprecedented. Dave Ramsden opened **Rogue** on Morrison Street in 2001 (*see p149*), while the other big arrivals that year were **Santini** in Conference Square (*see p147*) and **Oloroso** in Castle Street (*see p139*). In 2002 along came **Vermilion** in the Scotsman Hotel on North Bridge (*see p135*) and Harvey Nichols' **Forth Floor**, overlooking St Andrew Square (*see p135*). James Thomson, the man behind such classic local restaurants as the **Witchery** (*see p135*) and the **Tower** (*see p135*), wasn't going to be left out, however, and in autumn 2003 he opened **Rhubarb** in a 17th-century mansion south of Arthur's Seat (*see p146*). Meanwhile, the likes of chef Jeff Bland at **Number One** (*see p139*), and **Martin Wishart** at his

eponymous Leith restaurant (*see p150*) were earning Michelin stars. However, a reminder of the limits to Scottish restaurant tolerance came early in 2004 – and it came from the west. Gordon Ramsay, arguably the UK's top chef, was forced to close down his Glasgow venture, Amaryllis, due to a simple lack of business. Edinburgh, like Glasgow, has neither the population base nor the economic muscle to support the kind of restaurant scene enjoyed by London – so no equivalents to Restaurant Gordon Ramsay, Le Gavroche or Sketch up here. All the same, in terms of upmarket eating establishments Edinburgh has certainly never had it so good.

That's all fine and dandy for those who can afford terrine of foie gras and duck confit. When it comes to bums on seats, though, the

Edinburgh public will have noticed two much more obvious trends in the last couple of years. A wave of Thai restaurants hit the city in 2002 and 2003, catering to an obvious gap in the market that now feels saturated. Meanwhile, at the cheap 'n' cheerful end of things, Chinese canteens have made stuffing yourself at lunchtime more affordable than ever before (see p146 **The China syndrome**).

That's not to mention Edinburgh's excellent reputation for seafood, its wide range of ethnic restaurants, and all its many and varied cafés and café-bars (see p152). Bon appetit.

PRACTICALITIES

Few places have strict dress codes these days. As a general rule, the pricier the joint, the smarter the clientele: but if you're unsure, it's wise to call ahead first.

It's standard practice to pay ten per cent on top of the bill for service. Some restaurants will add this automatically (while insisting that it is 'optional'; so if service wasn't up to scratch, you should deduct the charge. Be wary of places that include service on the bill and still leave a space for a gratuity on your credit card slip.

Finally, during the Festival (August to early September; see p32) many restaurants are open much later than indicated in the year-round times; phone first to check.

Old Town

Fish & seafood

Creelers

3 Hunter Square (220 4447/www.creelers.co.uk). Bus 35/Nicolson Street–North Bridge buses. **Open** *June-Sept* noon-2.30pm, 5.30-10.30pm Mon-Thur, Sun; noon-2.30pm, 5.30-11pm Fri, Sat. *Oct-May* 11.30am-2.30pm, 5.30-10pm Mon-Thur; 11.30am-2.30pm, 5.30-11pm Fri, Sat; noon-3pm, 6-10pm Sun. **Main courses** £9.75-£30. **Credit** AmEx, DC, MC, V. **Map** p304 D3.
This is a light room with simple wooden tables and a panoramic artwork on one wall while there are more space through the back (non-smoking). The seafood lets the excellence of the raw materials shine through which means dishes like hake fillet with nori, or baked cod with Arran mustard. There are always one or two meat and vegetarian options for non-piscivorous diners.

Mediterranean

La Garrigue

31 Jeffrey Street (557 3032/www.lagarrigue.co.uk). Bus 30, 35/Princes Street buses. **Open** noon-2.30pm, 6-10.30pm daily. Closed Sun Jan-Mar. **Main courses** £9.50-£18. **Credit** AmEx, DC, MC, V. **Map** p310 G5.

This restaurant sneaked quietly on to the scene in mid 2001 with little fanfare. Chef-proprietor Jean Michel Gauffre was formerly at the city's Sheraton Hotel, but La Garrigue allows him more scope to pursue his interest in food from his home region, Languedoc, in southern France. The decor is high-class rustic, but the cooking is far from rough and ready: all the ingredients are top quality and well sourced. Unassuming, but one of Edinburgh's best French restaurants.

Igg's

15 Jeffrey Street (557 8184). Bus 30, 35/Princes Street buses. **Open** noon-2.30pm, 6-10.30pm Mon-Sat. **Main courses** £15-£20. **Credit** AmEx, DC, MC, V. **Map** p310 G5.
Igg's has been around since 1989. The decor is quietly classy and the waiting staff pad around discreetly. A generally Iberian approach comes with other European and international influences, there's a good wine choice, and desserts are well crafted. It's not young and buzzing, but its sister tapas establishment two doors down (Barioja, 19 Jeffrey Street; 557 3622) fulfils that role with gusto.

Maison Bleue

36-38 Victoria Street (226 1900/www.maison-bleue.co.uk). Bus 2, 23, 27, 28, 41, 42, 45. **Open** noon-3pm, 5-11pm Mon-Sat; noon-3pm, 5-10pm Sun. **Main courses** £6.90-£18.80. **Credit** DC, MC, V. **Map** p304 C3.
This is an atmospheric establishment on three floors, with a comfortable bar area, subdued lighting, and some bare stone. The menu is split into 'bouchées', 'brochettes' and 'bouchées doubles'. *Bouchées* are small (one for a starter, two or three for a full meal); *brochettes* are char-grilled meat skewers with couscous and yoghurt; *bouchées doubles* are more substantial. Once you're used to the menu structure, you'll love it.

Eat, Drink, Shop

Top five Restaurants

Atrium
Enduring and consistent (see p147).

Grill Room
Far from fashionable, but excellent (see p149).

Number One
A placid space to appreciate fine food (see p139).

Restaurant Martin Wishart
Some shine in Leith (see p150).

Vermilion
A new kid on the block at this level (see p135).

The Pompadour

Lunch: Tue-Fri 12.30pm-2.30pm
2 courses £15.95   3 courses £19.95
Dinner: Tue-Sat 7pm-10pm

Full a La Carte menu available

The Pompadour Signature Dish ~ **Châteaubriand**
Scottish beef fillet served with Château Potatoes Sauce
Bérnaise and Rich Wine Jus, prepared in front of you
on a traditional carving trolley   **£25.50pp**

Caledonian Hilton
Princes Street, Edinburgh EH1 2AB
0131 222 8777

Mexican

Viva Mexico

41 Cockburn Street (226 5145/www.viva-mexico.co.uk). Bus 35/Princes Street or Nicolson Street–North Bridge buses. **Open** noon-2pm, 6.30-10.30pm Mon-Sat; 6.30-10pm Sun. **Main courses** £9.50-£13.95. **Credit** AmEx, DC, MC, V. **Map** p304 D2.

Serving all the usual Mexican dishes (fajitas, chimichangas, and more) to Edinburgh's citizenry since 1984, the ground floor may perhaps look a tad sparse, but the basement is much more convivial and vibrant. The *calamares a la mexicana* are very popular, and the restaurant serves a decent Margarita. Much loved by many locals, including author Iain Banks.

Modern European

Doric Tavern

15-16 Market Street (225 1084/www.thedoric.co.uk). Princes Street buses. **Open** 11.30am-1am Mon-Sat; noon-1am Sun. **Main courses** £8.95-£15.95. **Credit** AmEx, MC, V. **Map** p304 D2..

The Doric is all very old-wood with menus and wine lists sketched up on blackboards. The dishes are sound bistro fare: it's the kind of place students bring their parents, and the atmosphere can be faintly boisterous (in a civilised way). It has been around for years and its popularity endures despite a potential scattiness about service when it's full.

Grain Store

30 Victoria Street (225 7635/www.grainstore-restaurant.co.uk). Bus 2, 23, 27, 28, 41, 42, 45. **Open** noon-2pm, 6-10pm Mon-Thur; noon-2pm, 6-11pm Fri; noon-3pm, 6-11pm Sat; noon-3pm, 6-10pm Sun. **Main courses** £6.50-£23. **Credit** AmEx, MC, V. **Map** p304 C3.

Tucked away upstairs off a winding Old Town street, the Grain Store has a few candelit recesses that come into their own during the evening, but has always seemed to excel as a place to while away an afternoon by a window, after lunch, and after a bottle or two of wine. For that lunch you can do a tapas-style pick 'n' mix with small dishes or have a proper main course. Also good for dinner, and the wine list is worth investigating.

North Bridge Brasserie

Scotsman Hotel, 20 North Bridge (556 5565/ www.thescotsmanhotel.co.uk). Nicolson Street–North Bridge buses. **Open** noon-3pm, 6-10pm daily. **Main courses** £6-£17.50. **Credit** AmEx, DC, MC, V. **Map** p304 D2.

Housed in the former offices of the *Scotsman* newspaper, this upmarket hotel opened for business in 2001. Its brasserie faces on to North Bridge and looks as grandiose and eclectic as only an Edwardian foyer possibly can. The menu is highly flexible, with starters, assorted salads, vegetarian mains, grills and puddings.

Never eat alone. **Outsider.**

Off The Wall

105 High Street (558 1497). Bus 30, 35/Princes Street buses. **Open** noon-2pm, 6-10pm Mon-Sat. **Main courses** £19.95-£22. **Credit** AmEx, MC, V. **Map** p304 D3.

From the moment the waitress brings an *amuse bouche* of cream of cauliflower soup with truffle oil, until the last impressions of mango and almond tart ebb from the palate, this establishment keeps its diners content. Off The Wall is a haven of quietly tasteful decor and fine cooking completely at odds with its souvenir shop Royal Mile neighbours.

Outsider

15-16 George IV Bridge (226 3131). Bus 2, 23, 27, 28, 41, 42, 45. **Open** noon-11am daily. **Main courses** £7.20-£15.20. **Credit** MC, V. **Map** p304 C3.

A bigger, more central, and snazzier sister restaurant to the Apartment (*see p145*). Very popular since it arrived on the scene in 2002, it has a similar menu to the Bruntsfield original but a more considered, minimalist decor.

Tower

*Museum of Scotland, Chambers Street (225 3003).
Bus 2, 23, 27, 28, 41, 42, 45.* **Open** noon-11pm
daily. **Main courses** £9.95-£25. **Credit** AmEx,
DC, MC, V. **Map** p309 F6.
The Tower is on the top floor of the Museum of
Scotland, a repository of Caledonian culture that
opened in late 1998. The views over the Old Town
can transport you back in time, while the chic interior would not look out of place in a bigger capital
city. Service is deft and the wine list affordable but
with some star bins for those looking to blow serious money. The menu is flexible (have a salad and
side dish if you like) and there's a trenchantly British
feel in places, but smart international flourishes too.

Vermilion

*Scotsman Hotel, 20 North Bridge (556 5565/
www.thescotsmanhotel.co.uk). Nicolson Street–North
Bridge buses.* **Open** 7-9.45pm Wed-Sun. **Main
courses** £16-£24. **Credit** AmEx, DC, MC, V.
Map p304 D2.
Expectations of excellence rise as diners descend
this designer hotel's grand marble staircase to the
dining room. Vermilion has the appearance of a contemporary oenological grotto: a subterranean space
with walls covered by wine bottles in semi-translu-
cent glass cabinets, subtly back-lit. Since it opened
in 2002, it has gone on to establish itself as one of
the city's best, with an ambitious and elaborate
menu. Roast halibut with linguini, morels, peas and
truffle butter anyone?

Witchery by the Castle/
Secret Garden

*352 Castlehill (225 5613/www.thewitchery.com). Bus
23, 27, 28, 35, 41, 42, 45.* **Open** noon-4pm, 5.30-
11.30pm daily. **Main courses** £13.95-£50. **Credit**
AmEx, DC, MC, V. **Map** p304 C3.
One owner (James Thomson), one venue, one huge
reputation, but two dining rooms. The Witchery is
a high-class, leathery/wooden affair just yards from
the Castle Esplanade, while the adjacent Secret
Garden oozes even more atmosphere (tapestries,
arched windows, candles) and is popular for major
romantic occasions. Destination dining? Absolutely.
(And you should see the wine list.) Hardly cheap, but
you can always try the bargain lunch menu if full-
on à la carte is too expensive. Thomson also has the
Tower (*see above*) and Rhubarb (*see p146*).

Vegetarian

Black Bo's

*57-61 Blackfriars Street (557 6136). Bus 35/
Nicolson Street–North Bridge buses.* **Open** 6-
10.30pm Mon-Thur, Sun; noon-2pm, 6-10.30pm Fri,
Sat. **Main courses** £9.50-£10.50. **Credit** MC, V.
Map p310 G5.
One of the city's longstanding vegetarian venues, in
early 2003 it bowed to 'customer demand' and introduced a few meat and fish dishes. Now, as you sit in
its simple bistro surroundings, you can choose the

likes of sirloin steak, or pepper stuffed with pista-
chio and cumin soufflé. It still feels vegetarian,
though, and its trademark remains a sense of adventure with fruit – which diners tend to love or loathe.
Its namesake bar is next door (*see p166*).

David Bann

*56-58 St Mary's Street (556 5888/www.david
bann.com). Nicolson Street–North Bridge buses.*
Open 11am-1am daily. **Main courses** £9.50-£10.50.
Credit AmEx, MC, V. **Map** p310 G5.
Well known on the local scene, David Bann is a minimal and tasteful space with dark wood fittings and
dark red decor. You can choose from starters and
snacks, light meals, salads, mains and sides – the
kitchen has a deft touch and service is smooth. There
are also appropriate wines and good beers. Simply
the best vegetarian restaurant in the city.

New Town

Asian

Dusit

49A Thistle Street (220 6846). Bus 13, 19A, 24, 28.
Open noon-3pm, 6-11pm Mon-Sat; noon-10pm Sun.
Main courses £7.95-£8.95. **Credit** AmEx, MC, V.
Map p304 B1.
In the last couple of years Edinburgh has seen a
wave of new Thai restaurants and Dusit is certainly among the best. It's the opposite of the usual Far
Eastern cliché: a self consciously modern environment that provides something beyond the boundaries of traditional Thai (guinea fowl with red curry,
venison with basil and chilli). Unassuming frontage,
dining space through the back, and be warned: while
some ethnic eateries provide a cheap night out, Dusit
is more upmarket.

Kweilin

19-21 Dundas Street (557 1875). Bus 23, 27. **Open**
noon-2pm, 5-11pm Tue-Sat; 5-11pm Sun. **Main
courses** £9.50-£14.75. **Credit** MC, V. **Map** p306 E3.
The Cantonese Kweilin has been a New Town institution since 1984, which is a long time on the local
restaurant scene. Given the longevity and the location, no surprise that it offers an aspirational atmosphere and it's really not the place to bring the kids
for dim sum. The menu is fairly adventurous. Decent
wine, and dare you try the duck feet?

Yo! Sushi/Yo! Below

*66 Rose Street (220 6040/www.yosushi.com). Princes
Street buses.* **Open** noon-10pm daily. **Main courses**
£5.50-£16.50. **Credit** AmEx, MC, V. **Map** p304 A1.
The same formula as the London original: seats at
the bar or in booths, and a moving conveyor belt
with plates carrying an astonishing variety of dishes prepared by the chefs in the central kitchen. Yo!
Sushi on the ground floor is the snack 'n' go part
while Yo! Below downstairs is a more full-on restaurant experience with extras like massage, tarot readings, music, and more.

Eat, Drink, Shop

Power lunch at the **Tower**. *See p135.*

Fish & seafood

Mussel Inn

*61-65 Rose Street (225 5979/www.mussel-inn.com).
Princes Street buses.* **Open** noon-3pm, 6-10pm Mon-
Thur; noon-10pm Fri, Sat; 12.30-10pm Sun. **Main
courses** £9.90-£15.50. **Credit** MC, V. **Map** p304 A1.
Edinburgh's seafood canteen *par excellence*. The signature dish is a kilo pot of mussels in a variety of
flavours from, 'natural' (unadorned) to 'Spanish'
(with tomato, green olives and chorizo). If mussels
aren't your thing, you could start with seafood chow-
der or crab spring rolls, then move on to grilled platters of scallops in various sauces. There are one or
two alternatives to shellfish, but not many.

Mediterranean

Le Café St Honoré

*34 North West Thistle Street Lane (226 2211). Bus
13, 19A, 24, 28.* **Open** *Sept-July* noon-2.15pm, 5.30-
10pm Mon-Sat. *Aug* noon-2.15pm, 5.30-10pm Mon-
Sat; 6-10pm Sun. **Main courses** £10-£19. **Credit**
AmEx, DC, MC, V. **Map** p304 B1.
The food is distinctly French, with an occasional
modern international twist. There might be grilled
oysters with crayfish, bacon and Gruyère to start for
example – but also warm salad of scallops, chicken
tikka and chorizo. Mains are a little more traditional. The establishment carries the double-edged plau-
dit of being somewhere that critic AA Gill would like
to have 'within walking distance'.

Café Marlayne

76 Thistle Street (226 2230). Bus 13, 19A, 24, 28.
Open noon-2pm, 6-10pm Tue-Sat. **Main courses**
£10.60-£13.90. **Credit** MC, V. **Map** p304 B1.
It can be a real relief to sneak in here for lunch to
escape the bustle of Frederick and George streets;
wicker chairs and solid wooden tables help along the
impression of a polite but relaxed environment. The
food can be accomplished and it is certainly affordable, but the restaurant is not large, so in general it's
wise to book ahead.

Cosmo

*58A North Castle Street (226 6743). Princes Street
buses.* **Open** 12.30-2.15pm, 7-10.45pm Mon-Fri; 7-
10.45pm Sat. **Main courses** £14.50-£21.90. **Credit**
AmEx, MC, V. **Map** p304 B1.
Appealing to the more mature and better-heeled customer, Cosmo is an Edinburgh institution, albeit one
that doesn't like to shout about its status. A million
miles away from the usual pizza and pasta joints,
it's all about classic Italian cooking here. Trainers
and T-shirts are definite sartorial no-nos.

Duck's at Le Marché Noir

*2-4 Eyre Place (558 1608/www.ducks.co.uk). Bus 13,
17, 23, 27.* **Open** 7-10pm Mon; noon-2.30pm, 7-10pm
Tue-Thur; noon-2.30pm, 7-10.30pm Fri; 7-10.30pm
Sat; 6.30-9.30pm Sun. **Main courses** £11.75-£20.50.
Credit AmEx, DC, MC, V. **Map** p306 E3.
Duck's offers an intimate and polite (but not overly)
setting on the fringe of Edinburgh's New Town,
with a lot of stress put on both good food and good
service. Mind you, the wine list is quite a wonder to
behold and although there are numerous affordable
bottles, there are also examples of top-end Bordeaux
that don't even carry a price.

Scalini

*10 Melville Place, Queensferry Street (220 2999).
Bus 19, 36, 37, 41.* **Open** noon-2pm, 6-10pm Mon-
Sat. **Main courses** £7.90-£15.50. **Credit** AmEx,
DC, MC, V. **Map** p308 C5.
Among the traffic and hassle of the West End, you
walk down Scalini's stairs and feel immediately
more peaceful. Silvio Praino is one of the city's
friendlier restaurateurs, and he runs an establishment where people really care about the food. The

Hold forth at the **Forth Floor**.

antipasti della casa will be brought over and shown
to you – it always looks good – while mains might
include dishes like thin-sliced salmon cooked with
balsamic vinegar. The wine list has some absolute
Italian gems dating from the 1950s.

Tapas Olé

10 Eyre Place (556 2754). Bus 13, 17, 23, 27. **Open**
noon-3pm, 6-10pm Mon-Thur; noon-10pm Fri, Sat;
1-10pm Sun. **Main courses** £2.75-£6.50. **Credit**
MC, V. **Map** p306 E3.
Tapas Olé is big and bright, red and yellow (the
colours of the Spanish flag). It looks more in tune
with large parties than intimate dining, although a
table for two won't be a problem. At the last count
there were around 40 different tapas to choose from
– but if you can't be bothered there's a set menu for
the indecisive. Puddings will appeal to kids.

Middle Eastern

Nargile

*73 Hanover Street (225 5755/www.nargile.co.uk).
Bus 23, 27, 28, 41, 42, 45.* **Open** noon-2pm, 5.30-
10pm Mon-Thur; noon-2pm, 5.30-11pm Fri, Sat.
Main courses £6.50-£20. **Credit** AmEx, MC, V.
Map p304 C1.

Welcome to the Turkish kitchen in the city centre.
Decor-wise, it's bright, modern and cliché-free, while
the extensive menu has meze as a big feature, but
also kebabs, couscous, seafood, veggie options and
specials – some Turkish wines too. Sit-down cuisine
from this corner of the world is rare in Scotland
(while kebab houses are not), so Nargile has managed to jam a welcome foot in the door.

Modern European

Forth Floor

*Harvey Nichols, 30-34 St Andrew Square (524 8350/
www.harveynichols.com). Princes Street buses.* **Open**
Brasserie 10am-6pm Mon; 10am-11pm Tue-Sat; noon-
6pm Sun. *Restaurant* noon-3pm Mon; noon-3pm,
6-10pm Tue-Fri; noon-3.30pm, 6-10pm Sat; noon-
3.30pm Sun. **Main courses** *Brasserie* £7.50-£11.
Restaurant £12.50-£18. **Credit** AmEx, DC, MC, V.
Map p304 D1.
The overall impression when you walk into the
swish people's posh eaterie is '1970s funky' moder-
ated by modern panache – imagine a high-class
Space 1999 canteen – with a lot of glass and a balcony, hence the cool views and a punning name (it's
on the fourth floor). There's a discreet, transparent

division between the all-day buzz of the bar-brasserie (the shoppers' favourite) and the more formal and expensive restaurant.

Martin's

70 Rose Street North Lane, between Frederick Street & Castle Street (225 3106). Princes Street buses. **Open** noon-2pm, 7-10pm Tue-Fri; 7-10pm Sat. Closed 23 Dec-23 Jan. **Main courses** £16-£23. **Credit** AmEx, DC, MC, V. **Map** p304 B1.

Not easy to find but worth the effort, Martin Irons' restaurant is a showcase for Scottish produce; he realised the value of attentive sourcing and organic ingredients years before most. From the vegetables to the meat and the fish, Irons insists that, as far as possible, everything is just as nature intended. The reward for such persistence has been an enviable reputation in the city – and beyond – since opening in 1983. The artisan cheeseboard is among the very best to be found in Edinburgh.

Number One

Balmoral Hotel, 1 Princes Street (557 6727). Princes Street buses. **Open** noon-2pm, 7-9.30pm daily. **Main courses** £16.50-£27.50. **Credit** AmEx, DC, MC, V. **Map** p304 B2.

Number One is the flagship restaurant of the Balmoral hotel. Away from the bustle of the city's main thoroughfare, you enter a placid and classy world of deft service and even more dextrous cuisine. There are red lacquer walls, there are scalloped banquettes, and there is a wine list to intimidate or delight. The food is among the very best in the capital and the set lunch actually represents excellent value for money. A Michelin star kind of experience.

Oloroso

33 Castle Street (226 7614/www.oloroso.co.uk). Princes Street buses. **Open** noon-2.15pm, 7-10.15pm daily (bar open till 1am). **Main courses** £17. **Credit** AmEx, MC, V. **Map** p304 B1.

The ground-floor entrance may be baffling – only a flat-screen video hints at what lies above – but once out of the lift everything becomes clear. This modern establishment occupies the top (fourth) floor of an office building, which means excellent all-round views. There's a very smart bar where you can drink or snack and a restaurant space for the full dining experience (including a grill menu with top-grade and top-price Highland beef). Experience the buzz of the beautiful people in the bar, then dust off the credit card for dinner.

Scottish

Haldane's

39a Albany Street (556 8407/www.haldanes restaurant.com). Bus 8, 13, 17. **Open** noon-1.30pm, 6-9.30pm Mon-Fri; 6-9.30pm Sat, Sun. **Main courses** £16-£22. **Credit** AmEx, DC, MC, V. **Map** p306 F4.

If a good Scottish restaurant is one that's run by Scots, uses the best of local ingredients, and serves dishes with a Scots slant (but no gimmickry), then Haldane's qualifies in spades. Some regard it as the best of its kind in the city. It has been steadily building a reputation and gathering a faithful clientele since it first opened in 1997. The decor is discreet and tasteful, the wine list is good and there are lots of single malts. Very fine indeed.

The late show

Getting a late meal in Edinburgh can be problematic: unlike in the great capitals of the world, Edinburgh's restauranteurs don't, by and large, believe in serving dinner after 10pm. After this genteel, but common, cut-off time hungry diners must normally search for one of the café-bars that stay open into the early hours (*see p152*).

However, there is one type of restaurant that seems to be associated more than most with a capricious post-midnight carbo-frenzy: the traditional, no-nonsense Italian. There are few frills to these, they're just the kind of longstanding establishments that have been fuelling locals with pasta and pizza since Silvio Berlusconi was in short trousers.

Right in the middle of the Old Town, **Gordon's Trattoria** (231 High Street, Royal Mile, Old Town; 225 7992) stays open until midnight Sunday to Thursday, but until 3am on Friday and Saturday. Meanwhile, in West

Edinburgh, **Bar Italia** (100 Lothian Road; 228 6379) keeps going until 3am daily. Down in Calton Hill and Broughton, **Giuliano's** (18-19 Union Place, Leith Walk; 556 6590) stays up until 2am daily. By contrast, the **North Bridge Pizza Express** (23 North Bridge, Old Town; 557 6411) wimps out at midnight, daily, but it's the most reliably 'late' branch of that chain in the city.

If pizza and pasta aren't your thing, though, you could try: **Favorit**: there are two branches of this café-bar and they keep going until 3am (*see p154*).

Loon Fung: north Edinburgh's dependable Cantonese, is open until 11.30pm most nights, but until 12.30am on Friday and Saturday (*see p141*).

Negociants: a café-bar where the main menu stops at 10pm but substantial snacks are available, daily, until much, much later (*see p154*).

FORTH FLOOR

RESTAURANT BAR & BRASSERIE

"...EXTRAORDINARILY GOOD, INCREDIBLE VIEWS,
FAULTLESS SERVICE." METRO

"...EVERYTHING ABOUT THIS RESTAURANT
IS A CLASS ACT." HERALD

LUNCH DAILY
DINNER TUESDAY - SATURDAY

HARVEY NICHOLS   30 - 34 ST ANDREW SQUARE
EDINBURGH   EH2 2AD
TEL 0131 524 8350 - FAX 0131 524 8351
forthfloor.reservations@harveynichols.com

Not so so. **Oloroso**. *See p139*.

Vegetarian

Henderson's Salad Table and Wine Bar

94 Hanover Street (225 2131). Bus 33, 37. **Open** 8am-10.30pm Mon-Sat. **Main courses** £4.60-£5.25. **Credit** AmEx, MC, V. **Map** p304 C1.

This establishment dates from 1963, when the idea of having a vegetarian canteen in Edinburgh was probably as amusing as telephones you didn't have to plug into the wall. In the 1960s and 1970s it really was way out on its own. Basically, you're looking at a self-service restaurant (robust veggie dishes, salads, and desserts) with seating on the counter level where people can eat-and-go, or wander down a few stairs into the cellar space to linger. Round the corner Henderson's also has a bistro with table service (25 Thistle Street; 225 2605).

Stockbridge

American

Bell's Diner

7 St Stephen Street (225 8116). Bus 19A, 24, 28. **Open** 6-10.15pm Mon-Fri, Sun; noon-10.30pm Sat. **Main courses** £6.50-£12.50. **Credit** MC, V. **Map** p306 D3.

This tiny eaterie in the heart of Stockbridge has been going strong since around 1972. There are two reasons for such unusual longevity: first, the burgers and steaks that form the bulk of the menu are pretty good; second, even if customers drift away to other restaurants, or even other countries, Bell's Diner is still there waiting for them when they drift back. Vegetarians get the best nutburger in the city, while pancakes with peaches and cream is a typical pudding. After more than 30 years, why change a winning formula?

Asian

Loon Fung

2 Warriston Place, Inverleith Row, near Canonmills (556 1781). Bus 8, 17, 23, 37. **Open** noon-11.30pm Mon-Thur; noon-1am Fri; 2pm-1am Sat; 2pm-midnight Sun. **Main courses** £6.90-£19. **Credit** AmEx, MC, V. **Map** p306 E2.

Down on Canonmills and handily placed for the Botanic Gardens, Loon Fung is one of Edinburgh's better Cantonese restaurants; the kind that Sino-Scots describe as a cut above. The decor is nothing to write home about, but there's a great selection of dim sum and specials. Often busy when everywhere else is deserted, it's been a stalwart of the scene for longer than anyone remembers.

Calton Hill & Broughton

Mediterranean

Jolly Pizzeria

9 Elm Row, Leith Walk (556 1588). Leith Walk buses. **Open** 11.45am-2.30pm, 5-11pm daily. **Main courses** £5.95-£14. **Credit** AmEx, DC, MC, V. **Map** p307 G3.

The maitre d' has an hallucinogenic waistcoat; the decor has evolved into kitsch by dint of doing nothing; and can you spot the *Serie A* club crests? The pizza toppings are unsophisticated but the wood burning oven here bakes the best pizza base in the city. That's reason enough for a visit – but also because in the 1960s and '70s, Italian restaurants like this made a huge impact on Scottish working class sensibilities. Pop in and pay your respects.

Santorini

32c Broughton Street (557 2012). Playhouse buses. **Open** 5.30-10.30pm daily. **Main courses** £9. **Credit** MC, V. **Map** p306 F3.

Eats with a view

Top five

Elephant House
From the back room of this popular café, you get an idea of what 17th-century Edinburgh was like (*see p161*).

Forth Floor
A bird's eye perspective of St Andrew Square and the city skyline, or you can watch the beautiful people eat (*see p138*).

Old Chain Pier
Great pub grub right on the sea wall; next stop, Fife (*see p173*).

Oloroso
Castle one way, coast the other (*see p139*).

Tower
Classic Old Town views from the Museum of Scotland's roof (*see p135*).

This address has seen a procession of restaurants try (and fail) over the last few years, so let's hope that this splendid little Greek establishment does better than all its predecessors. It's a bright, open space with a vaguely nautical feel to it; serves the best aubergine dip in the city; and although it won't win prizes for fine dining, Santorini is an excellent place to sit with friends and pick your way through a selection of small dishes. The big ones are here too though, like an excellent moussaka, and the simple yoghurt/nuts/honey dessert is a showstopper.

Tapas Tree
1 Forth Street (556 7118). Playhouse buses. **Open** 11am-11pm daily. **Main courses** £3-£11. **Credit** AmEx, DC, MC, V. **Map** p307 G3.
This is a down-home tapas bar – tables crowd, but it's a little more spacious downstairs. There are daily specials on the blackboard, and a goodly range of substantial tapas regulars: meat, vegetarian, fish/shellfish, and skewered things. The house bread is among the most substantial in Edinburgh, there are a few Spanish lagers, and the wine list has a few bottles that are better than you might imagine. The emphasis is definitely on fun, conversation and sharing – when the mood takes you, the Tapas Tree does just fine.

South Edinburgh

American

Buffalo Grill
14 Chapel Street (667 7427/www.buffalogrill.co.uk). Bus 41, 42. **Open** noon-2pm, 6-10.30pm Mon-Fri; 6-10.30pm Sat; 5-10.15pm Sun. **Main courses** £7.95-£15. **Credit** MC, V. **Map** p310 G7.
With every kind of steak, and as many burger variations as you care to dream of, this is where it's at if you want to get busy on the beef. Lots of Edinburgh restaurants offer a steak but this is the only place that offers them all. Although it isn't licensed (there's no charge if you take your own bottle), the original branch always seems fully booked, and the (licensed) Stockbridge outpost is pretty much the same way. Vegetarians are catered for.

Asian

Ann Purna
45 St Patrick Square (662 1807). Nicolson Street–North Bridge buses. **Open** noon-2pm, 5.30-11pm Mon-Fri; 4-11pm Sat, Sun. **Main courses** £5.50-£7.50. **Credit** MC, V. **Map** p310 G7.
Ann Purna has a wholly vegetarian menu and relaxed style (although the decor may be a little bright 'n' cheesy for some). It's a family-run business (the Pandyas) and the cooking has a Gujarati and south Indian flavour; exactly the kind of thing you won't find in many other allegedly Indian restaurants throughout Edinburgh. Business lunches are ludicrously cheap and there's Indian lager on tap. An unprepossessing wee gem.

Bonsai
46 West Richmond Street (668 3847/www. bonsaibarbistro.co.uk). Bus 2/Nicolson Street–North Bridge buses. **Open** noon-late daily. **Main courses** £2.50-£6. **Credit** MC, V. **Map** p310 G6.
Bonsai's Japanese team produce a range of dishes, many of which won't spook the Scots palate. There's assorted tempura for instance and user-friendly *makizushi* (rice rolled in seaweed), but if the diner wants roast eel *nigirizushi*, *umeboshi* plums, and some (raw) squid *sashimi* then that's available too. Vegetarians have no problem and there's Japanese lager to accompany the food.

Dragon Way
74-78 South Clerk Street (668 1328). Nicolson Street–North Bridge buses. **Open** noon-2pm, 5-11.30pm Mon-Sat; 4-11.30pm Sun. **Main courses** £7-£8. **Credit** MC, V. **Map** p310 H7/8.
Ornamentation is not a word that crops up in food guides very often, but then there are few places like Dragon Way. This restaurant has gilded birds and dragons on the walls, another lacquer dragon wrapped around a column, a small waterfall, and other elaborate design features. The menu is good too, with Peking, Sichuan and Cantonese cooking as well as seafood specialities that depend on the day's catch. A night with friends at one of Dragon Way's round tables is an experience on several levels.

Eat, Drink, Shop

Cafe Hub.
The kind of
place you
want to tell
your friends
about.

(But then decide to
keep to yourself.)

Dinner

Coffee

Lunch

Drinks

Terrace

Brunch

Celebrations

Castlehill, Royal Mile
Edinburgh
Open daily
Reservations 0131 473 2067
www.thehub-edinburgh.com

the hub

EDINBURGH'S FESTIVAL CENTRE

Kalpna

*2-3 St Patrick Square (667 9890). Nicolson Street–
North Bridge buses.* **Open** 11am-2.30pm, 5.30-11pm
Mon-Sat. **Main courses** £4.50-£15. **Credit** MC, V.
Map p310 G7.

The continuous stream of happy, chatty diners is
testament to Kalpna's enduring popularity. What's
more, the vegetarian menu is far from subcontinen-
tal cliché. The thali options give a nice spread of
dishes as an alternative to starter/main/sides, but
some specialities and traditional offerings on the
menu are just dandy in themselves. There's Indian
lager on tap and some overwhelmingly sweet puds.

Namaste

*15 Bristo Place (466 7061). Bus 2, 23, 27,
41, 42, 45.* **Open** 5.30-11pm daily. **Main
courses** £5-£10. **Credit** MC, V.
Map p309 F6.

The food here is decent enough – a fair-sized menu
of robust if predictable dishes (pakora, fish tikka,
rogan josh, or jalfrezi lamb, for example) and the odd
unexpected offering. But Namaste stands out by
serving dishes in a little brass pot. The north Indian
frontier theme and distressed wooden fixtures help,
but it really scores because it twists your head.
Despite arriving on the scene as recently as 2001, it
looks like a ramshackle hippy conception of India
from the time the Rolling Stones were recording
Beggar's Banquet. Meanwhile, the background music
can sound like Bollywood meets Massive Attack.

Suruchi

*14a Nicolson Street (556 6583). Nicolson Street–
North Bridge buses.* **Open** noon-2pm, 5-11.30pm
Mon-Sat; 5-11.30pm Sun. **Main courses** £7.50-
£12.95. **Credit** AmEx, MC, V. **Map** p310 G6.

Easily one of the best Indian restaurants in
Edinburgh, Suruchi distinguishes itself with regu-
lar food festivals and an eclectic menu (written in
Scots). Conservative diners might stick to tried and
tested mains or they could opt for nirvana: chicken
with lemongrass, mustard seeds, curry leaf, lemon,
and coconut. There's also a 'hame produce' section
on the menu drawing on key ingredients of the
Scottish larder, including haggis, salmon and trout.
The coconut rice is magical.
Other location: Suruchi Too, 121 Constitution
Street, Leith (554 3268).

Thai Lemongrass

*40-41 Bruntsfield Place (229 2225). Bus 10, 11, 15,
16, 17.* **Open** noon-2.30pm, 5-11.30pm Mon-Thur,
noon-11.30pm Fri, Sat; 1-11.30pm Sun. **Main
courses** £6.95-£14.95. **Credit** MC, V. **Map** p309 D8.

One of a new wave of Thai restaurants in the city,
Thai Lemongrass was praised from the outset. It is
spacious enough, with uplifting yellow walls and
dark wooden furniture. There are set banquets for
two to three people, or four to seven; there's also a
short vegetarian menu for those wanting to avoid
the fish, chicken or pork involved in most other dishes. Desserts are basic, but this is surely one of the
city's better Thai establishments.

Thaisanuk

21 Argyle Place (228 8855). Bus 24, 41. **Open**
6-11pm daily. **Main courses** £6-£10. **Credit**
MC, V. **Map** p309 F8.

A tiny restaurant, Thaisanuk has the kind of winning attitude that captures hearts and minds – so
book ahead. The menu is simple: starters, mains and
noodles. Ingredients are shipped in from as far afield
as Thailand itself, giving the traditional tom yum
soup an extra zing. Noodles, whether dry bowls or
soups, are generous and come in various Asian versions. If you can't get a seat, you can get a takeaway.

Fish & seafood

Sweet Melinda's

11 Roseneath Street (229 7953). Bus 24, 41. **Open**
7-10pm Mon; noon-2pm, 7-10pm Tue-Sat. **Main
courses** £12.50-£14.50. **Credit** MC, V. **Map** p309 F8.

Edinburgh's baronial tenement 'burb of Marchmont
is short on eateries, so the bright and compact Sweet
Melinda's is an oasis in the desert. Although it does-
n't bill itself as a fish restaurant, there's certainly a
lot of the creatures on the menu. Generally, first time
diners tend to walk in with little expectation ('Just a
wee place in Marchmont') and walk out with a smile
because of the standard of cooking. On Tuesday
evenings, diners pay what they think the meal is
worth – not a bad way of filling an establishment on
a traditionally quiet night.

Modern European

Apartment

*7-13 Barclay Place (228 6456). Bus 11, 15, 16, 17,
23, 45.* **Open** 6-11pm Mon-Fri; noon-3pm, 6-11pm
Sat, Sun. **Main courses** £6.50-£10. **Credit** MC, V.
Map p309 D8.

The Apartment's success obviously leans on the
food, but its status as a designer eaterie for middle
class Edinburgh hipsters owes a lot to location:
Bruntsfield, Merchiston and Marchmont are right
on the doorstep. Key dishes are solid healthy lines
(chargrilled chunks on a skewer, served with ample
amounts of pitta and coleslaw), and slabs (thick
crunchy home-made bread with 'stuff'). It's a riot of
flavour – but there are salads, grilled fish, steaks,
and pasta as alternatives.

Blonde

*75 St Leonard's Street (668 2917) Bus 2, 14, 21,
33.* **Open** 6-10pm Mon; noon-2.30pm, 6-10pm Tue-
Sun. **Main courses** £8-£11. **Credit** MC, V.
Map p310 H7.

The name comes from the blonde wood interior, and
this is more of a good-standard neighbourhood
favourite rather than destination dining. All the
same, it's been keeping the locals happy since its
2000 debut and anyone would be glad to have somewhere as nifty on their block. It's not Scottish per se,
but local ingredients are given a fine modern treatment, with an international spin. The wine list is
brief, and the waitresses are sharp as a tack.

The China syndrome

Back in 2002, someone with a sharp eye for a gap in the restaurant market decided that Edinburgh lacked a cheap Chinese buffet. Consequently, **China China** was born. It was effectively a canteen, with a nod to IKEA design values, that provided self-service dishes from catering vats (spare ribs, chicken curry, black bean beef and more). The food was hardly award-winning, but the most important thing was price: basically you could eat all you wanted and it was only around £5 per head at lunchtime, more expensive later in the day – but still a bargain (booze extra). China China became one of the most successful restaurant openings of the year, although not for food writers. But families loved it – the cost per child was even lower than for adults and there was fresh fruit as a dessert alternative.

What came next (2002-03) was a rash of similar establishments like **Buffet King Chinese Dining**, the **Jimmy Chung's** chain, and **Saigon Saigon** (to name but three). They all offer the same formula of cheap, filling food and can get packed out at peak times. Jimmy Chung's is near the financial district for example and the lunchtime turnover is incredible to witness.

If you want to eat something cheap and a little different, then the Chinese buffets are fine. If you're a family on a budget (or anyone on a budget) then they're a godsend. But generic beef curry that's been sitting under bright lights for a while won't gather many fine food awards – so don't set your culinary expectations too high.

Buffet King Chinese Dining, 6a Nicolson Street, South Edinburgh; 557 4567.

China China, 10 Antigua Street, Calton Hill & Broughton; 556 9791.

Jimmy Chung's, 30 Grindlay Street, West Edinburgh; 228 8688.

Saigon Saigon, 14 South St Andrew Street, New Town; 557 3737.

Howies

208 Bruntsfield Place (221 1777). Bus 10, 11, 15, 16, 17. **Open** noon-2.30pm, 6-10pm daily. **Main courses** £15.95 for 2 courses. **Credit** AmEx, DC, MC, V. **Map** p309 D8.

Howies fills a niche. It's the kind of place that young couples might use for an economical Friday night out, or where mums and dads take their university student kids for a relaxed Sunday lunch. The tables are big and wooden, and the walls bright with the odd bit of art. It's a formula, but more artisan than mass market, so all power to them. Scottish produce forms the foundation of the menus.
Other locations: 10-14 Victoria Street, Old Town (225 1721); 4 Glanville Place, Kerr Street, Stockbridge (225 5553); 29 Waterloo Place, Calton Hill & Broughton (556 5766).

Marque

19 Causewayside (466 6660). Bus 3, 5, 7, 8, 29, 31, 37, 42, 49. **Open** noon-2pm, 6-10pm Tue-Thur; noon-2pm, 6-11pm Fri; 12.30-2pm, 6-11pm Sat; 12.30-2pm, 6-10pm Sun. **Main courses** £12-£16. **Credit** MC, V. **Map** p310 H8.

The Marque is neat, has understated class and does its thing quietly at its original premises in Causewayside. It's very modern/international and local opinion has the Marque among Edinburgh's top dozen restaurants – local opinion is right. The younger Marque Central (next door to the Royal Lyceum Theatre) hits the same high standards, and offers good-value pre- and post-theatre menus.
Other location: 30b Grindlay Street, West Edinburgh (229 9859).

Rhubarb

Prestonfield, Priestfield Road (225 1333). Bus 30, 33. **Open** noon-3pm, 6-11pm daily. **Main courses** £13-£24. **Credit** AmEx, DC, MC, V.

James Thomson, the man behind the Witchery and the Tower (for both, *see p135*), has revamped the old Prestonfield House Hotel in the shadow of Arthur's Seat. The 17th-century mansion house is now known simply as Prestonfield, and its restaurant is Rhubarb (so called because this is where rhubarb was first grown in Scotland; *see p17* **Scatology in the city**). This establishment has taken contemporary minimalism and turned it on its head. It's lush: a bit Gaultier, a bit Greenaway and with Franco-Scottish cuisine. Worth the taxi ride.

West Edinburgh

Asian

Indian Cavalry Club

3 Atholl Place, off West Maitland Street (228 2974). Bus 3, 4, 12, 21, 25, 26, 31, 33, 44. **Open** noon-2.30pm, 5.30-11.30pm daily. **Main courses** £8-£9. **Credit** AmEx, DC, MC, V. **Map** p308 B6.

Waiters in quasi-military costume and set meals with names such as Our Regimental Banquet either appal or appeal. However, the Cavalry Club has a lot going for it. There's the usual Indian starters but also excellent fresh *poori* with fillings such as lamb, chicken, prawns and various veggie options. There are several set meals for two or more, and an à la carte menu including far from clichéd fare.

Jasmine

32 Grindlay Street (229 5757). Bus 1, 2, 10, 11, 15, 16, 22, 35. **Open** noon-2pm, 5-11.30pm daily. **Main courses** £7.60-£19.80. **Credit** MC, V. **Map** p304 A3.
This Cantonese-slanted establishment is good for seafood and, despite its longevity, has a fresh contemporary look with tasteful artefacts in the windows and no sense of fuss or clutter. Chinese is one of the city's most overcrowded restaurant sectors, so quite an achievement that this is rated by those in the know as Edinburgh's best.

Rainbow Arch

8-16A Morrison Street (221 1288). Bus 1, 2, 22, 28, 34. **Open** noon-midnight daily. **Main courses** £5-£12. **Credit** AmEx, MC, V. **Map** p308 C6.
This has the look and atmosphere of a plush and proper 'traditional' Chinese restaurant (with a friendly welcome from the waitresses, mind you), and a menu so wide in scope it could almost be intimidating. There are dozens and dozens of choices, and over 25 vegetarian dishes to pick from alone. The dim sum is acclaimed and the menu is sufficiently authentic to attract Chinese diners.

Thai Orchid

44 Grindlay Street (228 4438). Bus 1, 10, 11, 15, 16, 17, 22, 24, 34. **Open** noon-2.30pm, 5.30-10.30pm Mon-Fri; 5.30-10.30pm Sat. **Main courses** £7.50-£10.50. **Credit** AmEx, DC, MC, V. **Map** p304 A3.
This family-run eaterie has quietly built its reputation, predating a recent local vogue for Thai restaurants. Neither spectacular nor trendy, it takes care with the basic ingredients, has a predominantly green decor, and it's the kind of place that comes to nestle in your affections. Vegetarians have a good choice and there's a wide range of other dishes, including old reliables such as *goong chup peng todd* (tempura-style prawns) and *gaeng kiew wan* (green coconut milk curry with chicken or prawns).

Mediterranean

Santini/Santini Bis

1 Festival Square (221 7788/www.santini.5pm. co.uk). Bus 1, 10, 11, 15, 16, 17, 22, 24, 34. **Open** noon-2.30pm, 6.30-10.30pm Mon-Fri; 6.30-10.30pm Sat. **Main courses** £7-£16.50. **Credit** AmEx, DC, MC, V. **Map** p309 D6.
In the middle of the blockish architectural mêlée that is the city's financial district, there's a restaurant of impeccable repute. Santini arrived in 2001 and gathered plaudits before the first chargrilled baby cuttlefish had time to yelp, 'Mama!' Actually, there are two eateries: the more formal Santini, and the designery bistro Santini Bis. Both make excellent use of fresh ingredients and are among the city's top Italians. Not for scruffs though.

Modern European

Atrium

10 Cambridge Street (228 8882/www.atrium restaurant.co.uk). Bus 1, 10, 11, 15, 16, 17, 24, 34. **Open** noon-2pm, 6-10pm Mon-Fri; 6-10pm Sat. **Main courses** £16-£22. **Credit** AmEx, DC, MC, V. **Map** p304 A3.

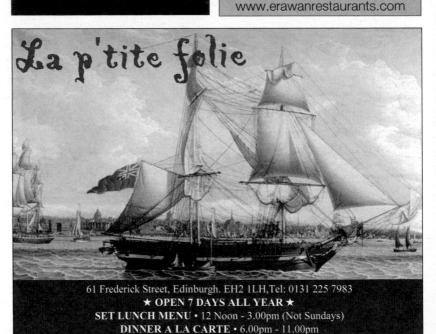

Eat, Drink, Shop

Top five Theatre eats

Jasmine
Good Cantonese, opposite the Royal Lyceum (*see p147*).

Marque Central
Next door to the Royal Lyceum (*see p146*).

Witchery by the Castle/ Secret Garden
Feast after Festival (*see p135*).

Santorini
Convenient for the Playhouse (*see p141*).

Suruchi
Opposite the Edinburgh Festival Theatre (*see p145*).

Andrew Radford's flagship restaurant changed the rules of the game as far as top Edinburgh eateries were concerned. Its design still looks contemporary – low key lighting, dark wood, copper fixtures and fittings all adding to a real sense of atmosphere and otherness. Destination dining that has stood the test of time, this is high calibre all round.

Channings
15 South Learmonth Gardens (315 2225). Bus 13. **Open** noon-2pm, 6.30-10pm Tue-Sat. **Main courses** £12.50-£22. **Credit** AmEx, DC, MC, V. **Map** p305 B4.
Channings, a smart hotel around 15 minutes' walk from the west end of Princes Street, has two basement eateries: an informal Mediterranean bistro (Ochre Vita; 556 3636) and an eponymous fine dining room. The latter is tastefully furnished with the odd contemporary touch to buttress a wooden-fixtured classicism. Its wine list is unpretentious, service friendly, and the cooking very good indeed. Excellent vegetarian options too.

First Coast
99-101 Dalry Road (313 4404). Bus 24, 34, 35. **Open** noon-2pm, 5-11pm Mon-Sat. **Main courses** £6.95-£12.95. **Credit** MC, V. **Map** p308 B7.
To say that Dalry Road is an unfashionable area for eats is a bit of an understatement. Or it was until First Coast arrived. This is a small, airy neighbourhood bistro, but the standard of cooking (sole in cheese and mustard sauce, lamb and mussel pie) is way in excess of expectation. Local critics have raved. Excellent venue, excellent value.

Grill Room
Sheraton Grand Hotel, Festival Square (221 6422/ www.sheraton.com/grandedinburgh). Bus 1, 10, 11, 15, 16, 17, 22, 24, 34. **Open** noon-2.30pm, 7-10pm Mon-Fri; 7-10pm Sat. **Main courses** £13.50-£22.50. **Credit** AmEx, DC, MC, V. **Map** p309 D6.

The Sheraton Grand is a big, blockish, modern edifice that has dominated its locale since it opened in the mid 1980s. But behind the bland façade, chef Nicholas Laurent has been consistently building a reputation that bears comparison with the city's best. In terms of decor, the Grill Room is a modern take on upmarket hotel classicism. In terms of food, it's in Edinburgh's top five.

Pompadour
Caledonian Hilton Hotel, Princes Street (222 8888/ www.hilton.com/caledonian). Princes Street buses. **Open** noon-2.30pm, 7-10pm Tue-Fri; 7-10pm Sat. **Main courses** £19.50-£25.50. **Credit** AmEx, DC, MC, V. **Map** p304 A2.
First impressions of the Pompadour leave you scrabbling for the right word ('rococo? baroque?'); you browse the menu in an ante-room, then a waiter escorts you to your table, carrying any unfinished G&Ts on a silver tray. The staff glide around soundlessly and the food is elaborate, with roots in *haute* (and haughty) French cuisine. Dining tip: dress smart.

Rogue
Scottish Widows Building, 67 Morrison Street (228 2700). Bus 1, 2, 28, 34, 35. **Open** noon-2.30pm, 6-10pm Mon-Sat. **Main courses** £6-£11. **Credit** AmEx, DC, MC, V. **Map** p308 C6.
Sumptuous. Given its location – firmly in the city's financial district – it's no surprise that its lunchtime clientele is drawn from local offices. Evenings are much more visually interesting for people-watchers. The menu is informal, offering everything from soups and starters to pizza and pasta, grills, seafood, meat, and a few vegetarian choices. If you want to sit in spacious, draped surroundings like these and just have spaghetti with baby clams and herbs, you could. A fuller exploration of the menu brings its own rewards however.

Leith

Asian

Britannia Spice
150 Commercial Street, Britannia Way (555 2255/ www.britanniaspice.co.uk). Bus 1, 16, 22, 35, 36. **Open** noon-2.15pm, 5-11.45pm Mon-Sat; 5-11.45pm Sun. **Main courses** £6.95-£13.95. **Credit** AmEx, DC, MC, V. **Map** p311 Jy.
This nautical-themed venue tries to cover the whole subcontinent rather than just India, with some Thai thrown in for good measure. The menu includes all the usual suspects of Indian cooking, but much more besides (Bangladeshi baked fish, Himalayan mince dumplings, stir-fried Thai seafood). The wine list is somewhat better than the average Asian restaurant.

Joanna's Cuisine
42 Dalmeny Street (554 5833). Leith Walk buses. **Open** 5.30-10.30pm Tue-Thur, Sun; 5.30-11.30pm Fri, Sat. **Main courses** £7.15-£10. **Credit** MC, V. **Map** p307 J2.

In the tenemental netherlands between Leith Walk and Easter Road, the last thing you expect to find is a tiny Chinese restaurant specialising in dishes from Peking. But Joanna's has been a city secret for years. It's considered brilliant in the neighbourhood, and has its fans who travel here. It is small, though – so call ahead and book – and the decor borders on sparse.

Palace Chine

Unit 11, Ocean Terminal Shopping Centre, Ocean Drive (555 4212). Bus 11, 22, 34, 35, 36, 49. **Open** noon-11pm daily. **Main courses** £6-£10. **Credit** MC, V. **Map** p311 Hx.

There's no two ways with restaurants in huge shopping malls. The diner is either appalled by the environment (no soul), or simply doesn't care. But even the retail-averse would do well to try our Palace Chine. The big innovation is a menu based on Chinese herbal medicine, said to have all kinds of health benefits (although there's a more traditional menu as a back-up). If you're shopping, or visiting the mall's cinema, Palace Chine can make for an interesting alternative meal.

Fish & seafood

Fisher's

1 The Shore (554 5666/www.fishersbistro.co.uk). Bus 1, 16, 22, 35, 36. **Open** noon-4pm, 6.30-10.30pm Mon-Sat; 12.30-10.30pm Sun. **Main courses** £10.50-£16.25. **Credit** AmEx, DC, MC, V. **Map** p311 Jy.

The nautical theme at Fisher's (decor, fittings) is pretty well justified by the fact that the harbour's on the doorstep and you can see real, working ships as you're walking down The Shore. Diners can eat in the bar, or the small raised area adjacent. It is essentially a seafood restaurant – generally regarded as one of the city's best – although there are a few meat choices; vegetarians should phone ahead.

Other location: 58 Thistle Street, New Town (225 5109).

Shore

3-4 The Shore (553 5080). Bus 1, 16, 22, 35, 36. **Open** noon-2.30pm, 6.30-10pm Mon-Sat; 12.30-3.30pm, 6.30-10pm Sun. **Main courses** £12.50-£17. **Credit** AmEx, MC, V. **Map** p311 Jy.

The Shore qualifies as a 'proper restaurant' since the smart dining space seems the main feature, although people do come just for a drink. In summer, there are even seats outside; the more adventurous walk across the street and sit on the edge of the dock. The bar's theme is nautical with wooden panelling, while the restaurant space is defined more by sparkling cutlery, white tablecloths, and a seafood slant.

Skippers

1a Dock Place (554 1018/www.skippers.co.uk). Bus 1, 16, 22, 35, 36. **Open** 12.30-2pm, 7-10pm Mon-Fri; 12.30-2pm, 6.30-10pm Sat; 12.30-2.30pm, 7-10pm Sun. **Main courses** £13-£21. **Credit** AmEx, MC, V. **Map** p311 Jy.

Skippers has been around for over 20 years and was a real pioneer in the pre-refurbished docklands of Leith. Ownership has changed in that time, but the reputation endures. The decor is attractively cluttered, with a nod to the sea, and dishes range from the simple to complex. This is fish heaven: watch for specials they've just pulled out of the ocean.

Waterfront

1c Dock Place (554 7427). Bus 1, 16, 22, 35, 36. **Open** noon-10pm daily. **Main courses** £8.50-£15.50. **Credit** AmEx, MC, V. **Map** p311 Jy.

The Waterfront is a class act: a wood-panelled, sea-themed bar, with booth seating, a bright, open conservatory and even a mini barge out the back where people can sit in summer. The wine list is pretty good and some customers come just to sip a bottle of red and munch olives for an hour or two. The kitchen, however, can also provide a well executed three-course meal in a seafood-bistro style.

Mediterranean

Daniel's

88 Commercial Street (553 5933). Bus 1, 16, 22, 35, 36. **Open** 10am-10pm daily. **Main courses** £6-£13. **Credit** AmEx, MC, V. **Map** p311 Jy.

The row of premises opposite Leith's intimidating Scottish Executive building has been a graveyard for restaurants and bars ever since it was constructed in the 1990s. Daniel Vencker's place, however, was among the first and has lasted the course. The decor is modern and the extensive and warming menu has an Alsatian slant; you won't find a special like *jarret de porc* (pork knuckle on the bone, slowly cooked) anywhere else in the city.

Modern European

Restaurant Martin Wishart

54 The Shore (553 3557/www.martin-wishart.co.uk). Bus 1, 16, 22, 35, 36. **Open** noon-2pm; 6.45-9.30pm Tue-Fri; 6.45-9.30pm Sat. **Main courses** £21.50-£24.50. **Credit** AmEx, MC, V. **Map** p311 Jy.

Since it opened in 1999, this diner has gained a stratospheric reputation. But, is it actually the best in Edinburgh? In foodie terms: yes, actually. Quality control is impeccable, service is confident enough to be relaxed, and although it's generally formal it's not uptight. The menu changes all the time, as you'd expect, and the sheer amount of craft displayed is astounding. There's even a separate veggie menu.

Vintners Rooms

The Vaults, 87 Giles Street (554 6767). Leith Walk buses. **Open** noon-2pm, 7-10pm Tue-Sat; 12.30-2.30pm Sun. **Main courses** £15-£19. **Credit** AmEx, MC, V. **Map** p311 Jy.

Housed in a highly atmospheric, 17th-century wine warehouse, the Vintners has tables by the bar (high ceiling, lots of space) and another room adjacent (more intimate, low-ceilinged, good for candlelit trysts). The daily changing menu has a French slant, and there's a good wine list. The Vintners is the kind of restaurant that makes a visit to Leith worthwhile.

MARTIN WISHART

WATERS CLOSE

The art of wishing.
Restaurant Martin Wishart.
See p150.

Café-bars & Cafés

It's a bar, it's a café, it's, er...

These are a few of my **Favorit** things. *See p154.*

It's 1pm. At the table to your left, there are two people engaged in earnest conversation while working their way down a bottle of Shiraz. To your right, a group of four office workers are concluding an early lunch. Meanwhile, you're sitting with a newspaper, a croissant and a latte. Six or seven hours later, and the very same space might be packed with gorgeous young things drinking bottled beer or Bacardi Breezers and talking loudly to make themselves heard over the music. Welcome to a typical café-bar.

Many visitors to the city would take such scenes for granted, as would younger natives. You don't have to go back too far in Edinburgh's history, though, to when the choices of food and drink were constrained by a service-sector apartheid. Pubs were for boozing; restaurants were for posh meals; unlicensed cafés were for tea, coffee, and snacks. But with the success of somewhere like **Negociants** (*see p154*) from the 1980s onwards, it became apparent that customers would take to flexibility and choice like ducks to the wet stuff. Having a menu, a drinks licence, and some

interior-design sense paid off handsomely. Of course, there are no hard and fast definitions of what constitutes a café-bar – but generally they all sell food and drink, and the majority will keep pub-like hours. Consequently, the first part of this chapter covers a range of establishments where you're as likely to find someone having a quiet lunch as four friends caning the chenin blanc. As for the more traditional café, *see p159.*

Café-bars

Old Town

Assembly
41 Lothian Street (220 4288/www.assemblybar. co.uk). Bus 15, 23, 27, 28, 41, 42, 45. **Open** 9am-1am daily. **Credit** MC, V. **Map** p309 F6.
Formerly known as the Iguana, Assembly got a makeover in early 2003. Given its proximity to Edinburgh University, Assmbly thrives as a place to dawdle with coffee during the day, and gets a lot jiggier in the evenings when DJs appear and the sound level is upped a notch. The environment is

style-bar rustic, with plasma screens, and the menu is all things to all people. During Scotland's brief summer, you can even sit outside.

Beluga

30A Chambers Street (624 4545). Bus 15, 23, 27, 28, 41, 42, 45. **Open** 11am-1am daily. **Credit** MC, V. **Map** p310 G6.
This fairly cavernous basement style-bar-with-food, and an attached ground-floor restaurant, is located in what used to be the city's dental hospital. On weekend nights, the bar is packed with a twenty-something crowd, high on music, atmosphere and hormones. But when quieter, it can be a relaxed and roomy place to enjoy a light meal, or just a coffee.

Café Hub

Castlehill (473 2067/www.eif.co.uk/thehub). Bus 15, 23, 27, 28, 41, 42, 45. **Open** 9.30am-6pm Mon, Sun; 9.30am-10pm Tue-Sat. **Credit** AmEx, MC, V. **Map** p304 C3.
This building was completed in 1845 and was originally an assembly hall and offices for the Church of Scotland. In 1999, it reopened as the headquarters for the Edinburgh International Festival (*see p32*). Café Hub only occupies part of the space here, but the high ceilings and church-like feel can be affecting when it's quiet. It gets stupidly busy in August of course. Flexible daytime menu, more dinner-like in the evenings, and there's a terrace.

City Café

19 Blair Street (220 0125). Nicolson Street–North Bridge buses. **Open** 11am-1am daily. **Credit** MC, V. **Map** p304 D3.

As much a part of Edinburgh as the Castle, the City Café has the look of a 1950s diner, has a downstairs DJ space, a pool table, serves all-day breakfasts, and caters to the pre-club crowd later. The food is fill-you-up stuff while those breakfasts (carnivore and vegetarian versions) really kick-start your morning (or afternoon or evening). But can you spot the legendary spelling error behind the bar?

Ecco Vino

19 Cockburn Street (225 1441). Nicolson Street–North Bridge buses. **Open** noon-11.30pm Mon-Thur; noon-1am Fri, Sat; 12.30pm-midnight Sun. **Credit** AmEx, MC, V. **Map** p304 D2.
The formula is so simple, it's genius. Create a basic Italian menu with some straightforward dishes and the odd daily special. Devise an Italian-slanted wine list. Store your wines up on one wall as a design feature, run the bar along the other side of the room, choose predominantly wooden decor, light candles and wait for clientele. And since it opened in autumn 2001, the clientele has come. Between the Royal Mile and Waverley Station in prime tourist country, but the opposite of a tourist trap.

EH1

197 High Street, Royal Mile (220 5277). Nicolson Street–North Bridge buses. **Open** 9am-1am daily. **Credit** AmEx, MC, V. **Map** p304 D3.
On a sunny day in August there's no better place than EH1 to sit out and watch the chaos of the Festival. The Royal Mile is pedestrianised at that time of year, and performers will likely be doing impromptu street theatre, juggling, fire eating and, most of all, trying to drum up business. Play hard

Switching on the wireless

Without dwelling on the technology, **wi-fi** (wireless networking) allows laptop and handheld PC users to surf the internet – at broadband speeds – without having to mess around with anything as tedious as bits of cable or USB ports; it's a radio thing. As long as you've got the right wireless card in your laptop, access rights, and you're in a wi-fi 'hotspot', then it's possible.

This really took off in Edinburgh in 2003 as a number of hotspots were installed. BT set up half a dozen, based around kiosks in the city centre. Internet access is possible up to 100 metres from a kiosk, so there are parts of Edinburgh where shops, pubs, offices, and even stretches of pavement have wi-fi. Then there are a number of hotels, pubs, and cafés that have made a specific effort to provide wi-fi too.

The rate of development of wi-fi, as with all things computer related, is such that the

entire city might be 'turned on' soon enough (*see p283*). Meanwhile, coffee and web surfing have always gone together well, so if you fancy an espresso as you wirelessly check your email, try these:
Beanscene: pay at the counter, £3 per hour. 67 Holyrood Road, Old Town (557 6549). 99 Nicolson Street, South Edinburgh (667 8159).
Caffè Nero: log on and follow payment instructions. 58 Rose Street, New Town (220 3577).
Kariba Coffee: free – as long as you buy a coffee. 1 Parliament Square, Royal Mile, Old Town (226 1214).
Starbucks: account with T-Mobile required, or log on and follow payment instructions. Exchange Crescent, 5-6 Conference Square, West Edinburgh (221 0687). 55 Forrest Road, Old Town (220 5543). 120B Princes Street, New Town (226 5881).

to get, relax and take it all in with a drink and some eats (small dishes, wraps, burgers, pasta, salads, sandwiches – and much more).

Favorit
19-20 Teviot Place (220 6880/www.favorit edinburgh.co.uk). Bus 23, 27, 28, 45. **Open** 8am-3am daily. **Credit** AmEx, MC, V. **Map** p309 F6.
With its long opening hours, Favorit provides everything from breakfast for workers in a hurry to nightcaps for clapped-out clubbers. It has an American diner flavour, and also acts as a delicatessen. The bacon butties are much loved. Formulaic, but a good formula (*see p173* **Drinking till dawn**).
Other location: 30-32 Leven Street, South Edinburgh (221 1800).

Negociants
45 Lothian Street (225 6313). Bus 23, 27, 28, 45. **Open** 9am-3am daily. **Credit** AmEx, MC, V. **Map** p309 F6.
If you ever want to hide in a café-bar until the small hours of the morning, nibbling nachos and drinking artisanal beer from Belgium or cheap house wine, this is the place. It seems to have been around forever and has a vaguely French feel; it's also spacious, with lots of mirrors and big windows. Don't be in a hurry though, as the slow service is legendary. There are seats outside in summer.

Oxygen Bar & Grill
3-5 Infirmary Street (557 9997/www.oxygen-edinburgh.co.uk). Nicolson Street–North Bridge buses. **Open** 10am-1am daily. **Credit** MC, V. **Map** p310 G6.
Oxygen opened with a flourish at the end of 1999 as the only establishment in Edinburgh to sell canisters of oxygen. As a gimmick, the gas was both short-lived and, given Scottish drinkers love of a good smoke, rather too flammable. But the style bar has endured, however, thanks to its proximity to the university and the club-packed Cowgate. Foodwise, expect light bites and more substantial 'plates'. Chilled place for an afternoon coffee.

New Town

Opal Lounge
51a George Street (226 2275/www.opallounge. co.uk). Princes Street buses. **Open** noon-3am daily. **Credit** AmEx, MC, V. **Map** p304 B1.
The Opal Lounge hit the city centre with a design flourish in 2002 and instantly became the place to see and be seen. Housed in a basement, it goes for a contemporary, cool and minimal look: dark chic. As a bar, it's big on cocktails, offers entire (and expensive) bottles of spirits, stays open late and has a roster of resident DJs. On the food front, it's predominantly oriental.

Rick's
55a Frederick Street (622 7800/www.ricks edinburgh.co.uk). Princes Street buses. **Open** 8am-1am daily. **Credit** AmEx, MC, V. **Map** p304 B1.

More than just a bar, Rick's is also a restaurant and a small boutique hotel (*see p53*). It tends to attract identikit girls (black clothes, straight blonde hair) and guys (black clothes, expensive haircuts). While maybe not as louche as Rick's Café Americain, and certainly not as self sacrificing as its proprietor, this northern version of Rick's is really a kind of bar-restaurant collision with lots of people coming for the booze – good tequila, decent cocktails – and the buzz. Just don't ask anyone to play it again.

Whighams Wine Cellars
13 Hope Street, Charlotte Square (225 9717/ www.whighams.co.uk). Princes Street buses. **Open** noon-midnight Mon-Thur; noon-1am Fri, Sat. **Credit** AmEx, MC, V. **Map** p308 C5.
Just off the west end of Princes Street, this is a well-established basement wine bar with a real 'cellar' feel. The small alcoves off the main bar space have candlelit atmospheric low ceilings, while the decor is minimal to the point of non-existence. The wine choice is excellent and the competent menu has a seafood slant. A good hideaway.

Stockbridge

Circus Café
15 North West Circus Place (220 0333/www. circuscafe.co.uk). Bus 23, 27. **Open** 10am-11pm daily. **Credit** MC, V. **Map** p306 D4.
If a café-bar is a contemporary solution to the old divisions between the food and drink service industries then what's Circus Café? Eclecticism gone mad, perhaps. This is a café-bar (half a dozen Loch Fyne oysters, yum), takeaway, delicatessen and bakery, while at nights it has the feel of a restaurant – a very tasteful one at that. The food on offer is very good indeed: try a dish, then buy the ingredients.

Hector's
47-49 Deanhaugh Street (343 1735). Bus 23, 27. **Open** noon-midnight Mon-Wed, Sun; noon-1am Thur-Sat. **Credit** AmEx, MC, V. **Map** p305 C3.
Once called Maison Hector, one of the city's pioneer designer restaurants, this venue has long since morphed into a less ostentatious style-bar-with-food. It's good for cosy chats by candlelight or nestling by the fire. The menu comprises all of the usual style-bar offerings (light bites, sandwiches, weekend brunch) and it's a handy stop after wandering around the Royal Botanic Gardens nearby.

Watershed
44 St Stephen Street (220 3774). Bus 23, 27. **Open** 11.30am-midnight daily. **Credit** MC, V. **Map** p306 D3.
A calm, personable venue in the quintessential Stockbridge street, the Watershed is a basement establishment with a distressed wooden floor, quiet colours and designer seating. Its drinks menu offers decent bottled lager as well as affordable wines and a reasonable cocktail list. Often quite quiet on weekday afternoons, later on it has the usual posse happily knocking back those happy-hour pitchers.

Un po di vino? **Valvona & Crolla Caffè Bar**. *See p157.*

Darling! *Kiss, kiss.* You were marvellous. **Traverse Theatre Bar**. *See p158.*

Calton Hill & Broughton

Baroque

*39-41 Broughton Street (557 0627). Bus 8, 17/
Playhouse buses.* **Open** 10am-1am daily. **Credit**
AmEx, MC, V. **Map** p306 F3.

A decor compromise makes Baroque a barometer of
changing mores. When it opened, it was a 1990s riot
of confused styles (Matisse prints, cracked tile
cladding on the pillars, bright colours). A refurbishment calmed it down a little, but it's impossible
to disguise the queasy metallic curves of the bar or
the odd flash of flamboyance that has still survived.
However, it's open to the street in summer, serves
all the basic booze choices, and the menu is functional. More a pre-club bar in the evenings, so don't
go then expecting a quiet night.

Basement

*10A-12A Broughton Street (557 0097/www.the
basement.org.uk). Bus 8, 17/Playhouse buses.* **Open**
noon-1am daily. **Credit** AmEx, MC, V. **Map**
p306 F3.

The original Broughton Street style bar, this place
still has an orange and blue decor and eccentric furniture made from old engineering discards. The bar
itself separates the establishment into two: one side
is more pubby, the other has tables for sit down dining. Either way, it's dark, atmospheric and can get
pretty party-like in the evenings, when the staffs'
shirts vie with the music over which is louder. The
kitchen has a good reputation for its Thai dishes on
Wednesdays and Mexican ones at the weekends.
Still hip after all these years.

Blue Moon Café

*36 Broughton Street (556 2788). Bus 8, 17/
Playhouse buses.* **Open** 11am-11pm Mon-Fri;
10am-midnight Sat, Sun. **Credit** MC, V.
Map p306 F3.

This gay-run but straight-friendly café-bar is a popular meet-and-eat place both during the idle days of
midweek and at evenings towards the weekend,
when the atmosphere steps up to accommodate the
clubbing brigade. The food tends to be simple and
filling (macaroni cheese, nachos, vegetarian haggis,
assorted burgers, big cakes), while there are some
good bottled beers and economy wines. If you want
to know anything about the city's gay scene, ask the
friendly waiting staff. There's even a small book and
accoutrement shop in the basement.

Outhouse

*12A Broughton Street Lane (557 6668). Bus 8, 17/
Playhouse buses.* **Open** 10am-1am Mon-Fri; 11am-
1am Sat, Sun. **Credit** MC, V. **Map** p307 G3.

The forgotten café-bar on the Broughton Street
scene. It's hidden halfway down a back lane and was
looking a little uncared for until a 2003 redecoration.
A functional menu, DJs towards the end of the week
and the added attraction of a 'garden space' out in
the back with a gazebo-style construction to keep
the rain off in summer.

Valvona & Crolla Caffè Bar

*19 Elm Row, Leith Walk (556 6066/www.valvona
crolla.com). Bus 7, 10, 12, 14, 16, 22, 25, 49.* **Open**
8am-6.30pm Mon-Sat; 11am-4.30pm Sun. **Credit**
AmEx, MC, V. **Map** p307 G3.

The best delicatessen in Scotland, and one of the best
in the UK. Its *caffè* bar is a simple and tasteful space
at the rear of the shop, with its white walls and
wooden beams. The food (breakfast, panatella sandwiches, and more substantial dishes) draws on the
quality of raw materials sold in the deli, shipped in
fresh from Italian markets. There's a great selection
of pricey Italian wines too. Peerless.

South Edinburgh

blue

*10 Cambridge Street (221 1222/www.bluebar
cafe.com). Bus 1, 10, 11, 15, 16, 17, 22, 24, 34.*
Open noon-midnight Mon-Thur, Sun; noon-1am Fri,
Sat. **Credit** AmEx, DC, MC, V. **Map** p304 A3.

Sister establishment to the grander Atrium downstairs (*see p147*), blue offers everything from a pint
of lager to a glass of house white with an elaborate
sandwich or a three-course Modern European experience. At lunchtime, suits predominate, but in the
afternoon and evening the diners and drinkers are a
more mixed lot. Still very good, but these days perhaps failing to match the very high standards it set
when it burst on the scene in 1997.

Borough

*72-80 Causewayside (668 2255/www.borough
hotel.com). Bus 41, 42.* **Open** 11am-1am Mon-Sat;
12.30pm-midnight Sun. **Credit** MC, V. **Map** p310 H8.

Even though it's only a mile or so south of Princes
Street, in Edinburgh terms Borough still feels a little
out of the way. All the same, it's a smart, contemporary boutique hotel with a public bar and restaurant
(*see p57*). The large space for drinking is also good
for lounging, with above-average food, and there's
an adjacent restaurant for more formal eats.

Centraal

*32 West Nicolson Street (667 7355/www.centraal.
co.uk). Nicolson Street–North Bridge buses.* **Open**
11am-1am daily. **Credit** MC, V. **Map** p310 G7.

Head downstairs into a clean-line designer basement
space split into two areas. There's the brickwork bar,
with its big leather sofas and TV screens for the football, then down another couple of steps there are the
dining tables. The main attraction here is the amazing beer menu, but the food can be tempting (wild
deer terrine, steaks, and roast chicken, for instance).

Filmhouse Bar

*88 Lothian Road (229 5932/www.filmhouse
cinema.com). Bus 1, 10, 15, 16, 17, 22, 24, 34.*
Open 10am-11.30pm Mon-Thur, Sun; 10am-12.30am
Fri, Sat. **Credit** MC, V. **Map** p304 A2.

The city's main art-house cinema (*see p206*), the
Filmhouse has been around for over 20 years, but
the bar was refurbished in 2002. It's the ideal place

Beware the attack of the killer croissant.
Pâtisserie Florentin.
See p161.

to meet friends before or after a movie, but also for snacks, light meals and drinks. The draught beer is pretty respectable and there's an industrious kitchen making pizzas, light curries, soup and salads.

Human Be-In
2-8 West Crosscauseway (662 8860/www.human be-in.co.uk). Nicolson Street–North Bridge buses. **Open** 11am-1am daily. **Credit** AmEx, MC, V. **Map** p310 G7.
A sharp-edged style bar close to the university with dark wood and clean lines. There are booths to the rear for the insecure, and low, comfortable seats in front of the big windows looking out to the street for the expansive. In summer you can sit outside. Many come in here just for a drink although food is served until 9pm. It's an impressive menu and a cut above the average Edinburgh café-bar, but also caters for those who just want a ciabatta sandwich.

Montpeliers
159-161 Bruntsfield Place (229 3115/www. montpeliersedinburgh.co.uk). Bus 11, 15, 16, 17, 23, 45. **Open** 9am-1am daily. **Credit** AmEx, MC, V. **Map** p309 D8.
Montpeliers has been around since 1992 but the odd refurb has made sure it still looks bang up-to-date: clean-cut, with dark wood and subdued red lighting. There's a great beer selection and the cocktails are better than average too. The dining area is slightly raised, off to one side, and offers a range of dishes from breakfast to the full three-course evening experience. It often gets very crowded, but Montpeliers is among Edinburgh's top café-bars.

Traverse Theatre Bar
10 Cambridge Street (228 5383). Bus 1, 10, 11, 15, 16, 17, 22, 24, 34. **Open** 10.30am-midnight Mon-Wed, Sun; 10.30-1am Thur-Sat. **Credit** MC, V. **Map** p304 A3.

One of the main venues for the Festival, with two theatre spaces, the Trav (*see p238*) gets very busy pre- and post-performance all year round. It's a modern, roomy establishment, refurbished in a minor way after the 2003 Fringe to provide more comfortable, low seating in one corner, and a few discreet booths in another. It still has that inside-out ceiling (ducts and conduits as a design feature) and attracts a typical café-bar crowd. The regular menu features ciabatta sandwiches, potato wedges, and more, with a nachos 'n' lager special offer in the evenings. Some decent beers on tap too.

West Edinburgh

Indigo Yard
7 Charlotte Lane (220 5603/www.indigoyard edinburgh.co.uk). Princes Street buses. **Open** 8.30-1am Mon-Fri; 9am-1am Sat, Sun. **Credit** AmEx, MC, V. **Map** p308 C5.
Indigo Yard made quite a splash when it hit the West End in the mid '90s, with its design values (canvas canopies, exposed brickwork, a balcony level) and aspirational menus. These days it has found a niche catering to a fairly mature but up-for-it crowd on weekend evenings, while classic Edinburgh business folk form the bulk of the clientele at lunch and after work. Brunch, sandwich, pint of beer, three course dinner, raspberry martini? The choice is yours.

Leith

Bar Sirius
7-10 Dock Place (555 3344). Bus 1, 6, 22, 35, 36, 49. **Open** 11.30am-midnight Mon-Wed; 11.30am-1am Thur-Sat; noon-1am Sun. **Credit** MC, V. **Map** p311 Jy.
When Sirius arrived in Leith in 1996, its like had never been seen before. Not locally, anyway. Since then, the original ostentatious design has been

calmed down a little, but the old place remains popular with an imaginative menu (including steaks, weekend brunch and ambitious salads), some decent vodkas and tequilas behind the bar, and comfortable leather seats for slumping. Hungover? Try the Bloody Mary breakfast fry up (but don't blame us if your head doesn't forgive you). Where other bars and restaurants around here have come and gone in the last few years, Sirius has survived.

Malmaison

1 Tower Place (468 5000/www.malmaison.com). Bus 1, 16, 22, 35, 36. **Open** 10am-11pm Mon-Thur, Sun; 10am-midnight Fri, Sat. **Credit** AmEx, DC, MC, V. **Map** p311 Jx.

The Malmaison name is well known now for its string of boutique hotels across the UK, but this was actually the very first. The ground floor bar is a fine, sharp, contemporary space (made over from its original raffish French look) to sit and linger, and has a pretty good short menu to boot. If you want the more formal dining experience, there's the even more designery brasserie adjacent.

Sugo

14-15 Albert Place, near Albert Street, Leith Walk (554 7282). Leith Walk buses. **Open** 11am-midnight Mon-Thur, Sun; 11am-1am Fri, Sat. **Credit** MC, V. **Map** p307 H2.

When Sugo opened in 2002, a lot of people in the neighbourhood gave thanks. At last, somewhere they could go for a glass of wine and some food without having to head to the city centre or the distant heart of Leith. Fitting snugly into its unusual surroundings – an adapted space on the ground floor of a tenement block – Sugo has dining tables and sofas to settle into, and the atmosphere here is relaxed and informal. Eats-wise, it's nothing elaborate but you'll find something appropriate to go with that bottle of red.

Cafés

COFFEE 'N' CAKE

The rise and rise of the café-bar (*see p152*) has been a boon for Edinburgh's citizens and visitors, but they don't suit every occasion. Sometimes, all you need is a pot of tea or a cappuccino, and a moist muffin; what you don't want is a DJ and exuberance. Under those circumstances, the choice is clear: head for a good old café. The city has been overcome with a glut of chains in recent years and there are now more Starbucks and Costa coffee houses than you can count (they're not in the main listings below but they're hardly tough to find). Fortunately, the big brand names have complemented the more individual local establishments rather than driven them out, so there is still space for old-school tearooms loved by generations of grannies (**Chatterbox**, *see p163*, or **Clarinda's**, *see p161*), more contemporary venues with excellent food (**Glass & Thompson**, *see p162*), and even the opportunity for a glimpse of grandeur (**Palm Court**, *see p162*).

Old Town

Always Sunday

170 High Street (622 0667/www.alwayssunday. co.uk). Nicolson Street–North Bridge buses. **Open** 8am-6pm Mon-Fri; 9am-6pm Sat, Sun; extended opening hours in summer. **Credit** MC, V. **Map** p304 D3.

Much as we like the name, we can only lament the passing, following a 2003 refit, of the magnificently – but of course unnecessarily – memorable moniker,

"I had authentic Italian food good enough for Pavarotti, for under a tenor."

Authentic Italian dishes cooked with love, at prices you'll adore.
Our bistro menu at Santini Bis is created with the finest ingredients direct from Italy. Or why not select from our award winning menu in our Santini Ristorante.

Santini Ristorante &
Santini Bis.
8 Conference Square,
Edinburgh EH3 8AN.
0131 221 7788

Elephant's Sufficiency. But Always Sunday is still handily placed on the city's main tourist drag, it's light, bright, pays attention to what it serves (Fair Trade coffee, for instance) and has the papers on Sunday. The place is custom-built for a wet weekend linger over a long breakfast.

Beanscene

67 Holyrood Road (557 6549/www.beanscene.co.uk). Bus 30, 35. **Open** 8am-10pm Mon-Sat; 10am-10pm Sun. **Credit** MC, V. **Map** p310 H5.

A real Scottish chain (hurrah!) with mod-groovy branches in Edinburgh and Glasgow, and more in the pipeline, serving the typical coffee, sandwiches and pastries combo. It's a nice place to hang out and has regular live music of the jazz/acoustic variety. Perhaps most notable these days for being an Edinburgh wi-fi pioneer (*see page 153* **Switching on the wireless**). Sit down, log on, and surf. Magic. **Other location**: 99 Nicolson Street, South Edinburgh; 667 8159.

Cafeteria

Fruitmarket Gallery, 45 Market Street (226 1843/ www.fruitmarket.co.uk/cafe). Princes Street buses. **Open** 11am-5pm Mon-Sat; noon-5pm Sun. **Credit** MC, V. **Map** p304 D2.

Big baguette melts are the order of the day in the Fruitmarket Gallery café. Fresh danishes keep the mid-morning grazers happy and there's a selection of gateaux for the leisurely afternoon browser. But it's at lunchtime that you'll witness the real action, with staff aiming to refuel customers with pasta and melts in under an hour. No smoking.

Clarinda's

69 Canongate, Royal Mile (557 1888). Bus 30, 35. **Open** 9am-4.30pm Mon-Sat; 10am-4.30pm Sun. **No credit cards**. **Map** p310 G5.

Not one to change merely for the sake of change, Clarinda's seems to have been a feature on the volatile Royal Mile catering scene forever. Home-baking is the name of the game here, and this place is sure to find approval in the hearts of those who appreciate the beauty of a well-turned-out bun.

Elephant House

21 George IV Bridge (220 5355/www.elephant-house.co.uk). Bus 23, 27, 28, 41, 42, 45. **Open** 8am-11pm Mon-Fri; 9.30am-11pm Sat, Sun. **Credit** MC, V. **Map** p304 C3.

A popular and busy café not far from the university, with a vaguely ethnic look and a fine fetish for pachyderms. The clientele ranges from tea-sipping students, to lecturers having a panini while lingering over the newspaper, to grandmothers. Some of the teas and coffees are first-rate (and organic to boot), there's a reasonable choice of good affordable wines, and the food on offer includes salads, baguettes and savouries. The main room through the back has some great views out over the Old Town (*see p143* **Eats with a view**). **Other location**: **Elephant & Bagels** 37 Marshall Street, Nicolson Square, South Edinburgh (668 4404).

Lower Aisle Restaurant

St Giles' Cathedral, High Street, Royal Mile (225 5147). Bus 23, 27, 28, 41, 42, 45/Nicolson Street–North Bridge buses. **Open** 8am-4.30pm Mon-Fri; 10am-1.30pm Sun; extended opening hours during Festival. **No credit cards**. **Map** p304 D3.

The Lower Aisle isn't exactly the place for a party, but it is handy for a simple and filling lunch while you're on the tourist trail, especially if you like baked potatoes. The big attraction in coming here is the history, though, rather than the victuals: you're in the High Kirk of Edinburgh – a sacred site since 854 (*see p77*). Relax, and pay your respects.

Pâtisserie Florentin

8 St Giles Street (225 6267). Bus 23, 27, 28, 41, 42, 45. **Open** 8am-6pm Mon-Fri; 9am-6pm Sat, Sun. **No credit cards**. **Map** p304 C3.

A bit of a refurb in 2002 spruced up this French-flavoured old place. It's a long-standing favourite among locals, and possibly the original Edinburgh home of the killer almond croissant. Famous, fantastic pâtisserie, and snacky savouries too.

Plaisir de Chocolat

251-253 Canongate (556 9524). Bus 30, 35/Nicolson Street–North Bridge buses. **Open** 10am-6pm daily. **Credit** MC, V. **Map** p310 G8.

The Plaisir opened in 2000 and instantly gained a reputation as one of the best cafés in the city. It's a salon with the biggest tea list in Christendom, brimming cups of hot chocolate that make grown women weep with joy, and there's a very capable kitchen too (serving French savouries). You can have a fulfilling lunch with wine, but it's the tea, hot chocolate and pâtisseries that enthrall. **Other location**: 270 Canongate, Royal Mile, Old Town (556 0112).

Spoon

15 Blackfriars Street (556 6922). Nicolson Street–North Bridge buses. **Open** 8am-6pm Mon-Sat; extended hours during Festival. **Credit** AmEx, MC, V. **Map** p310 G5.

A neighbourly but neat and modern café just off the main tourist strip, Spoon offers soup, sandwiches, cake, and even wine. So what's the big deal? In fact, the food's all very good and better than you might expect from such an apparently modest establishment. The cheese platter might involve Dunsyre Blue or Brie de Meaux for instance.

New Town

Au Gourmand

1 Brandon Terrace (624 4666). Bus 23, 27. **Open** 9am-10pm Tue-Sat; 9am-6pm Sun. **Credit** MC, V. **Map** p306 D2/3.

Newly arrived on the scene in 2002, this is essentially a very accomplished pâtisserie/boulangerie with a café space added at the rear. It's been stripped back to the bare stone walls, thus offering a fairly minimal environment, but that goes with some of the best French snacking in the city. Alcohol is limited to wine but there are assorted crêpes, and a fine choice of excellent ample sandwiches.

Glass & Thompson
2 Dundas Street (557 0909). Bus 23, 27. **Open** 8.30am-5.30pm Mon-Sat; 11am-4.30pm Sun. **Credit** AmEx, MC, V. **Map** p306 E3.
A cross between a deli and a café, Glass & Thompson sits on one of New Town's main thoroughfares. It has a modern look, a few tables (with a couple outside in summer) and offers some high-class snacks. That means tarts (asparagus and fennel; ricotta and pine nut) or one of the signature platters, such as Colston Basset stilton with pear, salad and bread. There's also assorted antipasti and a very small selection of wine and bottled beer. The cakes are simply amazing too.

Juniper
117a Hanover Street (225 1552). Bus 23, 27. **Open** 8am-5pm Mon-Wed; 8am-10pm Thur-Sat. **Credit** MC, V. **Map** p304 C1.
A green façade, a basement situation, homely decor (hippy meets IKEA), and a range of decent meals and snacks. Juniper looks like it might belong to the radical wing of the lentil tendency but the food on offer is thankfully a tad more interesting than that. Here you'll find everything from an adventurous soup to a filling French beef stew, and it all comes as a blessed relief from this part of the New Town's relentless retail outlets.

Palm Court
Balmoral Hotel, 1 Princes Street (556 2414). Princes Street buses. **Open** 10am-1am daily. **Credit** AmEx, DC, MC, V. **Map** p304 D2.
The Balmoral, which remains one of Edinburgh's grandest hotels (*see p49*), lays on a slap-up afternoon tea in its sumptuous Palm Court area. There are no crusts on the sandwiches and the cake selection can lead to agonies of glorious indecision. While the staff may not throw you out if you turn up dressed in jeans and a T-shirt, you'll be the only one there dressed that way.

Queen Street Café
1 Queen Street (557 2844). Bus 4, 8, 10, 11, 12, 15, 16, 17, 26, 44, 45. **Open** 10am-4.30pm Mon-Sat; noon-4.30pm Sun. **No credit cards. Map** p306 D4.
A venerable Edinburgh institution in a wild Victorian-Gothic building, the National Portrait Gallery (*see p94*) has a reassuring feel of tradition. The café is good for a gossip and a scone, or a light meal, even if the sight of stern Scottish founding fathers in the gallery can be a bit unsettling. Big windows, big space, nice refuge.

Stockbridge

Café Newton
Dean Gallery, 72 Belford Road (623 7132). Bus 13. **Open** 10am-4.30pm Mon-Sat; noon-4.30pm Sun. **No credit cards. Map** p308 A5.

Despite the fine feeling of space in this big classical building (refurbished and opened as a gallery in 1999), the ground floor Café Newton can get cramped. All the same, the café serves light meals, fabulous cakes, good soups and great focaccias as well as excellent coffee from one of the most impressive espresso machines in the city. And there will be some art on display as well, depending on what's showing.

Gallery Café
Scottish National Gallery of Modern Art, 74 Belford Road (624 6309). Bus 13. **Open** 10am-4.30pm Mon-Sat; noon-4.30pm Sun. **No credit cards. Map** p308 A5.
Perennially popular, and not just with the city's art hounds. There are light meals, cakes and usually a couple of decent cheeses but the real value of this place becomes apparent on fine summer days when people take their snacks outside and soak up the rays in peace. For details of the gallery, *see p101*.

Maxi's
33 Raeburn Place (343 3007). Bus 19A, 24, 28. **Open** 8.30am-6pm Mon-Sat; 10am-5pm Sun. **Credit** MC, V. **Map** p305 C3.
A happy and popular café-bar with a few delicatessen-style bits and bobs for sale. Located in a very bourgeois neighbourhood the space is airy and light, with blonde wood and blue paint; all very 'now' but in an accessible way. Stop for a fast coffee, or sit down and dawdle with a bargain bottle of Malbec, a panini and a salad.

Terrace Café
Royal Botanic Garden, Inverleith Row (552 0616). Bus 8, 17, 23, 27. **Open** 9.30am-6pm daily (earlier closing times Oct-Apr; phone for details). **Credit** MC, V. **Map** p305 C2.
The Botanics (*see p99*) are a popular spot for an afternoon wander, and the café next to Inverleith House (*see p99*) is a perfect handy pit-stop with seats inside and out, light lunches of the quiche and salad variety, plus sandwiches and cakes. Sitting outside, taking in the sun on a fine day, the view of central Edinburgh's skyline is unparalleled.

Calton Hill & Broughton

Embo
29 Haddington Place, near Annandale Street, Leith Walk (652 3880). Bus 7, 10, 12, 14, 16, 22, 25, 49. **Open** 7.30am-3.30pm Mon-Fri; 9am-4.30pm Sat. **No credit cards. Map** p307 G3.
The only gripe about this café is its short opening hours. If you catch it when it's open, perch yourself on a stool, watch the world go by on Leith Walk, and try a continental breakfast or tuck into a panini. A small, friendly and well cared-for spot.

Mediterraneo
73 Broughton Street (557 6900). Bus 8, 17/Playhouse buses. **Open** 8am-5.30pm Mon-Thur; 8am-9pm Fri, Sat; 9am-4pm Sun. **Credit** MC, V. **Map** p306 F3.

EdinBurgher Kevin Williamson

As pipe dreams go, the opening of Edinburgh's first cannabis coffee shop was always likely to suffer a quick and unhappy come-down. For Kevin Williamson, however, chief advocate of such enlightened moves, it was just one more power play in a lifetime mission combining political agitation with punk attitude and club-culture hedonism.

Highland-born Williamson first came to prominence via *Rebel Inc*, the literary fanzine he launched on May 1st 1992. The mag's name alone blew a breath of fresh air through the capital's tweedy literary scene, drawing inspiration from Glasgow writer James Kelman and Beat icon Alexander Trocchi.

The result was messy and provocative, the first issue featuring fresh work by then rookies Irvine Welsh and Alan Warner. *Rebel Inc* only lasted five issues, by which time *Trainspotting* fever was at its height. Contrary to popular belief, Williamson didn't publish *Trainspotting*. Nor was he the first to publish Welsh. That honour rests with fellow novelist Duncan McLean, whose Clocktower Press first showcased work by Welsh and others in a stream of now ultra-rare pamphlets later collected in the *Ahead Of Its Time* anthology. *Rebel Inc* incurred the wrath of the city fathers as their semi-spoof *A Visitor's Guide To Edinburgh* scoured alleyways other guide books feared to tread. Then, jumping into bed with Canongate (*see p119* **Books and bonking**), the *Children Of Albion Rovers* anthology captured the spirit of a series of packed, semi-legal *Rebel Inc* live events.

By this time, Williamson's political preoccupations had already put his picture on the cover of the tabloids, with his head being 'cradled' by a member of Dundee's constabulary in an effort to remove him from the Timex picket line. His book, *Drugs And The Party Line*, offered a timely polemic on the legalisation of all drugs, and in 1996 he founded Scotland Against Drugs Hypocrisy, later becoming drugs spokesman for the Scottish Socialist Party.

Williamson was last spotted being ejected from the Scottish Parliament while wearing a George W Bush mask after proffering muffled interjections during a debate on the Iraq war, and continues to agitate from the frontline of Edinburgh's underground.

A wonder: a café in a street of style bars. Not only does family-run Mediterraneo manage a thriving lunchtime trade in takeaway baguettes, but it also has a pleasant sit-down area. Most of the food displays the owners' Italian roots; the staff here can do things with grapes and a piccante sausage that your tastebuds wouldn't dare dream about.

South Edinburgh

Black Medicine Co.
2 Nicolson Street (622 7209). Nicolson Street–North Bridge buses. **Open** 8am-8pm daily. **Credit** MC, V. **Map** p310 G6.
The black medicine in question is coffee, which is served up in several varieties at this rather rugged-looking café. The walls are rough stone and the furniture is chunky and wooden, giving the place a bit of an outdoorsy feel. It's comfy enough and the large windows are excellent for talent-spotting.

Café Grande
184 Bruntsfield Place (228 1188). Bus 11, 15, 16, 17, 23, 45. **Open** 9am-11pm Mon-Thur; 9am-midnight Fri, Sat; 10am-11pm Sun. **Credit** AmEx, MC, V. **Map** p309 D8.
A cosy establishment with warm red tones behind its yellow façade, this place has something of a dual personality. By day, it's a two-roomed café selling cakes, pastries, burgers and pretty good breakfasts. At night, the menu switches to more substantial fare, with dishes such as seafood risotto and steaks.

Chatterbox Tea Room
1 East Preston Street (667 9406). Bus 3, 5, 7, 8, 14, 29, 31, 33, 37, 49. **Open** 8.30am-5pm Mon-Fri; 9am-5pm Sat; 11am-5pm Sun. **No credit cards**. **Map** p310 H8.
Millennia have come and gone, Scotland has gained its own parliament, but Chatterbox remains. Many of the locals are regulars, and swimmers from the nearby Commonwealth swimming pool often stop by to wet their insides after thoroughly soaking their outsides. An ideal venue for a scone or cake, and a pot of tea in the best old-fashioned style.

Elephants & Bagels
37 Marshall Street, Nicolson Square (668 4404/ www.elephant-house.co.uk). Nicolson Street–North Bridge buses. **Open** 8.30am-5pm Mon-Fri; 10am-5pm Sat, Sun. **Credit** MC, V. **Map** p310 G6.
The baby sister operation to the Elephant House (*see p161*), the E&B doesn't sell many elephants but it's big on the bagel side of the equation. Popular with students, who often take away their goodies for impromptu picnics in George Square during the brief but glorious Scottish summer.
Other location: Elephant House 21 George IV Bridge, Old Town (220 5355).

Engine Shed

19 St Leonard's Lane (662 0040). Bus 2, 21. **Open** 10.30am-3pm Mon-Thur; 10.30am-2.30pm Fri; 10am-4pm Sat. **No credit cards**. **Map** p310 H7.

This vegetarian wholefood café opened in 1990 in a former maintenance shed for the trains that used to run on the now defunct line out to East Lothian. It's a handy eastern alternative to the Sheep Heid Inn (*see p170*) after you've hiked round Arthur's Seat. The main dishes on offer (cashew nut pie or spinach bake, for example) are utterly wholesome, and the bread's excellent, but what sets this enterprise apart is that full-time staff supervise adults with learning difficulties in all aspects of the work.

Festival Theatre Café

13-29 Nicolson Street (662 1112). Nicolson Street–North Bridge buses. **Open** 10am-6pm daily; later on performance nights. **No credit cards**. **Map** p310 G6.

There are two ways to look at the Festival Theatre Café. Depending on your point of view, the huge plate glass windows that form the front the theatre (*see p239*) allow you a prime view of passers-by or they make you feel as if you're stuck in a goldfish bowl. Not possessed of the best-kept wine list in town, but popular with local workers for lunch. No smoking.

Luca's

16 Morningside Road (446 0233/www.s-luca.co.uk). Bus 11, 15, 16, 17, 23, 45. **Open** 9am-10pm daily. **Credit** MC, V.

Famed for the ice-cream at its Musselburgh café (*see p263*), this branch near the city's Holy Corner (so called because it boasts more churches per square foot than the Vatican City) also offers a range of club sandwiches, panini melts and pizzas. But who needs to eat sensible food when there are nut sundaes and Caribbean longboats to be enjoyed?
Other location: 28-32 High Street, Musselburgh (665 2237).

Metropole

29-33 Newington Road (668 4999). Bus 3, 5, 7, 8, 29, 31, 37, 49. **Open** 9am-10pm daily. **Credit** MC, V. **Map** p310 H8.

Deep in the heart of studentland, this converted bank lends an air of faded grandeur to the simple act of sipping a cappuccino. The Metropole sticks firmly to the belief that variety is better than cream and sugar: the adventurous customer could come in here every day for a month and still not sample all the speciality teas and coffees. No smoking.

Ndebele

57 Home Street (221 1141/www.ndebele.co.uk). Bus 10, 11, 15, 16, 17, 23, 27, 45. **Open** 10am-10pm daily. **Credit** AmEx, MC, V. **Map** p309 D7.

The city's only African café-deli, Ndebele has foods on offer that you'd be hard pushed to find anywhere else in Scotland, let alone Edinburgh. It's a nicely scruffy, student-style hangout with staff who seem to be on a mission to bring the likes of smoked ostrich, biltong shavings and *boerewors* (beef

sausage with coriander) to a new public. The menu is largely South African, and while soups and more substantial hot dishes are available, it's the sandwiches that are the mainstay.

Stromboli

20 Bruntsfield Place (229 7247). Bus 11, 15, 16, 17, 23, 45. **Open** 9am-5pm Mon-Sat. **Credit** MC, V. **Map** p309 D8.

Known as the Breadwinner bakery once upon a time, this establishment has happily reinvented itself as a café and takeaway. There are trendy-looking liquid-filled tables and an abstract expressionist painting of the eponymous volcano to keep you amused while you tuck into utterly fabulous pies (puff pastry filled with assorted stir-fries), as well as all kinds of baked-on-the-premises savouries, pleasant pâtisseries, soups and salads.

Two Thin Laddies

103 High Riggs (229 0653). Bus 10, 11, 15, 16, 17, 23, 24, 270. **Open** 8am-5pm Mon-Sat; 10am-5pm Sun. **No credit cards**. **Map** p309 D7.

This friendly café at the heart of Tollcross opens early for those seeking breakfast en route to work (unlike some of the café-bars with supposed breakfast menus that only open at something approaching lunchtime). Bright and wholesome, with a menu that also features bakes, salads and the legend that is Two Thin Laddies' macaroni cheese.

West Edinburgh

Cornerstone Café

St John's Church, corner of Princes Street & Lothian Road (229 0212). Princes Street buses. **Open** 9.30am-4pm Mon-Sat; extended hours during Festival. **No credit cards**. **Map** p304 A2.

This well located café is a popular lunch time haunt for many weary shoppers and hungry office workers. The Cornerstone (although this one has not been rejected) is housed in the vaults of the Episcopalian Church of St John's (*see p90*) and serves up reasonable salads, baked spuds and the stomach filling like. After refreshment, contemplation: upstairs is the best stained glass collection in Scotland. In the summer, people seem to like sitting on the terrace outside by the cemetery and peering at the adjacent gravestones, perhaps pondering mortality. No smoking.

Leith

Café Truva

77 The Shore (554 5502). Bus 1, 16, 22, 35, 36. **Open** 9am-6.30pm daily. **Credit** AmEx, MC, V. **Map** p311 Jy.

A wee Turkish delight of a café right down by the rejuvenated waterside in Leith. It's not big but it can serve the kind of light meals and sweets that might just remind you of holiday trips to that end of the Mediterranean (yes, moussaka, of course; but also alternative breakfasts, filo pastry savouries and teeth-melting baklava). Ideal for summer afternoons.

Pubs

It's a drinking thing.

Top
five

Unusual
boozers

Medina
Lie on a cushion in an Old Town basement, enjoy the North African-themed decor, chill out to the DJ, and – bliss – drink until 3am *(see p166)*.

Dome
Excess all areas with overblown Victorian splendour *(see p169)*.

Fopp
A tiny bar selling bottled beer and wine in the city's best CD emporium *(see p169)*.

Ocean Bar
Wonderful harbour views and retail-a-go-go in a Conran shopping centre *au bord de la mer* *(see p172)*.

Scotch Malt Whisky Society Members' Room
Club-like atmosphere with the rarest single malt whiskies on the planet *(see p173)*.

Twenty years ago, pointing out a pub in Edinburgh was a simple task. There were classics that had survived from the late Victorian era or before (**Bennet's**, *see p170*, or the **Guildford Arms**, *see p169*, for example), then there was a whole tranche of dull establishments where people went to drink mass-produced fizzy beers and lagers. Since the early 1980s, however, this scene has changed beyond recognition. The revival of cask ales has seen some bars taking a little more care with their beer for one thing – both in terms of selection and handling. A spin-off from this is that traditional bars have got more user-friendly. Meanwhile, the greater economic prosperity of the city in recent times has seen younger citizens looking for a way to dispose of their income – hence the growth of the style-bar phenomenon. The result? It can often be difficult to tell the difference now between a restaurant with an attached bar, a café-bar, and a pub that happens to sell decent food. All the establishments listed however have been chosen because they are good, entertaining, or just plain interesting places for a drink. Some may aspire to being grander than a simple 'pub' while others might have everything from live DJs to the best French lamb stew north of Calais. But mainly, it's a drinking thing.

Old Town

Bannermans

212 Cowgate (556 3254). Nicolson Street–North Bridge buses. **Open** noon-1am Mon-Sat; 12.30pm-1am Sun. **Food served** 6-10pm Mon-Thur; noon-10pm Fri, Sat; 12.30-10pm Sun. **Credit** AmEx, DC, MC, V. **Map** p304 D3.

The Cowgate is an urban canyon, dreary by day and bordering on the completely insane by night. In the middle of all this is Bannermans. Its nooks and crannies have seen some history and it is the best of the bunch down this street.

Bar Kohl

54-55 George IV Bridge (225 6936). Bus 23, 27, 28, 41, 42, 45. **Open** 4.30pm-1am daily. **Credit** MC, V. **Map** p304 C3.

Bar Kohl offers dance music, a regular clientele, and a vast range of different flavours and brands of vodka. You get the real deal here with imported Russian and Polish varieties.

Black Bo's

57-61 Blackfriars Street (557 6136). Nicolson Street–North Bridge buses. **Open** 4pm-1am daily. **No credit cards. Map** p310 G5.

A mainstay of any self-respecting local bohemian, the place is tiny and by about 10pm it's usually packed and enveloped in a thick fug of blue smoke. DJs play but the emphasis is on convivial, half-cut banter. There's a pool table and the pub's namesake restaurant is next door (*see p135*).

Bow Bar

80 West Bow (226 7667). Bus 23, 27, 28, 41, 42, 45. **Open** noon-11.30pm Mon-Sat; 12.30-11pm Sun. **Credit** MC, V. **Map** p304 C3.

The Bow offers one of the largest ranges of Scotch whiskies of any pub in the city, and backs this up with a selection of Scottish and English cask ales that includes real rarities.

Doric Tavern

15-16 Market Street (225 1084). Bus 23, 27, 28, 41, 42, 45. **Open** noon-1am Mon-Sat; 12.30pm-1am Sun. **Food served** noon-10pm daily. **Credit** AmEx, MC, V. **Map** p304 D2.

A ground floor pub with upstairs restaurant (*see p133*), the Doric is a simple establishment with decent pub grub. Just right, whether you're killing time before a train (Waverley station is across the street) or whiling away an afternoon.

Ensign Ewart

521 Lawnmarket, Royal Mile (225 7440). Bus 23, 27, 28, 35, 41. **Open** 11am-11pm Mon-Thur; 11am-midnight Fri, Sat; 12.30pm-midnight Sun. **Food served** 11am-9.30pm Mon-Thur; 11am-7.30pm Fri-Sun. **No credit cards. Map** p304 C3.

This pub sits at the top of the Royal Mile and it's often packed out with visitors seeking the authentic Scottish drinking experience. And yet there's something about this establishment. Try it on a quiet February night when there's no one around and frost has settled on the cobbles outside.

Medina

45-47 Lothian Street (225 6313). Bus 23, 27, 28, 41, 42, 45. **Open** 10pm-3am daily. **Credit** MC, V. **Map** p309 F6.

Downstairs from Negociants café-bar (*see p154*), Medina is half club, half bar, and 100% ersatz North African. Most nights there's a cover charge but it's never a bank-breaker and the music in this basement venue varies from hip hop to Latin to live acoustic sets. Pull up a cushion, kick back, and chill.

Royal Oak

1 Infirmary Street (557 2976). Nicolson Street–North Bridge buses. **Open** 9am-2am Mon-Fri; 11.30am-2am Sat; 12.30pm-2am Sun. **No credit cards. Map** p310 G6.

This celebrated folk-music pub has a tiny ground floor bar and a larger basement bar – both looking more plush these days following a bit of a clean up.

The best Alfresco drinks

Near the university

In the wild west of Lothian Street, both **Negociants** (*see p154*) and **Assembly** (*see p152*) have tables outside in summer. So do **Human Be-In** (*see p158*) and the capaciously beer-gardened **Pear Tree** (*see p171*).

Broughton Street

One of Edinburgh's prime people-watching patches with good alfresco drinking facilities. The **Outhouse** has a gazebo (*see p157*), and there are outside tables at **PopRokit** (*see p170*) and **Baroque** (*see p157*).

Leith

On the east side of the Water of Leith, try the **Shore** (*see p150*), **Malmaison** (*see p159*), or the **Lighthouse** (*see p172*). On the west side, there's the **Waterfront** (*see p150*).

The Grassmarket

Lots of pubs with pavement tables for an alfresco pint.

Around the Royal Mile

Particularly during August, try **Café Hub, EH1**, the **City Café** or **Ecco Vino** (for all of these, *see p153*).

A wee dram? A fine cigar? A helping of baroque excess? The **Dome**. *See p169.*

Entertainment consists of regular sessions in both from around 9.30pm (musicians just turn up, order a pint and play). There's also an afternoon music session on Sundays: ideal for a weekend linger.

Sandy Bell's

25 Forrest Road (225 2751). Bus 35/Nicolson Street–North Bridge buses. **Open** noon-1am Mon-Sat; 12.30-11pm Sun. **No credit cards**. **Map** p309 F6.
No frills, just a space for drink and music. There's a folk session every weeknight, from around 9pm, and also on weekend afternoons. You get the gist of the place from the bust of Hamish Henderson above the bar: Scottish cultural hero and the writer of 'Freedom Come All Ye' (the alternative national anthem).

Scotsman Lounge

73 Cockburn Street (225 7726). Nicolson Street–North Bridge buses. **Open** 6am-1am Mon-Sat; 12.30pm-1am Sun. **No credit cards**. **Map** p304 D2.
Have you ever woken up at 6am and thought, 'What I need is a pint of lager'? Hopefully not; but for night-shift workers, clubbers who haven't come down yet, and passing punters with a desperate thirst, the Scotsman opens when the rest of Edinburgh hasn't. It's far from salubrious, but it does have definite character and live music on some evenings.

Villager

49-50 George IV Bridge (226 2781). Bus 23, 27, 28, 41, 42, 45. **Open** noon-1am daily. **Food served** noon-9.30pm Mon-Thur, Sun; noon-9pm Fri, Sat. **Credit** AmEx, MC, V. **Map** p304 C3.
Almost every bar that has opened in Edinburgh in recent years could be described as a 'style bar'. And lo, in late 2003, along came Villager. For the moment, it's the happening new place, but does the city have too many formulaic style bars? The fate of Villager could answer that question.

Whistlebinkie's

6 Niddry Street (557 5114). Nicolson Street–North Bridge buses. **Open** 5pm-3am daily. **Credit** MC, V. **Map** p304 D3.
Edinburgh's late-night, pub-rock hangout par excellence. It doesn't even open until evening but then stays awake until 3am and there's always some sort of live band doing folk, covers, indie, ska, or Latino. It used to have a reputation as a real grungy cellar but a refurb tidied up the old place nicely, although there's still a subterranean feel.

New Town

Abbotsford

3 Rose Street (225 5276). Princes Street buses. **Open** 11am-11pm Mon-Sat. **Food served** noon-3pm Mon-Sat. **Credit** MC, V. **Map** p304 C1.
Rose Street was once a place for student pub crawls and stag parties. The crowds have moved on but the Abbotsford's simplicity and Victorian authenticity have endured. While its neighbours now include music stores and sushi bars, you can slide quietly in here for pint of cask ale and a steak pie at lunchtime, or just sit with a whisky during an afternoon. A real old school pub.

Café Royal Circle Bar

19 West Register Street (556 1884). Princes Street buses. **Open** 11am-11pm Mon-Wed; 11am-midnight Thur; 11am-1am Fri, Sat; 12.30-11pm Sun. **Food served** 11am-10pm daily. **Credit** AmEx, DC, MC, V. **Map** p304 D1.
The island bar dominates this attractive pub where the walls are decorated with 19th-century Royal Doulton tiles of famous inventors. It can get busy, especially in the early evening after work. High-standard snacks are available (including oysters).

Eat, Drink, Shop

Pubs

Clark's Bar
142 Dundas Street (556 1067). Bus 23, 27. **Open** 11am-11pm Mon-Thur; 11am-11.30pm Fri-Sat; 12.30-11pm Sun. **No credit cards. Map** p306 E3.
Sparse and traditional, this old 'howf' has red leather seats, shiny brass table tops and a dark red ceiling. It hasn't changed in years (probably since opening in 1899). Reasonable whisky selection, some cask ale, and basic food (toasties and baguettes). Clark's is a welcome find.

Cumberland Bar
1-3 Cumberland Street (558 3134). Bus 23, 27. **Open** 11am-1am Mon-Sat; 12.30pm-1am Sun. **Food served** noon-3pm daily. **Credit** MC, V. **Map** p306 E3.
One of Edinburgh's classic cask-ale pubs, this is a very well-kept establishment in the heart of the New Town. Its decor is predominantly wooden, with a nod to tradition, but light and spacious. It's no misogynistic drinking den, however; there's a selection of wine and a beer garden (sheer joy in summer). The nine or so cask ales on tap change regularly; bar food includes toasties and paninis.

Dome
14 George Street (624 8624). Bus 13, 19, 28, 40, 41, 42/Princes Street buses. **Open** *Main bar* 10am-late Mon-Wed, Sun; 11am-1am Thur-Sat, *Frazer's bar* 10am-late Thur-Sat. **Food served** noon-10pm Mon-Wed, Sun; noon-11pm Thur-Sat. **Credit** AmEx, DC, MC, V. **Map** p304 B1.
Underneath the vaulted cupola of this grandiose former bank building is a large central bar surrounded by carefully placed seating and plants. It's so extravagant, it's almost silly and therein lies the appeal. There's also a quite expensive restaurant.

Fishtank
16a Queen Street (226 5959). Bus 13, 19, 28, 40, 41, 42/Princes Street buses. **Open** 4pm-1am Mon-Sat; 6pm-1am Sun. **Credit** MC, V. **Map** p306 D4.
A basement, a bar, some seats, and some fish (in a small aquarium). Essentially, that's all there is to Fishtank: stylish in a lazy kind of way, slightly rough around the edges, and well hidden from passing impulse drinkers. It occasionally functions as a pre-club bar and has DJs doing the DJ thing.

Fopp
7-15 Rose Street (220 0310/www.fopp.co.uk). Princes Street buses. **Open** noon-9pm Mon-Sat; 1-6pm Sun. **Credit** AmEx, MC, V. **Map** p304 B2.
Fopp is the kind of music shop (cheap CDs, vinyl, pop culture books) people learn to love. In 2002, it opened its second branch in Edinburgh, but with something extra: a bar. It's in a corner of the first floor. So if you're dithering over which CD to buy, stop and have a drink instead. Genius.

Guildford Arms
1-5 West Register Street (556 4312). Princes Street buses. **Open** 11am-11pm Mon-Thur; 11am-midnight Fri, Sat; 12.30-11pm Sun. **Food served** noon-2.30pm, 6-9.30pm daily. **Credit** MC, V. **Map** p304 D1.

Established in 1898, with a few nooks and crannies, and a gallery dining space, the Guildford is bang in the city centre, but quite discreet given its position off the east end of Princes Street. It has an excellent, rotating selection of cask ales. It's ornate, it does pub food, but the beer's the thing.

Kays Bar
39 Jamaica Street (225 1858). Bus 13, 19A, 24, 28, 28A. **Open** 11am-midnight Mon-Thur; 11am-1am Fri, Sat; 12.30-11pm Sun. **Food served** noon-2.30pm daily. **Credit** MC, V. **Map** p306 D4.
This building housed a wine merchant for more than 150 years until it morphed into a pub in 1976 – so drink has been the mainstay here for nearly two centuries. It now has a reputation as a somewhat patrician New Town 'howf', with an excellent choice of around 50 single malt whiskies.

Oxford Bar
8 Young Street (539 7119/www.oxfordbar.com). Bus 13, 19, 29, 37, 41, 42. **Open** 11am-1am Mon-Sat; 12.30pm-midnight Sun. **No credit cards. Map** p304 A1.
The Oxford has one of the most cramped bars in the city, the walls in the side room are the colour of congealed mustard, and there's a general air of dowdiness that complements the establishment's odd bare lightbulb. So why drink here? Because it cussedly ploughs its own furrow and gives not a damn for the white noise of contemporary style. Also has minor celebrity status as a haunt of Inspector Rebus from the Ian Rankin novels.

Stockbridge

Antiquary
72-78 St Stephen Street (225 2858). Bus 23, 27. **Open** 11.30am-midnight Mon-Thur; 11.30am-1am Fri, Sat; 11am-midnight Sun. **Food served** noon-2.30pm Mon-Sat; 11am-2.30pm Sun. **Credit** MC, V. **Map** p306 D3.
A long, basement pub that is split into two sections by the bar; the old stone walls and other original features are rather upstaged by modern additions like flat-screen TVs. Big Sunday breakfasts though.

Avoca
4-6 Dean Street (315 3311). Bus 19A, 24, 28. **Open** 11am-midnight Mon-Thur, Sun; 11am-1am Fri, Sat. **Food served** noon-7.30pm daily. **Credit** MC, V. **Map** p305 C3.
Despite being named after *Ballykissangel's* village, Avoca is nothing like some of the 'Oirish' pubs that spread across Edinburgh in the 1990s. Instead, it's a modern neighbourhood bar in the city's most bourgeois *quartier*. Wooden fittings, friendly staff, a sense of warmth and decent bar food.

Bailie
2 St Stephen Street (225 4673). Bus 23, 27. **Open** 11am-midnight Mon-Thur; 11am-1am Fri, Sat; 11am-12.30am Sun. **Food served** 11am-5pm daily. **Credit** MC, V. **Map** p306 D3.

Eat, Drink, Shop

Time Out Edinburgh **169**

The Bailie is a basement space of cigarette smoke and quality beer that somehow manages to combine an atmosphere of old money and Stockbridge bohemia, with an island bar providing the focus. It hasn't changed in years. A good thing.

Calton Hill & Broughton

Barony
81-83 Broughton Street (557 0546/www.barony bar.co.uk). Bus 8/Playhouse buses. **Open** 11am-midnight Mon-Thur; 11am-1am Fri, Sat; 12.30-11pm Sun. **Food served** 11am-10pm Mon-Sat; 12.30-10pm Sun. **Credit** MC, V. **Map** p306 F3.
A very traditional looking pub, the Barony has cask ales with regular guest rarities, offers a menu of basic pub grub, and has live music on Sunday nights. The atmosphere wouldn't be entirely out of place in one of the neighbouring style bars though.

Cask & Barrel
115 Broughton Street (556 3132). Bus 8/Playhouse buses. **Open** 11am-12.30am Mon-Wed; 11am-1am Thur-Sat; 12.30-11.30pm Sun. **Food served** noon-2pm daily; *snacks* noon-late daily. **Credit** MC, V. **Map** p306 F3.
Beer heaven. As well as local brews, there are English and obscure Scottish artisan cask ales on tap, while the bottled beers come from Germany and the Low Countries. Wherever you are in the bar, you'll be able to see one of the TV screens, often showing the football.

Pivo Caffé
2-6 Calton Road (557 2925). Bus 30, 40. **Open** 4pm-3am daily. **Credit** AmEx, MC, V. **Map** p307 G5.
Despite its Czech theme, and lagers to match, Pivo's main selling point is that it's a late-night DJ bar. Some of the spinners (especially Thursday to Saturday) are well known on the Scottish scene.

PopRokit
2 Picardy Place (556 4272). Playhouse buses. **Open** 11am-1am Mon-Sat; noon-1am Sun. **Food served** noon-7pm daily. **Credit** MC, V. **Map** p307 G4..
A busy pre-club bar with minimalist decor. Hang out in the ground-floor area where the glass windows look out to Picardy Place or head downstairs to the big basement where DJs, funky lighting and coloured walls keep the party atmosphere alive in the evening. There's food available during the day, and seating outside during Scotland's brief summer.

Arthur's Seat

Sheep Heid Inn
43-45 The Causeway (656 6951). Bus 4, 44, 45. **Open** 11am-11pm Mon-Wed; 11am-midnight Thur-Sat; 12.30-11pm Sun. **Food served** noon-3pm, 6-9pm Mon-Fri; noon-8pm Sat, Sun. **Credit** AmEx, MC, V.
As close as you'll come to an authentic, historical country pub in Edinburgh. Legend has it that the pub received its name from the motif on a snuff box

Gordon **Bennet's**! A proper pub.

gifted by James VI of Scotland before he legged it to London to become James I & VI of Great Britain. The food's good, the beer's well kept, and there are few finer ends to a tramp over Arthur's Seat.

South Edinburgh

Bennet's
8 Leven Street (229 5143). Bus 11, 15, 16, 17, 23, 45. **Open** 11am-12.30am Mon-Wed; 11am-1am Thur-Sat; noon-11.30pm Sun. **Food served** noon-3pm, 5-8.30pm daily. **Credit** MC, V. **Map** p309 D7.
A Victorian design marvel. The long, wooden bar occupies one side of the main room, with alcoves along the top of the gantry for the huge selection of single malts (around 100), while the opposite wall has fitted red leather seats and more wooden surrounds. Some cask ales and hearty pub grub are available.

Canny Man's
237 Morningside Road (447 1484). Bus 11, 15, 16, 18. **Open** noon-11pm Mon-Wed; noon-midnight Thur, Sat; noon-1am Fri; 12.30-11pm Sun. **Food served** noon-3pm, 6.30-9pm Mon-Fri; noon-3pm Sat; 12.30-3pm Sun. **No credit cards**.
It looks as if it was decorated by a mad maiden aunt from the late Victorian era, it's been around since 1871, has the biggest selection of single malt whiskies of any Edinburgh bar, a good wine list and offers among the most ambitious pub food in the city. The sign by the door says, 'Dress smart but casual' – so don't say you weren't warned.

Cloisters
26 Brougham Street (221 9997). Bus 11, 15, 16, 17, 23, 45. **Open** noon-midnight Mon-Thur, Sun; noon-12.30am Fri, Sat. **Food served** noon-6pm daily. **Credit** MC, V. **Map** p309 D7.

A life on the **Ocean Bar**. *See p172.*

Housed in a former manse, and physically attached to a church, the decor is simple, but it's rare cask ale that's the big selling point here, not cutting-edge interior design. Does OK on the whisky front too, with around 40 on the shelf.

Meadow Bar

42-44 Buccleuch Street (667 6907). Bus 41, 42. **Open** 11am-1am daily. **No credit cards.** **Map** p310 G7.
A student paradise around the corner from the main university buildings, the Meadow has sofas for slumping, drinks promotions, cheap snack food and is slightly ramshackle. A good place to go to meet drunken English lit student.

Pear Tree House

36 West Nicolson Street (667 7533). Nicolson Street - North Bridge buses. **Open** 11am-midnight Mon-Thur; 11am-1am Fri, Sat; 12.30pm-midnight Sun. **Food served** noon-2.30pm Mon-Fri. **No credit cards. Map** p310 G7.
Literally over the road from Edinburgh University, the Pear Tree's cobbled beer garden has seen generations of thirsty students. Inside, the decor is traditional Scottish pub, apart from the big screen for the football. Out of term time, it is unusually placid.

Athletic Arms

1-3 Angle Park Terrace (337 3822). Bus 4, 28, 35. **Open** noon-midnight Mon-Thur; 11am-midnight Fri, Sat; 12.30-6pm Sun. **Food served** throughout day. **No credit cards. Map** p308 A8.
Before the cask ale boom and the style-bar trend there were few classic pubs in Edinburgh – but this was one. Everyone used to call it Diggers, as

gravediggers used to come here from the cemetery across the street. Then it was famous for serving the best pint of McEwan's 80/- in the city. Nowadays, its reputation has waned. Worth checking out, though, to see what a good pub used to be like.

Caledonian Ale House

1-3 Haymarket Terrace (337 1006). Bus 2, 3, 4, 21, 25. **Open** 11am-12.30am Mon-Sat; noon-12.30am Sun. **Food served** 11am-5pm Mon-Sat; noon-5pm Sun. **Credit** DC, MC, V. **Map** p308 B6.
Next to Haymarket Station, the Caledonian is a haven for travellers killing time before a train. With a bistro upstairs, the bar food is a cut above the usual standard. There are some decent cask ales and it's generally more gender mixed than the other robust drinking dens in these parts.

Caley Sample Room

58 Angle Park Terrace (337 7204). Bus 4, 28, 35. **Open** 11.30am-midnight Mon-Thur; 11.30am-1am Fri, Sat; 12.30pm-midnight Sun. **Food served** 11.30am-9pm Mon-Sat; 12.30-9pm Sun. **Credit** MC, V. **Map** p308 A8.
The Caley is red brick on the outside, roomy on the inside, with wooden benches in the middle of the room and a simple, functional decor. It's just a few minutes' walk from the Caledonian Brewery, so a good place to sample the beers brewed there.

Cramond Inn

30 Cramond Glebe Road (336 2035). Bus 41, 42. **Open** 11am-11pm Mon-Thur; 11am-midnight Fri, Sat; 12.30-11pm Sun. **Food served** 12.30-2pm, 6-9pm Mon-Fri; noon-9pm Sat; 12.30-9pm Sun. **Credit** MC, V.
Tucked away in Cramond, a conservation village on the coast, this pub is quite cramped, with nooks and crannies to get holed up in. It gets very busy on summer Sundays when Edinburgh folk go for a walk.

Sitting on the dock of the bar. **Starbank Inn**. *See p173.*

Golden Rule

28-30 Yeaman Place (622 7112). Bus 4, 28, 35.
Open 11am-11.30pm Mon-Thur; 11am-midnight Fri,
Sat; 12.30-11pm Sun. **Credit** MC, V. **Map** p308 B8.
A grand old-fashioned pub, the Golden Rule is much
respected for the quality of its drink, with as many
as eight cask ales on offer at one time. The western
reaches of Edinburgh tend to lose out when it comes
to good food and drink, so this is a bit of a gem.

Leith & Newhaven

Cameo Bar

*23 Commercial Street (554 9999). Bus 1, 6, 22, 35,
36, 49.* **Open** noon-1am daily. **Food served** noon-
10pm daily. **Credit** MC, V. **Map** p311 Hx.
Steadily building a name for itself, the Cameo has
everything from decent bar food to decadent velvet
booth seating, a big screen for the football, occasional live music and even a six-hole putting green
out the back. It's a fun place for a drink or bar snack.

Cougar Lounge

*28 Bernard Street (476 8080). Bus 1, 6, 22, 35, 36,
49.* **Open** 11am-1am daily. **Food served** 11am-6pm
daily. **Credit** MC, V. **Map** p311 Ky.
Over the last years, this establishment seems to have
gone through as many incarnations as Doctor Who.
No modern style bar in these premises has caught
on – perhaps because modern design flourishes were
being shoehorned into a very traditional building.

King's Wark

36 The Shore (554 9260). Bus 1, 6, 22, 35, 36, 49.
Open noon-11pm Mon-Thur; noon-midnight Fri,
Sat; 11am-midnight Sun. **Food served** noon-3pm,
6-10pm Mon-Sat; 11am-3pm, 6-10pm Sun. **Credit**
MC, V. **Map** p311 Jy.

This is definitely a pub – snug, neat, wooden-clad,
candlelit, and in premises dating from the early 17th
century. It serves good cask ale and fantastic bar
food (no surprise since it also has a tiny and capable restaurant). There's also a presentable wine list.

Lighthouse

*32-34 The Shore (554 9465). Bus 1, 6, 22, 35, 36,
49.* **Open** 11am-1am Mon-Sat; noon-1am Sun. **Food
served** 11am-9.45pm Mon-Sat; noon-9.45pm Sun.
Credit AmEx, MC, V. **Map** p311 Jy.
Another year, another style bar. The Lighthouse
landed in 2003, overlooking the Water of Leith itself.
There are a few restaurant tables on the mezzanine
floor, but on ground level the Lighthouse has more
the look and feel of a bright contemporary bar than
a destination diner. Upstairs, there's another bar
with a mellower ambience.

Noble's

*44A Constitution Street (554 2024). Leith Walk
buses.* **Open** 11am-midnight Mon-Wed, Sun; 11am-
1am Thur-Sat. **Food served** noon-3pm Mon-Fri.
Credit MC, V. **Map** p311 Jz.
Catch Noble's at a weekday lunchtime and office
staff will be tucking into basic bar food. On Friday
and Saturday nights it has live music. On a quiet
afternoon there's time to sit and watch the light flood
through the stained-glass windows. This is a classic, well-kept, wood 'n' leather Victorian-style pub
that aims for a new guest cask ale every week.

Ocean Bar

*Ocean Terminal, Ocean Drive (553 8073). Bus 1, 6,
22, 35, 36, 49.* **Open** noon-midnight Mon-Thur,
Sun; noon-1am Fri, Sat. **Credit** AmEx, MC, V.
Map p311 Hx.
On the first floor of the Ocean Terminal shopping
centre, the Ocean Bar has splendid views across the

harbour. The terrace and balconies are done out in slatted wood, reminiscent of a ship; inside, coloured booths and bar stools add to the bright and breezy atmosphere. This is one of the most unusual places to quaff in the whole city.

Old Chain Pier

32 Trinity Crescent (552 1233). Bus 10, 11, 16, 32. **Open** noon-11pm Mon-Wed, Sun; noon-midnight Thur-Sat. **Food served** noon-9.45pm Mon-Sat; noon-8pm Sun. **Credit** MC, V.

The bar with everything? The OCP is literally perched on the sea wall; on wild nights, when there's a high tide and the wind is up, spray even flecks the windows. The cask ale is well cared for, with usually five on offer, and the bar food is great. Watch the ships pass along the Forth by day and the lights flickering on the Fife coast at night; you might even see the occasional heron.

Pond

2 Bath Road (467 3825). Bus 12, 16, 35, 36. **Open** 1pm-1am daily. **No credit cards.**

The pub at the end of the universe. The Pond lies in an unlovely street between Leith Links and the docks. The interior resembles a hand-knitted university common room dumped in the middle of nowhere, That said, if you get a pint of German wheat beer, a bag of bombay mix and slump in one of the sofas, it can seem like a home from home.

Port O' Leith

58 Constitution Street (554 3568). Leith Walk buses. **Open** 9am-1am Mon-Sat; 12.30pm-1am Sun. **No credit cards. Map** pp311 Jz.

A legend. You could sit for hours looking at the detail: ships' flags, lifebelts, snuff for sale, and more. It's a small, oddly neat pub patronised by everyone from merchant mariners (the docks are nearby) to locals and students. Loads of character: essence of Leith.

Scotch Malt Whisky Society Members' Room

The Vaults, 87 Giles Street (555 2266). Bus 1, 22, 35, 36, 49. **Open** 10am-5pm Mon, Tue; 10am-11pm Wed-Sat; 11am-10pm Sun. **Food served** noon-2.30pm Mon-Sat; 12.30-2.30pm Sun. **Credit** AmEx, MC, V. **Map** p311 Jy.

This is a private club with the distinguished look of a crusty gentlemen's haunt in central London. Fortunately, the joining fee isn't prohibitive and the membership encompasses a wide range of ages, and both genders. Basically, it's the prime place in the city to drink the rarest single malt Scotch on the planet. The society buys single casks of whisky from distilleries, bottles it, then sells it to members only. You can buy bottles to take home, or just sample a range of drams. Whisky bliss.

Starbank Inn

64 Laverockbank Road (552 4141). Bus 10, 11, 16, 32. **Open** 11am-11pm Mon-Wed; 11am-midnight Fri, Sat; noon-11pm Sun. **Food served** noon 2.30pm, 6-9pm Mon-Fri; all day Sat, Sun. **Credit** MC, V. **Map** p311 Dx.

Set back on the other side of the road from the sea wall, and slightly raised, the Starbank arguably has better views of the Forth than the nearby Old Chain Pier (*see above*). Like its neighbour, it has a reputation for good pub food and well-kept cask ales.

Eat, Drink, Shop

Drinking till dawn

Can you drink in Edinburgh around the clock? More or less. Would you want to? Well, would you? There are a handful of bars on Leith Walk and the city centre that open at 5 or 6am – a quirk of the licensing laws that people usually explain with talk of night-shift workers, 'the docks', and the city's old industries. Whether or not anyone really emerges from a night-shift and then heads for a pint of lager before breakfast is a moot point: anyone who *needs* a drink at that time are should really be seeking professional help.

In any event, some of the early riser establishments are hardly the loveliest places to enjoy a pint, although one exception is the **Scotsman Lounge** (*see p167*). Once you've managed the first couple of hours, though, you can move on to the **Port O' Leith** (*see above*), which opens at 9am. By noon, virtually all the pubs and café-bars listed in this guide will have opened their doors, so

choosing where to go won't be a problem again until late. Most pubs close at 11pm or midnight, although a few like **Black Bo's** (*see p166*) keep going until 1am. **Whistlebinkies** (*see p223*) is open until 3am, as are café-bars like **Negociants** (*see p154*) or **Favorit** (*see p154*). After that, you're struggling. During the Festival, some pubs and bars extend their opening hours till 5am, but for the other 11 months of the year the options are limited. The well-heeled could try room service in a hotel, the desperate could try a park bench and a bottle of cider. The crafty might go somewhere like **Pizza Paradise** (4-6 South Bridge, Old Town; 557 4905), which stays open until 5am and serves wine or beer as long as you're eating. Red wine and a pre-breakfast pizza with extra anchovies to conclude a 24-hour drinking binge? Frankly, if you've been mad enough to drink round the clock it's all you deserve.

Shops & Services

Kilts, Scotch and whisky-flavoured condoms may be here in abundance, but you will also find food, fashion and other fripperies.

For all your tartan needs. The **Royal Mile**. *See p190.*

Princes Street is the retail heart of Edinburgh. Said to be the only major shopping street in the world to have outlets only on one side, it sports spectacular views over the Castle and the Scott Monument. Depressingly, however, much of what it has to offer can be found in the wallet-withering retail parks of any UK city: from Marks & Spencer through to Debenhams and H&M. The only real exception is the quintessentially Scottish **Jenners** (*see p175*). If we are what we buy, Princes Street is the route to a drone civilisation of identikit chino-wearing culture consumers.

But all is not lost. To find a bit of commercial class and individuality, take a stroll along George Street, parallel to Princes Street. There, upmarket chain stores such as Karen Millen and Pink can be found alongside branches of Bonhams, and Hamilton and Inches. For the truly 'Scottish' shopping experience, head out to Morningside, Bruntsfield and Stockbridge. Purchase a haggis from the high quality delicatessens scattered around these parts, such as **Peckham's** (*see p184*) in Bruntsfield, or

buy hand-crafted toys from the **Owl & the Pussycat** (*see p192*). Edinburgh is steeped in history (some would say stifled) and buying a little piece of it is easy (there's plenty to go round). There's no better place for take-away histori-junk than the Royal Mile. While tartan-tat and 'I'm a wee monster' T-shirts are available in ready supply, there are also some top notch goods in the form of fine Scottish whiskies from **Royal Mile Whiskies** (*see p186*), or Highland clobber from the flashy **Geoffrey (Tailor) Highland Crafts Shop** (*see p184* **The new Scotsman**).

If it's kooky originality you are looking for, stroll off the main thoroughfares and explore the independent shops and boutiques. Unconstrained by the tyranny of centrally generated sales targets and the fads of interior design, they are a haven of innovation and choice. Snaking back down the Mound towards Princes Street, Cockburn Street is best known for its array of independent music shops, including local favourites, **Fopp** (*see p189*) and **Underground Solu'shn** (*see p190*).

Eat, Drink, Shop

Victoria Street coils into the underbelly of the city from George IV Bridge, opening out on to the Grassmarket below. With a more vibrant, carnivalesque flair, it is a mecca for small trendy designer shops.

OPENING HOURS

Usual hours are from 9am to 6pm Monday to Saturday, but lots of places open late on Thursday and, despite the opposition of the churches and trades' unions, are also open on Sunday. Many shops keep longer hours during the Festival and before Christmas.

One-stop shopping

Department stores

The area around Princes Street has most of the major UK department stores but looking down its elegant classical nose at them all is Jenners, secure in its antiquity – it's passed its centenary, after all. John Lewis caters for everyday quality products, while the long awaited opening of Harvey Nichols adds a touch of class, and fun, to department store shopping in the capital.

Bhs

64 Princes Street, New Town (226 2621/ www.bhs.co.uk). Princes Street buses. **Open** 9am-5.30pm Mon-Wed; 9am-8pm Thur; 9am-6pm Fri, Sat; 11am-5pm Sun. **Credit** AmEx, MC, V. **Map** p304 B2.
Basic everyday fashion and household goods all available at reasonable prices.

Debenhams

109-112 Princes Street, New Town (225 1320/ www.debenhams.com). Princes Street buses. **Open** 9.30am-6pm Mon-Wed, Fri; 9.30am-8pm Thur; 9am-6pm Sat; 11am-6pm Sun. **Credit** AmEx, DC, MC, V. **Map** p304 B2.
Debenhams has hired fashion and interior designers to improve this branch in recent years, but the labyrinthine layout continues to baffle. Fashion, cosmetics and housewares can be found as expected.

Fraser's

145 Princes Street, New Town (225 2472/www. houseoffraser.co.uk). Princes Street buses. **Open** 9am-6pm Mon-Wed, Fri; 9am-7.30pm Thur; 9am-6pm Sat; 11am-5pm Sun (hours may vary according to season). **Credit** AmEx, MC, V. **Map** p304 B2.
Part of the reliable House of Fraser Stores, Fraser's sells a modest range of household appliances and fashion for all ages.

Harvey Nichols

30-34 St Andrew Square, New Town (524 8388/ www.harveynichols.com). Princes Street buses. **Open** 10am-6pm Mon-Wed; 10am-8pm Thur; 10am-7pm Fri, Sat; noon-6pm Sun. **Credit** AmEx, DC, MC, V. **Map** p304 D1.

The jewel of St Andrew Square, Harvey Nics brings Edinburgh shopping into the dizzying heights of cosmopolitan commerce. The best deals can be had on the top floor, where a truly imaginative international food-hall linked to the trendy Forth Floor bar (*see p138*) looks out across Princes Street and over to the flood-lit castle, offering spectacular glimpses of the Firth of Forth along the way.

Jenners

48 Princes Street, New Town (225 2442/ www.jenners.com). Princes Street buses. **Open** 9am-6pm Mon, Wed, Fri, Sat; 9.30am-6pm Tue; 9am-8pm Thur; 11am-5pm Sun (hours may vary according to season; phone for details). **Credit** AmEx, DC, MC, V. **Map** p304 B2.

Top five Designers

Cookie

29-31 Cockburn Street, Old Town (622 7260).
Eye-catching original designs alongside tortuously cute Yo! Japan dresses. Look out for the bright soft polka-dot bags from local designer Paperdoll.

Godiva

54 West Port, Old Town (221 9212).
Godiva buys in original designs from Edinburgh's College of Art. The designs tend to feature second-hand clothes torn and recycled into fairly priced exclusive styles. GSOH is essential.

Hatrix 13

Cowgatehead, Old Town (225 9222).
Redesigning the rules of millinery Fawns Reid's staggering array of hats are designed and hand-made onsite. A veritable wonderland of hats and accessories.

Impractical Clothes

5 East Fountainbridge, South Edinburgh (221 1722).
Supporting unknown Scottish designers Impractical Clothes for men and women is for the truly flamboyant. Denim G-strings by Cheekabo and the owner, Irene's, famous duffel bags to name a few choice items.

Joey D

54 Broughton Street, Broughton (557 6672).
Ripping the labels off jeans and shredding designer suits to strips, Joey D's is an alternative shopper's dream. Delicately crafted scraps create a sleek urban look.

Eat, Drink, Shop

The world's oldest independent department store, known as the Harrods of Scotland, Jenners opened its doors in 1895. Six stately floors brimming full of merchandise, including international designer wear, a huge toy department and a food hall specialising in Scottish and international delicacies. With an additional hair and beauty salon and a photographic studio, it's almost a self-contained village. A sight as well as a shop.

John Lewis
69 St James Centre, Leith Street, New Town (556 9121/www.johnlewis.com). Princes Street or Nicolson Street–North Bridge buses. **Open** *Jan-Nov* 9am-6pm Mon-Wed; 9.30am-8pm Thur; 9am-8pm Fri; 9am-6.30pm Sat; 11am-5pm Sun. *Dec* hours vary; phone for details. **Credit** MC, V. **Map** p307 G4.
Fairly priced, and modestly sized, John Lewis stocks everything from blank tapes to kitchen equipment, designer clothes, millinery and furniture.

Marks & Spencer
54 Princes Street, New Town (225 2301/ www.marksandspencer.com). Princes Street buses. **Open** 9am-6pm Mon-Wed, Fri; 9am-8pm Thur; 8.30am-6pm Sat; 11am-5pm Sun. **Credit** AmEx, MC, V. **Map** p304 B2.
Menswear, children's wear, housewares and food; for women's wear visit 91 Princes Street (225 2301). **Other location:** 21 Gyle Av, West Edinburgh (317 1333).

Shopping centres

Cameron Toll
6 Lady Road, South Edinburgh (666 2777/ www.camerontoll.co.uk). Bus 3, 8, 33, 80. **Open** 7.30am-10pm Mon-Sat; 8am-7pm Sun. **Credit** varies.
A large shopping complex about 15 minutes' bus journey south of the city centre dominated by Sainsbury's with around 50 other high-street outlets.

Fort Kinnaird Retail Park
Newcraighall Road, South Edinburgh (www.fort kinnaird.com). Bus 14. **Open** times vary. **Credit** varies.
Located 20 minutes' bus ride from the city centre, outlets include Next, Gap, H&M and Borders.

Gyle Centre
South Gyle Broadway, West Edinburgh (539 8828/ www.gyleshopping.com). Bus 2, 12, 18, 21, 22, 24, 38. **Open** 8am-10pm Mon-Fri; 8am-8pm Sat; 9am-7pm Sun. **Credit** varies.
Chain stores such as Marks & Spencer, Boots and Sainsbury's are laid out along with smaller fashion and gift shops in an attractive mall. The Centre is a 20-minute bus journey west out of the city.

Ocean Terminal
Ocean Drive, Leith (555 8888/www.ocean terminal.com). Bus 11, 22, 34, 35, 36, 49. **Open** 10am-8pm Mon-Fri; 10am-7pm Sat; 11am-6pm Sun. **Credit** varies. **Map** p311 Hx.

Ocean Terminal is the latest stage in the continuing transformation of Leith from former industrial wasteland to thriving commercial centre. High-street names dominate the shopping selection, but the centre itself is also worth visiting for the lovely views from its cruise-ship style balconies over the Forth (*see p172*).

Princes Mall
Princes Street (east end), New Town (557 3759/ www.princesmall-edinburgh.co.uk). Princes Street or Nicolson Street–North Bridge buses. **Open** *Jan-July, Sept-Nov* 8.30am-6pm Mon-Wed, Fri, Sat; 8.30am-7pm Thur; 11am-5pm Sun. *Aug, Dec* extended hours; phone for details. **Credit** varies. **Map** p304 D2.
On the site of an old fruit and veg market, this mall's crude exterior encroaches vulgarly on to the glorious vista from the east end of Princes Street. Inside are three bland floors of shopaholics' heaven.

St James Centre
Leith Street, New Town (557 0050/www.thestjames. com). Princes Street or Playhouse buses. **Open** 7.30am-6.30pm Mon-Wed, Sat; 7.30am-8.30pm Thur, Fri; 10.30am-5pm Sun. **Credit** varies. **Map** p307 G4.
Imprisoning a wide range of high-street shops in a depressing '70s-style concrete block, the St James Centre is in fact quite a busy and flourishing little mall with John Lewis at its heart.

Auctioneers & antiques

Look for the best selection of antique shops in Causewayside, sneaking a little glimpse along the Grassmarket on the way.

Architectural Salvage Yard
31 West Bowling Green Street, Leith (554 7077). Bus 8. **Open** 9am-5pm Mon-Fri; noon-5pm Sat. **Credit** MC, V. **Map** p311 Gz.
A plethora of trinkets and artefacts are stashed away in this giant warehouse in Leith.

Bonhams
65 George Street, New Town (225 2266/www. bonhams.com). Bus 28, 41/Princes Street buses. **Open** 9am-5.30pm Mon-Fri. **Credit** MC, V. **Map** p304 B1.
Upmarket antique dealer and valuer.

Books & magazines

At Festival time, the annual **Book Festival** is held on Charlotte Square in New Town, hosting talks and discussions with authors (*see p37*).

Analogue
102 West Bow, Victoria Street, Old Town (220 0601). Bus 23, 27, 41, 42. **Open** 10am-6pm Mon-Sat. *Aug, Dec* also noon-5pm Sun. **Credit** MC, V. **Map** p304 C3.
An interesting display of the latest in design and contemporary culture books. The friendly atmosphere and exclusive T-shirts make this shop an invaluable addition to Edinburgh's trendy Victoria Street.

Eat, Drink, Shop

Beyond Words

*42-44 Cockburn Street, Old Town (226 6636/
www.beyondwords.co.uk). Nicolson Street–North
Bridge buses.* **Open** 10am-6pm Mon-Sat; 1-5pm Sun.
Credit MC, V. **Map** p304 D3.

A small tranquil shop devoted to photography, with
titles covering topics from art and design to celebrity portraits. Also useful for finding more offbeat
visual mementos of Scotland.
Branch: 45 Broughton St, Broughton (556 3377).

Blackwell's

*53-62 South Bridge, Old Town (622 8222).
Nicolson Street–North Bridge buses.* **Open** 9am-8pm
Mon, Wed-Fri; 9.30am-8pm Tues; 10am-6pm Sat;
noon-5pm Sun. **Credit** AmEx, DC, MC, V.
Map p304 D3.

Predominantly an academic bookshop that caters
for university reading lists, Blackwell's also offers
a good selection of popular titles.

Deadhead Comics

*27 Candlemaker Row, Old Town (226 2774/www.
deadheadcomics.com). Bus 23, 27, 41, 42.* **Open**
10am-6pm Mon-Sat; 12.30-5.30pm Sun. **Credit** MC,
V. **Map** p309 F6.

Fans of mainstream Marvel and DC superhero titles
will find just what they want here. Deadhead also
stocks independent and small-press publications
and fantasy role-playing cards and figures.

International Newsagents

*351 High Street, Old Town (225 4827). Bus
35/Nicolson Street–North Bridge buses.* **Open**
Sept-July 6am-6pm Mon-Fri; 7am-7pm Sat; 7.30am-
5.30pm Sun. *Aug* 6am-11.30pm Mon-Fri; 6am-1am
Sat; 7.30am-5pm Sun. **Credit** MC, V.
Map p304 C/D3.

Does what its name says.

McNaughtons

*3a Haddington Place, Leith Walk, Broughton (556
5897). Playhouse buses.* **Open** 9.30am-5.30pm Tue-
Sat. **Credit** MC, V. **Map** p307 G3.

This gloomy-looking bookshop hides a haven of
high-quality second-hand literary treasures.

Ottakar's

*57 George Street, New Town (225 4495). Bus 28,
41, 42/Princes Street buses.* **Open** 9am-7pm Mon-
Wed, Fri, Sat; 9am-8pm Thur; 11.30am-5.30pm Sun.
Credit AmEx, MC, V. **Map** p304 B1.
Books etc.
Other location: 16 Cameron Toll, South Edinburgh
(666 1866).

Waterstone's

*128 Princes Street, New Town (226 2666/
www.waterstones.co.uk). Princes Street buses.* **Open**
8.30am-8pm Mon-Sat; 10.30am-7pm Sun. **Credit**
AmEx, DC, MC, V. **Map** p304 B2.

Book chain links with coffee chain – Starbucks – to
inject caffeine into biblio browsing.
Other locations: 13-14 Princes Street, New Town
(556 3034); 83 George Street, New Town (225 3436).

West Port Books

*145 West Port, South Edinburgh (229 4431). Bus 1,
2, 10, 11, 16, 17, 35.* **Open** 10.30am-5.30pm Mon,
Tue, Fri; noon-6pm Wed, Thur, Sat. **Credit** MC, V.
Map p309 E6.

A fantastically labyrinthine second-hand book shop
laid out in a veritable rabbit warren of rooms on two
floors, it over-flows with read and remaindered
books, classical records and sheet music (*see p119*
Books and bonking).

Word Power

*43 West Nicolson Street, South Edinburgh (662
9112/www.word-power.co.uk). Nicolson Street–North
Bridge buses.* **Open** *Jan-Nov* 10am-6pm Mon-Fri;
10.30am-6pm Sat; *Aug, Dec* also noon-5pm Sun.
Credit AmEx, DC, MC, V. **Map** p310 G7.

The only radical bookshop in Edinburgh is a vibrant
centre for the capital's alternative writing scene. The
owner hosts the annual Radical Book Fair in mid
May (*see p195*).

Dry-cleaners & launderettes

Johnsons Cleaners

*23 Frederick Street, New Town (225 8095/www.
johnsoncleaners.com). Princes Street buses.* **Open**
8am-5.30pm Mon-Fri; 8.30am-4pm Sat. **Credit** MC,
V. **Map** p304 B1.

Rapid dry-cleaning for last-minute tux disasters.
Other locations: 5 Drumsheugh Place, New Town
(225 8077); 12 Elm Row, Calton Hill (556 3802).

Kleen Cleaners

*10 St Mary's Street, Old Town (556 4337). Bus
35/Nicolson Street–North Bridge buses.* **Open** 1-5pm
Mon; 9am-5pm Tue-Fri; 10am-1pm Sat. **Credit** MC,
V. **Map** p310 G5.

Dry-cleaning, plus speedy repairs and alterations.

Sox in the City

*6 Jeffrey Street, Old Town (558 9605/www.ark.
ednet.co.uk). Nicolson Street–North Bridge buses.*
Open 9am-4pm Mon-Fri. **No credit cards.**
Map p310 G5.

This trendy launderette is a charitable organisation
that aims to cater for all the community by keeping
laundry prices cheap.

Fashion

For details of where to find independent
designers in Edinburgh, *see p175* **Top five**
Designers.

High fashion

Emporio Armani

*25 Multrees Walk, St Andrew Square, New Town
(523 1580/www.giorgioarmani.co.uk). Princes Street
buses.* **Open** 9.30am-6pm Mon-Wed, Fri, Sat; 9.30am-
8pm Thur; noon-5pm Sun. **Credit** AmEx, DC, MC, V.
Map p304 D1.

Analogue, not digital. See p177.

March 2004 saw the opening of the Emporio Armani store, the latest addition to Multrees Walk ('The Walk'), which is fast becoming one of the most prestigious shopping areas in the city.

Louis Vuitton

1-2 Multrees Walk, St Andrew Square, New Town (652 5900/www.vuitton.com). Princes Street buses. **Open** 9.30am-6pm Mon-Sat; noon-5pm Sun. **Credit** AmEx, DC, MC, V. **Map** p304 D1.

Spurred on by the arrival of the glitzy Harvey Nichols, the Louis Vuitton shop opened its doors in March 2003, just in time to celebrate the design house's 150th anniversary.

High street fashion

Big Ideas

96 West Bow, Grassmarket, Old Town (226 2532/ www.bigideasforladies.co.uk). Bus 2, 23, 27, 28, 42, 45. **Open** 10am-5.30pm Mon-Sat. **Credit** AmEx, MC, V. **Map** p304 B3.

A refreshingly bright and eye-catching range of day- and evening-wear for women of size 16 and upwards. Don't miss the permanent sales rails in the branch down the road.

Other location: 116 West Bow, Old Town (226 2532).

Corniche

2 Jeffrey Street, Old Town (556 3707). Bus 35/Nicolson Street–North Bridge buses. **Open** *Jan-July, Sept-Nov* 10am-5.30pm Mon-Sat. *Aug, Dec* also noon-4pm Sun. **Credit** AmEx, MC, V. **Map** p310 G5.

Bringing the latest trends from London and beyond, this hip little outlet does quietly what Harvey Nics has to shout about. Keep an eye out for Debbie Little's inspiring 'parachute dresses', and for the regular end-of-line specials. The branch next door stocks designer menswear.

Other location: 4 Jeffrey Street, Old Town (557 8333).

Crombie Retail

63 George Street, New Town (226 1612/www. crombie.co.uk). Bus 28, 41, 42/Princes Street buses. **Open** 9.30am-6pm Mon-Wed, Fri; 9.30am-7pm Thur; 9am-6pm Sat; noon-5pm Sun. **Credit** AmEx, MC, V. **Map** p304 B1.

Renowned worldwide for almost 200 years for the Crombie coat – beloved of American presidents, teddy boys and East End gangsters – the oak-panelled elegance of this gentlemen's outfitter sums up the classic, genteel side of the city. A classic Crombie, either single or double breasted, will set you back £499.

Cruise

14 St Mary's Street, Old Town (556 2532). Bus 35/Nicolson Street–North Bridge buses. **Open** 10am-6pm Mon-Wed, Fri; 10am-7pm Thur; 9.30am-6pm Sat; 11am-5pm Sun. **Credit** AmEx, DC, MC, V. **Map** p310 G5.

With designers such as Stone Island, Armani, Dolce & Gabbana and Hugo Boss – and prices to match – it's no wonder that this well established outlet is a fashion favourite for well-heeled clubbers and upmarket hipsters.

Eat, Drink, Shop

Browsing with the bull. **West Port Books**. *See p178.*

Cult Clothing

7-9 North Bridge, Old Town (556 5003). Nicolson Street–North Bridge buses. **Open** 9.30am-6pm Mon-Wed, Fri, Sat; 10am-7pm Thur; noon-5pm Sun. **Credit** AmEx, DC, MC, V. **Map** p304 D2.

Cult Clothing has become something of a fashion empire in its own right. Dressing every local university student in Bench wear and Carhartt gear, it is possibly the hippest shop in Edinburgh.

Jigsaw

49 George Street, New Town (225 4501). Bus 28, 41, 42/Princes Street buses. **Open** 10am-6pm Mon-Wed, Fri; 10am-7.30pm Thur; 9am-6pm Sat; noon-5pm Sun. **Credit** AmEx, MC, V. **Map** p304 B1.

This chain's stylish but wearable clothes (for the over-25s) remain perennially popular.

Karen Millen

53 George Street, New Town (220 1589/www.karenmillen.co.uk). Bus 28, 41, 42/Princes Street buses. **Open** 10am-6pm Mon-Wed, Fri, Sat; 10am-7pm Thur; noon-5pm Sun. **Credit** AmEx, MC, V. **Map** p304 B1.

Gorgeous dresses, jumpers and coats.

Momentum Surf Shop

22 Bruntsfield Place, South Edinburgh (229 6665/www.momentumsurfshop.com). Bus 10, 11, 15, 16, 17, 23. **Open** *Jan-July, Sept-Nov* 10am-6pm Tue-Sat; noon-4pm Sun. *Aug, Dec* also 10am-6pm Mon; 11am-5pm Sun. **Credit** MC, V. **Map** p309 D8.

Well-priced, high-quality skateboarding and surf-wear for all you dudes out there.

Odd One Out

16 Victoria Street, Old Town (220 6400/www.odd oneout.com). Bus 23, 27, 41, 42. **Open** 10am-6pm Mon-Sat; noon-5pm Sun. **Credit** AmEx, MC, V. **Map** p309 F6.

Fairly priced designer clothes for men with a little bit more flair and originality than most of the shops on Princes Street. There's also a reasonable selection of girls' clothes up the stairs.

Pie In The Sky

21 Cockburn Street, Old Town (220 1477). Bus 35/Nicolson Street–North Bridge buses. **Open** 9.30am-6pm Mon-Wed, Fri, Sat; 9.30am-7pm Thur; noon-5pm Sun. **Credit** AmEx, MC, V. **Map** p304 D3.

This student haunt has always been famous for its cheap tie-dye and rainbow clothes as well as its hats, bags, jewellery and incense. More recently it has branched out into the more feminine Funky Fish clothes label, selling flimsy dresses, floral boob-tubes and fitted hoodies.

TK Maxx

Meadowbank Retail Park, London Road, Calton Hill (661 6611/www.tkmaxx.co.uk). Bus 4, 5, 15, 44, 45. **Open** 10am-8pm Mon-Fri; 9am-6pm Sat; 11am-5.30pm Sun. **Credit** AmEx, MC, V.

A massive warehouse of end-of-line bargain-priced stock from such names as Prada, Red or Dead and Levi's. Men's, women's and children's clothing, plus a tumble of accessories, household goods and luggage. Be prepared to rake through rails and endure long queues, particularly at weekends.

Eat, Drink, Shop

Whistles

97 George Street, New Town (226 4398). Bus 28, 41, 42/Princes Street buses. **Open** 10am-6pm Mon-Wed, Fri; 10am-7.30pm Thur; 9am-6pm Sat; noon-5pm Sun. **Credit** AmEx, DC, MC, V. **Map** p304 B1.
Whistles' own range of fashionable, highly wearable and moderately expensive clothes sits well beside the other designer labels in stock.

Scottish casual fashion

For information on kilt hire, full Highland dress or accessories, *see p184* **The new Scotsman**.

Hawick Cashmere

71-81 Grassmarket, Old Town (225 8634/www. hawickcashmere.com). Bus 2, 23, 27, 28, 42, 45. **Open** *Oct-Mar* 10am-6pm Mon-Sat. *Apr-July, Sept* 10am-6pm Mon-Sat; 11am-4pm Sun. *Aug* 10am-7pm Mon-Fri; 10am-6pm Sat; 11am-4pm Sun. **Credit** AmEx, MC, V. **Map** p304 B3.
Although the minimalist appearance of this shop, topped with a few silently loitering sales assistants, may be a little intimidating at first sight, the factory made cashmere products do have quite a sense of humour. Made from Hawick Cashmere at the historic Trinity Mill, the products blend elegant, high quality, basic styles with diamante skulls or glittering explosions sewn boldly across the fronts and sides of the garments.

Isley Clothing

479 Lawnmarket, Old Town (225 4088). Bus 23, 27, 28, 35, 41, 42. **Open** 10am-6pm daily. Extended hours during Festival. **Credit** MC, V. **Map** p304 C3.
Tucked in between all the gimmicky shops along the Royal Mile, Isley Clothing has a colourful display of tartan skirts and stylish woollies for women of all ages. A subtle Scottish theme pervades, with high quality goods at reasonable prices.

Ness Scotland

367 High Street, Old Town (226 5227/www. nessclothing.com). Nicolson St–North Bridge buses. **Open** 10am-6pm daily; extended hours during Festival. **Credit** AmEx, MC, V. **Map** p304 C3.
Predominantly selling accessories such as bags, hats and scarves, most of the merchandise is made from 100% Scottish lambs' wool – ideal for friends and family back home.

Vintage

15 The Grassmarket

15 Grassmarket, Old Town (226 3087). Bus 2, 23, 27, 28, 35, 41, 42, 45. **Open** noon-6pm Mon-Fri; 10.30am-5.30pm Sat. **No credit cards**. **Map** p304 C3.
This cavern-like shop offers period lace, linen and velvet curtains, as well as clothing. Check out the pre-1950s men's suits, the tweed jackets and an impressive selection of trilby hats.

Herman Brown

151 West Port, South Edinburgh (228 2589). Bus 2, 28. **Open** 12.30-6pm Mon-Sat. **Credit** AmEx, MC, V. **Map** p309 E6.
Well-made second-hand and vintage clothes. Prices start from around £6 for tops and less than £15 for dresses, while authentic vintage items cost more. Herman Brown's eye-catching range of quirky jewellery and good selection of bags and accessories should complete the outfit.

Shoes

Carina Shoes

25 Jeffrey Street, Old Town (558 3344/ www.carinashoes.com). Bus 24, 35, 35A. **Open** 9.30am-5.30pm Mon-Sat. **Credit** AmEx, MC, V. **Map** p310 G5.
This intimate yet spacious shop provides a suitably plush backdrop to a range of high-class continental footwear. If prices are too steep, wait till the sales.

Jones Bootmaker

32 George Street, New Town (220 1029/www.jones bootmaker.com). Bus 28, 41/Princes Street buses. **Open** 9am-5.30pm Mon-Wed, Fri, Sat; 9am-7pm Thur; 11am-5pm Sun. **Credit** AmEx, MC, V. **Map** p304 B1.
An upmarket shop, with shoes for men and women. **Other location**: Unit 6, Princes Mall, New Town (557 0295).

Grazing the **Grassmarket**.

Eat, Drink, Shop

Office

79a Princes Street, New Town (220 4296/www.
office.co.uk). Princes Street buses. **Open** 9am-6pm
Mon-Wed, Fri, Sat; 9am-7pm Thur; 11.30am-5pm
Sun. **Credit** AmEx, MC, V. **Map** p304 B1.
A hedonistic display of the freshest funky fashions
in shoes, slippers and boots for women.

Schuh

6-6a Frederick Street, New Town (220 0290/www.
schuh.co.uk). Bus 13, 19A, 24, 28. **Open** 9am-6pm
Mon-Wed; 9am-8pm Thur; 9am-6pm Fri, Sat; 11am-
6pm Sun. **Credit** AmEx, MC, V. **Map** p304 B1.
The place to find cheaper versions of the latest
trends, or those thigh-high, spike-heeled PVC boots
you always wanted.
Other locations: 32 North Bridge, Old Town (225
6552); Ocean Terminal, Leith (555 3766).

Jewellery & accessories

For information on hats, *see p181*.

Craze

46a George Street, New Town (220 3450/www.the
craze.net). Bus 28, 41/Princes Street buses. **Open**
10am-6pm Mon-Sat; noon-5pm Sun. **Credit** AmEx,
MC, V. **Map** p304 B1.
Hidden in the recesses of George Street's sprawl,
Craze is a small treasure chest of costume jewellery,
flamboyant one-off dresses and sparkling hair and
head accessories from around the world.

Hamilton and Inches

87 George Street, New Town (225 4898/www.
hamiltonandinches.com). Bus 28, 41, 42/Princes
Street buses. **Open** 9.30am-5.30pm Mon-Fri; 9.30am-
5pm Sat. **Credit** AmEx, MC, V. **Map** p304 B1.
The reputation of this upmarket jeweler, which
opened in 1866, has been sealed by its new link with
Tiffany of New York. The late Georgian interior,
with its gilded columns and ornate plasterwork, is
as awe-inspiring as the glittering gems themselves.

Scottish Gems

24 High Street, Old Town (557 5731/www.scottish-
gems.co.uk). Bus 35/Nicolson Street–North Bridge
buses. **Open** *June-Aug* 10am-6pm Mon-Sat; 11am-
4pm Sun. *Sept-May* 10am-5.30pm Mon-Sat; 11am-
4pm Sun. **Credit** DC, MC, V. **Map** p304 C3.
Modern Scottish jewellery, including well-crafted
Celtic wedding-rings from £20 to over £300.
Other location: 162 Morningside Road, South
Edinburgh (447 5579).

Florists

Lily West

43 West Port, South Edinburgh (228 6003). Bus 1,
2, 10, 11, 16, 17. **Open** 9.30am-5.30pm Mon-Fri;
10am-4pm Sat. **Credit** MC, V. **Map** p309 E6.
Colourful, warm displays of blossoms and foliage
touched up with feathers, crystals and stones; a welcoming stop for visitors.

Narcissus

63 Broughton Street, Broughton (478 7447). Bus 8,
13, 17. **Open** 9am-6pm Mon-Sat; noon-4pm Sun.
Credit AmEx, DC, MC, V. **Map** p306 F3.
Sells a select range of simple but exotic blooms and
plants, including some impressively tall cacti.
International and national deliveries.

Stems

24 Grindlay Street, South Edinburgh (228 5575).
Bus 1, 10, 11, 15, 16, 17, 22, 24, 34. **Open** 9.30am-
5.30pm Mon-Fri; 10am-1pm Sat. **Credit** MC, V.
Map p304 A3.
A very sleek contemporary florist.

Food & drink

Finding groceries or a basic bite to eat in the
centre of Edinburgh, particularly in the New
Town, can be awfully difficult. **Marks &
Spencer**'s food hall provides a wide range of
tasty sandwiches, wraps and salads, available
all day. Slightly upmarket, **Jenners** food-
hall caters for the most exacting palette.
Sainsbury's on Charlotte Square, **Tesco
Metro** on Nicolson Street and **Scotmid** in
Tollcross are also convenient for a quick
inexpensive snack.

Delicatessens

Crombies of Edinburgh

97-101 Broughton Street, Broughton (557 0111/
www.sausages.co.uk). Bus 8, 13, 17. **Open**
8am-6pm Mon-Fri; 8am-5pm Sat. **Credit** MC, V.
Map p306 F3.
Top-quality meats from local farms are sold here,
but it's the extensive and inventive range of pies and
sausages that get the queues stretching out of the
door. Try a venison, wild boar and apple sausage.

Iain Mellis Cheesemonger

30a Victoria Street, Old Town (226 6215/www.
ijmellischeesemonger.com). Bus 23, 27, 28, 41, 42.
Open 9am-6pm Mon-Sat; noon-5pm Sun.
Credit MC, V. **Map** p304 C3.
Only the most olfactorically-challenged of passers-by
could miss the pungent odour from this small,
gallery-shaped cheesemonger, situated just a step
away from the Royal Mile. Organic food and vegetables are also sold. Try a piece of Gubbeen cheese.
Other locations: 6 Bakers Place, Stockbridge (225
6566); 205 Bruntsfield Place, South Edinburgh (447
8889).

Lupe Pinto's Deli

24 Leven Street, South Edinburgh (228 6241/
www.lupepintos.com). Bus 10, 11, 15, 16, 17.
Open 10am-6pm Mon-Wed, Sat; 10am-7pm Thur,
Fri; 12.30-5.30pm Sun. **Credit** MC, V. **Map** p309 D7.
Mexican, Spanish and Caribbean produce line the
walls. Authentic salsa, herbs and spices to perfect
any meal are available in abundance.

La Dolce Vita. **Valvona & Crolla.**
See p184.

The new Scotsman

Don't be fooled into thinking that Scottish kilts are merely the ultimate souvenir. A short amble down the Grassmarket, to a rugby match, or just into the right pub will soon tell another story. Recent years have seen the kilt-making industry enter a golden era of creativity. Even rock-hard film star Vin Diesel wasn't afraid to don a leather number at the MTV Europe awards in Edinburgh in 2003.

Leading the clan, **Geoffrey (Tailor) Highland Crafts** (57-59 High Street, Old Town; 557 0256/www.geoffreykilts. co.uk), has redrawn the Scottish fashion tradition to present the new-retro, metrosexual Scotsman: the fashion-conscious cosmopolitan Scottish male recapturing his heritage, in style. Designer, model and part-owner of the family-run business, Howie Nicholsby is a living example of this new Scotsman. He enjoys excessive media coverage in his pin-stripe kilt suit (among countless others), brushing shoulders with Robbie Williams, striding down LA catwalks in combat-style kilts, and hobnobbing with models in the *Playboy* mansion. Further boosting his profile, the Scots icon loaned Vin Diesel his leather number. Much to the media's amusement, the Next Big Thing almost forgot to return it. Harvey Nichols was quick to identify the

Macsweens of Edinburgh
Dryden Road, Loanhead (440 2555/www.macsween. co.uk). Bus 37. **Open** 8.30am-5pm Mon-Fri. **Credit** MC, V.
So dedicated are the Macsweens to their haggis that every single batch is tasted by one of the family. Vegetarian haggis is also available. Also stocked in Jenners and Peckham's.

Peckham's
155-159 Bruntsfield Place, South Edinburgh (229 7054/www.peckhams.co.uk). Bus 11, 16, 17, 23. **Open** 8am-midnight Mon-Sat; 9am-midnight Sun. **Credit** MC, V. **Map** p309 D8.
This old-style grocers has shelves stretching right up to the ceiling. Peckham's is a good one-stop shop for all manner of exotic sweet and savoury delicacies and drinks. It is also licensed to sell alcohol until midnight. **Other locations**: 48 Raeburn Place, Stockbridge (332 8844); 49 South Clerk Street, South Edinburgh (667 0077).

Valvona & Crolla
19 Elm Row, Leith Walk, Broughton (556 6066/ www.valvonacrolla.com). Bus 7, 10, 12, 14, 16, 22, 25, 49. **Open** 8am-6.30pm Mon-Sat; 11am-5.30pm Sun. **Credit** AmEx, MC, V. **Map** p307 G3.
Run by the families of Valvona and Crolla since the 1930s, this long and narrow Italian food shop is famed throughout Scotland for the mouthwatering range of Mediterranean edibles that are crammed onto the shelves. In recent years it has risen to the challenge of the big supermarkets by going upmarket, concentrating on speciality goods while keeping prices reasonable (*see p157*). A branch is planned.

Specialist

Casey's Confectioners
52 St Mary's Street, Old Town (556 6082). Bus 35/ Nicolson Street–North Bridge buses. **Open** 9am-5.30pm Mon-Sat. **No credit cards**. **Map** p310 G5.

trend: in September 2002, its grand opening was celebrated with an auction of 16 designer kilts, from Vivienne Westwood, Burberry and SAS, among others. Things have changed for kilts.

But the renaissance of the kilt has not escaped the fun-hating pen-pushers of the EU. They declared that the national dress was to be registered as women's clothing... it is, so the Eurocrats said, a skirt. The claim was easily quashed by Scotland's First Minister Jack McConnell.

Buying your own piece of tartan fashion isn't cheap though. The price of kilts is dependent on the number of yards used to create the pleats, and the detail on the garment. It can range from £120 for machine-sewn casual kilts to £550 for special-weave hand-sewn kilts. The **Woollen Mill** (453 Lawnmarket, Old Town; 225 1525) offers a full dress outfit for £559. Alternatively hire the outfit for the evening for just £44.50.

Romanes and Pattersons (62 Princes Street, New Town; 225 4966), is an equally reputable branch of the Woollen Mill to be found on Princes Street, offering a similar price and selection. Other distinguished kilt shops include **Kinloch Anderson** (Commercial Street/Dock Street, Leith; 555 1390/www.kinlochanderson.com) and **Nicholson Highland Wear** (189 Canongate, Old Town; 556 4763).

Only the prices have changed since this old-fashioned sweet shop first opened in 1954. It still has a picture-postcard, art deco exterior, while the interior is packed with row upon row of colourfully filled jars of mouthwatering sweets, all of which are handmade on the premises.
Other location: 28 Norton Park, Calton Hill (no phone).

Fudge House
197 Canongate, Old Town (556 4172/www.fudgehouse.co.uk). Bus 30, 35. **Open** 10am-5pm daily. **Credit** AmEx, MC, V. **Map** p310 G5.
Blocks of fudge are sold by weight in 24 flavours, including Highland cream, pecan and chocolate swirl, and Italian nougat; all made on the premises. Fudgeoholics beware – there may be no escape.

Nittiya Thai Market
39 Dalry Road, West Edinburgh (313 4888). Bus 26, 31, 33. **Open** 11am-7pm daily. **Credit** MC, V. **Map** p308 B7.

Delicate spices, flavourings, nuts and fruits are among the freshest things this bustling food shop has to offer.

Pat Chung Ying Chinese Supermarket
199-201 Leith Walk, Broughton (554 0358). Leith Walk buses. **Open** 10am-6pm daily. **Credit** MC, V. **Map** p307 G3.
For Chinese food.

Fruit & vegetables

Argyle Place
23 Argyle Place, Marchmont, South Edinburgh (228 1841). Bus 24, 41. **Open** 7am-7pm Mon-Sat; 9am-6pm Sun. **No credit cards**. **Map** p309 F8.
A busy strip of fruit and veg shops on the south side of the city, good for cheap, high quality fresh produce.

Health & vegetarian

Nature's Gate
83 Clerk Street, South Edinburgh (668 2067). Nicolson Street–North Bridge buses. **Open** 10am-7pm Mon, Wed-Fri; 10am-6pm Tue, Sat; noon-5pm Sun. **Credit** MC, V. **Map** p310 G7.
A wide range of vegetarian and vegan foods, both pre-packed and fresh, fill this wooden-shelved shop.

Real Foods
37 Broughton Street, Broughton (557 1911/www.realfoods.co.uk). Bus 8, 13, 17. **Open** 9am-7pm Mon-Wed, Fri; 9am-8pm Thur; 9am-6.30pm Sat; 10am-6pm Sun. **Credit** MC, V. **Map** p306 F3.
A supermarket for the vegetarian, vegan and organic enthusiast, even if the prices can be unreal. **Other location**: 8 Brougham Place, South Edinburgh (228 1201).

Late-night grocers

Scotmid
91-93 Nicolson Street, South Edinburgh (667 7481/www.scotmid.co.uk). Nicolson Street–North Bridge buses. **Open** 24hrs daily. **Credit** MC, V. **Map** p310 G6.
Satisfy those munchies here.
Other locations: throughout the city.

Costcutter
125 Lothian Road, South Edinburgh (622 7191/www.costcutter.co.uk). Bus 1, 10, 11, 15, 16, 17, 22, 24. **Open** 5am-3am daily. **Credit** MC, V. **Map** p304 A3.
A basic range of grocery and household supplies.
Other locations: throughout the city

Sainsbury's
185 Craigleith Road, Blackhall (332 0704/www.sainsburys.co.uk). Bus 24, 38, 41, 42. **Open** 7am-midnight Mon-Fri; 7am-10pm Sat; 8am-8pm Sun. **Credit** AmEx, MC, V.

This branch of Sainsbury's also has a coffee shop, three ATMs, SupaSnaps, Sketchley dry cleaners, and assistance for people with mobility difficulties. **Other locations**: 9-10 St Andrew Square, New Town (656 9377); Savacentre Cameron Toll (666 5200).

Drinks

Better Beverages Co

204 Morrison Street, New Town (476 2600/www. betterbeverage.co.uk). Bus 2, 11, 28, 34, 35. **Open** 11am-5pm Tue-Sat. **No credit cards. Map** p308 C6.
The quality range of coffee beans will satisfy even the most discerning connoisseur.

Noble Grape

21-27 Brandon Terrace, New Town (556 3133). Bus 8, 17, 23, 27. **Open** 9.30am-5.30pm Mon-Sat. **Credit** AmEx, MC, V. **Map** p306 D2/3.
Dereck Tang introduced Scotland's first Chinese wine shop to Edinburgh in 1997.

Peter Green

37a-b Warrender Park Road, South Edinburgh (229 5925/www.petergreenwines.com). Bus 24, 41. **Open** 10am-6.30pm Tue-Thur, Sat; 10am-7.30pm Fri. **Credit** MC, V. **Map** p308 E8.
Green's has a diverse selection of wines and over 100 whiskies. Tastings most Fridays 4.30 to 7.30pm.

Royal Mile Whiskies

379 High Street, Old Town (225 3383/www.royal milewhiskies.com). Bus 35/Nicolson Street–North Bridge buses. **Open** Sept-July 10am-6pm Mon-Sat; 12.30-6pm Sun. *Aug* 10am-8pm Mon-Sat; 12.30-8pm Sun. **Credit** AmEx, MC, V. **Map** p304 C3.
A traditional façade shields a classic range of whiskies, with over 300 varieties available. The free tastings on Sunday afternoons during peak season should whet the appetite.

Scotch Malt Whisky Society

The Vaults, 87 Giles Street, Leith (554 3451/www. smws.com). Bus 7, 10, 11, 12, 14, 16, 17, 22, 35 . **Open** 10am-5pm Mon-Tue; 10am-11pm Wed-Sat; 11am-10pm Sun. **Credit** AmEx, MC, V.
Unique malt whiskies, bottled directly from single casks, are available to members only. If you're a bit of a whisky buff, phone for a tasting programme and join the society. The resulting pleasure more than compensates for the fee of £75 for the first year (which includes a bottle of whisky with full tasting notes) and £25 per year thereafter (*see p173*).

Scottish Whisky Heritage Centre

354 Castlehill, Old Town (220 0441/www.whisky-heritage.co.uk). Bus 23, 27, 28, 35, 41, 42. **Open** 10am-6pm daily (licensed from 12.30pm on Sundays). **Credit** AmEx, MC, V. **Map** p304 C3.
Try before you buy from the broad range of commercial whiskies at the Centre's friendly bar and gift shop. Both the shop and bar are open whether or not you've taken part in the Centre's tour (*see p72*).

Hairdressers & barbers

Cheynes

46 George Street, New Town (220 0777). Bus 28, 41/Princes Street buses. **Open** 9am-6pm Mon-Wed, Fri; 9am-7.30pm Thur; 9am-5.15pm Sat. **Credit** MC, V. **Map** p304 B1.
Popular Edinburgh chain of unisex hairdressers.
Other locations: 57 South Bridge, Old Town (556 0108); 45A York Place, New Town (558 1010); 77 Lothian Road, South Edinburgh (228 9977); 3 Drumsheugh Place, Queensferry Street, New Town (225 2234).

Demon Barbers

36 Home Street, South Edinburgh (466 3232/ www.demon/barbers.com). Bus 10, 11, 15, 16, 17. **Open** 9am-6pm Mon-Wed, Fri; 9am-7pm Thur; 8.30am-4pm Sat. **No credit cards. Map** p309 D7.
Enjoys modest fame with the locals: a stylish haircut or shave is always guaranteed at the Demon Barbers. Prices are around £8 to £10.

Egg Hairdressing

23 Broughton Street, Broughton (556 6685/ www.egghair.co.uk). Bus 8, 13, 17. **Open** 10am-8pm Tue-Thur; 10am-6pm Fri; 9am-5pm Sat. **Credit** MC, V. **Map** p306 F3.
Winners of the European Hair Designer Awards, Egg Hairdressing offers a luxurious experience.

Medusa

6-7 Teviot Place, Old Town (225 6627/www.medusa-hair.co.uk). Bus 23, 27, 28, 45. **Open** 9am-6pm Mon-Wed, Fri; 9am-8.15pm Thur; 9am-4.30pm Sat. **Credit** MC, V. **Map** p309 F6.
Unisex hairdressers for the young and outrageous or the old and brave. Reasonable prices, friendly service and a complementary glass of wine to boot.
Other location: 26 Bread Street, South Edinburgh (622 7277).

Health & beauty

Jo Malone

93 George Street, New Town (478 8555/www.jo malone.co.uk). Bus 28, 41/Princes Street buses. **Open** 10am-6pm Mon-Wed; 10am-7pm Thur; 9.30am-6pm Fri, Sat; noon-4pm Sun. **Credit** AmEx, MC, V. **Map** p304 B1.
Highly covetable (and expensive) toiletries and perfumes. The fragrances are gorgeous and the skin care range (including the delectable orange and geranium night cream) should not be overlooked.

Lush

44 Princes Street, New Town (557 3177/ www.lush.co.uk). Princes Street buses. **Open** 9.30am-6pm Mon-Wed, Fri, Sat; 9.30am-7pm Thur; 11.30am-5pm Sun. **Credit** AmEx, MC, V. **Map** p304 B1.
Fresh ingredients are packed tightly into exploding bath bombs and soaps that unleash a host of harnessed energies as well as creams, oils and pretty much every other luxuriant bathroom product ever.

Men's where?

Not every man in Edinburgh has Mel Gibson's physique, or more importantly, his legs. Neither, it should be noted, do all the males in the city wish to appropriate a 'see-you-Jimmy' bonnet, or tartan trews. But even the aesthetically challenged man can find clothes to blend in with the upmarket city, while staying original enough to stand out (subtly) from the crowds.

Saunter along George Street – pockets well lined – and pick up a suit or two. Alternatively, **Cruise** (*see p179*) has a wide selection of designer casual wear, as do department stores like **Harvey Nichols** or **Fraser's** (for both; *see p175*).

If stiff collars and starched shirts feel a little conservative, there are always the hordes of skaters in Bristo Square by the university in their over-priced designer skatewear. Check out **Cult** on North Bridge or **Momentum Surf Shop** in Bruntsfield Place (for both; *see p180*).

If you're after a jumper of the non-hooded variety, there's a third option: a combination of the traditional and the original with the affordable at Edinburgh's impressive array of vintage and second-hand shops. **Flip of Hollywood** (56-91 South Bridge, Old Town; 556 4966) offers a fine selection of shirts, duffel coats and a little retro gear in the form of Adidas jerseys and 1950s mechanics' shirts. They also sell everything from new Bench clothes to rainbow striped slacks and tweed trench coats.

Student-staple the **Rusty Zip** (14 Teviot Place, South Edinburgh; 226 4634) assumes a slightly more sophisticated poise. Vintage two-piece suits, waistcoats and tails hang next to skinny-fit jumpers, smoking jackets

and sheep-skin coats. The vertical displays make for a bountiful range of clothes in this tall, narrow shop, yet it remains but a drop in the ocean compared to the empire of **Armstrongs** (83 Grassmarket, Old Town; 220 5557/www.armstrongsvintage.co.uk). A cluttered main room full of cravats, Biggles' jackets and ties explodes out into annexes of army gear, denim, tweed slacks, dinner jackets and cowboy hats (suitable for any occasion).

Neal's Yard Remedies
102 Hanover Street, New Town (226 3223/ www.nealsyardremedies.com). Bus 28, 41/Princes Street buses. **Open** 10am-6pm Mon-Wed, Fri, Sat; 10am 7pm Thur; times vary Sun (phone for details). **Credit** MC, V. **Map** p304 C1.
These fab-smelling alternative lotions and potions showcase the benefits of various herbs and oils. Book in at the treatment room for a good pamper.

Space NK
97-103 George Street, New Town (225 6371/ www.spacenk.co.uk). Bus 28, 41/Princes Street buses. **Open** 10am-6pm Mon-Wed, Fri; 10am-7.30pm Thur; 9.30am-6pm Sat; noon-5pm Sun. **Credit** AmEx, MC, V. **Map** p304 B1.

Upmarket purveyor of smelly stuff. The staff are perfectly turned out, the decor is minimalist and the pongs are dearer than vintage champagne.

Household

Concrete Butterfly
317-319 Cowgate, Old Town (558 7130/ www.concretebutterfly.com). Nicolson Street–North Bridge buses. **Open** *Jan-July, Sept-Nov* noon-6pm Tue-Fri; noon-5pm Sat. *Aug, Dec* noon-6pm daily. **Credit** MC, V. **Map** p304 D3.
Just along from Holyroodhouse, this exclusive shop specialises in designer household goods and the trendiest of kitchen wares.

  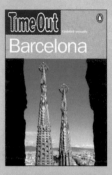
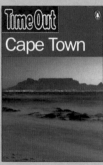  

Habitat

*32 Shandwick Place, New Town (225 9151/
www.habitat.net). Bus 3, 4, 12, 21, 25, 26, 31, 33,
44.* **Open** *9am-5.30pm Mon-Wed, Fri; 9am-7pm
Thur; 9am-6pm Sat; 11.30am-5.30pm Sun.* **Credit**
AmEx, MC, V. **Map** p308 C5.
Popular household chain store with affordable,
attractive furnishings and furniture.

Halibut and Herring

*89 Westbow, Old Town (226 7472). Bus 23, 27, 28,
35, 41, 42.* **Open** *9.30am-5.30pm Mon-Sat; 11am-
5pm Sun.* **Credit** MC, V. **Map** p304 C3.
Clockwork diving submarines, see-through shower
curtains and a colourful range of soaps and ceramics made in Musselburgh have established this as a
firm local favourite for quirky bathroom treats.
Other locations: 31 Raeburn Place, Stockbridge
(332 5687); 108 Bruntsfield Place, South Edinburgh
(229 2669).

Lakeland

*26 George Street, New Town (220 3947/www.
lakelandlimited.co.uk). Bus 28, 41/Princes Street
buses.* **Open** *9am-5.30pm Mon-Sat.* **Credit** MC, V.
Map p304 B1.
Two floors housing every kitchen accessory you
could ever need, plus many more eccentric inven-
tions you never even knew existed.

Markets

Fight against the winds, and you'll find
Edinburgh's various markets ideal sites for
bargain hunting and for finding the freshest
produce – a fun weekend adventure, well worth
getting up early for.

Farmers' Market

*Castle Terrace, South Edinburgh (no phone/
www.scottishfarmersmarkets.co.uk). Bus 1, 10, 11,
15, 16, 17, 22, 24.* **Open** *9am-2pm 1st & 3rd Sat of
the month.* **Credit** varies. **Map** p304 A3.
The market attracts over 40 specialist producers,
most of whom sell goods they have grown themselves. There's plenty of meat, with an emphasis on
organic produce, plus fish (and lobster in season),
free range eggs (including quail and duck), cheeses
and seasonal vegetables and fruit. Some home producers also take part in the market, providing
liqueurs, breads and chutney.

Ingliston Market

*Off Glasgow Road (A8), past Edinburgh Airport,
West Edinburgh (333 3801). Scottish Citylink service
900/902 to Glasgow.* **Open** *9.30am-3.30pm Sun.*
Credit varies.
Around 100 traders sell mostly clothes, household
and electrical goods, and hippy paraphernalia in an
outdoor field. There's a car boot sale alongside with
anything from 20 to 200 cars (depending on the
weather). If you want a cheap fleece, novelty clock
or lighter, then this place will offer the best prices.
Just make sure you check the quality first.

New Street Indoor Sunday Market

*Waverley Car Park, New Street, Old Town
(no phone). Bus 30, 35.* **Open** *10am-3pm Sun.*
No credit cards. **Map** p310 G5.
While away a Sunday morning and afternoon at this
extensive market.

Mobile phones

Carphone Warehouse

*27 North Bridge, Old Town (0870 168 2452).
Nicolson Street–North Bridge buses.* **Open** *9am-6pm
Mon-Sat; 11am-5pm Sun.* **Credit** MC, V. **Map** p304
D2.
Your mobile is broken. They'll fix it.
Other location: 25 Princes Street, New Town (0870
168 2026).

Music

CDs, records & tickets

Avalanche

*17 West Nicolson Street, South Edinburgh (668
2374/www.avalancherecords.co.uk). Nicolson
Street–North Bridge buses.* **Open** *9.30am-6pm Mon-
Sat.* **Credit** MC, V. **Map** p310 G6.
The original branch of music-loving entrepreneur
Kevin Buckle's record shop opened here in 1983 and
is now a Scottish indie institution and a respected
mini-chain.
Other locations: 28 Lady Lawson Street, South
Edinburgh (668 2374), 63 Cockburn Street, Old Town
(225 3939).

Backbeat

*31 East Crosscauseway, South Edinburgh (668
2666). Nicolson Street–North Bridge buses.* **Open**
*10am-5.30pm Mon-Sat; occasional Sundays (phone
for details).* **Credit** AmEx, MC, V. **Map** p310 G7.
Collectors of rare vinyl and obscure CD re-issues will
feel they've stumbled into aural heaven here.

Fopp

*55 Cockburn Street, Old Town (220 0133/www.fopp.
co.uk). Bus 2, 10, 11, 15, 16, 17, 22/Nicolson
Street–North Bridge buses.* **Open** *9.30am-7pm Mon-Sat; 11am-6pm Sun.* **Credit**
AmEx, DC, MC, V. **Map** p304 D3.
Scotland's largest independent record and CD retail-
er regularly sells chart releases at prices that are
markedly less then the big high-street chains
Other location: Rose Street, New Town (220 0310,
see p169).

McAlister Matheson Music

*1 Grindlay Street, South Edinburgh (228 3827/
www.mmmusic.co.uk). Bus 2, 10, 11, 15, 16, 17, 22,
24.* **Open** *9.30am-7pm Mon-Fri; 9am-5.30pm Sat;
Aug also 1-5pm Sun.* **Credit** AmEx, DC, MC, V.
Map p304 A3.
A quiet haven for classical music and opera CDs.
The stock reflects what's coming up in local perfor-
mances and during the Festival.

Ripping Music & Tickets

*91 South Bridge, Old Town (226 7010/
www.rippingrecords.com). Nicolson Street–North
Bridge buses.* **Open** 9.30am-6.30pm Mon-Wed, Fri;
9.30am-7pm Thur; 9am-6pm Sat; noon-5.30pm Sun.
Credit AmEx, MC, V. **Map** p304 D3.
Rock, pop, dance and indie CDs are all here, but
Ripping is best known as the place to buy advance
tickets (booking fee 50p per ticket) for rock, pop and
club nights (*see p220*).

Uberdisko

*36 Cockburn Street, Old Town (226 2134/
www.uberdisko.com). Bus 35/Nicolson Street–North
Bridge buses.* **Open** 10am-6pm Mon-Sat; noon-5pm
Sun. **Credit** MC, V. **Map** p304 D3.
Small, sparse and sometimes intimidating shop for
house and techno sounds.

Underground Solu'shn

*9 Cockburn Street, Old Town (226 2242/
www.undergroundsolushn.com). Bus 30, 35.* **Open**
10am-6pm Mon-Wed, Sat; 10am-7pm Thur, Fri; noon-
6pm Sun. **Credit** AmEx, MC, V. **Map** p304 D3.
Unbeatable for vinyl dance imports, with a huge
choice of house, garage, techno and jungle sounds.
The staff are happy to answer questions, play
requests and give insider tips for a top night of clubbing in the city (*see p227*).

Instruments & sheet music

Bagpipes Galore

*82 Canongate, Old Town (556 4073/www.bagpipe.
co.uk). Bus 30, 35.* **Open** 9.30am-5.30pm Mon-Sat.
Credit AmEx, MC, V. **Map** p310 G5.
A huge range of new and second-hand pipes. The
starter tutor kit is good value, with a chanter (the
reed pipe of a bagpipe on which the melody is
played), book and CD for £28. Those who feel a bit
more adventurous can try the practice pipes at £97.
Accessories include reeds and pipe bags.

Opticians

Dolland and Aitchison

*65 St James Centre, Leith Street, New Town (558
1149/www.danda.co.uk). Princes Street or Nicolson
Street–North Bridge buses.* **Open** 9am-5.30pm Mon-
Wed, Fri, Sat; 10am-6pm Thur. **Credit** AmEx, MC,
V. **Map** p307 G4.
Other locations: 56 Newington Road, South
Edinburgh (667 6442); 61 London Road, Greenside
(652 0806); Cameron Toll (664 2545).

Vision Express

*Units 12-14, St James Centre, Leith Street, New
Town (556 5656/www.visionexpress.co.uk). Princes
Street or Nicolson Street–North Bridge buses.* **Open**
9am-5.30pm Mon-Wed, Fri; 9am-7pm Thur; 9am-6pm
Sat; 11am-5pm Sun. **Credit** AmEx, MC, V. **Map**
p307 G4.
Other location: Gyle Centre, West Edinburgh (339
0176).

Pharmacies

There's no 24-hour pharmacy in the city.

Boots

*101-103 Princes Street, New Town (225 8331/
www.wellbeing.com). Princes Street buses.* **Open**
9am-6pm Mon-Wed, Fri, Sat; 9am-7.30pm Thur;
noon-5pm Sun. **Credit** MC, V. **Map** p304 B2.
This is Edinburgh's largest branch of the reliable
health, toiletries and cosmetics chain store. Optician
and chiropodist available upstairs.

Napier Dispensary

*18 Bristo Place, Old Town (225 5542/
www.napiers.net). Bus 2, 23, 27, 28, 41, 42.* **Open**
10am-6pm Mon; 9am-6pm Tue-Fri; 9am-5.30pm Sat;
12.30-4.30pm Sun. **Credit** MC, V. **Map** p309 F6.
An historic dispensary dating from 1860. Today it
is a medical herbalist, stocking homeopathic medicines, as well as running clinics in various forms
of complementary medicine, including acupunc-
ture, homeopathy and osteopathy.

Photography

There are numerous branches of photo-
processing shops such as SupaSnaps around
the city, but pharmacies are usually cheaper
and offer all the same services, including one-
hour processing (although this service normally
carries a premium).

Souvenirs

The Royal Mile pretty much has the monopoly
on souvenirs in Edinburgh, whether you're after
quality or kitsch (and there's plenty of the
latter). Princes Street also has numerous gift
shops selling tartan tea towels and other
touristy items, but overall you'll find better
bargains, not to mention tasteless gifts, on the
Royal Mile – with a few nice pubs scattered
around to help you on your way (*see p166*).

Wha'slikeus

*328 Lawnmarket, Old Town (225 4152). Bus 23, 27,
28, 35, 41, 42.* **Open** *Winter* 9am-8pm daily.
Summer 9am-late daily. **Credit** AmEx, DC, MC, V.
Map p304 C3.
If you can make it in tartan, you'll find it here.

Scotland Shop

*18-20 High Street, Old Town (557 2030/
www.scotlandshopdirect.com). Bus 35/Nicolson
Street–North Bridge buses.* **Open** *Winter* 10am-6pm
Mon-Sat; 11am-6pm Sun. *Summer* 9am-8pm daily.
Credit AmEx, MC. V. **Map** p304 C3.
Fearsome *Braveheart*-style swords, cutlasses and
equally scary tartan porcelain dolls bedeck the window of the Scotland Shop. But the neat interior also
contains a wide range of reasonably priced and
rather more low-key paraphernalia.

Eat, Drink, Shop

Edinburgh Floatarium. *See p192.*

Tartan Giftshop

54 High Street, Old Town (558 3187/www.tartan-kilts.org). Bus 35/Nicolson Street–North Bridge buses. **Open** *Winter* 10am-6pm daily. *Summer* 10am-11pm daily. **Credit** AmEx, MC, V. **Map** p304 C3.
A small, traditional shop aimed mainly at men, with a large stock of kilt-wear accessories, golf balls, engraved hip-flasks and ornamental knives.

Whigmaleeries Ltd

334 Lawnmarket, Old Town (225 4152/ www.whigmaleeries-ltd.com). Bus 23, 27, 28, 35, 41, 42. **Open** *Winter* 10am-6pm daily. *Summer* 10am-late daily. **Credit** AmEx, DC, MC, V. **Map** p304 C3.
Reproduction weapons, jewellery and a family history research service in elegant surroundings.

White Dove

140 High Street, Old Town (220 1566/www.white-dove.co.uk). Bus 35/Nicolson Street–North Bridge buses. **Open** *Jan-July, Sept-Dec* 9.30am-6pm daily. *Aug* 9.30am-11pm daily. **Credit** AmEx, MC, V. **Map** p304 C3.
A fine range of tacky novelties including the obligatory whisky-flavoured condoms.

Sport & outdoors

Blacks Outdoor Leisure

13-14 Elm Row, Broughton (556 3491/ www.blacks.co.uk). Bus 7, 12, 16. **Open** 9am-5.30pm Mon-Sat; noon-4pm Sun. **Credit** AmEx, MC, V. **Map** p307 G3.

Quality rucksacks, clothes, tents and equipment for hikers, skiers and ramblers.
Other location: 24 Fredrick Street, New Town (225 8686).

Boardwise

4 Lady Lawson Street, South Edinburgh (229 5887/ www.boardwise.com). Bus 2, 28. **Open** 10am-6pm Mon-Sat. **Credit** AmEx, MC, V. **Map** p309 E6.
If you are heading up to Hill End (*see p235*) for some snow-boarding or skiing, Boardwise is a good pit-stop to get kitted out in the season's trendiest gear. All the major skate-labels can be found among the relentless supply of baggy jeans and T-shirts.

Rent-a-Bike

29 Blackfriars Street, Old Town (556 5560/ www.cyclescotland.co.uk). Nicolson Street–North Bridge buses. **Open** *Summer* 9am-9pm daily. *Winter* 10am-6pm daily. **Credit** MC, V. **Map** p310 G5.
A simple, trustworthy outlet from which to rent your bike then cycle off on a tour arranged by the company around Edinburgh or the Highlands.

Tiso

123-125 Rose Street, New Town (225 9486). Princes Street buses. **Open** 9.30am-5.30pm Mon, Wed, Fri, Sat; 10am-5.30pm Tue; 9.30am-7.30pm Thur; noon-5pm Sun. **Credit** AmEx, MC, V. **Map** p304 A1.
Pretty much *the* department store for the outdoor type: the four floors of Tiso are packed with all manner of sports and survival equipment, clothes and accessories. The knowledgeable staff will advise.
Other location: 41 Commercial Street, Leith (554 0804).

Wind Things

11 Cowgatehead, Old Town (662 7032/ www.windthings.co.uk). Nicolson Street–North Bridge buses. **Open** 10am-5.30pm Mon-Sat; noon-5pm Sun. **Credit** AmEx, MC, V. **Map** p304 C3.
A perfect shop to buy your kite in and then join all the other enthusiasts out on Holyrood Park. An eye-catching display, ideal to pick up a new hobby.

Stationery & gifts

Aitken Dott

36 North Bridge, Old Town (225 1006/www.millers-graphics.co.uk). Nicolson Street–North Bridge buses. **Open** 9am-5.30pm Mon-Sat. **Credit** AmEx, MC, V. **Map** p304 D2.
A centrally located professional stationery supplier.

Crystal Clear

52 Cockburn Street, Old Town (226 7888). Nicolson Street–North Bridge buses. **Open** 10am-6pm Mon-Sat; noon-5pm Sun. **Credit** AmEx, MC, V. **Map** p304 D3.
Crystal Clear is a tiny but atmospheric Old Town shop packed with self-help, spiritual and occult books. Owner Thom McCarthy is often around to offer friendly and knowledgeable advice.
Other locations: Wildwood Books, 16 High Street, Old Town (557 4888); Golden, 109 High Street, Old Town (624 3777).

Eat, Drink, Shop

Eden

*37-39 Cockburn Street, Old Town (220 3372). Bus
35/Nicolson Street–North Bridge buses.* **Open**
9.30am-6pm Mon-Wed, Fri, Sat; 9.30am-7pm Thur;
noon-5pm Sun. **Credit** AmEx, MC, V. **Map** p304 D3.
Ethnic wooden crafts and textiles intermingle with
smiling furry monkeys, blow-up chairs and other
brightly coloured oddities.

Helios Fountain

*7 Grassmarket, Old Town (229 7884/www.helios-
fountain.co.uk). Bus 2, 23, 27, 28, 41, 42.* **Open**
10am-6pm Mon-Sat; noon-5pm Sun. **Credit** MC, V.
Map p304 B3.
You'll find Celtic jewellery, crafts, trinkets and a
huge selection of beads for necklaces or bracelets on
one side of the shop; vegetarian, vegan and New Age
books on the other. Plus – it surely goes without saying – a suitably old-fashioned hippie ambience.

Kick Ass

*34 Cockburn Street, Old Town (622 7318/
www.kickassposters.co.uk). Bus 35/Nicolson
Street–North Bridge buses.* **Open** 9.30am-6pm Mon-
Wed, Fri, Sat; 9.30am-7pm Thur; noon-5pm Sun.
Credit AmEx, MC, V. **Map** p304 D3.
Squeeze through the inevitable hordes of teenagers
flipping through posters to find a great supply of
postcards, featuring everything from the Simpsons
to saucy 3D winking ladies.

Paper Tiger

*53 Lothian Road, West Edinburgh (228 2790/www.
papertiger.ltd.uk). Bus 1, 2, 10, 11, 15, 16, 22, 35.*
Open 9.30am-6pm Mon-Wed, Fri, Sat; 9.30am-7pm
Thur; 11am-5pm Sun. **Credit** MC, V. **Map** p304 A2.
A small cavern jam-packed with cards that are just
a little bit different from those you'll find on the high
street. Hand-crafted designs which may cost a little
bit extra, but are sure to cater perfectly for even the
most unusual of situation.
Other location: Stafford Street, New Town (226
2390).

Studio One

*10-16 Stafford Street, New Town (226 5812). Bus 3,
4, 12, 21, 25, 26, 31, 33.* **Open** 9.30am-6pm Mon-
Wed, Fri; 9.30am-7pm Thur; 9.30am-5.30pm Sat;
noon-5pm Sun. **Credit** MC, V. **Map** p308 C5.
Studio One is a trendy subterranean shop full of
exotic gifts and household furnishings.
Other location: Studio One Cookshop 71
Morningside Road, South Edinburgh (447 0452).

Toys & games

Aha Ha Ha

*99 West Bow, Old Town (220 5252). Bus 23, 27, 28,
41, 42, 45.* **Open** *Jan-July, Sept-Nov* 10am-6pm Mon-
Sat. *Aug, Dec* also noon-4pm Sun. **Credit** MC, V.
Map p304 C3.
The oversized Groucho moustache and glasses over
the front door are only the tip of the chuckles to be
found in this cheap and infinitely cheerful shop.

Balloon & Party Shop

*3 Viewforth Gardens, off Bruntsfield Place, South
Edinburgh (229 9686/www.balloonandparty.co.uk).
Bus 11, 16, 17, 23.* **Open** 10am-6pm Mon-Fri; 10am-
5.30pm Sat. **Credit** MC, V. **Map** p309 D8.
An unassuming little shop selling banners and all
manner of balloons and accessories to make your
party go with a swing or even a bang.

Games Workshop

*136 High Street, Old Town (220 6540/www.games-
workshop.com). Bus 35/Nicolson Street–North Bridge
buses.* **Open** *Jan-Oct* 10am-6pm Mon-Sat; 10am-5pm
Sun. *Nov, Dec* 9am-6pm Mon-Sat; 10am-5pm Sun.
Credit MC, V. **Map** p304 D3.
War-gaming figures and accessories, plus regular
workshops and battle enactments.

Owl & the Pussycat

*166 Bruntsfield Place, South Edinburgh (228 4441).
Bus 11, 16, 17, 23.* **Open** 9am-5.30pm Mon-Sat; *Dec*
also 10am-4pm Sun. **Credit** MC, V. **Map** p309 D8.
Situated in the suburbs, the Owl & the Pussycat is
a toy shop of exquisite quality. Painted wooden toys
lollop from springs on the ceiling and cheerful animals line the wooden shelves.

Robot Shop

*26 St Mary's Street, Old Town (556 5500). Nicolson
Street–North Bridge buses.* **Open** 11am-5.30pm Tue-
Sat. **Credit** AmEx, MC, V. **Map** p310 G5.
Get whisked back in time to the days of wind-up tin
robots, and hurled into the future with the impres-
sive selection of AI toys.

Wonderland

*97 Lothian Road, South Edinburgh (229 6428/
www.wonderlandmodels.com). Bus 11, 15, 16, 17,
24, 34.* **Open** *Jan-Oct* 9.30am-6pm Mon-Fri; 9am-
6pm Sat. *Nov, Dec* also noon-5pm Sun. **Credit**
AmEx, MC, V. **Map** p304 A2.
A breathtaking range of model cars, trains and
planes, dinosaurs, monsters and skeletons, plus hor-
ror, sci-fi and cult-favourite action figures.

Treatments & therapies

See also p186.

Edinburgh Floatarium

*29 North West Circus Place, New Town (225 3350/
www.edinburghfloatarium.co.uk). Bus 13, 19A, 24,
28.* **Open** 9am-8pm Mon-Fri; 9am-6pm Sat; 9.30am-
4pm Sun. **Credit** MC, V. **Map** p306 D4.
The sea salt floats are the main attraction here. Bliss
out in a flotation tank for just £25. Beauty and health
treatments, crystals and gifts are all available.

Nail Factory

*32 Lady Lawson Street, South Edinburgh (221
1880). Bus 23, 27, 28, 45.* **Open** 9.30am-7pm Mon-
Wed; 9am-8pm Thur; 9am-5pm Sat.
Credit MC, V. **Map** p309 E6.
Highly professional beauticians who create art so
small it can fit on your fingertip.

Arts & Entertainment

Features

Festivals & Events

Outside of the Festival bunfight, Edinburgh has other seasonal delights.

Edinburgh isn't just for August: there's fun all the year round. With the long darkness of winter comes the light and festivity of Capital Christmas and Edinburgh's Hogmanay, while spring and autumn are traditionally quieter periods and probably the best seasons in which to experience the true essence of Edinburgh. For those events marked 'tbc', the exact date was yet to be confirmed as this guide went to press; always phone to check these first.

January

Burns Night

www.rabbie-burns.com. **Date** 25 January.
Robert 'Rabbie' Burns, Scotland's unofficial poet laureate, was born on this date in 1759. It is the custom of Scots the world over to gather, consume haggis, neeps and tatties, sup whisky, and recite the sacred texts. Meanwhile theatres and bookshops play host to readings of Burns's work. Some of the poems are extremely bawdy, although 'Tam o' Shanter' is a great story and the 'Address to a Haggis' a true celebration of the working man.

Turner Watercolours

National Gallery of Scotland, The Mound, New Town (624 6200/www.nationalgalleries.org). Princes Street buses. **Open** 10am-5pm Mon-Wed, Fri-Sun; 10am-7pm Thur. **Admission** free. **Credit** (Shop) AmEx, MC, V. **Map** p304 C2. **Dates** 1-31 Jan.
More than 40 Turner watercolours were bequeathed to the National Gallery of Scotland in 1900 by Henry Vaughan, who stipulated that they should only be exhibited in January when the light of this northern latitude is at its weakest and least destructive.

February

Six Nations Rugby

Tickets 0870 040 1925/www.6nations.net. Prices and dates vary.
Six nations, one game. Rugby internationals bring Edinburgh alive like no other sporting event, particularly for the Calcutta Cup. With Murrayfield (*see p232*) packed out, the atmosphere is electric. Watch the match, drink some beer, see the city.

March

Ceilidh Culture Festival

Various venues across the city (information 243 1442/box office 228 1155/www.ceilidhculture.co.uk). **Open** *Box office* 10am-8pm Mon-Fri; 10am-5.30pm

Sat. **Tickets** prices vary; phone for details. **Credit** MC, V. **Dates** 20 Mar-25 Apr 2004; 2005 dates tbc; 2006 dates tbc.
Gaelic song, traditional dance, harp playing, bagpipe blowing, it's all here in this five week long celebration of everything that is Celtic.

Edinburgh International Science Festival

Information & box office 557 5588/www.sciencefestival.co.uk). **Open** *Information & tickets* (from late Feb) 9.30am-5pm Mon-Sat (tickets also available online). **Tickets** prices vary; phone for details. **Dates** 2-12 April 2005; 2006 dates tbc.
The Science Festival began in 1989 and has become adept at putting an accessible, topical and controversial slant on scientific subjects without dumbing down. The UK's largest science festival, it has around 200 public events, attracting scientific heavyweights from around the world.

April

Beltane Fire Festival

Calton Hill (information 228 5353/www.beltane.org). Bus 30, 40. **Time** 10pm-dawn. **Map** p307 G4. **Date** 30 Apr.
One of the four major quarters of the Celtic year, Beltane is an old druidic tradition marking the transition from winter to spring which has been reborn, in a no doubt completely authentic fashion, after two millenia in hiatus. '80s industrial musical experimentalists – and metal abusers – Test Department, made an unlikely alliance with the School of Scottish Studies at Edinburgh University to set the flames burning. The event since has grown into a mass of fire, drumming and exhibitionists watched by an audience of around 15,000. There were plans to sell tickets for the event for the first time in 2004 in a move to cover costs. The druids would love it.

tripTych

Various city-centre clubs (tickets & information 0870 220 1116/www.triptych04.com). **Open** 10am-6pm Mon-Fri (tickets also available online and at Ripping Records; *see p190*). **Tickets** £5-£15.50. **Credit** MC, V. **Dates** 2005 dates tbc (probably May Day Bank Holiday).
Exploring the less mainstream corners of new music, tripTych presents five days of DJs, dance, electronica, roots, soul, and all-round experimentation, just staying the right side of pretentiousness. Franz Ferdinand and John Peel were set to headline in 2004; the festival also happens in Glasgow and Aberdeen on the same long weekend.

'Who are you calling hathead?'
T in the Park. *See p196.*

June

Royal Highland Show

*Royal Highland Centre, Ingliston (information &
tickets 335 6200/www.royalhighlandshow.org.uk).*
Tickets (available online) £15-£16; £5-£10
concessions. **Credit** MC, V. **Dates** 24-27 June 2004;
23-26 June 2005; 2006 dates tbc.
If sheep shearing is your thing (and it was for
150,000 people in 2003), then this is your festival.
The Highland Show celebrates the best of Scottish
rural life and features exhibitions of everything from
top-notch food producers through to tractor makers
and farm equipment suppliers.

Scottish Children's International
Theatre Festival

*Various city-centre theatres (information 225 8050/
box office 228 1404/www.imaginate.org.uk).* **Open
Information** 9am-5pm Mon-Fri. *Box office* 10am-6pm
Mon-Fri. **Tickets** prices vary; phone for details.
Credit MC, V. **Dates** 24 May-1 June 2005;
2006 dates tbc.
Indigenous children's theatre talent is on display
alongside respected international companies, often
performing newly written productions as well as
adaptations of classics like *The Selfish Giant*.

Meadows Festival

*The Meadows, South Edinburgh (620 9108/www.
meadowsfestival.co.uk).* Bus 24, 41, 42. **Admission**
free. **Map** p309 E/F7. **Date** 1st weekend in June.
An eclectic assortment of live music, family entertainment, stalls and fairground rides.

Edinburgh Independent
Radical Book Fair

*Assembly Rooms, George Street, New Town
(information 662 9112/www.word-power.co.uk).
Princes Street buses.* **Admission** charged for
some events; phone for details. **Map** p304 B1.
Dates 10-13 June 2004; 2005 dates tbc.
This event, organised by the Word Power bookshop
(*see p178*), consists of readings and book launches
– as well as some lively panel discussions – focusing on the promotion of books from small, independent and radical publishing houses. It's fair to say
that they're not usually very keen on President
George W Bush or the United States of America.

Arts & Entertainment

Pride Scotia

Information: 11 Dixon Street, Glasgow G1 4AL (www.pride-scotia.org). **Date** mid June.

Pride Scotia rose from the financial ashes of Pride Scotland in 2003, and, like gay pride events throughout the world, is really an excuse for a massive knees-up. Its location alternates between Glasgow and Edinburgh; it will be held in Edinburgh in 2005.

July

T in the Park

Balado Airfield, near Kinross, Perthshire (information 0870 169 6879/TicketMaster 0870 169 0100/www.tinthepark.com). **Tickets** £42.50-£88; see the website for details. **Credit** AmEx, MC, V. **Dates** 10, 11 July 2004; 2005 dates tbc.

T in the Park attracts luminaries from the British and international music scene, as well as around 50,000 eager music fans each day. Confirmed acts for 2004 include legends David Bowie and the Pixies, and pomp-rock upstarts Muse and the Darkness. The festival has benefited from dry weather in the last two years but nothing is guaranteed: invest in wellies, a cagoule and a nip of something warmer than Tennents, as well as sunglasses and a T-shirt.

August

Edinburgh Festivals (*see p32*).

September

Doors Open Day

Information: Cockburn Association, Trunk's Close, 55 High Street, Old Town (557 8686/www.cockburn association.org.uk). **Admission** free. **Date** 25 Sept 2004; 2005 date tbc.

On one day a year the Cockburn Association persuades the owners of many of Edinburgh's finest private buildings to join a Europe-wide movement and open their doors to the public. Ranging from disused sewage plants to stately homes, this is your chance to go *Through the Keyhole*.

October

Scottish Storytelling Festival

Various locations across both Edinburgh and Scotland (information & tickets 557 5724/ www.scottishstorytellingcentre.co.uk). **Tickets** approximately £5-£10. **Credit** MC, V. **Dates** 22-31 Oct 2004; 21-30 Oct 2005; 2006 dates tbc.

'This party rocks!' **Edinburgh's Hogmanay.** *See p197.*

Big blue inflatable balls: never leave home without 'em. **Edinburgh's Hogmanay**.

Hallowe'en: Samhuinn
From Castle Esplanade to Parliament Square,
High Street, Old Town (information 228 5353).
Date 31 Oct.
Samhuinn marks the end of the Celtic summer, six
months after Beltane. The Beltane Fire Society takes
to the streets once again (*see p194*), from Castle
Esplanade, down the Royal Mile to Parliament
Square, where the summer court, led by the Green
Man, is banished to the magical realm for winter.

November

Bonfire Night
Meadowbank Stadium, 139 London Road, Calton
Hill (661 5351). Bus 4, 5, 15, 19, 26, 34, 35, 44, 45.
Tickets £4. **Credit** MC, V. **Date** 5 Nov.
The fact that Guy Fawkes' gunpowder plot of 1605
was against Scotland's James IV is masked by the
fact that it was also meant to destroy the hated
Westminster Parliament. The biggest event takes
place at Meadowbank Stadium (*see p234*).

St Andrew's Day
Date 30 Nov.
As if you needed an excuse to come to Edinburgh,
take in its delights and go on an extended drinking
session. St Andrew's Day isn't quite as debauched
for the Scots as St Patrick's Day is for the Irish, but
as excuses for a good time go, it rates highly.

December

Capital Christmas
Various venues across the city
(www.edinburghscapitalchristmas.org).
What started out as a few events to brighten up the
month of December has grown into a full-blown festival. Capital Christmas is a mix of live entertainment, family attractions and other events. The

programme is published in October, but usually
includes Winter Wonderland, complete with fairground rides, mini-market and the largest outdoor
skating rink in Britain; and the Edinburgh Wheel, a
large Ferris wheel adjacent to the Scott Monument.

Edinburgh's Hogmanay
Information & passes: Hogmanay Box Office,
The Hub, Castlehill, Old Town (www.edinburghs
hogmanay.org). **Date** 29 Dec-1 Jan.
Scotland is the home of Hogmanay, and Edinburgh
is the best place to celebrate it. Hogmanay is New
Year's Eve; the night when the people of Scotland
take to the streets, kiss everyone in sight as the bells
ring out midnight, and afterwards go 'first footing'
with a lump of coal, a bun and a bottle of single malt.
If you see a house with open curtains and a light in
the window, knock on the door – tradition decrees
that uninvited guests are welcome.

Edinburgh's Hogmanay, now a four-day extravaganza, features an infamous street party, live music
in the gardens, ceilidh dancing, marching bands,
processions, street theatre and several events for the
hardiest of constitutions on Ne'er Day itself.

The city woke up reeling and punch-drunk for a
different reason on 1 Jan 2004 – the cancellation of
the Hogmanay concert and fireworks at the eleventh
hour because of high winds was a financial disaster
and a severe blow to Edinburgh's reputation.

Some 100,000 passes are offered on a ballot basis
and applications are normally opened to the public
in October. Members of the First Foot Club (around
£15 annual fee) are eligible for a pass, as are those
purchasing tickets for one of the major concerts. But
don't worry if you can't get hold of a pass – there is
still plenty of fun to be had on the streets outside the
cordon and you can see the extravagant and beautiful Seven Hills fireworks' display from many vantage points, including the Meadows and North
Bridge or, for the intrepid, Salisbury Crags.

Children

Edinburgh is an ankle-biter's paradise.

Clockwatching at the **Museum of Scotland**. *See p88.*

Spoilt – that's what Edinburgh children are. What with festivals cropping up year-round, galleries, museums and theatres on every corner, open green spaces across the city – not to mention a former volcano and a castle right in the centre – the danger is not boredom but cultural overload. That's even more the case in a city so easy to get around. Most of the key sites can be reached on foot, but when short legs get tired there's a good bus system: five- to 15-year-olds pay 50p and under-fives go free. Although the open-top tour buses are more expensive, they allow you to get on and off all day for the price of a single ticket and are a great way to get your bearings. Taxis are more expensive, but they seat five and pushchairs don't need to be folded. An invaluable guidebook is *Edinburgh for Under Fives*, available from most local bookshops (£5.95).

Events & entertainment

Many of Edinburgh's annual events (*see p194*) include activities for kids. The **Scottish Storytelling Centre** spins yarns year-round, focusing on October's Scottish International Storytelling Festival (*see p196*). Look out too for Easter's Puppet Animation Festival.

Most theatres have a Christmas children's show. The **Royal Lyceum** always has an excellent reinterpretation of a classic fairy story for five- to ten-year-olds; **Theatre Workshop** (for both; *see p238*) produces a small-scale alternative for the over-fives; and the **King's Theatre** (*see p237*) comes up trumps for traditional panto. The **City Art Centre** (*see p77*) hosts the sort of blockbuster exhibitions that will attract children and the **Filmhouse** (*see p206*) runs fortnightly morning screenings for parents and carers with babies, charmingly titled 'For Crying Out Loud!'

Exploring the city

Old Town, Arthur's Seat & South

There's plenty to keep even the most boisterous kids occupied at **Edinburgh Castle** (*see p70*). Get there in good time for the one o'clock gun salute; this is fired daily (except on Sunday) – with a satisfyingly big bang and a puff of smoke – by a stiffly marching bombardier.

South of the castle is the **Meadows** (*see p115*), a big grassy space with three playgrounds: one at each end, with a toddler park in the middle. Alternatively, the Royal Mile is riddled with alleyways and courtyards that are perfect for exploring – quite a few lead to open spaces that are good for a run-about or a picnic. **Dunbar's Close** (137 Canongate) conceals a replica of a 17th-century garden, and is a particularly peaceful spot.

At the bottom of the hill you'll find **Our Dynamic Earth** (*see p84*). You don't need to buy a ticket to visit its café, which is the only convenient place to fuel up before you make your assault on **Arthur's Seat** (*see p107*). The Park Rangers (140 Holyrood Road; open 10am-4pm Mon-Fri) will give you maps and suggest suitable walks.

New Town, Calton Hill, Stockbridge & West

For kids the unique attraction of **Princes Street** is that it has shops on only one side; the other is a rolling grassy park with steep winding paths leading up to the castle, bisected by a railway. If you wave like mad from the bridge behind the Ross Bandstand you get a whistle in return from passing train drivers. In the westernmost corner of the gardens are a snack bar, toilets and often a delightful Edwardian merry-go-round.

East of Princes Street is **Calton Hill** (*see p102*). A flight of steps from Waterloo Place will get you to the top in no time for splendid views of the city and beyond.

To the north of the New Town is the **Royal Botanic Garden** (*see p99*). Not only does it have acres of greenery and absolutely no dog mess, but there are also friendly squirrels and ducks to feed, glasshouses with huge goldfish, a pricey café with high chairs, an outdoor eating area and nappy-changing facilities.

In Dean Village to the south, the **Scottish National Gallery of Modern Art** and the **Dean Gallery** (for both, *see p101*) sit across the road from each other. The art in the Dean Gallery will probably appeal to youngsters most as it includes Paolozzi's massive metal giant and a replica of his chaotic studio.

A steep path from the rear of the Gallery of Modern Art takes you to the **Water of Leith Walkway**, a ribbon of riverside paths that meanders through the city to the docks. Maps and information can be obtained from the Water of Leith Visitors' Centre, where there are also interactive exhibits allowing children to examine the river and its plant and animal life in detail. Leith itself boasts the **Royal Yacht Britannia** (*see p125*).

Out of town

Eight miles (13 kilometres) south-east of town is **Dalkeith Country Park** (*see p264*), which has an adventure playground with elevated walkways for over-fours, a café, woodland paths and spooky Victorian riverside tunnels. The seabirds and ancient monastic ruins of **Inchcolm Island and Abbey** (*see p265*), together with the ferry boat trip to get there, are a sure-fire hit. The most exciting castles close to the capital are **Linlithgow Palace** (*see p266*) and **Tantallon Castle** (*see p263*). Both have dizzying drops, so watch the children.

Active kids

Also *see p230* **Sport & Fitness**.

Laserquest
56B Dalry Road, West Edinburgh (346 1919/www. laserquest.co.uk). Bus 3, 21, 22, 33, 44. **Open** 11am-11pm Mon-Sat; 11am-8pm Sun. **Admission** £4 per game. **No credit cards. Map** p308 B7.
You can zap them with laser fire and they can zap you back, and you all go home in one piece.

Leith Waterworld
377 Easter Road, Leith (555 6000). Leith Walk buses. **Open** *Summer* 10am-5pm daily. *Winter* 10am-5pm Fri-Sun. **Admission** £3.20; £2.65 concessions; free under-5s. **No credit cards. Map** p307 J1.
Edinburgh's best swimming pool for kids includes a gently sloping beach for toddlers, a wave machine, flumes, river rapids and bubble beds. Note the limited opening hours.

Top five Kids sights

Arthur's Seat
Imagine: a real-life dead volcano on your doorstep (*see p107*).

Edinburgh Castle
The best place in the world to play king (or queen) of the castle (*see p70*).

Edinburgh Zoo
Monkeys, camels, tigers, flamingos, sea lions, and penguins on parade (*see p120*).

Our Dynamic Earth
Journey back in time to the formation of the planet (*see p84*).

Royal Museum and Museum of Scotland
Everything from whale skeletons to personal computers (*see p88*).

Arts & Entertainment

Winter Wonderland

Princes Street Gardens, New Town. Princes Street buses. www.edinburghscapitalchristmas.org. **Map** p304 B/C2.

A fabulous outdoor skating rink gets rigged up here each December.

Animal encounters

Butterfly & Insect World

Dobbies Garden World, Lasswade, Midlothian (663 4932/www.edinburgh-butterfly-world.co.uk). Bus 3. **Open** *Summer* 9.30am-5.30pm daily. *Winter* 10am-5pm daily (last admission 4.30pm). **Admission** £4.70; £3.60 concessions, 3-15s; free under-3s; family £15-£19. **Credit** MC, V.

Butterflies are hatching all year round in this tropical greenhouse paradise. And, for the more adventurous of your offspring, the jovial keepers lead beastie-handling sessions, involving snakes, tarantulas, and very brave children, at noon and 3pm daily. A useful option if the weather turns.

Deep Sea World

North Queensferry, Fife (01383 411 880/www.deep seaworld.com). North Queensferry rail then 10min walk (down steep hill). Free bus in summer 01383 621249 for details. **Open** *Apr-Oct* 10am-6pm daily. *Nov-Mar* 10am-5pm daily. **Admission** £7.95; £6.50 concessions; £5.75 3-15s; free under-3s. **Credit** MC, V.

Aquariums, a feely fish pool where you can touch the piscine life, plus films, educational lectures and a café. You can even learn to dive to PADI accepted standards among the sharks and stingrays.

Edinburgh Zoo

Corstorphine Road, Murrayfield, West Edinburgh (334 9171/www.edinburghzoo.org.uk). Bus 12, 26, 31. **Open** *Apr-Sept* 9am-6pm daily. *Mar, Oct* 9am-5pm daily. *Nov-Feb* 9am-4.30pm daily. **Admission** £8; £5.50 concessions; £5 3-15s; free under-3s; family £24-£30. **Credit** MC, V.

While Edinburgh Zoo has all the favourite animals, its principal claim to fame is its army of penguins, the largest number assembled in captivity anywhere.

For a rainy day

Few tourists come to Scotland for the weather, and you shouldn't rule out the possibility of having to keep the family entertained in a downpour. It isn't difficult. Head first to the **Royal Museum** and its extension, the **Museum of Scotland** (for both, *see p88*). Entry is free, there are lockers to stash pushchairs and coats, and there's loads to look at, from stuffed animals and goldfish ponds to interactive displays. The cafés are dull and overpriced, but the children's Discovery Centre (in the Museum of Scotland) is terrific. Every weekend afternoon there are family performances and free talks.

On the Royal Mile, you can choose between the **Brass Rubbing Centre** (*see p79*), the **Museum of Childhood** (*see p82*) and the **People's Story** (*see p85*). Down the hill there are more gruesome distractions at **Edinburgh Dungeon** (*see p78*). Between Holyrood Palace and Arthur's Seat is the volcanic **Our Dynamic Earth** (*see p84*).

The **Museum of Flight**, a car journey away at East Fortune airfield (*see p263*) has 50 aircraft, from warplanes to microlights, and now its very own Concorde.

At Newhaven, you'll find the charming **Newhaven Heritage Museum** (*see p126*), where kids get to dress up as fishermen and fishwives; **Charlie Chalk's adventure play area** in Brewsters Pub (*see p201*); and the extraordinary Alien Rock **climbing centre** (*see*

p234), which holds children's classes at weekends. To burn off excess energy try Murrayfield **Ice Rink** (*see p234*) or for something a little more placid there's the **Ceramic Experience** (8 Hopetoun Street, Broughton; 556 0070) where you can paint your own pottery.

The penguin parade, held at 2.15pm every day between April and August (as long as the birds are in the mood), is one of the city's most bizarre sights.

Gorgie City Farm
Gorgie Road, South Edinburgh (337 4202). Bus 1, 2, 3, 21, 25, 33, 34, 38. **Open** *Mar-Oct* 9.30am-4.30pm daily. *Nov-Feb* 9.30am-4pm daily. **Admission** free.
This lovely informal spot has all the farmyard faves, plus a rabbits' cuddle corner, a playground and a good café with high chairs.

Scottish Seabird Centre
The Harbour, North Berwick (01620 890 202/www. seabird.org). North Berwick rail then 10min walk. **Open** *Apr-Oct* 10am-6pm daily. *Nov-Jan* 10am-4pm Mon-Fri; 10am-5.30pm Sat, Sun. *Feb-Mar* 10am-5pm Mon-Fri, 10am-5.30pm Sat, Sun. **Admission** £5.95; £3.95 concessions, 5-15s; under-5s free; family £12.50-£19.50. **Credit** MC, V.
Perched on the shore, this excellent museum lets you zoom in on nesting birds with live-action video cameras, watch them through telescopes or see short films indoors. Excellent loos and a nice café.

Rover's rest. **Edinburgh Castle**. *See p70.*

Indoor play centres

Charlie Chalks & the Fun Factory
Brewsters, Newhaven Quay, Newhaven, Leith (555 1570). Bus 7, 10, 11, 16, 32. **Open** 11am-9pm Mon-Sat; noon-9pm Sun. **Admission** £2 per hour session. **Credit** AmEx, MC, V. **Map** p311 Ex.
A large and exciting indoor play area attached to a pub/restaurant, with a safe section for toddlers.

Clambers
Royal Commonwealth Pool, 21 Dalkeith Road, South Edinburgh (667 7211). Bus 2, 14, 21, 33. **Open** *Children aged 3-8* 10am-6pm Mon-Fri; 10am-5pm Sat, Sun. *Accompanied under-3s* 10am-noon Sat, Sun. **Admission** £1.90 per 45min session. **No credit cards**. **Map** p310 J8.
A large, safe, enclosed play area.

Eating out

Pubs

Pubs that serve full meals are allowed to admit children until 8pm, at the bar staff's discretion. Among the better ones are: the **Cramond Inn** (Glebe Road, Cramond Village; 336 2035); **Ratho Park Hotel** (101 Dalmahoy Road, Kirknewton; 333 1242),

Fun & games

Umberto's (2 Bonnington Road Lane, Leith; 554 1314) has booth tables that form a train and there's an outdoor playground. Children can make their own pizzas at **Giuliano's on the Shore** in Leith (1 Commercial Street, Leith; 554 5272) and **Est Est Est** (135a George Street, New Town; 225 2555). **China China** (10 Antigua Street, Old Town; 556 9791), offers a buffet and you can keep going back for more. Under-fives eat free, under-12s for half-price.

Central eats

The **Filling Station** (235 High Street; 226 2488) is a large American-style diner with high chairs and nappy-changing area. Just off the High Street at 63a Cockburn Street is the **Southern Cross Café** (622 0622), which serves tasty adult food plus child friendly dishes. If pizza's the thing, head for North Bridge, where you'll find **Pizza Express** at No.23 (557 6411) and **Pizza Hut** on the other side (No.46; 226 3038). Pachyderm fans will love the **Elephant House** (21 George IV Bridge; 220 5355), a busy, informal café with elephants simply everywhere. The **Forest**, an activist café and gallery (3 Bristo Place; 220 4538), offers cheap healthy eats and runs a babies and toddlers group Tue from 10am to noon.

Practicalities for parents

Babysitting/childminding

Butterfly Personnel
7 Earlston Place, London Road, Calton Hill (659 5065). **Open** *Office* 24hrs daily. **No credit cards**.

Edinburgh Crèche Co-op
297 Easter Road, Leith (553 2116). **Open** *Office* 9am-4pm Mon-Fri. **No credit cards**.

Equipment hire

Baby Baby Equipment Hire
45 Glendevon Place, West Edinburgh (337 7016). **Open** no specific office hours; please phone at reasonable times. **No credit cards**.

Arts & Entertainment

Comedy

Laughter's last Stand.

If Edinburgh is the world capital of comedy during August, it's little more than a backwater for the rest of the year. But it is, at least, a backwater with a comedy HQ in the shape of the **Stand** (*see p203*). The New Town venue has nurtured a keen comedy audience and operates seven nights a week, with a programme featuring a mix of home-grown talent and luminaries from the international circuit. Big-name headliners might include Ross Noble, Daniel Kitson or Adam Hills, supplemented by resident compères and local support acts. The club is also increasingly being used as a venue for touring acts, including the Pub Landlord (Al Murray) and Ireland's freewheeling fruitcake, Jason Byrne. Weekday shows can offer delightful surprises: established performers like Miles Jupp, Des Clarke and Craig Hill cut their teeth at the weekly newcomers' Red Raw night, while the Wednesday night slot is devoted to more diverse forms of comedy including live sketch shows and topical satire.

Now that **Jongleurs** (*see p203*), the comedy equivalent of Starbucks, has just opened a few hundred yards away it remains to be seen whether the Stand can hold on to its king of comedy title. At the very least, the Stand has raised its game on Thursday night, which now – more than ever – is a highlight of the week.

Jupp to it

Who better than Edinburgh-based English toff and Perrier nominee **Miles Jupp** to give an outsider's view of comedy in the city from an insider's perspective? He tells us four things that make Edinburgh's comedy unique:

Audience
Edinburgh audiences tend to be highly comedy literate, consequently, there's a lot more variety on each bill. In London, there may be more clubs and comedians, but there is not as much choice, with the circuit there dominated by 'patter merchants'.

Environment
Everybody in the room is on the comedian's side. Obviously there can be exceptions, and what could be more enjoyable than to occasionally witness someone unexpectedly behave in a totally inappropriate fashion in front of an audience who all decide to follow suit?

The Stand
The atmosphere here is quite unique – you really feel like you are in Scotland without it being overtly 'Scottish'. The Stand's weekend compères, Jane Mackay and Susan Morrison, are both excellent and play a large part in creating this atmosphere, but everyone in the club contributes to it. I'll always play The Stand: it doesn't feel like work for me.

Talent
I'd recommend anyone who appreciates a broad range of comedy to go to one of Reg Anderson's gigs, if only to see the man himself. I think he's a genius. When I first moved to Edinburgh, my flatmate and I used to quote his act all day long. Or wrestle.

Any number of Scottish comedians could easily break through into the mainstream consciousness if they are given the opportunity. Des Clarke, Frankie Boyle, The Reverend Obadiah, Raymond Mearns, Craig Hill, Vladimir McTavish/Bob Doolally and Colin Ramone are all among the best acts I have seen anywhere.

Stand-up at the **Stand**.

While the Cowgate's Gilded Balloon popped in the fire of 2002 (*see p73* **Burning down the town**), the area will soon see the opening of the **Cowgate Central Theatre**. Outside the permanent venues, pub-based gigs come and go with a regularity that is quite unpredictable. The only certainty is that Reg Anderson – a legend among comedians, if not audiences – will be hosting a gig somewhere. Quality is variable, but they are always an experience. In addition to this indigenous activity, the big UK comedy guns periodically pass through, playing the **Queen's Hall** (*see p217*), the **Traverse** (*see p238*) or the **Festival Theatre** (*see p239*). See local listings for details.

Big Word Performance Poetry

The Tron, 9 Hunter Square, Old Town (226 0931/ www.dreamit.org/bigword). North Bridge–Nicolson Street buses. **Shows** fortnightly Thur. **Tickets** £3; £2 concessions. **No credit cards. Map** p304 D3.
Not strictly comedy, but laughter is high on the agenda at these fortnightly performances. Hosted by the ever-ebullient Jem Rolls and accomplished wordsmith Anita Govan, Big Word features serious poets and well-versed stand-ups. The Poetry Slam, held every three months at the Bongo Club, is a must-see (*see p221*).

Cowgate Central Comedy Club

Cowgate Central Theatre, Wilkie House, Cowgate, Old Town (478 5333/www.cowgate.com). North Bridge–Nicolson Street buses. **Shows** 8.30pm Thur-Sat; late night improv 11pm Sat. **Tickets** £8; £5 concessions. **Credit** MC, V. **Map** p304 D3.
The latest addition to Edinburgh's comedy scene, set to open in May 2004. Other clubs have tried – and failed – to pull punters in a city dominated for so long by a single venue, but with the promise of a permanent home at the Cowgate Theatre, this all looks very promising. Expect a Stand-style blend of up-and-coming local talent with more established acts in the headline spots.

Snatch Social

Liquid Room, 9C Victoria Street, Old Town (225 2564). Bus 23, 27, 28, 41, 42, 45. **Shows** 10.30pm Thur. **Tickets** £4; £3 concessions. **No credit cards. Map** p304 C3.
The antithesis of straight stand-up. Harry Ainsworth and Tony Carter (aka Garth Cruikshank and Will Andrews, winners of Perrier Best Newcomer and Tap Water Awards, respectively) continue to ply offbeat absurdity at their weekly club night.

Stand

5 York Place, New Town (558 7272/www. thestand.co.uk for online bookings). Bus 8, 12, 16, 17, 25, 25A **Shows** 8.30pm Mon; 9pm Tue-Sat; 1pm, 8.30pm Sun. **Tickets** £1 Mon; £5-£6 Tue, £4-£6 Wed; £5 Thur; £6-£7 Fri; £8 Sat; £3-£4 Sun (1pm show free). **No credit cards. Map** p306 F4.
Sunday afternoons find the Stand in a seriously chilled mood: battered sofas, intimate spaces and a simple menu create its laid-back café-bar vibe, with free improvised comedy from 1pm. Nightly, the basement venue is transformed into a comedy haven comprising two performance spaces. The snug studio, with its trademark *Looney Tunes* backdrop, is used for weekday shows, while the main cabaret bar, with capacity for 160 comedy-goers, hosts the weekend showcases. Arrive early for a good seat.

Jongleurs

Unit 6/7, Omni Centre, Greenside Place, Calton Hill (08707 870707/www.jongleurs.com). Bus 8, 12, 16, 17, 25. **Shows** 8.30pm Fri, Sat. **Tickets** £15 Fri; £16 Sat. **Credit** AmEx, MC, V. **Map** p307 G4.
Like most major chains, you always know exactly what you're going to get with Jongleurs – and this is both the best and worst thing about it. On the plus side, you can expect to find some of the biggest names in the business. But this is comedy for the masses, so even comedians known for dark, edgy stuff may jettison their riskier gags in favour of the crowd-pleasers. The price includes entrance to the post-gig club, for a comedy flavoured party night.

Arts & Entertainment

Film

Edinburgh: Hollywood comes to Holyrood.

Edinburgh straddles the gritty and the pretty, and it's the city's combination of inhospitable conditions and architectural charm that has made it the perfect backdrop for films. **Sean Connery**, perhaps the finest of the city's crop of actors (and unquestionably the best Bond ever; *see p208* **EdinBurgher Sean Connery**) is still adamantly attached to Edinburgh as a cinematic city. 'I've filmed in most of the world's great cities, which makes coming home all the better. To me, Edinburgh seems to have been built as a film set,' he says.

Edinburgh's biggest cinematic success, however, was about as unpretty as they come. *Trainspotting*, Danny Boyle's 1996 elegy to Edinburgh's smacked-up suburbs (*see p121*), launched the career of just about everyone in it: Robert Carlyle, Kelly MacDonald and Ewan McGregor. Boyle managed to outdo his previous film, *Shallow Grave*, in bringing the city's twisted side to cinema screens worldwide.

Trainspotting was swiftly followed by *Mary Reilly* (1996), a reworking of the Jekyll and Hyde story, for which Julia Roberts and John Malkovich spent a few days filming in Edinburgh. Unfortunately, *The Acid House* (1999), author Irvine Welsh's follow-up to *Trainspotting,* failed to emulate the success of its predecessor.

There is a small group of Edinburgh movies in which, as David Bruce points out in his book *Scotland the Movie*, the character of the city is integral to the feel of the film. In *The Battle of the Sexes* (1959), the depiction of the city as 'cold, hidebound, reactionary and harbouring homicidal tendencies' is used by Peter Sellers to great comic effect, with ominous undercurrents. This aspect of Edinburgh's character is also portrayed in the 1930s girls' school drama *The Prime of Miss Jean Brodie* (1968), adapted from the novel by Muriel Spark, which won Maggie Smith the Oscar for Best Actress in 1969.

There remains a healthy interest in adaptations of works by Edinburgh-based authors. Jonny Lee Miller played the lead in *Complicity* (2000), a big-screen version of Iain Banks's tale of gruesome murders in and around the city. Meanwhile, *Women Talking Dirty* (2001), an adaptation of Isla Dewar's novel portraying the unlikely friendship between an oddball single mother and a shy cartoonist, was marred by Helena Bonham Carter's dubious Scottish accent – but at least Edinburgh looked nice. Ewan McGregor returned in early 2002 to film an adaptation of Scottish beat writer Alex Trocchi's *Young Adam* on the canals between Edinburgh and Glasgow.

Filmmakers are currently chasing Sir Sean Connery and McGregor himself to star in *Mile High*, a new Edinburgh-based film about the life of James Tytler, Britain's first aeronaut and supposedly the first man to have sex in a hot-air balloon. Locals have also been agog over George Clooney's visit in 2004, while filming *The Jacket* which he is co-producing with Steven Soderbergh. The film, set in Dechmont, just west of Edinburgh, tells of a Gulf War veteran accused of a murder he does not remember, and will be bringing the Lothians to the big screen in 2005.

Beer Monsters, Inc

Top three pubs with a secret hidden cinema.

Brass Monkey

14 Drummond Street, Old Town (556 1961). A busy little bar with a Narnia-style twist – peep behind the curtain at the back of the bar and you'll stumble into a room full of cosy rug-covered beds, and a film flickering on the wall.

Forest Café

3 Bristo Place, Old Town (220 4538). No beers to be had here (it's BYOB, though, with £1 corkage per person), but if you check the chalk-board schedule you'll no doubt find all manner of obscure filmic delights to watch with a Rooibosch tea and a bowl of salsa.

Nicol Edwards

29 Niddry Street, Old Town (556 8642). Somewhere in the rabbit warren depths of this labyrinthine bar is a neat little pew-lined cinema room. Phone in advance to find out what's screening.

Arts & Entertainment

Cinema Paradiso? **Filmhouse.** *See p206.*

Bleu. **Odeon Lothian Road**. *See p206.*

The annual Edinburgh International Film Festival (*see p37*) always has a soft spot for local filmmaking talent – *Young Adam* opened the 2003 festival. It also manages to haul more glamorous international film premieres north of the border, for one month of the year at least.

Film-making in Edinburgh is pretty prolific thanks to Mediabase (25a South West Thistle Street Lane, EH2; 220 0220/www.edinburgh mediabase.com), a resource facility that showcases local short films on the first Monday of every month at the Cameo. Every screening of the event has sold out since it began in 2001, so tickets should be booked in advance.

PRACTICAL INFORMATION

Film programmes change on Fridays, and listings appear in the *Metro, Edinburgh Evening News, Scotsman, Herald,* the *List* and online (www.yell.co.uk, among others). Films are classified as: (U) – for universal viewing; (PG) – parental guidance advised for young children; (12a), where under-12s must be accompanied by an adult; (15) and (18) – no entry for those aged under 15 and 18 respectively. Most of the city's cinemas have disabled access and toilets, but it's best to phone to check first.

Cinemas

Necessity may well have spawned Edinburgh's healthy crop of cinemas: on days when the rain hits you horizontally, seeing a film becomes a most attractive option.

Cameo

38 Home Street, South Edinburgh (228 4141/ www.cameocinema.co.uk). Bus 10, 11, 15, 16, 17, 23. **Tickets** £3.50 Mon; £4.50-£5.50 Tue-Sun; £3.50 concessions. **Credit** MC, V. **Map** p309 D7. Nestled in Tollcross, this independent cinema is a real treat, picking four films from the edges of the mainstream every week. Screen One's impressive atmosphere more than makes up for the slightly uncomfortable seats. You can chat up the friendly staff at the bar and then take your pint through when the film starts. This can soak up Sunday, if you take in the weekly double-bill of classic cinema. All tickets cost less on Mondays and the cheapest concession seats in Edinburgh are to be found on a Wednesday, when the first screening of every film is £1.

Dominion

18 Newbattle Terrace, Morningside, South Edinburgh (box office 447 4771/information 447 2660/www. dominioncinemas.net). Bus 11, 15, 16, 17, 23. **Tickets** £4-£5.90; concessions all day Mon & before 6pm Tue-Sun. **Credit** MC, V.

The Dominion is family-run and family-friendly, although not overly hospitable to those unprepared for the fairly hefty ticket prices. Still, it's a pretty little place, with an art deco interior dating from 1938, and the decadent Pullman seats in Screen One are a joy. Hot snacks are available before 6pm in the basement café-bar, which stays open until the end of the last film; drinks may be taken into the auditorium.

Filmhouse

88 Lothian Road, South Edinburgh (box office 228 2688/information 228 2690/www.filmhousecinema. com). Bus 1, 2, 10, 11, 15, 16, 22. **Tickets** £3.50-£5.50; £1.20-£4 concessions. **Credit** MC, V. **Map** p304 A3.

Ah, the Filmhouse: where Edinburgh is treated to some of the most imaginative and obscure cinema to be found. You'd be hard pressed to find a day when they're not screening a classic, or midway

Chillin' crime. **Complicity.** *See p204.*

through some festival or other (the London Lesbian and Gay Film Festival screens here, for example, and recent retrospectives include one on Greek director Theo Angelopoulos). The slightly po-faced staff do nothing to ease the austere atmosphere of the front of house, but venture into the bar and you can relax with a quiet drink. Except, that is, on the second Sunday of each month, when you'll find yourself head-to-head with Edinburgh's cinema-going cognoscenti at the Filmhouse's notoriously competitive quiz night. The venue is also home to the Edinburgh Film Guild, whose regular Sunday screenings will please the purist with their always punctual start and no-trailer policy.

Odeon Lothian Road

118 Lothian Road, South Edinburgh (221 1477/ www.odeon.co.uk). Bus 1, 2, 10, 11, 15, 16, 22. **Tickets** £4.80-£5.80; £4.20 concessions. **Credit** MC, V. **Map** p304 A3.

Filling both a geographical and cultural gap between its independent neighbours, the Cameo and the Filmhouse, the newly-opened Odeon picks up where the ABC and the Regal before it left off in supplying the city centre with its diet of mainstream and family films. You can take your drinks down the aesthetically satisfying circular staircase and into the auditorium with you. Very civilised.

Odeon Wester Hailes

Westside Plaza, 120 Wester Hailes Road, Wester Hailes, West Edinburgh (453 1569/information & credit card bookings 0870 505 0007/www.odeon. co.uk). Bus 3, 3A, 18, 20, 28, 30, 32, 33. **Tickets** £3.50-£5.20; £3.20-£3.50 concessions. **Credit** AmEx, MC, V.

This eight-screen multiplex is west of the city centre, and visible from the train as you arrive. A licensed bar is open every evening and refreshments are also served in an ice-cream bar: coffee, soft drinks, ice-cream, snacks and sweets.

Ster Century, Ocean Terminal

Ocean Terminal, Ocean Drive, Leith (553 0700/ www.stercentury.co.uk). Bus 11, 22, 34, 35, 36. **Tickets** £4.60-£5.60; £3.30-£3.50 concessions. **Credit** AmEx, MC, V. **Map** p311 Hx.

On the second floor of the dense slab of commercial delights that is Leith's Ocean Terminal lies yet another multiplex. Don't let the surrounding shopping complex put you off, though: there are superb views of the Forth from the bar and grill opposite the cinema. Mainstream films dominate the programme, with cheap kids' matinées on weekday mornings. All tickets are £3 on Wednesdays.

UGC Fountain Park

Fountain Park, 130-133 Dundee Street, West Edinburgh (228 8788/information & credit card bookings 0870 902 0417/www.ugccinemas.co.uk). Bus 1, 28, 34, 35. **Tickets** £4.70-£5.50; £2.95-£3.40 concessions. **Credit** AmEx, MC, V. **Map** p308 B8.

Located in Sean Connery's old stomping ground of Fountainbridge, (*see p208* **EdinBurgher Sean**

Reel to real

You've seen the film, but now you want to be in it: here are the three best places in Edinburgh to recreate your favourite Scottish movie moments.

Princes Street – *Trainspotting*

Edinburgh's most bustling shopping street: the perfect location to make like Ewan McGregor in *Trainspotting*. To recreate the opening scene of Danny Boyle's drug-addled classic, your shoplifting extravaganza has to be followed by a marathon sprint down Leith Street to Calton Road, where you should really make every effort to narrowly avoid being run over at some point.

Edinburgh Academy, Henderson Row – *The Prime of Miss Jean Brodie*

The more masochistic of film fanatics may be pleased to learn that the Donaldson's building at the Edinburgh Academy in Stockbridge was the location used as the school in *The Prime of Miss Jean Brodie*. You could try strutting up to the building, lips pursed, hands balled into fists, announcing to passers-by in your best Maggie Smith accent: 'My gels are the crème de la crème.'

Heriot Row, New Town – *Shallow Grave*

Once you've developed a taste for the classier side of Edinburgh, the next step for any diehard film buff is to buy a Georgian flat in the New Town and interview potential flatmates, *Shallow Grave* style. Questions should be direct and straightforward: 'What on earth could make you think that we would want to share a flat like this with someone like you?' Let Danny Boyle's 1994 film serve as a reminder, though, that chopping up and burying your dead flatmates is probably not the best of ideas.

Connery) the UGC is as sprawling and comprehensive as Edinburgh cinemas get. It boasts 13 screens and there's ample leg-room – especially if you get there in time to nab the seats in front of the railings which serve as perfect footrests. It has an unappealing café-bar, and the usual food stalls, and you can round off your night at Fountain Park with a spot of bowling and a pint at Brannigans.

UCI Kinnaird Park

Kinnaird Park, Newcraighall Road, South Edinburgh (669 0777/information & credit card bookings 0870 010 2030/www.uci.co.uk). Bus 14, 32, 52. **Tickets** *£4.40-£5.40; £3.65-£4.75 concessions.* **Credit** *AmEx, MC, V.*

A modern 12-screen multiplex in the centre of the Kinnaird Shopping Park, about 20 minutes out from the centre of Edinburgh. It lacks the atmosphere of the older cinemas and shows almost solely mainstream films, but at least it has decent equipment and a good selection of sweets and the obligatory popcorn buckets for munchies during the films.

Vue Cinemas

Omni Centre, Greenside Place, New Town (0870 240 6020/www.myvue.com). Princes Street/Playhouse buses. **Tickets** *£4.60-£5.50; £3.30-£4 concessions.* **Credit** MC, V. **Map** p307 G4.

The corporate fairy waved its magic wand and, Lo! Warner Village became Vue Cinemas. This giant glass cheesecake that has sprung up at the top of Leith Walk is home to the cinema closest to the bustling crowds of Princes Street. There are 12 screens, the seats are perfectly comfy, and although the regular programme does not stray away from the well-trodden blockbuster path, there are signs that the cinema may not be averse to accommodating more innovative events (self-portraitist Cindy Sherman's *Billboard Commission* graced the side of the Omni Centre early in 2004, and it was home to the Blue Box, a mini-cinema screening local short films). Outside the cinema, you'll find yourself surrounded by all manner of chain pubs and cheesy discos (*see p228* **Saturday night fevers**).

EdinBurgher Sean Connery

He is, perhaps, the most famous Edinburgh man alive today. He might even be the most famous Scot alive today. He's been voted 'Sexiest Man Alive'. His voice has been voted the sexiest of any man living. He has an Oscar. He has a knighthood. He was James Bond. To some, he always will be.

But more than any of these things, Sir Sean Connery is Scottish and he wants people to know it. Scotland's self-appointed president of people's hearts is very proud of his country of birth – he just doesn't want to live here. From the 'Scotland Forever' tattoo on his forearm, to his vocal support for the Scottish National Party, Sir Sean does everything he can to prove that the haggis spirit runs true in his veins. Some would say that he is merely Scotland's fair-weather film star friend, and little more than a part-time patriot, but even when he isn't around, he exerts an influence. It seems that almost every chip shop, post office and butcher has a framed photo hung in pride of place, that depicts a touching scene wherein Edinburgh's own celluloid icon bonds with his people while tarrying a while over the purchase of a stamp.

He may now call Spain his home, but Connery's roots in Edinburgh run deep. Born in Fountainbridge in 1930, he earned his first few pennies working as a milkman. After a spell in the Navy, he returned to Edinburgh and took his body (freshly toned from his new interest in bodybuilding) along to the Edinburgh College of Art, where he posed as a life model.

It was his continued interest in bodybuilding that finally led him away from Edinburgh. While in London for the 1953 Mr Universe competition, he rather stumbled upon an interest in the theatre. From there, he went on to various small parts in film and television, and then – a leading role as a certain roguish spy. Thereafter, Auld Reekie would be little more than a memory, but many chip shop and post office owners would tell you that the memory of Sean is far from bad for business.

Galleries

Out of the frame and into the future.

Ramona by Camilla Løw
at **doggerfisher**. *See p211.*

Moyna Flannigan's *Debutant.*
doggerfisher. *See p211.*

Scottish-based artists are forging an identity
above and beyond the crafts and traditional
schools expected of them in fusty old Scotland.
None more so than the industrious and
inventive artists of Edinburgh.

The city's distinguished reputation used to
rest on the elegant laurels of the Enlightenment.
In recent years, however, attention has lingered
too long on the Scottish Colourists, a group of
painters influenced by the wild palettes of
the Fauves and the loose brushes of the
Impressionists. While there's no doubt that they
started the shockwaves that put Scotland on the
map way back when, what was once outrageous
is now very much part of the mainstream.

The city has long been seen as the reserved
elder sibling to vibrant Glasgow, but its visual
culture is gaining momentum. The first phase
of the Royal Scottish Academy's ambitious
renovation project was unveiled in 2003, and a
five-year £30 million development will link the
building to the adjacent National Gallery in

2005. At the time of writing plans were also underway for a new £2 million gallery to be built on a donated former industrial site at Granton in North Edinburgh. Meanwhile artist-run spaces like the Collective on Cockburn Street, Out of the Blue in Leith and Total Kunst in the side room of the Forest Café are proving what can be done with imagination, energy and decidedly modest resources.

There are high hopes too for the National Galleries' upcoming programmes, which will include Titian at the **National Gallery** (*see p93*), and Jasper Johns and Lucien Freud retrospectives at the **National Gallery of Modern Art** (*see p101*), in 2004 alone. World-class shows can also be expected from the extensive national collections, such as the precious Turner watercolours that are so delicate that a condition of their bequest to the nation is that they can only be displayed once a year, in January, when the northern light is at its weakest (*see p194*).

On the Old Town side of the Bridges, be sure to visit the **Fruitmarket**, which showcases modern art in an intimate setting. Sample the latest in photographic and video work at **Stills** on Cockburn Street.

If you're after a piece of art to take home, check out the capital's numerous commercial galleries. Elegant Dundas Street in the New Town has long been the heart of the market for traditional Scottish painting, housing **Bourne Fine Art** and the rather unimaginatively titled **Scottish Gallery** among others. Recent years have seen some younger contemporary galleries muscling in on the selling game, such as the **Patriothall Gallery @ WASPS** in the New Town and both **doggerfisher** and **Merz** down in Broughton. Those out on the prowl for hot young talent should also check out shows at the Edinburgh College of Art (Lauriston Place, South Edinburgh; 221 6000/www.eca.ac.uk).

Art in Edinburgh isn't all about galleries though: there are plenty of non-traditional spaces where the city's creative zest is also in evidence. The **Roxy Art House** (2 Roxburgh Place, South Edinburgh; 556 9222), is slowly transforming into a year-round arts hub while **Sleeper** sticks its neck out from under the bedclothes and blinks blearily at the passing world with interesting shows in the basement of an architect's office (Reiach and Hall Architects, 6 Darnaway Street, New Town; 225 8444).

Detailed information on what is showing and where is available in the fortnightly *List* magazine or in daily papers such as the *Scotsman* or *Herald*. See also the **Dean Gallery** (*see p101*), **Inverleith House** (*see p99*), the **Portrait Gallery** (*see p94*) and the **Royal Scottish Academy** (*see p93*).

Bourne Fine Art

6 Dundas Street, New Town (557 4050). Bus 23, 37. **Open** 10am-6pm Mon-Fri; 11am-2pm Sat. **Admission** free. **No credit cards**. **Map** p306 E3.

Spacious, elegant and decorous, this long established gallery is a Dundas Street veteran with a strong reputation for trading in traditional Scottish landscapes and portraiture from the 1700s onward. A prestigious selection of watercolours and sketches by Scottish masters including Sir David Wilkie are displayed on two floors, tastefully set among mahogany tables and white lilies. Works from a range of artists and designers including the Scottish colourists, the Glasgow Boys and Charles Rennie Mackintosh are all on display.

City Art Centre

2 Market Street, Old Town (529 3993/www.cac. org.uk). Princes Street buses. **Open** *Sept-June* 10am-5pm Mon-Sat. *July-Aug* 10am-5pm Mon-Sat; noon-5pm Sun. **Admission** free, charge for occasional exhibitions. **Credit** MC, V. **Map** p304 D2.

This is one of several buildings dotted around the city that was designed for the *Scotsman* newspaper but has now found another use, having been converted into the City Art Centre in 1979. Its airy galleries reach up six floors (though not all are in use) and the focus is mostly on Scottish art. There is a predilection for the conceptual and while the scope is mostly local, it does occasionally attract big overseas shows. Cultural consumerism is encouraged in the gallery's shop, and relaxation in the licensed café, which can provide tea or a three-course meal.

Collective

22-28 Cockburn Street, Old Town (220 1260/fax 220 5585/www.collectivegallery.net). Bus 35/Nicolson Street–North Bridge buses or Princes Street buses. **Open** noon-5pm Tue-Sat. **Admission** free. **Credit** MC, V. **Map** p304 D3.

Edinburgh Printmakers. *See p211.*

Barbara Rae takes the *Sea Path – Ballinskelligs* at **Scottish Gallery.** *See p212.*

This artist-run gallery remains a dynamic centre for art in Edinburgh and is one of the best places in town to spot upcoming talent. The gallery has a track record for guest-curated shows that bring together established artists from further afield. The shows are perhaps not consistently strong but they can be relied upon to be adventurous. The small Project Room has also carved out a niche for itself by hosting a programme of debut solo shows.

doggerfisher

11 Gayfield Square, Broughton (558 7110/ www.doggerfisher.com). Playhouse buses. **Open** 11am-6pm Wed-Fri; noon-5pm Sat or by appointment. **Credit** AmEx, MC, V. **Map** p307 G3.
In the Georgian splendour of Gayfield Square, Susanna Beaumont champions Edinburgh's contemporary scene from her modern gallery and art agency. When not exhibiting at prestigious art fairs including the Armory in New York, this former tyre garage houses cutting edge contemporary work. Expect to see group and solo shows by established and upcoming Scottish artists such as Keith Farquahar and Louise Hopkins. Already scheduled for 2004 are shows by Bergen born but Glasgow resident, Hanneline Visnes, and her fellow Glaswegian and frequent collaborator, Lucy Skaer.

Edinburgh Printmakers

23 Union Street, Broughton (557 2479/www. edinburgh-printmakers.co.uk). Playhouse buses. **Open** 10am-6pm Tue-Sat. **Credit** MC, V. **Map** p307 G3.
The UK's first open-access print studio combines a workshop and two-floor gallery dedicated to displaying and selling contemporary fine-art prints. Local experimental artists rub shoulders in the racks with John McClean, Donald Urquhart and Eduardo Paolozzi, Scotland's most famous printmaker. At this cosy and welcoming space you can pick up an original piece of artwork for £40. If you are in Edinburgh for a longer visit, you can try out printmaking for yourself on one of the in-house courses.

Fruitmarket Gallery

45 Market Street, Old Town (225 2383/www.fruit market.co.uk). Princes Street buses. **Open** 11am-6pm Mon-Sat; noon-5pm Sun. **Admission** free. **Credit** MC, V. **Map** p304 D2.
The Fruitmarket Gallery was revamped in 1992 by the high-profile Edinburgh architect Richard Murphy and now puts the neighbouring Waverley Station entrance to shame. Laid out over two levels, it uses a small space well to accommodate the best of local art, as well as regular shows from all over

the world including Jeff Koons, Matthew Dalziel and Louise Scullion. Over the years the Fruitmarket has also established a tradition of bringing non-Western works to Britain, often for the first time, including a hugely popular show of paintings by Chinese artists. The lower floor is partly given over to a stylish café and a well-stocked bookshop selling everything from exhibition catalogues to philosophical treatises.

Ingleby Gallery

6 Carlton Terrace, Calton Hill (556 4441/ www.inglebygallery.com). Bus 30, 35. **Open** 10am-5pm Wed-Sat or by appointment. **No credit cards.** **Map** p307 J4.

Behind the façade of a smart town house lies the quiet pine-floored Ingleby, set up in 1998 by Richard and Florence Ingleby, who still live above the shop on the upper floors. Despite its homely atmosphere, this is a world-class David to the National Gallery Goliaths, regularly holding shows for big names including Callum Innes, Andy Goldsworthy, Thomas Joshua Cooper and Howard Hodgkin. Ian Davenport's poured paint works are characteristic of the gallery's focus on chic abstraction.

Merz

87 Broughton Street, Broughton (558 8778/ www.merzart.com). Bus 8/Playhouse buses. **Open** noon-6pm Tue-Sat. **Credit** MC, V. **Map** p306 F3.

Perched on a Broughton Street corner, Calum Buchanan's latest venture is housed in the premises of an old junk shop. The ephemeral and eclectic philosophy of the previous tenant still pervades and it is not unusual to find paintings stacked on the floor as well as the walls. Plans are afoot to include more sculpture, but painting is the major medium and the gallery's average ten-day turnover guarantees fresh fare. As well as representing the margins of the art world, Merz is also a place to uncover early works by big names like Tracey Emin and Jenny Saville. A one-room treasure trove.

Open Eye and I2

34 Abercromby Place, New Town (557 1020/558 9872/www.openeyegallery.co.uk). Bus 23, 27. **Open** 11am-6pm Mon-Fri; 10am-4pm Sat. **No credit cards.** **Map** p306 E4.

Recently merged, these two galleries have taken brighter, more spacious premises. They are a vivid and mischievous pair, with Open Eye displaying the output of established contemporary Scottish painters and sculptors from Alan Davies' prints to Calum Colvin's disorientating large-scale photographs. I2 specialises in international prints – expect to see a portfolio including Picasso, Chagall and Warhol alongside a wide range of delicate handmade jewellery and applied arts.

Patriothall Gallery @ WASPS

Patriothall Studios, off Hamilton Place, Stockbridge (225 1289). Bus 24, 28, 36. **Open** noon-5pm Mon-Fri; noon-6pm Sat. **No credit cards.** **Map** p306 D3.

Having lobbied the city councillors, the artists of WASPS have not only succeeded in keeping their studios and gallery but have amassed the funds to buy the premises outright and continue their open-minded programme of Scottish and European art. In addition to painters, sculptors and installation artists, the venue hosts community projects. The current programme of ten day shows may develop to longer runs but Patriothall will remain dedicated to its task of providing artist-led space free of heavy curation, open to new and emerging artists.

Red Door Gallery

42 Victoria Street, Old Town (477 3255/ www.edinburghart.com). Bus 23, 27, 28, 41, 42, 45. **Open** 12.30-5.30pm Mon-Wed, Fri; 1.30-5.30pm Thur; 11am-5.30pm Sat; noon-5pm Sun. **Credit** MC, V. **Map** p304 C3.

Everything's for sale in the lovely little Red Door Gallery, with prices ranging from a wholly affordable £10 right up to £1,000. A real option if you want to return home with a piece of the new Scotland in your luggage. As well as paintings and sculptures by recent graduates, there is a gorgeous selection of original jewellery. Small, but pleasingly formed.

Scottish Gallery

16 Dundas Street, New Town (558 1200/ www.scottish-gallery.co.uk). Bus 23, 27. **Open** 10am-6pm Mon-Fri; 10am-4pm Sat. **Credit** MC, V. **Map** p306 E3.

Trading since 1897, the oldest and largest private gallery in Scotland was active in launching the careers of the Scottish Colourists and the more iridescent works of their contemporaries, the Edinburgh School painters. A century later it still nurtures artists carefully through their careers with a range of 20th-century pieces from recent college graduates and established artists. The colourist style that characterises the Highland landscapes remains well represented. Wide windows and the split-level open format make for a welcoming and colourful haven. The applied arts rooms downstairs are excellent for jewellery, glass, silver and wood crafts, and contemporary sculpture, such as the light-hearted figure vignettes of Adam Paxton.

Stills Gallery

23 Cockburn Street, Old Town (622 6200/ www.stills.org). Bus 35/Nicolson Street–North Bridge or Princes Street buses. **Open** 11am-6pm daily. **Admission** free. **Credit** MC, V. **Map** p304 D3.

Across the road from the Collective Gallery (*see p210*), Stills has a similar feel but specialises in photographic and video work: two levels of cutting-edge exhibitions of little-known but often exceptionally good modern artists. There are regular events providing the opportunity to meet local artists and like-minded enthusiasts. Revamped and enlarged, the gallery is a clean-cut, concrete-floored rectangular space. The widening of the exhibitions policy has enabled Stills to bring some exciting European artists to Scotland, as well as to show work by artists based here. The gallery also offers photography and digital imaging courses.

Gay & Lesbian

Cruisin' without attitude.

Into orbit at **Planet Out**. *See p215*.

Whether you're looking for a big gay love or just a big gay night out, the gayer side of Edinburgh is more diverse now than ever. There are R&B and (finally!) lesbian nights springing up among the usual cheeky pop and house-til-it-hurts affairs, and more new bars seem to be realising that you don't need leopard-print interiors and ear-crushing music to draw in a decent crowd. Broughton has been the home of Edinburgh's gay community for many years now, and the area defined by Broughton Street, Picardy Place and the top of Leith Walk (*see p102*) is still considered Edinburgh's pink triangle. Sure, it's no Soho, but the close proximity of its bars and clubs does mean your gay nights out are less strenuous if your boots aren't made for walking.

Refreshingly, Edinburgh's gay scene does not have too much of an attitude problem. Your T-shirt doesn't have to be nipple-chafingly tight to avoid raising the more carefully-plucked eyebrows around you, and bouncers are not going to be checking your footwear, labels and paperwork confirming your 'alternative lifestyle choice' at the door. All the bars and clubs are open to gay men and women equally, except the new lesbian club night Velvet and the leather bars, which only really cater for men.

During the Edinburgh Festival and Hogmanay gay venues are open throughout the day and are mobbed into the wee small hours. The Lesbian & Gay Switchboard's fundraising ceilidhs on Valentine's Day and Hallowe'en draw some of the biggest crowds of the year, while **Pride Scotia** in June (*see p196*), held alternately in Glasgow and Edinburgh, is a chance for the LGBT communities in both cities to take to the streets. What's more, since the creation of a new Scottish parliament, there has been a strong sense in Edinburgh's gay scene that grass-roots campaigning can really lead to positive change. Active gay groups include the Stonewall Youth Group, a police liaison team and Parents Enquiry Scotland (for all, *see p280*). Edinburgh is also home to Scotland's only gay rugby team, the Caledonian Thebans (www.thebans-rfc.co.uk), who welcome players of all sexual persuasions and ability.

See you at CCs. **CC Blooms**. *See p216.*

INFORMATION

Free magazine *Scotsgay* can be found in most gay bars. The gay section of the *List* has fortnightly listings of club nights and gay-related events, and the **LGBT Centre** on Broughton Street (No. 60; 478 7069) might be the place to start if you're looking for more information. The new **LGBT Centre for Health and Wellbeing** (9 Howe Street, New Town; 523 1100) should be able to help with any specific medical problems. Alternatively, telephone the **Gay Switchboard** or **Lesbian Line** (for all, *see p280*).

Arts & entertainment

Edinburgh is never gayer than when the Fringe takes over (*see p32*). The festival season brings a glut of gay theatre, as well as swarms of gay tourists and actors. The rest of the year, new gay writing is often to be found at theatres like the **Traverse** (*see p238*) while the **Filmhouse** (*see p206*) hosts the annually exported London Lesbian and Gay Film Festival in late August.

OOT: On Tuesday

The Stand, 5 York Place, New Town (558 7272/ www.thestand.co.uk). Bus 4, 8, 10, 11, 12, 15, 16, 17, 26. **Open** 9pm 2nd Tue of month. **Admission** £5; £4 concessions. **Credit** MC, V. **Map** p306 F4.
This intimate basement venue hosts monthly gay stand-up comedy from the best entertainers around,

usually compered by cheeky camp scamp Craig Hill. Previous headliners include Scott Capurro and that mix of Dolly Parton and Lily Savage: Tina C.

Bars

Edinburgh doesn't do too badly for gay bars, but most half-decent bars in the city have a pretty open-minded clientele. The most gay-friendly of these are **Black Bo's** (*see p166*), the **Outhouse** and the **Basement** (for both; *see p157*), and the bars at the **Filmhouse** cinema (*see p206*) and **Traverse Theatre** (*see p238*).

Claremont

133-135 East Claremont Street, Broughton (556 5662/www.claremont-bar-edinburgh.co.uk). Bus 8, 13, 17. **Open** 11am-1am daily. **Credit** MC, V. **Map** p306 F2.
Denim and skinheads and bears: oh my! Every night is leather night at the Claremont, and as cruise bars go this is pretty welcoming. Food is available every day – one of the co-proprietors is a French, leather-clad pastry chef. Those with a taste for the more hirsute man will enjoy the BearScots club night, held the first Saturday of every month.

Frenchies

89 Rose Street North Lane, New Town (225 7651). Princes Street buses. **Open** 2pm-1am Mon-Sat; 2pm-midnight Sun. **No credit cards.** **Map** p304 B1.
The oldest gay bar in Edinburgh. The boarded-up windows and tucked-away location are a reminder

of the days when gay venues were neither seen nor heard. Still, it's an oddly cute wee place, if a little off the beaten track. Happy hour is from 6 to 8pm daily.

Habana

22 Greenside Place, Leith Walk, Calton Hill (558 1270). Playhouse buses. **Open** noon-1am Mon-Sat; 12.30pm-1am Sun. **No credit cards. Map** p304 G4.
Cheap, chirpy and chart-music-heavy, Habana is the Dannii Minogue kid sister to nearby Planet Out's Kylie. Drinks are cheapest Monday to Wednesday.

Bar Java

48-52 Constitution Street, Leith (553 2020). Bus 1, 16, 22, 35, 36. **Open** 11am-1am daily. **Credit** MC, V. **Map** p311 Jz.
It may only be officially gay on Wednesdays, but Bar Java is sufficient reason to hop on the bus and head out to Leith any night of the week for a quiet pint in friendly, comfy surroundings.

Laughing Duck

24 Howe Street, New Town (220 2376). Bus 13, 19A, 24, 28. **Open** noon-midnight Mon-Thur, Sun; noon-1am Fri, Sat. **Credit** AmEx, DC, MC, V. **Map** p306 D4.
A hub of gay life as far back as the '80s, the Duck is a clean-cut, relaxed bar with a slightly older, but not cruisier, mix of people than at the other end of Princes Street, and cosy booths at the back. Brilliantly, it also hosts the monthly gathering of Kilts, the club for men who have a thing for... well, kilts.

New Town Bar

26B Dublin Street, New Town (538 7775). Bus 4, 8, 10, 11, 15, 16, 17, 20. **Open** noon-1am Mon-Thur, Sun; noon 2am Fri, Sat. **Credit** MC, V. **Map** p306 F4.
A popular cruise bar that attracts gay men of all types, sizes and ages. The upstairs bar is busy, with a friendly ambience. The anything-goes downstairs club stays open late at weekends.

Planet Out

Greenside Place, Calton Hill (524 0061/www.planet out.8m.com). Playhouse buses. **Open** 4pm-1am Mon-Sat; 2pm-1am Sun. **Credit** MC, V. **Map** p307 G4.
The place where all big gay nights out should begin. Pout, as it has become affectionately known, is easily the best gay bar in Edinburgh. Open to anyone, funny, busy and friendly, it's the place where you're most likely to get talking to someone and not spend the rest of the evening trying to get rid of them. On Monday all drinks cost £1 (after the £1 entry fee) and the soundtrack (courtesy of *la grande dame* Trendy Wendy) is proper pop. Prepare to have a crush on at least three of the bar staff.

Regent

2 Montrose Terrace, Calton Hill (661 8198). Bus 30, 35. **Open** 11am 1am Mon-Sat; 12.30pm-1am Sun. **Credit** MC, V. **Map** p307 J4.
The Regent is an unpretentious, friendly pub with decent music that you don't have to shout over. It's the location of choice for folk still bracing themselves to hit the sticky dancefloors in town.

Stag & Turret

1 Montrose Terrace, Calton Hill (661 6443). Bus 4, 5, 44, 45. **Open** 11am-1am Mon-Sat; 12.30pm-1am Sun. **Credit** MC, V. **Map** p307 J4.
It may not be the freshest-faced of bars and it may not be the busiest, but with pints this cheap and as much '80s pop as one jukebox could possibly contain, you can't complain too much.

Cafés

Blue Moon Café

1 Barony Street, New Town (556 2788/www. broughtonstreet.co.uk/theblue). Bus 8, 13, 17. **Open** 11am-12.30am Mon Fri; 9.30am-12.30am Sat, Sun. **Credit** MC, V. **Map** p306 F3.
Another of the essential places, the Blue Moon is cosy and tasteful, with an impressively varied menu. The coal fire puts a bit of heat back into Edinburgh's winter nights out, and the chatty staff will point you in the right direction for nearby pubs and clubs.

Sala

60 Broughton Street, Broughton (478 7069). Bus 8, 13, 17. **Open** 11am-1pm daily. **Credit** MC, V. **Map** p306 F3.
An excellent, neat and new café-bar, fronting the Broughton Street LGBT centre, Sala seems to have become one for the ladies, although anyone is welcome. The bar staff are usually on good form, the atmosphere is refreshingly down-to-earth, and there is a good little tapas menu too.

The best Venues for

Dancefloor shape-throwing

Tuesday's Vibe (*see p216*) is the best venue to stage your shameless ass-shaking exhibition.

Watching girls go by

The big sofa in Sala (*see above*) means you can people-watch from behind your plate of tapas.

Karaoke *schadenfreude*

Habana's regulars prove their oral talents, or lack thereof, every Thursday night at 9pm (*see left*).

Dress-code-bending clubbing

The monthly theme at Tackno (*see p216*) gives you a chance to dust off your dressing-up box.

Pocket-friendly pints

Monday's Pink Pounder at Planet Out (*see left*) ensures you go home with a bulge in your trousers: all drinks are £1.

Arts & Entertainment

Clubs

CC Blooms is still Edinburgh's only permanent gay club open seven nights a week, although Ego is edging up behind it with weeknight alternatives. Keep an eye out in bars for flyers that will get you into clubs cheaper, and don't worry too much about dress code – none of the clubs are particularly strict.

CC Blooms

23-24 Greenside Place, Calton Hill (556 9331). Playhouse buses. **Open** 10.30pm-3am daily. **Admission** free. **Credit** MC, V. **Map** p304 G4.

Oh, CCs, where great romances start and end (often in the same evening), and Edinburgh's gayest groove and squirm to the sound of bad pop. The capital's only permanently gay club may be offensive on the eye and on the ear, but CC's cheeky charm is undeniable to girls and boys alike. Monday nights are best, when things quieten down and there's breathing room on the dancefloor. The weekend queues to get downstairs provide the perfect opportunity to make your move; as soon as you get down there, the pair of you will be itching to leave, and... bingo! No matter what you said after the last time, you'll be back, mark my words.

Club nights

BootyLUSHous

Medina, Lothian Street, Old Town (07736 936650). North Bridge–Nicolson Street buses. **Open** 10pm-3am Sun. **Admission** £2-£3. **No credit cards.** **Map** p309 F6.

Charged with the task of bringing proper R&B to the house ridden gay masses, BootyLUSHous has strolled over from Ego to a new, more intimate home: Medina, whose bed-strewn interior will please anyone looking for a relaxing Sunday evening to wind down the weekend.

Joy

The Venue, 15-17 Calton Road, Calton Hill (557 3073/www.clubjoy.co.uk). Bus 30, 35. **Open** 11pm-3am Sat monthly. **Admission** £8-£10. **No credit cards.** **Map** p310 G5.

It may be the oldest and priciest gay night out in Edinburgh, but Joy continues to reel in masses of folk hungry, after their month long dance music fast, for a night of uninhibited house action. DJs Alan and Maggie Joy are no strangers to waving a glow stick or two, it's fair to say.

Luvely

Liquid Room, 9c Victoria Street, Old Town (225 2564). Bus 23, 27, 28, 41, 42, 45. **Open** 10pm-5am Sat monthly. **Admission** £8-£10. **No credit cards.** **Map** p304 C3.

A truly luuuurvely two-room clubbing extravaganza with DJs Jared, GP, Tommy K and Newton & Stone playing everything from the inevitable house music, to chart and party tunes.

Mingin'

Studio 24, 24-26 Calton Road, Calton Hill (558 3758). Bus 24, 25, 35, 35A. **Open** 11pm-3am Sat monthly. **Admission** £6. **No credit cards.** **Map** p310 G5.

Your monthly dose of dirrty house and trance is supplied in the intimate confines of Studio 24's first floor. You might need to tone down your dance moves as elbow room becomes an issue later in the night.

Tackno

Massa, 36-39 Market Street, Old Town (226 4224). North Bridge–Nicolson St buses. **Open** 10.30pm-3am Sun monthly. **Admission** £4-£6. **Map** p304 D2.

A giant, glittery behemoth of a club night. Tackno is a sequin-strewn monthly group therapy session for those who harbour a secret yearning to slip into their spangliest shoes and throw their arms in the air to Tiffany's 'I Think We're Alone Now'. The entry fee may seem a little hefty, but it's peanuts for the perma-grin that DJ Trendy Wendy's camp classics will cement on your face.

Taste

Liquid Room, 9c Victoria Street, Old Town (225 2564). Bus 23, 27, 28, 41, 42, 45. **Open** 11pm-3am Sun. **Admission** £5-£8. **No credit cards.** **Map** p304 C3.

Taste is gay-friendly rather than exclusively gay, which makes for a better night out all round. Whether you like your house music deep, American or just plain ready-salted, the resident DJs Fisher and Price, Martin Valentine and Steven Wanless are all quite happy to sort you out.

Velvet

Commplex, 39-40 Commercial Street, Leith (555 5600/www.clubvelvet.co.uk). Bus 1, 6, 22, 35, 36, 49. **Open** 10pm-2am Sat monthly. **Admission** £5-£6. **No credit cards.** **Map** p311 Hx.

The Commplex may be bafflingly hard to find, but once you've got into Edinburgh's sole women-only club night you'll be pleasantly surprised by this busy, pop-friendly venue. Good boys are allowed in as guests of their girl-friends.

Vibe

Ego, Picardy Place, New Town (478 7434). Playhouse buses. **Open** 11pm-5am Tue. **Admission** £3. **No credit cards.** **Map** p307 G4.

Conserve some of your ass energy over the weekend, because you'll be needing it on Tuesdays to shake your thing to some proper non-camp pop. Vibe is a good laugh: cheap as you like and always packed out with bouncing boys and grooving girls.

Wiggle

Ego, Picardy Place, New Town (478 7434). Playhouse buses. **Open** 11pm-3am Sat monthly. **Admission** £6. **No credit cards.** **Map** p307 G4.

Trendy Wendy suppresses her natural pop instincts and puts on something a little housier on the main floor, while downstairs the promised 'alternative' playlist turns out to be mainstream R&B pop.

Music

From trad folk to electro cool, Edinburgh's music scene is in rude health.

Henry's Jazz Cellar.
See p224.

Classical & Opera

Classical

Edinburgh's rarefied façade is perfect for the plethora of classical concerts on offer. This has been the case since the 18th century, when the Edinburgh Musical Society caused an upsurge in instrument making and music publishing, moving into the purpose-built St Cecilia's Hall on the Cowgate in 1762. Despite outbreaks of fire, plague and urban regeneration, St Cecilia's still hosts concerts today (Niddry Street, Cowgate, Old Town; 650 2805).

Nowadays, there is a high profile classical scene that revolves around regular visits from Scotland's two main orchestras, the **Royal Scottish National Orchestra** (RSNO – www.rsno.org.uk) and the **Scottish Chamber Orchestra** (SCO – www.sco.org.uk). These divide their time between Usher Hall and Queen's Hall, with a season that runs between October and May. The RSNO's Pops concerts in March are a precursor to their Proms series in June, while the SCO presents more intimate

works. Also regular visitors are the **BT Scottish Ensemble** and the **BBC Scottish Symphony Orchestra**, while groups such as the innovative **Paragon Ensemble** jostle for space on a relatively small circuit.

A fantastic offshoot of such activity has been the rise of **Mr McFall's Chamber**, a splinter group of SCO players who originally gathered together to play their cheeky reinterpretations of prog rock legends King Crimson (with musical saw, cor anglais and electric violin) and Pink Floyd in club-based cabarets.

Venues

Queen's Hall

Clerk Street, South Edinburgh (box office 668 2019/administration 668 3456/www.queens halledinburgh.co.uk). North Bridge–Nicolson Street buses. **Open** *Box office* 10am-5.30pm Mon-Sat (or until 15mins before concert). **Tickets** prices vary. **Credit** AmEx, MC, V. **Map** p310 G7.
Although renovations are continually mooted by the management, this former church remains suitably sepulchral for all forms of music. Go for the full ecclesiastical vibe by sitting in one of the pews that line the auditorium. The SCO and the BT Scottish

Arts & Entertainment

Ensemble perform here, as have Philip Glass and Julian Lloyd Webber. Also used regularly for jazz and rock concerts (see p224).

Reid Concert Hall

Bristo Square, Old Town (650 2423/www.music. ed.ac.uk). Bus 2, 41, 42/Nicolson Street–North Bridge buses. **Open** *Office* 9am-5pm Mon-Fri. **Concerts** (in term-time) 1.10pm Tue, Fri; please see website for details of other events. **Tickets** free. **Map** p310 G6.

The University of Edinburgh Faculty of Music is a hotbed of young talent. On most Tuesdays and Fridays during term time you can wander in to enjoy a free lunchtime concert at 1.10pm. Whether showcasing the Edinburgh Quartet or more contemporary fare (Arab Strap and Barbara Morgenstern have appeared), the future face of music is here.

Usher Hall

Lothian Road, South Edinburgh (box office 228 1155/administration 228 8616/www.usherhall.co.uk). Bus 1, 10, 11, 15, 16, 17, 22, 24, 34. **Open** *Box office* 10am-8pm Mon-Fri (counter from 5.30pm); 10am-5.30pm Sat or until 15mins after the start of performance. **Tickets** prices vary. **Credit** AmEx, MC, V. **Map** p304 A3.

This grandest of spaces is back in business following the first phase of its £9-million refit in 2003, although the next stage is currently ongoing. Only minor disruptions to the rolling programme are envisaged, however. Also a major festival venue and home to the RSNO.

Churches

Edinburgh has two cathedrals and many wonderful old churches, some of which are used as concert venues, particularly during the Fringe. The 1688-built **Canongate Church** (153 Canongate, Old Town, call the Queen's Hall on 668 2019 for tickets) provides a home for choral groups and chamber orchestras, and becomes the local place of worship for the Queen when she's in residence at Holyroodhouse. As well as holding free concerts at 6pm most Sundays, **St Giles' Cathedral** (see p77) also plays host to travelling choirs and guest musicians letting rip on the cathedral's acclaimed Rieger organ, or there's **Greyfriar's Kirk** (see p88).

St Mary's Episcopal Cathedral

Palmerston Place, New Town (225 6293/www. cathedral.net). Bus 3, 4, 12, 13, 21, 25, 26, 33. **Open** *Services with music* Sung Eucharist 10.30am Sun. Evensong 5.30pm Mon-Fri; 3.30pm Sun. **Concerts** phone for details. **Tickets** (concerts) prices vary; phone for details. **No credit cards**. **Map** p308 B6.

St Mary's is unique in Scotland in maintaining daily sung services. Regular recitals on the Father Willis organ at 4.30pm each Sunday are just one of the musical highlights at this magnificent church.

Opera

When Scottish Opera performed Wagner's Ring Cycle in its entirety during the 2003 Edinburgh International Festival, the whole run was sold out before even being advertised. Edinburgh **Festival Theatre** (see p239) is the main venue for such work, thanks to its capacious orchestra pit and fine acoustics. The **Edinburgh Playhouse** (see p237) also plays host to large-scale works. There is no dedicated opera house in the city.

Rock, Folk & Jazz

Rock, pop & dance

Somewhere between the sad-lad bubblegum of the Bay City Rollers and desperate failed *Pop Idol* Darius, Edinburgh has been in possession of a pretty spiffy music scene. Not that viewers watching 2003's MTV Europe Music Awards would have gleaned any knowledge of this, so enthralled were they by the showbiz glitz of Christina, Beyoncé, Kylie and co (see p122 **Star for a night**).

Ever since punk broke upon an unsuspecting world, Edinburgh has leaned towards the artier end of the spectrum. These days the city has a horde of record labels highlighting a slew of maverick talents, their DIY approach to doing business proving that the means of production are within the grasp of all. The template was set in the late 1970s by the now legendary Fast Product Records, which provided homes for early incarnations of the Human League and the Gang of Four.

In the mid-1980s, Edinburgh became the focus for 'shambling' bands such as the Shop Assistants and Jesse Garon and the Desperados. The '90s were left to more corporate fare such as Garbage, featuring former Stockbridger Shirley Manson as iconic frontwoman (see p220 **EdinBurgher Shirley Manson**). Oh, and the Proclaimers and Finley Quaye have done rather well for themselves too.

Today, umpteen cottage industry record labels have picked up Fast's baton. Human Condition (www.humancondition.co.uk) has been on the go for more than a decade, and released Idlewild's first single, as well as the *Handbags At Dawn* compilation of Edinburgh labels.

More experimental fare can be heard via the thriving electronic scene highlighted by KFM, Benbecula and MRW44 (see p219 **Sonic boom**). ballboy's magnificently named song, 'I Hate Scotland', is perhaps the best

Sonic boom

'Christ. on Benbecula? How often can you say that?' Immortal DJ John Peel there referring to Christ., Edinburgh's premier exponent of annoyingly punctuated electronica. Christ., a one-man laptop god who releases records on the Benbecula label (named, for the non-geographers, after the remote Scottish island), has certainly got about of late. Since releasing his album, *Metamorphic Reproduction Miracle,* in 2003, he has appeared everywhere from Barcelona's Sonar festival to Cannes.

Christ. is at the forefront of a wave of electronic and experimental musical activity that has kept bubbling away in Edinburgh for several years and now encompasses a host of cottage-industry record labels, club nights and live shows. On Benbecula alone, records by screen-based auteurs such as Operator, Frog Pocket, Reverbathon and Greenbank have all oozed out of the ether.

Two other labels, KFM and MRW44, are equally responsible for creating a buzz. David Jack's two KFM albums of hip hop based soundscapes (*Texture Freak* and *Without Vocabulary*), work just as well in a live environment, while the angry young men of the Magnificents sound like Suicide and the Stooges bludgeoning each other to death. Meanwhile, label MRW44's ongoing series of *No Rewind* music compilations embraces more traditionally instrumented left-field provocateurs such as Nimrod 33 and Giant Tank.

CDs by most of the artists mentioned here are available in the small record section of **Analogue**, the coolest emporium in town (*see p177*). Benbecula artists and others appear infrequently at both the **Bongo Club** and **Cabaret Voltaire** (for both; *see p221*), where club nights such as Dffnt Drm consistently showcase the most inventive acts in town.

Curiously, all three labels mentioned are based in Portobello (*see p127*). Whatever form of electricity is crackling in the water out there, Christ. – and the rest – are clearly walking tall on it.
Benbecula: www.benbecula.com
KFM: www.kfmrecords.com
MrW44: www.mrw44.co.uk

Arts & Entertainment

contemporary expression of a generation blighted by the lingering insecurity and parochialism of the little-Scotlander mentality.

Hip hop has long enjoyed a ferocious following in the city. First port of call for those wishing to large it, or indeed small it, is **Underground Solu'shn** (*see p190*).

Information & tickets

The best way to find out about all this activity is via the **Jockrock** website (www.jockrock. org), particularly its venomous yet informative message board. Check out also *Is This Music?*, Scotland's only dedicated music magazine, available at Edinburgh's record shops

Avalanche and **Fopp** (for both, *see p189*). The *List* magazine also has a decent gig guide, as does Radio One's website www.bbc. co.uk/radio/scotland

The main ticket outlets in Edinburgh are **Ripping Records** (91 South Bridge, Old Town; 226 7010) and **Tickets Scotland** (127 Rose Street, New Town; 220 3234).

Venues

Many venues serve a variety of functions. For example, the **Queen's Hall** (*see p217*), as well as holding regular classical and jazz performances, is used for rock and pop gigs, Nick Cave having once basked in its basilican

EdinBurgher Shirley Manson

When Stockbridge-stropster Shirley Manson sang 'Only Happy When it Rains' a decade back, anyone in thrall to such a sulky little madam had little choice but to believe her lest they get a smack in the mouth. Such was the iconic wham of the debut single by Garbage.

An ex-pupil of Broughton High School, Manson was an archetypal troubled teen long before Avril Lavigne watered down her angst. Taunted for what is now considered a stunning flame-haired, green-eyed assemblage, Manson's low self-esteem while working as a Saturday girl in Miss Selfridge resulted in violent reactions to the constant bullying. Such energy eventually found an outlet onstage at Edinburgh Youth Theatre.

It was here she joined Goodbye Mr Mackenzie, a band who never quite hit the big time, despite considerable industry push over several albums. Even when the band reconvened as Angelfish, with Manson finally shoved up front, only ex-Nirvana producer Butch Vig noticed. And Garbage was born. Lucky he did, because both *Garbage*, and its follow-ups, *Version 2.0* and *beautifulgarbage*, have given the music industry some well-honed sass to play with.

Since 2001's release of *beautifulgarbage*, much of Manson's energy has been devoted to AIDS charities. While she may be the

feistiest poster-girl mouthpiece for the most streetwise of worthy causes, she isn't averse to a spot of proper glamour, having joined the ranks of pale waifs posing for Calvin Klein ads.

Manson has also played the perfect homecoming queen on more than one occasion: first when Garbage headlined Princes Street Gardens to commemorate the opening of the Scottish Parliament on 1 May 1999; more recently when she co-hosted – albeit briefly – 2003's MTV European Music Awards in Leith (*see p122* **Star for a night**). With a fourth Garbage album pending, Manson looks a whole lot happier these days, whatever the weather.

splendour. As well as being ideal for jazz and classical, the **Usher Hall** (*see p218*) has played host to Belle & Sebastian, the Flaming Lips and Yo La Tengo. Cavernous nightclub **Arena** (*see p228*) was poised to host live music at the time of writing.

Bannermans

212 Cowgate, Old Town (556 3254). Nicolson Street–North Bridge buses. **Open** noon-1am Mon-Sat; 12.30pm-1am Sun. *Gigs* 9pm Mon, Wed-Sun. **Admission** £3. **Credit** AmEx, DC, MC, V. **Map** p304 D3.

The surprisingly sprawling arched room at the back of Bannermans pub was once the ultimate haven for old folkies. Changing its name to Thee Underworld on gig nights, the venue's promters have taken it upon themselves to book every spunky noisenik in town. The likes of Biffy Clyro and Franz Ferdinand all cut their broken teeth here.

Bongo Club

37 Holyrood Road, Old Town (558 7604/ www.thebongoclub.co.uk). Nicolson Street–North Bridge buses. **Open** times vary. *Gigs* see website. **Admission** £3-£9. **No credit cards**. **Map** p310 H5.

Since moving to the spick-and-span confines of the spruced up former Edinburgh University students' union in 2003, the Bongo has become more gig-friendly. This is pretty much on account of a semi-circular stage that can adapt to both dancefloor sweatbox and more intimate candlelit table affairs. Of the local crowd, the Magnificents, the Aphex Twin and David Jack have all showed face here.

Cabaret Voltaire

36 Blair Street, Old Town (220 4638). Nicolson Street–North Bridge buses. **Open** 10pm-3am daily. **Admission** £2-£10. **No credit cards**. **Map** p310 G5.

The most interesting venue to have opened in Edinburgh for years, even though it looks more or less the same as when it was the tacky old Peppermint Lounge. Founded post-Cowgate fire at the fag end of 2002, it has hosted gigs by pretty much anyone innovative on the local scene. As the venue's retro-cool moniker suggests, there's also been a strong electronic and experimental input, including the cream of the Benbecula roster (*see p219* **Sonic boom**). Jazz, folk, dub and hip hop acts have also all been showcased here.

Café Royal

17 West Register Street, New Town (557 4792). Princes Street buses. **Open** 11.30am-1pm daily. *Gigs* times vary; please phone for details. **Admission** free. **Credit** MC, V. **Map** p304 D1.

Old men get dewy-eyed when they recall legendary performances by ex-Lemonhead Evan Dando and others in this upstairs, 280-capacity function room. It was really jumping in the 1980s but more recently, alas, a lack of PA has left the room to wedding parties and rather wonderful Northern Soul nights.

Caledonian Backpackers

3 Queensferry Street, New Town (476 7224/ www.caledonianbackpackers.com). Princes Street buses. **Open** *Gigs* Fri, Sat 8.30pm. **Admission** free Fri; £4-£5 Sat. **No credit cards**. **Map** p308 C5.

One of the more imaginative additions to the scene, this is essentially the rough and ready bar of a backpackers' hostel at the west end of Princes Street. Under the auspices of Baby Tiger promotions (www.baby-tiger.net), however, such acts as Fence Records' the Lone Pigeon have played in an eclectic series of weekend bills.

Commplex

30-40 Commercial Street, Leith (555 5600/ www.thecommplex.co.uk). Bus 1, 6, 22, 35, 36, 49. **Open** *Gigs* fortnightly; monthly alternate Fri, Sat. **Admission** free Thur; £6, £4 concessions Fri, Sat. **No credit cards**. **Map** p311 Hx.

If rough and ready local band nights are your thing, you could do worse than take the Leith-bound bus to check out this regular series of guitar-friendly triple bills.

Corn Exchange

11 Newmarket Road, South Edinburgh (477 3500/ box office 443 0404/www.ece.co.uk). Bus 4, 28, 35, 44. **Open** times vary; see website for details. **Admission** £7-£22. **Credit** AmEx, MC, V.

It'll never be anywhere near as good as Glasgow's Barrowlands (*see p255*), simply because it's too far out of town and doesn't have the width to feel entirely comfortable. Nevertheless, this converted slaughterhouse has still proved itself essential to the scene. It has played host to the likes of Primal Scream, as well as the now legendary N.E.R.D MTV aftershow, which featured an impromptu guest slot from Justin Timberlake.

Forest

3 Bristo Place, Old Town (220 4538/www.theforest. org.uk). Bus 23, 27, 28, 41, 42, 45. **Open** *Café* 10.30am-10pm. *Gigs* times vary. **Admission** free. **No credit cards**. **Map** p309 F6.

You can regenerate a city as much as you like, but Edinburgh's hippy spirit never fully goes away. Want proof? Then check out this self-funding, not-for-profit arts café and exhibition space, settled in the open-wide expanse of a converted church. The heroic Wee Black Skelf records (www.wee-blackskelf.co.uk) launched the debut single by nu-folk experimentalists Lucky Luke in here, and there is a regular Ugandan xylophone workshop. Events are sporadic, so a regular check of the chock-a-block notice board is essential.

Liquid Room

9c Victoria Street, Old Town (225 2564/www.liquid room.com). Bus 23, 27, 28, 41, 42, 45. **Open** times vary; phone for details. **Admission** £4-£15. **No credit cards**. **Map** p 304 C3.

On a busy night the Liquid Room is as claustrophobic as a prison cell riot, which probably didn't make Love's Arthur Lee feel at home when he

They hate Scotland. **ballboy**. *See p218.*

played his first UK date here after being released
from six years in chokey. Other old-timers who have
performed here include John Cale and Jimmy Cliff.
The upstairs bar and gallery give a great view of the
stage – provided you're the soundman, that is. Also
in residence is an under-18s goth night called Live
At The Witch Trials. Ace.

Subway

*69 Cowgate, Old Town (225 6766/www.subway
clubs.co.uk). Nicolson Street–North Bridge buses.*
Open times vary; please phone for details.
Admission prices vary. **No credit cards.**
Map p304 D3.
Used sporadically over the years (Idlewild played
their first ever gig here, trivia fans), this spit 'n' saw-
dust dive has nevertheless proved spacious enough
to host country singer Laura Cantrell and other
Lonesome Highway gigs, though these days the people behind MRW44 records are pushing it towards
a more experimental bent.

Studio 24

*24-26 Calton Road, Calton Hill (558 3758). Bus 24,
25, 35, 35A.* **Open** times vary; please phone for
details. **Admission** £2-£10. **No credit cards.**
Map p310 G5.

Formerly known as Calton Studios, at one time the
likes of Pere Ubu and Teenage Fanclub held noisy
court here. Now only used occasionally, which is a
shame, because it's still a cracking unkempt space
that's popular with fetish clubs (check out the man-
acles in the upstairs rooms).

Venue

*17-21 Calton Road, Calton Hill (557 3073/
www.edinvenue.com). Bus 30, 35.* **Open** times vary;
please phone for details. **Admission** £2-£10.
No credit cards. Map p310 G5.
You name 'em, they've played here on their way up
to the concert hall and stadium world domination
circuit. Blur, the Stone Roses, Nirvana and, more
recently, the Strokes, have all graced the original
grizzled black-painted dive. At time of writing, the
Venue looks set to be sold as another victim of
Edinburgh's ludicrous predilection for building luxury flats on any patch of ground going. This will,
however, take until 2008 to materialise.

Wee Red Bar

*Edinburgh College of Art, Lauriston Place, South
Edinburgh (229 1442). Bus 23, 27, 28, 45.* **Open**
Club nights 11pm-3am Fri, Sat. **Admission** £4. **No
credit cards. Map** p309 E6.

The bijou, scarlet-painted Edinburgh College of Art student union has long played host to indie and '60s nights so busy you could believe you're frugging your way into a triptastic movie. Despite having no stage to speak of, it's also popular with some of the more interesting bands in town.

Wheatsheaf Inn

207-209 Balgreen Road, West Edinburgh (346 9801). Bus 10, 27, 38. **Open** 11am-11pm Mon-Thur; 11am-midnight Fri, Sat; 12.30-11pm Sun. *Gigs* times vary; please phone for details. **Admission** £4-£5. **Credit** MC, V.

This is punk central, presenting occasional nights of spiky-topped thrash from across the globe. An annual European punk festival congregates in this off-the-beaten-track bar, though it's probably worth checking out what's on before re-sugaring your Mohican and practising pogoing.

Whistlebinkies

4-6 South Bridge, Old Town (557 5114/ www.whistlebinkies.com). North Bridge–Nicolson Street buses. **Open** 5pm-3am daily. *Gigs* 9pm, midnight daily. **Admission** free Mon-Thur, Sun and before midnight Fri, Sat; £3 after midnight Fri, Sat. **Credit** MC, V. **Map** p304 D3.

Whistlebinkies used to be just a cavernous labyrinth of folk-based pursuits with a late licence. These days its brief has been widened to include workaday indie bands and just passing through singer-songwriters, who all seem to enjoy forcing passing trade to shout over each other by using a PA that would be deemed too loud for Knebworth.

Folk & roots

It was poet Hamish Henderson (the composer of 'Freedom Come All Ye', which most agree should be the Scots anthem) who spearheaded the Scottish folk revival in the 1960s by founding the Edinburgh Folk Club.

Since then, a younger generation of artists has picked up on other World traditions and influences to create a mongrel hybrid of ethnocentric sounds. While Martyn Bennett marries his virtuoso pipe playing to club beats and dub rhythms, the likes of Shooglenifty, Burach and the Tartan Amoebas will have you burling round the floor until you're sick. The nearest descendants of the 1960s generation, however, come from the Fence Collective (www.fencerecords.com), a raggle-taggle bunch of ex-pat Fifers currently making waves with a defiantly loose-knit approach to making music.

The best way to discover the late-night thrills of folk is to get your hands dirty in the pub sessions listed below. Taken with the right blend of whisky, a night at **Sandy Bell's** (*see p167*) or the **Royal Oak** (*see below*) will leave you reeling. Besides the regular sessions, evening gigs take place at the **Central Bar** in

Leith (7 Leith Walk, Leith; 467 3925), with Wednesday nights at the **Shore Bar** on the Shore, Leith (553 5080). Thursday to Sunday nights at the **Hebrides** on Market Street in the Old Town (No.17; 220 4213) are also interesting. While there are plenty of other bars, any room containing hirsute men banging out singalonga versions of the dreadful 'Flower of Scotland' should be avoided like a cross-town night bus.

The newly constituted **Ceilidh Culture** festival picks up where the old Edinburgh Folk Festival left off, with gigs and sessions great and small every March and April (*see p194*).

Venues

Cabaret Voltaire

36 Blair Street, Old Town (220 4638). North Bridge–Nicolson Street buses. **Open** *Gigs* 11pm-3am Mon. **Admission** £2-£3. **No credit cards.** **Map** p304 D3.

Monday nights host Acoustica, a weekly night for singer-songwriters performing original material. In case you're getting any thoughts of showing up to play an out of tune cover of 'Blowin' in the Wind', forget it: cover versions are outlawed.

Canon's Gait

232 Canongate, Old Town (556 4481). Nicolson Street–North Bridge buses. **Open** *Gigs* 8.30-11.30pm Tue. **Admission** free. **No credit cards.** **Map** p310 G5.

On Tuesdays, and down the road from the Cab, is Folk 'n' Friends, another session of trad excess.

Pleasance

60 Pleasance, South Edinburgh (556 6550/ www.edinburghfolkclub.co.uk). Nicolson Street– North Bridge buses. **Open** *Gigs* 8pm Wed (not Aug). **Admission** £6; £5 concessions. **No credit cards.** **Map** p310 G6.

Home of the Edinburgh Folk Club, which holds sessions here every Wednesday in the Cabaret Bar, except during the Festival.

Royal Oak

1 Infirmary Street, Old Town (557 2976/www.royal-oak-folk.com). Nicolson Street–North Bridge buses. **Open** *Gigs* 9.30pm-1.30am Mon-Sat; 3-7pm, 9.30pm-1.30am Sun. **Admission** free. **No credit cards.** **Map** p310 G6.

Fall through the doors of this tiny two floor bar, and you're guaranteed to be regaled with a highly charged session of impromptu fiddles, squeezeboxes and guitars, all under the banner of the Wee Folk Club. The effect is intoxicating enough to make you feel you've stumbled onto a highland bothy. Just don't make the mistake of talking over the music.

Waverley

3-5 St Mary's Street, Old Town (556 8855/ www.outofthebedroom.co.uk). North Bridge–Nicolson Street buses. **Open** *Gigs* 9pm-midnight Thur. **Admission** free. **No credit cards.** **Map** p310 G5.

This quiet upstairs room in an even quieter bar was a major venue during the 1960s folk revival. These days, it plays host to Out of the Bedroom, a weekly Thursday night showcase for singer-songwriters to perform original material. As with Acoustica, croaky cover versions are banned. Phew.

Jazz

Up until the end of 2002, Edinburgh had three of the coolest jazz venues in the country. One, the only recently opened **Bridge Jazz Bar**, perished in the now legendary Cowgate fire (*see p73* **Burning down the town**). A second, the **Beat Jazz Basement**, was transformed by its owners in order to recoup losses from the blaze. A third, more upmarket, affair was mooted on the site of the old BBC building by a consortium that included Jools Holland, though at time of writing this appears to have fallen by the wayside. That leaves only **Henry's Jazz Cellar**, which had already lost its edge since being taken over by Assembly Direct.

Even so, Edinburgh has long been in possession of a thriving jazz scene, though in the last few years a younger set of hepcats have been making their mark beyond the circuit of trad pub gigs. Wester Hailes born saxophonist Tommy Smith has become a major figure on the international mainstream scene and an ambassador for jazz, even if his own work is a bit dull.

Far more interesting than the elder statesmen are the younger school of players, such as the ubiquitous drums and saxes of Trio AAB. Others born in such a melting pot atmosphere, such as Toby Shippey's Salsa Celtica, have outgrown clubland to be a main draw on the concert hall circuit. Vocal jazz, too, has a bright new face in the form of Nikki King, who can do funk and nu-jazz alongside more mainstream baladeering. Such virtuosity is probably why she picked up the 2001 Perrier Young Jazz Vocalist of the Year award. Many of these artists can be heard on albums released by Caber Music (www.cabermusic.com).

If it's trad you're after, look hard enough in Saturday lunchtime boozers and a Dixieland banjo band is bound to appear. More formally speaking, the **Scottish National Jazz Orchestra** (01555 860599/www.snjo.co.uk) keeps the big band flag flying.

Festival season kicks off at the end of July with the **Edinburgh Jazz and Blues Festival**, a fairly safe ten-day array of concerts featuring the likes of Courtney Pine and Jools Holland's Rhythm and Blues Orchestra (*see p37*). The **Leith Jazz Festival** (www.jazz-in-scotland.co.uk) is a much more modest event but has a convivial atmosphere.

Venues

Cellar Bar
*1a Chambers Street, Old Town (225 3598).
Nicolson Street–North Bridge buses.* **Open** 9pm-3am Mon, Tue, Fri; 10pm-3am Wed, Thur, Sat, Sun. **Admission** £2-£5 (free Mon, Tue). **Credit** MC, V. **Map** p310 G6.
One of the casualties of the Cowgate fire in 2002 was the Blue Note, the Chambers Street jazz club named after, and with sponsorship from, the most famous jazz record label in the world. Now, however, it's back as the Cellar Bar, and Trouble, the most swinging Friday night showcase of nu-jazz inflections, is open for business again.

Henry's Jazz Cellar
8-16 Morrison Street, West Edinburgh (467 5200/ www.jazzmusic.co.uk). Bus 1, 2, 28, 34, 35. **Open** *Gigs* 8.30pm Tue-Sun. **Admission** £5-£8. **Credit** MC, V. **Map** p308 C6.
Once upon a time, this magnificently scruffy basement establishment was party central, with live funk packing out its tiny dancefloor. Since Assembly Direct took over, however, much of the edge has gone. This isn't the artists' fault, as a steady stream of local talent, including trumpeter Colin Steele, John Rae and the excellent Bancroft brothers, regularly play alongside acts from America and Europe.

Eighty Queen Street
80 Queen Street, New Town (226 5097/www.eighty-queen-street.com). Princes Street buses. **Open** *Gigs* 8.30pm Mon; 9pm Thur-Sat. **Admission** free. **Credit** MC, V. **Map** p306 D4.
A relative newcomer to the scene, the spacious cellar bar beneath this office-friendly haunt presents nightly sets of unobtrusive modern bop, with guest artistes on Saturdays.

Oxygen Bar
3-5 Infirmary Street, Old Town (557 9997/www. oxygen-edinburgh.co.uk). Nicolson Street–North Bridge buses. **Open** *Gigs* times vary; phone for details. **Admission** free. **Credit** MC, V. **Map** p310 G6.
Since the loss of the Bridge Jazz Bar, drummer Bill Kyle has shifted operations to this minimalist chichi bar with an ongoing series of midweek sessions.

Queen's Hall
Clerk Street, South Edinburgh (668 3456/www. queenshalledinburgh.co.uk). Nicolson Street–North Bridge buses. **Open** *Gigs* times vary; see website for details. **Admission** £6-£25. **Credit** AmEx, MC, V. **Map** p310 G7.
Considered the spiritual heart of Edinburgh jazz, Friday night gigs here have become a fixture on every aficionado's calendar. In the past, Sonny Rollins, Art Blakey and Don Cherry all played here before passing on to the great blowout in the sky. Enthusiasts either sit in wooden pews at the side, or, for an extra couple of quid, book a table where they can nod along while checking out the cut of their polo neck by candlelight. Nice.

Arts & Entertainment

Nightlife

Edinburgh might not be an obvious clubbing destination, but its clubs and bars party to an eclectic mix of beats.

Edinburgh's reputation as a party city derives more from its festivals and pubs than its club scene. Recent years have seen the closure of scruffy techno den Wilkie House, the relocation of the Bongo Club, and the Old Town fire of December 2002, which destroyed La Belle Angele. Unlike Manchester, London and Glasgow, Edinburgh isn't really somewhere you would travel to for its dance music scene, but it is far from a city in crisis. Most of the club nights in Edinburgh are driven by enthusiasm rather than the profit motive and suffer from few pretensions. The best are friendly and relaxed and almost all are within walking distance of each other: keep your eyes open and your ears wide and you won't go wrong.

Pre-club bars

The term pre-club is misleading: for starters, you don't have to go clubbing afterwards. Edinburgh's relaxed licensing hours mean most city-centre bars are open till 1am, and some stay open till 3am. North African lounge bar **Medina**, West End hideaway **Berlin** and glossy rockers' haunt **Opium** all have 3am licenses, as does **Pivo** (*see p170*), which has house-orientated DJs seven nights a week and an Eastern European theme that's validated by a decent bottled beer selection. The nearby Broughton Street harbours funky style bar **PopRokit** (*see p170*) and the laid-back **Outhouse** (*see p157*).

The mass of Edinburgh's DJ bars, though, hang in the Old Town's dark corners. The city's classic pre-club bar is the **City Café** (*see p153*), an American-style diner with pool tables, decent grub and a basement that, when open, hosts DJs from the likes of **Manga** (drum 'n' bass) and **Progression** (progressive house). The shiny new **Assembly** (*see p152*) goes for sweet house music, poky but charming **Black Bo's** (*see p166*) plays a mix of electronica and funk, while **Wash** (*see below*) combines retro furnishings with classic soul, and the bistro-esque **Human Be-In** (*see p158*) offers a mix of DJs and laid-back live performances.

Berlin Bierhaus

3 Queensferry Street Lane, New Town (467 7215/ www.berlin.com). Princes Street buses. **Open** 5pm-3am Mon-Thur, Sat; 4pm-3am Fri. **Admission** £5 after 11pm Fri, Sat. **No credit cards. Map** p308 C5.

Medina

45-47 Lothian Street, Old Town (225 6313/ www.medinaedinburgh.co.uk). Bus 23, 27, 28, 45. **Open** 10am-3pm daily. **Admission** £2-£3. **No credit cards. Map** p309 F6.

Opium

71 Cowgate, Old Town (225 8382/www.opium rocks.com). Nicolson Street–North Bridge buses. **Open** 8pm-3am daily. **Admission** free. **Credit** AmEx, MC, V. **Map** p304 D3.

Wash

11-13 North Bank Street, Old Town (225 6193). Bus 23, 27, 41, 42. **Open** noon-1am daily. **Admission** free. **Credit** MC, V. **Map** p304 C3.

The best Club nights

For getting back in black
Studio 24's fortnightly club night **Mission** has been going on almost as long as the goth scene, and now has a junior wing at 7pm every Saturday (*see p229*).

For midweek frolics
Motherfunk at the Honeycomb is the biggie – a Tuesday night funkathon always rammed with students keen to forget about the day's lectures (*see p228*).

For brainmelting techno
Dogma at Studio 24 occasionally flirts with the lighter, electro side of things, but supercharged mentalism is arguably what it does best. Monthly Fridays (*see p229*).

For wearing a safari suit
Easy-listening night **Vegas** at Ego sees showgirls, cravat-clad gents and wastrels mingle with the usual revellers (*see p227*).

For hearing the Stone Roses
Party like it's 1990 at **Evol** every Friday at the Liquid Room (*see p228*).

For drum 'n' bass
Past guests at **Manga** have included Goldie and Bad Company. Monthly Fridays at Honeycomb (*see p228*).

The **Gaia** hypothesis: look stupid, pull birds. *See p228.*

Clubs

The closure and re-launch of several venues in the last few years has seen nights dart from space to space like fireflies. Genres take longer to rise and fall: the predicted demise of house music now seems a rather melodramatic claim. **Massa's** stable of clubs focus on the glossy, commercial end of the market, while nights like **Progression** and the Glasgow-born **Colours** (both at the Liquid Room) turn their attention to big guests and progressive beats. **Ultragroove** (at Cabaret Voltaire) keeps things deep and funky, while **Do This Do That** regularly attracts the likes of Darren Emerson and Tim Deluxe to the Honeycomb.

For trance fans, **Majestica** (at the Venue) and **Nuklear Puppy** (at Ego) cater, respectively, for the frisky and mentalist ends of the spectrum, while gay and gay-friendly nights like **Joy** and **Mingin'** (the Venue) and the legendary **Taste** (at the Liquid Room) mix trance, hard house and unbridled hedonism.

These days, the techno scene is defiantly underground, and largely rooted in the decidedly minimalist setting of Studio 24: **Dogma** is the longest running and perhaps the finest. The one constant in the drum 'n' bass scene is **Manga** (at the Honeycomb), where anyone who is anyone has played at some stage. Hip hop is another surprisingly potent force in the capital, with **Scratch** (at the Venue) offering breaking, scratching and a whole lot of worthy head-nodding.

If none of that appeals, you may want to check out **Motherfunk** (long-running Tuesday night funk), **Dr No's** (ska), **Messenger** (dub reggae), the **Go-Go** ('60s and soul), the **Egg** (indie and soul) or **Evol** (indie). If you're a fan of the dark stuff, meanwhile, the **Mission** is Edinburgh's classic goth night.

Despite the best efforts of the purists, these genres have a tendency to collide, and you'll find some of Edinburgh best music in these chaotic twilight zones. The newly relocated Bongo Club hosts **Pogo Vogue**, a tasty fusion of techno and electro, and **Headspin**, which mixes hip hop, house and funk, while Cabaret Voltaire hosts an impressively diverse and relatively cheap set of club nights.

INFORMATION AND PRICES

The ever-evolving nature of the nightlife scene means that venues and club nights change from one week to the next. For detailed, up-to-date listings, check out fortnightly entertainment guide the *List*. Information and previews are also available on Thursdays in free sheet *Metro* and in the *Herald* newspaper's 'Going Out' supplement, and on Fridays in the *Edinburgh Evening News*, while monthly dance mags like *DJ*, *Mixmag* and *Jockey Slut* round up the highlights. Flyers stacked up in style bars and record shops help promote one-off events, and **Underground Solu'shn** (*see p190*) is a good place to hang out if you want the inside track on Edinburgh's club scene – the staff are friendly and know their stuff.

Club admission prices vary wildly (from £2 to £20), with most venues charging little, if at all, during the week. The higher prices are for non-members on Fridays and Saturdays. Expect to pay even more during the Festival, when many clubs extend their opening hours until well into the early hours.

Bongo Club

37 Holyrood Road, Old Town (558 7604/ www.thebongoclub.co.uk). Nicolson Street–North Bridge buses. **Open** times vary; please see website for details. **Admission** £3-£10. **No credit cards**. **Map** p310 H5.

The clubbing arm of arts organisation Out of the Blue, the Bongo Club is a wonderfully welcoming venue that offers an impressive range of underground club nights, from techno to dub and hip hop. The club's current (post-2003) site lacks some of the cosily battered charm of its New Street predecessor, but it is substantially better appointed, with a pleasant bar area that sits above the main dancefloor. Come along and learn to swing or break dance at the regular classes, then show off your skills later.

Cabaret Voltaire

36 Blair Street, Old Town (220 4638). Nicolson Street–North Bridge buses. **Open** 10pm-3am daily. **Admission** £2-£10. **No credit cards**. **Map** p304 D3.

It may not be quite as radical as its name suggests, but this intimate, engaging club (known to regulars as 'the Cab') still hosts a fair mix of music alongside gigs and arty events. Electronica, funk, house and world rhythms dominate.

Cellar Bar

1a Chambers Street, Old Town (225 3598). Nicolson Street–North Bridge buses. **Open** 9pm-3am Mon, Tue, Fri; 10pm-3am Wed, Thur, Sat, Sun. **Admission** £2-£5 (free Mon, Tue). **Credit** MC, V. **Map** p309 G6.

This compact underground space has had a turbulent few years – previously a jazz bar under the sponsorship of the most famous record label around, Blue Note, it subsequently became a commercial disco, and then reopened in early 2004 as a laid-back club. It now offers hip hop, house, reggae and funk nights, with live gigs promised during the week.

Citrus Club

40-42 Grindlay Street, South Edinburgh (622 7086/ www.citrus-club.co.uk). Bus 1, 10, 11, 15, 16, 17, 22, 24, 34, 35. **Open** 11pm-3am Thur, Sat; 10.30pm-3am Fri. **Admission** £2-£5. **No credit cards**. **Map** p304 A3.

Small and sweaty club that hosts inexpensive retro and alternative nights, including Planet Earth ('80s, Fridays) and Tease Age (indie, Saturdays).

Ego

14 Picardy Place, Broughton (478 7434/www.club ego.co.uk). Playhouse buses. **Open** times vary; phone for details. **Admission** £2-£10. **No credit cards**. **Map** p307 G4.

Once a dancehall, then a casino, Ego retains the faded grandeur of its former identities with long red velvet curtains, antique chandeliers and dramatic wall murals. These camp surroundings would not be suited to every club night, but easy-listening night Vegas flourishes here. Downstairs, the Cocteau Lounge is sometimes used as a chill-out zone for the main event or hosts its own nights.

Dance music's not dead... it's live

It's long been one of dance music's key distinctions: you can be a great DJ, and make great records, without being able to cut it in the traditional live arena. Not any more – not in Edinburgh, anyway, as here the lines drawn between gigging and DJing are becoming increasingly blurred, giving more experimental club nights room to breathe.

Edinburgh's clubbing heroes have often been unsung, playing in small venues far from the spotlight, and from the commercial pressures that might blunt their radicalism. It's a culture that has helped produce acts like nu-jazz man **Jo Malik** (signed to hip

German label Compost) and electropunk *NME* faves the **Magnificents**, as well as a host of irregular, entertaining gigs at the likes of the Venue and Cabaret Voltaire.

So called "decks 'n' fx" and laptop sets, meanwhile, allow DJs to move from playing records to shaping them live: sounds can be sampled, looped and manipulated. It's less showy than scratching, although the effects can be even more impressive – check out **Moving Through** (breakbeat and funk at Cabaret Voltaire), **Pogo Vogue** (electro and house at the Bongo Club) or the trance-orientated **Colours Live!** at the Liquid Room.

Saturday night fevers

If you're sober, the idea of squeezing yourself into a garish boozehole where hip hop means 'Jump Around' and disco means 'Stayin' Alive' may not be a tempting one. Get a few drinks down your throat, though, and your music taste will decay, your eyes will rove, and you won't go home till you've re-enacted *Dirty Dancing* under neon lights.

Edinburgh's many party dens have pretty much the same soundtrack as mainstream clubs nationwide. The city's substantial student population means that the usual atmosphere is more dressed-down, while weekends see shirted and skirted locals fill the bars and kebab queues, and you may need nice shoes to get in.

Most discos are grouped on the rowdy stretch of the Cowgate, and the still rowdier corridor of shame that is Lothian Road. Of special note are **Revolution** (big and tacky, with acres of exposed flesh), the **Subway** (with a relaxed dress code and DJ requests), the **Subway West End** (a separate enterprise, with enticing themed nights that include 'Pole Idol' and 'Office Idol'), **Gaia** (studenty, with a multitude of midweek deals), the **Cavendish** (for an older crowd), **Faith** (a two-level club with an R&B slant located in a converted church), **Arena** (part of a huge amusement centre in the West End) and **City** a new development just by Waverley Station whose illusions of class are almost matched by its shiny, glass-ridden interior. The **Opal Lounge** on George Street in the New Town (*see p154*) is a late-night bar with substantial dancefloor. To reflect its upmarket aspirations there is a cover charge at weekends to go with its usual funky soundtrack.

Arena

Fountainpark, 65 Dundee Street, West Edinburgh (228 1661/www.edinburgh-arena.com). Bus 28, 34, 35. **Open** 10pm-3am Fri, Sat. **Admission** £5; £4 concessions. **Credit** MC, V. **Map** p308 B8.

Cavendish/Diva

3 West Tollcross, South Edinburgh (228 3252/www.thecav.co.uk). Bus 10, 11, 15, 16, 17. **Open** 10pm-3am Tue, Wed, Sat, Sun; 4pm-3am Fri. **Admission** £2-£6. **No credit cards. Map** p309 D7.

City: Edinburgh

1a Market Street, Old Town (226 9560/www.clg.co.uk). Nicolson Street–North Bridge buses. **Open** 11pm-3am Mon, Wed, Fri-Sun. **Admission** £3-£7. **No credit cards. Map** p304 D2.

Faith

207 Cowgate, Old Town (225 9764/www.faithclub.co.uk). Nicolson St–North Bridge buses. **Open** 10pm-3am Mon, Tue, Thur-Sun. **Admission** £2-£6. **Credit** MC, V. **Map** p304 D3.

Gaia

28 King's Stables Road, South Edinburgh (229 9438). Bus 2, 35. **Open** 10pm-3am Tue, Thur-Sat. **Admission** £2-£4. **No credit cards. Map** p309 E6.

Revolution

31 Lothian Road, West Edinburgh (229 7670). Bus 1, 10, 11, 15, 16, 17, 22, 24, 34. **Open** 10.30pm-3am Mon, Thur-Sat. **Admission** £4-£7. **No credit cards. Map** p304 A3.

Subway

69 Cowgate, Old Town (225 6766/www.subwayclubs.co.uk). Nicolson Street–North Bridge buses. **Open** 9pm-3am daily. **Admission** (Fri, Sat only) £2; £1 concessions. **No credit cards. Map** p304 D3.

Subway West End

23 Lothian Road, West Edinburgh (229 9197/www.subwaywestend.co.uk). Bus 1, 10, 11, 15, 16, 17, 22, 24, 34. **Open** 7pm-3am Mon-Thur, Sat, Sun; 4pm-3am Fri. **Admission** £1-£5. **No credit cards. Map** p304 A3.

Honeycomb

15-17 Niddry Street, Old Town (556 2442/www.the-honeycomb.com). Nicolson Street–North Bridge buses. **Open** 11pm-3am Tue, Fri, Sat; occasional events on other nights – please phone for details. **Admission** free Tue; £10 Fri, Sat. **No credit cards. Map** p304 D3.

The main bar may be a little cramped, but with a cracking sound system and refurbished interior, Honeycomb has dripped into a decent groove, with

underground nights including drum 'n' bass bash Manga and groovy house nights Do This Do That and Audio Deluxe. Plans are afoot to build a new bar at the front of the club, ideal for more intimate events.

Liquid Room

9c Victoria Street, Old Town (225 2564/www.liquidroom.com). Bus 2, 23, 27, 28, 41, 42, 45. **Open** 10.30pm-3am Wed-Sun. **Admission** £3-£15. **No credit cards. Map** p304 C3.

Getting sticky and sweet at the **Honeycomb**. *See p228.*

This subterranean, two-roomed space (complete with a balcony for people-watching) is turned over to club-goers after gigs finish. Its club programme is far from an afterthought, though, with house nights Colours and Progression, indie institution Evol and gay/mixed Sunday nighter Taste dominating its weekend schedule.

Massa

36-39 Market Street, Old Town (226 4224). Bus 23, 27, 28, 41, 42, 45/Nicolson Street–North Bridge buses. **Open** 10.30pm-3am Wed, Thur, Sun (only last Sun of month); 5pm-3am Fri; 11pm-3am Sat. **Admission** £3-£7. **No credit cards.** **Map** p304 D2.

The name may have changed (pre-2003 this was Club Mercado), but the emphasis – commercial house for a moderately dressy crowd – is the same. Cheap post-work drinks are offered on Fridays, but the highlight is Tackno, a kitsch-fest run by legendary DJ Trendy Wendy on the last Sunday of the month.

Studio 24

24 Calton Road, Calton Hill (558 3758). Bus 24, 25, 35, 35A. **Open** 11pm-3am Wed; 10pm-3am Thur; 10.30pm-3am Fri, Sat. **Admission** £1-£7. **No credit cards.** **Map** p310 G5.

Rumours of its closure have been circulating for some time, but this minimal warehouse-like venue pulls the crowds in, its genuinely alternative vibe suiting a seemingly bizarre mix of nights (mostly hardcore techno and full-on goth).

Venue

17-21 Calton Road, Calton Hill (557 3073/ www.edinvenue.com). Bus 30, 35. **Open** *Gigs* 7pm. *Club nights* 10pm-3am Fri, Sat; phone for details. **Admission** phone for details. **No credit cards.** **Map** p310 G5.

This three-floor live-music and club venue is scheduled for closure in 2008, although things certainly seem to be on the up. Friday nights have seen the venue take advantage of its layout to run three underground clubs with one entry fee, while Saturdays offer a rotating line-up of house, techno and trance.

Wee Red Bar

Edinburgh College Of Art, Lauriston Place, South Edinburgh (229 1442). Bus 23, 27, 28, 45. **Open** *Club nights* 11pm-3am Fri, Sat. **Admission** £4; £3 concessions. **No credit cards.** **Map** p309 E6.

The most charming of Edinburgh's student unions, this compact space holds occasional gigs and events as well as a weekend clubs programme. Its mainstay is the Egg, a retro/indie Saturday nighter, while Fridays are a mix of reggae, drum 'n' bass and private functions. It's open to students (at any university), students' guests or members.

Arts & Entertainment

Sport & Fitness

18 holes, round ball, oval ball, no balls: the choice is yours.

Three! **Prestonfield**. *See p233*.

Edinburgh's sporting scene struggles to compete with neighbouring Glasgow, particularly in football, as Glasgow's Rangers and Celtic totally dominate the Scottish Premier League. More humiliatingly, Edinburgh has twice seen teams move down the M8 to Glasgow: in 2000, American football club the Scottish Claymores switched Murrayfield for Hampden Park, and two years later, the Edinburgh Rocks basketball side also moved.

Nevertheless, Edinburgh has a proud sporting history and the atmosphere is always raised a notch when the Scotland rugby team play their home matches in the Six Nations Championship at Murrayfield Stadium. If that gets you hooked, check out resident team Edinburgh Rugby at Meadowbank Stadium. Football also vies for local affection: the city is divided between the green of Hibernian and the maroon of Heart of Midlothian. If you prefer doing to watching, Edinburgh's first-rate exercise facilities can more than offset the city's consumption of deep-fried Mars bars. Edinburgh's golf courses are among the world's oldest and most scenic, though you may have to book some time in advance to play at the more prestigious. The K2 of Edinburgh's sporting facilities, however, is the newly opened **National Rock Climbing Centre of Scotland** (*see p234*), which boasts the world's largest climbing arena. For dance and related activities, *see p239*. Sport-Scotland's website (www.sportscotland.org.uk) is a useful link to find out more about local events, clubs and governing bodies, while www.godoscotland. com is an excellent website for extreme sport in Edinburgh and the rest of Scotland.

Spectator sports

Cricket

Under the banner of the Scottish Saltires, the Scottish national side competes with English and Welsh clubs in Division Two of the Norwich Union League. Their entry into the English domestic league in 2003 was a huge boost for Scottish cricket, as was the capture of legendary Indian batsman Rahul Dravid. The season runs from mid April to September.

Scottish Saltires

Grange Club, Portgower Place, Stockbridge (313 7420/www.scottishcricket.co.uk). Bus 24, 29, 36, 42. **Open** 9am-5pm Mon-Fri. **Tickets** £10; £5 concessions. **Credit** MC, V. **Map** p305 B3.
The Grange is a picturesque ground with a capacity of 3,000. It is also home to one of Scottish sport's most relaxed atmospheres: where else can you read the paper while watching the match?

Football

Edinburgh's two main football teams, Heart of Midlothian (Hearts) and Hibernian (Hibs), hail from opposite ends of the city (Gorgie in the south and Leith in the north, respectively). Derbies are always passionate but largely good natured affairs and lack the violence and bigotry that has plagued their Glasgow equivalents. Recently Hearts have been the capital's stronger team: in the 2002-2003 season they finished a creditable third behind the Old Firm (the collective name for Rangers and Celtic). A dilemma was posed in spring 2000 when European football's governing body UEFA deemed Hearts' pitch too small to host European level matches. At the time of writing they face the choice between leaving, substantially redeveloping their historic Tynecastle home, or ground sharing with Hibs at a new site in the south west, with the first option being the more likely.

Heart of Midlothian FC

Tynecastle Stadium, Gorgie Road, West Edinburgh (200 7200/tickets 200 7201/www.heartsfc.co.uk). Bus 1, 2, 3, 21, 25, 33, 34. **Open** *Shop* 9.30am-5.30pm Mon-Fri; 9.30am-3pm matchdays. **Tickets** £16-£20; £10 concessions. **Credit** AmEx, MC, V.
If you haven't bought tickets by phone, you can usually get them on match days from the ticket sales booths in McLeod Street (not at the turnstiles). The Wheatfield Stand is a good place to watch the game.

Hibernian FC

Easter Road Stadium, 12 Albion Place, Leith (661 2159/tickets 0870 840 1875/www.hibernianfc.co.uk). Bus 1, 4, 5, 15, 19, 25, 35. **Open** *Shop* 9am-5pm Mon-Fri; 9.30am-3pm, 4.45-5.15pm matchdays. *Ticket office* 9am-5pm Mon-Fri; (non-matchday) 9am-3pm Sat (matchday) 9am-kick-off. **Tickets** £18-£24; £10 concessions. **Credit** AmEx, MC, V. **Map** p307 J2.
Tickets can be bought over the telephone, or at the ticket office until an hour before kick-off on matchdays; after that, pay at the turnstiles. Top spots in the stadium are the West and Famous Five stands.

Livingston FC

West Lothian Courier Stadium, Alderstone Road, Livingston (01506 417000/www.livingstonfc.co.uk). **Open** 9am-5pm Mon-Fri; 10.30am-3pm matchdays. **Tickets** £17-£19; £10 concessions. **Credit** AmEx, MC, V.

Golf

Scotland is home to some famous golf courses, which regularly host major tournaments. **Royal Troon** hosted the 26th British Open in 2004. In 2005 the competition goes to **St Andrews**, the home of golf's governing body the Royal & Ancient (01334 460000/www.randa.org). For tickets, either book online at www.opengolf.com or phone the R&A ticket office on 01334 460 010. Prices range from £470 for a composite ticket including car-parking, to £40 to watch a championship day (though you can watch Tiger Woods and co in action on their practice days for as little as £5).

Horse racing

The sport of kings takes place at five courses in Scotland, with around 80 days of racing a year. These are **Ayr** (01292 264179/www.ayr-racecourse.co.uk), **Hamilton Park** (01698 283806/www.hamilton-park.co.uk), **Kelso** (01668 280800/www.kelso-races.co.uk), **Musselburgh** (665 2859/www.musselburgh-racecourse.co.uk) and **Perth** (01738 551597/www.perth-races.co.uk). See www.scottish racing.co.uk for more information.

Rugby Union

Edinburgh's club scene is historically linked to a group of prestigious, fee-paying schools like Edinburgh Accies, Heriot's, Watsonians and Stewart's-Melville though those ties have weakened lately.
Edinburgh's pro-team, **Edinburgh Rugby**, nicknamed 'the Gunners', play their home games at Meadowbank Stadium (*see p234*). They compete with Glasgow and The Borders in the Celtic League against Welsh and Irish sides and their season runs from September to April. The Gunners team contains many Scottish internationals, including Simon Taylor (*see p232* **EdinBurgher Simon Taylor**).
Scotland's national team is based at Murrayfield. The Six Nations Championship (February to April) and the Autumn Test matches (November) are a huge draw.

Edinburgh Rugby

Meadowbank Stadium, 139 London Road, Leith (661 5351/tickets 0870 272 6600/www.edinburgh rugby.com). Bus 4, 5, 15, 19, 26, 34, 35, 44, 45. **Open** *Ticket office* 9am-9pm daily. **Tickets** £10-£20; £5-£10 concessions. **Credit** MC, V. **Map** p307 J3.
Tickets can be bought by phone and online, but you should have no problem buying tickets before kick-off, which is usually 7.30pm Fridays. Supporters normally sit in the 6,000 capacity main stand, so get there early if you want to get a good view.

Arts & Entertainment

Murrayfield Stadium

7 Roseburn Street, West Edinburgh (SRU 346 5000/ shop 346 5044/www.scottishrugby.org). Bus 12, 12A, 26, 31. **Open** *Office* 9am-5pm Mon-Fri & matchdays. **Tickets** from Ticketmaster (0870 900 9933). **Credit** *Shop* MC, V.

Murrayfield seats 67,500 and is one of the world's finest rugby stadiums. Stadium tours are run 10am-3pm Monday to Thursday. Details can be obtained from the marketing department of the SRU.

Gogar Park

Gogar Station Road, West Edinburgh (339 1254/www.gocurling.co.uk). Bus 100. **Open** 10am-11.45pm Mon-Fri; 10am-10pm Sat; 11am-9pm Sun. **Admission** *Peak* (5.45-9.45pm Mon-Fri; all Sat, Sun) £8.25; £4 children. *Off-peak* (10am-5.30pm, 9.45-11.45pm Mon-Fri) £7.75; £4 children. **Credit** MC, V.

A purpose-built curling rink used by over 35 clubs. Phone or e-mail to book a two hour session. You'll be supplied with curling stones and brushes (charged at £1 per session). Prices are based on eight people using a sheet of ice. Coaching is available.

Active sports

Curling

Olympic gold for Britain (though won by an all-Scottish team) in 2002 brought a lot of attention, and even a little glamour, to the sport of curling. You can also get your broom out at Murrayfield Ice Rink (*see p234*).

Cycling

The velodrome at Meadowbank Sports Centre (*see p234*) is home to the Scottish Cyclists' Union (652 0187/www.scuonline.org), which can advise on all the cycling sports and will have news of non-competitive family cycling events,

EdinBurgher Simon Taylor

Simon Taylor is the golden boy of Scottish rugby. His rise to international rugger stardom through the ranks of Edinburgh's clubs has been one of the few glimmers of hope in an otherwise gloomy outlook for the oval ball game north of the border. Still a young pup, blonde-haired, blue-eyed Taylor has amassed admirers both on and off the pitch – thanks in no small part to his racy ads for Sloggi underpants. The slogan? 'Top tackle. TopPants.' Fans please take note: he was also Mr September in Scottish Rugby's 2002 calendar.

His international debut came in 2000 in an autumn test victory over the USA and, after only four Scottish caps, he joined the British and Irish Lions in their 2001 tour of Australia. He made a try-scoring debut during the 116-10 rout of Western Australia before a knee injury cut his tour short. Instead of wallowing in self-pity, the plucky lad used the time to study for and complete his law finals at Edinburgh University.

Since then his international career has gone from ruck to driving maul as he established himself as Scotland's No 8. In the 2002-2003 season he was named Scotland's Player of the Season.

At 6ft 4in and weighing in at over 16 stone, Taylor's athleticism around the pitch and power with ball in hand makes him a threat to any opposition. He demonstrated his toughness (or foolhardiness, perhaps) when, during his second ever test match, aged just

21, against the then world champions Australia, he played for 75 minutes with a double fracture of his left hand. With his game still improving, it would be a major surprise not to see him in the starting line up when the British and Irish Lions tour New Zealand in 2005.

including the Edinburgh Cyclefest (mid June) and the Pedal for Scotland Glasgow to Edinburgh cycle (mid September). Spokes (313 2114/www.spokes.org.uk) and Edinburgh Bicycle Cooperative (331 5010/www.edinburgh bicycle.com) both offer useful information on biking in Edinburgh including local cycling clubs. On the web, **www.sustrans.org** is the best place to find cycling routes in Edinburgh and throughout Scotland.

Golf

Scotland is the home of golf, and East Lothian has some of the world's finest links courses, including **Muirfield** (www.golfingedinburgh. com/eastlothian/muirfield.htm). There are some 20 courses near the city centre and 70 others within easy driving distance. While there are a few snooty clubs, the majority welcome visitors with open arms. It is even possible to fly up from London for the day to play: first flight out in the morning and last back at night, with eighteen holes in between. But don't turn up to a course and expect to play straight away because demand often outstrips supply; be sure to book in advance. The website www.golfing edinburgh.com is the best source of information about golf in and around the city. For less serious golfers, the **Bruntsfield Links**, next to the Meadows, is a free, fun, pitch and putt.

Braid Hills

22 Braid Hills Approach, South Edinburgh (447 6666). Bus 11, 15, 16, 17. **Open** dawn-dusk daily. **Green fee** (per round) £14 Mon-Fri; £16 Sat, Sun. **Club hire** £15; £15 deposit. **Credit** MC, V.
Not one, but two, municipal courses. Situated against the backdrop of the Pentland Hills to the south and the Firth of Forth to the north, Braid One provides perhaps the most stunning views in Edinburgh. Book at least a week in advance.

Duddingston

Duddingston Road West, Arthur's Seat (661 7688/ www.duddingston-golf-club.com). Bus 4, 44, 45. **Open** dawn-dusk daily. **Green fee** (per round) £35. **Club hire** £10. **Credit** MC, V.
A demanding, tree-lined course set in undulating parkland towards the south-east of Arthur's Seat. The Braid Burn (stream) winds throughout the course and is in play on a disturbing number of holes. Within walking distance of the city centre.

Lothianburn

106a Biggar Road, Hillend, South Edinburgh (445 2206/shop 445 2288). Bus 4. **Open** dawn-dusk daily. **Green fee** (per round) £16.50 Mon-Fri; £22.50 Sat, Sun. **Club hire** £12.50 per set. **Credit** AmEx, MC, V.
A hillside course perched around 900ft (270m) above sea level, again affording great views of the city. One of the cheaper private courses.

National Rock Climbing Centre. *See p234.*

Murrayfield

43 Murrayfield Road, West Edinburgh (337 3479). Bus 12, 22, 26, 31. **Open** (to visitors) 8am-4.30pm Mon-Fri. **Green fee** (per round) £30. **Club hire** £14. **Credit** Shop MC, V.
Legendary, but closed to unaccompanied visitors at weekends and with limited access on weekdays.

Musselburgh Old Links

Balcarres Road, Musselburgh (665 5438/www. musselburgholdlinks.co.uk). Bus 15. **Open** dawn-dusk daily. **Green fee** (per round) £8.50-£9; £5-£5.50 concessions. **Club hire** £14. **Credit** MC, V.
Musselburgh is worth a visit simply to pay homage to the world's oldest active golf course. You can hire a set of hickory clubs and guttie balls for £24 for a taste of the 19th-century game.

Prestonfield

6 Priestfield Road North, Prestonfield (667 8597). Bus 2, 14, 30, 33. **Open** dawn-dusk daily. **Green fee** (per round) £18; £33 day ticket. **Club hire** £10. **Credit** MC, V.
A not too taxing scenic parkland course that is within easy reach of the city centre.

St Andrews

West Sands Road, St Andrews, Fife (01334 466666/ www.standrews.org.uk). **Open** dawn-dusk daily. **Green fee** (per round) varies according to course & time of year; consult the website for details. **Club hire** £20-£30. **Credit** MC, V.

Arts & Entertainment

Europe's biggest golf complex, with six courses. There are also two non-members' clubhouses and a driving range. Starting times on 18-hole courses should be reserved at least one month in advance, except for Saturday play, which can only be booked 24 hours in advance. The nine-hole Balgove course cannot be pre-booked: turn up and take the next available tee-time. For the Old course, the minimum handicap required is 24 (men) and 36 (women), but you must be prepared to endure a complicated booking system – as well as a two year wait.

Gyms & fitness centres

In addition to the gyms listed below there are also extensive work out and fitness facilities at the **Craiglockhart Tennis & Sports Centre** (*see p235*).

Holmes Place

Omni Centre, Greenside Place, Calton Hill (550 1650/www.holmesplace.com). Bus 1, 5, 7, 14, 19, 22, 25, 34, 49. **Open** (members & their guests only) 6.30am-10.30pm Mon-Fri; 8am-8pm Sat, Sun. **Rates** membership only; phone for details. **Credit** AmEx, MC, V. **Map** p307 G4.
This stylish members-only complex was opened in January 2003 and is Scotland's largest health club. Facilities include separate male and female sauna and steam rooms, spa baths, a dedicated health and beauty clinic and a restaurant. The centrepiece is the 25m stainless steel UVA treated swimming pool. Five minute walk from Princes Street.

Meadowbank Sports Centre

139 London Road, Abbeyhill, Leith (661 5351). Bus 4, 5, 15, 19, 26, 34, 44. **Open** 7.30am-10pm daily. **Rates** vary according to activity & time of day; phone for details. **Credit** MC, V.
Opened for the Commonwealth Games in 1970, this public centre has facilities for athletics, badminton, squash, basketball and football, as well as a velodrome. There are classes for children, adults and the over-50s in everything from archery to martial arts.

One Spa

8 Conference Square, West Edinburgh (221 7777/ www.one-spa.com). Bus 10, 11, 16, 17. **Open** 6.30am-10pm Mon-Fri; 7am-9pm Sat, Sun. **Rates** from £55 half-day package; from £187 full-day package. Membership also available. **Credit** AmEx, DC, MC, V. **Map** p309 D6.
One Spa claims to be the most advanced urban spa in Europe. Aside from the gym and typical treatments, the top-floor ozone-infused pool and its outdoor hydrotherapy area is a distinctive feature.

Pleasance Sports Centre

46 Pleasance, South Edinburgh (650 2585/www. sport.ed.ac.uk/facilities/pleasance). Bus 2, 21, 30. **Open** 8.30am-9.30pm Mon-Fri; 8.50am-5.30pm Sat; 9.50am-5.30pm Sun. **Rates** (non-members) £4 per session; £2 concessions. Membership also available. **Credit** MC, V. **Map** p310 G6.

Attached to the University of Edinburgh; during term time the Pleasance is open only to students, members and their guests, but during vacations it's open to all. There are facilities for badminton, basketball, indoor football, netball and squash, as well as an impressive gym.

Ice-skating

Murrayfield Ice Rink

Riversdale Crescent, West Edinburgh (337 6933). Bus 12, 26, 31. **Open** 2.30-4.30pm, 7-9pm Mon, Tue, Thur; 2.30-4.30pm, 7.30-10.30pm Wed; 2.30-4.30pm, 7.30-10.30pm Fri; 10am-noon, 2.30-4.30pm, 7.30-10.30pm Sat; 2.30-4.30pm Sun. **Admission** (includes skate hire) £2.50-£4. **No credit cards**.
As well as being home to the Edinburgh Capitals ice hockey team, this large rink is used for public skating sessions and curling. The evening session on Fridays and Saturdays attracts a young crowd for disco skating. A family session takes place on Thursday evening and Saturday morning, while the Sunday noon-1.45pm session is set aside for the popular group skating lessons.

Rock climbing

Meadowbank Sports Centre (*see above*) has a climbing wall constructed mainly of brick.

Alien Rock

8 Pier Place, Leith (552 7211/www.alienrock.co.uk). Bus 10, 11, 16, 32. **Open** *Summer* noon-10pm Mon-Fri; 10am-7pm Sat, Sun. *Winter* noon-11pm Mon-Thur; noon-10pm Fri; 10am-9pm Sat, Sun. **Admission** £4-£5.50; £3-£5 concessions. **Credit** MC, V. **Map** p311 Ex.
A 30ft (10m) surface with 50 ropes located in a former church and ten different walls. There are 180 different routes, which are changed every four months to present new challenges. All the necessary equipment can be hired, including footwear. A two-hour introductory course for novices costs £25, including equipment hire.

National Rock Climbing Centre of Scotland

Ratho Quarry, West Edinburgh (333 6333/www. adventurescotland.com). **Open** *Climbing arena* 12.30-10.30pm Mon-Fri; 9.30am-8pm Sat, Sun. *Gym* 6.30am-10pm Mon-Fri; 8am-8pm Sat, Sun. **Admission** (non-member) £10 day climbing pass; £8.50 concessions. **Credit** MC, V.
This £24 million project in a disused quarry is the largest indoor climbing arena in the world and, in December 2003, hosted the Climbing World Cup. It boasts 8,200ft (2,500m) of indoor surfaces, 16,400ft (5,000m) of outdoor surfaces, three free-standing boulders, a huge suspended assault course and a specialist gym for adventure sports. But maybe it's all too much of a good thing: at time of writing the centre had gone into receivership, although the management hope to continue under a new owner.

In the North Sea this is extreme sport. *See p230.*

Skiing

Midlothian Ski Centre

*Biggar Road, Hillend (445 4433/http.//ski.
midlothian.gov.uk/). Bus 4.* **Open** *May-Aug* 9.30am-
9pm Mon-Fri; 9.30am-7pm Sat, Sun. *Sept-Apr*
9.30am-9pm Mon-Sat; 9.30am-7pm Sun. **Rates**
Main slope £7.50 1st hr plus £3 per extra hr; £5
concessions plus £2 per extra hr. *Nursery slopes*
£4.60 1st hr plus £2.30 per extra hr; £2.90
concessions plus £1.60 per extra hr. **Ski hire**
£13.70 per day; £9.90 concessions. **Credit** MC, V.
Situated to the south of Edinburgh, the Midlothian
Ski Centre is in proud possession of the longest artificial ski slope in Europe, at 1,150ft (400m), which
includes a learning slope and a selection of jumps.
Prices include the hire of boots, skis and poles and
use of the chairlift. There's an additional charge for
snowboards or specialist skis. For younger skiers,
age 7-12, there's Sno' Cats, meeting Saturday 2-4pm.

Swimming

For swimming pools *see p127* and *p199*.

Tennis

Craiglockhart Tennis & Sports Centre

*177 Colinton Road, Craiglockhart (444 1969/
www.edinburghleisure.co.uk). Bus 10, 10A, 27, 45.*
Open 9am-11pm Mon-Fri; 9am-10.30pm Sat, Sun.
Rates phone for details. **Credit** MC, V.

Scotland's most comprehensive tennis centre has six
indoor and eight outdoor courts and also provides
coaching to all standards. The sports centre has a
fitness room, badminton and squash courts, and a
crèche. It also runs step and aerobics classes.

Meadows Tennis Courts

*East Meadows, Melville Drive, South Edinburgh (444
1969). Bus 41, 42.* **Open** *Summer only*; phone for
details. **Rates** £4-£5.50 per session. **No credit
cards. Map** p310 G8.
There are a number of public tennis courts around
the city, the largest of which are the Meadows
Tennis Courts. This facility has sixteen tar courts
and is open each year from April to September.
Phone 444 1969 for opening hours and rates.

Track & field

Most track and field activities are organised
around the public **Meadowbank Sports
Centre** (*see p234*) which caters for athletics,
badminton, basketball, football and squash.
Edinburgh Leisure (650 1001) can provide
details of activities and venues, while
SportScotland (317 7200/www.sport
scotland.org.uk) holds a database of governing
sports' bodies in Scotland. The **Meadows**
(*see p115*), in south Edinburgh and located
off Melville Drive, is the centre for most
unorganised sporting activities and during the
summer months buzzes with a host of different
games being played under the broad banner
of sport and recreation.

Arts & Entertainment

Theatre & Dance

It all goes mad in August, but Edinburgh is an all-year luvvie land.

What would Aristotle think? **Royal Lyceum**. *See p238.*

Theatre

Visit Edinburgh in August, when the biggest arts festival in the world engulfs the city (*see p32*), and theatre-loving party animals could be forgiven for thinking that they've reached nirvana. But while travelling north during the rest of the year might be quieter (certainly) and colder (probably), it is still worthwhile.

Yet Edinburgh, remember, is where the late-20th-century renaissance of indigenous playwrighting found its natural home, long before its near neighbours picked up the slack. In the 1970s, both the **Royal Lyceum** and especially the **Traverse** theatres (for both, *see p238*) were hotbeds of change and activity, in which a new generation of writers, directors and actors learnt their trade before making waves elsewhere.

But creativity isn't just about bricks and mortar, and real innovation has come from ad hoc companies surviving on a shoestring without any real supportive framework. Site-specific maestros **Grid Iron** (*see p238* **Theatres: who needs 'em?**), for instance,

have grown from modest beginnings to become one of the most inventive companies around.

Much hot air from politicians and pundits of late has been devoted to the task of setting up Scotland's national theatre, a move that is set to bear its first fruits in 2005. The Lyceum and the Traverse, meanwhile, situated almost back-to-back off the rough and ready Lothian Road, are still really the only main venues for regular home-grown activity. If it's starry-eyed glitz and West End transfers you're after, the **Edinburgh Playhouse** (*see p237*) should be a first point of call.

Tickets

Tickets for many major venues can be booked through the **Ticketline** network (0870 748 9000; 10am-8pm Mon-Sat; 11am-6pm Sun). **Showstoppers** (558 9800) provides tickets for the Church Hill Theatre, while **Ticketmaster** (0870 606 3424; 24 hours daily) sells for the Edinburgh Playhouse. In other cases contact the individual box offices listed under the relevant venues.

Venues

Bedlam Theatre

*11b Bristo Place, Old Town (information 225 9873/
box office 225 9893/www.bedlamtheatre.co.uk). Bus
23, 27, 28, 41, 42, 45.* **Open** *Box office* 45mins
before performance. **Tickets** £2.50-£7.50 **Credit**
(during Festival only) MC, V. **Map** p309 F6.

Home to the Edinburgh University Theatre
Company, which produces a rolling programme of
student drama fare, as well as showcasing work
penned by fledgling undergraduate writers. EUTC
alumni include *Chariots of Fire* star Ian Charleson
and teen soap *Hollyoaks'* blonde bombshell, Elize Du
Toit. If you look hard enough in the theatre's poster
strewn foyer café, you can see Ms Du Toit once
appeared in a production of David Mamet's *Sexual
Perversity in Chicago.* Phwoar!

Brunton Theatre

*Bridge Street, Musselburgh (665 2240). Bus 15, 26,
44.* **Open** *Box office* 10am-7.30pm Mon-Sat (10am-
6pm Mon-Sat when no performance).* **Tickets** £5-
£10.50. **Credit** MC, V.

Up until recently, this theatre, a 20-minute bus ride
out of town, had its own thriving company, producing a regular repertory of classics alongside new
work. The good burghers of East Lothian, alas,
decided money could be better spent elsewhere, and
the company was scrapped. These days the Brunton
is a more localised civic affair, taking in one-night-
stands from companies on the touring circuit.

Church Hill Theatre

*Morningside Road, South Edinburgh (447 7582).
Bus 11, 15, 16, 17, 23.* **Open** *Box office* only on
performance days.* **Tickets** (available from
individual companies or Showstoppers) £3-£10.
No credit cards.

Deep in the heart of suburbia, the Church Hill is a
mecca for wobbly amateur dramatics societies
across the land. Occasionally used professionally: it
actually housed the British debut of New York
experimentalists The Wooster Group, who count
Willem Dafoe as a regular collaborator. The show?
LSD – Just the High Points.

Counting House

*Upstairs at the Counting House, West Nicolson
Street, South Edinburgh (07969 163065/
silencio@talk21.com). Nicolson Street–North Bridge
buses; please phone for details.* **Tickets** £3; £2 concessions. **No credit cards.**

Once an occasional annexe of the Gilded Balloon
comedy empire (somewhat declined since the
Cowgate fire, *see p73* **Burning down the town**),
this is now the nearest thing to a pub theatre venue
in Edinburgh. Though not widely used, it is the current home of Silencio, an ongoing series of monthly
cabaret nights that combine music, performance art
and comedy. Its founders are key players in the
freshly constituted Highway Diner company (*see
p238* **Theatres: who needs 'em?**).

Edinburgh Playhouse

*18-22 Greenside Place, Calton Hill (0870 606 3424/
www.ticketmaster.co.uk). Playhouse buses.* **Open** *Box
office* 10am-8pm Mon-Sat (6pm on non-performance
days). *Telephone bookings* 24hrs daily. **Tickets**
£7.50-£35. **Credit** AmEx, MC, V. **Map** p307 G4.

Now run by global entertainment conglomerate
Clear Channel, the Playhouse's 3,000-seat auditorium is the natural home for touring West End musicals. Recent years have seen productions of *Saturday
Night Fever* and *Cats* keep the box office tills tinging.
The Edinburgh International Festival also utilises
the space for its more lavish dance and opera productions, while grown-up rock stars use the venue
as a stopping off-point. Ageing Beach Boy Brian
Wilson played here, and it's apparently Lou Reed's
favourite venue ever.

Gateway Theatre

*Elm Row, Leith Walk, Broughton (information 317
3900/box office 317 3939). Playhouse buses.* **Open**
Box office (during term time) noon-2pm Mon-Fri;
45mins before performance. *Telephone bookings*
10am-4pm Mon-Fri. **Tickets** £4-£8. **Credit**
AmEx, MC, V. **Map** p307 G3.

You'll see many a budding thespian skipping their
way down Leith Walk en route to Queen Margaret
University College's drama department on the site
of this former TV studio. This is your chance to see
talent in the raw in regular productions directed by
professionals who invariably use the venue to talent
spot. In 2002 QMUC also presented the world pre-
miere of Irvine Welsh's 1980s set musical, *Blackpool.*

King's Theatre

*2 Leven Street, Tollcross, South Edinburgh (529
6000/www.eft.co.uk). Bus 10, 11, 15, 16, 17.* **Open**
Box office 1 hr before performance. *Telephone
bookings* 11am-8pm Mon-Sat (until 6pm when no
performance); 4pm-curtain (performance days only).
Tickets (also available from the Edinburgh Festival
Theatre) £4-£16. **Credit** AmEx, DC, MC, V.
Map p309 D7.

Built in 1905, this elegant old-time Edinburgh institution is now managed (with the Edinburgh Festival
Theatre) under the auspices of the Festival City
Theatres Trust. The programme features tours by
the likes of the Royal Shakespeare Company and the
Royal National Theatre, as well as lavish productions of Oscar Wilde plays that habitually feature
some of the *grandes dames* of TV and stage. Recent
years have seen Tara Fitzgerald in Ibsen's *A Doll's
House,* and Diana Rigg in *Suddenly Last Summer.*

North Edinburgh Arts Centre

*15a Pennywell Court, Stockbridge (315 2151/
www.northedinburgharts.co.uk). Bus 27, 32A, 37,
37A, 42.* **Open** *Box office* 8am-4pm Mon-Fri; 10am-
3pm Sat. **Tickets** £2-£8. **No credit cards.**

Off the main drag, but an essential resource for a
part of town otherwise starved of any theatrical
activity, North Edinburgh Arts Centre regularly produces its own community shows, as well as being a
new addition to the small-scale touring circuit.

Theatres: who needs 'em?

A welter of hip Edinburgh gunslingers have proved that you don't need stacks of money to create theatre that makes the more seasoned establishments sit up and take notice. Shunning the high gloss (and high prices) of established theatre buildings, the new kids have set up shop in unconventional spaces which they incorporate into the heart of their work.

Cream of this new breed of site-specific companies is **Grid Iron** (www.gridiron.org.uk), founded by producer Judith Docherty and director Ben Harrison while they were still students at Edinburgh University in the early 1990s. They first made their mark with *The Bloody Chamber*, an Angela Carter adaptation that was performed in the dank dungeons and long hidden passageways of Mary King's Close. Now a tourist attraction in its own right, the Close was once a burial site for 17th-century plague victims (*see p77*).

Following their debut, they went even further underground, into the labyrinthine network of rooms beneath George IV Bridge. The Underbelly, now a major Festival venue (*see p34*), was christened with a Fringe performance of the Rabelaisian *Gargantua*. Blinking into the light, Douglas Maxwell's superb *Decky Does a Bronco* was performed in an outdoor swing park and was Grid Iron's most successful show to date. In the 2003 Festival, the company proved themselves a major force once again with the hugely succesful one-woman show, *Those Eyes, That Mouth*, performed over the three floors of a New Town tenement building.

Other theatre companies going beyond bricks and mortar are **Boilerhouse** (www.boilerhouse.org.uk), who began life as purveyors of what became known as in-yer-face theatre – particularly in the club-based Irvine Welsh collaboration, *Headstate* – but who have since reconstituted themselves as producers of open-air spectacles; the mime-based **Benchtours** (www.benchtours.com) and **Highway Diner**, a new company – as yet not seduced by the internet – founded by some of the people behind the Silencio series of cabaret nights at the **Counting House** (*see p237*).

Royal Lyceum

Grindlay Street, South Edinburgh (248 4848/ www.lyceum.org.uk). Bus 1, 10, 11, 15, 16, 17, 22, 24, 34. **Open** *Box office* 10am-6pm Mon-Sat (or until curtain performance days). **Tickets** £1-£17.50. **Credit** AmEx, MC, V. **Map** p304 A3.

At its peak in the 1970s, the Lyceum was at the vanguard of a renaissance of indigenous culture in Edinburgh. By the 1980s, however, the Lyceum was just one more workaday rep. After the best part of a decade in the creative doldrums, a new regime was ushered in during 2003 by artistic director David Mark Thomson, who has continued the Lyceum's safety-first repertory of classics. He did, however, score a considerable coup in 2004 by tempting Dundee-born Hollywood resident Brian Cox back onto the stage in *Uncle Varick*, John Byrne's reworking of Chekhov's *Uncle Vanya*.

Theatre Workshop

34 Hamilton Place, Stockbridge (226 5425). Bus 23, 27. **Open** *Box office* 9.30am-5.30pm Mon-Fri (only during show run). **Tickets** £8. **Credit** MC, V. **Map** p238 D3.

Those who recall this small, boho establishment as an epicentre of Stockbridge life could be forgiven for thinking that it's hardly used most of the year round. Once a thriving receiving house of radical touring theatre, the building's focus is now with its own professional company, which is the first professional mixed physical ability ensemble in Europe. Its shows tackle single-issue politics head-on, from anti-globalisation marches to disabled activism. Aesthetic sensibilities, alas, are often buried in the desire to get the message across.

Traverse Theatre

10 Cambridge Street, Old Town (228 1404/ www.traverse.co.uk). Bus 1, 10, 11, 15, 16, 17, 22, 24, 34. **Open** *Box office* 10am-6pm Mon; 10am-8pm Tue-Sat (until 6pm when no performance); 4-8pm Sun (performance days only). **Tickets** £4-£14. **Credit** MC, V. **Map** p304 A3.

Born in the 1960s as the brainchild of freethinking ex-GI Jim Haynes, the Traverse has come a long way from its counter-cultural roots to its current status as a major player on the world stage. Originally housed in a former brothel on the High Street, a legend was born on its second night of business when actress Colette O'Neill was accidentally stabbed in a production of Sartre's *Huis Clos*. By the time it moved to its second home in the Grassmarket, the emphasis on European experimentalism was shifting towards more homegrown fare. The 1970s saw a rise in new plays by writers such as John Byrne and Tom McGrath, and hosted early work by the likes of Steven Berkoff. By the mid 1980s, actors such as Robert Carlyle and Tilda Swinton were cutting their teeth in ambitious programmes. The Traverse moved to its current home in 1992, in to a purpose-built subterranean expanse housed beneath a complex of offices. Two performance spaces showcase a lively diet of new plays from writers developed by the Traverse Theatre Company itself, as well as a rolling programme of touring shows.

Dance

The fan base for ballet and dance in Edinburgh is a devoted one. It's also young, hip and colourful enough to appreciate regular visits from the likes of Mark Morris, Nederlands Dans Theater and Michael Clarke, as well as Scottish Ballet. Smaller companies regularly tour to the Traverse and the Brunton, though the biggest initiative has been the opening of the very lovely Dance Base, a purpose built network of studios providing space for both professionals and amateur enthusiasts alike.

Venues

Dance Base

14-16 Grassmarket, Old Town (225 5525/ www.dancebase.co.uk). Bus 2, 23, 27, 28, 41, 42, 45. **Open** *Administration & bookings* 10am-5pm Mon-Fri; 10am-1pm Sat. **Tickets** (during Festival only) phone for details. **Credit** MC, V. **Map** p304 B3.
This beautifully airy purpose-built venue in the shadow of Edinburgh Castle has become a state-of-the-art focus for the capital's thriving dance community. With four studios housing an extensive programme of classes and workshops, all levels and areas of interest are catered for. Ever wanted to learn Highland or gumboot dancing? Feldenkreis and

Alexander technique? This is the place. Regular performances have yet to happen here, though during the Edinburgh Fringe, BBC Radio 3 broadcast live concerts from the building.

Edinburgh Festival Theatre

13-29 Nicolson Street, South Edinburgh (box office 529 6000/administration 662 1112/www.eft.co.uk) Nicolson Street–North Bridge buses. **Open** *Box office* 10am-8pm Mon-Sat (6pm when no performance); 4pm-curtain Sun (performance days only). *Telephone bookings* 11am-8pm Mon-Sat (6pm when no performance); 4pm-curtain Sun (performance days only). **Tickets** £5.50-£55. **Credit** AmEx, DC, MC, V. **Map** p310 G6.
There's a wonderfully flamboyant sense of camp behind the revitalised glass façade of the Festival Theatre that is perfect for doyens of the dance scene. While sharing management with the King's Theatre, the Festival however seems more like a glammed-up kid sister. But it wasn't always so. Having begun life as the Empire Palace Theatre and played host to the biggest of old-time variety stars, by the mid 1980s it was the Empire bingo hall, run-down enough to put on gigs by the likes of trash-sleaze merchants the Cramps. When the bingo hall decamped to the old porn cinema across the street, major restoration saw the new Festival Theatre reborn as the most opulent of commercial receiving houses. Alongside appearances by Scottish Opera and others throughout Edinburgh International Festival, the Festival Theatre was also the venue of choice for the 2003 Royal Variety Performance, a top pop extravaganza hosted by children's TV presenter Cat Deeley – the first time in its history the show has played outside London.

Prose and verse at the **Traverse**.
See p238.

HOTELGALLERY
RESTAURANTBAR

63 BEDROOMS
1 RESTAURANT
2 BARS
PRIVATE DINING
MEETING ROOMS
CONFERENCES
FUNCTIONS
HAIR & BEAUTY

ARTHOUSE HOTEL > 129 BATH STREET > GLASGOW G2 2SY
T 0141 221 6789 > F 0141 221 6777 > info@arthousehotel.com

WWW.ARTHOUSEHOTEL.COM

Trips Out of Town

Getting Started

Away from Edinburgh, there's wilderness within reach.

Yes, it's a capital city, but Edinburgh is also small and compact. That gives it two great advantages: one is that it's easy to explore, the other is that it's easy to escape. In less than an hour you can find yourself in the open countryside of East Lothian, the pretty fishing villages of Fife or the cosmopolitan bustle of Glasgow. With a little more time, you can reach places that feel utterly remote and are in fact the nearest approach in the British Isles to genuine wilderness.

This section of the guide focuses on the areas that make a comfortable day trip from Edinburgh by car, train or bus. Many of them are attractive holiday destinations in their own right, and you might well be tempted to stay longer than a day. In the following pages, we concentrate in particular on **Glasgow**, which has a long-standing and generally healthy cultural rivalry with Edinburgh. It's a vibrant place, Scotland's biggest city with an important industrial heritage. In the past 15 years, it has managed to reinvent itself as a fashionable destination for the arts, entertainment, clubbing, shopping and eating.

On a less frenetic note, we highlight the attractions of the **Lothians**, **Stirling**, **Fife** and the **Borders**, with some hints about how to get further afield (*see p262*). Most of this is pitched at the independent traveller, but if you don't want to strike out alone, there are plenty of organised trips and group tours to destinations all around Scotland, varying from guided coach tours to group backpacking and hill-walking trips (*see p268* **Trips and tours**). The more intrepid visitor, by contrast, will be attracted to the Highlands, which offer ideal terrain for a number of adventure and winter sports.

PLANNING A TRIP

The **Edinburgh & Lothians Tourist Board** on Princes Street (*see p290* and www.edinburgh.org) can provide information on travel, sightseeing and accommodation throughout Scotland. It's also worth investing in a good map. Ordnance Survey (OS) has the whole of Great Britain mapped in intimate detail. The two series that are likely to prove of greatest use are the Landranger (scale 1:50,000) and the Explorer (scale 1:25,000). Ordnance Survey maps can be bought at TSO Scotland (71 Lothian Road, South Edinburgh; 0870 606 5566) and most major bookshops.

GETTING AROUND

Public transport to the more rural regions of Scotland can sometimes be a problem, so hiring your own car is often the best option. (For details of hire firms, *see p277*). Having said that, the rail system is fairly efficient and provides a network of trains to most of the larger towns. **Scotrail** (08457 550033/ www.scotrail.co.uk) also has some flexible travel passes that allow you to roam using trains, buses and ferries. These include the **Freedom of Scotland Travelpass** (£89 for four days' travel over eight days, or £119 for eight days' travel over 15 days). If you just want to cover the Highlands, then get an eight-day **Highland Rover** pass (£59 for four days' travel, including ferries to, and bus travel on, Mull and Skye) and discover some stupendous country that isn't accessible by car. For further details of rail travel, *see p275*.

Bus travel is another possibility, although bear in mind that services in more remote areas may be as infrequent as twice a week. Buses from Edinburgh usually depart from **St Andrew Square Bus Station** (*see p274*).

PRECAUTIONS

Scotland's mountain scenery is one of the country's greatest assets but is also potentially dangerous for hillwalkers and climbers who do not observe these basic safety precautions.

● Don't overestimate your ability and fitness.
● Always tell someone where you are going and what time you plan to get back.
● Take a map, a compass and a torch.
● Wear suitable footwear and always take waterproofs with you.
● Carry a water bottle and emergency rations.
● The weather can change very quickly; if it looks like turning bad, get off the mountain.

If you're travelling to the Highlands, you should also be prepared for midges: tiny flying insects with a voracious appetite for fresh human blood. Midges breed on boggy ground, prefer still days and are at their worst between late May and early August. Their bites make you itch, and a cloud of them are enough to drive you mad. No one has yet found a repellent for them that works; however, they are deterred by citronella and herb oils such as thyme or bog myrtle. They are also attracted to dark-coloured clothing, so there is an argument for going with a Goth while wearing a white T-shirt yourself.

Glasgow

With its superlative nightlife and edgy charm, Scotland's largest metropolis is always a winner.

Glasgow's soul. For sale or hire. **Barrowland** and the **Barras**. *See p255 and 256.*

The rain falls on Glasgow two days out of three, the clouds rolling in from the low pressure systems of the North Atlantic to hang around over Scotland's largest city. But Glasgow remains undaunted. This town – pronounced 'toon' – has absorbed every shock and adapted to every change without breaking stride or losing heart. If plagues, fires, cholera epidemics, the boom and bust of colonial trade and the collapse of local industry haven't really spoiled the general good mood, then a few drops of water will never bring the place down.

Glasgow seems to convert adversity and rivalry into energy, continually redefining itself in proud, progressive opposition – not only to Edinburgh, its smaller, prettier, bureaucratic senior, but also to mighty London. Once the second city of the British Empire, Glasgow is arguably becoming a viable lifestyle alternative to that bigger smoke way down South – an enclave for the cultured and creative, offering up its own range of urban diversions and possibilities with a little more flavour, spirit, and room to breathe. Between 1990, when it was nominated European City of Culture, and 1999, when it was appointed UK City of Architecture and Design, Glasgow spent serious time and money on remodelling, redirection and rebranding. A dark period of post-industrial decline – with poverty and unemployment giving rise to drug addiction, razor gangs and grim council towerblocks – was painstakingly shifted into a brighter future of high-tech business, service-based commerce and hyperactivity in the arts and media. And if anything, the rate of change is accelerating.

These days, the whole town is image-conscious to the point of vanity. At the upper end of the market, there is an infatuation with designer clothing labels – heavily represented around the **Merchant City** (*see p245*). At the lower end, there is an obsession with curing the natural Glaswegian pallor – this city has more tanning salons per head than anywhere else in the world. Indeed, much of this change is cosmetic. Older problems haven't been solved, they've just been pushed to outer estates and overspill towns as the centre becomes busily middle-class. Conditions in certain areas of South and East Glasgow are still defined by abysmal poverty. Young people from these communities are regarded as both troubled and trouble-making, known collectively as 'Neds' – 'non-educated delinquents'. Generally identified by their almost tribal sportswear outfits, they are feared and patronised by the urbane.

Glasgow's history of sectarianism, a lingering product of antagonism between Irish Catholic and Scottish Protestant workers and unions, still finds ugly expression in the 'Old Firm' clashes between Celtic and Rangers football teams. But any fears the city might be forgetting its long traditions of industriousness, socialism, free-thinking and fun-loving have so far proven unfounded. Glasgow is once again adapting to the times, but its physical character remains essentially unchanged, a compact grid of grand, bold architecture – exemplified by the magnificent work of Charles Rennie Mackintosh and Alexander 'Greek' Thomson.

Glasgow's personality remains progressive, curious, innovative, and wildly sociable: it's a tremendously exciting place to be. Entertainment is prized and thrillingly indulged every night of the week, without any of the self-consciousness that can often make fashionable city-dwellers reluctant to be seen to have a good time. A Wednesday in the **Ben Nevis** bar (*see p253*), listening to awesomely talented folk musicians, is just as worthwhile an experience as a Saturday at the **Soundhaus** (*see p258*), listening to awesomely talented DJs.

While Glasgow's reputation for toughness and drunkenness isn't unjustified, reports of its good humour and friendliness aren't necessarily exaggerated either. Every citizen, from kids to old folks, seems to be ready with a casual, truthful, hilarious remark. And their honest, realist brand of *joie de vivre* is infectious. Other cities are likeable, or admirable, but Glasgow is just plain lovable.

Sightseeing

Waterfront

Start your exploration down by the Clyde – that's where Glasgow began when St Mungo settled here in the sixth century, and where the city is most visibly regenerating itself with huge new development schemes. The **Clyde Walkway** runs underneath the numerous city-centre bridges along the north bank. Beginning at the west end of Glasgow Green, head westwards along the Broomielaw, home to Glasgow's burgeoning financial district, and you'll soon see one of the city's new sci-fi riverside landmarks, Foster and Partners' **Clyde Auditorium** (*see p255*), known locally as the 'Armadillo'. The hard, funky glisten of the Armadillo has recently been eclipsed by the spectacular shine of the new **Glasgow Science Centre**, across the Clyde at Pacific Quay (*see right*). Within the centre, the

titanium-encased IMAX cinema and Science Mall are hip examples of leading-edge design, and provide classy edu-tainment for all. The Centre's Glasgow Tower will provide unsurpassed views as soon as those hip designers sort it out – due to ongoing technical problems, you still can't go up there. Which is Glasgow all over – progressive, but prone to glitches. Still, the Science Mall's glass front offers a good view of the **Tall Ship** at Glasgow Harbour (*see below*), the *SV Glenlee*, one of the few Clyde-built sailing ships still in existence. In summer you can see the **Waverley**, the world's only sea-going paddle steamer (*see below*), cruising to the Isle of Bute and other west coast locations. Then there's the **Clyde Waterbus** (*see p261*), ferrying shoppers to Braehead, or to the nearby Clydebuilt Museum.

Clydebuilt Maritime Museum

King's Inch Road, Braehead, G51 (0141 886 1013/ www.scottishmaritimemuseum.org). Bus 23, 101. **Open** 10am-6pm Mon-Sat; 11am-5pm Sun. **Admission** £3.50; £1.75 concessions. **No credit cards**.
One of the Scottish Maritime Museum's three sites, Clydebuilt tells the worthwhile, intertwined story of Glasgow and the Clyde, from trading to shipbuilding. Double the fun by taking the Clyde Waterbus from the city centre (*see p261*).

Glasgow Science Centre

50 Pacific Quay, G51 (0141 420 5000/www.glasgow sciencecentre.org). Exhibition Centre rail. **Open** *Science Mall* 10am-6pm daily. *IMAX* Nov-Mar noon-6pm daily; Apr-Oct 10am-6pm Mon-Thur, Sun; 10am-8pm Fri, Sat. **Admission** prices vary; please phone for details. **Credit** MC, V.
Since opening in 2001, the GSC Mall has become deservedly popular with kids and armchair scientists for its well-run exhibits and planetarium. It also houses an IMAX cinema.

Tall Ship at Glasgow Harbour

100 Stobcross Road, G3 (0141 222 2513/ www.thetallship.com). Exhibition Centre rail. **Open** *Mar-Oct* 10am-5pm daily. *Nov-Feb* 11am-4pm daily. **Admission** £4.50; £3.25 concessions. **Credit** MC, V. Map p314 A2.
The tall ship *SV Glenlee* is one of only five Clydebuilt sailing ships remaining afloat. Launched in 1896, she stands as an impressive reminder of the Clyde's shipbuilding legacy.

Waverley Paddle Steamer

Waverley Excursions, Waverley Terminal, G3 (0141 243 2224/www.waverleyexcursions.co.uk). Anderston rail. **Sailings** *July, Aug* 9.30am Mon; 10am Fri-Sun. No sailings Sept-June. **Admission** varies. **Credit** MC, V.
Built in 1947, the *Waverley* paddle steamer is a unique summer attraction. The breezy, Huckleberry charm of a quiet churn down the water has been known to cure hangovers and shopping-exhaustion.

City centre

The wealth generated by Glasgow's once-great place in the world of trade and commerce transformed the semi-rural old medieval city into one of the most elegant urban centres in the country. It's a small but perfectly formed arrangement of decorative stone canyons; laid out in a grid like old New York or Chicago, but definitively Victorian. The River Clyde, the main historic channel for the city's income,

leads into the city, whose heart is **George Square**, a former swamp that now hosts a year-round programme of public events, including the city's wildly rowdy Hogmanay celebrations. The magnificent **City Chambers** to the east of the square, which were opened by Queen Victoria in 1888, are a potent reminder of Glasgow's former importance in the British Empire. Spreading away from the south-east of George Square is the **Merchant City**, formerly the centre for Glasgow's sugar and tobacco

Top seven Sights

Burrell Collection
A staggering display of artistic and cultural booty, hoarded from a rich variety of times and places (*see p248*).

Glasgow School of Art
Charles Rennie Mackintosh's finest building (pictured) is itself art, expressing the earthy, lofty spirit of Glasgow in stone (*see p247*).

Glasgow Science Centre
A shining shell beside the Clyde, the place to watch Glasgow's granite shell hatching into something more futuristic (*see p244*).

Kelvingrove Park
Elegant green haven, sweeping across from Park Circus to the cloud-capped University spires (*see p251*).

Necropolis
Beautifully gloomy resting place for long-dead Victorian industrialists, with a grand view allowing them to keep watch over the city they built (*see p248*).

People's Palace/Winter Gardens
A much-loved repository for Glasgow's collective memory, the whole of the city's life and history are written up on the walls (*see p248*).

St Mungo Museum of Religious Life and Art
Home to Salvador Dali's most popular, most passionate and most mesmeric painting, his inspired interpretation of a vision of *Christ of St John on the Cross* (*see p248*).

Down in the tube station at midnight.

traders. The boom years of the 1990s began the area's renaissance, which is still giving birth to new bars, cafés and boutiques.

The main thoroughfare of Ingram Street connects the Merchant City to the centre proper, leading to the great **Gallery of Modern Art** (GOMA, *see p247*) at Royal Exchange Square. The Candleriggs area, a few streets east, is home to **Café Gandolfi** (*see p251*), an essential Glasgow pitstop with a wooden interior designed by the brilliant sculptor and furniture-maker Tim Stead. To the south lies Trongate, marked by the Tolbooth Steeple, at the intersection of five roads dividing the city centre from the East End. The clock steeple belongs to vital local playhouse the **Tron Theatre** (*see p256*). Just off the shabby Argyle Street shopping drag is the **Argyle Arcade**, an airy Victorian glass-roofed passage, lined with jewellers' shops, which links on to Buchanan Street, the increasingly upmarket candy-lane for tasteful shoppers. Further south, Chisholm Street and Parnie Street are composed of an eye-catching fusion of red and yellow sandstone tenements and an unlikely mix of emporia – you can get a tattoo and buy some rare comics, signed footballs and tropical fish within yards of each other.

The adjoining King Street is a mini art-district, featuring the **Transmission Gallery** (No.28, 0141 552 4813/www.transmission gallery.org), **Glasgow Print Studio** (No.22, 0141 552 0704/www.gpsart.co.uk) and **Street Level Gallery** (No.26, 0141 552 2151/www.sl-photoworks.demon.co.uk) and **Art Exposure** on nearby Parnie Street (No.19, 0141 552 7779). With a number of studios above the galleries, this is one of the cutting edges of Glasgow. King Street swerves and culminates in King's

Court, a homecoming for the wandering vintage clothes shopper. Paddy's Market, a rundown palace of junk, lies just over the road. Following the curve of the railway line towards the Clyde, you'll find three of Glasgow's longest-standing bars. The **Stockwell Triangle** – consisting of the Victoria Bar, the Clutha Vaults and the 250-year-old Scotia Bar (for all, *see p252*), all around Stockwell Street – is a hub of folk music and ancient drinkers, giving off a more palpable, atmospheric sense of Glasgow's history than any of the city's museums. Just off the pedestrianised drag of Buchanan Street, with its stylish blue streetlamps, is Mitchell Lane, and the first public building designed by Charles Rennie Mackintosh, constructed in 1895 to house the Glasgow *Herald*. An ultramodern makeover has transformed it into the **Lighthouse**, Scotland's Centre for Architecture, Design & the City (*see p247*).

The **Willow Tea Rooms** (*see p252*), was designed by Mackintosh and commissioned by the formidable Kate Cranston, a pioneer of the genteel tearoom society prevalent in 19th-century Glasgow. The **Centre for Contemporary Arts** (CCA, *see p247*), housed in a building by Glasgow's other visionary architect, Alexander 'Greek' Thomson, is one of the country's most stylish venues for visual and performance art.

A sharp incline to the north leads up **Garnethill**, a mainly residential area that is not only the centre of Glasgow's small Chinese community but also contains Garnethill Synagogue, the oldest Jewish place of worship in the city. The **Glasgow School of Art** (*see p247*), Mackintosh's masterpiece, balances on this perilously steep hill, which students can sometimes be seen ill-advisedly but amusingly rolling down after hours. And the view south takes in the exotic spire of **St Vincent Street Church** designed by Alexander Thomson – even now, these two great architects contend for mastery of Glasgow's skyline.

Centre for Contemporary Arts (CCA)

350 Sauchiehall Street, G2 (0141 352 4900/ www.cca-glasgow.com). Cowcaddens tube. **Open** *Centre* 11am-11pm Tue-Thur; 11am-midnight Fri, Sat; 11am-6pm Sun. *Gallery* 11am-6pm Tue, Wed, Fri-Sun; 11am-8pm Thur. **Admission** free; ticket prices vary. **Credit** MC, V. **Map** p314 C2.
Achingly cool forum for modern art in the city. The exhibitions are always worth a look, though the courtyard bar and restaurant space is a little chilly and bland. But New York disco legend Dave Mancuso has warmed up the atmosphere considerably with his performances in recent years.

Gallery of Modern Art

Queen Street, G1 (0141 229 1996/www.glasgow museums.com). Buchanan Street tube/Queen Street rail. **Open** 10am-5pm Mon-Thur, Sat; 11am-5pm Fri, Sun. **Admission** free. **Map** p315 D3.
Glasgow architect David Hamilton was responsible for the portico addition to the Cunninghame Mansion (1778), now home to a lively, eclectic and controversial modern art collection. The two-tier café offers terrific views of the city's skyline and good-value food.

Glasgow School of Art

167 Renfrew Street, G3 (0141 353 4500/www. gsa.ac.uk). Cowcaddens tube/Charing Cross rail. **Open** *Tours* July, Aug 11am, 2pm Mon-Fri; 10.30am, 11.30am, 1pm Sat, Sun; Sept-June 11am, 2pm Mon-Fri; 10.30am, 11.30am Sat. *Shop* 10am-5pm Mon-Fri; 10am-1pm Sat. **Admission** *Tours* £5; £4 concessions; free under-10s. **Credit** AmEx, MC, V. **Map** p314 C2.
An icon of 20th-century design by Charles Rennie Mackintosh. The best angles on this fantastic building are around the façades of the north and west wings, and the library beyond. The interior is only open to guided tours but it is well worth booking for a trip that includes a visit to the extraordinary library and its wonderful lights and desks.

Lighthouse

11 Mitchell Lane, G1 (0141 221 6362/www. thelighthouse.co.uk). St Enoch or Buchanan Street tube/Central Station rail. **Open** 10.30am-5pm Mon, Wed-Sat; 11am-5pm Tue; noon-5pm Sun. **Admission** £3; £1.50 concessions. **Credit** MC, V. **Map** p315 D3.
Mackintosh's Glasgow *Herald* building has metamorphosed into the Lighthouse, Scotland's Centre for Architecture, Design & the City. With an evolving programme of exhibitions and events, it's a lively addition to Glasgow's cultural scene. It includes the Mackintosh Interpretation Centre, a state-of-the-art facility providing three-dimensional insights into the man's visions of the city.

Old Town & East End

Moving east from the arty exclusivity of the Merchant City, you're travelling back toward Glasgow's historic heart; this was the centre of the city before the 19th-century surge westwards and remains a living source of landmarks and stories for anyone interested in Glasgow's rich social history.
The city was effectively founded at the point where the Molendinar Burn flowed into the Clyde, now the site of the High Court. The **McLennan Arch**, facing the court, marks the entrance to the city's most famous public space, **Glasgow Green**. This stretch of parkland, recently given a facelift, is Europe's oldest public park, and it supports over 800 years of memories and experiences. It doubled as both fairground and hanging place, although these days it's more famous for hosting the annual Bonfire Night fireworks display, Glasgow Fair Festival in July and the Download music festival (formerly Big Day Out), which in June 2004 was due to feature Metallica and Linkin Park. The **People's Palace** and the **Winter Gardens** (for both, *see p248*) are the main permanent attractions of the Green.
Just where the Green where it borders on Greendyke Street is the **Homes for the Future** development, a cornerstone project of Glasgow's year as the UK City of Architecture and Design, replacing some of the wasted urban spaces north of the Green with attractive, imaginative housing designs. Also north is **St Andrew's in the Square** (*see p252*), a former church that now hosts traditional Scottish music events. Further north still are the twin thoroughfares of Gallowgate and London Road, forming the boundary of Glasgow's monumental weekend market, the **Barras** (*see p252* **Bargain hunters**); the legendary **Barrowland Ballroom** is next door (*see p255*). The Ballroom's gigantic trademark neon sign was temporarily taken down during World War II, when it was realised that German bombers were using it as a guiding light. Up the High Street, north of Gallowgate, are **Glasgow Cathedral**, the **Necropolis** and the **St Mungo Museum of Religious Life & Art** (for both *see p248*). They are all that's left of the medieval city, and seem increasingly strange and wonderful in this 21st-century metropolis.

Glasgow Cathedral

Castle Street, G4 (0141 552 6891/www.glasgow cathedral.org.uk). High Street rail. **Open** *Apr-Sept* 9.30am-6pm Mon-Sat; 2-5pm Sun. *Oct-Mar* 9.30am-4pm Mon-Sat; 2-4pm Sun. **Admission** free. **Map** p315 F2.
Glasgow's patron saint, St Mungo, whose tomb can be found in the crypt, founded Glasgow Cathedral

in 543 on the site of a burial ground consecrated by St Ninian. Parts of the current building date from the 12th century, making it one of Scotland's oldest medieval churches.

Necropolis

Glasgow Necropolis Cemetery, 50 Cathedral Square, G4 (0141 552 3145). High Street rail. **Open** 24hrs daily. **Admission** free. **Map** p315 F2.
The first non-denominational 'hygienic' graveyard in Scotland was inspired by the famed Père Lachaise cemetery in Paris. It was intended to provide the industrialists and merchants of the 19th-century city with a suitably grand resting place.

People's Palace/Winter Gardens

Glasgow Green, G4 (0141 554 0223/www.glasgow. gov.uk). Bridgeton rail. **Open** 10am-5pm Mon-Thur, Sat; 11am-5pm Fri, Sun. **Admission** free.
Map p315 F4.
The red sandstone People's Palace, which was built in 1898, originally served as a municipal and cultural centre for the city's working class. It now houses one of Glasgow's most cherished exhibitions, covering all aspects of Glaswegian life, particularly the city's social and industrial history. The adjoining Winter Gardens is one of the most elegant Victorian glasshouses in Scotland.

Provand's Lordship

3 Castle Street, G4 (0141 552 8819/www.glasgow. gov.uk). High Street rail. **Open** 10am-5pm Mon-Thur, Sat; 11am-5pm Fri, Sun. **Admission** free.
Map p315 F2.
Glasgow's last medieval house was built in 1471.

St Mungo Museum of Religious Life & Art

2 Castle Street, G4 (0141 553 2557/www.glasgow museums.com). High Street rail. **Open** 10am-5pm Mon-Thur, Sat; 11am-5pm Fri, Sun. **Admission** free. **Map** p315 F2.
The main reason to visit this museum is to see Dali's awesome *Christ of St John on the Cross.* But it's also a refuge from Glasgow's unpleasant sectarianism – a museum that records and respects the articles of every faith, with its own Zen garden outside.

South Side

The West End may be the city's bohemian quarter, but the South Side is much more cosmopolitan – diverse, fascinating, and under-visited. Most of it is residential, composed of many districts, from affluent **Newton Mearns** to the rather less monied housing estates, such as **Castlemilk**. The **Gorbals**, previously one of the most moribund areas of the city, is fast becoming a respectable address, thanks to a wide ranging regeneration programme. The area also boasts one of the best theatres in Britain. The **Citizens' Theatre** (*see p256*) was founded in 1943 by James Bridie as a theatre for the people, and it is justly world

famous for its angry, aware and exhilarating productions – with ticket prices remaining fittingly egalitarian. The **Tramway** (*see p256*), an impressive open space for ambitious local art and performance, is also close by, and recently opened its own garden of tranquillity.

Some of the best examples of Alexander 'Greek' Thomson's architecture can also be found on the South Side. The **Caledonia Road Church** (1856) on Cathcart Road was inspired by the Acropolis. A fire in 1965 destroyed the painted interior, leaving only the portico and tower intact, but it's still worth seeing. The Thomson-designed terraces of Regent Park, in the district of Strathbungo, have been designated a conservation area since the 1970s. Both Thomson and Mackintosh lived here.

The South Side opens out into Glasgow's largest parks; in fact, the city as a whole boasts more parks per head than anywhere else in Europe. These include **Bellahouston**, where you'll find **House for an Art Lover** (*see p249*), a modern construction based on plans submitted by Mackintosh in 1901. In **Pollok Park** – Glasgow's largest at 146 hectares – you'll find the main South Side attractions: **Pollok House** (*see 249*) and the wonderful phantasmagorical **Burrell Collection** (*see below*). But most visitors to the South Side are heading to **Hampden Park** (*see p249*), home to Scotland's national football team. A Football Museum has been added to the stadium, with permanent displays and temporary exhibitions on Scottish football's finest moments – most of them, alas, long in the past.

Burrell Collection

Pollok Park, 2060 Pollokshaws Road, G43 (0141 287 2550/www.glasgowmuseums.com). Pollokshaws West rail, then 10min walk. **Open** 10am-5pm Mon-Sat; 11am-5pm Sun. **Admission** free.
Sir William Burrell gave his prodigious collection of art and artefacts to the city of Glasgow in 1944. One of the jewels in Glasgow's cultural crown, the collection encompasses treasures from ancient Egypt, Greece and Rome, and ceramics from various Chinese dynasties, as well as European decorative arts, including rare tapestries and stained glass. It also boasts one of the finest collections of Impressionist and post-Impressionist paintings and drawings in the world. Try to come on a sunny day, when the reflected light in the interior glass-roofed courtyard is breathtaking.

Holmwood House

61-63 Netherlee Road, Cathcart, G44 (0141 637 2129/www.nts.org.uk). Cathcart rail. **Open** *Apr-Oct* noon-5pm daily; access may be restricted at peak times. Groups must pre-book. **Admission** £3.50; £2.60 concessions. **No credit cards.**
Thomson's most elaborate villa, with a newly renovated, richly ornamental classical interior.

It doesn't rain every day.

House for an Art Lover

Bellahouston Park, 10 Dumbreck Road, G41 (0141 353 4770/www.houseforanartlover.co.uk). Dumbreck rail. **Open** 10am-1pm Sat, Sun; midweek times vary, phone to check. **Admission** £3.50; £2.50 concessions. **Credit** AmEx, MC, V.

Built according to plans Mackintosh submitted to a German architecture competition in 1901, the house has been recently completed to mixed reactions.

Pollok House

Pollok Park, 2060 Pollokshaws Road, G43 (0141 616 6410/www.nts.org.uk). Pollokshaws West rail, then 10min walk. **Open** 10am-5pm daily. **Admission** *Apr-Oct* £6; £4 concessions. *Nov-Mar* free. **Credit** MC, V.

This magnificent 18th-century mansion displays the Stirling Maxwell collection of Spanish and European paintings, including some beautiful works by Goya, and an extensive selection of William Blake.

Scotland Street School Museum

225 Scotland Street, G5 (0141 287 0500/www. glasgow.gov.uk). Shields Road tube. **Open** 10am-5pm Mon-Thur, Sat; 11am-5pm Fri, Sun. **Admission** free. **Map** p314 B4.

A real Mackintosh treat, this majestic school building is now a newly refurbished museum offering an insight into Glaswegian schooling in the first half of the 20th century.

Scottish Football Museum

National Stadium, Hampden Park, G42 (0141 616 6100/www.scottishfootballmuseum.org.uk). King Park or Mount Florida rail. **Open** 10am-5pm Mon-Sat; 11am-5pm Sun. **Admission** *Museum* £5; £2.50 concessions. *Stadium tours* £2.50; £1.25 concessions. **Credit** MC, V.

The Scottish national side hasn't troubled Brazil, England, or even the Iceland for a while, but names like Dalglish, Law, Shankly and Stein – all well-documented here – still inspire a nostalgic pride.

West End

Beginning at the huge dome and imposing façade of the **Mitchell Library**, the West End has a character all of its own – it's Glasgow all right, but doesn't really seem to fit with the rest of the city. Leafy, hilly, prettier and lazier than the city's other quarters, the West End remains a middle-class enclave, populated mainly by students, rich folks and creative types, and catering for their tastes with a quality range of bars, coffee shops, delis and record stores.

The main artery is the long, straight Great Western Road, built in 1836 for Glasgow's bourgeois, who wanted a route out of the crowded, soot-blackened city centre. Now, the road itself is often a choked snarl of traffic, heading out to Loch Lomond. South are domestic terraced buildings from the same period, which are among the city's most beautiful features. Highlights are **Park Circus** (1857-63) and **Park Terrace** (1855). Further west, flanking Great Western Road, **Great Western Terrace** (1867) is the definitive Glasgow terrace designed by Alexander 'Greek' Thomson. The **Botanic Gardens** is the place to lay on the grass during Glasgow's summer.

But **Byres Road**, just beyond the Garden's gates, is the heart of the West End, the mainline of shopping and students. It leads off into several charming little lanes, including Dowanside and Cresswell, scattered with stores for vintage clothes and unusual gifts. Ashton Lane is home to the recently modernised **Loft/Grosvenor** bar and cinema complex, as well as a host of older cafés and bars, which are generally attractive and flavoursome.

The **University of Glasgow** dominates the whole West End with its dark fairytale neo-

Trips Out of Town

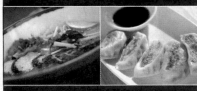
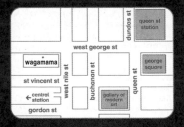
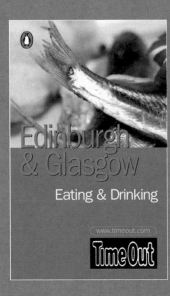

Gothic tower. And the bizarre concrete façade of the Mackintosh House at the **Hunterian Art Gallery & Museum**, next door, helps shape a strange and beautiful skyline. To the east of the University is the 34-hectare **Kelvingrove Park**. First laid out as pleasure grounds in the 1850s, on a hot day it becomes instantly packed with dogs, bongo-players and cheerful displays of public drunkenness (the open stretch of grass is known locally as 'The Green Beach'), but for the rest of the year it's a cold or wet oasis. The striking red Victorian palace that is the Kelvingrove Art Gallery & Museum was built to hold the 1901 International Exhibition and dominates the end of the park, but is closed until 2006 for renovation. On those rare evenings when the sunset hits it, Glasgow takes on an exotic, storybook magic.

Botanic Gardens & Kibble Palace

730 Great Western Road, G12 (0141 334 2422/ www.glasgow.gov.uk). Hillhead tube. **Open** *Palace* Apr-Oct 10am-4.45pm daily; Nov-Mar 10am-4.15pm daily. *Gardens* 7am-dusk daily. **Admission** free. **Map** p314 B1/C1.

The gardens are dominated by the huge dome of Kibble Palace, a marvel of Victorian engineering that has been recently restored.

Hunterian Museum & Art Gallery

University of Glasgow, Hillhead Street, G12 (0141 330 5431/www.hunterian.gla.ac.uk). Hillhead tube. **Open** 9.30am-5pm Mon-Sat. *Mackintosh House* 9.30am-12.30pm, 1.30-5pm Mon-Sat. **Admission** free.

Scotland's largest print collection is housed in the Hunterian Art Gallery. The gallery leads on to the Mackintosh House, and includes a recreation of the architect's home in Southpark Avenue, where he lived from 1906 to 1914. Built in 1807, the Hunterian is Scotland's oldest public museum, and among its archaeological treasures are several dinosaurs – as befits the Scottish Centre for Dinosaur Research.

Mitchell Library

North Street, G3 (0141 287 2999/www.mitchell library.org). Charing Cross rail. **Open** 9am-8pm Mon-Thur; 9am-5pm Fri, Sat. **Map** p314 B2.

Containing over one million books and documents, the high-roofed main reading room is a beautiful place to sit quietly. The library also has a huge collection of photographic prints and lithographs that vividly illustrate Glasgow's past.

Museum of Transport

1 Bunhouse Road, Kelvinhall, G3 (0141 287 2720/ www.glasgowmuseums.com). Kelvinhall tube/Partick rail. **Open** 10am-5pm Mon-Thur, Sat; 11am-5pm Fri, Sun. **Admission** free.

The Clyde Room, where Glasgow's long-gone foundational shipbuilding industry is celebrated and mourned, makes this one of Britain's more involving transport museums.

Top five Cafés

Café Gandolfi

Busy, handsome Merchant City establishment, immersing patrons in a collective good mood (*see p251*).

Tchai Ovna

Calming quasi-Tibetan tea-house sitting quietly above the River Kelvin. Serves over 80 varieties of tea (*see p253*).

University Café

Beautiful art deco institution, grinding good coffee and churning excellent ice-cream (*see p253*).

Where The Monkey Sleeps

Lazy but vibrant young lounge with its own small, dynamic art space (*see p252*).

Willow Tea Rooms

The exquisite interiors, designed by Charles Rennie Mackintosh, are best appreciated slowly over cream tea and scones (*see p252*).

Where to eat & drink

Glasgow has an extraordinary selection of restaurants, pubs and bars. We list a range of main course prices for restaurants.

City centre

Café Gandolfi

64 Albion Street, G1 (0141 552 6813). Argyle Street or High Street rail. **Open** 9am-11.30pm Mon-Sat; noon-11.30pm Sun. **Main courses** £6.50-£16. **Credit** AmEx, MC, V. **Map** p315 E3.

The finest institution in the Merchant City, with a devoted clientele. Sculptor and furniture-maker Tim Stead's rich natural wood interior is a good excuse to hang around longer than you need to over coffee and cake, lunch, or a robust Scottish dinner.

Arta

62 Albion Street, G1 (0141 552 2101). Argyle Street or High Street rail. **Open** *Restaurant* 5-11pm daily. *Bar* 5pm-1am Mon-Thur, Sun; 5pm-3am Fri, Sat. **Main courses** £8. **Credit** MC, V. **Map** p315 E3.

Staggeringly opulent villa complex developed by the G1 Group, who are currently converting many of Glasgow's grandest spaces into studiously trendy eating, drinking and dancing facilities. The vast second floor restaurant is well served by a Spanish-tinged menu rich with pleasant details, down to the warm home-made breads and desserts.

Nice 'n' Sleazy does it every time. *See p258.*

Fratelli Sarti

121 Bath Street, G2 (0141 204 0440). Buchanan Street tube. **Open** 8am-10.30pm Mon-Fri; 10am-10.30pm Sat; noon-10.30pm Sun. **Main courses** £6-£11. **Credit** AmEx, MC, V. **Map** p314 C2/D2.
Family-run and "100% authentic Italian" restaurant/bistro/deli. Often busy, especially at weekends.
Other locations: 133 Wellington Street, G2 (0141 248 2228); Il Gran Caffè, 42 Renfield Street, G2 (0141 572 7000).

Horseshoe

17 Drury Street, off Renfield Street, G2 (0141 229 5711). Buchanan Street tube. **Open** 11am-midnight Mon-Sat; 12.30pm-midnight Sun. **Main courses** £2.95-£3.50. *Lunch menu* (Mon-Sat) 3 courses £3.20. **Credit** MC, V. **Map** p315 D2.
The pub that best expresses Glasgow. According to the *Guinness Book of Records*, it boasts the longest continuous bar in the UK. More impressive is the atmosphere – this is a genuine mixer for every stripe of Glasgow citizen. Famed also for its cheap three-course lunches and its passionate karaoke nights, which are for talented and sincere singers only.

Wee Curry Shop

7 Buccleuch Street, G3 (0141 353 0777). Cowcaddens tube. **Open** noon-2pm, 5.30-10.30pm Mon-Sat. **Main courses** £5.50-£6.95. **Credit** MC, V. **Map** p314 C1.
In a city renowned for its Indian restaurants, this is the best – and smallest – a little living room tucked away behind Sauchiehall Street. Everything on the menu is excellent, and genuinely original, but trust the chefs – who cook in a kitchen space right in front of you – and order off the daily specials board.
Other location: 23 Ashton Lane, G12 (0141 357 5280).

Where The Monkey Sleeps

182 West Regent Street, G2 (0141 226 3406/ www.wherethemonkeysleeps.com). Buchanan Street tube. **Open** 7am-5pm Mon-Fri; 10am-6pm Sat. **Credit** MC, V. **Map** p314 C2.

Youthful coffee lounge combined with an art-house, displaying good taste in relaxing music and a nice line in creative soups and sandwiches.
Other location: 77 Hanson Street, East End (0141 556 6733).

Willow Tea Rooms

217 Sauchiehall Street, G2 (0141 332 0521/www. willowtearooms.co.uk). Cowcaddens tube. **Open** 9am-5pm Mon-Sat; 11am-5pm Sun. **Credit** DC, MC, V.
Drink tea, admire Mackintosh's art. He designed everything you know, including the teaspoons and the waitresses' dresses. Afternoon tea, with sandwiches, scone and cake, is a fairly hefty £8.95.
Other location: 97 Buchanan Street, G1 (0141 204 5242).

Old Town & East End

Café Source

1 St Andrew's Square, off Saltmarket, G1 (0141 548 6020/www.cafesource.co.uk). St Enoch tube/High Street rail. **Open** 11am-11pm Mon-Thur; 11am-midnight Fri, Sat; 12.30-9pm Sun. **Main courses** £4.25-£9.95. **Credit** MC, V. **Map** p315 E4.
Downstairs from the wonderful St Andrew's church hall, this cosy basement bar has a folksy feel, reflected in the hearty Scottish menu. But an injection of contemporary style keeps the place from slipping into a pit of tartan tweeness.

Scotia

112 Stockwell Street, G1 (0141 552 8681). St Enoch tube/Argyle Street rail. **Open** 11am-midnight Mon-Sat; 12.30pm-midnight Sun. **Main courses** £2.25-£3.95. **No credit cards**. **Map** p315 D3/E3.
By all accounts the oldest pub in Glasgow. It is the busiest and most famous of the three bars that make up the so-called Stockwell Triangle – also including the Victoria Bar (159 Bridgegate; 0141 552 6040) and the Clutha Vaults (167 Stockwell Street; 0141 552 7520). Skilled live musicians play at all three, and the regulars will tell you half-true stories for free.

South Side

Heraghty's

708 Pollokshaws Road, G41 (0141 423 0380).
Pollokshields East rail. **Open** 11am-11pm Mon-
Thur; 11am-midnight Fri, Sat; 12.30-11pm Sun.
No credit cards.
Authentic Irish bar, figuratively and literally far
removed from the theme pubs of the city centre. An
ideal place to watch a Celtic match.

1901

1534 Pollokshaws Road, G43 (0141 632 0161).
Shawlands rail. **Open** *Bistro* noon-2.30pm, 5-9.30pm
Mon-Fri; noon-9.30pm Sat; 12.30-9.30pm Sun. *Bar*
11.30am-11pm Mon-Fri; 11.30am-midnight Sat; 12.30-
11pm Sun. **Main courses** £10-£15. **Credit** MC, V.
This bar/bistro has established a loyal regular
crowd, with its consistently relaxed vibe and nice-
ly-done Mediterranean nosh. Live jazz on Sundays.

West End

Ben Nevis Bar

1147 Argyle Street, G3 (0141 576 5204). Kelvinhall
tube. **Open** 11am-11pm Mon-Thur; 11am-midnight
Fri, Sat; 12.30-11pm Sun; extended hours Jan, Dec.
Credit MC, V. **Map** p314 A1/B2/B3.
Legendary little room, attracting folk musicians of
extraordinary ability and affability to play just for
the hell of it. Wednesday nights are essential.

Firebird

1321 Argyle Street, G3 (0141 334 0594). Kelvinhall
tube. **Open** *Restaurant* 11.30am-10pm Mon-Sat;
12.30-10pm Sun. *Bar* 11.30am-midnight Mon-Thur;
11.30am-1am Fri, Sat; 12.30pm-midnight Sun.
Main courses £8.50-17.50. **Credit** MC, V.
Map p314 A1/B2/B3.
Airy, subtly fashionable bar and restaurant, shifting
between afternoon reverie and clubby excitability.
The menu is exotic but nourishing – even the pizzas
– and the staff are masters of customer rapport.

Stravaigin

28-30 Gibson Street, G12 (0141 334 2665/www.
stravaigin.com). Kelvinbridge tube. **Open** *Café-bar*
11am-midnight daily. *Restaurant* 5-11pm Tue-Thur;
noon-11pm Fri-Sun. **Main courses** *Café-bar* £5.25-
£16.95. *Restaurant* £13.45-£21.50. **Credit** AmEx,
DC, MC, V.
Downstairs in the restaurant or up in the bar and
mezzanine, the food is astonishing whether the dishes are local or exotic: did you know that catfish have
digits? Catfish fingers will prove they have. And
don't forget the haggis. The beers are good too, and
the atmosphere bright and convivial.
Other location: 28 Ruthven Lane, G12 (0141 334
7165).

Tchai Ovna

42 Otago Lane, G12 (0141 357 4524/www.tchai
ovna.com). Kelvinbridge tube. **Open** 11am-11pm
daily. **No credit cards.**
Brilliant little teahouse with a staggering menu of
international teas, providing a snug forum for storytelling sessions and live jazz nights.

Ubiquitous Chip

12 Ashton Lane, G12 (0141 334 5007/
www.ubiquitouschip.co.uk). Hillhead tube. **Open**
Restaurant noon-2.30pm, 5.30-11pm Mon-Sat; 12.30-
3pm, 6.30-11pm Sun. *Brasserie* noon-11pm Mon-Sat;
12.30-11pm Sun. **Main courses** £8-£14. *Dinner*
menu 3 courses £34.95. **Credit** AmEx, DC, MC, V.
A converted mews stable, with wall murals by the
great local writer and artist Alasdair Gray (*see p260*
GlasWegian Alasdair Gray), the Ubiquitous
Chip is a mighty Glasgow institution. The upstairs
bar, and corner "wee bar", attract an older crowd,
prone to esoteric, involving and illuminating con-
versations. The menu revolves around seasonal
Scottish produce and there's an excellent wine and
whisky selection too.

University Café

87 Byres Road, G11 (0141 339 5217). Hillhead or
Kelvinhall tube. **Open** 9am-10pm Mon, Wed, Thur;
9am-10.30pm Fri, Sat; 10am-10pm Sun. **Main**
courses £2-£4. **No credit cards.**
Famous for both its fabulous 1950s-style decor and
reliably hearty food. Ice-cream is a speciality.

Arts & entertainment

Glaswegians live for the hours after work, and
have strong, broad and clear ideas of a good
time and how to get it, taking a feverishly
passionate interest in sports, culture and
entertainment of every kind.

TICKETS AND INFORMATION

For listings information, peruse the fortnightly
List or the *Glasgow Evening Times*. Glasgow
City Council's website (www.glasgow.gov.uk)
has a relatively useful events page divided into
sections for theatre, music, sport, visual arts,
family and festivals.

The Glasgow music Mafia

The old heavy-industry cities of northern Britain tend to carry an endemic strain of music-wildness, and the people of Glasgow have still got it bad. Bad, meaning good. In the 1930s and '40s, Glasgow boasted more dancehalls per head than any other city in the world. Throughout the '50s and '60s, crates of American blues, soul and rock records were offloaded from ships in the port, firing up hundreds of local R&B and beat combos. And a distinctive, independent attitude to guitar music emerged in the aftermath of the punk era – a lingering compulsion to experiment with melody, intelligence and thrilling noise that has sustained a legacy of influential local bands, from Orange Juice, the Vaselines, the Pastels and the Jesus and Mary Chain, through to Primal Scream and Teenage Fanclub, recent upstarts Mogwai, the Delgados, Belle and Sebastian (pictured), Snow Patrol, and hotshots Franz Ferdinand.

The city remains infected with a deep love of loud music, spread across a hungry mainstream and a tirelessly keen and sharp underground scene, fed by a constant supply of musicians, DJs and students who come to be part of Glasgow's ongoing sonic history. **Nice 'n' Sleazy** (*see p258*) remains a key breeding ground, a dimly red-lit bar with a superlative jukebox where elder indie gods

play records and buy pints for future rock heroes. Many of the patrons might trek up the steep hill to **Glasgow School of Art** (*see p247*), where the kids know their music, and act like it. Newer venues Stereo and its East End sister Mono are now the primary hangouts for bands you haven't heard of yet. **King Tut's Wah Wah Hut** (*see p255*) attracts the early disciples of acts on the verge of fame, and the **Barrowland Ballroom** (*see p255*), tatty and tacky as it is, remains hallowed ground, consecrated by a million life-changing gigs. Almost any band is worth watching in that space, if only for the inclusive delirium of the crowd. That warmth is the essence of Glasgow audiences. It tempers the sneering coolness of the inevitable purists and poseurs, and fosters a rare, open-eared and open-hearted sense of community. A disproportionately large number of the city's residents now seem to have rich and varied record collections and an eager readiness to play them in public, which has given rise to a recent rash of semi-legal warehouse parties along the Clyde and under the railway lines. You may or may not hear whispers about them in the **Variety Bar** or at the **Soundhaus** (for both *see p258*). Listen out – the Glasgow music mafia is keen to induct new members.

Trips Out of Town

Football

The Old Firm rivalry between Celtic and Rangers is still furious, and the religious bigotry of their fans still a boorish and unpleasant affectation: Celtic's are almost uniformly Catholic, Rangers' are Protestant. Celtic play at Celtic Park, Rangers at Ibrox. The national team plays at the recently refurbished Hampden Stadium, which has much less character than those two volatile grounds.

Celtic Park

95 Kerrydale Street, G40 (0141 551 8653/www. celticfc.net). Bus 12, 62, 64/Bellgrove rail. **Open** *Museum & tours* 11am, noon, 2.30pm daily (depending on matches); phone for details. *Shop* 9am-5pm Mon-Wed, Fri, Sun; 9am-7pm Thur; 9am-1pm Sat. **Tickets** *Match* £21-£24; £14-£17 concessions. *Stadium tours* £8.50; £5.50 concessions. **Credit** AmEx, MC, V.

The state-of-the-art stadium also features a museum and the Celtic Superstore.

Hampden Park

Hampden Park, G42 (information 0141 620 4000/ www.scottishfa.co.uk). King Park or Mount Florida rail. **Open** for matches or by guided tour only; phone for details. **Tickets** *Stadium tours* £5; £3.50 concessions. **Credit** MC, V.

Match tickets are not sold at the stadium. For details of guided tours around the ground, contact the Scottish Football Museum (*see p249*).

Ibrox

Edmiston Drive, G51 (ticket hotline 0870 600 1993/ www.rangers.co.uk). Ibrox tube. **Open** *Shop* 10am-5.30pm Mon-Fri; 9am-6pm Sat; 11am-5pm Sun. *Tickets* 10am-7pm Mon-Fri; 10am-4pm Sat. *Stadium tours* Mon, Fri, Sun; phone for details. **Tickets** *Match* £18-£24; £10-£15 concessions. **Credit** MC, V.

As well as the Ibrox Superstore, there are tours of the stadium on Mondays, Fridays and Sundays.

Music: classical

Royal Concert Hall

2 Sauchiehall Street, City centre, G2 (0141 353 8000/www.grch.com). Buchanan Street tube/Queen Street rail. **Open** *Box office* Non-concert days 10am-6pm Mon-Sat; concert days 10am-9pm Mon-Sat; 1-6pm Sun. *Phoneline* 9am-9pm Mon-Fri; 10am-9pm Sat; 10am-6pm Sun. **Tickets** £7.50-£25. **Credit** MC, V. **Map** p315 D2.

Home to the Royal Scottish National Orchestra and, for the last three weeks of January, to the prestigious Celtic Connections festival.

Royal Scottish Academy of Music & Drama

100 Renfrew Street, City centre, G2 (0141 332 4101/box office 0141 332 5057/www.rsamd.ac.uk). Cowcaddens tube. **Open** *Box office* 9am-8.30pm Mon-Fri; 9am-4.30pm Sat (until 8.30pm on performance evenings); noon-4.30pm Sun. **Tickets** prices vary; please phone for details. **Credit** MC, V. **Map** p315 D2.

Recitals, masterclasses and guest soloists feature regularly at the concert hall of the Royal Scottish Academy of Music and Drama.

Music: rock, pop, roots & country

Barrowland

244 Gallowgate, East End, G4 (0141 552 4601/ www.glasgow-barrowland.com). Argyle Street rail/ High Street rail. **Open** *Box office* 7pm-performance starts (performance days only). **Tickets** £11-£25. **No credit cards. Map** p315 F3.

One of the greatest live music venues in the world – ask any new or established rock band where they most love to play, and they'll probably scream 'Barrowland'. Apart from the garish, gigantic neon sign, it's not much to look at, but the crowd regard it as their historical duty to go electrifyingly wild.

Grand Ole Opry

2-4 Govan Road, South Side, G51 (0141 429 5396). Shields Road tube. **Open** 7pm-1am Fri, Sat. **Admission** £4. **No credit cards. Map** p314 A3.

A South Side institution for Glasgow's legions of country-music fans. They gather every weekend in this tacky hall, decorated in confederate memorabilia, to imbibe cheap liquor, line-dance, witness the fake shoot-out and – yee-ha! – play bingo.

King Tut's Wah Wah Hut

272A St Vincent Street, City centre, G2 (0141 221 5279/www.kingtuts.co.uk). Central Station rail. **Open** noon-midnight Mon-Sat; 6pm-midnight Sun. **Tickets** £5-£14. **No credit cards. Map** p314 B2/C2.

The Hut punches way above its weight in terms of riotous performances by new and cult indie acts.

Glasgow Carling Academy

121 Eglinton Street, G5 (0141 418 3000/ www.glasgow-academy.co.uk). West Streettube. **Open** times vary; please phone for details. **Admission** £10-£27.50. **Credit** AmEx, MC, V. **Map** p314 C4.

First an art deco cinema, then a bingo hall, now it's Glasgow's newest mid-sized live music venue, a pleasantly grubby space reminiscent of London's Brixton Academy. Has hosted triumphant performances by Public Enemy and the Flaming Lips.

Scottish Exhibition & Conference Centre and Clyde Auditorium

Exhibition Way, G3 (0141 248 3000/box office 08700 404000/www.secctickets.com). Exhibition Centre rail. **Open** *Box office* 10am-6pm Mon-Fri; 10am-5pm Sat. *Phoneline* 9am-9pm daily. **Tickets** prices vary. **Credit** MC, V. **Map** p314 A3.

This soulless aircraft hangar of an arena is the main venue for the biggest touring bands who come to Scotland, while the 3,000-seater Clyde Auditorium, or 'Armadillo', provides the sit-down atmosphere sought by more mature performers (and audiences).

Bargain hunters

The character of warm, dry European cities is often best expressed in their marketplaces. Cold, wet Glasgow has its own equivalent in the Barrowland, better known as 'The Barras', a riotous run of stalls spilling over with clothes, antiques, old records, modern electronics, local curios, useless artefacts and deep-fried foodstuffs. All of it is going cheap and sold with idiosyncratic cheer.

Founded in the 1920s near the historical heart of Glasgow, the market has survived as an institution, a tradition and a good story. It is the legacy of one woman's businesslike response to the vagaries of Scottish weather. Maggie McIver, 'The Queen of the Barras', was an industrious street trader who rented out horses, carts and stall-spaces to fellow hawkers from a yard in the Calton area of the East End. Noticing that certain goods were prematurely ruined by Glasgow's almost perpetual rainfall, she had the idea of a permanent, covered site.

Her chosen location was problematic – the estate of the late Marion Gilchrist, which had been subject to legal wrangling since Gilchrist's mysterious murder 20 years before (one Oscar Slater, a local gambler, was wrongfully convicted of the crime; Sir Arthur Conan Doyle, creator of Sherlock Holmes, investigated personally). But McIver made a roaring success of it, expanding the lot to house over 300 vendors and developing the **Barrowland Ballroom** (*see p255*) next door. She was a multi-millionaire by the time she died, and the Barras was a daily diorama of Glasgow life, from the nearby slums and beyond. Older residents still remember it as a noisy congregation of traders, drunks, tarts, pimps, musicians, fakirs and snake-oil salesmen, where the earliest rock 'n' roll records were heard long before BBC radio ever played them.

The market is still lively these days – employing 2,000 people and visited by 30,000 every weekend, the whole place ringing with barely comprehensible local lingo. But, like the rest of the city, it's a little less rambunctious than it used to be. Lawlessness has been confined to the copyright theft common in the digital age, and recent police raids on unlicensed traders have seized thousands of pounds worth of pirated music and films. Even so, a browse around the Barras remains a definitive Glasgow experience, mixing every kind of citizen together in search of a bargain.

The Barras
244 Gallowgate, East End, G4. Argyle Street rail/High Street rail. **Open** 10am-4pm Sat, Sun. **No credit cards. Map** p315 F3.

Theatre

Citizens' Theatre
119 Gorbals Street, South Side, G5 (administration 0141 429 5561/box office 0141 429 0022/ www.citz.co.uk). Bridge Streettube. **Open** *Box office* 10am-6pm Mon-Sat (until 9pm on performance days). **Tickets** £5-£16; £2-£12 concessions. **Credit** MC, V. **Map** p315 D4.

Risk-taking productions of new theatre are the mandate of the 'Citz'. The main theatre concentrates on British and foreign work, while the smaller Circle and Stalls studios cram the audience right up next to the actors for sometimes brilliant, sometimes awful, but always interesting, new or obscure plays.

King's Theatre
297 Bath Street, City centre, G2 (0141 240 1111/ www.theambassadors.com/kings). Charing Cross rail. **Open** *Box office* 10am-8pm Mon-Sat. *Phoneline* 10am-8pm Mon-Sat. **Tickets** prices vary; phone for details. **Credit** AmEx, MC, V. **Map** p314 C2/D2.
Glasgow's home to musicals, where amateur shows alternate with large-scale touring productions.

Theatre Royal
282 Hope Street, City centre, G2 (0141 332 9000/ www.theatreroyalglasgow.com). Cowcaddens tube. **Open** *Box office* 10am-6pm Mon-Sat (until 8pm on performance days). **Tickets** prices vary. **Credit** AmEx, MC, V. **Map** p315 D2.
Home to Scottish Opera and Scottish Ballet, and destination for larger touring productions by the likes of the Royal Shakespeare Company.

Tramway
25 Albert Drive, Pollokshields, G41 (0141 422 2023/ www.tramway.org). Pollokshields East rail. **Open** *Box office* 10am-8pm Tue-Sat; noon-6pm Sun. *Phoneline* 10am-8pm Mon-Sat; noon-6pm Sun. **Tickets** prices vary. **Credit** MC, V.
Cutting-edge art, theatre and performance, plus a new year-round garden of tranquillity. Brilliant local companies such as Magnetic North make continually exciting and enriching use of this space.

Tron Theatre
63 Trongate, City centre, G1 (0141 552 4267/ www.tron.co.uk). St Enoch tube. **Open** *Box office* 10am-6pm Mon-Sat (until 30mins before curtain on

performance days); open 1hr before curtain on performance Sundays. **Tickets** prices vary; please phone for details. **Credit** MC, V. **Map** p315 E3.
This vital theatre puts on an esoteric variety of smaller touring productions, along with its own shows, which are usually of a high standard. The restaurant and bar here are also highly recommended, murmuring with the chat of local dramatists.

Nightlife

Venue to venue, funk to funky, Glasgow is one of the most spirited cities in the world after dark. The vibrations can be felt as far away as Edinburgh – residents of the capital tend to be both envious and embarrassed about their inferiority in this regard.

Clubs

Arches

30 Midland Street, City centre, G1 (administration 09010 220 300/box office 0141 565 1023/www. thearches.co.uk). St Enoch tube/Central Station rail.
Open times vary; please see website for details. *Box office* (253 Argyle Street) 9am-8pm Mon-Sat; noon-6pm Sun. **Admission** prices vary. **Credit** MC, V.
Housed in renovated railway supports beneath Central Station, the Arches is monumental, and rightly famous for hosting techno nights such as Colours and the ever-astonishing Pressure. Dare you enter the Death Disco? The queue to get in suggests that a great many are prepared to do so.

Glasgow School of Art

168 Renfrew Street, City centre, G3 (0141 353 4531/www.artschool.co.uk). Cowcaddens tube/ Charing Cross rail. **Open** *Club nights* 11pm-3am Thur, Fri; 10pm-3am Sat. **Admission** Thur £3, £2 concessions; Fri £8, £6 concessions; Sat £7, £6 concessions. **No credit cards**. **Map** p314 C2.
Infinitely cooler and a little more smug than any other student union you've ever been in, and with a music remit that extends from Northern Soul, through hip hop to thundering techno, often in different rooms on the same night. If you're not a student, the doormen will pair you up with one for signing-in purposes.

Step on the pedal at **King Tut's Wah Wah Hut**. *See p255.*

Polo Lounge

84 Wilson Street, City centre, G1 (0141 553 1221/
www.pololounge.co.uk). Buchanan Street tube/Queen
Street rail. **Open** 5pm-1am Mon-Thur; 5pm-3am Fri-
Sun. **Admission** free Mon-Thur; £5 after 11pm Fri-
Sun. **Credit** MC, V. **Map** p315 E3.
The polestar of the local gay and lesbian scene, with
a palatial interior. The weekend club nights are
tremendous; carnal, yes, but always tasteful.

Soundhaus

47 Hydepark Street, Anderston, G3 (0141 221
4659/www.soundhaus.co.uk). **Open** 8.30pm-1am
Thur; 11pm-4am Fri, Sat. **Admission** £4.50 Thur;
£6-£10 Fri, Sat. **No credit cards. Map** p314 B3.
Hidden in a warehouse, in an industrial estate,
beside the motorway, this place looks, feels and,
vitally, sounds underground. The music is a curious
selection of house, funk and disco that is, at worst,
tolerably cheesy and at best obscure and fantastic.
One hitch – a member must sign you in.

Pre-club bars

Bar 10

10 Mitchell Lane, City centre, G1 (0141 572 1448).
St Enoch tube. **Open** 10am-midnight Mon-Sat; noon-
midnight Sun. **Credit** MC, V. **Map** p315 D3.
The grandaddy of the Glasgow style bars, Bar 10
remains a beautiful place to drink, designed in the
'80s by Ben Kelly, who also created the Hacienda.

Variety Bar

401 Sauchiehall Street, City centre, G2 (0141 332
4449). Cowcaddens tube. **Open** 11am-midnight Mon-
Sat; 11.30am-midnight Sun. **No credit cards.**
Map p314 C2.
Dark, a bit grotty and massively charming. The elegantly wasted staff will play dub music at rib-quak-
ing volume on a hungover Sunday afternoon if they
feel like it, and that somehow goes toward creating
a tremendous sense of well being.

Nice 'n' Sleazy

421 Sauchiehall Street, City centre, G2 (0141 333
0900/www.nicensleazy.com). Cowcaddens tube.
Open 11.30am-11.45pm Mon-Sat; 12.30-11.45pm
Sun. **No credit cards. Map** p314 C2.
The spiritual home of Glasgow rock action, still fre-
quented by members of the Pastels, Arab Strap and
Mogwai. It's as dark and loud as it should be –
sleazy but nice.

Where to stay

City centre

ArtHouse Hotel

129 Bath Street, G2 (0141 221 6789/fax 0141 221
6777/www.arthousehotel.com). Buchanan Street
tube/Central Station rail. **Rates** £115-£155 double.
Credit AmEx, DC, MC, V. **Map** p314 C2.
Hip city-centre address – bling-bling enough for
Eminem and his crew, who stayed recently.

Malmaison

278 West George Street, G2 (0141 572 1000/fax
0141 572 1002/www.malmaison.com). Buchanan
Street tube. **Rates** £100-£165 double. **Credit** AmEx,
DC, MC, V. **Map** p314 C2/D2.
Stylishly converted Greek Orthodox church, this is
a clean, gleaming model of a modern city hotel –
each room individually designed, some with mezza-
nines and French windows, all slinkily decked out
with good art, dataports and CD players.

Rab Ha's

83 Hutcheson Street, G1 (0141 572 0400/fax 0141
572 0402/www.rabhas.com). Buchanan Street tube.
Rates £75 double. **Credit** AmEx, MC, V. **Map**
p315 E3.
Thrillingly lively city inn named after Robert Hall,
the legendary Glasgow glutton who was insatiably
hungry from birth and the invariable winner of eating contests with other local gourmands. The bar is

Trips Out of Town

always packed and chatty – with excellent bar meals served by pleasingly cheeky staff – the restaurant downstairs is a dimly lit delight, and the bedrooms upstairs are affordable, clean and subtly stylish.

Old Town & East End

Cathedral House Hotel
28-32 Cathedral Square, G4 (0141 552 3519/fax 0141 552 2444). High Street rail. **Rates** £80 double. **Credit** MC, V. **Map** p315 F2.
This chic and minimalist hotel began its life in 1877 as a halfway house for a local prison, before being transformed into the diocesan headquarters of the Catholic Church. The split-level café bar downstairs is now a popular lunching spot for professionals.

South Side

Sherbrooke Castle Hotel
11 Sherbrooke Avenue, Pollokshields, G41 (0141 427 4227/fax 0141 427 5685/www.sherbrooke.co.uk). Bus 59/Dumbreck rail. **Rates** £75-£110 double. **Credit** AmEx, MC, V.
One of the most impressive-looking hotels in the city – from its hilltop position it looks almost like a Caledonian Addams Family mansion.

Dream your dreams away underneath the **Arches**. *See p257.*

West End

One Devonshire Gardens
1 Devonshire Gardens, G12 (0141 339 2001/fax 0141 337 1663/www.onedevonshiregardens.com). Hillhead tube. **Rates** £145-£485 double. **Credit** AmEx, DC, MC, V.
It appears that not even Glasgow's *bon vivants* are sufficiently numerous to support Gordon Ramsay. His restaurant here, Amaryllis, had to close recently due to a simple lack of business. Unfortunately, cameras were not on hand to record the famously bad tempered super-chef's reaction to this snub by his native city. But even stripped of its exotic bloom this remains a beautifully quiet and comfortable place to stay at the leafier end of Great Western Road. George Clooney sent hearts fluttering when he took up residence while on a recent film shoot.

Hostels, flats & seasonal lets

Glasgow Youth Hostel (SYHA)
7-8 Park Terrace, West End, G3 (administration 0141 332 3004/fax 0141 332 5007/bookings 0870 155 3255/www.syha.org.uk). Bus 11, 44, 59; then 5min walk. **Rates** (per person per night) £12-£14; £10-£11.50 concessions. **Credit** MC, V.
A Georgian townhouse that was formerly a hotel, which accounts for the en-suite-as-standard facilities. It's now a popular SYHA hostel with five to eight beds in most rooms. You have to be a YHA member to stay, but that can be arranged on the spot. But note that new members pay an extra £1, and rates increase by £1 during July and August.

University of Glasgow
3 The Square, University Avenue, West End, G12 (0141 330 3123/fax 0141 334 5465/www.cvso. co.uk/accommodation). Hillhead tube, then 5min walk. **Open** *Office* 9am-5pm Mon-Fri. **Rates** *Self-catering* from £14.65. *B&B* from £22.50. **Credit** MC, V.
The University has a wide range of affordable student accommodation to let, generally available during the holidays.

University of Strathclyde
50 Richmond Street, G1 (0141 553 4148/fax 0141 553 4149/www.rescat.strath.ac.uk). Queen Street rail. **Open** *Office* 9am-5pm Mon-Fri. **Rates** *Self catering* prices vary; please phone for details. *B&B* from £22. **Credit** MC, V. **Map** p315 E2.
Most accommodation is available to rent during student holidays.

West End Apartments
401 North Woodside Road, West End, G20 (0141 342 4060/fax 0141 334 8159/www.glasgow hotelsandapartments.co.uk). Kelvinbridge tube. **Open** *Office* 9am-10.30pm daily. **Rates** £315-£588 per wk; daily rates on request. **No credit cards.**
Four fine apartments in an elegant sandstone building at Kelvinbridge, just off the Great Western Road.

Trips Out of Town

GlasWegian Alasdair Gray

Fiery wordsmith, fantastical painter, visionary socialist republican – author and artist Alasdair Gray continues to represent his home city of Glasgow more powerfully and imaginatively than any member of the new Scottish Parliament. Born in East Glasgow in 1934, Gray's name was made with the publication of his first novel *Lanark,* in 1981. A magnum opus almost 30 years in the writing, it intertwines the stories of a struggling artist who transmits his frustrations into an epic church mural, and the unhappy saviour of some dank otherworldly dystopia.

Anthony Burgess hailed Gray as 'the greatest Scottish novelist since Sir Walter Scott'. But he was already a familiar and well-liked figure in Glasgow; as a painter of local portraits, theatrical scenes and murals for various public buildings, and as a truly great conversationalist. So great, in fact, that one theatre director offered him a salary just to sit in the bar every night, drinking whisky and entertaining the customers. Gray impolitely declined, having always been guided only by his own all-consuming muse and his

artistic/political/philosophical principle of 'equality of opportunity for everybody'. He has, however, accepted regular free meals as payment for the mural he once painted along the staircase of the Ubiquitous Chip bar and restaurant (*see p253*), near his home in the city's West End.

Many of Gray's early public murals have been lost to Glasgow's often over-zealous urban renewal schemes, but he has committed himself to restoring or completing certain works he began in the 1960s and '70s. Surviving pieces can be viewed at the aforementioned Chip, and outside the city at Palacerigg Country Park in Cumbernauld (01236 720047), awash with magnificent images of utopian gardens, cosmic constellations and dark industrial futures.

This hard-working polymath has recently suffered ill health, and resigned his post as creative writing co-ordinator at Glasgow University. But he remains hopeful that he will finish his newest, grandest mural in the former Kelvinside Parish Church, thus returning in art to the theme of *Lanark*.

Resources

Communications

Post offices

There are post offices throughout the city, the majority open for usual shop hours. To get information about the nearest one, call 08457 223344 (8.15am-6pm Mon-Fri; 8.30am-7pm Sat). There's a late-opening post office at 1606 Great Western Road, G13; 0141 954 8661; open 8am-10pm Mon-Sat; 9am-8pm Sun.

Telephones

The area code for Glasgow and its environs is 0141.

Health

Glasgow Dental NHS Trust

378 Sauchiehall Street, City centre, G2 (0141 211 9600). Cowcaddens tube. **Open** *Emergency clinic* 9-11am, 1.30-2.30pm Mon-Fri. **Map** p314 C2.

Glasgow Royal Infirmary NHS Trust

84 Castle Street, G4 (0141 211 4000). High Street rail then Bus 2, 37. **Open** *Accident & emergency* 24hrs daily. **Map** p315 F2.

Western Infirmary NHS Trust

Dumbarton Road, G11 (0141 211 2000). Kelvinhall tube. **Open** *Accident & emergency* 24hrs daily.

Getting there

From the airports

Glasgow Airport (0870 040 0008) is 8 miles (14km) south-west of the city, at Junction 28 of the M8. Buses leave the airport for the city every 15mins during the day, and about every 30mins after 6pm and on Sun. The 25min journey costs £3. A taxi will take about 20mins and cost about £16. Cheap flights operated by Ryanair arrive at Glasgow Prestwick, 32 miles southwest of the city. There's a regular train service to the airport and, handily, upon presentation of the relevant plane tickets, all passengers receive 50% off the ticket price to and from anywhere in Scotland.

By car

Despite its all-ensnaring motorway system, Glasgow is actually easy to access by car. The M8 from Edinburgh delivers you into the heart of the city. Take Exit 15 for the East End and Old Town, 16 for Garnethill, 18 for the West End, 19 for the City centre and 20 for the South Side.

By bus or coach

Long-distance buses arrive at and depart from Buchanan Street Bus Station (0141 333 3780) at Killermont Street. Buses to and from Edinburgh every half hour and from London every hour.

By train

Glasgow has two mainline train stations. Queen Street Station (West George Street) serves Edinburgh (trains every 15mins) and the north of Scotland.

Central Station (Gordon Street) serves the West Coast and south to England. The stations are centrally located and are within walking distance of each other. For all rail enquiries call the national number (08457 484950).

Getting around

Central Glasgow is easy to negotiate on foot, but you'll need to use public transport or hire a car if you're going further afield. Nearly all the listings in this chapter refer only to the underground or train network for reasons of space. However, the frequent bus service that runs throughout the city is well signposted at the regular bus stops. Glasgow is also served by a fleet of capacious black taxis. They're cheap, but elusive in the early hours. As for trains, besides the inter-city services, there is a good network of low-level trains serving Glasgow's suburbs, which is run by Scotrail. The slightly ramshackle underground system, affectionately known as the Clockwork Orange, is a single, circular line that loops between the centre and the West End. To enjoy another view of Glasgow, or to travel to Braehead shopping centre or the **Scottish Maritime Museum** (*see p244*), hop on the waterbus at Central station bridge.

Clyde Waterbus

07711 250969/www.clydewaterbusservices.co.uk. **Ferry services** 10am-6.15pm Mon-Fri; 10.30am-5.15pm Sat; 11am-5.45pm Sun. **Tickets** (single) £3; £2 concessions. **No credit cards.**

Europcar/BCR

Terminal Building, Glasgow Airport, Inchinnan Road, Paisley (0141 887 0414/www.europcar.co.uk). **Open** 7.30am-10pm daily. **Credit** AmEx, DC, MC, V. Rentals (subject to change) start from £59 per day or £179 per week.

Traveline Scotland

0870 608 2608/www.travelinescotland.com. **Open** 8am-8pm daily.

Tourist information

Greater Glasgow & Clyde Valley Tourist Information Centre

11 George Square, City centre, G2 (0141 204 4400/fax 0141 221 3524/www.seeglasgow.com). *Buchanan Street tube.* **Open** *Oct-Mar* 9am-6pm Mon-Sat. *Apr, May* 9am-6pm Mon-Sat; 10am-6pm Sun. *June, Sept* 9am-7pm Mon-Sat; 10am-6pm Sun. *July, Aug* 9am-8pm Mon-Sat; 10am-6pm Sun. **Credit** MC, V. **Map** p315 D/E3.

The Tourist Information Centre will take credit card bookings for accommodation throughout the city (£2, plus 10% deposit). It also answers general enquiries about sightseeing and local events, and supplies details of special rates in its brochure.

Around Edinburgh

Glens of glory, abandoned abbeys and haar-haunted hills: this is Scotland.

Sandy beaches, clear skies, azure sea. And it hardly ever rains. **East Lothian**.

East Lothian

North of the A1

Just off the A1, and almost seamlessly attached to Edinburgh, is **Musselburgh**, known since the early 14th century as the 'honest toun', a sobriquet gained when townsfolk refused to claim the reward for recovering the body of the Earl of Moray. Don't miss **Inveresk Lodge**, a National Trust property located behind the town; the lodge is private but the gardens are sublime, sloping down to the River Esk's peaceful riverside walks. The National Trust also owns **Newhailes** (off Newhailes Road, the A6095), a 250-year-old house with rococo interiors and an 18th-century garden.

After the Musselburgh Race Course, the coast road turns off along the B1348. Beyond the village of Longniddry, the full picturesque roll of the East Lothian coast takes off. The **Aberlady Wildlife Sanctuary** is reached by crossing the footbridge from the car park just east of the village of Aberlady. Its sandy

mudflats and dunes are a good spot to see wading birds. The clean beach at Gullane is a summer time favourite with families, while golf fanatics will recognise the Muirfield course, where the Scottish Open is sometimes played.

Five miles on, at the heart of the pretty village of Dirleton, is **Dirleton Castle**. Its grounds still contain an old bowling green as well as an early 20th-century Arts and Crafts garden. Further east again is the **National Museum of Flight** at East Fortune Airfield, a popular destination for family outings. Exhibits range from an 1896 glider to Concorde (from summer 2004).

North Berwick is a quaintly traditional seaside town only 40 minutes away from Edinburgh by train. Two clean, sandy beaches with splendid rock pools flank the old harbour area, where you'll find the award-winning **Seabird Centre**; control your own live video camera to see nesting birds a mile away. In the summer boats leave North Berwick harbour (01620 892838, book in advance) for trips to the gannet-smothered **Bass Rock**, a vast offshore lump of volcanic basalt that has been a prison, fortress and monastic retreat. The coast between North Berwick and the attractive seaside nature reserve of **Tyninghamme Links** is dominated by **Tantallon Castle**, a formidable, mainly 14th-century, cliff-edge fortification.

Dirleton Castle & Gardens

Dirleton (01620 850330/www.historic-scotland. gov.uk). **Open** *Apr-Sept* 9.30am-6.30pm daily. *Oct-Mar* 9.30am-4.30pm Mon-Sat; 2-4.30pm Sun. **Admission** £3; £1-£2.30 concessions. **Credit** AmEx, MC, V.

Inveresk Lodge

24 Inveresk Village, Musselburgh, East Lothian (01721 722502/www.nts.org.uk). Bus 40. **Open** 10am-6pm (or dusk) daily. **Admission** £2; £1 concessions; free under-16s. **Credit** MC, V.

National Museum of Flight

East Fortune Airfield, East Fortune (01620 880308/www.nms.ac.uk/flight). **Open** *Jan-Oct* 10am-5pm daily. *Nov, Dec* 11am-4pm Sat, Sun. **Admission** £3; £1.50 concessions; free under-16s. **Credit** MC, V.

Newhailes

Newhailes Road, Musselburgh, East Lothian (653 5599/www.nts.org.uk). **Open** *Apr-Sept* noon-5pm Mon, Thur-Sun. *Oct* noon-5pm Sat, Sun. **Admission** £7, £5.25 concessions, £5.60 adult group.

Scottish Seabird Centre

The Harbour, North Berwick (01620 890202/ www.seabird.org). **Open** *Apr-Oct* 10am-6pm daily. *Nov-Mar* 10am-4pm Mon-Fri; 10am-5.30pm Sat, Sun. **Admission** £4.95; £3.50 concessions; £13.50 family. **Credit** AmEx, MC, V.

Tantallon Castle

off A198, 2 miles east of North Berwick (01620 892727/www.historic-scotland.gov.uk). **Open** *Oct-Mar* 9.30am-4.30pm Mon-Wed, Sat; 9.30am-12.30pm Thur; 2-4.30pm Sun. *Apr-Sept* 9.30am-6.30pm daily. **Admission** £3; £1-£2.30 concessions. **Credit** AmEx, MC, V.

South of the A1

The royal burgh of **Haddington** is a well-heeled market town, 13 miles east of Edinburgh on the A1 and boasting 284 listed buildings. The 14th-century **St Mary's Collegiate Church** is particularly impressive. To the east of Haddington is the 13th-century **Hailes Castle**. South of Haddington is the toy-town-like model village of **Gifford**, built by the Marquis of Tweeddale in the 18th century for his estate workers. An interesting eaterie is the **Goblin Ha'** (*see below*), which is signposted by a yogic levitating goblin. It derives its name from an underground chamber at the now ruined **Yester Castle**. The **Lammermuir Hills** are easily accessible from Longyester.

Hailes Castle

1.5 miles south-west of East Linton (Historic Scotland 668 8800/www.historic-scotland.gov.uk). **Open** *Apr-Sept* 9.30am-6pm daily. **Admission** free.

Where to eat

Luca's (34 High Street, Musselburgh; 665 2237) is home to the best ice-cream on the east coast.

In North Berwick the sea air is likely to make you ravenous for chips and the best places are the **North Berwick Fry**, in Quality Street, or the **George Café**, in the High Street. Finer fare is available at **Miller's Bistro** (Douglas Court, 17 Market Place, main courses £6.50-£14.50), or, for an Edwardian atmosphere, try the grand **Macdonald Marine Hotel** (Cromwell Road; 01620 892406; three course set meal £22.50) with putting green, snooker and open air swimming pool.

For more hearty fare head south to the **Goblin Ha' Hotel** in Gifford (Main Street, 01620 810244, main courses £5-£12.25). The **Waterside Bistro** (Waterside, Nungate, 01620 825674, main courses £15) is a popular spot for Sunday lunch on the banks of the River Tyne.

Where to stay

In North Berwick, the **Tantallon Inn** (4 Marine Parade, 01620 892238, closed 2wks Oct) has double rooms for £30-£34 per person. Or try **Browns Hotel** in Haddington (1 West Road, 01620 822254, rates £108 double).

Top five Out of town

1 Falkirk Wheel
Watch in wonder as the world's only rotating boat lift links the Union Canal with the Forth & Clyde Canal (*see p266*).

2 Stirling Castle
Perfectly preserved combination of palatial halls and fortifications (*see p272*).

3 Fife fishing villages
Collect the set: Elie, St Monance, Pittenweem, Anstruther and Crail (*see p268*).

4 Linlithgow Palace
Atmospheric ruin full of intriguing nooks and crannies (*see p266*).

5 Rosslyn Chapel
Pagan secrets meet Christian symbolism in this 15th-century church (*see p264*).

Trips Out of Town

South of the A1, the **Eaglescairnie Mains** (01620 810491) in Gifford is a lovely old farmhouse bed and breakfast; rates are from £25 to £35 per person.

Getting there

By bicycle

Cycling is a viable mode of travel in this area, with signposted routes and trails (mostly along disused railway lines) leaving Edinburgh.

By car

Take the A1 out of Edinburgh towards Haddington. The coastal trail is signposted.

By train

A branch line runs regular services from Edinburgh's **Haymarket station**, through **Waverley station**, to Musselburgh, Prestonpans, Longniddry, Drem and North Berwick.

By bus

East Lothian is served by buses from **St Andrew Square** in Edinburgh. For further information consult www.lothianbuses.co.uk or contact **First Bus** (663 9233/www.firstgroup.com).

Tourist information

Dunbar

143a High Street (01368 863353). **Open** *Oct-May* 9am-5pm Mon-Fri. *June* 9am-5pm Mon-Sat; 11am-4pm Sun. *July* 9am-7pm Mon-Sat; 11am-6pm Sun. *Aug* 9am-8pm Mon-Sat; 11am-6pm Sun. *Sept* 9am-5pm Mon-Sat; 11am-4pm Sun.

Musselburgh

Old Craighall, Granada Service Station, off A1 (653 6172). **Open** *Apr, May* 9am-6pm Mon-Fri. *June, Sept* 9am-6pm Mon-Sat; 10am-3pm Sun. *July* 9am-7pm Mon-Sat; 11am-6pm Sun. *Aug* 9am-8pm Mon-Sat; 11am-6pm Sun; *Oct-Mar* 9am-5pm Mon-Fri.

North Berwick

1 Quality Street (01620 892197). **Open** *Oct-Mar* 9am-5pm Mon-Sat. *Apr, May* 9am-6pm Mon-Sat. *June, Sept* 9am-6pm Mon-Sat; 11am-4pm Sun. *July* 9am-7pm Mon-Sat; 11am-6pm Sun. *Aug* 9am-8pm Mon-Sat; 11am-6pm Sun.

Midlothian

The graciously curving Pentland Hills cover 22,000 acres just south of the city on the A702. The area forms the **Pentland Hills Regional Park**. From here you can travel further along the A702 to reach the Iron-Age fort of **Castle Law Hill** and explore even more genuine Scottish unadulterated ruralness.

It is possible to do some serious hill-walking in the Pentlands (always observe suitable safety precautions, *see p242*), but there's also the **Glencorse Reservoir** for those who don't

fancy putting in much effort. A five-minute stroll up the gentle incline from the reservoir car park plunges you straight into the heather covered hills that form the image of classic Scottish countryside worldwide. Ready and waiting for you on the return trip is the inviting **Flotterstone Inn** (*see below*).

Rosslyn Chapel, an intensely and ornately carved demonstration of medieval religious syncretism is six miles (ten kilometres) south of Edinburgh at Roslin. The ruins of Rosslyn Castle lie in the nearby woodlands of **Roslin Glen Country Park**, accessed from the B7003 Roslin–Rosewell road. The country park hugs the steep-sided valley of the river Esk, where there are many cliffs and caves, one of which is said to be the site of Robert the Bruce's famous encounter with the spider.

Where to eat & stay

The **Allan Ramsey Hotel** in Carlops (01968 660258) is an old inn with accommodation (rates £50 double), bar meals and a restaurant (main courses £12-£14.50). Just a few minutes' walk from Rosslyn Chapel is the **Original Hotel** in Roslin (440 2384, rates £75 double). It also has a restaurant (main courses £10.50-£16). Dalkeith's **County Hotel** (152 High Street; 663 3495, rates £80 double) is a luxury townhouse hotel. If you're in the Pentland Hills, don't miss the food at the **Flotterstone Inn** (01968 673717, main courses £10-£15) on the A702 at Milton Bridge.

Getting there

By car

Take the A701 to Roslin or the A702 to the Pentland Hills. Dalkeith is on the A7.

By bus

Buses leave from **St Andrew Square**, Edinburgh, for the Pentland Hills and Roslin. For Glencourse and Flotterstone Inn ask for buses to Milton Bridge.

Tourist information

Check **www.midlothian-online.com**.

West of Edinburgh

Just south of the airport, the village of Ratho is home to the **Edinburgh Canal Centre**. The centre recollects the Union Canal's construction and the waterway's heyday in the 19th century. New to the area is the **National Rock Climbing Centre** (*see p234*), with the highest climbing walls in Europe.

The best parts of West Lothian, however, are closer to the Forth. Along the A90, and just off the B924 towards South Queensferry, is the

Watch the birdie. The **Scottish Seabird Centre**. *See p263*.

village of Dalmeny, where you'll find **St Cuthbert's**, one of the finest Norman churches in Scotland. Overlooking the Forth is **Dalmeny House**, a Gothic revival mansion designed by William Wilkins in 1814 and home of the Earls of Rosebery. It boasts the obligatory grand interior and, incongrously, an extensive collection of Napoleonic memorabilia. **South Queensferry** lies just beyond the house. It is an excellent place to view the two Forth bridges. The *Maid of the Forth* ferry sails from South Queensferry to **Inchcolm Abbey**. Founded in 1123, it comprises a fine clutch of monastic buildings and is spectacularly located on Inchcolm Island in the Firth of Forth. Seal sightings are common during the boat trip.

West of South Queensferry is the self-consciously grandiose **Hopetoun House**, designed by William Bruce in 1699 and enlarged by William Adam in 1721. Further west still is **Blackness Castle**, used by Zefferelli in his film version of *Hamlet*. Its stark walls have crumbled since they were built in the 1440s, but the view across the Forth from the castle promontory is still spectacular.

Four miles south, just off the M9, is the attractive royal burgh of **Linlithgow**, famed for its royal palace where Mary, Queen of Scots, was born in 1542. The beautiful, ruined **Linlithgow Palace** overlooks the Loch and the Peel – a grassy lochside parkland. A walk around the bird-filled loch takes about an hour and gives you a real sense of the countryside. Behind the station is the **Canal Basin**, where you'll find the **Linlithgow Canal Centre**, which includes a museum and tearoom.

Just north of Linlithgow lies the once-thriving town of **Bo'ness**, which today looks more than a little frayed at the edges. It does, however,

boast a major attraction for steam fanatics in the iron and steam of the **Bo'ness & Kinneil Railway**, along which trains run the seven-mile round trip to the **Birkhill Claymines**, where there is a guided tour.

Falkirk, west of Bo'ness, has a popular landmark in the form of the **Falkirk Wheel**, a magnificent bird-like lift, which scoops boats from the Forth & Clyde Canal and pops them down again into the Union Canal, thus connecting the waterways between Glasgow and Edinburgh.

Blackness Castle

Blackness, 4 miles north of Linlithgow on the A904 (01506 834807/www.historic-scotland.gov.uk). **Open** (last admission 30mins before closing) *Apr-Sept* 9.30am-6.30pm daily. *Oct-Mar* 9.30am-4.30pm Mon-Wed, Sat; 9.30am-12.30pm Thur; 2-4.30pm Sun. **Admission** £2.50; 75p-£1.90 concessions. **No credit cards.**

Bo'ness & Kinneil Railway

Bo'ness (01506 822298/www.srps.org.uk/railway). **Open** *Apr, May, Sept, Oct* Sat, Sun. *July, Aug* Tue-Sun. Phone for train times and events at other times of year. **Tickets** £4.50; £2-£3.50 concessions; £11 family. **Credit** AmEx, MC, V.

Dalmeny House

South Queensferry (331 1888/www.dalmeny.co.uk). **Open** *July, Aug* 2-5.30pm Mon, Tue, Sun. Closed Sept-June. **Admission** £5; £3-£4 concessions. **No credit cards.**

Edinburgh Canal Centre

27 Baird Road, Ratho (333 1320/www.bridge inn.com). **Cruises** *June-Aug* 2.30pm daily. *Apr, May, Sept, Oct* 2.30pm Sat, Sun. Closed Nov-Mar. **Admission** £6; £4 concessions; £15 family. **Credit** AmEx, DC, MC, V.

Trips Out of Town

One of the last of the few. A Spitfire at the **National Museum of Flight**. *See p263.*

Trips Out of Town

Falkirk Wheel

Lime Road, Tamfourhill, 1.5 miles from centre of Falkirk (booking line 0870 050 0208/www.falkirkwheel.com). **Tickets** £8; £4-£6 concessions; £21 family. **Credit** AmEx, MC, V.

Hopetoun House

South Queensferry (331 2451/www.hope tounhouse.com). **Open** *Apr-Sept* 10am-5.30pm daily (last admission 4.30pm). Closed Oct-Mar. **Admission** £6.50; £3.50-£5.50 concessions. **Credit** MC, V.

Inchcolm Abbey

Inchcolm Island, Firth of Forth (01383 823332/www.historic-scotland.gov.uk). **Open** *Apr-Oct* 9.30am-6.30pm daily. Closed Nov-Mar. **Admission** £3; £1-£2.30 concessions. **Credit** AmEx, MC, V.

This beautiful and mysterious island can be reached by sailing on the *Maid of the Forth* ferry from South Queensferry (*see p267*).

Linlithgow Canal Centre

Canal Basin, Manse Road, Linlithgow (01506 671215/www.lucs.org.uk). **Open** (museum & cruises) *Easter-June, Sept, Oct* 2-5pm Sat, Sun; *July, Aug* 2-5pm daily. Closed Nov-Easter. **Admission** *Museum* free. *St Magdalene cruise* £6; £3 concessions; £15 family. *Victoria cruise* £2.50; £1.50 concessions. **Credit** MC, V.

Linlithgow Palace

Kirkgate, Linlithgow (01506 842896/www.historic-scotland.gov.uk). **Open** *Apr-Sept* 9.30am-6.30pm daily. *Oct-Mar* 9.30am-4.30pm Mon-Sat; 2-4.30pm Sun. **Admission** £3; £1-£2.30 concessions. **Credit** AmEx, MC, V.

Maid of the Forth

Ferry leaves from: Hawes Pier, South Queensferry (331 4857/www.maidoftheforth.co.uk). **Open** *Apr-Oct* phone for details. Closed Nov-Mar. **Admission** *Ferry & abbey* £11; £4.50-£9 concessions; £27 family. **Credit** AmEx, MC, V.

Where to eat

In South Queensferry, the **Hawes Inn** (6 Newhalls Road; 331 1990) was immortalised by Robert Louis Stevenson in *Kidnapped* as the site of the abduction of David Balfour, and serves food every day (main courses £5.95-£13.50). The **Bridge Inn** (333 1320) in Ratho, has two canal boat dining rooms (for parties) and a restaurant on land (main courses £6.95-£17). The **Hopetoun House** teashop near South Queensferry (331 4305, closed Nov-Feb) is very well thought of by cake aficionados.

There are plenty of pubs and restaurants with decent food along the High Street in Linlithgow, including **Livingston's** at No.52 (01506 846565, closed Mon, Sun, 1st 2wks Jan and 1st wk June, set meals £25-£30), which is very popular for deliciously cooked Scottish beef and fish dishes. A good quality alternative is the **Star & Garter Hotel** at No.1 High Street, Linlithgow (01506 846362, main courses £7-£15).

Where to stay

Houston House in Uphall (01506 853831) has double rooms from around £110. A cheaper option is the **Thornton** in Edinburgh Road, Linlithgow (01506 844693), a spacious Victorian house with B&B rates of £25-£28 per person.

Getting there

By car

Take the A902 west of Edinburgh, then the B974 for South Queensferry. Take the M9 for Linlithgow and Falkirk.

By bus

A regular bus service departs from **St Andrew Square**.

By train

Trains regularly depart from **Waverley** and **Haymarket** stations in Edinburgh for South Queensferry, Bo'ness, Linlithgow and Falkirk. Linlithgow is on the main Glasgow–Edinburgh line, with four trains every hour from Edinburgh.

Tourist information

Bo'ness

Seaview car park (01506 826626). **Open** *Apr-Aug* 10am-5pm daily. *Sept* noon-5pm daily. Closed Oct-Mar.

Falkirk

2-4 Glebe Street (01324 620244). **Open** *Apr, May* 10am-5pm daily. *June-Aug* 9.30am-6pm Mon-Sat; noon-4pm Sun. *Sept* 9.30am-6pm Mon-Sat. *Oct-Mar* 10am-4pm Mon-Sat.

Linlithgow

Burgh Halls, The Cross (01506 844600). **Open** *Easter-Sept* 10am-5pm daily. Closed Oct-Easter.

Scottish whisky

Two hints: don't call it Scotch if you're ordering it in a bar and don't spell it with an 'e'. Whiskey is what they drink in Ireland. If that strikes you as pedantic, you might want to stop reading now. With more than 100 distilleries across Scotland, malt whisky is a drink of connoisseurs and pedantry is their speciality. Foremost among Scotland's whisky pedants is writer Iain M Banks, who recently dropped the M in favour of his other nom de plume, took a break from detailing the Culture and set out to tour the country writing about a different but even more involved and involving culture in his book, *Raw Spirit*.

After all, there's plenty there for him to explore. The flavour of a malt whisky depends on any number of factors: the way the key ingredient, malted barley, is dried; the quality of the water that flows into the distillery; the shape and size of the copper pot-still where distillation takes place; and the oak casks where the drink is matured for anything from five to fifty years. So many variables produce a vast range of whiskies, from the peaty Laphroaig to the smooth Isle of Jura (for a mini whisky tour in Edinburgh itself visit the Scottish Whisky Heritage Centre, *see p72*).

One thing to clarify: a single malt whisky is the produce of just one malt whisky distillery and will have a unique flavour; a blended malt, such as the Famous Grouse, Bells and Johnny Walker, is a mixture of malt and grain whiskies, and has a less distinct character.

There are distilleries throughout Scotland, with a particular concentration in Speyside. The closest to Edinburgh is the **Glenkinchie Distillery** (Pencaitland, Tranent, East Lothian; 01875 342004).

Further north, is **Blair Atholl Distillery** (Perth Road, Pitlochry; 01796 482003), which dates from 1798, and offers guided tours and samples of its Blair Atholl 12 year old single malt. Your health!

Trips Out of Town

Fife

Looking north from Edinburgh, you will see Fife on the far shore of the Firth of Forth. After North Queensferry and **Deep Sea World** – where a huge aquarium full of rays and sharks stretches over your head – the coast comes into its own around Largo Bay. This stretch of coastline up to St Andrews is known as **East Neuk**, but also goes by the name 'fringe of gold' because of its wonderful sandy beaches and the rich fishing grounds offshore. Its fishing villages are lovely, with tiny colourful houses huddled round each harbour and plenty of boats still working from them. Elie, St Monance, Pittenweem, Anstruther and Crail in particular are all delightful.

According to legend, the university town of **St Andrews** is home to the bones of the apostle Andrew, the brother of St Peter. Now it trades more on being Prince William's place of study. St Andrews is also where the **Royal & Ancient Golf Club** has determined the rules of the game since 1754.

Trips and tours

Sightseeing tours

Celtic Trails
477 5419/www.celtictrails.co.uk
Ancient sites near Edinburgh are this company's speciality with a particular emphasis on the mythical and medieval. The Rosslyn Chapel Trail lasts half a day and costs £27 (£17 children).

Rabbie's Trail Burners
226 3133/www.rabbies.com
Mini-coach tours of between one and five days. A trip from Edinburgh to Skye for three days costs £99 (peak season). Accommodation is extra.

Scot Tracks
01383 820208/www.touringscotland.co.uk
Personalised tours of Scotland for groups. Scot Tracks lets you choose your own itinerary based on tours of cities, castles, whisky trails, walking or sailing. Phone for up to date prices.

Timberbush Tours
226 6066/www.timberbush-tours.co.uk
Off-the-peg or tailor-made tours for groups of up to 24 in mini-coaches with your driver doubling as your guide.

Backpacking tours

Celtic Connections
225 3330/www.thecelticconnection.co.uk
Backpacking tours for groups of 10-12 people, combining Scotland, Ireland and Wales in a complete Celtic tour. Prices start at £79 for a three-day one-way trip.

Haggis Adventures
557 9393/www.haggisadventures.com
Haggis will take you from Edinburgh to destinations in the Highlands and across the sea to the Isle of Skye.

MacBacpackers
558 9900/www.macbackpackers.com
A variety of Highland tours. The seven-day Grand Tour, leaving from Edinburgh and taking in Inverness, Fort William, Oban and the Isle of Skye, costs £145.

Wild in Scotland
478 6500/www.wild-in-scotland.com
Wild in Scotland offers a number of tours, including a six-day trip to Skye and the Hebrides for around £220.

Hill-walking

See www.walkingwild.com.

Make Tracks Walking Holidays
229 6844/www.maketracks.net
Guided walks along the main hill-walking trails, including the Southern Upland Way, St Cuthbert's Way and the Great Glen. The company will transport your luggage. Prices start from £105 for two nights.

Walkabout Scotland
661 7168/www.walkaboutscotland.com
Guided hill-walking tours from Edinburgh to the Highlands. There are day tours, weekend breaks and longer walking holidays – and you don't have to be an experienced hill-walker to join in. Day tours from £40.

Wild about Scotland
478 0435/www.wildaboutscotland.co.uk
Tailored, eco-friendly minibus tours to Sandwood Bay on the far north west coast, offering a taste of the wilderness. Available in the summer months. Call to discuss prices.

The great escape. **Forth Road Bridge**. *See p265.*

Deep Sea World

Battery Quarry, Fife (01383 411880/www.deepseaworld.com). **Open** *Mar-Oct* 10am-6pm daily. *Nov-Feb* 10am-5pm Mon-Fri; 10am-6pm Sat, Sun. **Admission** £7.95; £5.75-£6.50 concessions. **Credit** MC, V.

Where to eat

For hot and hearty lunches **Brambles**, at No.5 College Street, St Andrews; 01334 475380 (main courses £6.50-£13.25) is unbeatable. Seafood lovers will enjoy the **Cellar** in Anstruther (24 East Green, 01333 310378, closed Mon, Tue in winter, three course set meals £28-£35) or **Anstruther Fish Bar** (42/44 Shore Street), held by many to be the best fish and chip shop in Scotland. The massive queues testify to its fish frying supremacy.

Where to stay

In Dunfermline, the **Davaar House Hotel** (126 Grieve Street, 01383 721886) has double rooms for £75-£80. The **Inn at Lathones** (Lathones, by Largoward, 01334 840494, rates £55-£75 per person) is a 400-year-old former coaching inn; its restaurant uses local produce where possible (main courses £13.50-£17.50). In Falkland, the highly recommended **Covenanter Hotel** (The Square, 01337 857224, rates £54 double) is another comfortable former coaching inn.

Getting there

By car

Take the A90 out of Edinburgh, then the M90. Turn onto the A823 for Dunfermline; or the A921 for the coastal route. For St Andrews take the A91 off the M90.

By bus

Buses depart from Edinburgh's **St Andrew Square** for Dunfermline and St Andrews. Many buses in the area are run by **Stagecoach Fife** (01383 621249/www.stagecoachbus.com/fife).

By train

Trains depart Edinburgh's **Waverley station** for Dunfermline, Kirkcaldy and Leuchars.

Tourist information

See **www.standrews.co.uk**.

Dunfermline

1 High Street (01383 720999). **Open** *Mid Sept-June* 9.30am-5pm Mon-Sat. *July-mid Sept* 9.30am-5.30pm Mon-Sat; 11am-4pm Sun.

St Andrews

70 Market Street (01334 472021). **Open** *Apr-June* 9.30am-5.30pm Mon-Sat; 11am-4pm Sun. *July, Aug* 9.30am-7pm Mon-Sat; 10.30am-5pm Sun. *Sept* 9.30am-6pm Mon-Sat; 11am-4pm Sun. *Oct-Mar* 9.30am-5pm Mon-Fri.

The Borders

Pastoral landscapes, a handsome coastline, picturesque towns and a host of abbeys make the Borders a most fascinating stretch of Scotland. **Peebles** is the closest Borders town to Edinburgh and offers up some surprising sights as well as the obligatory woollen shops. East of Peebles is the handsome, 1,000-year-old **Traquair House**. Acclaimed as the oldest inhabited house in Scotland, it has served as a court for William the Lion, a hunting lodge for Scottish royalty, a refuge for Catholic priests and a stronghold of Jacobite sentiment. Close by are the ruins of **Melrose Abbey**, founded by St Aidan in about 660AD and the reputed

The High country

The Lowlands of Scotland are picturesque and rich in history, but it's the Highlands where the drama really begins. With awesome peaks of sandstone and granite reaching to 4,406ft (1,343m), the region takes up half of the country's land mass. There are 790 islands, 130 of which are inhabited. If you have an opportunity to travel further afield and discover more of Scotland's staggering scenery, you should grab it. Here are some pointers to help plan trips to three of the most popular destinations. For details of organised tours to these and other areas, *see p268* **Trips and tours**.

The Trossachs

The Highlands converge with the Lowlands in the Trossachs, an area of lochs, rivers and hills. It takes about an hour and a half to reach the region from Edinburgh and you'll need a car to explore it thoroughly. Loch Lomond, to the west of the Trossachs, is Scotland's largest, and jostles with Ness for the title of most famous loch. The Trossachs' website (**www.trossachs.org.uk**) has lots of general information, while the Loch Lomond website (**www.loch-lomond.net**) has a comprehensive list of accommodation, boat-hire firms and maps. There are tourist information centres in Callander (Rob Roy & Trossachs Visitor Centre, Ancaster Square; 01877 330342) and Aberfoyle (Trossachs Discovery Centre, Main Street, Aberfoyle; 01877 382352).

The Highlands & Isle of Skye

Fort William is a good point from which to explore the Highlands, as many of the major mountains and glens are within striking distance: Glen Coe, Ben Nevis, Glen Nevis, the West Highland Way and Loch Ness. The Road to the Isles (more prosaically known as the A830) takes you from Fort William on a dramatic 46-mile journey through lochs, forests and mountains to Mallaig, where you can board a boat for Skye. A number of websites can help you plan your trip: **www.gael-net.co.uk**; **www.ecossenet.com**; **www.skye.co.uk** and **www.visitscotland.com** are all worth a look. There are tourist information centres at Fort William (Highlands of Scotland Tourist Board, Cameron Square; 01397 703781) and on Skye (2 Lochside, Dunvegan; 01470 521581). For more information about Fort William, see **www.visit-fortwilliam.co.uk**.

Isle of Mull

Mull is the easiest major island to get to because its mainland ferry port, Oban, is only three hours' drive or four and a half hours on the train from Edinburgh. Mull has it all: castles, heathery hills, glistening sandy beaches, miniature train trips and boat excursions to Staffa and Fingal's Cave – not to mention the world's smallest theatre (one, incidentally, with an adventurous programme and a highly professional reputation) and its own unique cheese and whisky. The main

resting place of Robert the Bruce's heart. Restored in 1822 by Sir Walter Scott, this is one of the most evocative sites in all the Borders.

It is not surprising that the history-packed Borders should have appealed to Sir Walter Scott, the tireless promoter of Scotland's past. **Abbotsford** was his home and is an appropriately romantic baronial pile. Scott frequently praised the nearby **Eildon Hills**, the legendary burial ground of King Arthur. You can see what he saw by visiting 'Scott's View', a few miles east of Melrose. Nearby, another hero, William Wallace, is celebrated by the gargantuan **Wallace Statue**.

Abbotsford

Melrose (01896 752043). **Open** *Mar-Oct* 9.30am-5pm Mon-Sat; 2-5pm Sun. Closed Nov-Feb. **Admission** £4.50; £2.50-3.50 concessions. **No credit cards**.

Dawyck Botanic Garden

Stobo, on B712 (01721 760254/www.www.rbge.org. uk/rbge/web/visiting/dbg.jsp). **Open** *Feb, Nov* 10am-4pm daily. *Mar, Oct* 10am-5pm daily. *Apr-Sept* 10am-6pm. Closed Dec, Jan. **Admission** £3.50; £1-£3 concessions; £8 family. **Credit** MC, V.

Melrose Abbey

Abbey Street, Melrose (01896 822562/www. historic-scotland.gov.uk). **Open** (last entry 30mins before closing) *Apr-Sept* 9.30am-6.30pm daily. *Oct-Mar* 9.30am-4.30pm Mon-Sat; 2-4.30pm Sun. **Admission** £3.50; £1.20-£2.50 concessions. **Credit** AmEx, MC, V.

Traquair House

Innerleithen, Peebleshire (01896 830323/ www.traquair.co.uk). **Open** *Apr, May, Sept* noon-5pm daily. *June-Aug* 10.30am-5.30pm daily. *Oct* 11am-4pm. Closed Nov-Easter. **Admission** £6; £3-£4 concessions. **Credit** DC, MC, V.

town, Tobermory, is the setting for the BBC's popular children's series *Balamory*, a fact that has produced a surge in family tourism. It is a picturesque huddle of multi-coloured houses and, according to the TV, remarkably multi-cultural inhabitants, grouped around a harbour. Mull has a comprehensive website (**www.isle.of.mull.com**) that lists all kinds of accommodation, and there is a tourist information office on the island (Main Street, Tobermory; 01688 302610), as well as one in Oban (Albany Street; 01631 563122).

Where to eat

A picturesque choice is the **Tibbie Shiels Inn** (St Mary's Loch, 01750 42231, closed dinner Sun, closed Mon-Wed in winter, main courses £3.50-£10), an old haunt for writers that overlooks the water. **Kailzie Gardens**, near Peebles (01721 720007, open daily), has a tea shop that serves good home baking. Also try the **Ship Hotel** (Harbour Road, Eyemouth, 01890 750224, main courses £5-£8).

Where to stay

In Peebles, the **Peebles Hydro Hotel** (01721 720602, rates £65-£74 per person) has great views of the town and good facilities. For B&B in an 18th-century farmhouse, contact Mrs Debby Playfair at **Morebattle Tofts**, Kelso (01573 440643, closed Nov-Mar, rates £50

double). The Best Western **George & Abbotsford Hotel** (High Street, Melrose, 01896 822308, closed Christmas and New Year) has doubles for around £70, while the four-star **Philipburn Country House Hotel** in Selkirk (01750 720747, closed 1st 2wks Jan) has double rooms for £120.

Getting there

By car
Take the A701, followed by the A703 to Peebles.

By train
It is almost impossible to reach the Borders by train. The nearest train station is in Berwick-upon-Tweed, from where there are connecting buses to Galashiels and other destinations.

By bus
Buses depart from **St Andrew Square**, Edinburgh.

Trips Out of Town

Tourist information

Also, try online at **www.scot-borders.co.uk**.

Jedburgh
Murray's Green (01835 863435). **Open** 9.30am-4.30pm Mon-Sat.

Kelso
Town House, The Square (01573 223464). **Open** 10am-2pm Mon-Sat.

Melrose
Melrose Abbey House, Abbey Street (01896 822555). **Open** 10am-2pm Mon-Sat.

Peebles
23 High Street (01721 720138). **Open** 9.30am-4.30pm Mon-Sat.

Stirling

For centuries Stirling's position just above the River Forth at the meeting of Scotland's Highlands and Lowlands made it into a key strategic stronghold. Two of the most significant battles against English rule took place nearby: in 1297 William Wallace defeated the English at the Battle of Stirling Bridge and, in 1314, Robert the Bruce conquered Edward II's forces at **Bannockburn**. (There's a heritage centre on the battle site.)

Castle Rock was probably first occupied in the 600s, yet today's **Stirling Castle** dates mainly from the 15th and 16th centuries and combines a robust fortress with a royal palace. Below it, on Castle Wynd, is **Argyll's Lodgings**, one of Scotland's most stunning examples of a 17th-century grand townhouse. Over the way is **Mar's Wark**, the impressive stone remains of what was once a grand Renaissance-style house built by the Earl of Mar. Next door is the **Church of the Holy Rude**, which has one of the few surviving medieval timber roofs in Scotland, the intended rebuild having been halted by the Reformation.

Beyond Stirling Old Bridge, and about a mile north-east of the town, an oddly shaped tower dominates the skyline. It is the **National Wallace Monument** commemorating the hero of the Battle of Stirling Bridge, and the subject of the film *Braveheart*. Built in 1860, it houses Sir William Wallace memorabilia, including his double-edged sword.

Argyll's Lodging
Castle Wynd (01786 461146/www.historic-scotland.gov.uk). **Open** (last entry 30mins before closing) *Summer* 9.30am-6pm daily. *Winter* 9.30am-5pm daily. **Admission** *Argyll's Lodging & Stirling Castle* £8; £2-£6 concessions. *Argyll's Lodging only* £3; £1.20-£2.25 concessions. **Credit** AmEx, DC, MC, V.

Bannockburn Heritage Centre
Glasgow Road, Stirling (01786 812664/www.nts.org.uk). **Open** *Feb, Mar, Nov-late Dec* 10.30am-4pm daily. *Apr-Oct* 10am-5.30pm daily. Closed late Dec-Jan. **Admission** £3.50; £2.60-£2.80 concessions; free under-18s; £9.50 family. **Credit** MC, V.

National Wallace Monument
Abbey Craig (01786 472140). **Open** *Apr, May, Oct* 10am-5pm daily. *June* 10am-6pm daily. *July, Aug* 9.30am-6.30pm daily. *Sept* 9.30am-5pm daily. *Nov-Feb* 10.30am-4pm daily. **Admission** £3.95; £2.75-£3 concessions; £10.75 family. **Credit** AmEx, MC, V.

Stirling Castle
Castle Esplanade, Stirling (01786 450000/www.historic-scotland.gov.uk). **Open** (last entry 45mins before closing) *Summer* 9.30am-6pm daily. *Winter* 9.30am-5pm daily. **Admission** £8; £2-£6 concessions. **Credit** AmEx, MC, V.

Where to eat

Stirling has the very reasonably priced **Barnton Café** (3 Barnton Street; 01786 461698, main courses £3.20-£5.25); **Hermann's** at the Tolbooth near Stirling castle (Broad Street; 01786 450632, main courses £11.50-£17); and the **Tolbooth Restaurant and Café/Bar**, which is part of the city's newest arts centre (The Tolbooth, Jail Wynd; 01786 274101).

Where to stay

The **Golden Lion Flagship Hotel** (8 King Street; 01786 475351, rates £97 double) dates from 1876. A cheaper option is the **youth hostel** on St John Street (01786 473442, rates £11.50-£13.50 adult, £5-10.50 child). It's for SYHA members only, but you can join at the hostel. Membership costs £6 and is valid at all SYHA hostels for one year.

Getting there

By car
Stirling is 40 miles north of Edinburgh on the A91.

By train
There are hourly trains from Edinburgh's **Waverley** station. The journey takes about 55mins.

By bus
The M9 express bus run by **Citylink** (08705 505050) leaves hourly from **St Andrew Square**. Slower buses to Stirling are run by **First Bus** (663 9233).

Tourist information

For more information, see **www.stirling.co.uk**.

Stirling
41 Dumbarton Road (01786 475019). **Open** *May, June, Sept, Oct* 9am-5pm daily. *July, Aug* 9am-7pm daily. *Nov-Apr* 10am-5pm daily.

Directory

Directory

Getting Around

Arriving & leaving

By air

Edinburgh Airport (0870 040 0007) is about 10 miles (16km) west of the city centre, north of Glasgow Road. The airport is about 25 minutes' drive from Princes Street and services flights from international and English airports. **Continental Airlines** (0845 607 6760/www.continental.com) runs daily direct flights from Edinburgh and Glasgow to New York's Newark airport. The main low cost airlines are **Easyjet** (0870 600 0000/www.easyjet.com) and **bmibaby** (0870 6070 555/www.bmibaby.com). They fly to Edinburgh from airports in England and Ireland. Both face stiff competition from **British Airways**, who have significantly reduced their prices (0870 9850 3377/www.ba.com) and fly to Edinburgh from most London airports. If you're planning on taking in other European cities from Edinburgh, **Air-Scotland** (0141 222 2362/www.air-scotland.com) and **Flyglobespan** (www.flyglobespan.com) service a number of popular holiday destinations, while **Ryanair** (0871 246 0000/www.ryanair.com) flies direct to Dublin. Flights also leave Edinburgh for the north and Highlands and islands of Scotland.

TO AND FROM THE AIRPORT

The cheapest and quickest way to travel to and from the airport is the dedicated bus service **Airlink 100** (555 6363). These modern buses stop at Maybury, Corstorphine, Edinburgh Zoo, Murrayfield and the West End. Services leave the airport 4.50am-12.20am Mon-Sat, 5am-midnight Sun; the service from Waverley Bridge runs 4.20am-11.46pm Mon-Sat; 5.20am-11.26pm Sun. There's also a night bus, **Night Service 22**, that runs every hour from 12.15am-4.15am daily. Buses are low-floor double-deckers with ample luggage space and easy access for wheelchair users and buggies. Tickets cost £3.00 adult (£2 5-15s) one way; £5 adult (£3 5-15s) open return; free under-5s. The Airlink Day Saver, £4.20 adult (£2.50 5-15s) allows one journey to or from the airport and unlimited travel for the whole day on the Lothian Buses network (*see p275*). Ridacards (*see p275*) are also valid on Airlink 100.

Skycab Taxis (333 2220) also cover the distance quickly. The service meets every flight in and out of the airport (from approximately 5am-11pm); the journey time is 20-25 minutes, rising to 30 minutes during rush hours (7.30-9.30am and 4.30-7pm Mon-Fri). The fare is around £12-£14, depending on the time of day and the number of passengers. Most taxis in the city have one seat adapted for disabled passengers (*see p279*).

By bus/coach

St Andrew Square Bus Station

Elder Street, New Town. Princes Street buses. **Open** 6am-midnight daily. **Map** p304 D1.

Coaches arriving in Edinburgh from England and Wales are run by Britain's most extensive coach network, National Express (0870 580 8080/www.nationalexpress.com). Coaches serving the whole of Scotland are run by Scottish Citylink (0870 550 5050/www.citylink.co.uk). Both services run from the brand new St Andrew Square Bus Station, in the city centre, which opened in February 2003 after extensive refurbishment. Alternatively, Mega Bus (www.megabus.com) runs services from Edinburgh Waterloo Place (along from Princes Street, just past the top of Leith Street) to Glasgow, Dundee and St Andrews, with prices starting from £1 single, although you have to book online in advance.

By train

Waverley Station

Waverley Bridge, New Town (train information 0845 748 4950/www.thetrainline.co.uk). Princes Street buses. **Map** p304 D2.
Edinburgh's central railway station serves the East Coast main line to London and Aberdeen. Scotrail services leave for destinations throughout Scotland, including a shuttle service (every 15mins) to Glasgow and connections to the West Coast. Local services go to East and West Lothian.

Haymarket Station

Haymarket, West Edinburgh (train information 08457 484950). Bus 2, 3, 4, 12, 25, 26, 31, 33, 44, 44A, Airlink. **Map** p308 B6.
On the main line to Glasgow. Most trains travelling north and west from Waverley stop here, as do local services to West Lothian.

Getting around

To fully appreciate the beauty, elegance, charm and contrasts of the city centre and its environs, Edinburgh is best explored on foot. Walking around the city is safe and can provide a rewarding experience, but exercise the usual caution at night, particularly around the areas of the city with abundant and rowdy nightlife such as Lothian Road and the Cowgate. A useful way to orient yourself and get an overview of the major tourist sights is on one of the guided bus tours (see p67) or themed walking tours (see p80). Getting around the centre of Edinburgh by bus is reasonably fast and reliable, and passes – Daysavers and Ridacards – are available (see below). Driving in town can be stressful and more hassle than it's worth, especially as city-centre parking can be problematic. Taxis are numerous, if rather pricey. Cycling, on the other hand, is a fast and efficient way of getting around, both in the city centre and further afield, as long as you don't mind a few cobbled streets and the odd hill along the way.

For information on getting around **Glasgow**, see p261. Travel information for other destinations is given in the **Around Edinburgh** chapter (see p262).

Public transport

Buses

Edinburgh has extensive bus networks that give ready access to most of the city, day and night. The ubiquitous maroon and white buses (some now being displaced by harlequin red, gold and white low floor buses) are run by **Lothian Buses** (voted Britain's best bus company 2003), which has a seven-day, 24-hour telephone enquiry line, on 555 6363. Also, check the website: www.lothianbuses. co.uk. Lothian Buses' city centre Travelshops (see below) provide details and maps of all Lothian Buses services in Edinburgh and the Lothians.

Throughout this guide, we have listed Lothian Buses only, as they cover the majority of

bus services throughout Edinburgh and into Mid and East Lothian. As parts of town are served by many different routes, we have grouped buses for three of the busiest streets or areas together in our listings.

Below are the groupings used, together with a list of bus routes that serve those streets or areas:
Princes Street buses (not all routes travel the full length of street) 1, 3, 4, 8, 10, 11, 12, 15, 16, 17, 19, 22, 23, 24, 25, 26, 27, 28, 29, 30, 31, 33, 34, 36, 37, 37A, 41, 42, 44, 44A, 45.
Nicolson Street–North Bridge buses
3, 5, 7, 8, 14, 29, 29A, 31, 33, 37, 37A, 49.
Playhouse buses
1, 4, 5, 7, 8, 10, 11, 12, 14, 15, 15A, 16, 17, 19, 19A, 22, 25, 26, 34, 44, 44A, 45, 49.

Edinburgh's other main bus company is FirstBus (www.firstbus.co.uk), which incorporates SMT, Eastern Scottish, Lowland Omnibuses and Midland Scottish. Although both Firstbus and Lothian Buses run parallel services along some routes at similar prices, day tickets are unfortunately not transferable between the companies. For information on Firstbus services and routes, call 663 9233. For sightseeing tours, see p67.

Lothian Buses Travelshops

27 Hanover Street, New Town (554 4494/www.lothianbuses.com). Bus 23, 27, 28, 41, 42, 45/Princes Street buses. **Open** 8.30am-6pm Mon-Sat. **Map** p304 C1.
Other locations: 7 Shandwick Place, New Town. Waverley Bridge, New Town.

Night buses

Night buses, operated by Lothian Buses, run seven days a week and depart from Waverley Steps at 12.15am, 1.15am, 2.15am, 4.15am Sun-Thur and 12.15am, 1.15am, 2.15am, 3.15am Fri, Sat. There is a flat fare of £1.60, which allows one passenger to make one transfer to another night service at Waverley Bridge, on production of a valid ticket. A free map and timetable can be picked up at Lothian Buses Travelshops.

Fares

Bus fares are based on a stage system; fares and fare stages are listed on individual service timetable leaflets and at bus stops. Bus drivers don't give change, so ensure you have the correct fare before boarding. Prices, offers and concessions are subject to change, so contact a Lothian Buses Travelshop or phone for information.

Adult fares

Single journey tickets start from 80p which will carry you from 1 to 8 stages in your journey; if the trip goes to 9 or more stages then it costs a flat fare of £1. You can buy a **Daysaver** multiple journey ticket from the driver of the first bus you board (or from Travelshops). This costs £2.50 and allows unlimited travel around the Lothian Buses network for a day (not Airlink or tours). It's worth waiting till 9.30am to get an off-peak Bargain Daysaver, which costs £1.80 and is valid for the rest of the day.

Child fares

Children under 5 travel free (up to a maximum of two children per adult passenger). The children's fare is charged for ages 5 to 15 inclusive: a flat fare of 60p per journey. A **Child Daysaver** ticket is £1.80.

Ridacard

The GoSmart! Electronic Ridacard gives unlimited travel on normal Lothian Buses services (but not tours). For adults, a one week Ridacard costs £11; 4wks £33. Junior Ridacards (ages 5-15 inclusive) are £7 for 1wk; £21 for 4wks. Buy from Lothian Buses Travelshops (see left).

Trains

Most rail services in Scotland are run by **Scotrail**. Details of services and fares are available from National Rail Enquiries (08457 484950, 24hr) or can be found on the website: www.thetrainline.co.uk. Specific Scotrail information can be found at www.scotrail. co.uk. The information desk at Waverley station (see p274) has timetables and details of discount travel, season tickets and international travel.

As well as Waverley and Haymarket (see p274), the city has several suburban stations including South Gyle, Slateford and Edinburgh Park.

Directory

Taxis

Black cabs

Most of Edinburgh's taxis are black cabs. They take up to five passengers and have facilities for travellers with disabilities. When a taxi's yellow 'For Hire' light is on, you can stop it in the street. Many taxi companies take credit cards, but check when you book or get in. After midnight taxis are scarce, in demand, and charge more. If you want to phone for a taxi, use the *Yellow Pages*; larger companies with facilities for the disabled traveller and a 24-hour service are **Central Radio Taxis** (229 2468), **City Cabs** (228 1211) and **Computer Cabs** (272 8000).

Private hire cars

Minicabs (saloon cars) are generally cheaper than black cabs and may be able to accommodate more passengers (some use people carriers for up to eight passengers). Reputable private-hire companies include **Bluebird Private Hire** (621 6666), and **Persevere Private Hire** (554 8222). It's a good idea to call around first to get the best price. Complaints or compliments about a taxicab or private hire company journey can be made to the Licensing Board, 343 High Street, Edinburgh EH1 1PW (529 4260). Be sure to make a note of the date and time of the journey and the licence number of the vehicle.

Cycling

Edinburgh is a great, if tiring, place to cycle around, thanks to some successful lobbying by the local cycle campaign Spokes (232 Dalry Road, EH11 2JG, 313 2114/www.spokes. org.uk). The city council has invested in some off-road cycle paths and road-edge cycle lanes. Although it is not compulsory for motorists to observe the latter, the lanes ease the flow of cyclists during rush hours and make some roads safer. Cyclists can travel freely along bus lanes.

Be sensible when tethering a bike in the street: the Grassmarket, Rose Street and other pub-infested areas are prone to vandalism and theft is a problem. Otherwise, the only real worries for cyclists not on mountain bikes are the steep and cobbled streets around the Old Town.

One of the joys of cycling in Edinburgh is that you can fly from one side of town to the other in minutes, even when the roads are blocked during the Festival – vital if you're to get to that show in time. A bike can also help to make areas outside the centre remarkably accessible. Spokes produces three cycle maps that show all the cycle routes and paths for Edinburgh, Midlothian and West Lothian (all £4.95). Other good sources of information on cycling in Edinburgh and beyond can be found on the websites: www.edinburghbicycle.com and www.sustrans.org.

Bike hire

BikeTrax Cycle Hire

7-11 Lochrin Place, South Edinburgh (228 6633/www.biketrax.co.uk). Bus 11, 15, 16, 17. **Open** *May-Oct* 9.30am-6pm Mon-Fri; 9am-5.30pm Sat; 12-5pm Sun. *Nov-Apr* 9.30am-5.30pm Mon-Sat. **Hire** from £10 per day; £60 per week. **Deposit** £100 per bike. **Credit** MC, V. **Map** p309 D7.

Edinburgh Cycle Hire

29 Blackfriars Street, Old Town (556 5560/www.cyclescotland.co.uk). Nicolson Street–North Bridge buses. **Open** *May-Oct* 9am-9pm daily. *Nov-Apr* 10am-6pm daily. **Hire** £10-£15 per day; £50-£70 per wk. **Deposit** credit card details. **Credit** AmEx, MC, V. **Map** p310 G5.
Also organises Scottish cycle safaris, and in the summer there are daily tours of Edinburgh city centre.

Driving

The city centre has an expanding network of one-way streets and pedestrian-only areas. This can make driving in the centre a frustrating experience. Princes Street has limited access for private vehicles and is best avoided. A knock-on effect of this is that the surrounding roads are becoming increasingly busy: slow-moving traffic is the norm, especially during rush hours (7.30-9.30am, 4.30-7pm Mon-Fri). In addition to overcrowded roads, circuitous one-way routes and traffic jams, there are stringent parking restrictions, so the whole driving process may leave you feeling harassed and frustrated.

The City of Edinburgh Council intends to hold a referendum in late 2004 on the possible introduction of London-style congestion charges, where you would have to pay to enter the city centre in your car; although, if approved, the eventual introduction of the scheme would be some way off.

The council employs a notoriously efficient private company to keep the streets clear of illegally parked cars. So if you park illegally, it is highly probable that you will get a parking fine. For the purposes of on-street car parking, the city is divided up into central and peripheral zones. In the central zone you must pay for parking between 8.30am and 6pm Mon-Sat. In the peripheral zone, payment must be made between 8.30am and 5pm Mon-Sat. Payment is either by parking meter or on-street pay-and-display ticket vending machines. Outside these zones, on-street parking is free.

The fine for parking illegally is £60 (reduced to £30 if it is paid within a fortnight). Worse, if your car is causing an obstruction, it can be towed away and impounded (*see below*). The good news is that, in Scotland, the clamping of vehicles has been ruled illegal; don't let that lull you into a false sense of security, however, as zealous traffic wardens patrol the city centre.

During August, the Festival makes things even worse. The High Street is pedestrianised, while Chambers Street and others are also used as coach parks for the Tattoo: cars left here will be impounded.

Vehicle removal

If your car has been impounded, a fee of £105 is levied for removal, plus a £12 storage fee for every day the vehicle remains uncollected. This is in addition to the £60 parking ticket. Impounded cars are taken to the Edinburgh Car Compound, which keeps a log of all cars held. If your car has been stolen you should report it at once to the police.

Edinburgh Car Compound
57 Tower Street, Leith (555 1742). Bus 13, 36. **Open** 7am-9pm Mon-Sat; 8.45am-11.30am Sun. **Credit** MC, V. **Map** p311 Kx.

24-hour car parks

Greenside Car Park
Greenside Row, Broughton (558 3518). **Map** p307 G4.

Morrison Street Car Park
Morrison Street, West Edinburgh (no phone). **Map** p308 C6.

National Car Parks
Castle Terrace, Old Town (229 2870). **Map** p304 A3.

National Car Parks
Potterrow, South Edinburgh (668 4661). **Map** p310 G6.

St James Centre
Leith Street, Broughton (556 5066). **Map** p307 G4.

Waverley Car Park
6 New Street, Old Town (557 8526). **Map** p310 G5.

Breakdown services

If you are a member of a motoring organisation in your home country, check to see if it has a reciprocal agreement with a British organisation. The principle UK organisations are:

AA (Automobile Association)
Fanum House, Basing View, Basingstoke, Hampshire, RG21 4EA (enquiries 0870 600 0371/emergency breakdown 0800 887766/insurance 0800 444777/www.theaa.com). **Open** 24hrs daily. **Credit** MC, V.
If you break down you can call the AA and become a member on the spot for £144. Its information line (08705 500600) gives information on International Driving Permits and route maps. The AA also offers a premium rate service for Roadwatch and Weatherwatch on 09003 401100.

Environmental Transport Association
68 High Street, Weybridge, Surrey, KT13 8RS (0800 212810/www.eta.co.uk). **Open** 8am-6pm Mon-Fri; 9am-4pm Sat. *Breakdown service* 24hrs daily. **Credit** MC, V.
The green alternative, if you don't want part of your membership fee to be used for lobbying the government into building more roads, which is what happens with the AA and RAC.

RAC
Great Park Road, Bradley Stoke, Bristol, BS32 4QN (enquiries 08705 722722/breakdown 0800 828 282/motor insurance 08453 000 755/new membership 0800 722822/www.rac.co.uk). **Open** Office 8am-9pm Mon-Fri; 8.30am-5pm Sat, 10am-4pm Sun. *Breakdown service* 24hrs daily. **Credit** AmEx, MC, V.

Car hire

To hire a car, you must have at least one year's driving experience and be in possession of a current full driving licence with no serious endorsements. Most firms insist you be over 21 and book by credit card. Overseas visitors, particularly those whose national driving licence is not readily readable by English speakers, are recommended to acquire an

International Driving Licence before travelling.

Prices for car hire vary considerably between companies, and may be subject to change, so it's a good idea to ring around to find the deal that suits you best. A few of the more reputable companies are given below. Be sure to check exactly what insurance is included in the price. Also ask about deals when booking.

Arnold Clark
Lochrin Place, Tollcross (228 4747/www.arnoldclark.co.uk). Bus 1, 10, 11, 15, 16, 17, 23, 24, 27, 28, 45, 34, 35, 15a. **Open** 8am-7pm Mon-Fri; 8am-6pm Sat; 11am-6pm Sun. **Credit** DC, MC, V (no cash). **Map** p309 D7.
A full range of vehicles is available for hire. Free courtesy coach to and from Edinburgh Airport (from Bankhead Drive branch only). Cheapest rental rates are £19 per day; £44 weekend; £95 seven days. You must be aged between 23 and 75 to hire here. £100 deposit necessary. The Lochrin Place branch is most convenient for central Edinburgh car hire.
Other locations: 38 Seafield Road East, Duddingston (669 5030); 16 Bankhead Drive, West Edinburgh (458 1501).

Hertz
Edinburgh Airport (333 1019/central reservations 0870 599 6699/www.hertz.co.uk). **Open** Phone line 24hrs daily. Office 6.30am-11pm Mon-Fri; 8am 11pm Sat, Sun **Credit** AmEx, DC, MC, V.
A wide range of manual and automatic vehicles. Cheapest rental, all inclusive, is £53 per day; £74 weekend; £179 seven days. It is cheaper to hire in town than at the airport. You must be 25 or over.
Other location: 10 Picardy Place; New Town (556 8311).

National Car Rental
Edinburgh Airport (333 1922/central reservations 0870 600 6666/freephone 0800 263263/www.nationalcar.com). **Open** Phone line 24hrs daily. Office 7am-10pm Mon-Fri; 8am-10pm Sat, Sun. **Credit** AmEx, DC, MC, V.
A wide range of manual and automatic vehicles, one-way rates and a delivery and collection service. The cheapest rental, all inclusive, is £36 per day; £55 weekend; £164.75 seven days. You must be 21 or over and have a credit card.
Other location: 39 Roseburn Street, Murrayfield (337 8686).

Directory

Resources A-Z

Age restrictions

You have to be 18 to drink in Scotland, though there are some bars and clubs that admit over-21s only. Seventeen is the legal age for driving, though most car rental companies won't hire cars to people under 21. Sixteen is the legal age of consent.

Business

Conferences & conventions

Edinburgh Convention Bureau

4 Rothesay Terrace, New Town, EH3 7RY (473 3666/fax 473 3636/www. edinburgh.org/conference). Bus 13, 19, 29, 36, 37, 41, 42. **Open** 9am-5pm Mon-Fri. **Map** p308 B5.
The ECB offers advice on finding a conference venue and help with the necessary organisation.

Edinburgh International Conference Centre

The Exchange, 150 Morrison Street, West Edinburgh, EH3 8EE (300 3000/www.eicc.co.uk). Bus 1, 2, 22, 28, 34. **Open** *telephone enquiries & office* 8am-6pm Mon-Fri. **Map** p308 C6.
In the modern surroundings of the city's new financial centre, the Exchange, the EICC can accommodate up to 1,200 delegates and offers in-house catering as well as business services.

Couriers & shippers

All the major international couriers are active in Edinburgh. See the Edinburgh telephone directory or *Yellow Pages* for further details. All companies listed below can arrange pick-up.

DHL

Unit 15/4-15/5 South Gyle Crescent, South Gyle Industrial Estate, West Edinburgh (08703 661200/www. dhl.com). **Open** *Phone line* 24hrs daily. **Credit** AmEx, DC, MC, V.
Worldwide express delivery service. Next-day deliveries can be made

within the EU (not guaranteed), and for documents to the USA if booked before 2pm.

Federal Express

1/16 Spitfire House, West Edinburgh Cargo Airport (0800 123800/www. fedex.com/gb). **Open** *Phone line* 7.30am-7.30pm daily. **Credit** AmEx, MC, V.
FedEx can deliver next day by 8am (premium service) or 10.30am (standard service) to certain destinations across the USA (mainly New York and other major cities). More than 210 countries served.

UPS

30 South Gyle Crescent, South Gyle Industrial Estate, West Edinburgh (08457 877877/www.ups.com). **Open** 8am-8pm Mon-Fri; 8am-1.30pm Sat. **Credit** AmEx, MC, V.
UPS offers express delivery to more than 200 countries; cheaper, slower services are also available. Deliveries to some destinations can be guaranteed to arrive by 9am or 10.30am the next day.

Equipment hire

Sound & Vision AV

11B South Gyle Crescent, West Edinburgh, EH12 9EB (334 3324/ www.sound-and-vision.co.uk). Bus 2, 12, 18, 21, 22, 24. **Open** 8.30am-5.30pm Mon-Fri. **Credit** MC, V.
Will hire out anything required for a presentation, including PCs, and can produce graphics. Keeps a van full of equipment ready to come to the rescue in case of emergencies.

Import & export

Companies House

Argyle House, 37 Castle Terrace, South Edinburgh, EH1 2EB (0870 333 3636/www.companieshouse. gov.uk). Bus 11, 15, 16, 34, 35. **Open** *Office* 9am-5pm Mon-Fri. *Telephone enquiries* 8.30am-6pm Mon-Fri. **Map** p304 A3.
Companies House incorporates new limited companies and partnerships. In order to export goods you must be registered here. It also has information on Scottish companies and foreign companies registered in Scotland.

Customs & Excise

Glasgow office: 21 India Street, Glasgow G2 4PZ (0845 010 9000/www.hmce.gov.uk). **Open** *Phone line* 8am-8pm Mon-Fri. *Office* 9am-4.30pm Mon-Fri.

The Glasgow office deals with all Scottish import/export licences and information, as well as enquiries about VAT.

Office hire & business centres

Edinburgh Office Business Centre & Conference Venue

16-26 Forth Street, Broughton, EH1 3LH (550 3700/fax 550 3701/www. edinburghoffice.co.uk). Bus 8, 17. **Open** 8.30am-5.30pm Mon-Thur; 8.30am-5pm Fri. **Map** p307 G3.
Over 60 office spaces, ranging from 85 to 775sq ft, with prices starting from £175 per month.

Regus

Conference House, The Exchange, 152 Morrison Street, West Edinburgh, EH3 8EB (200 6000/ fax 200 6200/www.regus.com). Bus 2, 28. **Open** 8.30am-6pm Mon-Fri. **Map** p308 C6.
Conference House contains one- to 67-person office suites, starting at £1,000 per month. A fully furnished office can be provided, with phones, PCs, secretarial support and catering. Conference space can also be hired.

Rutland Square House

12 Rutland Square, New Town, EH1 2BB (228 2281/fax 228 3637/www. braemore.co.uk). Bus 3, 12, 25, 31, 33. **Open** 8.30am-5.30pm Mon-Fri. **Map** p308 C6.
Twelve fully furnished offices, from £400 per month. All are hired out on a three-month minimum basis.

Secretarial services

Office Angels

95 George Street, New Town, EH2 3ES (226 6112/fax 220 6850/www. office-angels.com). Bus 28, 37, 41, 42/Princes Street buses. **Open** 8.45am-5.30pm Mon-Fri. **Map** p304 B1.
Hires out office staff at all levels, although it doesn't deal with accountants or IT specialists.

Reed Employment Solutions

13 Frederick Street, New Town, EH2 2BY (226 3687/fax 247 5900/ www.reed.co.uk). Bus 28, 37, 41, 42/Princes Street buses. **Open** 8am-6pm Mon-Fri. **Map** p304 B1.
Temporary and permanent office, secretarial and call centre staff.

Translators & interpreters

Berlitz
26 Frederick Street, New Town, EH2 2JR (226 7198/www.language centres.com). Bus 28, 41, 42/Princes Street buses. **Open** 9am-7.30pm Mon-Fri. **Map** p304 B1.
Berlitz will translate from or into any language. Phone for rates.

Integrated Language Services
School of Languages, Heriot-Watt University, Riccarton, EH14 4AS (451 3159/www.hw.ac.uk/ils). Bus 25, 34, 35, 45. **Open** 9am-5pm Mon-Fri.
All European languages, and most others, can be translated. ILS also supplies interpreters and interpreting equipment for conferences. Rates available on request.

Useful organisations

Edinburgh Chamber of Commerce & Enterprise
27 Melville Street, West Edinburgh, EH3 7JF (477 7000/www.ecce.org). Bus 2, 26. **Open** 8.30am-5.30pm Mon-Fri. **Map** p308 C5.

Scottish Enterprise Edinburgh & Lothian
Apex House, 99 Haymarket Terrace, West Edinburgh, EH12 5HD (SIS 4000/www.scottish-enterprise.com/edinburghandlothian). Bus 3, 3A, 21, 25. **Open** 9am-5pm Mon-Fri. **Map** p308 A6.
A government-funded economic development agency. The Small Business Gateway division specialises in helping small businesses start up.

Scottish Executive
St Andrew's House, Regent Road, Calton Hill, EH1 3DG (556 8400/www.scotland.gov.uk). Bus 3, 7, 8, 14, 19, 19A. **Open** 8.30am-5pm Mon-Fri. **Map** p307 H4.
This is a good starting point from which to reach the relevant government departments, such as Enterprise and Tourism, or Economic and Industrial Affairs.

Consumer

If you pay with a credit card, you can cancel payment or get reimbursed if there is a problem. Consider travel insurance that protects you against financial loss. The local trading standards office at the **Advice Shop**, or the **Citizens Advice Bureau** (for both, *see p282*), can advise if there is a problem.

Customs

When entering the UK, non-EU citizens and anyone buying duty-free goods have the following import limits:
● 200 cigarettes or 100 cigarillos or 250 grams (8.82 ounces) of tobacco.
● 2 litres still table wine plus either 1 litre spirits or strong liqueurs (over 22% alcohol by volume) or 2 litres fortified wine (under 22% abv), sparkling wine or other liqueurs.
● 60cc/ml perfume.
● 250cc/ml toilet water.
● Other goods to the value of: £75 for EU citizens purchasing from another EU country or £145 for travellers arriving from outside the EU.

No one under 17 is entitled to make use of the alcohol or tobacco allowances.

The import of meat, poultry, fruit, plants, flowers and protected animals is restricted or forbidden; there are no restrictions on the import or export of currency. People over the age of 17 arriving from an EU country have been able to import unlimited goods for their own personal use, if bought tax-paid (ie not duty-free). However, the law sets out guidance levels for what is for personal use (and it's not as much as you might expect or hope), so if you exceed them you must be able to satisfy officials that the goods are not for resale. Just remember, they've heard it all before. For all other enquiries phone 0845 010 9000 or check the website www.hmce.gov.uk.

HM Customs & Excise
Edinburgh Airport (344 3196). **Open** 6am-11pm daily.

Disabled

Listed buildings are not allowed to widen their entrances or add ramps, and parts of the Old Town have very narrow pavements, making it hard for wheelchair users to get around. However, equal opportunity legislation requires new buildings to be fully accessible – step forward the **Festival Theatre** (*see p239*), the **Omni Centre** (*see p208*) and the new **Museum of Scotland** (*see p88*).
The newer black taxis can all take wheelchairs, as can some private hire cars. Lothian Buses is replacing its buses with low-floor versions, with easy access for wheelchairs. Bus routes using low-floor buses at the time of writing are 3, 13, 16, 20, 22, 24, 26, 29, 30, 35, 36, 37, 37A, 38, 44, 44A, 49, Airlink 100 and all night buses (ring 554 6363 for up-to-date details).

Edinburgh City Council publishes a booklet, *Transport in Edinburgh: A Guide for Disabled People*. This gives information on transport accessibility, and services and assistance available to people with disabilities; it also includes a list of useful contact addresses and phone numbers. The booklet is free and can be requested on 469 3891.

Most theatres and cinemas are fitted with induction loops for the hard of hearing – ask when you're booking.

For more information, contact the following:

Grapevine
Norton Park, 57 Albion Road, Calton Hill, EH7 (475 2370/grapevine@lcodp.demon.co.uk). **Open** *Telephone enquiries* 10am-4pm Mon-Fri.
Publishes the free *Access Guide to Edinburgh*.

Drugs

Despite confusion over cannabis's reclassification as a Class C drug early in 2004, both hard and soft drugs are illegal in Scotland, as they are in the rest of the country (*see p163* **EdinBurgher Kevin Williamson**).

Directory

Electricity

The UK electricity supply is 220-240 volt, 50-cycle AC rather than the 110-120 volt, 60-cycle AC used in the US. Plugs are standard three-point. Adaptors for US appliances can be bought at airports. TV and video employ different systems to the US, so it will not be possible to play back American camcorder footage till you get home.

Embassies & consulates

For a full list of consular offices in Edinburgh, consult the *Yellow Pages* under Consuls and/or Embassies.

American Consulate General
3 Regent Terrace, Calton Hill, EH7 5BW (556 8315/www.usembassy. org.uk/scotland). Bus 1, 3, 5, 19, 19A, 25. **Open** *Phone enquiries* 8.30am-noon, 1-5pm Mon-Fri. *Personal callers* (emergencies only) 1-5.30pm Tues or by appointment. *After hours emergency* call 01224 857097. **Map** p307 H4.
A limited consular service; no visas or passport replacement.

Australian Consulate
37 George Street, New Town, EH2 (624 3333). Bus 28, 37, 41, 42/Princes Street buses. **Open** phone for times. **Map** p304 B1.
Offers basic services where a personal appearance is required, such as the witnessing of documents.

Consulate General of the Federal Republic of Germany
16 Eglinton Crescent, New Town, EH12 5DG (337 2323/german. consulate@btconnect.com). Bus 12, 13, 26, 31. **Open** 9am-noon Mon-Fri. **Map** p308 A6.
A comprehensive service including issuing visas.

French Consulate General
11 Randolph Crescent, New Town, EH3 (general enquiries only 225 7954/visa enquiries 220 6324/visa enquiry line 0891 600215/passports 225 3377/legal 220 0141). Bus 13, 19, 29, 29A, 37, 37A. **Open** *Visas* 9.30-11.30am Mon-Fri. *Passports/ID*

cards 9.30am-1pm Mon-Fri; by appointment 2-5pm Mon-Fri. **Map** p308 C5.

Italian Consulate General
32 Melville Street, New Town, EH3 7HA (226 3631/220 3695/fax 226 6260). Bus 3, 4, 12, 25, 25A, 41, 42. **Open** *Phone enquiries* 9.30am-5pm Mon-Fri. *Personal callers* 9.30am-12.30pm Mon-Fri. **Map** p308 B5.

Spanish Consulate
63 North Castle Street, New Town, EH2 3LJ (220 1843/fax 226 4568). Bus 28, 37, 41, 42/Princes Street buses. **Open** *Phone enquiries* 9am-3pm Mon-Fri. *Personal callers* 9am-noon Mon-Fri.* **Map** p304 B1.

Emergencies

In the event of a serious accident, fire or incident, call 999 and specify whether you require an ambulance, the fire service or the police. *See also* **Helplines**, *p282.*

Gay & lesbian

Help & information

Lesbian Line
557 0751. **Open** 7.30-10pm Mon, Thur.
A helpline for lesbians.

Lothian Gay & Lesbian Switchboard
556 4049. **Open** 7.30-10pm daily.
Advice on sexual health and HIV/AIDS for gay men and lesbians.

Groups & organisations

Edinburgh Gay Women's Group
Meets 8pm Wed at Sala (LGBT Centre, 58A & 60 Broughton Street, Broughton– *see p215*).
A weekly social group for women.

Gay Dads Scotland
www.gaydadsscotland.org.uk. **Meets** 8pm last Thur of month at LGBT Centre, 58A & 60 Broughton Street, Broughton.
Monthly meeting for gay fathers.

Icebreakers
Information 556 9331. **Meets** 7.30pm every 2nd Wed, CC Blooms (*see p216*).

Group for lesbians, gay men, bisexuals and transgendered people who want to meet similar.

Juice
Information 661 0982. **Meets** 2-4pm Fri at Solas, 2-4 Abbeymount, Calton Hill.
Gay men effected by HIV and AIDS meet every Friday in a group offering information, activities and support. A similar group for women, Isis, meets at the same place, 1-3pm Tue.

LGBT Youth Project
Information 0845 113 0005/ www.lgbtyouth.org.uk. **Meets** 7-9pm Tue LGBT Centre.
Project for young lesbians, gay men, bisexuals and transgendered people under the age of 26.

Health

National Health Service (NHS) treatment is free to those who fall into one of the following categories:
● European Union (EU) nationals, plus those of Iceland, Norway and Liechtenstein.
● European Economic Area (EEA) nationals living in an EEA state.
● Nationals/residents of countries with which the UK has a reciprocal agreement.
● Anyone who at the time of receiving treatment has been in the UK for the previous 12 months.
● Anyone who has come to the UK to take up permanent residence.
● Students on full-time recognised courses of study from anywhere in the world.
● Refugees and others seeking refuge in the UK.
● Anyone formally detained by the Immigration Authorities.
There are no NHS charges for any of the following services:
● Treatment in accident and emergency departments.
● Emergency ambulance transport.
● Diagnosis and treatment of certain communicable diseases, including STDs.
● Family planning services.
● Compulsory psychiatric treatment.
If you do not fit into any of the above categories, but you want to find out if you still qualify for free treatment, then contact:

Primary Care Department
Lothian Health, Stevenson House, 555 Gorgie Road, West Edinburgh, EH11 3LE (536 5200).

Directory

Accident & emergency

The 24-hour casualty department serving Edinburgh is located at:

Royal Infirmary of Edinburgh
51 Little France Crescent, EH16 (536 1000). Bus 8, 18, 24, 32, 33, 38, 49.

Chemists

Many drugs cannot be bought over the counter. A pharmacist will dispense medicines on receipt of a prescription from a doctor. An NHS prescription costs £6.30 per item at present. A late-opening dispensing chemist is **Boots** (46 Shandwick Place, New Town; 225 6757; open 8am-8pm Mon-Fri; 8am-6pm Sat; 10.30am-4.30pm Sun). For other pharmacies, *see p190.*

Complementary medicine

Edinburgh has a thriving alternative medicine scene. Some of the more established and reliable outfits are listed below – they will provide appointments for everything from chiropractors and osteopaths to herbalists and acupuncturists.

Napiers Dispensary and Clinic
18 Bristo Place, Old Town (225 5542/www.napiers.net). Bus 23, 27, 28, 41, 42, 45. **Open** 10am-6pm Mon; 9am-6pm Tue-Fri; 9am-5.30pm Sat; 12.30-4.30pm Sun. **Map** p309 F6.
A long established herbalist that stocks a wide range of herbs and remedies. The dispensary also has a clinic staffed by a variety of alternative practitioners.

Whole Works
Jackson's Close, 209 High Street, Old Town (225 8092/www.the wholeworks.co.uk). Bus 35/Nicolson Street–North Bridge buses. **Open** 9am-8pm Mon-Fri; 9am-5pm Sat. **Map** p304 D3.
Busy city centre clinic providing a wide range of different therapies.

Contraception & abortion

Abortions are free to British citizens on the National Health Service (NHS). This also applies to EU residents and foreign nationals living, working or studying in Britain. Two doctors must agree that an abortion is justified within the terms of the Abortion Act 1967, as amended, whether it is on the NHS or not. If you decide to go private, contact one of the organisations below. Edinburgh operates a system to provide free condoms to all who sign up. Again, contact the below organisations for more information.

Caledonia Youth (formerly the Brook Advisory Clinic)
5 Castle Terrace, South Edinburgh (229 3596). Bus 1, 10, 11, 15, 16, 17, 22, 34. **Open** noon-6pm Mon-Thur; noon-3.30pm Fri; noon-2.30pm Sat. No appointment necessary. **Map** p304 A3.
Advice on contraception, sexual problems and abortion, with referral to an NHS hospital or private clinic. Contraception, sexual advice and counselling for young people under 25, including pregnancy advice and emergency contraception. For visitors based outside Scotland, a £25 consultation fee is payable, plus any prescription costs.

Family Planning & Well Woman Services
18 Dean Terrace, Stockbridge (332 7941). Bus 19, 19A, 24, 29, 36, 42. **Open** *Switchboard* 8.30am-7.30pm Mon-Thur; 8.30am-4pm Fri; 9.30am-noon Sat. *General clinics* 9.30am-7.30pm Mon, Tue, Thur (by appointment); 9.30am-1pm, 5-7.30pm Wed. *Young people's clinic (under-20s)* 3.30-4.15pm Mon-Wed. *Young people's clinic (under-25s)* 9.30-11.30am Sat. **Map** p305 C4.
Confidential advice, contraceptive provision, pregnancy tests and abortion referral. As an NHS-run clinic, covered under the European Union E111 scheme, it provides most services free, though some charges may apply to overseas visitors. Post-abortion, pre-menstrual syndrome, menopause and psychosexual counselling is also offered. Note that, except in emergencies, you must make an appointment first.

Dental services

Dental care is free only to UK citizens in certain categories. All other patients, NHS or private, must pay; certain categories of people from some countries may be eligible for reduced dental costs. For advice, and to find an NHS dentist, contact the Primary Care Department (*see p280*). Emergency dental treatment can be obtained at:

Edinburgh Dental Institute
Lauriston Building, Lauriston Place, South Edinburgh (536 4955). Bus 23, 27, 28, 45. **Open** 9am-3pm Mon-Fri. **Map** p309 E7.
Free walk-in emergency clinic.

Western General Hospital
Crewe Road South, Stockbridge (537 1338). Bus 19, 19A, 28, 29, 37, 37A, 38. **Open** 6.30-8.30pm daily; 9.30am-11.30am Sat, Sun. Walk-in emergency clinic, for tourists/Lothian residents only; NHS charges and exemptions apply.

Doctors

If you're a British citizen or working in the city, you can go to any GP for diagnosis and treatment. People who are ordinarily resident in the UK, such as overseas students, can also register with an NHS doctor. For a list of names of GPs in your area, contact the Primary Care Department (*see p280*).

If you are not eligible to see an NHS doctor, you will be charged the cost price for medicines prescribed by a private doctor.

Hospitals

The Royal Infirmary moved from the centre of the city in Lauriston Place to newly built premises on the southern perimeter of the city at Little France in 2003. However, the Eye Pavilion, Dental Hospital and GUM clinic will remain in Lauriston Place (*see above*).

Royal Infirmary

51 Little France Crescent, EH16 (536 1000). Bus 8, 18, 24, 32, 33, 38, 49.

Opticians

For dispensing opticians, *see p190.*

Princess Alexandra Eye Pavilion

Chalmers Street, South Edinburgh (536 3755). Bus 23, 27, 28, 45. **Open** 8.30am-5pm Mon-Fri. **Map** p309 E7.
The Eye Pavilion operates a free walk-in service for emergency eye complaints; otherwise you will need an appointment.

STDs/HIV/AIDS

The Genito-Urinary Medicine (GUM) clinic (*see below*) is affiliated with the Royal Infirmary of Edinburgh. It provides free, confidential advice and treatment of STDs and non-sex related problems, such as thrush (yeast infections) and cystitis (urinary tract infections). It also offers information and counselling on HIV and STDs, and the clinic can conduct a confidential blood test to test for HIV status.

Solas

2-4 Abbeymount, Calton Hill (661 0982/fax 652 1780/www.waverley care.org). Bus 30, 35. **Open** *Drop-in & café* 11am-4pm Mon-Wed, Fri; 11am-5pm Thur. *Phone enquiries* 9am-5pm Mon-Wed, Fri; 9am-7pm Thu. **No credit cards.**
Map p307 J4.
The city's HIV/AIDS information and support centre. A wide range of support services are offered (including counselling, arts workshops, and support for children and young people).

Genito-Urinary Medicine Clinic

Lauriston Building, Lauriston Place, South Edinburgh (536 2103). Bus 8, 24, 33, 45. **Open** 8.30am-1pm, 2-5pm Mon-Thur; 8.30am-1pm, 2-4.30pm Fri. *Walk-in clinic* (emergencies only) 8.30-10am Mon-Fri; otherwise by appointment. **Map** p309 E7.
Free and confidential service that offers counselling for people who are HIV positive.

Advice Shop

South Bridge, Old Town (225 1255). Nicolson Street–North Bridge buses. **Open** *Phone lines* 8.30am-5pm Mon-Thur; 8.30am-4.40pm Fri. *Drop-in service* 9.30am-4pm Mon-Thur; 9.30am-3.30pm Fri.
Advice on consumer problems and welfare benefits.

Alcoholics Anonymous

(225 2727/www.alcoholicsanony mous.org.uk). **Open** 24hrs daily.
Confidential, round-the-clock help and advice on drinks problems.

Childline

(0800 1111/www.childline.org.uk). **Open** 24hrs daily.
Free and confidential national helpline for children and young people in trouble or danger.

Citizens Advice Bureau

58 Dundas Street, New Town (557 1500/fax 557 3543/www.cas.org.uk/ www.adviceguide.org.uk). Bus 23, 27. **Open** 9.30am-4pm Mon, Tue, Thur; 9.30am-12.30pm, 6.30-8pm Wed. **Map** p306 E3.
Citizens Advice Bureaux are independent, offering free advice on legal, financial and personal matters. The only city-centre branch is at the above address. The Wednesday afternoon sessions specifically deal with money advice. Check the phone book for other branches. The Citizens Advice Scotland website has contact details for all bureaux in Scotland.

Drinkline

0800 917 8282. **Open** 7am-11pm Mon-Fri; 24hrs Sat, Sun.
For help with drink and related problems.

Edinburgh Rape & Sexual Abuse Centre

556 9437.
Free, confidential rape counselling. If there's no answer, leave a message and someone will call you back as soon as possible.

Edinburgh Women's Aid

4 Cheyne Street, Stockbridge (229 1419). Bus 19, 19A, 24, 29, 36, 42. **Open** 10am-3pm Mon, Wed, Fri; 2-7pm Thur; 10am-1pm Sat.
Refuge referral for women and children experiencing domestic violence. An after-hours answerphone gives numbers for immediate help.

Gamblers Anonymous

(08700 508880/www.gamblersanony mous.org.uk). **Open** 9am-8pm daily.
Advice is offered by members of the fellowship. Referrals to meetings.

Know The Score Helpline

(0800 587 5879/www.knowthescore. info). **Open** 24hrs daily.
A free and confidential service giving advice and information on drugs.

National AIDS Helpline

(0800 567123). **Open** 24hrs daily.
A free and confidential information service on AIDS and sexual health.

NHS Helpline

(0800 224488). **Open** 8am-10pm daily.
A free telephone information service giving details about local NHS services, waiting times, common diseases and conditions.

Rights Office

Southside Community Centre, Nicolson Street, South Edinburgh (667 6339). Nicolson Street–North Bridge buses. **Open** 10am-3.45pm Mon, Wed. **Map** p310 G6.
Walk-in centre giving free, confidential advice and advocacy.

The Samaritans

(National 08457 909090/Edinburgh 221 9999/www.samaritans.org). **Open** 24hrs daily.
The Samaritans will listen to anyone with an emotional problem.

Victim Support

(Edinburgh helpline 0845 603 9213/national helpline 0845 303 0900). **Open** *Edinburgh helpline* 9am-3.30pm Mon-Fri. *National helpline* 9am-4.30pm Mon-Fri.
Victims of crime are put in touch with a volunteer who provides emotional and practical support, including information on legal procedures and compensation. Interpreters can be arranged.

ID

ID is not widely used in the UK, although there are plans for compulsory identity cards. You will need your passport for changing money, travellers' cheques and so on. When driving, carry your International Driving Licence in case you're stopped; if you don't have it you'll need to produce it at a police station within seven days.

Directory

Insurance

You should arrange insurance to cover personal belongings before travelling to Edinburgh, as it is difficult to organise once you have arrived.

Non-UK citizens should ensure that medical insurance is included in their travel insurance. If your country has a reciprocal medical treatment arrangement with the UK you will have limited cover, but you should make sure you have the necessary documentation before you arrive. If you cannot access the information in your own country, contact the Primary Care Department in Edinburgh (see p280).

Internet

Internet access is abundant in Edinburgh. Some public libraries have internet access and more is planned. Most payphones have internet kiosks attached. There are also plenty of internet cafés see below.

Internet access

easyInternetcafé

58 Rose Street, New Town (220 3577/www.easyinternetcafe.com). Princes Street buses. **Open** 8am-10pm daily.
Sharing floor space with Caffè Nero (see p153) creates a relaxed atmosphere, and with over 400 computers available you should not have a problem getting on the web.

Electronic Corner Ltd

Unit 4, Platform 1, Waverley Station, New Town (558 7858). Princes Street buses. **Open** 7.30am-9pm Mon-Fri; 8am-9pm Sat; 9am-9pm Sun.

Galleryinternet.com

44 West Preston Street, Newington (466 7767). **Open** 10am-6pm Mon-Fri.

Inter.net Café ltd

60 Clerk Street, Newington (466 5332). South bridge/Clerk street buses. **Open** 9.30am-10pm Mon-Sat; 11am-10pm Sun.

Micro Computer Centre

7 St Patrick Street, Newington (476 5600). Nicolson Street–North Bridge buses. **Open** 10am-6.30pm Mon-Sat; (June-Dec only) noon-5pm Sun.
Rates start at £1 per half hour. Also specialises in selling computer parts.

Pallas-Athene Internet Café Ltd

28 Marchmont Crescent, Marchmont (667 7711). Bus 5, 24, 42. **Open** 10am-8pm Mon-Sat; 11am-8pm Sun.

Web13

13 Bread Street, South Edinburgh (229 8883/www.web13.co.uk). Bus 2, 28, 35. **Open** 9am-6pm Mon-Sat; noon-6pm Sun; extended hours during festival. **Map** p309 D6.

Wireless internet connection

Wireless internet connection (or WiFi) provides wireless broadband connection to a laptop or PDA. However, it is only available in certain locations (hotspots) that are in range of a transmitter. Currently there are two main providers of WiFi in the United Kingdom, T-Mobile and BT. Payment differs between the two but generally you have to set up a personal account at a hotspot, before buying units of time (an hour, a day, a month) either at the hotspot or online beforehand.

WiFi is only just taking off in Europe after huge success in America. At the time of writing, Edinburgh has about 40 hotspots, where WiFi is available. These are mainly located in coffee houses, especially along the Royal Mile and in some hotels. Both www.wi-fihotspotlist.com and http://intel.jiwire.com both have up to date lists of hotspots in Edinburgh and the UK see p153.

Left luggage

Edinburgh Airport

(344 3486). **Open** 5am-11pm daily.
Located in the check in hall, opposite parking zone E.

St Andrew Bus Station

There are lockers in the station.

Waverley Station

(550 2333). **Open** 7am-11pm daily. Adjacent to Platform 11.

Legal help

If a legal problem arises, contact your embassy, consulate or high commission (see p280). You can get advice from a **Citizens Advice Bureau** (see p282), the **Rights Office** (see p282) or one of the organisations listed below. Ask about Legal Aid eligibility. For leaflets explaining how the system works, write to the **Scottish Legal Aid Board** (see below). Advice on problems concerning visas and immigration can be obtained from the **Immigration Advisory Service** (see below).

Edinburgh & Lothians Race Equality Council

14 Forth Street, Broughton, EH1 3LH (556 0441/admin@lrec.demon. co.uk). Playhouse buses. **Open** *Office* 9am-5pm Mon Fri. **Map** p307 G3.

Immigration Advisory Service

115 Bath Street, Glasgow, G2 (0141 248 2956). **Open** 10am-4pm Mon-Fri. **Map** p314 C2.

Law Society of Scotland

26 Drumsheugh Gardens, New Town, EH3 7YR (226 7411/www. lawscot.org.uk). Bus 13, 19, 29, 29A, 37, 37A, 41, 42. **Open** 9am-5pm Mon-Fri. **Map** p308 C5.

Scottish Legal Aid Board

44 Drumsheugh Gardens, New Town, EH3 7SW (226 7061/ www.slab.org.uk). Bus 13, 19, 29, 29A, 37, 37A, 41, 42. **Open** *Office* 9am-5pm Mon-Fri. *Switchboard* 8.30am-5pm Mon-Fri. **Map** p308 C5.

Libraries

Central Library

George IV Bridge, Old Town (242 8000/www.edinburgh.gov.uk/libraries). Bus 23, 27, 28, 42, 42, 45. **Open** 10am-8pm Mon-Thur; 10am-5pm Fri; 9am-1pm Sat. **Map** p304 C3.

Directory

The library stocks a selection of American and European publications and also has a large reference section (242 8060). You have to be a Lothian resident to join the lending library (242 8020). The Edinburgh Room (242 8030) and the Scottish Room (242 8070) are dedicated to local and Scottish material; staff will show how to use the library to trace their ancestors.

National Library of Scotland

George IV Bridge, Old Town (226 4531/www.nls.uk). Bus 23, 28, 41, 42, 45. **Open** 9.30am-8.30pm Mon, Tue, Thur, Fri; 10am-8.30pm Wed; 9.30am-1pm Sat. **Map** p304 C3.
The National Library of Scotland is a deposit library, entitled to a copy of all works published in the UK and Ireland. It receives as many as 350,000 items annually, including books, pamphlets, periodicals, maps and music. The Reading Rooms are open for reference and research; admission is by ticket to approved applicants. There's also a varied programme of exhibitions on a range of Scottish subjects.

University of Edinburgh Main Library

George Square, South Edinburgh (650 3384/www.lib.ed.ac.uk). Bus 41, 42. **Open** *Term-time* 8.30am-10pm Mon-Thur; 9am-7pm Fri; 9am-5pm Sat; noon-7pm Sun. *Holiday time* 9am-5pm Mon, Tue, Thur, Fri; 9am-9pm Wed. **Map** p310 G7.
With a valid matriculation card or ISIC, international students who aren't studying at the University may use the library for reference purposes only. Alternatively, full membership is available at £30 for 3 months, £55 for 6 months or £110 for 12 months for reference only, and £60/£100/£160 for reference and borrowing.

Lost property

Always inform the police if you lose anything (to validate insurance claims). A lost passport should also be reported at once to your embassy/consulate (*see p280*). The main lost property offices for items left on public transport are:

Edinburgh Airport

(344 3486). **Open** 5am-11pm daily. The lost property office is located in the check in hall. For items lost on the plane, contact the airline or handling agents.

Lothian Buses

Lost Property Office, Annandale Street, Broughton (558 8858). Bus 7, 10, 11, 14, 22, 49. **Open** 10am-1.30pm Mon-Fri. **Map** p307 G2.

Taxis

Edinburgh Police Headquarters, Fettes Avenue, Stockbridge (311 3141). Bus 19, 19A, 28, 29, 29A, 37, 37A, 38. **Open** 9am-5pm Mon-Thu; 9am-4.45pm Fri. **Map** p305 A3.
All property that has been left in a registered black cab, as well as in the street or in shops, gets sent here.

Trains

If items have been lost in railway stations or trains in Scotland, contact the individual station (see the phone book for numbers).

Media

Most of Scotland's newspapers – and much of its TV output – operate on a quasi-national basis pitched somewhere between the regional media and London's self-styled 'national' press.

The attitudes and arguments on display both reflect and illuminate the current state of that nebulous beast known as Scottish identity. From the time-honoured east/west rivalry for the title of Scotland's national daily broadsheet – perpetuated in the battle between the *Scotsman*, published in Edinburgh, and the Glasgow-based *Herald* – to the thorny question of the tabloid *Daily Record*'s Rangers affiliations; from Radio Scotland's Sony Award-winning output to the famously surreal couthiness of the *Sunday Post* letters page, the cultural divergences that impelled the long campaign for devolution continue to pervade the Scottish media.

The battle rages on at the BBC as to whether Scotland should have its own separate six o'clock news slot. Where devolution has had a more pronounced effect is the tartanisation of much of the London-based press, which now publishes special Scotland editions. The list below names the main Scottish papers, although the London nationals are available in Scotland.

Newspapers

The Scotsman

www.scotsman.com
Edinburgh-based broadsheet. Has gone downmarket, with film star stories and trashy features, and has abandoned its traditional devolutionary bias for a markedly opposing stance. The editorial line tends to the right, while the arts and features have an east coast bias.

The Herald

www.theherald.co.uk
Glasgow-based broadsheet. Has the edge in terms of news coverage (though many argue the opposite, and the balance shifts back and forth). Any Glasgow bias in its arts and features coverage complements the *Scotsman*'s east coast orientation.

Daily Record

www.dailyrecord.co.uk
Glasgow-based tabloid. Scotland's best-selling daily is published by the Mirror Group and shares its celebrity obsession. Lots of froth.

Evening News

www.edinburghnews.com
Edinburgh's daily evening tabloid. The latest headlines from around the world are combined with a strong local Edinburgh flavour, with a strong emphasis on transport issues.

Scotland on Sunday

www.scotlandonsunday.com
The *Scotsman*'s sister publication.

The Sunday Herald

www.sundayherald.com
Sister paper to the *Herald*, the *Sunday Herald* combines good news reporting and analysis, and award-winning environmental coverage, with intelligent arts coverage.

Sunday Mail

www.sundaymail.co.uk
Sunday sister to the *Daily Record*, with which it shares strong sports coverage and a campaigning instinct.

Magazines

Scotland's thriving literary scene is reflected in the disproportionate number of literary magazines per head of population. But there are also style and satirical magazines.

Cencrastus

Subtitled 'Scottish and International Literature, Arts and Affairs', this thrice-yearly publication has moved in a more satirical direction, and is not afraid to take the odd broadswipe at the Scottish Parliament. Also includes poetry and short stories.

Chapman

www.chapman-pub.co.uk
Established for more than a quarter of a century, and currently appearing four times annually, *Chapman* is a highly regarded platform for new writing (fiction and poetry) as well as reviews and general debate on contemporary Scottish culture.

Edinburgh Review

www.englit.ed.ac.uk/edinburghreview
By far the oldest of Edinburgh's literary magazines, founded in 1802, the *Review* now appears twice a year and features fiction, poetry, criticism and literary/cultural argument.

Is This Music?

www.isthismusic.com
For the finest in jock rock, this is your rag.

Product

www.product.org.uk
Scottish pop culture magazine that likes to think of itself as cutting edge.

Scots Magazine

www.scotsmagazine.com
In continuous publication since before Culloden, this is a magazine with a real history (first published in 1793). *Scots Magazine* sells more than 50,000 copies a month, and has pretensions to being a Scottish *Reader's Digest*.

Scottish Field

www.scottishfield.co.uk
Describes itself as 'Scotland's quality lifestyle magazine' and has been going for over a century.

Listings

The List

www.list.co.uk
Fortnightly listings magazine for Edinburgh and Glasgow (published on Thursdays). It gives details of everything from mainstream cinema releases to readings by local writers and concerts of all sizes and genres. Weekly during the Festival.

Scotsgay

www.scotsgay.co.uk
This Edinburgh-based magazine appears monthly and is distributed free in gay venues. It covers events related to the lesbian, gay and bisexual community, and also includes comprehensive entertainment listings.

Television

On the broadcasting front, both the BBC and ITV in Scotland opt in and out of the UK-wide output. BBC Scotland and the independent Scottish Television (STV) also contribute regularly to their respective networks. Since devolution, the ongoing debate has been as to whether or not BBC Scotland should have a six o'clock news slot of its own – with London saying that there's not enough Scottish news to fit the slot and Scotland, for its part, disagreeing vehemently. The debate continues.

Radio

Listed below are four renowned Scottish stations but you can easily pick up most nationwide radio stations.

BBC Radio Scotland

92-95 FM & 810 MW.
Enjoys widespread popularity and respect for its mix of talk and music-based programming, Radio Scotland's news coverage offers an illuminating alternative to the reports from London, while its arts, documentary, sports and short-story strands are all worth listening to. The nightly rotation of music shows includes folk and traditional-based sounds in Celtic Connections and Travelling Folk.

Beat 106

105.7-106.1 FM (*www.beat106.com*).
A relatively new and lively addition to the Scottish music scene. Beat FM bills itself as Scotland's radio revolution, despite being more of the MOR same old, same old. The excellent Beatscene sessions on Wednesday evenings, showcasing the latest indie and alternative (specifically Scottish) sounds, are well worth a listen, however.

Forth 1

97.3 FM (*www.forth1.co.uk*).
Edinburgh-based music-oriented commercial station that has a very charty playlist. Features local and Scottish acts and is a must for travel and festival news.

Real Radio

100-101 FM.
Launched in January 2002, a mix of music from the last 30 years and 'personality radio' has succeeded in making it the most listened to commercial station in Scotland.

Money

Britain's currency is the pound sterling (£). One pound equals 100 pence (p). 1p and 2p coins are copper; 5p, 10p, 20p and 50p coins are silver; the £1 coin is yellowy-gold; the £2 coin is silver with a yellowy-gold surround. There are three Scottish clearing banks, all of which issue their own paper notes: the Bank of Scotland, the Royal Bank of Scotland and the Clydesdale Bank. The colour of paper notes varies slightly between the three, but an approximation is as follows: green £1 (Scotland only; England and Wales have done away with the £1 note); blue £5; brown £10; purple/pink £20; red or green £50; and, unique to Scotland, a bold red £100. You can exchange foreign currency at banks or bureaux de change. It's a good idea to try to use up all your Scottish banknotes before leaving the country; the further south you go, the more wary people will be of accepting it, although it is legal tender.

While the euro is legal currency in the rest of Europe, in the UK the debate goes on. The euro is not used in the UK but is accepted in some shops, particularly in tourist areas.

Banks

Minimum opening hours are 9am-4pm Mon-Fri, but some are open until 5.30pm. Cashpoint machines (ATMs), usually situated outside a bank or building society (most building societies also operate as banks), give access to cash 24 hours a day. Most will also allow you to draw money on a credit card. All you need is an

ATM with a major national/ international network – such as Cirrus or Plus – and your PIN number to type in (check with your card issuer before leaving home).

Banks generally offer the best exchange rates, although these can vary considerably from place to place, and it pays to shop around. Commission is sometimes charged for cashing travellers' cheques in foreign currencies, but not for sterling travellers' cheques, provided you cash them at a bank affiliated to the issuing bank (get a list when you buy your cheques). Commission is charged if you change cash into another currency. You will always need identification, such as a passport, when cashing travellers' cheques.

There are branches of the three Scottish clearing banks and cash machines throughout the city. There are, however, few branches of the English clearing banks. These are located as follows:

Barclays Bank
1 St Andrew Square, New Town (0845 600 0180). Princes Street buses. **Open** 9am-5pm Mon, Tue, Thur, Fri; 10am-5pm Wed. **Map** p304 D1.

HSBC
76 Hanover Street, New Town (0845 740 4404) Bus 23, 27/Princes Street buses. **Open** 9am-5pm Mon-Fri; 9.30am-12.30pm Sat. **Map** p304 C1.

Lloyds TSB Bank
28 Hanover Street, New Town (0845 303 0109). Bus 28, 41, 42/Princes Street buses. **Open** 9am-5pm Mon, Tue, Fri; 10am-5pm Wed; 9am-6pm Thur; 9am-12.30pm Sat. **Map** p304 C1.

National Westminster Bank
8 George Street, New Town (0845 609 0000). Bus 28, 41, 42/Princes Street buses. **Open** 9am-5pm Mon, Tue, Thur, Fri; 9.30am-5pm Wed. **Map** p304 B1.

Bureaux de change
You will be charged for cashing travellers' cheques or

buying and selling foreign currency at a bureau de change. Commission rates, which should be clearly displayed, vary. Banks, travel companies and the major rail stations have bureaux de change, and there are many in tourist areas. Most are open standard business hours (9am-5.30pm Mon-Fri), but one that is open longer is FEXCO Ltd (Open 9am-5pm Mon-Wed; 9am-6pm Thur-Sat; 10am-5pm Sun), situated inside the tourist office for Edinburgh & the Lothians (*see p290*).

Lost/stolen credit cards
Report lost or stolen credit cards immediately to both the police and the 24-hour services listed below. Inform your bank by phone and in writing.

American Express
Personal card 01273 696933/ corporate card 01273 689955.

Diners Club
General enquiries & emergencies 0800 460800.

MasterCard
0800 964767.

Visa
0800 891725.

Money transfers
The Information Centre above the Princes Mall can advise on Western Union money transfer. Or call Western Union direct on 0800 833833. Alternatively contact your own bank to find out which British banks it is affiliated with; you can then nominate an Edinburgh branch of that bank to have the money sent to.

Opening hours
In general, business hours are 9am-5.30pm Mon-Fri. Most shops are open 9am-5.30pm Mon-Sat and 11am-5pm on Sun. Banks open at 9am and

close at 5pm on weekdays. Restaurants generally open 11am-2pm and 6-11pm. Many restaurants are open all day and some stay open well beyond 11pm. Officially closing time for pubs is 11pm; but Scottish pubs (unlike those south of the border) can apply for licenses to sell alcohol till 1am.

Police stations
The police are a good source of information about the locality and are used to helping visitors find their way around. If you have been robbed, assaulted or the victim of any crime, look under 'Police' in the phone directory for the nearest police station, or call directory enquiries (*see p289*). There is a **police information centre** at 188 High Street, Old Town (226 6966). In an emergency, and only in an emergency, dial 999.

If you have a complaint to make about the police, be sure to take the offending officer's ID number, which should be prominently displayed on his or her epaulette. You can then register a complaint at any police station, visit a solicitor or Citizens Advice Bureau, or contact the Complaints Department, Police Headquarters, Lothian and Borders Police, Fettes Avenue, Stockbridge, Edinburgh, EH4 1RB (311 3377).

Postal services
The UK has a fairly reliable postal service. If you have a query on any aspect of Royal Mail services, contact Customer Services on 08457 740740. For business enquiries contact the Royal Mail Business Centre for Scotland on 08457 950950.

Undeliverable mail can be collected in person from the sorting office at 10 Brunswick Road, Broughton (550 8141,

Directory

map p307 H3). Post office opening hours are usually 9am-5.30pm Mon-Fri; 9am-12.30pm Sat, with the exception of the **St James Post Office**. Listed below are two other main central offices. Consult the phone book for other post offices.

Frederick Street Post Office
40 Frederick Street, New Town (226 6937). Bus 28, 37, 41, 42/Princes Street buses. **Open** (as above except closed Sat). **Map** p304 B1.

Hope Street Post Office
7 Hope Street, New Town (226 6823). Bus 28, 37, 41, 42/Princes Street buses. **Map** p308 C5.

St James Post Office
8-10 Kings Mall, St James Centre, New Town (0845 722 3344). Princes Street buses. **Open** 9am-5.30pm Mon; 8.30am-5.30pm Tue-Fri; 8.30am-6pm Sat. **Map** p308 F4

Stamps

You can buy stamps at post offices and at any newsagent that displays the appropriate red sign. Stamps can be bought individually (at post offices only) or, in the case of first class or second class, in books of four or 12, at post offices, supermarkets and some shops. First class letters (for next-day delivery within mainland Britain), up to 60g, or 20g to EU countries, cost 28p. Second class letters (two- to three-day delivery in mainland Britain) up to 60g are 21p (April 2004). Postcards cost 38p to send to another country in the EU and 42p anywhere else in world. Rates for other letters and parcels vary according to the weight and destination.

Poste restante

If you intend to travel around Britain, friends from home can write to you care of a post office, where mail will be kept at the enquiry desk for up to one month. The envelope

should be marked 'Poste Restante' in the top left-hand corner, with your name displayed above the address of the post office where you want to collect your mail. Take ID when you collect your post. The St James Post Office (*see left*) offers this service.

Public holidays

Edinburgh shares some holidays with the rest of the UK, others with the rest of Scotland and has some of its very own.

On public holidays and bank holidays many shops remain open, but public transport services are less frequent. On Christmas Day and New Year's Day most things close down.
New Year's holiday.
Sat 1 Jan 2005, Mon 3 Jan, 2005 Tue 4 Jan; Sun 1 Jan 2006, Mon 2 Jan 2006, Tue 3 Jan 2006.
Spring holiday.
Mon 18 Apr 2005; Mon 10 Apr 2006.
Good Friday.
Fri 25 Apr 2005; Fri 14 Apr 2006.
Easter Monday.
Mon 28 Apr 2005; Mon 17 Apr 2006.
May Day.
Mon 2 May 2005; Mon 1 May 2006.
Victoria Day (Edinburgh only).
Mon 23 May 2005; Mon 22 May 2006.
August bank holiday.
Mon 20 Sept 2004; Mon 19 Sept 2005.
Christmas Day.
Sat 25 Dec 2004; Sun 25 Dec 2005.
Boxing Day.
Sun 26 Dec 2004; Mon 26 Dec 2005.
Christmas bank holiday.
Mon 27 Dec 2004, Tue 28 Dec 2004; Tue 27 Dec 2005.

Religion

Baptist
Charlotte Baptist Chapel, *204 West Rose Street, New Town (225 4812/www.charlottechapel.org). Princes Street buses.* **Open** *Office* 9am-5pm Mon-Fri. **Services** 11am, 6.30pm Sun; phone for details of weekday prayer meetings. **Map** p304 A1.

Buddhist
Edinburgh's Zen Buddhist community has a **priory** in Portobello (27 Brighton Place, Portobello; 669 9622/www.portobello buddhist.org.uk) with daily meditation, a resident monk and lay followers. The **Edinburgh**

Buddhist Centre, 10 Viewforth, Marchmont (228 3333/www. edinburghbuddhistcentre.org.uk) is run by the Friends of the Western Buddhist Order. Other Buddhist groups in Edinburgh have no central meeting place and tend to share space with other faiths or organisations. Phone 332 7987 for information.

Catholic
St Mary's Cathedral, *61 York Place, Broughton (556 1798/ www.stmaryscathedral.co.uk). Playhouse buses.* **Open** 7am-6pm Mon-Fri, Sun; 7am-7pm Sat. **Services** 10am, 12.45pm Mon-Thur; 7.30am, 10am, 12.45pm Fri; 10am, 6pm (*vigil mass*) Sat; 9.30am, 11.30am, 6pm (*vigil mass*), 7.30pm Sun. **Confessions** heard 10.30am-noon, 5-5.45pm Sat. **Map** p307 F4.

Church of Scotland
St Giles' Cathedral, *High Street (225 4363). Bus 23, 27, 28, 35, 41, 42, 45.* **Open** *Easter-Sept* 9am-7pm Mon-Fri; 9am-5pm Sat; 1-5pm Sun. *Sept-Easter* 9am-5pm Mon-Sat; 1-5pm Sun. **Services** 8am, noon Mon-Fri, noon, 8pm (*Holy Communion*) Sat; 8am (*Holy Communion*), 10am (*Holy Communion*), 11.30am, 8pm Sun. **Map** p304 D3.

Episcopalian
Cathedral Church of St Mary, *Palmerston Place, New Town (225 6293). Bus 3, 4, 12, 25, 31, 33.* **Open** 7.15am-6pm Mon-Sat; 7.30am-6pm Sun (9pm in summer). **Services** Phone for details. **Map** p308 B6.

Hindu
Edinburgh Hindu Mandir & Cultural Centre, *St Andrew Place, Leith (440 0084). Bus 1, 16, 25.* **Open/services** 2-4pm on 2nd Sunday and noon-2pm on 4th Sunday of the month. **Map** p311 Jz.

Islamic
Mosque & Islamic Centre, *50 Potterow, South Edinburgh (667 1777). Bus 41, 42.* **Open** dawn-dusk daily. **Services** phone for details. **Map** p310 G6.

Jewish
Synagogue Chambers, *4 Salisbury Road, South Edinburgh (667 3144). Bus 3, 7, 8, 29, 31.* **Open/services** phone for details. **Map** p310 H8.

Methodist
Nicolson Square Methodist Church, *Nicolson Square, South Edinburgh (667 1465). Nicolson Street-North Bridge buses.* **Open** Basement chapel & café 8.30am-3.30pm Mon-Fri. **Services** 11am, 6.30pm Sun. **Map** p310 G6.

Directory

Quaker

Quaker Meeting House, *7 Victoria Terrace, Victoria Street, Old Town (225 4825).* Bus 23, 27, 28, 41, 42, 45. **Open** 9am-10pm daily. **Services** 12.30pm Wed; 11am Sun. Map p304 C3.

Sikh

Sikh Gurdwara, *1 Mill Lane, Leith (553 7207).* Bus 1, 7, 10, 14, 32, 34. **Open/services** phone for details. Map p311 Hy.

Safety & security

Violent crime is relatively rare on the streets of Edinburgh, but, as in any major city, it is unwise to take risks. Thieves and pickpockets specifically target unwary tourists. Use common sense and follow these basic rules:

● Keep your wallet and purse out of sight. Don't wear a wrist wallet (they are easily snatched). Keep your handbag securely closed.
● Don't leave a handbag, briefcase, bag or coat unattended, especially in pubs, cinemas, department stores or fast food shops, on public transport, at railway stations and airports, or in crowds.
● Don't leave your bag or coat beside, under or on the back of your chair.
● Don't wear expensive jewellery or watches that can be easily snatched.
● Don't put your purse down on the table in a restaurant or on a shop counter while you scrutinise the bill.
● Don't carry a wallet in your back pocket.
● Don't flash your money or credit cards around.
● Avoid parks after dark. Late at night, try to travel in groups of three or more.

Despite the still-popular stereotype of the red-blooded Scottish male, and that of the country's macho drinking culture, Edinburgh is a pretty safe and civilised place. There's generally a reasonable safety-in-numbers feel on the streets throughout Edinburgh's main drag and its immediate hinterland, even into the wee small hours (the lively entertainment scene of central Edinburgh means the streets are rarely deserted).

The main areas best avoided on your own at night are the Cowgate (mad and quite threatening when the clubs and pubs spill out across the streets) and Lothian Road (a preponderance of decidedly laddish pubs and a history of violence at chucking-out time). For women in particular, the dockside and back street areas of Leith, particularly Coburg Street, one of Edinburgh's main red-light districts – and the Meadows – are best avoided. The latter's paths look safe and brightly lit, but prove deceptively long and tree-screened once you actually set off down them; it has been the scene of several assaults. The Royal Mile, too, perhaps more unexpectedly, has seen its share of such incidents, mainly because of the cover provided by the innumerable narrow alleys, or wynds, leading off it: it's highly picturesque by day, but it can seem spookily dark and shadowy at night.

Further afield, if you go to one of the city's big peripheral housing schemes, take local advice, and get your directions firmly sorted. The geographical layout of these areas is frequently bewildering, to say the least, and the levels of social deprivation to be found in some of them present a starkly different face of Edinburgh to the economic and architectural wealth of the centre.

Smoking

Scotland is the last bastion of smoking, with the highest rates for heart disease and lung cancer in Europe to show for it. Many Scots still smoke and smoking is permissible in more public places than in the rest of the UK and far more than the US, though the Scottish Parliament has been debating banning smoking in public places. Smoking is not allowed in cinemas or theatres and many restaurants are now banning the evil weed.

Study

Edinburgh has four universities (Edinburgh, Heriot-Watt, Napier and Queen Margaret) and numerous colleges. Edinburgh University is the city's largest and most prestigious university. Founded in 1583, it is renowned worldwide and has an unbeatable reputation, in particular for medicine and scientific research; its degrees carry real academic kudos. Edinburgh University has three main schools, with departments scattered all over the town, and the Old College boasts some truly stunning architecture.

Universities/colleges

Edinburgh College of Art

Lauriston Place, South Edinburgh (221 6000/www.eca.ac.uk). Bus 23, 27, 28, 45. **Map** p309 E6.
One of the most prestigious art colleges in the UK: competition for places here is stiff. Studies on offer range from film to textiles and sculpture.

Heriot-Watt University

Riccarton Campus, Currie (449 5111/www.hw.ac.uk). Bus 25, 34, 45.
A vocational university specialising in business, finance, languages, science and engineering subjects.

Napier University

Craiglockhart Campus, 219 Colinton Road, South Edinburgh (444 2266/ www.napier.ac.uk). Bus 4, 10, 27, 45.
Founded in 1964 and named after mathematical genius John Napier, this former polytechnic with a reputation for a more varied (and down-to-earth) student body than Edinburgh University was granted university status in 1992. Offering predominantly vocational courses, its employment record for graduates is second to none.

Queen Margaret University Campus

Corstorphine Campus, Clerwood Terrace, West Edinburgh (317 3000/www.qmuc.ac.uk). Bus 26.
An assortment of predominantly degree courses – you can study everything from nursing, nutrition and tourism to management, business and drama.

University of Edinburgh

Old College, South Bridge, South Edinburgh (650 1000/www.ed.ac.uk). Nicolson Street–North Bridge buses. **Map** p308 G6.

One of the UK's oldest and most reputable universities offers a staggering range of academic degree courses. There's also a good selection of part-time extramural courses run during the day and in the evening. Its international office is at 57 George Square, South Edinburgh (668 4565).

Language courses

A full list of the vast number of schools offering English language courses can be found in the *Yellow Pages*. The following is a small selection of some of the best and most well known establishments. Some also offer TEFL courses; phone for rates.

Berlitz

26 Frederick Street, New Town (226 7198/www.languagecentres.com). Bus 28, 41, 42/Princes Street buses. **Map** p304 B1.

Edinburgh Language Centre

10B Oxford Terrace, New Town (343 6596/www.edinburgh languagecentre.co.uk). Bus 19, 29, 29A, 36, 37, 37A. **Map** p305 B4.

Institute for Applied Language Studies

21 Hill Place, South Edinburgh (650 6200/www.ials.ed.ac.uk). Nicolson Street–North Bridge buses. **Map** p310 G6.

Regent Edinburgh

29 Chester Street, New Town (225 9888/www.regent.org.uk). Bus 13. **Map** p308 B5.

Stevenson College

Sighthill Campus, Bankhead Avenue, Sighthill (535 4700/www.stevenson. ac.uk). Bus 3, 20, 25, 34.

Telford College,

Telford College, Crewe Toll (332 2424/www.ed-coll.ac.uk) Bus 19, 27, 42, 29 37, 37A, 38, X31, X37.

Student travel

STA Travel

27 Forrest Road, Old Town (226 7747/www.statravel.co.uk). Bus 23, 27, 41, 42, 45. **Open** 10am-6pm

Mon-Wed, Fri; 10am-7pm Thur; 10am-5pm Sat. **Map** p309 F6.
Other location: 2 Bristo Square, South Edinburgh (668 9437).

Telephones

The telephone code for Edinburgh is 0131. If you're calling from outside the UK, dial the international code, followed by 44 (code for Britain), then the ten-digit number starting with 131 (omitting the first 0). The code for Glasgow and its environs is 0141.

International dialling codes

Australia 00 61; **Belgium** 00 32; **Canada** 00 1; **France** 00 33; **Germany** 00 49; **Ireland** 00 353; **Italy** 00 39; **Japan** 00 81; **Netherlands** 00 31; **New Zealand** 00 64; **Spain** 00 34; **USA** 00 1.

Mobile phones

Mobile phones in the UK work on either the 900 or 1800 GSM system used throughout much of Europe. If you're travelling to the UK from Europe, check whether your service provider has a reciprocal arrangement with a UK-based provider and that your phone has a built-in roaming capacity.

The situation is more complex for US travellers. If your service provider uses the GSM system, it will probably run on the 1900 band; this means you will need a tri-band phone, and your provider must have a reciprocal arrangement with a UK provider.

The simplest option may be to buy a 'pay as you go' phone (about £40-£200). There's no monthly fee and calls are charged by buying (widely available) cards that have numbers that you type into your phone to activate the money the card cost, in amounts of £10 and up. Check first that the phone is capable of making and receiving international calls.

Public phones

Public payphones take coins, credit cards or prepaid phonecards (and sometimes all three). The minimum cost is 20p. BT phonecards are available from post offices and many newsagents in denominations of £2, £5, £10 and £20. Most public phones in the city centre also have now an integrated internet facility (*see p283*).

Operator services

Call 100 for the operator in the following circumstances: when you have difficulty in dialling; for an early-morning alarm call; to make a credit card call; for information about the cost of a call; and for international person-to-person calls. Dial 155 if you need to reverse the charges (call collect) or if you can't dial direct. Be warned, though, as this service is very expensive.

Directory enquiries

The simple 192 directory enquiries number has been replaced by a host of competing operators. All numbers begin with 118. Rates for different requests vary but here are some of the more well-known companies. See www.118info.org.uk for an impartial comparison of the various services.
British Telecom – 118 500.
The Number – 118 118.
Yellow Pages – 118 247.
Directory Enquiries – 118 800.
'11' 88' '88' – 118 888.

Telephone directories

The phone directory for Edinburgh lists business and commercial numbers in the first section, followed by private phone numbers, and is available to consult at post offices and libraries. Hotels will also have a copy. The *Yellow Pages* directory lists businesses and services.

Directory

Telemessages & telegrams

Call 0800 190190 to phone in your message and it will be delivered by post the next day (rates vary, so phone for details). Call the same number to arrange domestic or international telegrams.

Time

Edinburgh operates on Greenwich Mean Time. Clocks go forward for British Summer Time on the night of the last Saturday in March and back to rejoin GMT on the last Saturday in October.

Tipping

In Britain it is accepted that you tip in taxis, minicabs, restaurants (some waiting staff are forced to rely heavily on gratuities), hairdressers, hotels and some bars (not pubs) – ten percent is normal. Be careful to check whether service has been added automatically to your bill – some restaurants include service and then also leave the space open for a gratuity on your credit card slip.

Toilets

It's not generally acceptable to use the toilets of cafés or bars unless you're a customer or have a small and rather desperate child. However, there are a good number of public toilets and the major department stores all have clean and available lavatories. Below are some of the city's public toilets.
Hunters Square *(by the Tron),* *Old Town.* **Open** 10am-10pm daily. **Map** p304 D3.
The Mound *Princes Street, New Town.* **Open** 10am-10pm daily. Disabled access 24hrs using National Key Scheme. **Map** p304 C2.
Princes Mall *Waverley Bridge, New Town.* **Open** 10am-6pm daily. **Map** p304 D2.
West Princes Street Gardens *Princes Street, New Town.* **Open**

10am-10pm daily. Disabled access from Princes Street Gardens only. **Map** p304 B2.

Tourist information

Scottish Tourist Board
19 Cockspur Street (just off Trafalgar Square), London, SW1Y 5BL (0845 225 5121/www.visit scotland.com). **Open** *May-Sept* 9.30am-6.30pm Mon-Fri; 10am-5pm Sat (mid June to mid Sept). *Oct-Apr* 10am-6pm Mon-Fri; noon-4pm Sat. The Edinburgh & Lothians Tourist Board operates the information centres listed below. There is also a 24hr electronic information unit at the Edinburgh and Scotland Information Centre. The tourist board website at www.edinburgh.org has further information. For other useful websites, *see p292.*

Edinburgh & Lothians Tourist Board
Above Princes Mall, 3 Princes Street, New Town, EH2 2QP (473 3800/ www.edinburgh.org). Princes Street buses. **Open** *Nov-Mar* 9am-5pm Mon-Wed; 9am-6pm Thur-Sat; 10am-5pm Sun. *Apr, Oct* 9am-6pm Mon-Sat; 10am-6pm Sun. *May, June, Sept* 9am-7pm Mon-Sat; 10am-7pm Sun. *July, Aug* 9am-8pm Mon-Sat; 10am-8pm Sun. **Map** p304 D2.

Edinburgh Airport Tourist Information Desk
Edinburgh Airport (473 3800). **Open** *Apr-Oct* 6.30am-10pm daily. *Nov-Mar* 7.30am-9.30pm daily.

Visas & immigration

Citizens of EU countries do not require a visa to visit the UK; citizens of some other countries, including the USA, Canada and New Zealand, require only a valid passport in order to be able to visit for up to six months.

To apply for a visa, and to check your visa status before you travel, you should contact the British Embassy, High Commission or Consulate in your own country. A visa allows you entry to Britain for a maximum period of six

months. For more help and information concerning work permits, *see p291.*

Home Office
Immigration & Nationality Department, Lunar House, 40 Wellesley Road, Croydon, CR9 2BY (08706 067766/www.homeoffice. gov.uk). **Open** *Phone enquiries* 9am-4.45pm Mon-Thur; 9am-4.30pm Fri. The Home Office deals with all queries about immigration matters, visas and work permits for citizens from the Commonwealth and a few other countries.

Weights & measures

As part of Europe, Scotland uses kilos and metres – but only nominally. The natives still tend to think in Imperial measures. Most goods are also weighed in pounds (lb) and measured in feet and inches.

When to go

There's not really a best time to visit Edinburgh. It all depends on what you want – if it's festivals, then take your pick; if it's weather, don't bank on it. Christmas and Hogmanay (that's New Year to you) have their own festivals, the International Science Festival is held in April and the city explodes into life in August with the various arts festivals. For more on festivals, *see p32* and *p194.*

Weatherwise Edinburgh is difficult to call. Average January temperatures range between 0° and 6° centigrade. July is the warmest month, with a 10°-19° centigrade average range. Winter days can be cold and wet but are equally likely to be sunny and crystal clear. There's no guarantee of good weather at any time, but between the months of May and October – when the days get longer and you can finally get your thermals off – Edinburgh's a great place to be.

In summer the streets are thronged with tourists and it can be difficult to find an inch of pavement. Unless you're coming to visit the Festival, then autumn and spring may be better times to visit.

Women

Women travelling on their own face the usual hassles, but generally Edinburgh is a safe city to visit. Take the same precautions you'd take in any big city. See p288 for where best to avoid and you should be fine.

The bigger chain hotels, of which Edinburgh boasts several, tend to be well geared to the needs of lone female guests, while many of the abundant B&Bs and guest-houses offer single rooms along with the kind of welcome that has made Scottish hospitality famous.

For a relaxed solo meal, though, cafés can often be a better (and cheaper) bet for women than restaurants, with several good city-centre ones opening late into the evening. Many of the city's (black) taxi firms have now signed up to a policy of giving priority to lone women, whether they're phoning up or flagging down. Bear in mind, though, that taxis are often like gold dust between midnight and 3am at weekends; book in advance or be prepared to wait or walk.

Working in Edinburgh

Finding a summer job in Edinburgh, or temporary employment if you are on a working holiday, can be a long, drawn-out process. If you can speak English and at least one other language well, and are an EU citizen or have a work permit, you should probably be able to find something in either catering, bar/restaurant or

shop work. Graduates with an English or foreign-language degree could try teaching. Other ideas can be found in *Summer Jobs in Britain*, published by Vacation Work, 9 Park End Street, Oxford (£8.99 plus £1.50 p&p). The Central Bureau for Educational Visits & Exchanges has been incorporated into the Scottish office of the British Council (The Tun, 4 Jackson's Entry, Holyrood Road, EH8 8PJ (524 5700/www.britishcouncil.org).

To find work, look in the *Scotsman*, other local and national papers, and newsagents' windows. Alternatively, you can write to, phone, or pound the pavement and visit employers. There is often temporary and unskilled work available; look in the *Yellow Pages* under 'Employment Agencies'. Bars and restaurants often advertise casual work with signs in their windows – be warned though: this is sometimes an attempt to get away with not paying the minimum wage (£4.50 per hour for those over 22 and £3.80 for 18-21 year olds, changing to £4.85 for those over 22 and £4.10 for those aged 18-21, from Oct 2004).

For office work, sign on with temp agencies. If you have good shorthand, typing or word-processing skills, such agencies may be able to find you well-paid assignments.

Work for foreign visitors

With few exceptions, citizens of non-European Economic Area (EEA) countries need a work permit before they are legally able to work in the UK. One of the advantages of working is the opportunity to meet new people, but for any job it is essential that you speak reasonable English. For office work you need a high standard of English and relevant skills.

Work permits

EEA citizens, residents of Gibraltar and certain categories of other overseas nationals do not require a work permit. However, others who wish to come to the UK to work must obtain a permit before setting out.

Prospective employers must apply for a permit to Customer Relations, Work Permits (UK), Immigration and Nationality Directorate, Home Office, Level 5, Moorfoot, Sheffield, S1 4PQ (0114 259 4074/www.working intheuk.gov.uk). Permits are only issued for jobs that require a high level of skill and experience. The employer must be able to demonstrate that there is no resident/EEA labour available.

There is a Training and Work Experience Scheme that enables non-EEA nationals to come to the UK to undertake training for a professional or specialist qualification, or to undertake a short period of managerial level work experience. Again, this should be applied for before leaving for the UK.

Voluntary work

Voluntary work in youth hostels provides board, lodging and some pocket money. For advice on voluntary work with charities contact the Home Office (see p290).

Working holidaymakers

Citizens of Commonwealth countries, aged 17-27, may apply to come to the UK as a working holidaymaker. This allows them to take part-time work without a work permit. They must contact their nearest British Diplomatic Post to obtain the necessary entry clearance before travelling to the UK.

Further Reference

Books

Fiction

Banks, Iain *Complicity.*
A visceral, body-littered thriller, with spot-on characterisation of both the city and the protagonists.
Butlin, Ron *Night Visits.*
'Edinburgh at its grandest, coldest and hardest... as if nothing less than such a stony grip and iron inflexibility were needed to prevent unimaginable pain,' as the *TLS* magisterially put it.
Hird, Laura *Born Free.*
Family life on a modern Edinburgh housing estate. So well observed and humorous, it hurts.
Hogg, James *Confessions of a Justified Sinner.*
An ironic jibe against religious bigotry in the 17th and 18th centuries, set in the turmoil of Edinburgh at that time.
Johnston, Paul *Body Politic, The Bone Yard, Water of Death.*
Future detective fiction set in a nightmare vision of Edinburgh as a city state with a year-round Festival, where the impoverished populace lives to serve the needs of the tourists. Nothing much changed there, then.
Rankin, Ian *Inspector Rebus* novels.
Quality detective fiction. Hardbitten Detective Rebus inhabits a city that is the reality for most of its inhabitants. The earlier novels are best for a strong sense of place (*see p74* **EdinBurgher Ian Rankin**).
Scott, Sir Walter *The Heart of Midlothian.*
Contains, among many other things, an account of the Porteous lynching of 1736.
Stevenson, Robert Louis *Edinburgh: Picturesque Notes.*
Perceptive, witty and the source of many subsequent opinions about Edinburgh.
Spark, Muriel *The Prime of Miss Jean Brodie.*
Practically the official Edinburgh novel. Schoolteacher Jean Brodie makes a stand against the city's moral intransigence.
Warner, Alan *The Sopranos.*
Spot-on story about a group of badly behaved teenage choir girls on a school trip in the capital.
Welsh, Irvine *Trainspotting.*
The first and best of Welsh's novels focuses on the culture of drugs, clubs and unemployment that more genteel Edinburgh residents do their best to ignore (*see p127* **EdinBurgher Irvine Welsh**).

Non fiction

Bruce, George *Festival of the North.*
Story of the Edinburgh International Festival, from its conception and its birth in 1947 until 1975.
Daitches, David *Edinburgh.*
A highly readable and academically sound history.
Lamond & Tucek *The Malt Whisky File.*
All the distilleries and nearly every malt that's sold is reviewed, with useful tasting notes.
Prebble, John *The King's Jaunt.*
Everything you could want to know (and more) about George IV's agenda-setting visit of 1822.
Youngson, AJ *The Making of Classical Edinburgh.*
An exhaustive account, with superb photos and plans, of the building of the New Town.

Films

Chariots of Fire
David Puttnam (1981).
Based on the true story of the 1924 Olympics, where Edinburgh sportsman Eric Liddell ran for Britain, David Puttnam's film has spectacular shots of Salisbury Crags.
The Prime of Miss Jean Brodie
Ronald Neame (1969).
Oscar-winning Maggie Smith will be forever Edinburgh's best-known schoolmarm – in her prime, of course.
Shallow Grave
Danny Boyle (1994).
Darkly humorous feature about three Edinburgh yuppies who find themselves landed with a suitcase full of drug money and a dead body.
The 39 Steps
Alfred Hitchcock (1935).
Hitchcock's loose adaptation of John Buchan's novel introduced what would become one of his enduring themes: the innocent man framed by circumstantial evidence. Shots of Edinburgh are scarce but evocative.
Trainspotting
Danny Boyle (1996).
Pitch-black comedy in this portrayal of Edinburgh's heroin culture, based on Irvine Welsh's novel.

Websites

Scotland & Edinburgh

For newspaper websites, *see p284.*
www.edinburgh.gov.uk/libraries/living inedinburgh/LivingInEdinburgh.html
A mine of useful information provided by the City Council. See also www.edinburgh.gov.uk, the council's homepage.
www.edinburgh.org
The Edinburgh Tourist Board's comprehensive list of attractions, hotels and entertainments.
www.historic-scotland.gov.uk
Home pages for the government body in charge of Scotland's historic monuments. There are strong databases on listed buildings, tourist attractions, literature and events.
www.nts.org.uk
The National Trust for Scotland's site provides the opening times, prices and details of all its properties.
www.visitscotland.com
Scottish Tourist Board site, with information on accommodation, restaurants, arts, events, nightlife. Online booking and useful links.

Entertainment

www.theoracle.co.uk
This really is the works, not particularly designer-web, but it delivers the goods – the most up-to-date and extensive set of listings for Edinburgh to be found on the net.
www.edinburgh-galleries.co.uk
This site will tell you what's on at the main Edinburgh galleries, and take you on a virtual tour around one or two of them.
www.electrum.co.uk/pubs
A virtual jaunt through Edinburgh's watering holes in the company of a wasted youth, a history geek or an architecture appreciator.
www.edinburghfestivals.co.uk
Full details of all Edinburgh's nine annual festivals. Links to the Fringe and Festival programmes online.
www.jockrock.org
Scottish music site with a good gig guide and witty, sometimes vicious message boards.

Politics & business

www.scotland.gov.uk
The Scottish Executive website.
www.scottish.parliament.uk
The Scottish Parliament's website is a user-friendly guide to tell you all about itself.
www.scotweb.co.uk
Primarily an online sales forum, but there's a lot more interesting stuff, too: read Piping World or browse Whisky Web or the Scotweb history site.
www.gro-scotland.gov.uk
General Register House has information on how to trace your Scottish ancestors online, as does www.scotlandspeople.gov.uk.

Directory

Index

Note Page numbers in **bold** indicate section(s) giving key information on a topic; *italics* indicate photographs.

Advertisers' Index

Please refer to the relevant sections for contact details

Place of interest and/or entertainment	
Railway station	
Park	
College/Hospital	
Neighbourhood	LEITH
Pedestrian street	
Tube station (Glasgow)	

Maps

Street Index

Edinburgh by Area

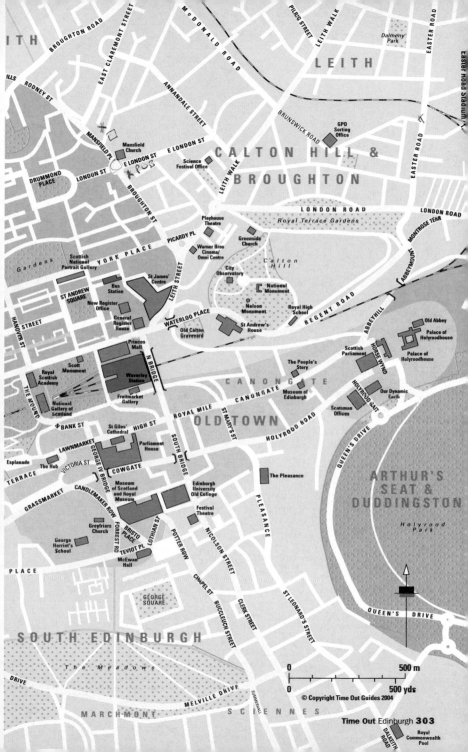

LEITH

Dalmeny Park

Easter Road Stadium

CALTON HILL & BROUGHTON

LONDON ROAD

Royal Terrace Gardens

LONDON ROAD

MONTROSE TERR

Calton Hill

National Monument

Nelson Monument

Royal High School

St Andrew's House

Old Abbey

Palace of Holyroodhouse

Palace of Holyroodhouse

Scottish Parliament

Our Dynamic Earth

Scotsman Offices

CANONGATE

OLD TOWN

The People's Story

Museum of Edinburgh

HOLYROOD ROAD

ARTHUR'S SEAT & DUDDINGSTON

Holyrood Park

The Pleasance

QUEEN'S DRIVE

QUEEN'S DRIVE

SOUTH EDINBURGH

The Meadows

GEORGE SQUARE

MARCHMONT

SCIENNES

0   500 m
0   500 yds

© Copyright Time Out Guides 2004

Time Out Edinburgh **303**

Royal Commonwealth Pool

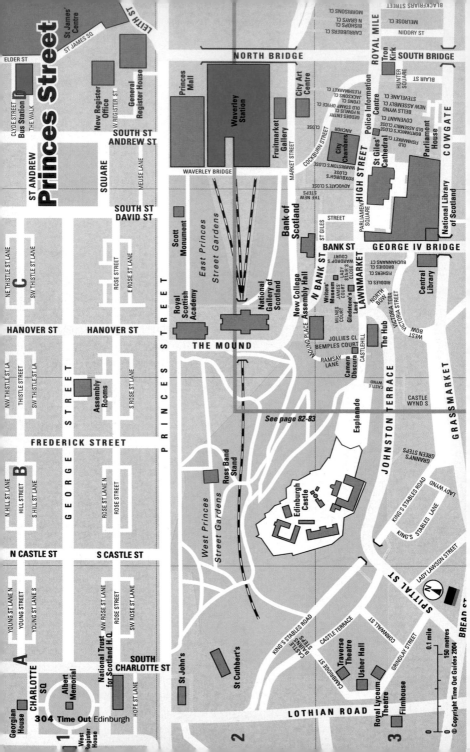

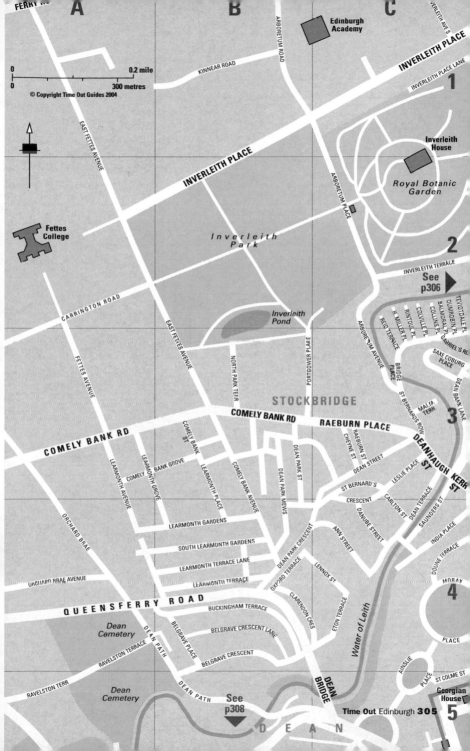

See
p306

See
p308

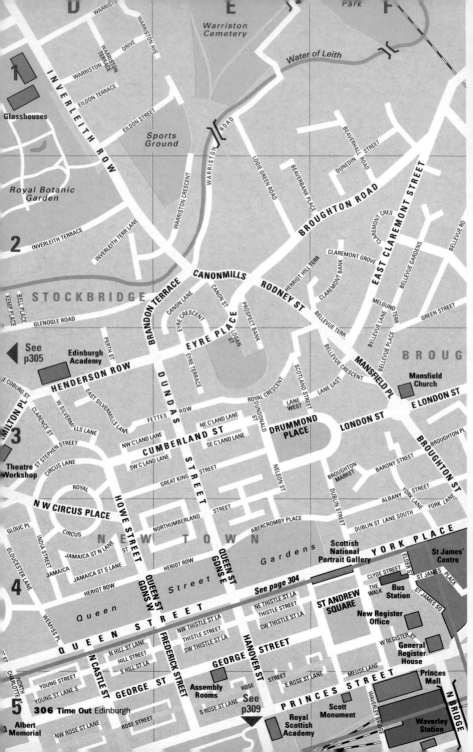

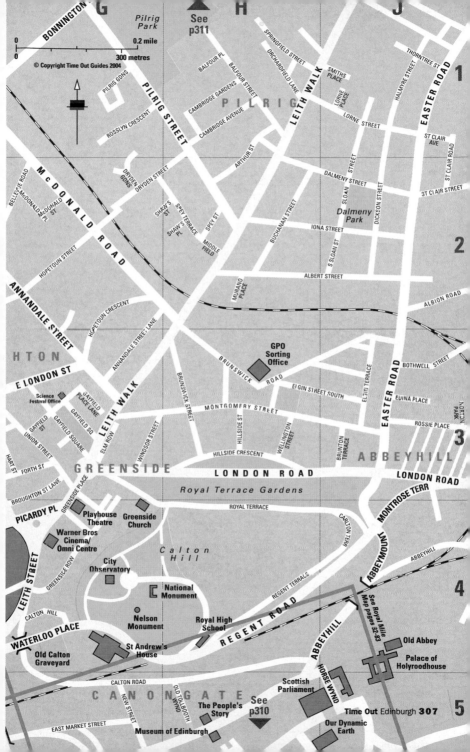

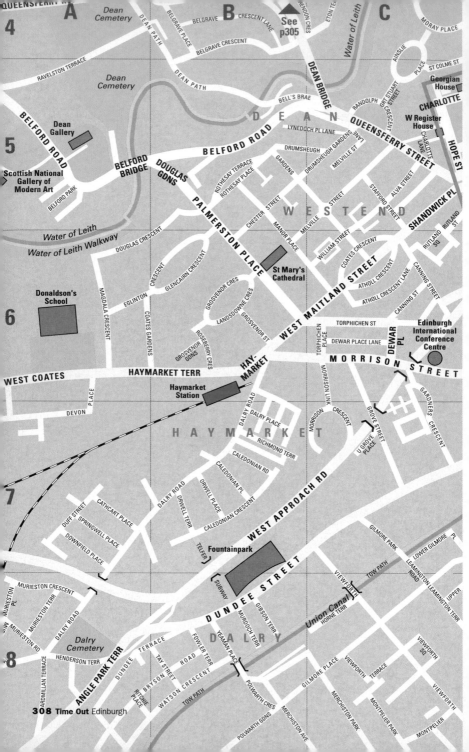

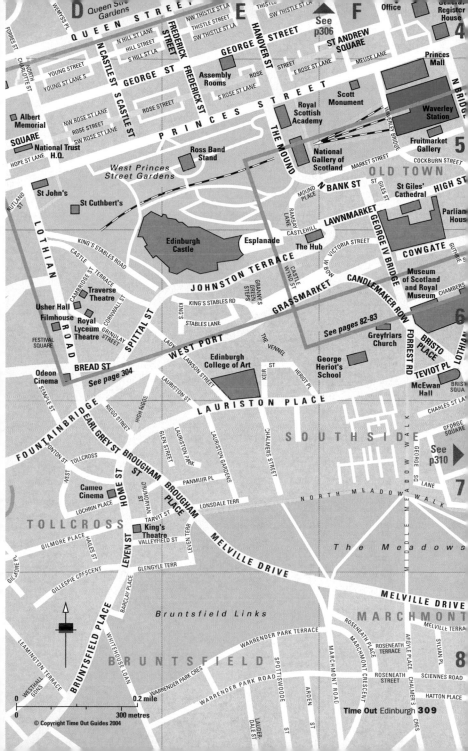

© Copyright Time Out Guides 2004

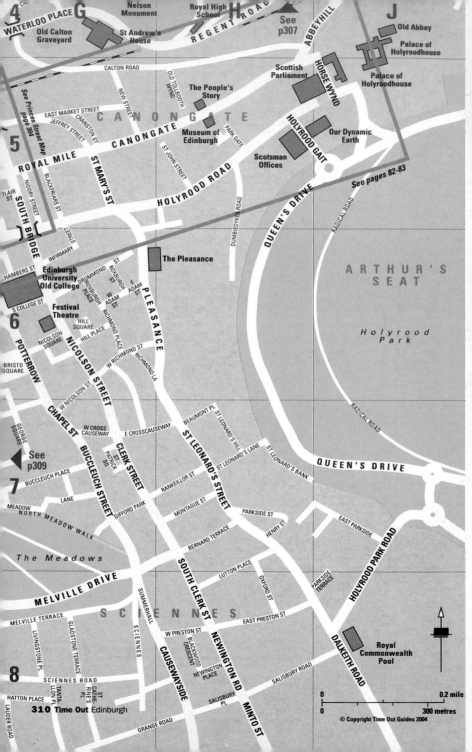

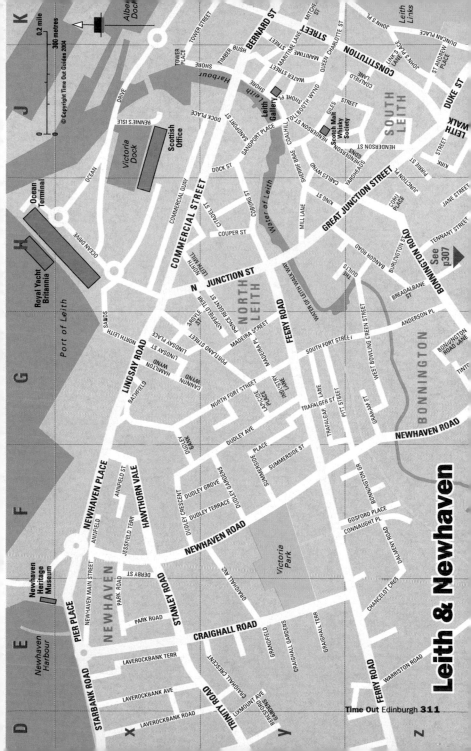

Leith & Newhaven

See p307

© Copyright Time Out Guides 2004

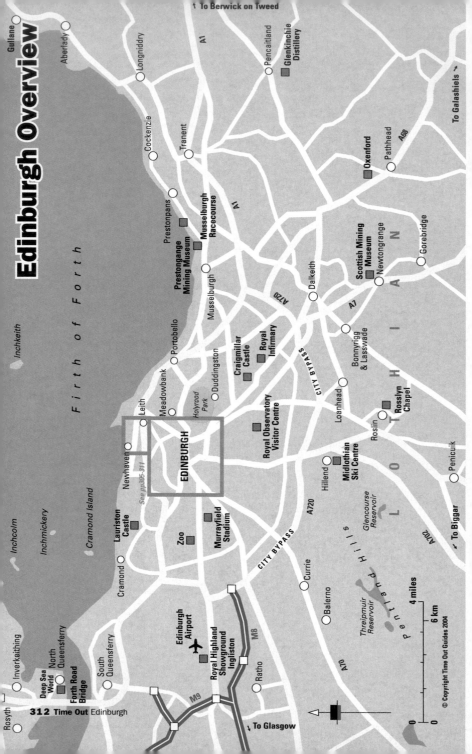

Edinburgh Overview

↑ To Berwick on Tweed

To Galashiels →

To Biggar ←

↓ To Glasgow

Firth of Forth

EDINBURGH

See pp305-311

LOTHIAN

Pentland Hills

Gullane
Aberlady
Longniddry
Cockenzie
Tranent
Pencaitland
Glenkinchie Distillery
Oxenford
Pathhead
A68
Gorebridge
Newtongrange
Scottish Mining Museum
A7
Bonnyrigg & Lasswade
Dalkeith
A720
Musselburgh
Musselburgh Racecourse
Prestonpans
Prestongange Mining Museum
Portobello
Meadowbank
Leith
Newhaven
Cramond
Lauriston Castle
Zoo
Murrayfield Stadium
Duddingston
Holyrood Park
Craigmillar Castle
Royal Infirmary
CITY BYPASS
Royal Observatory Visitor Centre
Loanhead
Rosslyn Chapel
Roslin
Midlothian Ski Centre
Hillend
Penicuik
Currie
Balerno
Glencourse Reservoir
Threipmuir Reservoir
A70
A720
A702
CITY BYPASS
A703
Ratho
Royal Highland Showground Ingliston
Edinburgh Airport
M8
M9
South Queensferry
North Queensferry
Forth Road Bridge
Deep Sea World
Inverkeithing
Rosyth
Inchcolm
Inchmickery
Inchkeith
Cramond Island

A1

4 miles
6 km

0
0

© Copyright Time Out Guides 2004

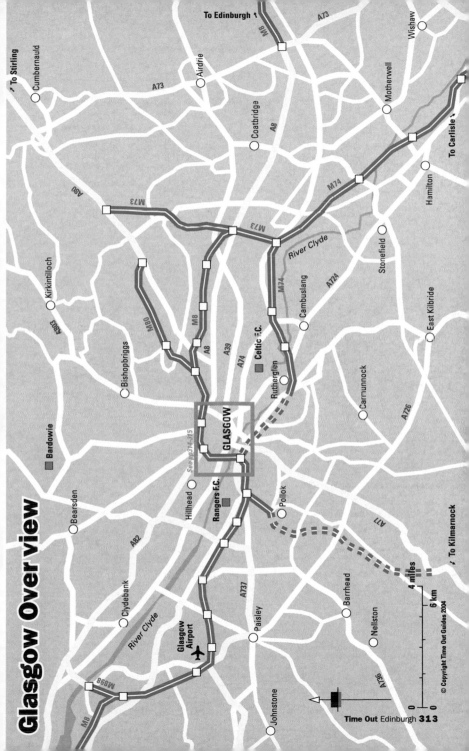

Glasgow Overview

To Edinburgh

To Stirling

Cumbernauld

A73

A73

Wishaw

Airdrie

Motherwell

Coatbridge

A8

To Carlisle

M74

Hamilton

A80

M73

M73

River Clyde

Stonefield

Kirkintilloch

A803

M80

M8

A8

M74

Cambuslang

A724

East Kilbride

Bishopbriggs

A39

A74

Celtic F.C.

Rutherglen

Carmunnock

A726

Bardowie

GLASGOW

See pp 314-315

Bearsden

Hillhead

Rangers F.C.

Pollok

A77

To Kilmarnock

A82

Clydebank

A737

Paisley

Barrhead

Neilston

River Clyde

Glasgow Airport

4 miles

6 km

A736

M898

M8

Johnstone

© Copyright Time Out Guides 2004

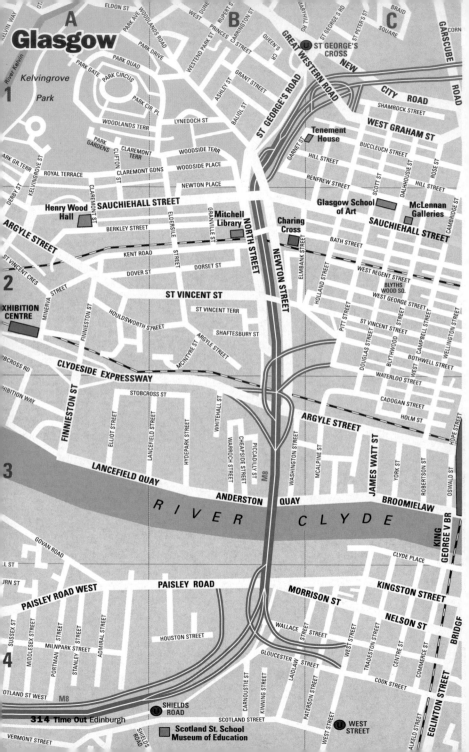

Glasgow

A   **B**   **C**

River Kelvin

Kelvingrove Park

1

KELVIN WAY · OTT... · ELDON ST · WOODLANDS ROAD · WEST DUNE · PRINCES ST · RUPERT S · CARRINGTON ST · QUEEN'S CR · ST GEORGE'S RD · ST PETER'S ST · BRAID SQUARE · CORN · GARSCUBE

PARK AVE · WOODLANDS ROAD · WESTEND PARK ST · ASHLEY ST · GRANT STREET · BALIO ST · GARNET ST · GREAT WESTERN ROAD · NEW · CITY · ROAD · ROAD

St George's Cross

PARK GATE · PARK QUAD · PARK DRIVE · PARK CIRCUS · PARK CIR PL · LYNEDOCH ST · WOODSIDE TERR

PARK GARDENS · CLAREMONT TERR · CLAREMONT GDNS · WOODSIDE TERR · WOODSIDE PLACE · NEWTON PLACE

ST GEORGE'S ROAD

SHAMROCK STREET

WEST GRAHAM ST

Tenement House

BUCCLEUCH STREET

HILL STREET · RENFREW STREET · SCOTT ST · DALHOUSIE ST · ROSE ST · HILL ST

ARK GR TERR · DERBY ST · KELVINGROVE ST · ROYAL TERRACE · CLAREMONT ST · CLIFTON ST

Henry Wood Hall

SAUCHIEHALL STREET

Glasgow School of Art

McLennan Galleries

BERKLEY STREET · ELDERSLIE · GRANVILLE ST · Mitchell Library · NORTH STREET · Charing Cross · BATH STREET · **SAUCHIEHALL STREET**

ARGYLE STREET

KENT ROAD · DORSET ST · DOVER ST · ELMBANK STREET · NEWTON STREET · HOLLAND STREET · CAMBRIDGE ST

ST VINCENT CRES

2

MINERVA STREET

ST VINCENT ST

ST VINCENT TERR

WEST REGENT STREET

BLYTHS WOOD SQ.

WEST GEORGE STREET

EXHIBITION CENTRE

HOULDSWORTH STREET · FINNIESTON ST · ARGYLE STREET · SHAFTESBURY ST · MCINTYRE ST · PITT STREET · DOUGLAS STREET · ST VINCENT STREET · BLYTHWOOD · CAMPBELL STREET · WEST · BOTHWELL STREET · WELLINGTON STREET

BCROSS RD

CLYDESIDE EXPRESSWAY

WATERLOO STREET

HIBITION WAY

FINNIESTON ST · STOBCROSS ST · ELLIOT STREET · LANCEFIELD STREET · HYDEPARK STREET · WHITEHALL ST · CHEAPSIDE STREET · WARROCH STREET · PICCADILLY ST · M8 · WASHINGTON STREET · MCALPINE ST · CADOGAN STREET · HOLM ST

ARGYLE STREET

JAMES WATT ST · YORK ST · ROBERTSON STREET · OSWALD ST · HOPE STREET

3

LANCEFIELD QUAY

ANDERSTON   **QUAY**

BROOMIELAW

KING GEORGE V BR

R I V E R   *C L Y D E*

GOVAN ROAD · L ST · JRN ST

CLYDE PLACE

PAISLEY ROAD

MORRISON ST

KINGSTON STREET

PAISLEY ROAD WEST

NELSON ST

BRIDGF

SUSSEX ST · MIDDLESEX STREET · MILNPARK STREET · PORTMAN STREET · STANLEY STREET · ADMIRAL STREET · HOUSTON STREET · WALLACE STREET · STREET · WEST STREET · TRADESTON STREET · CENTRE ST · COMMERCE ST · EGLINTON STREET

4

GLOUCESTER · STREET · LAIDLAW STREET

OTLAND ST WEST · M8 · VERMONT STREET · SHIELDS ROAD · CARNOUSTIE ST · KINNING STREET · SCOTLAND STREET · PATERSON STREET · WEST STREET · COOK STREET · ALKELD STREET

Shields Road

Scotland St. School Museum of Education

West Street

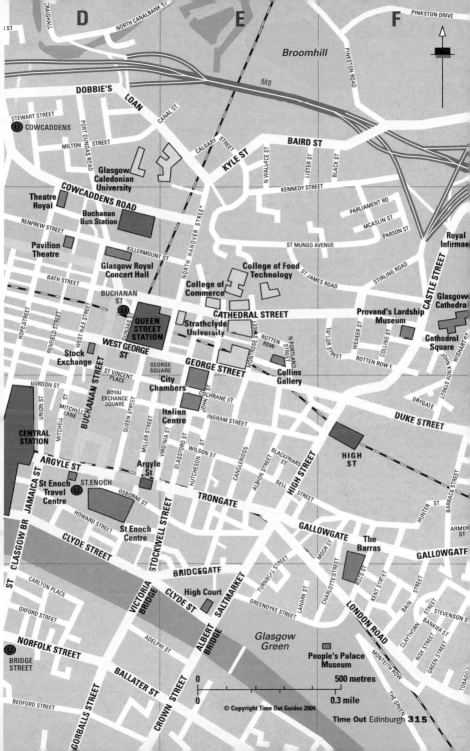

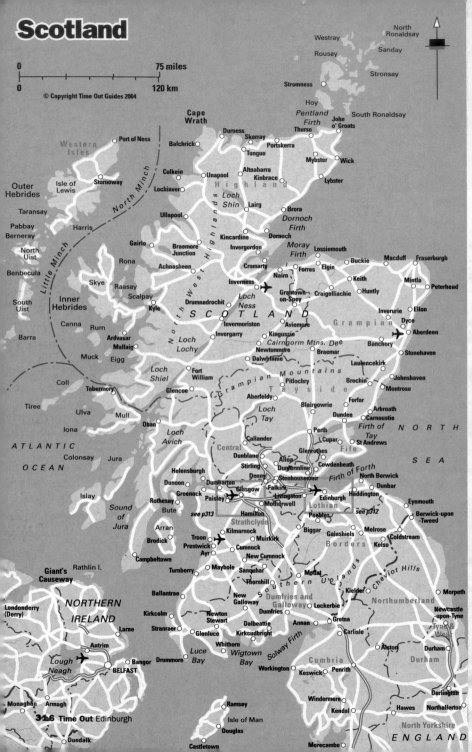

Scotland

0 —————————— 75 miles
0 —————————— 120 km
© Copyright Time Out Guides 2004

Western Isles

Outer
Hebrides

Taransay
Pabbay
Berneray

North
Uist

Benbecula

South
Uist

Barra

Isle of
Lewis

Port of Ness
Stornoway

Harris

North Minch

Little Minch

Rona

Skye
Raasay
Scalpay

Canna
Rum

Inner
Hebrides

Ardvasar
Mallaig

Muck
Eigg

Coll

Tiree

Ulva
Mull

Iona

ATLANTIC

OCEAN

Colonsay
Jura

Islay

Sound
of
Jura

Bute

Arran

Campbeltown

Rathlin I.

Giant's
Causeway

Londonderry
(Derry)

NORTHERN
IRELAND

Lough
Neagh

BELFAST

Monaghan
Armagh

316 Time Out Edinburgh

Cape
Wrath

Balchrick
Culkein

Lochinver

Ullapool

Gairlo
Braemore
Junction
Achnasheen

Kyle

Drumnadrochit

Loch
Lochy

Loch
Shiel

Glencoe

Oban

Loch
Avich

Helensburgh
Dunoon
Greenock
Rothesay
Paisley

Brodick

Troon
Prestwick
Ayr

Turnberry

Ballantrae

Kirkcolm
Stranraer
Glenluce
Drummore

Antrim
Bangor

Dundalk

Durness
Skerray
Tongue
Portskerra

Altnaharra
Kinbrace
Lairg

Loch
Shin

Kincardine
Invergordon
Dornoch
Cromarty

Inverness

Loch
Ness

Invermoriston
Invergarry

Newtonmore
Dalwhinnie

Fort
William

Aberfeldy

Loch
Tay

Callander
Dunblane
Stirling
Denny
Dumbarton
Glasgow
Falkirk
Motherwell
Hamilton

see p313

Kilmarnock

Muirkirk
Cumnock
New Cumnock
Sanquhar
Maybole

Thornhill

New
Galloway

Newton
Stewart
Dalbeattie
Kirkcudbright
Whithorn

Luce
Bay

Wigtown
Bay

Workington

Westray
Rousay

Stromness

Hoy

Pentland
Firth

North
Ronaldsay

Sanday

Stronsay

South Ronaldsay

John
o' Groats

Thurso
Mybster
Wick
Lybster

Brora

Dornoch
Firth

Moray
Firth

Forres
Nairn
Grantown-
on-Spey

Aviemore

Kingussie

Cairngorm Mtns.

Braemar

Lossiemouth
Elgin
Buckie
Keith
Craigiellachie
Huntly

Macduff
Fraserburgh

Mintla
Peterhead

Inverurie
Ellon
Dyce
Aberdeen

Banchory
Stonehaven

Laurencekirk
Johnshaven

Brechin
Montrose

Forfar
Arbroath
Carnoustie

Dundee

Firth of
Tay

St Andrews

Perth
Cupar
Glenrothes
Alloa
Cowdenbeath
Dunfermline
Stenhousemuir

Firth of Forth

North Berwick
Dunbar

Livingston
Edinburgh
Haddington

Peebles

Biggar
Galashiels
Melrose
Kelso
Coldstream

Eyemouth
Berwick-upon-
Tweed

Cheviot Hills

Kielder

Northumberland

Morpeth

Newcastle-
upon-Tyne

Tyne &
Wear

Dumfries and
Galloway

Lockerbie
Annan
Gretna
Carlisle

Alston

Durham

Cumbria

Keswick
Penrith

Windermere

Kendal

Hawes

Darlington
Northallerton

North Yorkshire

ENGLAND

Ramsey

Isle of Man

Douglas

Castletown

Morecambe